Book of Edward
Christian Mythology

Volume III

Itching Christian Ears

Broken Covenant

Why will some Christians actually go to Hell? If you are a Christian, this book may save your eternal soul and the eternal souls of your family. Who is Jesus talking about when he said: "I never knew you" in Matthew 7:21-23? Christians! So, which Christians have broken the covenant of Jesus' blood on the cross? Why are they headed to Hell instead of Heaven? The answers are inside.

The Apostle Edward

Introduction

Book of Edward
Christian Mythology

Copyright © 2005 by Edward G. Palmer
Published by JVED Publishing
Elk River, Minnesota 55330

    ISBN 0-9768833-2-5 (Volume III: Itching Christian Ears)
    ISBN 0-9768833-4-1 (4 Volume Set)

Palmer, Edward G.
    1. Faith—The Apostle Edward   2. Bible Prophecy—Christian Mythology
    3. Christianity—Christology

Printed in the United States of America.

All rights reserved. No portion of this book may be reproduced in any form without the written permission of the Author.

Notice. This book and its entire contents represents the sole opinion of Edward G. Palmer based upon his twenty-five plus years of in-depth Bible studies, his actual life experiences, his personal diaries and readily available public records. No part of this book is intended to offer professional counseling of any type especially that of legal advice. Persons involved in cultic churches, those in need of spiritual counseling, medical, legal or any other advice should seek competent professional help.

Capitalization Protocol. On all Bible citations, regardless of the translation used, and where the context clearly points to God Almighty or to Jesus Christ, this book makes the distinction between the two by using either small cap characters or lower case characters. For God Almighty, a small capitalized style protocol is followed and reflected in the format: CREATOR, FATHER, GIVER, HE, HIS, HIM, HIMSELF, YOU, YOUR, ME, MINE, MOST HIGH, MY, MYSELF, LORD and SAVIOR, ETC. For Jesus Christ, a lower case protocol is used except for Lord and Son. Hence, when these pronouns are used for Jesus, they show up as: he, his, him, himself, you, your, me, my, myself, savior, Lord, or Son. This has generally been followed throughout the book, but is not the case with every cited verse. It is used for those verses in which the context cannot be easily disputed or in the case of citing a quality or attribute, which belongs solely to God. For those interested in the original translation capitalization, the author refers them to the actual Bible version used for the cited text. A list of Bible translations is shown on the next page. In some other cases, capital letters used within the cited sentence structure were also changed on common words for ease of reading or modern grammar. In other cases, the capitalized letters were left as shown in the original translation. Hence the original Bible phrase "; Because" might appear as "; because." In all instances, Apostle Edward maintains complete integrity of translation and the writings herein can be traced back to the original Bibles to confirm the accuracy of presentation. While not perfect, the capitalization protocol is fairly consistent and enhances the reading and value of Apostle Edward's teachings.

Copyright 2005 Edward G. Palmer, All Rights Reserved.

Book of Edward—Foreword

Introduction

Translation Notice

The following Bible translations were researched for this book along with three Hebrew texts and one or more ancient manuscripts such as the Book of Enoch (ENO). Except where otherwise indicated and in regards to capitalization of words, all Scripture quotations are taken from the Holy Bible, New King James Version © 1979, 1980, 1982 by Thomas Nelson, Inc., Publishers. Verses that are followed by a two, three or four-letter capitalized identifier are from the following Bible translations or reference works.

Abbreviation	Bible Definition
KJV; NKJV	King James Bible[1]; New King James Bible[2]
AMP	Amplified Bible[3]
ASB; NASB	American Standard[4]; New American Standard Bible[5]
DB	Darby Bible[6]
ENO	Book of Enoch — Richard Laurence 1883 Edition[7]
GN; GNB	Good News[8]; Good News Apocrypha[9]-Today's English Bible
GW	God's Word Bible[10]
HEB	Hebrew Bible — English Translation JPS 1917 Edition[11]
JSB	Jewish Study Bible[12] - Jewish Publication Society 1985, 1999
LIV; NLT	Living Bible[13]; New Living Translation[14]
MB	MicroBible[15]
MLT	Morris Literal Translation[16]
MOF	James Moffatt Translation, Final Edition[17]
NIV	New International Bible[18]
NCV	New Century Bible[19]
NJB	New Jerusalem Bible[20]
REB	Revised English Bible[21]
RSV; NRSV	Revised Standard Bible[22]; New Revised Standard Bible[23]
SET	Simple English Translation[24]
TAN	Tanach - The Stone Edition 1996[25]
TB	Transliterated Bible[26]
WEB	Webster's Bible[27]
WEY	Weymouth's NT[28]
YLT	Young's Literal Translation[29]

Copyright 2005 Edward G. Palmer, All Rights Reserved.

Book of Edward—Foreword

Table of Contents

                                                                                    Page

Dedication vi

Foreword viii

Prophecies Fulfilled... x

Volume I
Matters Of The Heart

Chapter 1: It Starts With The Heart 1

Chapter 2: God Speaks To The Heart.. 11

Chapter 3: Repentance From The Heart 28

Chapter 4: God's Call Of The Heart 59

Chapter 5: Practice From The Heart... 72

Chapter 6: The Heart Of An Apostle 93

Chapter 7: Choices From The Heart 131

Volume II
God Does Not Change

Chapter 8: Understanding God's Word 171

Chapter 9: Rationalization of Mankind 204

Chapter 10: The False Trinity Doctrine 242

Chapter 11: God's Eternal Character 312

Chapter 12: The False Salvation Doctrine................................. 382

Chapter 13: A Light On My Path 416

Chapter 14: The Gift of Jesus 452

Introduction

Volume III
Itching Christian Ears

Chapter 15: Myth — God Heals Everyone 492

Chapter 16: Myth — God Owns Solid Rock 545

Chapter 17: Myth — Giving 10% Is A Tithe 615

Chapter 18: Myth — Abortion Doesn't Matter 678

Chapter 19: Myth — Sexuality Doesn't Matter................................ 749

Chapter 20: Myth — Politics Doesn't Matter 897

Chapter 21: Myth — Everybody Gets To Go 977

Epilogue.. 1039

Volume IV
Appendixes—Reference

Appendix A: A Real Salvation Prayer 1043

Appendix B: Baptism Doctrine 1046

Appendix C: Doctrinal Statement 1049

Appendix D: Jackie's Final Thoughts 1069

Appendix E: Ed's Goodbye Eulogy 1072

Appendix F: Cancer Killing Protocols 1083

Appendix G: Illustrations, Tables & Lists 1092

Appendix H: Notes & Bibliography.. 1099

Appendix I: Bible Verse Cross Reference 1134

Appendix J: Index 1177

Introduction

Dedication

This book is dedicated to my beloved wife Jacqueline Lee (Bowers) Palmer whose love I was privileged to have on this earth for the thirty-nine years of our marriage and the four years of our teen love that preceded it from 1960-1964. On June 3, 2003, God gave Jackie her heavenly wings. This book was started during our thirty-seventh year of marriage and finished in what would have been our fortieth year.

In the forty-three years of earthly love that we shared, God used Jackie to teach me the simplicity of a genuine faith and the resulting earthly righteousness, which is manifested by that faith. Christian mythology has distorted the righteousness message of Jesus Christ. This book sets the record straight again about what it really means to accept God's Son.

Introduction

God also used Dean H. Mattila, Jacqueline Mattila and Vernon Enstad to teach me. They are the three righteous people whom God chose for me, from within the church, to share the spiritual journey of this book with. These three alone had the courage to stand tall for the truth and stand by my side when we left a fellowship of Christians who long ago decided to turn their back on the truth and embrace mythology.

Then there is Michael and Maureen Gill, two righteous people whom God brought into my life uncommitted to Christ at the time and used by God to illustrate as HE did to Peter in Acts 10:34-35 NIV that, "How true it is that God does not show favoritism but accepts men from every nation who fear HIM and do what is right."

Jesus confirms the kingdom requirement of righteousness in Matthew 25:46 with his words: "Then they will go away to eternal punishment, but the righteous to eternal life." In Luke 5:32, Jesus further clarifies this by saying: "I have not come to call the righteous, but sinners to repentance."

This book is also dedicated to the memory of my first son Glen; to daughter Paula & husband James Kantorowicz; daughter Patty & husband Jon Morin; son Brian & wife Brandee Palmer; grandchildren Christopher, Paul, Kathryn, Bradley, Benjamin, Luke, Braiden, Bronson, those yet to arrive and to the memory of grandson Dylan.

This book is also dedicated to the memory of my parents and sister Barbara and all others whom have passed on, to my younger brother James Stanley, his wife Denise and sons Jimmy, John and Nick. This book is also dedicated to Karen and Amy whom God brought into my heart and who will always be like a daughter and granddaughter to me.

Finally, this book is dedicated to the Christian family that my wife and I were raised in. How wonderful to have lived life in a fellowship of people not afraid to talk about the Holy Bible, our God and what it means to have a genuine faith. To those in the family who have wondered why I chose to accept God's calling, the answers will be found in this book. I will always be grateful for all of these special people who shared in my life and I trust that our LORD will find them excellent members of HIS kingdom, even while on this earth and in this present existence. The Apostle Edward

Copyright 2005 Edward G. Palmer, All Rights Reserved.

Book of Edward—Foreword

Introduction

Foreword

It was a strange scene for me as I found myself watching television on a recent Sunday morning. As I prepared to leave to open the doors of my own church, I found myself instead surfing with the remote for a few moments. TV is not a high priority for me, but I was interested in seeing what was on the tube in the way of church services. Perhaps for my dear wife who would be taking care of grandkids at home that morning? Perhaps for my grandkids? Perhaps simply for some good content for my own church teachings? It didn't matter.

All of a sudden, I found myself watching the worship service of a church I had heard much about. It was an Assembly of God church in the Minneapolis metro area. The name is not important. What was important to me at the time was what I saw. I was watching a praise and worship service on television and it captivated my spirit. The church was reported by some to be "hot." You know, filled with the Holy Ghost and with signs and wonders. The service was "spirit-filled." I can tell you this by just watching as the people were giving their hearts to God in song, dance, praise and worship.

For years, it was wonderful for me to go up to the altar area, lift my head and arms as high as I could, and praise the LORD. I would sing and dance around the altar getting "drunk" in the Holy Spirit [see Acts 2:15-21]. The object of praise and worship for me was to press into God's Spirit and presence. We are taught in the Bible that through Christ Jesus, we are given the Spirit of truth. We are also taught that it is our ticket to step into the Holy of Holies to be with God.

For me, the worship service was very captivating to watch. I felt myself desiring to "sing, dance, praise and worship" God among those worshippers I saw. The "praise and worship" looked genuine and as my spirit was drawn in further, I sensed my heart crying out: "Make room for me!" There is simply something wonderful worshipping God. We are taught in the Bible that "In HIS presence" is fullness of joy. For me, that is exactly what "praise and worship" is all about—getting into company with HIM. I have never known the level of joy I feel with God in anything of this worldly existence. That isn't to say the world cannot provide you and I with joy. It can, but that kind of joy is short lived. With God, it is always there, it's eternal in nature: you just have to "press-in" to HIM.

Copyright 2005 Edward G. Palmer, All Rights Reserved.

Introduction

As much as I wanted to join the praise and worship service, I couldn't help but wonder: "Who in the crowd was worshipping God in vain?" Who in this particular crowd was going through the motions but inside were not "lovers of the truth?" Who in this particular crowd was still going to Hell yet thinking they were saved? The truth has been perverted from many pulpits and Paul's prophecy in 2 Timothy 4:3-4 was now fulfilled.

You see I recently left a church with this same type of "inviting" praise and worship service. However, Solid Rock Church turned out to be a den of thieves, filled with wicked and unrighteous people [Luke 19:46]. People who consider themselves Christian; yet, who routinely and without much thought ignore the truth. Turning their backs, God saw the fullness of their false witness.

God reminded me of HIS word in Matthew 15:8-9 "These people draw near to ME with their mouth, and honor ME with their lips, but their heart is far from ME, and in vain they worship ME, teaching as doctrines the commandments of men." And again it is written in Mark 7:7 that "They worship ME in vain."

Do you worship God in vain? Many, who call themselves Christians, and who think of them selves as being saved by the blood of Jesus, are simply deluding themselves on the way to their eternal home in Hell. Jesus tells us of this fact. Why? Does it have to be this way?

The message I received from God is to tell those who call themselves Christians that many of them will be going to Hell and that Jesus will serve up a very rude announcement to them as they plead for their eternal soul. However, by that time, it will be too late. So, who are these Christians?

Who is Jesus speaking to in Matthew 7:22-23? Jesus says: "Many will say to me in that day, 'Lord, Lord, have we not prophesied in your name, cast out demons in your name, and done many wonders in your name?' And then I will declare to them, I never knew you; depart from me, you who practice lawlessness." Jesus' message is clearly to those who call themselves Christian. To those who say: "I am saved by the blood of Lamb" or "I know Jesus." This book is a warning to Christians. Many of you are headed to Hell. Why?

The Apostle Edward

Copyright 2005 Edward G. Palmer, All Rights Reserved.

Book of Edward—Foreword

Introduction

Mythology Prophecy

"For the time will come when men will not put up with sound doctrine. Instead, to suit their own desires, they will gather around them a great number of teachers to say what their itching ears want to hear. They will turn their ears away from the truth and turn aside to myths."

2 Timothy 4:3-4 NIV

Truth Prophecy

"The coming of the lawless one will be in accordance with the work of Satan displayed in all kinds of counterfeit miracles, signs and wonders, and in every sort of evil that deceives those who are perishing. They perish because they refused to love the truth and so be saved. For this reason God sends them a powerful delusion so that they will believe the lie and so that all will be condemned who have not believed the truth but have delighted in wickedness."

2 Thessalonians 2:9-12 NIV

Prophecies Are Fulfilled

"The prophecies in 2 Timothy 4:3-4 and 2 Thessalonians 2:9-12 are fulfilled. Today, mythology is routinely taught from the pulpits of many Christian churches instead of God's Holy Word and many people attending Christian churches have turned away from the truth. These people are headed toward Hell unaware of their lost souls."

The Apostle Edward

Copyright 2005 Edward G. Palmer, All Rights Reserved.

Itching Christian Ears

Volume III

Chapter Fifteen
Myth—God Heals Everyone

— Jackie's Last 98 Days On Earth —
— Instruction On Cancer, Healing & Death —

"But those who seek the LORD shall not lack any good thing."
Psalm 34:10

"But if they refuse to listen to [God], they will perish … and [they will] die from [a] lack of understanding." Job 36:12 NLT

"He [or she] shall die for lack of instruction." Proverbs 5:23

"MY people are destroyed for lack of knowledge." Hosea 4:6

"I will be gracious to whom I will be gracious, and I will have compassion on whom I will have compassion." Exodus 33:19

"I will have mercy on whom I will have mercy." Romans 9:15

David said: "Who can tell whether the LORD will be gracious to me, that [my] child may [be healed]? But now [that] he is dead; why should I fast? Can I bring [my son] back again? I shall go to him, but he shall not return to me." 2 Samuel 12:21-23

"Nor can they die anymore, for they are equal to the angels and are sons [and daughters] of God, being sons [and daughters] of the resurrection." Luke 20:35-36

"When I sent you without money bag, knapsack, and sandals, did you lack anything?" So they said, "Nothing." Luke 22:35

Myth—God Heals Everyone

May God's grace, peace and mercy be with you this day and always. This chapter is written for those who will stand with God's Word. These are people who have made a conscious choice to walk in God's light and now realize that they are destined for HIS eternal life. If you are not one of these people, you are reading someone else's mail from God penned through this apostle of righteousness. Some secular people and some who carry the name of Christian may object to this chapter in part or in whole. However, the purpose herein is to teach God's people what HIS Word *really* says about divine healing. Will God always heal people because of prayer? No.

Did you just start reading at this myth? If so, you should stop now and read chapters one to fourteen. You should be more concerned about where your heart is with God than what is in this chapter. When your heart is right with God, HE will give you understanding about divine healing.

It's now November 29 and about two weeks since I finished the last chapter. To some extent I have been procrastinating. I know that to write what God wants me to write here, I will suffer great emotional stress. I have already had tears just counting the days Jackie lived after February 26. That was the worse day of my life. It was the day that Jackie and I were told of her inoperable pancreatic cancer. It wasn't the worse day because of that diagnosis. Listen, I believe in divine healing and I had already prayed Jackie through two separate times where she was coughing up blood clots from her lungs. Both of those events were life threatening and scary. No, this was the worse day of my life because God had confirmed to me, as HE had to Jackie, that her remaining time on earth was now very short.

Jackie looked at me with somber eyes and said: "My job on earth is done and it is time for me to go home." Just the thought of those words coming from her mouth has me in tears once again. As I looked into her eyes, I also knew that her time on earth was nearly over as God confirmed the same thing to my spirit. There would not be another miraculous healing in Jackie's life. The doctor said she might have as little as 10 days.

Myth—God Heals Everyone

If we were lucky, she might have a few months. Stunned, we drove silently back to our home in Elk River from the Hennepin County Medical Center in Minneapolis where she had the internal ultrasound and biopsy test.

That night I found myself gasping for air, as I couldn't breathe. I also couldn't sleep and the pain on my chest was over whelming. It felt like the rear axle of a truck was sitting on top of my chest. I didn't even know if my body could breathe without having Jackie next to my side. For that matter, I didn't even know if I really cared. For the moment, thoughts of checking out myself flowed freely through my mind. I knew I was ready to go home to be with God. I had been ready for twenty-five years. Now, I wondered if I could even live without Jackie.

Indeed, it seemed like my worse fear in this earthly life had now manifested itself. God had set Jackie and I on a path of physical separation. It was a path that would return me to my own flesh; a path that no longer would include Jackie and I as one flesh. As events progressed, I could feel the cords that held our flesh together as one begin to separate. She was being prepared for a heavenly journey. I was being prepared for a life without her. I knew she would be fine. Myself? There were a lot of tears and lonely thoughts at that moment. We both had our life flash in front of us and together we cried a lot. I began to think about what could be done.

The big question of this chapter is: "Will God always heal as a result of prayer?" I've already told you the answer. This chapter will explain the basis for that answer from God's Word. I will use Jackie's life, cancer and death to illustrate for you what God wants you to know about healing.

First let me cover some final thoughts God gave me about the last chapter. Consider the issue of being a Christian who professes a belief in the trinity doctrine. Does this belief preclude them from getting into Heaven? The answer is *yes* — IF that trinity belief leads them to conclude that they can freely sin in this earthly life *and/or* if they worship Jesus instead of God. The answer is *no* — IF that trinity belief does not involve unrighteousness, willful sin and idolatry. In other words, they worship Jesus' God, not Jesus.

Copyright 2005 Edward G. Palmer, All Rights Reserved.

Book of Edward—Chapter 15

Myth—God Heals Everyone

In the first case, the unrighteous *Christian* is firmly condemned to Hell exactly for their belief that sin is now somehow okay through Jesus Christ. They have literally treated the blood of Jesus Christ as a common thing and insulted God's Spirit of grace. Go back and study Hebrews 10:26 if this is still unclear to you. Continued sin should be a "fearful thing" for believers. Even worse are those who engage in idolatry worshipping Jesus.

In the second case, the righteous Christian is just one more example of another child of God who is confused about Jesus. They are no different than a Jewish or Muslim child of God who also does not understand Jesus. Remember that to "practice righteousness is to be righteous just like Christ."

> **"Children, do not be misled: anyone who does what is right is righteous, just as Christ is righteous." 1 John 3:7 REB**

When you walk in God's light as Jesus Christ did, you have escaped the pollutions of this world. There is no going back. It is a one-way street.

> **"People can know our Lord and savior Jesus Christ and escape the world's filth. But if they get involved in this filth again and give in to it, they are worse off than they were before." 2 Peter 2:20 GW**

I want to mention all of this to make something very clear to you. Accepting Jesus Christ in your heart should be a new beginning for you with God. It is a time to grasp God's hand and let HIM guide you. It should not be the end of some spiritual quest. I.E. Some churches put people through a confirmation process. At the end of that process, they accept Christ and become a member of the church. The next duty is usually to make a pledge to the church. In many instances, this is the last time the person picks up a Bible. Such a church has failed God. Instead of teaching the beginning of a new life with God, confirmation classes teach young people that they have learned all they need to know about God. When you really accept Christ, you begin a new walk with God for the rest of your life. That is salvation!

Christ Is A New Beginning, Not The End Of A Journey!

Myth—God Heals Everyone

I have been told several times that I am fearless. Indeed, I stopped fearing man some time ago. However, I do sincerely fear my God. What is often mistaken, as fearlessness, is simply a strong confidence in God.

"In the fear of the LORD there is strong confidence, and HIS children will have a place of refuge." Proverbs 14:26

When you reach this level of confidence with God, it won't matter what your checkbook looks like or how the world is treating you. It also won't matter if your truck gets a dented driver's side door because you hit someone's bumper. Nor will it matter if you just think you are unlucky and that others get all the breaks in life. Strong confidence in God is what you get when you walk in HIS light.

I tell you this because today I have exactly $76.62 cash to my name. Yes, it can cause some stress if you let it. My daughter Patty also informed me this afternoon that she dented the passenger's door on her husband's new Chevrolet truck. Yes, that too can cause some stress if you let it. If you walk in God's light, you have to look upward and not around you from an earthly perspective. My friend Robert taught me during times of trouble, you need to pray it up to God and play it down on this earth. Those are good words of advice for as long as you focus on God, you will have peace. This is what Isaiah has taught us. Take it to heart and see what God will do.

"God will keep you in perfect peace, when your mind is stayed on HIM, because you trust in God." Isaiah 26:3
                              [Paraphrased by Edward]

When you seek God, you can understand why the Psalmist teaches that you will not lack any good thing in Psalm 34:10. You will also understand why Jesus asked the question to his apostles: "Did you lack anything?" The answer was no, even when Jesus sent them out without any money. I have lived through a cycle of almost zero cash with God several times. I bear witness to you that God has always made a way where there seemed to be no way. Admittedly, such times will test your faith in God.

Myth—God Heals Everyone

Despite my strong confidence in the LORD and in HIS ability to take me through yet another cash flow crunch, I have learned something of this physical realm. I have learned that even though I think I am doing well, my body might inform me that I am not doing so well. To the degree we can walk with our spirit, all is well. But, if the flesh gets some control, stress will manifest itself in our bodies. This is true whether or not we will admit it or for that matter whether we even realize it. Do you listen to your body? I personally can absorb an incredible amount of stress. I will still be standing when all around me are totally stressed out. Why I am like this I do not fully understand. I have a natural desire to trust in God and operate in faith. This is not to say that stress doesn't rack my body at times. It does. I have also experienced a mind-body separation. This happens when you think you are well, but your body tells you something different with a cold or illness.

Therefore, low stress is an attribute of healing. Jackie and I were under enormous stress the last three years. There is little doubt that it impacted her more than I even if she hid it somewhat. In the realm of cancer invading our bodies, stress is one of the contributing factors. Your peace in this earthly life will be in direct proportion to your ability to simply yield your life over to God's control. It is not easy and not necessarily related to whether one is saved or has obtained eternal salvation. It's strong faith.

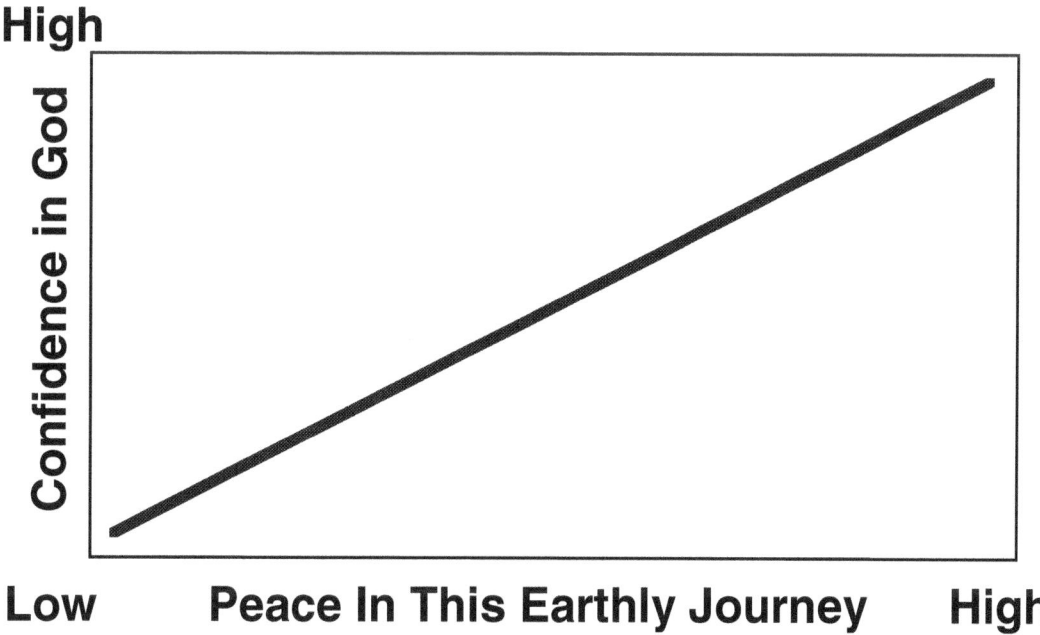

Copyright 2005 Edward G. Palmer, All Rights Reserved.

Myth—God Heals Everyone

As shown in the preceding graph, your peace in this earthly journey will be in direct proportion to your confidence in God. High confidence in God brings you perfect peace. Low confidence in God will bring anxiety and uncertainty. And no matter where you think you are at with your spirit and mind, the body you possess may have some different thoughts. I wish I could tell you that I always operate as I do this time where I have a perfect peace knowing that God is in control; I can't. At times, I too suffer. The difference for me, however, is I know that to the degree I do suffer a lack of peace, it is only because I am not in HIS presence. When I become aware of a lack of peace in my life that is when I get back into prayer and worship. It is my spiritual cue that I am "in the world" and not "in HIS peace." It is a time to mentally refocus on God and get out of myself or out of this world.

If life is getting you down, maybe its because you are too focused on yourself or the things of this world. Pick up a Holy Bible and start to read. Shift your thoughts towards God. If you do not know where to start in the Bible, start at Psalm 34. When you are hurting and in trouble, this Psalm is good place to meditate on. Listen to a part of this Psalm of David.

> **"The righteous cry out, and the LORD hears, and delivers them out of all their troubles. The LORD is near to those who have a broken heart, and saves such as have a contrite spirit. Many are the afflictions of the righteous, but the LORD delivers him [or her] out of them all." Psalm 34:17-19**

My friend Norman taught me that problems constitute a sign of life. When confronted by a member of his congregation that complained of his many problems, Norman asked him if he would like to move to a place where 100,000 people lived and not a single one of them had a problem. The man answered yes, he would like that. Norman replied: "Okay, but its Woodlawn Cemetery in the Bronx and everyone is dead." Norman went on to conclude that it was then logical that problems constituted a sign of life. I can add that if you choose to walk with God in HIS light and righteousness that "many will be your afflictions." That is what God teaches us. Why? It is simple. Satan doesn't care if you are "into yourself" or "into this world." He only cares about those who are "into righteousness" and belong to God.

Myth—God Heals Everyone

Do not be concerned about your afflictions if you are righteous. God will be near to your broken heart and HE will comfort you and deliver you out of your troubles. You should be concerned when life is peaceful and you have no trouble and everything seems to be going your way. As my friend Norman says: "You might be on your way out." Or, at the very least, you are of no concern to Satan. Lack of troubles in this earthly life is a sign that you might live on the wrong side of the fence of righteousness. It may be a sign that you are of the world and not of God's light. Check your priorities.

God Will Comfort Your Broken Heart!

When I think that Jackie will not be available to share life anymore, I experience a broken heart and unimaginable sadness. I cannot live with those kinds of thoughts because to do so is to live in the past with all the continued pain of Jackie's death. I can only live in the present moment of time. Jackie is not a part of my life anymore and I must move on in life and put her death behind me. I can take comfort from God knowing that she is now with HIM. When the sad thoughts arrive, I replace them with the good memories of our life together and the blessing that I know she was to me.

"Blessed be the God and FATHER of our Lord Jesus Christ, the FATHER of mercies and God of all comfort, who comforts us in all our tribulation, that we may be able to comfort those who are in any trouble, with the comfort with which we ourselves are comforted by God." 2 Cor. 1:3-4

When it comes to healing in our body, you have got to move beyond your problems and allow God to deal with them. Many times in my life I have not been able to understand something. During those moments in time I was left with the option to go nuts or to give the issue up to God to handle. I chose to put the issue(s) in a gunnysack labeled—"I can't handle it LORD!"

Now I imagine you may have already mentally collected many such objects and you don't know what to do with them. I can also imagine that you carry the objects in a gunnysack over your shoulder and that they are now a heavy burden on your life. You may even have become quite irritable

Copyright 2005 Edward G. Palmer, All Rights Reserved.

Myth—God Heals Everyone

about these issues or problems in your life. Maybe you feel unlucky and that everything seems to just happen to only you. Frustrated and angry you might even be lashing out at those who love you. If this sounds like you, then you have a high level of stress in your life and you need to unwind it a little. Norman taught me another lesson that I adopted over two decades ago. It has never failed me once over the years.

Imagine for the moment that all of your troubles, irritations and afflictions in life are in that sack on your back in the form of pots and pans. Each pot and pan represents a serious issue that increases your stress in this earthly life. Each item represents something over your head and something you just can't understand or make sense out of. Now imagine that Jesus Christ is standing in front of you and asks you to just take on his yoke so you can have rest. Christ is trying to tell you that there is more to life than what you can realize with your human senses.

In that moment, Christ is also asking that you give him all of your pots and pans, everything that burdens and troubles you in this earthly life. You take one item at a time out of your gunnysack and give it to Christ. Eventually your gunnysack becomes empty and all the troubles of your life are now taken off of your back. You are not free of problems. However, you now have some heavenly help from God and His Son Jesus.

> **Jesus said: "Take my yoke upon you and learn from me, for I am gentle and lowly in heart, and you will find rest in our FATHER [God] for your souls." Matthew 11:29** *Paraphrased*
>
> **"Give all your worries and cares to God, for HE cares about what happens to you." 1 Peter 5:7 NLT**
>
> **"When troubles come ... sing HIS praises [from within your heart] with much joy." Psalm 27:5-6 LIV**
>
> **"My brethren, count it all joy when you fall into various trials." James 1:2**

Myth—God Heals Everyone

Those Who Endure Life Are Counted Blessed!

"Indeed we count them blessed who endure [life]. You have heard of the perseverance of Job and seen the end intended by the LORD — that the LORD is very compassionate and merciful." James 5:11

If you want healing in your own life or more peace, a good place to start is to lower the level of stress you are experiencing. One of the greatest joys of my life occurred during Jackie's illness. It was watching her settle into the loving arms of God. I watched Jackie literally transcend all the cares of this world and only look forward to the joy of her heavenly home. The transformation that took place before my eyes brought both joy and tears. The joy I felt came from watching Jackie experience the perfect peace of God's presence. Indeed, the whole family experienced God's presence in our home and is a witness to Jackie's perfect peace. The tears came from just knowing that her earthly life was nearing its end.

Just reflecting on what I witnessed grabs my throat and causes even more tears to flow. Yet I know that these are both tears of joy and tears of sadness. I spent 43 years loving this woman and in this earthly life I could never give her the peace that God brought to her during the last 98 days of her life. Verily I say to you that at any given moment in your own earthly existence the level of peace you can experience with God will range from virtually none to virtually perfect peace. The choice will be yours to make.

Jackie had struggled to understand how to get to that area of perfect peace, but in the end God gave it to her during the last 98 days of her life. To the degree you can have high confidence in God, you can shed your earthly concerns. It comes from a heart that totally surrenders itself into God's hands. Jackie was like Martha in Luke 10:41. She was a servant of God, but she was always concerned about hospitality issues. Making sure everyone was fed, etc. She was the quintessential caregiver to my children, grandchildren, family and friends. However, in the end she was able to give herself completely over to our God and let HIM take over all of her concerns.

Myth—God Heals Everyone

The peace Jackie exhibited while dying was only matched by the unbelievable bravery she showed. I do not recall her ever expressing a concern about herself. I only recall her expressing concerns about others. The 98 days God gave us allowed all of us to say our good byes. In the end, there was no fear in her — only peace! To which, with tears in my eyes, I praise the God that I serve for the awesome gift HE gave to Jackie.

Of course our individual faith plays a role in healing and I am always conscious of the fact that the prayers of a righteous man counts a lot with our God. I remember looking at Jackie's somewhat emaciated body towards the end wondering how our grandson Christopher was coping. He was the first grandson and spent his first 24-months with us. It established a soul-bond with Jackie as if he was her son. At age 15 he fought back the tears and kept praying. I remember thinking towards the end what an excellent healing story this would be to see her suddenly get up having experienced yet another miracle. I could almost read Christopher's mind as he thought the same thing I did: "It's not over yet. God still has time to heal her." It wasn't over yet and who knew whether God would be gracious in this situation? To paraphrase King David, "Who knows what God will do at this time?"

I have lived a high-tension entrepreneurial life and studied the issue of stress reduction more than once. My top three methods of dealing with the issue of stress are simple. It starts with my spiritual connection to God.

1. Prayer
2. Nutrition
3. Exercise

The power of your own individual prayer is mainly dependent upon the degree to which you can surrender your heart to God. Draw near to God and witness that HE will draw near to you. Give God 100% of your heart and you will witness miracles happen. It doesn't always mean your prayers will be answered exactly the way you want them to be answered. Certainly mine wasn't. Yet I understand that all of this was God's will even if I do not understand what happens next in my life. I understand that Jackie's death is something that must be placed into the "I can't handle it LORD" gunnysack.

Myth—God Heals Everyone

For me, God will have to deal with every aspect of Jackie's death and absence from my side. I will get my chance to understand when I go to join Jackie in Heaven. God has said: "Do not lean on your own understanding." Make God an integral part of your own life and you'll find His peace.

Stress takes over life just like pain takes over life. When your body is in pain, all of your body's resources are working to just deal with the pain. I am happy to say that Jackie was relatively pain free except for two really bad days. This in itself is unusual for pancreatic cancer, which can be quite horrific. A variety of pain medications were used to keep Jackie pain free so her body could do its best with its God given innate healing powers. She was conscious until the last 24 hours of life when it became necessary to dramatically increase her pain narcotics. Did her pancreas burst open or start to leak? The chemicals inside the pancreas cannot exist outside of it except within the intestinal area. It is like an acid that would literally eat through all of the other organs.

About four hours before Jackie took her last breath, our dog Annie jumped up on the bed next to Jackie and howled aloud. She immediately left the bed and never came back. It was the first time our cocker spaniel ever howled and it left all of us wondering at the time what it was all about. She is almost nine years old and was Jackie's dog. By spiritual reckoning, we believe that Jackie's soul left her body at that very moment. The event that her dog Annie signaled was the departure of her spirit-soul. It took about four more hours before her body stopped breathing on its own.

If you can understand that Jackie's soul actually left her body before her body physically stopped functioning in all respects [stopped breathing, heart stopped, etc.], you can understand why Jesus told the thief next to him that he would be in Paradise that very day with Jesus. The soul doesn't need transportation to Heaven nor does it wait for all bodily functions to cease. When the soul leaves the body, it takes off for home. We knew that Jackie's essence [her spirit-soul] was nowhere to be found in the bedroom by the time her body ended its last physical function. It was very obvious she had gone home. The fact we observed this spiritual reality gives credence to a statement in the Gospel of Phillip about Jesus' own physical death.

Myth—God Heals Everyone

From the Gnostic Gospel of Philip [1], we read the following:

"Those who say that the Lord died first and then rose up are in error, for he rose up first and then died. If one does not first attain the resurrection will he not die? As God lives, he would already be dead." ...

"While we are in this world it is fitting for us to acquire the resurrection for ourselves, so that when we strip off the flesh we may be found in rest." ...

"Those who say they will die first and then rise are in error. If they do not first receive the resurrection while they live, when they die they will receive nothing."

If you can understand why Jackie rose before she died, you will also understand these words of Jesus Christ concerning our entering into life at the point of the spirit-soul leaving our body. It should be sufficient enough for you to understand that our resurrection will occur at death. The new resurrection body like Christ had will be a gift at a later appointed time.

Jesus said: "If your hand or foot causes you to sin, cut it off and cast it from you. It is better for you to enter into life lame or maimed, rather than having two hands or two feet, to be cast into the everlasting fire. And if your eye causes you to sin, pluck it out and cast it from you. It is better for you to enter into life with one eye, rather than having two eyes, to be cast into Hell fire." Matthew 18:8-9

Christ makes it abundantly clear that we enter eternal life at the time we die. The Gospel of Philip makes it clear that you better get your "life" here while on earth because you won't get it after you leave the earth. So the essence of life is what lies inside us. Our bodies are like a glove worn on our hand during cold weather. When the hand is inside the glove, the glove becomes animated and appears to be alive. Take the hand [our spirit-soul] out of the glove [our body] and the glove [our body] becomes lifeless.

Myth—God Heals Everyone

Philip's Gospel clarifies the separation of our spirit-soul from our physical body even further with the following statement about Jesus Christ.

"My God, my God, why, O LORD, have you forsaken me?" To which Philip teaches us: "It was on the cross that [Jesus] said these words, for it was there [on the cross that] he was divided."

Note: Philip teaches us that Christ's spirit-soul was "divided" and separated from his body [and rose] prior to the death of his physical body. Christ's separation of spirit-soul from his body is an example of what we can expect at the time of our death. The resurrected body was given to Christ at a later time, just like ours will be given to us at a later [appointed] time.

It was some time in the mid 1960's that Jackie and I were asked by her Uncle Earl to go to the hospital and help make a decision as to whether or not he should pull the life support from his wife, Jackie's Aunt Bernice, who had been in an accident. This was in San Diego, California when I was in the Navy. It was our first experience with life support machines and we were young adults. I can still remember the hospital room and Aunt Bernice lying in the bed with a mechanical respirator. She could not breathe for herself and she had no brain activity. Her heartbeat was strong.

I remember that I could clearly see that Bernice exhibited no essence or life force. It was because Aunt Bernice's spirit-soul had simply left to go home. It only took a few minutes to agree to turn off the respirator that kept her lungs working. Aunt Bernice stopped breathing a few moments after the respirator was shut down. Her heart stopped beating shortly thereafter. I knew at the time it was the right decision. Nothing has changed in forty years that would alter that decision. She, like Jackie, had simply left her earthly body and just wasn't there even though we could artificially keep her body going. I can imagine that just as Jackie took her last two breaths we could have attached a respirator to her body to keep it artificially breathing, but why? She wasn't there. To keep her body parts functioning just because we couldn't cope with her "shedding her flesh" would have been ungodly.

Myth—God Heals Everyone

Today, medical science has advanced far ahead of where it was in the 1960's. Place a feeding tube directly into the stomach of an almost dead body and combine it with IV fluids, meds, antibiotics and oxygen machines and you can keep a human body going almost indefinitely. This is very true if there exists no pathological disease eating away at the human body such as pancreatic cancer. We even have machines to keep the heart going if needed shocking it back into operating condition or forcing it to contract and expand with electrical signals as needed. In essence, all that is left to do is to keep moving the body periodically to prevent skin ulcers from forming. After our experience with Aunt Bernice, Jackie and I agreed that neither of us would want machines to keep our bodies going over a protracted period of time. It is a hideous and even odious thing that people do when they simply cannot let go of a loved one whose spirit has left the body or is unduly entrapped in a body that can no longer function with a mind as God designed.

The controversy over keeping a human body going indefinitely was center stage in the societal debate over whether or not to remove the feeding tube from Terri Schiavo in Florida. The debate was likened to starving her to death by "refusing" to give her food. However, if God wanted us fed with a stomach tube supplied externally with food, HE would have equipped our bodies with such a tube and provided attendants 24 hours a day to meet our needs. If the idea of dehydration during the death process seems repulsive to you, it is because you are ignorant of the body's natural dying process. It is a natural thing that the spirit rejects food and nutrition as it begins to shut down the body in the death process. In fact, food can cause more pain in the body as the spirit-soul attempts to shut things down and exit this earth, shedding its human flesh. Medical intervention can unduly restrain a spirit.

Do you believe it is righteous to keep someone on a feeding tube indefinitely? For fifteen years? It is unrighteous and self-serving to those who cannot cope with death. It is also shameful to state that it is wrong in the eyes of God to remove a feeding tube kept in for so long. This isn't a right to life issue like abortion, which kills a fully functioning human. This is about the right to die a natural death with some amount of dignity after a period of exhaustive medical intervention in the mechanically un-tethered body that God Almighty gave us. *Terri died on March 31, 2005, 13 days after her tube was removed for a third time. This section was updated.*

Myth—God Heals Everyone

If you think it was wrong in God's eyes to remove Terri's feeding tube, I want you to show me a single case in the Bible where it took God fifteen years to heal someone. God doesn't need hours, days, weeks, months and years to heal anyone. Every case of biblical healing was instantaneous in nature. Yet Terri's body was kept artificially alive for fifteen years by medical intervention. A body like hers could be kept going for another 40 years if no pathological disease attacks it. Terri lived a God given natural life for 26 years. Then, people who claim to love her, refuse to let her die a God given natural death after eight years of exhaustive medical intervention and seven years of subsequent litigation. Some people even want to keep her mindless brain damaged body artificially alive indefinitely using medical technology. Is that love? No, it is sick, perverse, and odious. It is the action of spiritually ignorant people who lack a true faith in God. After her feeding tube was removed on March 18, 2005, Congress passed a law to *save* her by authorizing Federal Court intervention. At one point, Florida's Governor even considered a plan to have state agents seize her and reinsert the feeding tube. All the political efforts failed. Can you rejoice for Terri's *new* life?

The second time Terri's feeding tube was removed, Florida passed a law forcing it to be reinserted; it was declared unconstitutional. There is no reason to involve the government or court in a family's end of life decision. They will only prolong your grieving process. Many organizations & people have used Terri Schiavo for *political* purposes; God will repay! Only the godly love of all family members can release an entrapped spirit-soul and let its artificially fed body die. Was Terri inside her body? Some say yes and some say no. Did it matter? If she was still inside her body, her family and society long ago lost any spiritual perspective about a natural death for her. They unduly entrapped her spirit-soul on this earth in a body that lacked a cognitive mind, a body artificially kept alive. In the other case, she was long gone and probably wondered why it took so long to stop the artificial means of keeping her earthly shell and pseudo life alive. Yes, a lot of controversy surrounded the participants in Terri's real life and death drama. However, there was really only one central truth in the drama. Terri Schiavo's body was kept artificially alive by means that the CREATOR never intended to be used over a protracted period of time. Without medical intervention, Terri would have died a natural death 7-15 years earlier in 1-2 weeks. There is a natural [nonintervention] death process of spirits shedding their flesh.

Myth—God Heals Everyone

Here is some startling medical truth. If you have good insurance and you are unlucky enough to get a feeding tube placed in your comatose or vegetative state body, you are likely to remain that way until the insurance runs out of money, the family runs out of money or the state refuses to pay. Especially if a loved one thinks he or she is applying a standard of true love.

Verily I say to you that true love can place a comatose or vegetative state loved one in the hands of God after reasonable medical care has been exhausted. If you choose artificial means for keeping their body alive, you do so for yourself not for them. It would be different if they were cognitive and gave those medical instructions, but then it wouldn't be your decision. Many quadriplegics have lived a meaningful life as a result of their own cognitive choices; Christopher Reeves is one example. However, it is their own spirit-soul that is directing their physically impaired life choices. God certainly may have a role in helping *them* make meaningful decisions.

"Let love be without hypocrisy. Abhor what is evil. Cling to what is good." Romans 12:9

Take a deep breath and put yourself into the body of your comatose or vegetative state loved one. Ask yourself how long it would be reasonable to keep yourself in that state. What would godly love do? If you think that love would be "long suffering" in such instance, you are misinterpreting the Bible. Keeping someone artificially going is simply cruel. It didn't take Jackie and I long to realize we needed to place her Aunt Bernice into God's loving hands. The condition was beyond our ability to understand and also beyond the medical systems ability to cure. Bernice's life belonged in the category of "I can't handle it LORD." Putting her into God's hands with prayer lets HIM make the decision about healing, life and death. It is no more complicated than simply yielding over to God what is beyond us.

When the Living Will became available in Minnesota, I completed one and gave a copy to the clinics I used. In that Living Will, I have said that it is okay to use machines on me for seven days if I am unable to speak for myself. After seven days, I have asked that the machines be taken off of my body and that I be left in the arms of the God that I trust. Should God desire me to stay on this earth, I know that HE can perform the healing that

Myth—God Heals Everyone

my body needs. Should it be my time to go, I am more than ready. When you know your God, you also know that there is truly an appointed time for you to die. There is no need to fear an earthly death by keeping your body artificially alive.

"And as it is appointed for men [or women] to die once, but after this the judgment." Hebrews 9:27

We see in Strong'S Concordance[2] that the word "appointed" as used in Hebrews 9:27 comes from the Greek word ***apokeimai*** (ap-ok'-i-mahee), which means to be reserved; fig. To await —be appointed, (be) laid up.

The word "appointed" means precisely what it says. God has an appointed a time for every one of us to die a natural death. This is the time when our spirit-soul sheds off its flesh and goes home. We are able to keep God's appointed time when our bodies are not subjected to artificial life support over a protracted period of time. This is man's way of trying to cheat death, but it never works. However, it does feed bank accounts.

As I was writing last night, December 1, news of the sudden death of the 11-year old son of a friend of my family reached me. The boy was struck dead by a car while returning from the mailbox outside of his rural home only a few miles from my home. It is nothing short of a Greek tragedy when such a young person dies. *Hear my prayer LORD!*

FATHER God, YOU see the immense pain we suffer when death strikes any family member. As YOU have comforted me, I pray for Connie and her family now that YOU would comfort them as in death there is no real comfort other than YOURS. FATHER, I also pray for the families of everyone whose body is being kept alive by artificial means to delay death. Guide these families to make the right spiritual decision for their loved ones so that these souls may not be trapped needlessly on this earthly plane by a love that fails to acknowledge the eternal rest that awaits for all righteous souls. Surely YOU are in control of these life and death matters. Surely they both fit into the gunnysack we all carry that says: "I can't handle it LORD!"

Myth—God Heals Everyone

Who can know our appointed time except God? When our oldest daughter Paula was 12-years old, Jackie's cousin lost their 12-year old son in a cruel accident. It was one of the saddest funerals I have ever attended. It didn't take long for Jackie and I to project this onto Paula. "My God, what if that would have been Paula?" Life has a way of offering up a lot of things to think about when it comes to healing and death. Verily I say unto you that you will never know if today is your last day. God knows the timing.

Often riches get our egos going and we think we can escape the misery of living by buying our way out of life's troubles. Perhaps this is one reason why people are kept artificially alive so long. They've got the money. When Jackie became ill, our options were limited because our funds were non-existent. We chose to trust in God and do the best with what we had available. I shudder to think of what I might have put Jackie through had I been a multimillionaire with unlimited resources. That is the main problem with wealth. Man will trust in wealth before he trusts in God.

Jesus makes it clear that trusting in our wealth to live life or to rely upon our own resources instead of God's doesn't work. Here's an example.

"But God said to him, 'Fool! This night your soul will be required of you; then whose will those things be which you have provided?'" Luke 12:20

When it comes to death, no amount of money and medical technology you can muster will be able to alter God's decision even if you can keep a body artificially alive. What we can do is choose the direction we are going. For the young boy who just died, there is only one place you will find him. It will be in the loving hands of God who understands his short life. A few more years would have required that he make a conscious spiritual choice. His behavior in life would have demonstrated which side he chose, just like yours does. I attended the funeral of Connie's son yesterday. I can tell you that her son had already chose God. In his short life he touched many other lives and was loved by many; the funeral home was packed. Yet can we say that the death of this boy was at God's appointed time? Hardly. As I will explain further, there are other factors involved in the length of our days.

Myth—God Heals Everyone

Note: It's now December 6. The funeral was Friday, Dec 5.

King Hezekiah's story demonstrates that we simply do not know God's plan or timing for our death. It also demonstrates that sincere prayer from a dedicated and loyal heart can result in healing from God.

"In those days Hezekiah was sick and near death. And Isaiah the prophet, the son of Amoz, went to him and said to him, 'Thus says the LORD: Set your house in order, for you shall die, and not live.' Then he turned his face toward the wall, and prayed to the LORD, saying, 'Remember now, O LORD, I pray, how I have walked before YOU in truth and with a loyal heart, and have done what was good in YOUR sight.' And Hezekiah wept bitterly. And it happened, before Isaiah had gone out into the middle court, that the word of the LORD came to him, saying, 'Return and tell Hezekiah the leader of MY people, Thus says the LORD, the God of David your father: I have heard your prayer, I have seen your tears; surely I will heal you. On the third day you shall go up to the house of the LORD. And I will add to your days fifteen years.' " 2 Kings 20:1-6

Hezekiah's sincere prayer not only got his healing from God it also got him an additional fifteen years added to his life, a longer time on this earthly plane. That is the power of a righteous individual's prayer.

A list of issues involved with cancer, healing and death has already taken shape in my mind. Here are some attributes of healing that need to be considered for understanding what our human body is up against on earth. Some items have already been discussed; I will try to touch on all of them.

1. Stress
2. Pain
3. Our Faith
4. Other's Faith
5. Our Prayer

Myth—God Heals Everyone

6. Other's Prayer
7. God's Sovereignty
8. God's Grace
9. God's Mercy
10. God's Healing
11. God's Glory
12. God's Bigger Picture
13. God's Protection
14. Good Habits
15. Bad Habits
16. Sin
17. Repentance
18. Age or Youth
19. Lack of Faith
20. Lack of Knowledge
21. Nutrition
22. Body's Innate Healing Ability
23. Health Laws
24. Food Laws
25. Sanitation
26. Doctors
27. Traditional Medicine
28. Alternative Medicine
29. Anointing With Oil
30. Call To Elders
31. Pray For Yourself While Healthy
32. God's Call to Pray for Someone Else

I believe that the issue of cancer, healing and death are affected by all of the items listed above. I also believe that God's Word speaks directly to most of these items. Please note that no attempt has been made to prioritize the above list or to make it all-inclusive. You can see that prayer is only a part of a longer list of items that will affect our bodily healing.

I remember a time when I would have told you that if I am sick, do not bring anyone to me that would pray a prayer with the words to "heal me if it be THY will LORD." This was biblical ignorance for me at that time.

Myth—God Heals Everyone

In fact, I was one of those Charismatic folks who would have been insulted if you even suggested that God might not want to heal my sickness. Why, for heaven's sake man [woman], don't you know the word of God? Yes, I would have uttered those words. I was programmed with mythology instead of the Word. Instead, I would say: "Bring me people who will pray knowing that it is God's will for me to be healed." Perhaps you are one of my Charismatic or Pentecostal brothers or sisters who currently hold to that opinion? Well, guess what? If you do hold to that opinion, it does not represent the truth of God's Word for you and you should keep on reading.

I have altered my thinking as a result of some in depth understanding given to me by God. Today, I would have people pray for my healing if it were God's will. I know that sometimes it is not HIS will for healing, as we like to think of healing, it being a longer life on earth. It might be that the healing that God wants for us is to take us to our heavenly mansion and to give us rest from this earthly life and all its incumbent struggles. That is what God did with Jackie. In God's bigger picture, it was her appointed time to go home. Her healing was the gift of eternal rest for her soul in a heavenly mansion God prepared. Can you understand that such a transition and shedding of the flesh is also a blessing? If not, why? Jackie's death was not the answer I sought from my prayers, yet it was still a great blessing to her from God. I had come to spiritual maturity and was able to condition my prayers to God with the words: "THY will be done O LORD!"

Jesus said: "If you loved me, you would rejoice because I said, 'I am going to the FATHER.'" John 14:28

Do you rejoice when a loved one goes to the FATHER? Jesus makes it clear that if you knew he was going to the FATHER *and* you really loved him, you would rejoice. Perfect peace, perfect joy and rest. We have long ago lost the ability to rejoice when a righteous person sheds his or her flesh to go back to the FATHER. Yet that is exactly what we should do. I know that some family members might think I didn't grieve enough over the loss of Jackie. However, exactly how much should I grieve when God's Word tells me to rejoice? The answer might surprise you and it is also in God's Word. You'll find instructions on grieving in the book of Sirach chapter 38.

Myth—God Heals Everyone

> "My child, let your tears fall for the dead, and as one in great pain begin the lament. Lay out the body with due ceremony, and do not neglect the burial. Let your weeping be bitter and your wailing fervent; make your mourning worthy of the departed, for one day, or two, to avoid criticism; then be comforted for your grief.
>
> For grief may result in death, and a sorrowful heart saps one's strength. When a person is taken away, sorrow is over; but the life of the poor weighs down the heart. Do not give your heart to grief; drive it away, and remember your own end.
>
> Do not forget, there is no coming back; you do the dead no good, and you injure yourself. Remember his fate, for yours is like it; yesterday it was his, and today it is yours.
>
> When the dead is at rest, let his remembrance rest too, and be comforted for him when his spirit has departed."
>
> Sirach 38:16-23 NRSV

Be Comforted For Them When Their Spirit Departs!

It is clear that we should rejoice and be comforted at the death of our loved ones when we know they are in the hands of our God. I can tell you that I am not done with suffering over Jackie's loss. Even so, life gives no respite from further heartache. Connie's son's death was also close to my heart. She is almost like another daughter having been raised with my kids in the neighborhood and my having known her thirty-years. To see her and her family suffer in such pain is almost unbearable. Yet I am getting close to "letting Jackie's remembrance rest" as Sirach teaches. What does Sirach mean? He means that I should stop constantly thinking about her during my daily life. It means that I put Jackie out of my mind. That has happened when everyone close has died. After a period of grieving, I realized that I had to move on mentally. God and time *will* heal our broken hearts; I know!

Myth—God Heals Everyone

Sirach also contains important instructions on using the help of medical doctors and pharmacists. Listen to Sirach.

> "Honor physicians for their services, for the LORD created them; for their gift of healing comes from the MOST HIGH, and they are rewarded by the king. The skill of physicians makes them distinguished, and in the presence of the great they are admired.
>
> The LORD created medicines out of the earth, and the sensible will not despise them. Was not water made sweet with a tree in order that its power might be known?
>
> And HE gave skill to human beings that HE might be glorified in [their] marvelous works. By them the physician heals and takes away pain; the pharmacist makes a mixture from them. God's works will never be finished; and from HIM health spreads over all the earth." Sirach 38:1-8 NRSV

You can clearly observe that we are not to ignore medical resources when it comes to our illnesses. Nor are we to treat our bodies poorly. Many people today violate biblical health and food laws and cram stuff into their bodies that we are not supposed to. There are many excellent books written about biblical nutrition. Get some to read and start observing what you are doing to your own body. If you smoke and drink alcohol, you are slowly poisoning your body. This has led many to a premature death. Instead of the natural death God had planned, many intervene with poor health habits. When asked if smoking would keep someone out of Heaven, a pastor I know answered, "No!" He then emphatically added: "In fact, it will help get you to Heaven faster!" When you treat your body poorly, you sin against your own body and accelerate your own earthly "shedding of the flesh."

> "Or do you not know that your body is the temple of the Holy Spirit who is in you, whom you have from God, and you are not your own?" 1 Cor. 6:19

Myth—God Heals Everyone

If you are a sharp reader, you might deduce that such sins against the body are both willful and continuous within many people. You might ask: "So will these sins which are willful now keep us out of Heaven?" This is a good question and the answer is also in the Bible. Consider these verses.

"Parents must not be put to death for the sins of their children, nor the children for the sins of their parents. Those worthy of death must be executed for their own crimes [sins worthy of death]." Deut. 24:16 NLT

"If anyone sees a fellow-Christian committing a sin which is not a deadly sin, he should intercede for him, and God will grant him life—that is, to those who are not guilty of deadly sin. There is such a thing as deadly sin, and I do not suggest that he should pray about that. Although all wrongdoing is sin, not all sin is deadly sin." 1 John 5:16-17 REB

Apostle John makes it clear that we can intercede with God for others when their sin is not a "deadly sin." Further, John says that God will grant them "life" when we intercede for them. I guess the idea that all sin is the same in God's eyes is really the stuff of Christian mythology. Obviously, there are some nuances with God. Rahab and the discussion earlier about the Nazi's and lying is another example of a nuance with God regarding sin. I believe that one of the cases where we can intercede with prayer for a loved one is when someone is hurting his or her body by a bad health habit.

Jackie and I started smoking when we were young. In our youth, we were told smoking was good for us. I managed to quit early. She struggled with cigarettes until the end albeit she had slowed way down to about 6-7 cigarettes a day for years. The last few weeks she smoked 1-3 cigarettes a day. Her smoker's cough stopped years ago when she slowed dramatically down and even quit smoking completely for a while. A few years ago, she encountered a health problem and she suddenly started coughing up blood clots about the size of a nickel. To say we were both horrified is an under statement. As she went through various medical tests, I kept interceding for divine healing. I prayed for each test to come back negative and they did.

Myth—God Heals Everyone

I believe my prayer for Jackie fit in the framework of what Apostle John taught. Jackie was healed and we never did find out what was wrong. I was gleeful because I knew it was the power of God that healed her. About 2-3 years later another bout occurred which was even worse. The blood clots were larger this time, about the size of a quarter. Again I went into a prayer mode and she was healed. Jackie had undergone a series of very sophisticated tests and they all came back negative. The final one was to go down into her lungs with a scope and look. I prayed that God would make her lungs look exactly like she had never smoked in her life. Smoker's lungs look real black compared to the pinkish tissue of a non-smoker's lung. I was in the room as the doctor went down into her lungs investigating the tissue. I remember how befuddled he looked as all he could see was normal healthy lung tissue. I specifically asked him: "What did you see?" He told me that he only saw healthy lung tissue and did not find anything. Again Jackie was healed and the doctor surmised that she probably had a tear on the lung tissue that was responsible for the blood. The doctor never really found anything solid. I knew that once again God healed her.

How did I pray? I got close to God in my spirit and I envisioned God's hands going over every area of Jackie's body and organs that needed to be healed. As I saw HIS hands touching her organs and body, I saw HIS healing over those areas that needed a healing touch. I have used the same method to pray for several other healings. I also meditated and spoke God's Word about healing from a list I have written in my Bible.

In the hospital on February 26, I was reading my healing verses and studying the Bible for one of the chapters I was writing. I kept focused on the Word in Luke 8:50. Jesus says: "Do not be afraid; only believe, and she will be made well." As I waited for Jackie to return from her invasive tests, I kept praising God and saying — "I believe FATHER." This time, it was not to be a divine healing. Like Apostle Paul, my prayers ran up against God's grace. And like Paul, God's grace would have to be sufficient for I did not have any answers that made sense to my limited human understanding. This time, Jackie's sickness would have to be stuffed into the "I can't handle it LORD" gunnysack. We never stopped praying for Jackie's healing right up to the end. We also never stopped praising God for the gift of Jackie's life.

Myth—God Heals Everyone

Smoking is a contributing factor in cancer and so is any form of alcohol. Jackie liked to have a Bacardi rum and diet-coke drink. She was a social drinker who finally stopped drinking prior to Christmas last year. Over 75% of pancreatic problems are associated with alcohol. It usually results in pancreatitis, a particularly serious illness in which the pancreas stops functioning to some extent. Smokers also have a 2-4 times risk of developing pancreatic cancer than nonsmokers. In Jackie's last words she writes: "Could I have caused the cancer? Maybe! But not on purpose." Not one of us knows. Jackie led a pretty healthy and clean life overall. She was also a very healthy eater. It could be that her pancreatic cancer could have been prevented if we had just planted her garden the year before. We had her pancreas tested early on and all its functions were within normal zones. Go figure. It can certainly all boil down to a lack of nutrients at the cellular level within Jackie's body. I will talk about this shortly.

We can contrast our typical bad habits and the sins against the temple of our body [over eating, obesity, smoking, moderate drinking, purging, lack of exercise, etc.] with what the Apostle Paul refers to as the "works of the flesh" in Galatians 5:19-20. Paul teaches us that those who practice the works of the flesh "will not inherit the kingdom of God." Here is Paul's list. One can observe that the world is filled with people who live in these works of the flesh. In fact, ministries even teach that some of these works are okay with God. Note that the list does not reflect what we would generally think of as bad health habits. This is a list of sins leading to death.

Adultery	Fornication (unmarried intercourse)
Uncleanness	Licentiousness (sexual immorality)
Idolatry	Sorcery
Hatred	Contentions
Jealousies	Outbursts of wrath
Selfish ambitions	Dissensions
Heresies	Envy
Murders	Drunkenness
Revelries	Etc. (the like)

DON'T LET BAD HABITS EVOLVE INTO SIN THAT LEADS TO DEATH!

Myth—God Heals Everyone

List Of Healing Verses I Use For Your Own Prayers!

    Exodus 15:26   Matthew 8:17
    Exodus 23:25-26   Matthew 18:18-19
    Deut. 7:15   Mark 10:52
    Psalm 34:17   Mark 16:17-18
    Psalm 107:20   Luke 8:50
    Psalm 118:5   Luke 10:19
    Isaiah 53:4-5   Romans 8:11
    Malachi 4:2   1 Peter 2:24

In the case of a sin against someone's own body, it is not generally a sin that leads to immediate death. However, it is a slow killer of our own flesh. It is akin to the mythical story of a frog placed in a pan of cold water. According to the story, when the water is slowly heated, the frog will be lulled to sleep and eventually get cooked alive. It could prevent its death if it were smarter. The story is illustrative of what happens in our human bodies, but many are not able to stop bad habits. Like the mythical frog, we think that nothing is amiss with how we are living our lives. We are wrong.

In our teens and twenties, we get away with beating our bodies pretty badly with a variety of health habits. As we get into our thirties, we then observe that some of our health habits are a cause of physical pain. Maybe it is something small like the Italian hot sauce that we always liked, but which is no longer tolerated by our stomach? Maybe it is that persistent cough which we know is linked to our smoking? Maybe it is the slow buildup of the alcoholic drinks, because we no longer get a buzz very easily. Now we need 3-4 drinks instead of 1-2 because our body is building up a tolerance for the alcohol. If we don't change our bad health habits by the time we are in the mid forties, it is payback time. Verily I say to you that I bear witness to many premature deaths beginning at age 45 and many are linked directly to bad health habits that were sins against the body. Jackie and I had cousins who both drank themselves to death at an early age. It was not God's plan!

Think Habits, Change Habits!

Myth—God Heals Everyone

We like to think of ourselves as an island unto ourselves. What we do is our own business. Right? Wrong! What we do affects everyone we love. If your bad habits lead to your premature death, you deprive your children and grandchildren of precious love. It is clear in God's Word that your body is HIS temple once you begin to walk in HIS light. God owns a part of your flesh. It is also clear in the Word that as husband and wife we own a part of each other's bodies. Therefore, if you are married and claim to walk with God and abuse your body with bad habits, you also abuse a body that belongs to both God and your spouse. Think habits and change habits was good advice I heard three decades ago. The truth of that maxim still reigns.

The saying to simply "listen to what your body tells you" is also true. As we age, our bodies change. If we don't alter calorie intake as we get into the thirties, the excess calories our bodies no longer need will be expressed on our guts, thighs or hips. The plain truth is our bodies are in a constant state of change. Literally billions of cells die each day inside our bodies and new cells are created. If you learn what happens at the cellular level of the body each day, it will astound you. The body requires more attention as we age. Learn to listen to what your body is trying to tell you. Learn to alter your habits to improve your own health. What is the best insurance policy you can own? It is a temple of the living God where the caretaker knows what a precious gift it is to own and learns how to properly take care of it.

My advice to you is to simply dump your bad health habits before they become a factor in your need for healing. And don't bother praying for the healing of your lungs if you are not willing to stop smoking. Don't bother praying for your diseased liver if you are a chronic alcoholic who refuses to stop drinking. Don't tell me that you can't stop. I know for a fact that you *will* eventually stop. The big question is whether you will have the courage to help yourself before it is too late. Note also that you can pray for God's help to give you the courage to quit. God does expect you to exert some common sense over the health issues of your own body. After all, God has built into your body some amazing healing powers on a cellular level.

This is to say that you have a direct role to play in your own healing. When you accept that fact, you'll understand God's medical health plan.

Myth—God Heals Everyone

You must exert your own will power to change your own bad habits. No one can do it for you. If your bad health habits lead to your premature death, you only have yourself to blame. Systematically killing your own body is not God's plan. HIS is a natural death, an appointed time. Likewise, the 11-year old boy just killed had his own life cut short by an adult driver exercising her own 66-year old free will. Killing that boy with her car was not God's plan. To the extent your free will intersects with another's and it results in their premature death, it is not the plan of God Almighty! HIS plan is defined in Genesis in which HE says we can live to be 120 years old and in Jeremiah where a future with hope is promised. Of course, this assumes you are smarter than the mythical frog and are also not accidentally killed.

> **"For I know the plans I have for you, says the LORD. They are plans for good and not for disaster, to give you a future and a hope." Jeremiah 29:11 NLT**

Don't blame all the evil in this earth on God Almighty. Man's sin, free will, ignorance and errant ways are responsible for a lot of it and the balance of the evil is Satan at work. Aside from the long life and future of hope, God also provides us with good things. That is God's nature.

> **"Every good gift and every perfect gift is from above, and comes down from the FATHER of lights, with whom there is no variation or shadow of turning." James 1:17**

> **"And we know that all things work together for good to those who love God, to those who are the called according to HIS purpose." Romans 8:28**

We Have A Responsibility For Our Own Heath!

So we can influence our longevity by our health habits. Our life can also be cut short by events beyond our control. However, in both cases, a life ends prematurely; it does not end by God's design. God's plan was to have us reach our "appointed time." Now, let's examine some graphics.

Myth—God Heals Everyone

Prior to yesterday's funeral, God gave me three illustrations to explain why some deaths are not at HIS appointed time. To start with, we can imagine that in God's design our spirit-souls were to move smoothly through life in the right direction peacefully coexisting with all other souls. This is represented in the graphic below showing seven lines with arrows pointing to the right. Each line is representative of a spirit-soul on this earth. The loops around the individual spirit-souls represent one or more groups of spirit-souls that fellowship and share life together. People might belong to more than one group and in this way our society grows by sharing life with each other. Sometimes there is a loner that likes to stay to his or her self [bottom arrow]. In God's design, we all get along. Now enters sin.

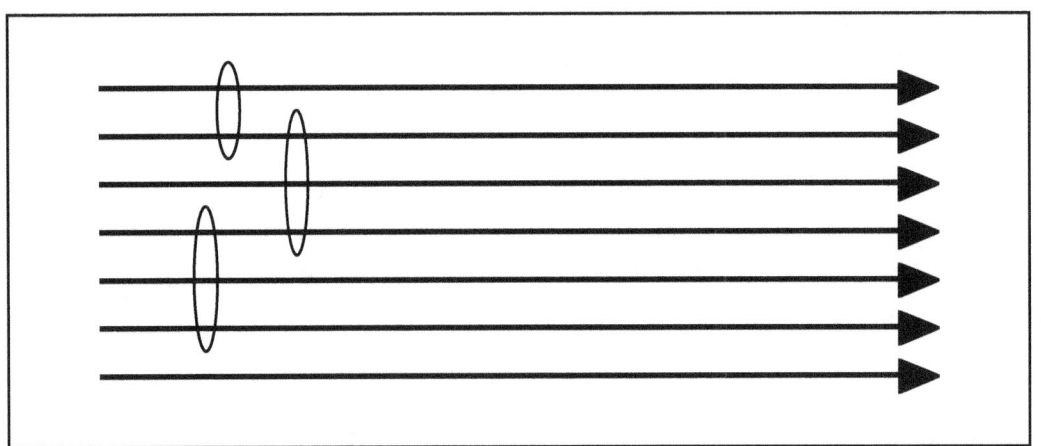

The Spirit-Soul Life As God Designed

The perfect plan of God did not unfold as HE intended once man had sinned and the knowledge of evil entered man's thoughts. You've already learned that Satan is the winner of the massive amount of spirit-souls on this earth. What happened in Noah's time is set to happen once again. Few follow the narrow path and are saved according to Jesus. As a direct result of the knowledge of evil, this world belongs to Satan [at least temporarily] and we do live in a life of literal chaos. Instead of all spirit-souls moving in the "right" direction like God had intended, some move all over the place crisscrossing one another and in essence crashing into one another. Some move in direct opposition to God's will. This causes many contentions.

Copyright 2005 Edward G. Palmer, All Rights Reserved.

Myth—God Heals Everyone

All the arrows that move in a direction not intended by God represent the chaos in this life that confronts our spirit-souls. The dots are areas of conflict and contention, because of opposing forces at work. It is one reason that someone dies prematurely because of the influence of a bad habit force that cannot be overcome. It is one reason that a 66-year old female driver crashes into an 11-year old boy standing at the end of his driveway and kills him. We were supposed to peacefully co-exist, live a long life and then die a natural death at God's appointed time. Now, however, all bets are off *unless* we get close to God and take advantage of HIS protection to the maximum degree possible. God will protect HIS people, but remember that HE has a bigger picture in which we only see a small amount. Go back to the graphic on page 380 in chapter 11 if you haven't fully grasped God's bigger picture.

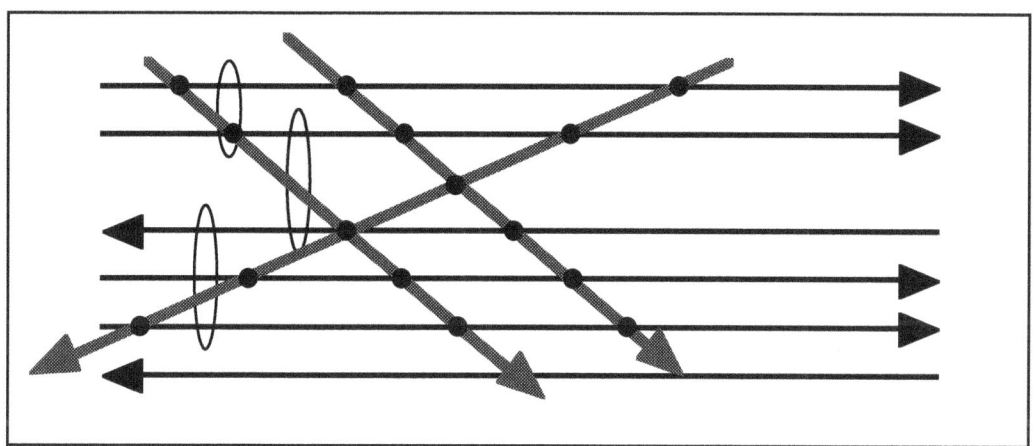

The Spirit-Soul Life In Satan's World

When God says that HIS grace is sufficient—you will never fully understand why. Like Paul and myself, where healing did not result from prayers, it may be a bitter pill to swallow. Yet God knows what is best for us and our understanding will be fulfilled at a later date when we see our LORD and HIS Son. For now, ponder the graphic above and try to understand that we live in a world that we were never supposed to live in. It is a world of evil desires and works of the flesh that conflict with God's ways. God has drawn a line down the middle of all cultures; choose a side. Suffering will increase worldwide as sin increases and morality sinks further.

Myth—God Heals Everyone

From the Gnostic Gospel of Philip [3] we read the following concerning God's protection given to sincere believers.

> "The powers do not see those who are clothed in the perfect light, and consequently are not able to detain them. One will clothe himself in this light sacramentally in the union."

For years I have felt the protection of God on my life. It is an unusual feeling of security that moves with you wherever you go. Listen to some Bible verses that speak of the protection that God provides.

> **Satan said: "Have YOU not made a hedge around him, around his household, and around all that he has on every side? YOU have blessed the work of his hands, and his possessions have increased in the land." Job 1:10**

> **Jesus said: "I do not pray that YOU [FATHER] should take them out of the world, but that YOU should keep them from the evil one [and protect them]." John 17:15**

> "For HE shall give HIS angels charge over you, to keep you in all your ways." Psalm 91:11

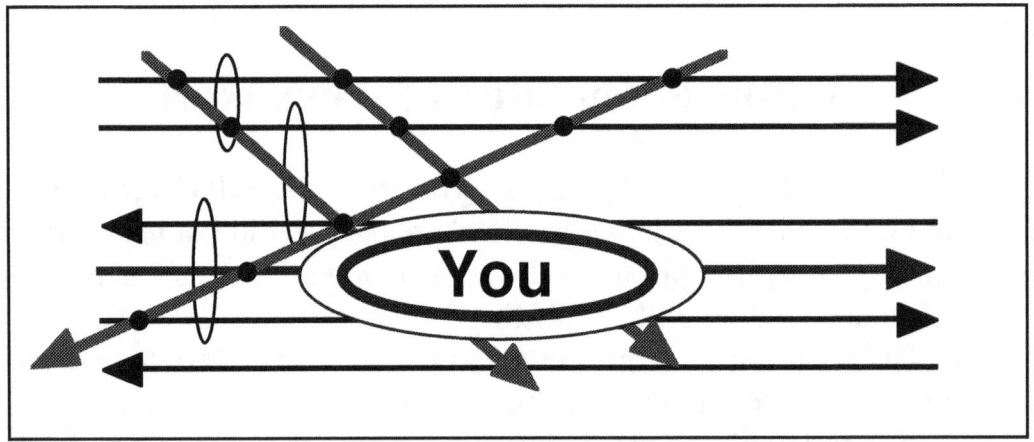

You In Satan's World With Holy Spirit

Myth—God Heals Everyone

It is possible to move through this world with a high degree of God's protection. The graphic above shows a hedge of protection that surrounds God's servant. Think of it as a force field that is able to deflect the evil of this world so that its full impact is not felt. It is the result of putting on the full armor of God. I have seen many examples of God's protection.

Just a few weeks ago, my adopted granddaughter Amy survived a near fatal car accident in which the state patrol officer said was unbelievable and almost 100% fatal. Her car was hit head on by a drunk driver driving down the interstate highway in the wrong direction. The rescue workers had to literally cut her out of the car with a machine. The femur bone on each leg was broken in two and she had to have them pinned and screwed together. She is only 20-years old and had a lot of other physical damage, but I am happy to report she is now doing fine and will heal and walk again soon. Where did God's protection come in? It came in the form of surviving the crash. Youth also plays a role in the healing of our bodies. When Amy was just a little girl, both her and I lost our big toe nail. Hers grew back in only three weeks. Mine took a year to grow back. As we age, the length of our years becomes a factor in healing. Make no mistake about it.

Like Amy, God offered similar protection for Jesus and his disciples. It often came in the form of survival or getting out of the way just in the nick of time. It often involved pain and suffering too. Study Paul's travels for some classic illustrations of trouble coupled with divine protection.

Last week my nine-month old grandson Braiden started choking on a bottle-cap sized chunk of jagged glass at the back of his throat. Brandee, my daughter-in-law managed to get it out. To all of our amazement, Braiden did not have as much as a scratch. We believe that this is divine protection and an answer to our weekly prayers. We ask God for protection on our family every time we pray in our Bible study and we have seen many such miracles.

Healing is a sticky point for many Christians who would still assert that God always heals. Usually there is a caveat indicating that of course it depends upon one's faith. And if there is sin in your life, all bets are off. Does the Word teach us that healing always comes as a result of prayer?

Myth—God Heals Everyone

Suppose for a moment that a Charismatic fellow claims that God will always heal him. To illustrate the point, he jumps out in front of a semi truck with 18 wheels and gets mangled. After months in the hospital and two years of physical therapy, he says to you that it proves he was right. I'll tell you what it proves. It proves he was stupid and that God was gracious. When he says he can do it again to prove the truth of the point, do you think he has much upstairs in the brain department? If he does, do you think God will still be gracious? God's grace is at the center of all divine healing.

> **Jesus said to them, "When you pray, say YOUR [Yahweh, God Almighty, FATHER] will be done on earth as it is in Heaven." Luke 11:2**

Prayer. LORD, teach us to understand YOUR sovereignty, grace and mercy. Teach us to pray like Jesus did and seek YOUR will and not ours.

One only needs to carefully study the story of King David. He fasted and prayed while his son was stricken. In the end, the child died. When asked why he stopped his grieving, he gives us an enlightening illustration of God's sovereignty. Go back and study this lack of healing in 2 Samuel 12:21-23 despite the sincere prayer of King David. Therefore, between King David and King Hezekiah, we have both situations when it comes to healing as a result of prayer. In one case healing was denied and in the other healing took place. But in both cases, it was the grace of God. Both David and Hezekiah acknowledged God's sovereignty over their life and death. Do you? If not, death will not make much sense to you and your suffering will continue unabated when a loved one dies. You will not understand like King David and I do that you too will go to see your loved one some day, but that your loved one will not come back to earth to see you.

But Edward you say, Jesus always healed people! To which I would reply: "You are misinformed of biblical facts." Consider the following Bible verse if you think Jesus always healed everyone.

> **"Now he did not do many mighty works there because of their unbelief." Matthew 13:55-58 NKJV**

Myth—God Heals Everyone

> "And he did not do many miracles there because of their unbelief." Matthew 13:58 NASB

> "And he did not work many miracles there because of their lack of faith." Matthew 13:58 NJB

> "He didn't work many miracles there because of their lack of faith." Matthew 13:58 GW

Here is the full context from the NLT translation.

> " 'He's just a carpenter's son, and we know Mary, his mother, and his brothers-James, Joseph, Simon, and Judas. All his sisters live right here among us. What makes him so great?' And they were deeply offended and refused to believe in him. Then Jesus told them, 'A prophet is honored everywhere except in his own hometown and among his own family.' And so he did only a few miracles there because of their unbelief." Matthew 13:55-58 NLT

I heard a radio preacher illustrate this verse in which he proclaimed: "God *refused* to do miracles in HIS hometown because of their lack of faith." Note the confusion of who Jesus is. His teaching was that *God chose* not to do miracles in HIS hometown. The interpretation is an error. The correct reading should be that Jesus [not God] was unable to do even more miracles because of the lack of faith in *his* hometown. You can learn two things from this verse. First of all, Jesus did not heal everyone. At least he did not in his own hometown, because that much is implicit. Secondly, our individual and even collective faith plays a role within our healing.

Jesus asks the poignant question: "Do you want to be healed?"

> "When Jesus saw him lying there, and knew that he already had been in that condition a long time, he said to him, 'Do you want to be made well?' " John 5:6

Myth—God Heals Everyone

Personal Desire & Will Power Matters To God!

Clearly our faith or lack of faith plays an important role in healing. Jesus gives us plenty of illustrations where faith was a direct attribute in achieving a miraculous healing. However, listen, personal desire for healing and individual will power also play a role. Isn't that why Jesus asked the question: "Do you want to be healed?" The plain truth is that many people do not want to be healed, but would not openly say that to love ones.

Some people, in long-term disabilities, want to continue to live in the misery because unbelievably they have come to look forward to the attention and pity of others. Not to mention they have grown accustomed to some very low expectations for their life. Yet there are many other people who just want to move on to their heavenly home. They are put out about this earthly life. Some even feel the "pull" from the heavenly side as being much stronger than the "pull" from this earthly side. To put it simply, they want to just check out in as natural way as possible in God's eyes.

I had the chance to talk to a banking acquaintance of mine named Carolyn. At one time, we had attended the same church. A mutual friend told me that she had cancer and only a short time to live. God told me to call her and tell her about the nutritional supplements that I had uncovered for healing cancer at the cellular level. There are, surprisingly, many natural cures available for cancer that are being stifled and kept hidden from the public's view. Perhaps Carolyn could use some of them, even though we had only a limited amount of success with Jackie?

As it turned out, Carolyn was not in the slight bit interested about any potential cancer cures on the cellular level. She had a strong faith and was intent on moving on. In fact, she told me that the heavenly pull was much stronger for her than anything on this earth. That included family. She indicated to me that she was trying to prepare the family so they would understand. It sounded like the family wanted her to undergo various treatment options, which she was soundly rejecting. She was ready for her heavenly mansion that she knew was already prepared for her.

Copyright 2005 Edward G. Palmer, All Rights Reserved.

Myth—God Heals Everyone

Virtually everyone in front of Jackie and I on her side of the family has already died and moved on except one aunt. Jackie also looked forward to moving on and this was an undeniable attribute that impacted her healing. When my small church group laid hands on her, she said the magical words of "thank you Jesus" and that very night began to arise again. The following two weeks were astonishing to me. Clearly God had touched her body that night and we all knew it. Yet, it was the proverbial last gasp of energy that flowed out of her. I enjoyed watching Jackie have some fun once again.

In our many talks and cries together, Jackie always told me that she did not want to leave me. Yet she persistently prepared my life for her absence. Like her father Archie did for her mother, she prepared me for her death. God prepared my heart for the separation of our flesh.

All of this is tough stuff for me and once again I am back in tears just thinking about the events that took place. At one point, I would estimate that at a minimum there were over 10,000-20,000 people praying for Jackie along with numerous churches. Virtually everyone I came into contact with was asked if they would have their church, synagogue or mosque pray for Jackie. I even received notice that her name was placed on a saint's list for prayer in perpetuity. Wow, perpetuity? Well, Jackie *was* special! That should have given me another clue; she is the only person I know on the list.

Pray earnestly in great faith for your own healing. There is no doubt this helps. You can even wear sackcloth and fast like many biblical people did during times of sickness and grieving. Yet there is still the sovereignty issue of God's graciousness and mercy as explained by Moses, King David, and Apostle Paul. Come to God with a loyal heart having walked by HIS definition of righteousness. That is my best advice to you in these matters in which divine healing is needed and is sought. Simply get as close to God as you can. True faith begins by accepting the reality into our hearts that we do serve a living God. Here are more verses where faith is an attribute.

Strong Faith & A Loyal Heart Matter To God!

Myth—God Heals Everyone

> "But Jesus turned around, and when he saw her he said, 'Be of good cheer, daughter; your faith has made you well.' And the woman was made well from that hour." Matthew 9:22

> "Then he touched their eyes, saying, 'According to your faith let it be to you.'" Matthew 9:29

> "Then Jesus answered and said to her, 'O woman, great is your faith! Let it be to you as you desire.' And her daughter was healed from that very hour." Matthew 15:28

> "Then Jesus said to him, 'Go your way; your faith has made you well.' And immediately he received his sight and followed Jesus on the road." Mark 10:52

It is not just your faith that matters when it comes to healing prayer. God makes it clear that those who pray for you can influence the outcome. Therefore, join your faith with others who trust in God for the outcome you need. Again, this doesn't always get you what you want. However, if you ask anything according to God's will, it is sure to come true.

> "Now this is the confidence that we have in HIM, that if we ask anything according to HIS will, HE hears us. And if we know that HE hears us, whatever we ask, we know that we have the petitions that we have asked of HIM."
> 1 John 5:14-15

Likewise, if you ask anything not in God's will, it will not come true.

> "You ask and do not receive, because you ask amiss." James 4:3

What should you do when *you* are sick? Follow James' instructions.

> "Is anyone among you sick? Let him [this is you] call for the elders [prayer warriors] of the church, and let them pray over him, anointing him with oil in the name of the Lord."

Myth—God Heals Everyone

> **"And the prayer of faith will save the sick, and the Lord will raise him up. And if he has committed sins, he will be forgiven." James 5:14-15**

> **"Confess your trespasses to one another, and pray for one another, that you may be healed. The effective, fervent prayer of a righteous man avails much." James 5:16**

A Prayer Of Faith Will Save The Sick!

Your healing goal in terms of prayer should be to get into an effective and fervent prayer. This should be with one or more righteous persons whose hearts are loyal to God. Many who read the above verses would say to me that they prove God *will* heal us. I cannot emphasize a singular fact enough. You simply cannot lift single verses out of the context of the entire Bible. To do so ignores God's bigger picture and His eternal character that I discussed in chapter 11. You cannot assume that God will heal you unless you also recognize His sovereignty and that He might not heal you. Your job is to exercise your faith to the best of your ability and then to simply put your fate into the hands of God Almighty. Having done all, stand on faith.

> **"Therefore take up the whole armor of God, that you may be able to withstand in the evil day, and having done all, to stand." Ephesians 6:13**

I have witnessed both wild success in the realm of divine healing and also some sad disappointments. I can never really say why healing comes to some and why it doesn't come to others, except for God's bigger picture. I say this because I have witnessed the strength of powerful prayer in both of these outcomes. Therefore, I know that the prayer of faith was answered in some cases and was not answered in other cases.

To my young friends at a local Charismatic church that claims God will always heal, I say: "Go check and find out how many people died in your 10,000 member church this last year and come tell me the same thing."

Myth—God Heals Everyone

If God always healed, we would not suffer so many losses each year within the Church at large despite many solid prayers of faith. Real prayers of faith are made in the manner of how Jesus taught us to pray. Jesus taught us to pray that God's will be done. Ultimately, God is not a slot machine whereby one simply makes a demand upon the anointing and gets what he wants. That is the stuff of Christian mythology in the "name it and claim it" crowd. Real sincere faith will yield to God in every situation and we are taught nothing less than that in the Holy Bible we profess to believe in. This doesn't mean you should not exercise your faith. It is just the opposite, exercise your faith and then trust in God to deal with the outcome.

What should you do if you get that subtle message inside of you to pray for someone? You should pray regardless of the time of day or night that you get that unction from God's Spirit. Your prayer may make the difference between life and death. What should you do if you get the message to go down to a hospital or nursing home to pray for someone? Get up and go down and pray for them, even if you do not know why. Too many people ignore the unction of the Holy Spirit in their lives. It is one reason our families suffer needlessly in this life. Here are some prayer examples.

A Healed Heart
Our friend Kathryn was purging her food with an over the counter syrup used to induce vomiting. She was bulimic. By the time we learned of the problem, she crashed and was on her deathbed in the hospital. Her heart had expanded physically to four times its normal size as a result of her eating disorder and uncontrolled bad habit. She was placed on a heart machine for a longer period of time than anyone in history; she was given less than a 5% chance of survival when the machine was removed. Our family mounted a prayer vigil at the hospital and spoke healing over her body using some of the verses shown earlier. Eventually, she was healed and is an example to others about the eating disorder. It was divine healing and no one can deny what had happened to her and how God *intervened* to save her life.

Legs Untouched
Prayer for my dear friend's wife was met with virtually no change. She is still restricted to a wheel chair and both legs are still totally dysfunctional.

Myth—God Heals Everyone

Many Wheel Chairs Untouched

My personal observation is that people in wheel chairs usually remain there if it has been many years. I have never witnessed a physically reconstructive healing such as a spinal regeneration or the growth of new bones, etc. We know that this kind of healing did occur in the Bible. Therefore, I personally believe in such healings and have thrown my faith into prayer many times. I myself have witnessed only those whose bodies were deathly sick healed by the prayer of faith as the Apostle James taught. Why healing occurs in some cases and not in others may be related to God's glory as Jesus explains.

> **Jesus said: "Go and tell John the things which you hear and see: The blind see and the lame walk; the lepers are cleansed and the deaf hear; the dead are raised up and the poor have the gospel preached to them." Matthew 11:4-5**

> **"As Jesus was walking along, he saw a man who had been blind from birth. 'Teacher,' his disciples asked him, 'why was this man born blind? Was it a result of his own sins or those of his parents?' 'It was not because of his sins or his parents' sins,' Jesus answered. 'He was born blind so the power of God could be seen in him.' " John 9:1-3 NLT**

Sometimes a serious physical abnormality exists in people simply so God's power can be seen in that person. It is a witness to all when someone who suffers physical limitations is still able to magnify God. Their faith is a huge testimony because of their physical limitations. Many blind are able to do things those with sight cannot do. Many lame are able to do things the physically able cannot do. I know of blind people who play music even though they cannot read music sheets. I know of people without arms who play guitars with their feet. Many such examples can be illustrated. How does this happen? It is accomplished through faith in God and all of the success of the disabled is a living testimony to the able bodied that God does exist and inspires people to lead remarkable lives despite serious limitations.

It is a sad commentary that the able bodied often cannot deal with bad health habits while the physically disabled accomplish wondrous things.

Myth—God Heals Everyone

Death Cheated

I remember the moment I got the message to go down to the hospital and lay hands on my good friend Al for his healing. I can't recall that I had ever laid hands on someone who was on a deathbed before. Al was close to death from hepatitis destroying his liver. My son-in-law James a man of similar faith, worked with me at the time. I said to him: "James, God gave me the message to go down tonight and pray for Al, do you want to come with?" James responded: "I got the same message, what time do you want to go?"

> *You might ask exactly how either one of us got a message from God? It is simple, the Spirit of Yahweh spoke within us as explained by Jesus. Get used to listening to HIS sweet soft voice and learn to understand when it is HE who speaks in you. If it is good, makes complete sense and lines up with the Word, you can be confident that the voice you hear inside is from God.*

"Do not worry about how or what you should speak. For it will be given to you in that hour what you should speak; for it is not you who speak, but the Spirit of your FATHER [Yahweh] who speaks in you." Matthew 10:19-20

By the time James and I arrived on the isolation ward that Al was in, he was looking pretty bad. His skin was darkened as if he had been sunbathing for months and his eyes were yellow. There was little doubt his body was stricken with a deadly disease. Al explained that he was unable to move much and was very weak. He could barely lift his arm up. I asked if his parish priest had laid hands on his body for divine healing. Al explained that the priest had been there three times and prayed. I ascertained from the conversation that no one had yet laid hands on him for healing, even though many had prayed for him over several weeks. I knew we would be deep into the Spirit as we laid hands on him and prayed; it meant speaking in tongues. I told Al that when we were done, he would know that hands had been laid on him for divine healing. I also told him to not pay attention to what we were doing or what we were saying. I said: "Close your eyes Al and simply reach out and grab the healing that God wants you to have. Thank God for your healing, because it is not your time to die."

Myth—God Heals Everyone

I started the prayer and for about twenty minutes James and I altered praying in and out of tongues for Al's healing. To this day I still remember God's awesome presence in that hospital room. All I could see in my spirit were bright lights and fireworks going off. At the end, God gave my spirit total satisfaction that healing was done. I told James it was time to go. God healed Al and in only a few hours he was up and shaving. Moving for the first time in days. But that is not the most amazing part of the story.

Earlier that very day, Al underwent another liver test. The results this time showed his liver was in need of a transplant. It was no longer functioning. As the doctor came into the room to give Al the bad news, he found Al sitting upright in a chair looking revived from death. Once again, a medical doctor was left befuddled.

Death Cheated Temporarily

It was a few years later that my sister Barb wound up in the ICU ward of a hospital in northern Minnesota after scheduled surgery went awry. When my brother and I got the message of her condition, she was near death. We decided to go up and lay hands on her for healing. I was terrified at the time that my own faith would not be good enough. This time, I was so emotional and in tears over her impending death, I simply did not even know if I could pray a "prayer of faith." I was shook. I asked James to come with his faith.

By the time we got to Barb's ICU room, the death rattle was already on her body. Her kidneys had both stopped functioning for days and her lungs were now almost filled up with fluid. Death was imminent and there was little doubt about it. As we prayed and cried, I was not given all the input from God that occurred during Al's healing prayer. We went back to her home for the night having placed her firmly into God's loving hands.

The next morning when we got back to the hospital, both kidneys had started working again and Barb's lungs were now clear. I was stunned. I asked the nurse when her lungs had cleared up. The attending nurse didn't have any answers. While she was in the hospital, it was my privilege to pray with her to receive the Holy Spirit. I watched Barb recover and go home. It gave me a chance to visit with her at length and to let her know how much I loved her and what she had meant to me in this life. We were able to share a lot.

Myth—God Heals Everyone

I remember the last time I visited with her. She explained how much pain she was in and I told her to give everything over to God. That night as she lay in bed and I was studying in the living room, I remember hearing her cry out in pain to God for relief. It was a heart-breaking cry from the bowels of Barb's soul. She screamed out loud: "Oh God, please help me!" The tears flow freely in my eyes again as I remember joining with her in a prayer for God to heal her hurting body. Barb died about three months after we resurrected her body in the ICU ward. I will always be grateful for the extra time that God gave me with her. When she died, I knew it was her time. God had indeed honored the family by giving us time to share and say goodbye.

Of course there are many more details to the events I am relating to you in this chapter. If I tried to cover all of them, each event would be worthy of its own book. This morning as I was talking with God, HE gave me this simple formula for HIS divine healing. Take it to heart. In addition, God gave me the illustration of Jesus' prayer, which follows.

Prayer of Faith = Belief in Healing + Trust in God's Bigger Picture

When you go to exercise your "prayer of faith" — the two ingredients you need are true belief that God will heal someone coupled with a trust that if God does not, it is because of HIS bigger picture. I mention this here, as there are different levels of faith and belief within Christianity. You must act in faith "as-if" God will deliver your loved one's healing. Many people do not believe in divine healing today. There are even people who do not believe in the resurrection. Unbelievable for Christians in both cases, but they do exist. Do not bring someone into the "prayer of faith" who does not believe in divine healing. If you do, they can literally "suck" the spiritual energy out of the prayer. It is better to have people who believe totally in healing than it is to have "anyone" who doesn't believe in healing but thinks the prayer motions are good therapy for the family.

Employ God's "As-If" Principle In "Prayers Of Faith!"

Myth—God Heals Everyone

The power of your prayers is enhanced when you deploy the biblical "as-if principle" explained by Paul in Romans 4. You literally envision in your mind and spirit the healing that God is delivering. This is to say that you do not see things as the world sees them. You know that two realities exist. One is the reality our senses detect; the other is God's reality. In God's reality, HE calls things into existence that did not exist before. In the present case, healing. Therefore, be like God and call healing into existence.

"This happened because Abraham believed in the God who brings the dead back to life and who brings into existence what didn't exist before." Romans 4:17 NLT

I flipped through two old tattered and marked up Bibles to find the "as-if" principle. My friend Norman taught it to me almost three decades ago. It works in all areas of life in situations where God doesn't have another plan for you. In any case, you should never stop praying regardless of what your senses tell you. Sometimes the nature of prayer might change like mine did with Jackie's father who died of colon cancer. We fought earnestly in prayer for healing for many months. However, his body became severely emaciated and his pain became intolerable. Eventually the nature of my prayer changed. God showed me that it was time for me to pray for mercy. That is what we then prayed for. We also told Archie that it was okay to go home. In the realm of dying and "shedding our flesh" it can get obvious that healing is not in God's bigger picture. Remember, God does not need months or years. At that moment, we need to spiritually release our loved ones. More than one person has suffered endlessly because he or she was afraid to leave a loved one. A lack of release held them in their body.

Listen. Do not unduly hold your loved ones on this earthly plain. To do so simply increases their pain and suffering. It is a very self-centered thing to do and we are taught not to live for ourselves by Christ. As a father or mother needs to give their child wings to leave the house, we all need to give our dying family members their wings to go home. My daughter asked Connie: "Do you know what to say when someone asks how many kids you have?" Connie said no. Patty replied: "Tell them you have two that can walk and one that can fly." Patty knows what it means to let go.

Myth—God Heals Everyone

Jesus Said: "Always Pray & Do Not Lose Heart!"

"Then [Jesus] spoke a parable to them, that men [and women] always ought to pray and not lose heart."
                                                    Luke 18:1

Your spiritual understanding should include the entire word of God and not just narrow sections of the Bible. God's context is the entire Word. That is why the healing of Jesus talked about in Matthew 9:35 is not applicable to Nazareth. Did not God teach us something else about that particular "hometown?" The miracles of Jesus were done at the direction of Yahweh. Therefore, pray to Yahweh your God just like Jesus did. Realize like Jesus did that not all prayers are answered, as we want them to be.

"When things go well, be glad; but when they go ill, consider this: God has set the one alongside the other in such a way that no one can find out what is to happen afterwards [next]." Ecclesiastes 7:14 REB

Spiritual translation: You never know what life will bring next!

I believe I have talked about this before; Jesus did not want to leave us. He did not want to die on that cross and his prayer to God reflected that clear thought in his mind. His willingness to do so was a result of his love for Yahweh [his FATHER and God]. Listen again to a prayer from Jesus that was not answered the way he wanted. If God did not answer all of Jesus' prayers in the manner he wanted, why should you be surprised if some of your prayers are not answered in the way you want them to be answered?

Jesus said: "Abba, FATHER, all things are possible for YOU. Take this cup away from me; nevertheless, not what I will, but what YOU will." Mark 14:36

Are you willing to yield to God's will just like Jesus Christ did? If not, why? Are you not supposed to follow the example of Christ?

Copyright 2005 Edward G. Palmer, All Rights Reserved.

Book of Edward—Chapter 15

Myth—God Heals Everyone

It is evening of December 8 now and I am at the final area of this chapter that God wanted me to discuss—the area of instruction, knowledge and nutrition. God says that His people die for lack of instruction and lack of knowledge. So, let's discuss the area of nutrition and its impact at the cellular level. God has placed inside our body tremendous healing power at the cellular level. Each cell is akin to a small manufacturing plant. Like the electricity and utilities that keep our homes functioning, our cells require various nutrients so that they can properly function. Literally billions of cells die each day we live; new ones are created. This cycle of cellular death and life in our bodies keeps us alive. However, if something goes awry at the cellular level, sickness and disease set in. In fact, it is possible that nutrition can make our body friendly to disease. Likewise, it is possible that nutrition can make our body extremely resistant to disease.

A few days ago, I caught a television special on alternative nutrition. One example on the show was a man who had pancreatic cancer and was sent home to die. As he and his wife searched for an alternative healing option, they wound up in the New York City office of an alternative doctor. These are doctors who use nutraceutical products instead of or in addition to pharmaceutical products. Let me explain. When I talk about nutrition in the cellular sense, I am talking about the nutrition found in vitamins, herbs, greens and other food supplement formulations. Instead of pushing drugs from pharmaceutical companies, alternative medical doctors specialize in treating the body's needs at a cellular level with natural nutrients.

When finished, the pancreatic cancer patient left the doctor's office with instructions to consume about 100 pills per day. He was also told to take four coffee enemas daily to keep his colon clean. Strangely enough, my research came to similar conclusions and I crafted a daily game plan for Jackie. She ruled out enemas and I had to restrict the pill intake to about 50 per day at a maximum. For someone who never consumed a lot of vitamins, this was a mountain for Jackie to climb. God has given me a couple of insights about this. First, pray for yourself while you are healthy, because when you are sick and on a deathbed—you may have to rely on others. It may be difficult during those times to pray. Secondly, when sick, it is often very hard to consume any volume of pills. Especially 50-100 per day!

Myth—God Heals Everyone

Jackie couldn't deal with the volume of nutrients needed daily. The man traveling to New York died after five months. He also couldn't take in the volume of nutrients needed? I was sick a couple of weeks ago and I can tell you that I myself couldn't take in the 30 or so nutrients [pills] I take in the mornings at the current time. My stock is low now or else this would be closer to 50 in the morning and another 20 at night. Therefore, one major problem when stage IV cancer sets in is the sheer volume of nutrients that are needed to counteract the onslaught of the disease at the cellular level.

I won't be able to discuss much here, but I want to point out a few things I have learned. I literally have a two-inch thick three-ring binder on cancer cures. It is too much to talk about here. However, I have included a list of nutrients I found for Jackie in the appendix for you. You will also find some additional instructions and cancer resources.

Today there is an attack from pharmaceutical companies and various government agencies against both alternative medical technologies and most nutritional supplements [nutraceuticals]. I know of one individual thrown into jail for selling apricot seeds and the drug form of its vitamin B17, a known cancer-fighting nutrient. I know of two alternative medicine doctors that the FDA is trying to shut down because of their cancer fighting practices. It is a sad commentary that if you want the best in cancer fighting treatments, you may have to go to Mexico. If the drug companies have their way, you will need a prescription to purchase any vitamins, minerals or other nutraceuticals that are readily available over the counter to you now.

Don't think for a moment I am joking. I am not. Nutrient knowledge, which is very limited in the area of public know how is being threatened with extinction through powerful and evil forces. It is Satan at work in the realm of our healing. The first time you hear about laws affecting vitamins, contact your politicians and tell them not to mess with availability. Laws have been passed in Europe that take effect soon and may make therapeutic doses of vitamins and minerals available only with a doctor's prescription. Drugs are dumped on society with as little as 3,000 human trials. When they kill people, no one finds out until a drug company insider blows the whistle. Yet many nutritional products used by millions are now being threatened.

Copyright 2005 Edward G. Palmer, All Rights Reserved.

Myth—God Heals Everyone

This is a warning for you and your family. Keep a watchful eye out. Why are nutraceuticals needed? They are needed because the nutrients we used to get in food have been stripped away. This has occurred by topsoil erosion, chemical fertilizers and various pre-shelf treatments such as food irradiation that kill every single enzyme the food used to have. Here are some things to consider.

1. Our bodies need enzymes for various cellular tasks. They have been stripped out of our food sources. While our bodies create enzymes, as much as 50% of what we need is no longer available from the foods that we eat.
2. Some nutraceuticals are now available in liquid form, which allow us to consume therapeutic amounts and reduce the "pill intake."
3. Empty gel capsules can be obtained and nutrients can be ground up and stuffed in the gel capsules for easier intake.
4. These filled gel capsules can be taken rectally if they cannot be tolerated in the stomach.
5. Medicines can also be taken rectally in gel capsules if they cannot be taken orally or tolerated in the stomach.
6. A properly functioning body can have a bowel movement after almost every meal.
7. When the colon is cleansed, it can eliminate 7-21 pounds of waste material stuck to its sides. A clean colon allows the liver to more easily dispose of body waste and toxins.
8. Disease can flourish on the inside walls of our colon. Cleansing the colon on a regular basis minimizes this disease-breeding zone.
9. Just eating fruit seeds can be a cure for cancer. Most fruit seeds contain vitamin b17 and all fruit seeds have the same taste. Bite into apple seeds you eat so the vitamin is absorbed in your body.
10. The Internet is functioning as a knowledge base for people to communicate and many cures for cancer are being documented.
11. A simple Ph test of your saliva can tell whether or not your body is friendly or resistant to disease. Your body should test alkaline.
12. The combination of L-Lysine and vitamin C in large volumes can prevent cancer from spreading by strengthening collagen fibers. This can help with stage IV cancers when metastasis has occurred.

Myth—God Heals Everyone

Most medical doctors remain uninformed on nutraceutical approaches to treating cancer. You have to know that cancer treatment is big business in the United States. It is literally a multi-billion dollar industry. Do you think that the industry wants you eating fruit seeds and taking other nutraceuticals to heal your body? Absolutely not. Their best business strategy is to stifle the availability of who knows such information. They use the government as an enforcer to limit the introduction of alternative nutritional cures.

Apricot seeds and its chemical equivalent laetrile are sources of vitamin b17.[4] This is natural to the body and we used to get the ingredients in the fruit seeds that were mixed into jams and jellies, etc. Cultures exist in the world where cancer is unheard of and vitamin b17 consumption is one major reason. I started to eat apricots seeds, a rich source of b17, years ago. The first thing I noticed was a black growth on my right leg shrunk and fell off. Some of my friends had similar experiences. I got Jackie on the seeds immediately and resumed my intake. One seed per day per 10 pounds of body weight was stated as safe and up to six seeds in an hour. When Jackie and I were up to 15 seeds a day, both of our blood pressures dropped by 25 points. Unbelievable. I also had another growth on my shoulder shrink up and disappear. Jackie had wanted me to see a doctor about it. Apricot seeds and laetrile was our number one weapon to fight the cancer.

A good daily vitamin and mineral package with greens is also useful. I chose Dr. David Williams' <u>Daily Advantage</u>[5] for its contents. Jackie was unable to take the number of pills required and never fully got onto this regiment. However, I would highly recommend it and have used it myself.

Keeping the spread of cancer minimized is a function of L-lysine and vitamin C in high volumes. Daily therapeutic doses of 12,000 to 25,000 mg of each nutrient are suggested. I located a source of liquid vitamin C that proved useful in getting volume down. I also located liquid vitamin A & E that allowed therapeutic doses of those nutrients to be taken.

I found many other nutraceuticals like MGN3, Ambrotose and liquid oxygen. Cancer cells do not like an oxygenated body or high temperatures. Locally applied heat can elevate body temperature and kill cancer cells.

Book of Edward—Chapter 15

Myth—God Heals Everyone

One of the more interesting discoveries was the Budwig diet designed by Dr. Johanna Budwig. The combination of organic cottage cheese and flaxseed oil has been shown as a powerful cure by oxygenating the body and supplying it with an abundance of free electrons. The recipe is to consume three tablespoons of flaxseed oil mixed with eight ounces of organic cottage cheese daily. I will stop with this nutritional cure, as I am sure you get the picture. There are many nutraceutical approaches to curing cancer.

When your loved one is condemned to death by traditional medicine, why should it matter what you do in terms of seeking a cure? It shouldn't. However, if the public at large suddenly learned how to keep their bodies healthy and eliminate or even cure disease, powerful drug companies and the medical industry would lose out in a huge way. You might be surprised that when your body is healthy at the cellular level, you don't even have any cravings for junk food. In other words, a healthy body has fewer bad habits. This is another chicken and egg scenario for you to think about.

Cancer thrives on sugars and junk food because those foods feed a fermentation growth process. Deny the body access to the nutrients that cancer wants and supply it with the nutrients your cells need to fight cancer and healing is generated at the cellular level. This was God's plan when HE taught us in Genesis what we should eat as our food.

> **"And God said, 'See, I have given you every herb that yields seed which is on the face of all the earth, and every tree whose fruit yields seed; to you it shall be for food.'"**
> **Genesis 1:29**

Catch the part about seeds? I believe Jackie could have been naturally healed by food from her garden had it been planted last year. Her source of the body nutrients she needed came from the garden she tended each year. Mine came from nutraceutical products. I took the position that I usually ate junk food and needed nutraceuticals. She took the position that she usually ate good foods. Ultimately, ongoing cellular health is achieved by giving the body God gave us the nutrition its cells need. If you need healing, you should also stop eating processed food. If God didn't make it, don't eat it!

What a journey this chapter has been with God. There have been many tears as I forced myself to go back in time and relive the suffering I have witnessed. In some respects, I feel like I have truncated some valuable information that you need. Perhaps for your own healing of cancer or another disease. However, I take satisfaction that additional information on cancer is in the appendix. I studied cancer for three weeks fulltime and was amazed by the many alternative-healing nutrients and strategies I found.

Don't wait until you are confronted with a stage IV metastasized cancer in your body to change. Start your healing today by changing your lifestyle and adopting better health habits before you get sick. God said we could live to 120-years of age. HE also said we could have a life with a future and a hope. Yet verily I say to you that it is you yourself that is in the driver's seat when it comes to your own health and longevity. If you want the best of God's grace and mercy, give HIM your best health habits.

It is mythology that prayer will always bring healing. You can see that prayer is an important part of healing, but it cannot be the only part. There are many attributes of healing in the word of God. HIS sovereignty, grace and mercy play a role. Solomon taught: "Have two goals: wisdom —that is, knowing and doing what is right—and common sense. Don't let them slip away, for they fill you with living energy." Proverbs 3:21 LIV

"Wisdom gives: A long, good life; Riches; Honor; Pleasure; and, Peace." Proverbs 3:16-17 LIV

"When you submit your life and will to God, HE will take care of you in ways that you cannot imagine. That includes the gift of healing and also the gift of eternal life in a heavenly mansion." The Apostle Edward

If God's Spirit Dwells In Your Heart, Your Spirit-Soul Knows That It's A …

Myth—God Heals Everyone

Book of Edward

Chapter Sixteen
Myth—God Owns Solid Rock

"This is how we know who the children of God are and who the children of the devil are: Anyone who does not do what is right is not a child of God." 1 John 3:10 NIV

"Satan himself masquerades as an angel of light. It is not surprising, then, if his servants masquerade as servants of righteousness." 2 Cor. 11:13-15 NIV

"On the outside you [William Neal Matthews] appear to people as righteous but on the inside you are full of hypocrisy and wickedness." Matthew 23:28 NIV

"Woe to you ... hypocrite! You travel over land and sea to win a single convert, and when he becomes one, you make him twice as much a son of Hell as you are." Matthew 23:15 NIV

"But now I am writing you that you must not associate with anyone who calls himself a brother but is ... a swindler. With such a man do not even eat." 1 Cor. 5:11 NIV

But to the wicked, God says: "What right have you to recite my laws or take my covenant on your lips? You hate my instruction and cast my words behind you. When you see a thief, you join with him; you throw in your lot with adulterers. You use your mouth for evil and harness your tongue to deceit. ... These things you have done and I kept silent; you thought I was altogether like you [William Neal Matthews]. But I will rebuke you and accuse you to your face." Psalm 50:16-21 NIV

Myth—God Owns Solid Rock

This chapter is about the theft of the Elk River Assembly of God Church in Elk River, Minnesota. When it accepted William N. Matthews as senior pastor, the congregation did not know it had ushered in a servant of Satan who would steal the church over the course of the next three-four years. The church was renamed Solid Rock Church during Matthews first year as senior pastor. It was a ruse to begin the theft of the church. Verily I say to you that all of the opening verses of this chapter and countless other Bible verses apply directly to William Neal Matthews, aka Pastor Bill and others as yet unknown who profess to serve Jesus Christ, the Son of God.

Could it be that his wife, Pastor Mary Beth Matthews is innocent and ignorant of her husband's theft of Solid Rock Church? I doubt it. However, I trust that God will deal with all of those who are involved and especially those who hide in the shadows. Without question, Satan owns this church and others even if their congregations are ignorant and don't have a clue.

This chapter asks an odd question. Does God really own the church that you attend? It sounds like an oxymoron, doesn't it? Put another way, does your church *really* serve God? How do you know? It may surprise you if you look deeper into the organizing structure of your church. It could be that you are actually unsuspectingly worshipping in a den of Satan. After years of attending Solid Rock Church in Elk River, Minnesota, that is what I was surprised to find out about the place that God sent me. I unknowingly attended a church that was not owned by God; Satan owned it. It was a den of thieves. God had sent me as a witness to the theft of Solid Rock Church.

Jesus said: "[God's] house will be a house of prayer; but you have made it a den of robbers." Luke 19:46 NIV

At this point, you might think it is unfair to name names and yet that is exactly what Satan would have you believe. There is a perverse doctrine in many churches that says: "Don't say anything, let God take care of it." This is a lie from Satan. God does not want you to remain silent as sin then remains un-addressed. When you remain silent about pastoral and priestly sin, those sins are perpetuated in the church. It is the primary reason why so much abuse within the church goes un-addressed.

Copyright 2005 Edward G. Palmer, All Rights Reserved.

Myth—God Owns Solid Rock

Furthermore, if you keep your mouth shut about crime, you are a servant of Satan and there is no truth in you. That is right, keep silent about church crimes and you yourself are lawless in God's eyes! You will be one of those who are rudely informed by Jesus Christ: "I never knew you."

Mr. Matthews has already had 10 years to repent of his crimes, return various properties that he has stolen and get right with God. It has yet to be done and so I will tell you that he is simply an unrepentant servant of Satan. Harsh words yes, but his church theft is documented in Minnesota public records. If you think that anyone really cares in and out of the church, the answer may shock you in the details that follow.

This chapter will explain to you how this church was stolen from its denomination first and then from its congregation second and what you can do to ensure that you are actually worshipping in God's house. I will also tell you how the crime is being perpetuated and why William N. Matthews knew he could pull it off. Yet, has William N. Matthews really gotten away with stealing God's property?

> **"For there is nothing hidden that will not be disclosed, and nothing concealed that will not be known or brought out into the open." Luke 8:17 NIV**

> **"No one who wants to become a public figure acts in secret. … Show yourself to the world." John 7:4 NIV**

> **"Rather, we have renounced secret and shameful ways; we do not use deception, nor do we distort the word of God. On the contrary, by setting forth the truth plainly we commend ourselves to every man's conscience in the sight of God."**
> **2 Cor. 4:2 NIV**

> **"Have nothing to do with the fruitless deeds of darkness, but rather expose them. For it is shameful even to mention what the disobedient do in secret." Ephesians 5:11-12 NIV**

Myth—God Owns Solid Rock

To fully understand the theft, let's take a look at how it came about that God told me to go to the Elk River Assembly of God Church. This theft was not conducted in a vacuous context. No, in fact the theft was enabled because Satan had already taken a strong foothold within the church. The only thing Satan needed was to consolidate his control.

When Jackie and I arrived in the small town of Elk River thirty years ago, we had leaned towards the Presbyterian Church as the faith we would raise our children in. That is because, quite frankly, I didn't have a real faith at the time. For that matter, I didn't even care about the church. I had my fire insurance I guess and didn't need a "real" relationship with God. For that matter, I could not even explain what that was. Nor did I know that I needed it. Like many men, I shirked my spiritual responsibilities to God and dumped them onto Jackie. She was taking the spiritual lead at the time and knew that we needed to get our children into the faith. The Reverend David Searfoss from her Bryn Mawr Presbyterian Church was a Pentecostal preacher of righteousness. He was the pastor that developed Jackie's faith. Praise God for righteous women, especially when their husband's are really clueless about the substance of true faith in God like I was at the time.

We looked for a Presbyterian church, but couldn't find one in town. As it turns out, there was a United Church of Christ [UCC] assembly in Elk River. Apparently, when a UCC church is in a small town, a Presbyterian church isn't and vice versa. I don't know if that is always the case. It is just what we were told by the local UCC pastor at the time. So, we decided to worship at the Union Church in Elk River since we were told it was similar to the Presbyterian Church.

At one point, I filled out a survey at Union Church indicating I only went there because of Jackie and I wasn't getting much out of it myself. I was brutally honest in the survey. I didn't want any confusion about the fact I wasn't really into this church stuff. Jackie became involved and served as a member on the board of Christian education. Eventually, I found God in the epiphany I talked about in chapter 13. Let's pick the story up from the point where I gave God my heart. It was the spring of 1978 that I let God into the bowels of my very soul. Remember? Life changed …

Copyright 2005 Edward G. Palmer, All Rights Reserved.

Book of Edward—Chapter 16

Myth—God Owns Solid Rock

I immediately began reading the Holy Bible. I was thirsty to know everything I could about God. Where once Genesis had been a stopping point in my reading of the Bible, nothing could stop me now. I read the Bible front to back and then got the Apocryphal books and read all of them. I became comfortable in the word of God. That is when I started teaching Sunday school to high school students at Union Church. It was months later that things started to get dicey for me mentally inside the church. I would read and study my Bible. However, when I got to church, I often heard messages that seemed opposite of what my Bible taught. I would run home and study the Bible on the issue that was just preached in the church. I often found that the pulpit message did not line up with God's Word.

Let me tell you that this will be your first big test with God. Will you adhere to what HIS Word says? Or, will you accept only what the pulpit teaches? Satan hopes that religious authorities will intimidate you to simply leave your Bible on the bookshelf at home. Ever wonder why it is that many people who go to church never carry a Bible? This is no doubt their main reason. They are ignorant of the Word and thus unable to confront apostasy. Better to accept the pulpit teaching, even if you do not agree with it? If you accept the Bible as the source of truth, you will not be able to accept the apostasy of any pulpit that contradicts it. You will be forced to move on to another church and another and another. You might eventually end up in a small fellowship group like I did, which stands solely on the word of God.

Our pastor at Union Church in Elk River was the Reverend Richard Scheerer. Our family attended this UCC Church for nine years until one fateful day in the fall of 1982. I can still remember the pastor's statement, which would turn out to be a milestone in my walk of faith with God. He said: "Many of you might have seen the statement in the Minneapolis paper yesterday. The Minnesota Council of Churches issued a statement backing Gay and lesbian relationships. You should know that our church is a part of this council and agrees with the statement." The pastor didn't explain precisely what was said in the paper. If anyone had questions about it, we were to see him. Immediately the spiritual alarm bells went off. I had already experienced several instances of where pulpit teaching ran counter to biblical teaching. I knew I had to get Saturday's paper and read the article.

Myth—God Owns Solid Rock

> # Minnesota Council of Churches statement backs gays, lesbians
>
> **By Ellen Foley**
> Staff Writer
>
> The Minnesota Council of Churches issued a strong statement in support of gay and lesbian people Friday.
>
> The council's 18 member organizations represent about a million people, 45 percent of the state's religious population. They include some divisions of the the Lutheran Church in America, the American Lutheran Church, the United Methodist Church and the United Church of Christ.
>
> The council's statement urged its members to welcome gays and lesbians into their congregations and support legislation that protects their rights.
>
> The Rev. Willis J. Merriman, executive director of the council, said the statement is the most far-reaching made by an ecumenical organization in the nation. He said the statement was not designed to speak for congregations but to prompt discussion.
>
> The statement approved unanimously by the council's 55-member board of directors contains strong language condoning homosexuality.
>
> "There may be creative and whole expressions of one's sexuality at various levels in relationships between men and women, between men and other men, and between women and other women," the statement said.
>
> While it stops short of saying that homosexuality is a natural phenomenon, it says it is "not necessarily a matter of choice. Evidence continues to suggest that there is a givenness about it."
>
> Churches continued on page 9A

Reference: The Minneapolis StarTribune, Sat. Oct. 30, 1982 page 2A.

Surprised that I can dig up a twenty-two year old article from my files? Don't be. I am a literal pack rat when it comes to documents. I can even show you some of the apostasies that I taught to high school students at Union Church as a result of being falsely programmed myself with orthodox Christian trinitarian dogma. It took a twenty-five year walk with God in the spirit to clear out programming errors in my mind and refocus on HIS Word.

You've got an inherent advantage now with the clear Scriptures that God is providing in this book that contradict the teachings of most pulpits. Now, as I heard the Reverend Scheerer talk about the above article, I began to reflect on what the Holy Bible taught. I remember distinctly thinking that somewhere in the Holy Bible I had read homosexuality was an abomination unto God. I found myself in a church that was openly condoning what God condemns. I did get the article and was shocked by the nature of its content and the unanimous support for the statement from the 55-member board of directors of the Minnesota Council of Churches. In case the above print is too small, listen to the clarity of the statement and understand that the gays and lesbians started on their political agenda within the church of God first.

Myth—God Owns Solid Rock

1982 Minnesota Council Of Church Statement!

"There may be creative and whole expressions of one's sexuality at various levels in relationships between men and women, between men and other men, and between women and other women."

To say that Jackie and I were flabbergasted is an understatement. On Monday, I told Jackie that we could no longer attend Union Church, as it no longer represented biblical truth. I called the church office and told them to take my family off of the church membership roles; we would not be back. Our family made a clear statement about God's Word being supreme; we would not tolerate biblical apostasy. Not for any church. I don't recall giving Jackie much to think about concerning the decision to leave Union Church. First, I didn't have to as we were of one spirit by then. However, it was clear that I had stepped up to the plate for my family. I had come to the point of accepting the spiritual responsibility that God wanted of me.

I have since witnessed other people taking the same stand on apostasy. If a church preaches opposite of God's Word, a few people will leave to find another fellowship. However, those who will stand with God on HIS Word are very few. My witness to this fact is an observation of the reality of the words of Jesus that few will walk the narrow path that does lead to eternal life. I was beginning God's lessons that would teach me who Jesus planned to tell: "I never knew you." For one, it would be people who did not value HIS Word over the pulpit's opinion or the church's doctrine.

I didn't know that God would provide twenty more years of training before HE would call me to apostleship. I had no clue about the future and the decisions that God would ask me to make. I only knew that I chose God over my very life on this earth. I knew that in the end it would be the right choice even if it caused problems during this earthly existence.

Jackie and I moved onward to the Nowthen Alliance Church located about seven miles from the house. Oddly enough, when we got there, we

Myth—God Owns Solid Rock

found four other families we knew from Union Church that had already made the same move. Like us, they decided not to tolerate the apostasy. I think it was comforting to us to know that we were not alone. Plus, we had some instant friends we already knew. We found a spiritual home for many years under the tutelage of Pastor Paul Frederick and his wife Lois. These two godly people stuck to the word of God and they opened up their arms to my family. Our stay at Nowthen Alliance would be interrupted by a job change in late 1984. However, during the two years we were there, we came to love this Bible believing ministry.

Life changed as God called us to California in December 1984. Our stay in the Santa Barbara area would be short lived and we returned to Elk River in September 1985. We spent nine months living in Goleta, which is next door to Santa Barbara. I had accepted a job of Director of Quality for a computer parts manufacturer. We located a church in Santa Barbara; it was the Living Faith Center. They didn't advertise it, but it was an Assembly of God Church. My faith started to deepen as I got into a higher form of worship than I had previously experienced. Our family had gone from a mainline church where the word "Amen" spoken out loud wasn't welcomed, to a church where it wasn't so unusual and now we attended a church where it just wasn't such a big deal. We were introduced to speaking in tongues and the lifting up of hands in worship. Both are biblical; listen to the Word.

> **"And these signs will accompany those who believe: In my name they will drive out demons; they will speak in *new* tongues." Mark 16:17 NIV**

> **"Now to each one the manifestation of the Spirit is given for the common good. To one there is given through the Spirit the message of wisdom, to another the message of knowledge by means of the same Spirit, to another faith by the same Spirit, to another gifts of healing by that one Spirit, to another miraculous powers, to another prophecy, to another distinguishing between spirits, to another speaking in different kinds of tongues, and to still another the interpretation of tongues." 1 Cor. 12:7-10 NIV**

Copyright 2005 Edward G. Palmer, All Rights Reserved.

Myth—God Owns Solid Rock

> **"If I come to you and speak in tongues, what good will I be to you, unless I bring you some revelation or knowledge or prophecy or word of instruction?" 1 Cor. 14:6 NIV**
>
> **Paul said: "I thank God that I speak in tongues more than all of you." 1 Cor. 14:18 NIV**
>
> **"Tongues, then, are a sign, not for believers but for unbelievers; prophecy, however, is for believers, not for unbelievers." 1 Cor. 14:22**
>
> **"So if the whole church comes together and everyone speaks in tongues, and some who do not understand or some unbelievers come in, will they not say that you are out of your mind?" 1 Cor. 14:23**
>
> **"Do not forbid speaking in tongues." 1 Cor. 14:39**

You can observe that speaking in tongues is very biblical even if many in the church do not understand it. Is this some kind of babble? It can certainly sound like that if you are in the flesh. However, this is a spiritual language and protocols exist for its use within the church. Look them up.

In our search for a church in Santa Barbara, we stopped at a small Four Square Church where we had a couple of very interesting experiences. First, my oldest daughter Paula felt it was time to make a public confession of her faith. That was exciting. Secondly, on cue, the entire congregation all started speaking in tongues. That is, everyone except our family, as we did not understand what was going on. Like Paul said in 1 Cor. 14:23, we thought they were all out of their minds and we never went back.

While at Living Faith Center, I concluded that they had gotten Apostle Paul's instructions on tongues correct. After returning to Minnesota, I also started to speak in tongues. The first time was while jogging and praying to God for the gifts of His Spirit. Tongues came out of my mouth in a way that I felt I was choking or throwing up. However, it was just the gift of tongues.

Myth—God Owns Solid Rock

Still, it startled me and was unexpected. Often we resist the very idea of speaking of tongues and we restrain it from happening. Weird or not, just let it happen. You'll know if it is a gift of tongues because the words (or babble sounds) will flow freely and effortlessly from your spirit to God. If you have to "force" tongues from your mouth, it is not the gift of tongues. It is only you pretending. A lot of Christians do pretend to have this gift, as they want to be part of the local "in crowd." This is especially true in some Charismatic churches that believe you are not saved unless you do speak in tongues. This is not biblical. Listen to Paul.

> **"Do all have gifts of healing? Do all speak in tongues? Do all interpret?" 1 Cor. 12:30 NIV**

> **"I wish you all had the gift of speaking in tongues, but even more I wish you were all able to prophesy." 1 Cor. 14:5 NLT**

Instruction: Not every Christian will speak in tongues and the Apostle Paul makes this fact clear. Therefore, tongues are a gift of the Spirit as are other items. It is not a sign of salvation, as many Charismatics believe. Want the clearest sign of salvation? It is standing for God's truth regardless of the impact it has on your life! Tongues are just another form of communications from our spirit to God's Spirit.

> **"I want men everywhere to lift up holy hands in prayer, without anger or disputing." 1 Tim. 2:8 NIV**

Something magical happens when you start to lift up your hands in prayer to worship God. Try it sometime. I experienced a deepening of my faith at Living Faith Center. I remember closing my eyes, lifting my hands and also thanking Jesus for all that he had done for us. God had some very important lessons to teach me. One of them occurred shortly after arriving in our new Goleta home. A friend of the family had lost his executive job and this was a serious thing at the time in the computer industry, which was in a recession. He was a Christian and told me that everything would work out fine. I wondered to myself what I would do if I lost my job. It was the wrong thing to wonder. Soon afterwards, the company I worked for laid off

Myth—God Owns Solid Rock

about ten of its executives and I was one of them. Suddenly, what I had wondered about materialized. Why I had taken the family out of our Minnesota roots to California is a long story. I suspect it was an answer to the prayers of at least two people. Even more important and looking back now I know it was part of God's spiritual training for my earthly life.

For my children who may still wonder what it was about, let me say that God was taking our family on a spiritual adventure to train dad in HIS ways. It would be a time to learn to rely upon HIS grace and not on our own resources. Remember in the last chapter where Jesus sent his apostles out without a moneybag? Well, God was also sending our family without one. Indeed, we would learn to trust in HIS ability to keep our family functioning. We couldn't afford any luxuries, but the family lacked little in terms of actual needs. We had a roof over our heads, electricity, heat and food. We had clothes on our backs. We also had a future with hope and knew that God's plan was still unfolding.

We returned to Nowthen Alliance in late 1985 and spent the next seven years there. During our stay, I became more grounded in God's Word as a result of Pastor Frederick's teachings. I have an entire NKJV Bible marked up with notes from his teachings during those years. Thanks for the great teachings Paul! God was using you to anchor this apostle in HIS Word. Indeed, this was a time for me to grow in depth concerning real knowledge of God's Word. This growth came about by detailed studies and application of the Word to my life. Remember, I had long ago read the whole Bible.

While at Nowthen Alliance I was baptized by immersion. It was almost ten years from the time of my epiphany before I was baptized as an adult. The issue of baptism by immersion weighed heavily on my mind. For me it was just another step away from the prior church programming. I was baptized as a baby in a Lutheran church, yet I know that it was the stuff of Christian mythology. When baptized, Pastor Frederick asked me what my testimony was. I said: "God had asked me what I was waiting for?"

"And now what are you waiting for? Get up, be baptized [by immersion] and wash your sins away, calling on his name [the name of Jesus Christ]." Acts 22:16 NIV

Copyright 2005 Edward G. Palmer, All Rights Reserved.

Myth—God Owns Solid Rock

Getting baptized by immersion was taking another step closer to the God that I love. I had already been given His Spirit, now I made an official declaration of my faith. My message to all is that I belonged to God. Note that this baptism did not mean I was unsaved at the time. That too is the stuff of Christian mythology. No, for me it was, "Take me deeper O Lord!" Until you take the bowels of your own soul underwater with God in an adult baptism, you will never fully understand the spiritual significance of what it all means and what I am talking about.

"Can anyone keep these people from being baptized with water? They have [already] received the Holy Spirit just as we have. So he ordered that they be baptized in the name of Jesus Christ." Acts 10:47-48 NIV

"Or don't you know that all of us who were baptized into Christ Jesus were baptized into his death?" Romans 6:3 NIV

Instruction. Get baptized as an adult. It will take you closer to God and you will never regret this declaration of your faith. Does this proclaim that you belong solely to Christ? No, it proclaims that you also belong to the Father [Yahweh] and that Christ [His human begotten Son] has brought you back to Him. You honor Christ by being baptized in his name unto God.

Pastor Paul Frederick and his wife Lois were transferring to a smaller church in Iowa in the early 1990's. There existed some behind the scenes conflict within Nowthen Alliance, which I am not privy to. I believe it was one of the reasons why Paul and Lois were moving on. Anytime a pastor change occurs, some people assess whether they want to continue attending the church. It is a sad fact, but true. My family was also reassessing church options. Just leaving a church can take on the same level of trauma that a divorce presents to a family. Changing churches is a very serious family event not taken lightly. Fortunately, there are times when a switch is more easily made. A change of pastors is one of those times. I had felt drawn to the local Elk River Assembly of God Church. I was interested in exploring a deeper level of worship; the kind that I was first introduced to at the Living Faith Center in Santa Barbara.

Copyright 2005 Edward G. Palmer, All Rights Reserved.

Book of Edward—Chapter 16

Myth—God Owns Solid Rock

I had watched the Elk River Assembly of God Church build itself up into a very powerful influence in our community. They had full-fledged food, clothing and other ministries. Each year they put on Passion plays. To use a common phrase, the church was "hot" in the spiritual sense. That is until some time in 1991 when news of sexual impropriety came to light.

Senior Pastor James Hoogenboom was accused of having sex with three married women whom he counseled. In one case, he was counseling both husband and wife separately. He told them to stay away from each other according to one newspaper article. How convenient and self-serving to take advantage of the wife. How evil is this? This Assembly of God church was literally exploding for God in our small city. How does Satan take out a big church on fire for God? He takes out the leader of the church. And what the heck, why not use sex? It works, doesn't it? Listen — if any pastor counsels you or your spouse to stay sexually apart from one another, it is ungodly counsel. God's Word teaches us differently. Again, let me point out that if you are ignorant of the Word, you can be led around like a cow with a ring in its nose. How would you know if you are being misled?

Of course, I assume that both spouses are healthy and that some disease does not interfere with your sexual intimacy. Listen to the Word.

> **"The husband should fulfill his marital duty to his wife, and likewise the wife to her husband. The wife's body does not belong to her alone but also to her husband. In the same way, the husband's body does not belong to him alone but also to his wife. Do not deprive each other except by mutual consent and for a time, so that you may devote yourselves to prayer. Then come together again so that Satan will not tempt you because of your lack of self-control." 1 Cor. 7:3-5 NIV**

From 39-years of marriage, I can tell you that there are always events that will make you distant from your spouse. Likewise, I can tell you that sexual intimacy with one another will always bring you back closer to each other. If you willy-nilly deny your spouse sex, you give Satan a foothold. The following article[1] is one of many written about the pastor's misconduct.

Copyright 2005 Edward G. Palmer, All Rights Reserved.

Book of Edward—Chapter 16

Myth—God Owns Solid Rock

Pastor Hoogenboom's Sexual Misconduct!

> **District Court News**
>
> ### Hoogenboom's attorney asks judge to change trial location
>
> Judge Gary Meyer is expected to make a ruling today (Wednesday, Dec. 9) or Thursday on a motion made by Dennis Miller, attorney for former Elk River Assembly of God pastor James Hoogenboom who now lives in Arizona.
>
> Citing what he feels has been extensive local pre-trial publicity surrounding three complaints charging Hoogenboom with 52 counts of criminal sexual conduct, Miller has requested the trial be moved to the Wright County courthouse in Buffalo. Considering the high level of interest in the case here, and the relatively small population in Sherburne County, Miller said the question is whether a fair and impartial jury can be found here.
>
> "It would be easier to get jurors who have not formed an opinion in Wright County," said Miller. "From what I've seen, there seems to be quite a bit of interest in this case."
>
> The complaints, filed last May, June and October by three women who are former members of the Assembly of God

I had felt God's call to start attending the Elk River Assembly of God Church for about three years before I actually went there. By the time I did go, the church had undergone a self-destruction and was in disarray. Only a fraction of the members remained after the pastor's sexual misconduct hit the news. To say that Elk River was abuzz with the sordid details would be an understatement. In fact, the whole Minneapolis-St. Paul metro area was abuzz. Sex sells papers and the falling out of grace of any pastor is a big deal and something the mainstream media eats up. Remember Swaggart?

Jackie and I were in disagreement about attending this church. She didn't want any part of it. She was always more perceptive than I was when it came to church matters. Still, I had ignored God for three years and now I felt I absolutely had to go even if I did not understand why. I remember asking God several times why I was supposed to attend this church. God told me more than once: "You are here to worship and observe. You are my witness." God, what should I witness? "Just observe Edward!"

Copyright 2005 Edward G. Palmer, All Rights Reserved.

Book of Edward—Chapter 16

Myth—God Owns Solid Rock

Jackie did not attend this church with me. I rationalized that I would help rebuild the church. And I did want to deepen my worship experience. However, I did not want the conflict that the church represented to our family. Jackie told me to go, since God was asking me. I started to attend the church by myself in about July of 1992 prior to the time that William Neal Matthews presented himself as a candidate for senior pastor. At that time, the church was in chaos having experienced the fall of its senior pastor. I remember that after I had attended the church for a few weeks, God gave me some strange instructions. Its current pastor was leaving and a temporary one was appointed to serve until a new senior pastor was found.

God told me: "Go tell them to change the name of the church." Of course I protested and said: "I'm only visiting the church. Why should I tell them to change the name of the church?" God said: "Go tell them because I asked you to." This conversation went on daily for about three weeks. It seemed like every morning as I shaved and looked into the mirror that God would remind me I had still not done what HE asked of me. Sometimes the voice was so loud, I would be tempted to look around and see who was messing with my mind. However, I knew it was God. The church sat at a crossroads of four separate communities and a different name made sense.

I understood the logic of changing the name. The church name with the city in it was limiting its appeal to the surrounding area of several other small towns. God never told me what to name the church. I eventually caved in and told the interim pastor Paul Johnson what God told me to say. You've always got to preface this stuff. Who knows if you are simply a whacko? I told Pastor Johnson: "Please take this for what it is worth. I am only relaying to you what God told me to say. This church needs to change its name because it is limiting its appeal to the surrounding area. Do with this information as you want." I left satisfied that I had finally done what God had asked. HE left me alone. I didn't realize that the incoming pastor had a similar agenda and planned to take over the church and its property. Reflecting back, God was giving Matthews some spiritual fodder for his crime. A new name would be an excellent launch point to start altering the corporation's Articles and to seize legal control of its property. It would a spiritual test of righteousness for William Neal Matthews that he failed.

Myth—God Owns Solid Rock

Matthews eventually manipulated the church into becoming an AFCM affiliated church. This is known as a *Word of Faith* church [WOF]. I will explain it shortly. For now, however, let me discuss a church illusion that is often presented to Christians. Do you remember that Satan masquerades as an angel of light and his servants as righteous ministers? If not, go back to the opening page of this chapter and study those verses. What does this mean? It means you can literally be in a church that you think is with God and is righteous, yet actually be in a den of thieves. Jesus said that you would know them by their fruits. Don't rely on just what comes out of the minister's mouth, as it is supposed to appear very sound and righteous. No, instead, you must also look at what is happening. Step back for some clarity and objectivity to see the whole picture [forest v. trees]. Do not get so close to your pastor that you cannot see what is happening. If you are myopic in your spiritual vision you will operate, as Satan wants. He knows you won't see what is really going on because you are too close and your focus is way too narrow. As I moved to each new church, I had a feeling I was somehow getting closer to God. Was I? Let's look at the issue of church types with some graphic illustrations. My church path is shown in this first graphic.

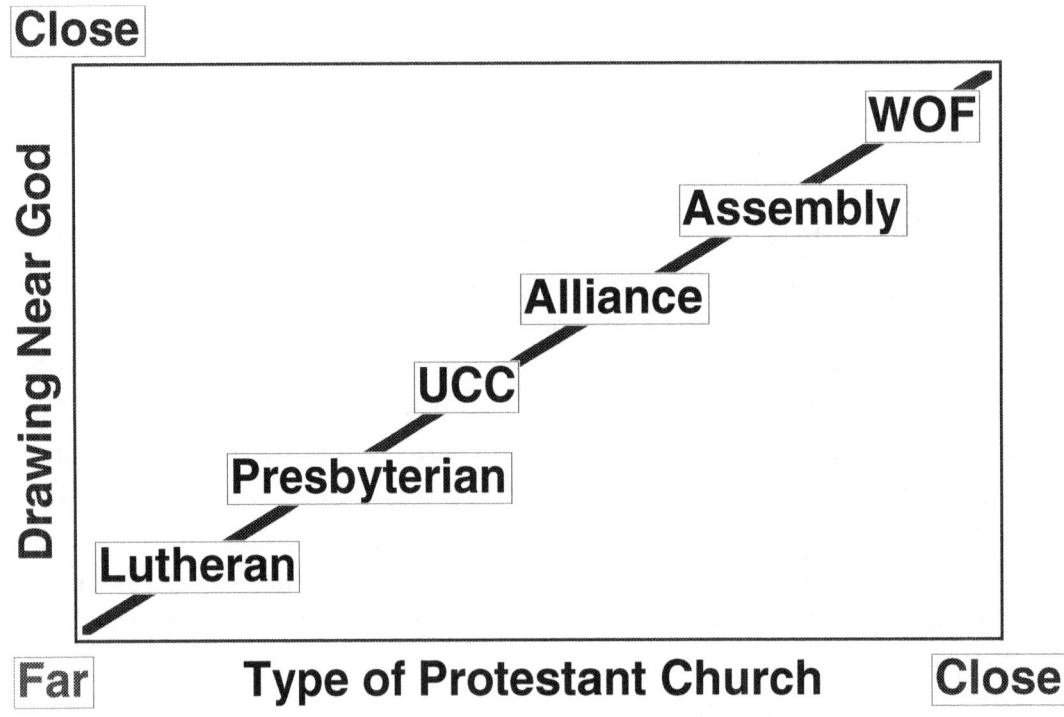

Myth—God Owns Solid Rock

I am not alone in seeking to get close to God. Drawing near to God is the objective of many sincere believers. As I changed denominations and churches, I was not aware of actually getting closer to God until I made the move from the UCC church to the Alliance church. That was a very clear move in my mind that got me closer to God, because one church supported what the Bible taught in Scripture and the other didn't. So, at the time, I knew I was moving closer to God and there was little doubt about it. I had a similar awareness of moving closer to God in the new worship experience at Living Faith Center. For the first time in my life, I was allowed to express myself in the form of individualized worship from my spirit to God's. This was a clear move closer to God. It was the same with tongues, lifting up of hands, kneeling prayer and water baptism. Each act took me closer to God.

As I got deeper into *Pentecostal* and *Word of Faith* churches, I did not have the same awareness. The thought of moving closer to God via a church change started to become an illusion. Listen—don't you think Satan knows you might want to move closer to God? Sure and guess what, Satan has a perfect church for you. In the Bible sense, there are really only two basic church zones. Bible believing churches and non-Bible believing churches.

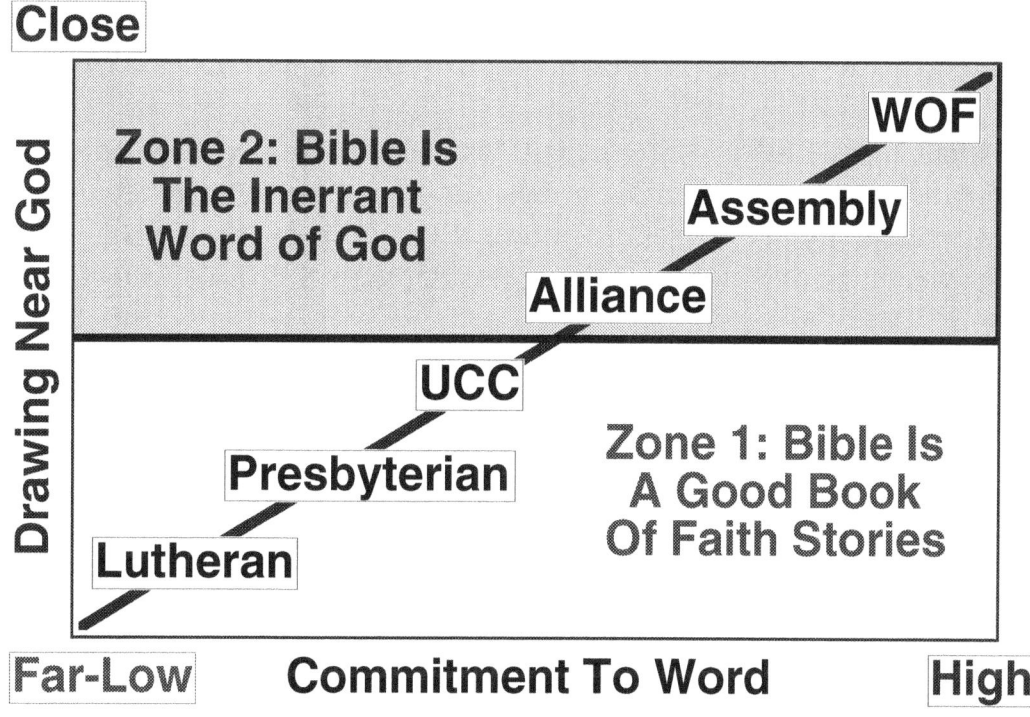

Copyright 2005 Edward G. Palmer, All Rights Reserved.

Myth—God Owns Solid Rock

In the above graphic, mainline churches, which tend to be more liberal in nature, are separated from churches that are more conservative. The most distinguishing feature of the two groups is how they treat the Bible and its text. At one extreme, the Bible simply represents a great storybook of faith. At the other extreme, it represents the inerrant word of God. Of course, there are various degrees within each group. Let me remind you that it is clear from my prior discussions that there are errors located in the Bible. Likewise, it is also clear that those who do not accept the teachings of the Bible in totality have little ground to stand on by accepting Jesus Christ's salvation. Hence the words: "Why do you call me Lord and do not do what I say?" The above grouping of churches into Bible zones is interesting; it also appears as a solid and basic distinction amongst different churches.

Now let me add a caveat here. It would be unfair to simply lump all of the various churches into only two categories. Quite frankly, you just never know what church really stands for God and what one doesn't based upon denomination alone. Listen—there are now many Episcopal churches that are dropping out of their denomination because of the sheer lack of Bible adherence recently demonstrated by the consecration of an activist homosexual as a bishop. Certainly the Episcopal Church would fall inside zone one in the above graphic. I also personally know of zone one Catholic and Lutheran churches that are filled with the Spirit and on fire for God.

Since the Antichrist started 2,000 years ago according to Scripture, can you understand that Satan's servants masquerading with righteousness are almost certainly in every church now? Even in Jesus' time, Satan's servants were teaching in the pulpits. Consider these words of Jesus Christ.

> **Then Jesus said to the crowds and to his disciples: "The teachers of the law and the Pharisees sit in Moses' seat. So you must obey them and do everything they tell you. But do not do what they do, for they do not practice what they preach. They tie up heavy loads and put them on men's shoulders, but they themselves are not willing to lift a finger to move them. Everything they do is done for men to see."**
> **Matthew 23:1-5 NIV**

Myth—God Owns Solid Rock

"Woe to you ... you hypocrites! You shut the kingdom of Heaven in men's faces. You yourselves do not enter, nor will you let those enter who are trying to." Matthew 23:13

Verily I say to you that I have lived and witnessed the above facts in today's churches. And why not, Satan began infiltrating the church over 2,000 years ago. Does anyone think he has stopped his objectives? The practice of Satan's servants is more sophisticated or easier today depending upon your perspective. Satan also has to contend with righteous believers leaving mainline churches in search of spiritual truth. Be aware that most of the dropping away of churches from biblical truths has occurred within the last fifty years or so since 1950. Clearly no mainline church would dare even propose the consecration of homosexual bishops or the condoning of divorce and fornication in 1950, which are just three obvious illustrations.

The further away from truth that any church moves, the faster some believers will exit in search for a new church centered on Bible truth. In this new millennium, there is a clear dichotomy when it comes to Bible text. It was not always that way. It would appear we just underwent a 2,000-year setup by Satan. The false trinity and salvation doctrines are key in ignoring Bible truth. If you "claim" Christ with your mouth, you don't need a Bible, do you? Another line is drawn like the one Moses drew after coming down from the mountain with the Ten Commandments. Choose carefully, which side of the line to stand on. One recognizes Bible truth, the other doesn't.

Observe these nine facts about religious teachers that Jesus taught:

1. Teachers "appeared righteous" in their teachings.
2. Teachers "performed" for the congregation [for men to see].
3. Teachers did not practice what they preached.
4. Teachers did not personally observe God's Word in their lives.
5. Teachers imposed heavy burdens on the people.
6. Teachers would not lift a finger to help with those burdens.
7. Teachers shut the doors to God's kingdom in men's faces.
8. Teachers refused to enter God's kingdom themselves.
9. Teachers said one thing and did another; they were hypocrites.

Myth—God Owns Solid Rock

Verily I say unto you, it is my testimony that William Neal Matthews exhibited virtually every one of the above nine traits identified by Jesus. Yes, Satan is alive and well in today's church. How will you know if you are sitting in a church of Satan instead of God given the fact that both will appear righteous to you? Here are some basic questions to answer.

1. Does the church stand for all biblical truth or does it selectively choose which biblical truth it likes while ignoring others?
2. Whose definition of righteousness is being used? God's or men's?
3. What exactly is going on behind the scenes inside the church from a governance and ownership perspective? Does one person or one family basically own and legally control the church?
4. Are there two classes of citizens in church by-laws? One with voting rights and the other without voting rights?
5. Does a board of deacons composed of men and women who know God's Word supervise the pastor? Is the board independent and only accountable to the congregation or is it a lapdog of the pastor doing his or her bidding?
6. Does the church teach that God is a slot machine and all you need to do is call on the "anointing" to get what you want in life?
7. Does the church bring you closer to men's ways or God's ways?

The clearest sign that you are in a church of Satan is when teaching is obviously opposite of what is written in the Bible. Now, listen, if you and I are looking at a blue sky and I tell you that the sky is azure blue in color and you look up thinking that it is more of a baby blue color, does the difference matter? No, it really doesn't. There are many times when a teaching can take on some subtleties and a clear case of apostasy is not taking place. On the other hand, what if we both looked at the same sky and I told you that it was red. Would you then believe it? Of course not. Yet that is exactly what people do when they stay in a church that teaches opposite of God's Word *and they know it*. They do not challenge it even when they possess first hand knowledge knowing it is false. What is this first hand knowledge they possess? It is their very own experiences reading the Holy Bible. We base our entire salvation on statements in this book. Why not be obedient to what it tells us? Want some easy examples to consider? Okay, here are a few.

Myth—God Owns Solid Rock

You read that "God hates divorce" and your pastor teaches divorce is "okay." You read that "men sleeping with other men sexually are worthy of death" and your pastor teaches, "It is no big deal." You read that "keeping the Ten Commandments leads to eternal life" and your pastor teaches you "don't have to keep the Ten Commandments." You read "to test God with your tithe and see if HE won't open the windows of Heaven for you" and suddenly your pastor ignores those verses and begins to teach that you "can't expect anything from God by simply tithing. Instead, you must now begin to give gifts and offerings beyond the tithe to get anything from God."

Not a single one of the examples above are a debate similar to which color of blue the sky is. No, instead, one position is like saying the sky is blue and the other position is like saying the sky is red. Yet, year after year, Christians put up with false teachings when they have firsthand knowledge from their own Bible studies that the teaching is wrong. Why? Is it because they are just in the crowd that Jesus will reject? Even if you don't think you are acting in a lawless manner, you are when you support lawlessness in any form. God will hold you lawless in HIS eyes when you knowingly accept and or ignore the lawlessness of others. In God's eyes it is the same thing. Jesus will execute judgment on every Christian that is lawless; there will be no excuses. That is the teaching of Jesus Christ, not mine!

Another way to know if you are in a house of Satan is by the outreach ministries of the church. Your first hand Bible knowledge might have taught you the following ways of directly serving the Lord. According to Matthew 25:35-46, these six activities are tantamount to giving directly to God and HIS Son. What are the ministries of your church? What are your ministries? You give directly to God and HIS Son when …

1. You feed the hungry.
2. You give drink to the thirsty.
3. You take in [and are hospitable to] strangers.
4. You clothe [those in need and] the naked.
5. You visit [and take care of] the sick.
6. You visit [and pray for] those in prison.

Myth—God Owns Solid Rock

I went out to lunch and when I reviewed these six items again, God told me that they were not just physical items. They are also spiritual items. Many people are hungry and thirsty for the word of God. Does your church feed the people God's Word and allow them to drink of God's Spirit?

Many people are in a spiritual prison of Satan's design. This could be a church that creates a social net supporting one another's sinful lifestyles or inside evil secrets such as adulterous relationships or theft, which makes the church difficult to leave. Think of a congregation of lesbians and gays who support one another and assure each other that everything is okay with God despite what the Bible actually says? Is such a church easy to leave? No, it is not easy to leave such a church without a change of heart towards God and the turning away [repenting] from the sinful lifestyle. Don't tell me that such churches don't exist. I know for a fact that they do exist. I also know that they are an abomination unto God Almighty. Such churches are filled with spiritually naked people who think it is safe to ignore God's Word.

They are spiritual strangers to God in need of true spiritual hospitality. Yes, we like to think of the above list in only the physical sense, but God says it is also a list of spiritual needs. God expects us to give spiritual food, water, clothes and hospitality. Especially to those who are spiritually sick or in a spiritual prison and for whom souls are spiritually naked. Therefore, we have an obligation to God to take care of body and spirit needs. Spiritually naked people need to be clothed in all the truth of God's Word to get saved.

When William Neal Matthews came to the Elk River Assembly of God Church in Elk River, it had food, clothing and other ministries that reached out to those in need within our community. Over the course of four years, Matthews systematically shut down all ministries serving the needs of people. In their stead, he placed advertisements seeking to draw people into his satanic lair and collect money for his international travels. The church moved from a focus on local outreach ministries in compliance with God's Word, to a ministry focused on Matthews' family and their itinerant travel plans outside of the local community. O LORD GOD, I bear witness that this church at one time served YOU. However, Satan's servant turned it into a satanic lair by deceiving YOUR people with the appearance of righteousness.

Copyright 2005 Edward G. Palmer, All Rights Reserved.

Myth—God Owns Solid Rock

Therefore, don't worry about subtle shades of color where differences in opinions should be respected and tolerated. Instead, worry about those teachings that are clearly opposite or disparate to what is written in the Holy Bible. Such teachings are only found in a house of Satan and it does not matter what denomination the church is. Remember, I am not talking about subtle theological teachings where reasonable people can disagree. I am talking about clear and diametrically opposite or disparate positions. If you are able to eliminate the false teachings, you should do so. Otherwise, get out fast as the souls of you and your family are at stake. You also need to inform every person in the church that you know so they are not left in a lair of Satan by your unwillingness to share the truth. If you know of evil inside the church and do not share it with others in a public way that exposes it, you are lawless. Indeed, "exposing the evil" is exactly what Apostle Paul teaches us to do. For it is shameful to talk about it in secret.

"Have nothing to do with the fruitless deeds of darkness, but rather expose them. For it is shameful even to mention what the disobedient do in secret." Ephesians 5:11-12 NIV

Remember, whoever does what is right is righteous like Jesus Christ. Therefore, it is not what we can mouth out loud about Jesus Christ that will ultimately count. It will be our behavior and whether or not we obeyed the instructions of God or were lawless in His eyes. Who did Jesus first reject? It was those who were lawless! Who was in the second group rejected? It was those who did not care about the bodily and spiritual needs of others. Both groups of rejected Christians went through life ignoring the needs of others and thinking that their mouth had provided eternal life; it hadn't.

I spent four years in Matthews' ministry at Solid Rock Church. Right from the start, I felt that there were odd things that did not make total sense to me. These were things in the nature of the color of sky discussion, but on one day everything changed. This pastor started teaching a clearly apostate message that was opposite to what was written in the word of God. It wasn't just opposite the Word; it was exactly opposite his own four years of pulpit teachings out of the book of Malachi. As I read my Bible and listened to Matthews repeat his apostate message three times, I again heard from God.

Myth—God Owns Solid Rock

God said: "Edward, it is now time for you to choose. It is MY Word or his. Go ask Matthews why he has preached opposite of MY Word." I did confront Matthews immediately after the service. I asked him point blank why he now taught in opposition to God's Word. He denied it and tried to pull a spiritual power play on me, but I obtained a tape of his message and studied the matter at length. I even transcribed the tape. I left the church that day and refused to come back until Matthews explained his apostasy.

It took four weeks before he would see me. When I went in to talk with him, he immediately began accusing me of not supporting his ministry. You've already learned from God's Word about the issue of godly wisdom. James 3:17 explained that godly wisdom contains the ability to reason with one another. You know, from the strong mind that God gives us. Simply put, if you can dialogue and reason directly with God as taught in Isaiah, you should be able to do so with your own pastor. If you cannot, it is time to leave the church. It is another sign you are in a house of Satan. God had shown me James 3:17 prior to the meeting. During the meeting and amidst the false accusations, a huge light bulb was lit in my mind and God said it was now time to leave. God had showed me the nature of Satan's lair.

You might find yourself suddenly on the outside of the church like I did and are unable to easily contact people in the church. Now what? You can take out an ad in the local paper, call people, write letters, set up a post office box, or even create a web site to dispense information. I have done all of these and I can tell you that I am satisfied that anyone whom God wanted to let know had the ability to learn the truth about this evil church.

If a ministry has converted your property by fraudulent means, you can also sue. If you assemble 10% of the membership, you can also file suit under most non-profit corporation acts, if the church was formed under that law. Don't sue a brother in Christ is what the Word says. Be aware I am not talking about some minor issues, which are best ignored. How is your love different if every little thing that bothers you winds up a lawsuit?

"But instead, one brother goes to law against another—and this in front of unbelievers!" 1 Corinthians 6:6 NIV

Myth—God Owns Solid Rock

Keep reading Paul at 1 Corinthians 6:6 and you will get the picture that brothers in the Lord would willy-nilly go to law over anything with each other. The theft of Solid Rock Church falls into a very different category. It is an evil crime. To show a brother your godly love and allow some minor cheating or wrongs to be forgiven is the right thing to do—as long as they have gotten the message that you are aware of those wrongs or cheating. However, let me ask you this question. Do you think this section of Paul's writings also applies to the swindler, which Paul taught at 1 Cor. 5:11? We are not even "to eat with such a person!" Believers can make molehills into mountains inside the church. However, sheer evil is also ignored despite the fact that God has told us to purge evil from among us and Paul also teaches us to "expose the evil." When it comes to dealing with satanic forces in the church and where you have first hand knowledge of evil, a lawsuit may be the most appropriate course of action or at least contact civil authorities.

Get the picture? There are many things you can do when confronting evil. God will expect you to do something when you yourself have the first hand knowledge of events. The level of what you need to do will be based upon James 4:17. To each individual, God will hold up a standard based upon what they know and the resources they have available. Don't think you can just walk away from evil and ignore it. This is not what the Bible teaches; it is the stuff of Christian mythology. Ignoring evil and turning your back will only wreak havoc on other unsuspecting Christians who are not in the know. Yet, I can tell you over 100 members of this congregation did exactly that. They left the church and said nothing of the evil that they knew about. Quite frankly, many of us were taken advantage of by evil for months and years needlessly, because Christians were programmed with the satanic message "Don't say anything to anyone, let God take care of it."

God has given you ears, hands, feet and a mouth. We are supposed to be HIS servants. If we are witnesses to crime, we are not to turn our backs. However, this is the nature of the church today at large. Many have been programmed to simply turn their backs. Is it any wonder why evil prospers in the church? Nobody remembers that God instructed us to purge all evil from our midst. Simply put, do not tolerate apostasy and kick evil people out of the church. You've already learned that biblical truth didn't you?

Copyright 2005 Edward G. Palmer, All Rights Reserved.

Book of Edward—Chapter 16

Myth—God Owns Solid Rock

We live in an age where access to knowledge and information is made incredibly easy. Take any subject you want to learn more about and head to the Internet with your computer. Don't have one? Go to the library and use one of theirs. Spend a day or two and maybe as little as eight hours and you can become more knowledgeable in any one-subject area than most experts. This is especially true in complex areas such as medicine and law. They have become so incredibly complex and vast in terms of knowledge that tiny bits of these industries are now broken down into specialty practices. That is why some medical doctors only treat eyes, feet, noses, ears, etc. Go ahead and name any body part; you will find a specialist in it. That is why you are shuffled from one doctor to another if you are seriously ill.

You will also find highly specialized lawyers who work in real estate, divorce, bankruptcy, etc. The days of the general practitioner are long gone simply because the volume of information now exceeds what any one person can reasonably be expected to deal with. You don't go to a family doctor for brain surgery. You don't go to a real estate lawyer to help you with export laws. However, instead of easy access to information freeing our people, as logic would dictate, the information overload is shutting people's minds down. The sheer volume of news and information are resulting in us relying increasingly upon second hand knowledge to formulate our opinions. The limited time families have also results in their reliance upon what is simply said in the news or spoken from the pulpit. In essence they rely on hearsay.

Therefore, even though access to first hand knowledge has never been easier, it has also never been so ignored. Verily I say unto you that there has never been a time when people were so easily manipulated by the media and ministries. This is difficult to believe until one realizes that we are not just relying upon second hand sources, we are also formulating our opinions on that second hand knowledge. I have said do not just believe what I say in this book, believe the scriptures I cite and only after you look them up for yourself in the Bible. Yet, if you are like a lot of programmed Christians, a pastor can simply tell you not to read this book and that is all you will need to form an opinion about it. That is how easy it is to manipulate Christians today from the pulpit. But would you be surprised if I also told you that you were just as easily manipulated in news stories?

Myth—God Owns Solid Rock

We either don't have the time or we don't take the time to check whether the news or the pastor's facts are actually true. We just assume they are true. That is why we accept them and formulate our opinions based on that second hand knowledge. In fact, society has gotten very adept at just formulating opinions based on second hand knowledge and hearsay. So much so that people willingly go to bat and argue their positions with one another based solely upon that second hand knowledge. I tried to explain a biblical aspect of righteousness a while ago to a 19-year old. His attitude exemplifies that of society at large. Even though he had not read the Bible and did not possess a first hand knowledge of Scripture, he argued that it was I who did not know what I was talking about since his pastor had taught him differently. He quoted Paul who said: "No one is righteous." It's a common false teaching in the church that no one is righteous. Paul's teaching is taken out of a larger Bible context. Do you remember my prior discussion on this?

I asked the young man to explain to me why the Apostle Luke taught us that Zacharias and Elizabeth "were both righteous before God, walking in all the commandments and ordinances of the LORD blameless." Besides being able to listen and reason with one another, when an elder speaks, all should listen carefully. Do so for a variety of reasons. Wisdom dictates that much. What is the difference in our discussion? It is simple. I possess first hand knowledge of what the Scriptures actually say from over 25 years of in depth studies and I only offer up Scripture for you to consider. Isn't that what Jesus did when he said: "It is written?" On the other hand, the young man was willing to argue based solely upon what another man had taught him. He did not possess first hand knowledge of Scripture to any degree.

Everything I write about in this book is based upon in depth first hand knowledge and experience. I do not write about a new theory or speculate about what the Bible says. When you come at me with your second hand knowledge, I will respond to you by quoting Scripture. If you have some limited first hand knowledge of Scripture, it will not be good enough, as I will use all of the Scripture. It is only through the use of all of God's Word that you can understand HIS character and intentions. If you have a conflict in your mind like the one above, because you read Paul's statement, your mind should be open to a larger dialogue from God's Word on the subject.

Myth—God Owns Solid Rock

Another illustration is that of politics. I suspect that at some point in our U.S. history, we could recognize the validity of the statement that our President must have more facts than we do in the general public. Therefore, we are not usually in a position to really debate the merits of his decisions. That said, it is really remarkable how the public can be whipped up into a frenzy by political demagoguery that misstates facts or leaves some unsaid. People get angry and rant and rave without knowing anything except second hand knowledge and hearsay. You know—"So and so said this and that and I know for sure it must be fact." Therefore, I have the right to be mad. Do you really know for sure? I doubt it. The manipulation of the minds of the public is an unmistakable fact in our society. Likewise pulpit manipulation of the minds of Christians is also an unmistakable fact.

Writer Lonny Kocina in his book *Media Hypnosis: Unleashing The Most Powerful Sales Tool On Earth*, (Mid-America Entertainment, Inc., 2002), speaks from over 15 years of direct experience in staging news stories for various companies. Yes, I said staging news stories. We are not just getting bombed with information from the pulpit and media; product advertisements of all type are also bombing us. Simply put, our minds are shutting down to most product ads. Society has become incredibly noisy to our minds with everything that is going on. One hundred years ago, people did operate mainly off of first hand knowledge that everyone shared. Today, however, the sheer level of sensory input each one of us is exposed to is literally 200-1,000 times larger than our ancestors were exposed to. No one can keep up mentally and most of us no longer make any attempt to try.

Ads are the ultimate turn off to our minds. We now have machines like the TIVO recorder that will not only record the television, cable or satellite shows we like, they also give us the convenience of skipping all the advertisements of the show. A three-hour Titanic movie just ran on regular television two nights ago in a four-hour time slot. Therefore, you had to endure one hour of advertisements if you watched the show. Do the math here and you'll find that your senses are being assaulted 25% of the time with paid commercials. Kocina's company, Media Relations, Inc. has found another way to penetrate your mind with product information. Instead of placing advertisements, his company converts product ads into news stories.

Myth—God Owns Solid Rock

Kocina documents in his book that we are more receptive to product information when we learn about a product in any newspaper, television or radio story. In short, we believe there is more objectivity to the information about the product because it does not come directly from the company. In contrast, many such stories are staged so the information can get into our minds, which now easily rejects an "obvious ad." In fact, companies are directly behind these news campaigns. Disappointed? Don't be, it is just one more way our minds are manipulated. Advertisements themselves are getting incredibly creative just to capture our attention. Some of them are ingenious. However, the ability of those ads to generate sales is low due to our information overload, even if we do enjoy a one-minute anecdote.

Satan is alive and in all of the churches to some extent or another and tries to manipulate your mind at every opportunity. Yet, verily I say to you this fact: "Your mind cannot be manipulated away from the truth of God's Word when you actually have first hand knowledge of that truth." It means that you must read the Bible yourself and hold everyone accountable to what it says. Leave any church that contradicts "obvious" Bible truth. Anything less and you are easily manipulated and controlled like a ringed-nosed cow.

Christ's own ministry was not immune from the influence of Satan. Consider that Judas Iscariot was a servant of Satan who masqueraded as a righteous man amongst Christ's apostles. And consider these words of Jesus Christ. Who do you think Christ was talking to, Peter or Satan? Jesus was speaking to Peter, but his rebuke was directed towards Satan. Peter was just the human instrument Satan was using as a front for his thoughts at the time.

> **Jesus turned and said to Peter, "Get behind me, Satan! You are a stumbling block to me; you do not have in mind the things of God, but the things of men." Matthew 16:23 NIV**

Both God And Satan Influence Man!

Wondrous thoughts from God flow into our minds, but Satan also tries to get in and influence us. So, how do you know if it is God or Satan?

Myth—God Owns Solid Rock

Jesus explains clearly that Satan will influence you with the things of men and of this world. Instead of a heavenly focus, you will get influenced to focus on this earthly life and the things of men. This is another way you will know who you are dealing with. Is the focus on this world or is the focus on Heaven? If one pulpit teacher says: "The anointing belongs to you for your health and wealth on earth" — and another says: "You will suffer on earth like Christ suffered" — which one is of God? Figure out which one is a heavenly focus and you'll have the answer. Unfair question? I don't think so. Not when you consider some other things that Christ taught us.

Now let's return to another graphic illustration of my church travels for further discussion. Set aside the two-zone analysis where one group or zone adheres to Bible instructions and the other doesn't. This time, let's separate out the churches I traveled through into three separate zones based upon their use of emotion during the worship service. Don't get mad at me by the church identities below. Remember, this is just the path I traveled and it is for illustrative purposes. I will use my own life to explain three new zones and why Satan may also be waiting for you in a WOF church.

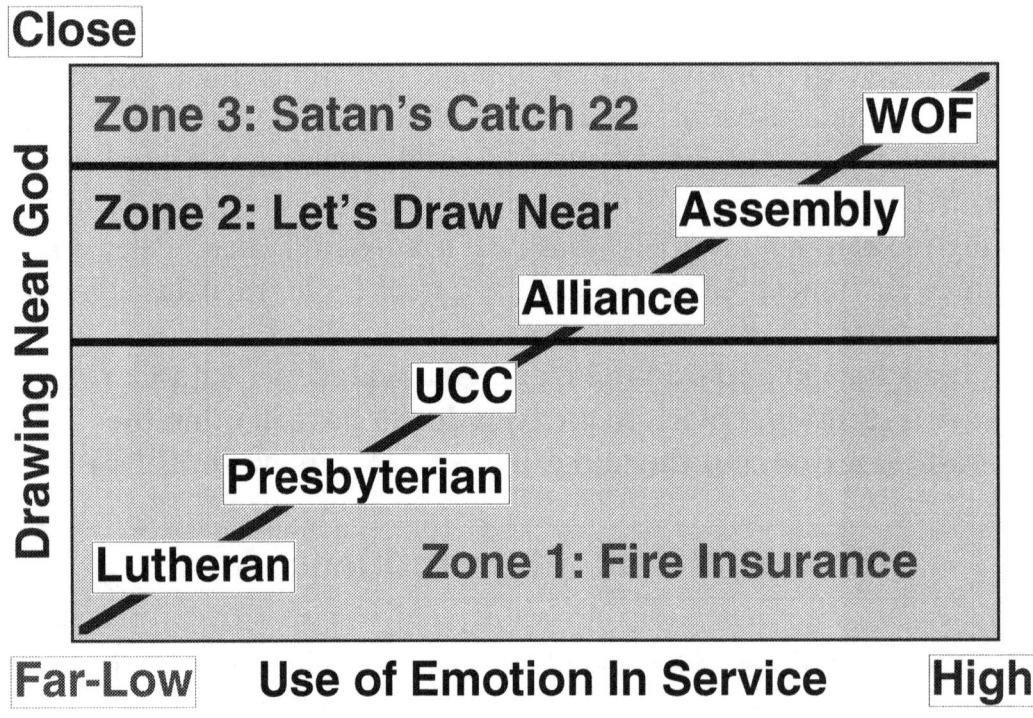

Myth—God Owns Solid Rock

Itching Christian Ears!

If the above graphic, three separate zones are now developed. Zone 1 is the fire insurance zone and is basically the same zone shown as Zone 1 in the prior graphic. Not every church located in Zone 1 will be a non-Bible adhering church by virtual of denomination. Also, remember the sea change that occurred in all mainline churches since 1950. Having said that, the lack of adherence to all of the word of God is a salient feature of churches located in this zone. Not submitting to God's Word is the big giveaway in this zone that you are *really* not in a house of God.

Once someone has caught the Spirit of God into the bowels of their soul where their heart resides they will become hungry and thirsty for all of His Word. They will find it illogical to profess a belief in the Holy Bible without then believing what it actually says. Likewise, they will find it very illogical to profess belief in the salvation of Christ without doing exactly what Christ told us to do "if we called him Lord." Having caught the wind of the Spirit, such a person will pour himself or herself into the Word, which is our sole basis of faith and salvation. I know. That is exactly what I did.

The Zone 1 conflict occurs when the pulpit teachings contradict in an obvious way what the Bible presents as truth. At that time you leave what can only be termed an apostate church. You then enter Zone 2, which I have termed "Let's draw near [to God]." You enter into a Bible based church that has a righteousness focus built into its teachings. This may still be a trinity believing church, yet it is not confused about the need for righteousness. As you get thirstier for the Word, you seek out other Bible churches and find some that offer a stronger worship experience. As in the first graphic, you have the general impression that you are evolving your way closer to God as you leave behind any church that is "not fully with it." Unbeknownst to you is that as you move upward in this perception of getting closer to God, you are being increasingly drawn into more of an emotional experience within the church. Your mind's input is being supplanted by an emotional input. Where your mainline church service kept you for one hour total, your new WOF church thinks nothing of a 4-6 hour emotional worship experience.

Myth—God Owns Solid Rock

You eventually evolve to Zone 3, which is labeled Satan's Catch 22 zone. Did I not warn you that Satan knows you will want to get closer to God and that you might find him waiting for you? In Zone 3 your emotions are brought into play in a way that makes you feel special and part of God's last day remnants. "It's the true church, unlike those apostate ones." This is the path that I traveled and watched others travel. I left a church that was obviously an apostate church because it was open about its unwillingness to obey the word of God. I traveled through strong Bible based churches that adhered to the Word. Eventually I wound up in a church where God's Word was carefully manipulated so that the obvious apostasy found in the Zone 1 church would not be so apparent. Instead of moving closer to God, I found myself in yet another den of Satan. This time, emotion would be used as the method of controlling people and the Word would be carefully twisted so as not to seem so obvious. The pulpit teachings shifted to health and wealth and the other things of men. What Jesus indicated when he spoke to Peter and rebuked Satan I saw manifested in WOF churches. This group would also feed the "itching ears" of their congregations exactly what they wanted.

True Worship Involves Our Emotions!

We are taught by Jesus Christ to worship God "in spirit and truth." The truth aspect involves the entire Bible. The spirit aspect must engage our emotions, because it must originate from the bowels of our soul—our heart. Therefore, I do not say you shouldn't get involved with your emotions during worship. It is the opposite. You will never experience the depth of worship possible unless you do engage your emotions and the fullness of your heart. Yet, verily I say unto you that your emotions cannot supplant the truth of God's Word. Your emotions must be tied to the truth. Only then can you experience what Christ refers to as "true worship" of the FATHER.

> **"Yet a time is coming and has now come when the true worshipers will worship the FATHER in spirit and truth, for they are the kind of worshipers the FATHER seeks. God is spirit, and HIS worshipers must worship in spirit and in truth." John 4:23-24 NIV**

Myth—God Owns Solid Rock

If you think it is hard to leave a church when a new pastor arrives because of the friends you've made, try leaving a church when emotions are also engaged. In such a church there is a new level of control deployed. It will work too, except against those who are truly committed to God's Word. My emotions were engaged, but I still became very upset when Matthews revealed his true allegiance to Satan by manipulating the word of God to suit his financial needs. Any questions I had over the nuances of color shades in Matthews' teachings were answered completely when his mouth obviously denied what was written in God's Word. I had to once again move on. A few of us visited different churches for about a year seeking a new home.

God eventually called us together to form a small Bible based church group. That became our new home for spiritual fellowship. After two years of leading services and in depth Bible studies, our group officially ordained my ministry. Everyone knew that God had called us into something special. Yet it would be another two years before this book would start to take shape. First, God had to move all of us out of the Christian mythology that we were programmed with and anchor us back into just the truth of His Word.

Regardless of what your beliefs are in Christianity, Satan has a church designed to be attractive to you unless you are grounded in God's Word. It is a place where your itching ears can be satisfied. It is a place where you will be literally fed exactly what you and others like you want to hear and nothing of biblically sound doctrines. It will be a place where like-minded believers will help reinforce each other's beliefs. Remember the illustration of an entire Gay and lesbian church reinforcing each other in the belief that their sexual sins are okay? If you are a practicing homosexual or lesbian and want the support of a Christian church that will teach you the Bible supports this sexual sin, you will find such a church. Try the Episcopal Church in your area first. That is what I am talking about. Regardless of what sin you want to have endorsed, Satan has an assembly of believers just for you.

If you believe abortion is okay, you will find a church to support your belief in abortion. I have even heard that some churches teach that abortion can be considered as a sacrifice unto God. Literally whatever sin you'd like to have endorsed by a clergyman, a church meeting your criteria awaits you.

Myth—God Owns Solid Rock

Do you remember the two prophecies I opened this book with? Think about them once again now that you have a more full perspective of the many different types of churches. Is the clarity of God's Word in these two prophecies coming through to your mind? I certainly hope so. Remember, I have taught you that both of these prophecies are now fulfilled. Exactly what type of church are you going to? Which zone represents it?

> **"For the time will come when men will not put up with sound doctrine. Instead, to suit their own desires, they will gather around them a great number of teachers to say what their itching ears want to hear."** 2 Timothy 4:3 NIV

> **"The coming of the lawless one will be in accordance with the work of Satan displayed in all kinds of counterfeit miracles, signs and wonders, and in every sort of evil that deceives those who are perishing. They perish because they refused to love the truth and so be saved. For this reason God sends them a powerful delusion so that they will believe the lie and so that all will be condemned who have not believed the truth but have delighted in wickedness."**
> 2 Thessalonians 2:9-12 NIV

I never cease to be amazed at how God has shifted every single page of this book into what HE wants to talk about. This chapter is no exception. I originally thought it would be more focused on the theft of Solid Rock Church, but God is choosing instead to have me instruct you on what you need to look out for in these various churches. First is the obvious lack of adhering to God's Word. It doesn't take much brainpower to just leave such a church. Can we *really* have it both ways mentally? That is to say, where is the common sense in attending a church that bases its salvation on a book that it really doesn't entirely believe in? Except for a few select passages?

A short while ago God refocused my mind on the word "counterfeit" in the second prophecy above. There is a clear distinction to be made. Zone 1 churches that do not adhere to the Bible are not really counterfeiting in the sense of Paul's teaching, are they? These are dry churches. Miracles?

Myth—God Owns Solid Rock

Clearly Zone 1 churches benefit from the false trinity and salvation doctrines talked about earlier, but these are not something they counterfeit since they are orthodox teachings. These two false doctrines are reasons the Bible's text can be so easily ignored. However, there is usually no attempt in Zone 1 churches to work at "miracles, signs and wonders." On the other hand, *Word of Faith* [WOF] churches specialize in these three areas.

Indeed, the WOF church seeks to convince you that it is behind all of God's Word. Yet it carefully crafts a message to be ever so deceptive and enticing. It is the WOF church that we now need to consider further. Let's contrast God's Word against WOF church practices to see if they line up with biblical truth. You may be surprised if you are into such a church with your emotions today. Have I told you that the difficulty of leaving any church is also in direct proportion to the length of time that you and your family have attended it? What if your children are grown adults with their own families attending the same church in which you've just discovered is not telling the truth? Do you think they will leave with you as you exit the church just taking your word for it? If the WOF church has done its job programming your family members and drawing in everyone's emotions, anyone who leaves will be looked down upon as not saved or even evil. Be aware of these words of Jesus concerning family conflict.

> **"Do not suppose that I have come to bring peace to the earth. I did not come to bring peace, but a sword. For I have come to turn man against his father, a daughter against her mother, a daughter-in-law against her mother-in-law—a man's enemies will be the members of his own household." Matthew 10:34-36 NIV**

Jesus goes on to point out that he must be first over family members. Conflict arises when both sides claim that this is true, but one side states the church is evil. I bear witness to such family conflicts. These disputes would resolve themselves if everyone just submitted to the word of God. They don't. Many in the family will take sides with a so-called "anointed" pastor over their very own mother and father. Why? It is because they have been regularly programmed that they should not "mess with God's anointed!"

Myth—God Owns Solid Rock

Verily I say to you that if you dishonor your parents in the process of taking sides with any pastor, you are lawless in the eyes of God Almighty. A good approach would be to work out the spiritual conflict from within the family using the Holy Bible as the final arbitrator. Keep the "anointed" pastor out of the discussion group when his or her ministry is the spiritual issue being discussed. You get lawful when you stick to the word of God and let it determine the outcome. You get lawless when you ignore the word of God. One of HIS key commandments is to honor your mother and father. HIS Word doesn't teach you to dishonor parents and honor the pastor. That is truly the stuff of Christian mythology as taught in WOF churches.

Fifteen Spiritual Warnings!

- ❑ Ministers having the appearance of righteousness [2 Cor. 11]
- ❑ Ministers' traveling around the world to win converts [Matthew 23].
- ❑ Ministers gathering a great number of speakers to speak [2 Tim. 4].
- ❑ Speakers teaching what itching Christian ears want to hear [2 Tim. 4].
- ❑ Many prophecies done in the name of Jesus [Matthew 7].
- ❑ Many demons cast out in the name of Jesus [Matthew 7].
- ❑ Many wonders done in the name of Jesus [Matthew 7].
- ❑ Counterfeit miracles, signs and wonders to wow people [2 Thess. 2].
- ❑ All sorts of evil deceiving those destined to perish [2 Thess. 2].
- ❑ A powerful delusion for those who do not love truth [2 Thess. 2].
- ❑ Congregations that refuse to "put up" with sound doctrine [2 Thess. 2].
- ❑ Lawlessness behind the scenes, not obvious to people [Matthew 7].
- ❑ Teaching the things of men and not the things of God [Matthew 16].
- ❑ A focus on worldly things instead of heavenly things [James 4].
- ❑ Emotions used to lure people away from God's Word [Edward 16].

Check off the characteristics of your church!

Copyright 2005 Edward G. Palmer, All Rights Reserved.

Myth—God Owns Solid Rock

It is easy to spot a WOF church because everything on the ministry side is usually first class from a worldly perspective. Look at the monthly ministry magazine and you may find a four-color booklet that would put major for profit corporations to envy over its professionalism. The message is clear: "Anything the world can do, we can do better in our church." You can even find coffee shops, bookstores and other merchants within these kinds of churches.

"Jesus entered the temple area and drove out all who were buying and selling there. He overturned the tables of the moneychangers and the benches of those selling doves. It is written, he said to them, '[God's] house will be called a house of prayer,' but you are making it a den of robbers [crooked merchants]." Matthew 21:12-13 NIV

Verily I say unto you that God's house is supposed to be a house of prayer and spiritual sanctuary. The peddling of doves and other sacrifices for use in the house of God is certainly of the past. Today, it is cappuccino, books, instructional tapes, music tapes, compact discs and other merchandise of the "modern day peddlers." Who peddles the merchandise? It is the great number of speakers called to feed the itching ears of the congregation things they want to hear. These speakers reinforce local teachings and sell onsite a variety of stuff for use in the house of God. Listen, have you read the Bible yet? I doubt it. Why not stop buying all the merchandise of these peddlers until you at least know what God's Word actually has to say?

The most glaring aspect of a WOF church is not the obvious speaking against God's Word as this church knows you have evolved out of Zone 2 and are on the alert for obvious apostasy. No, the big sign of Satan's Zone 3 church is its focus on the things of men and of this world. You can observe this focus in health and wealth messages, the coffee shops, the bookstores, the audio and CD sales booths, etc. You can even observe it in the private planes, personal pilots and Cadillac cars that are owned by these "anointed" ministers of God. Yes, I know, they say they are just blessed, but where do you think these blessings came from? Do you think they originated from Jesus Christ who told his followers to travel light without a moneybag?

Myth—God Owns Solid Rock

Jesus ... drove out all who were buying and selling [in the church]. Matthew 21:12 NIV

Here is a novel question for each church to consider. If Jesus did not tolerate the buying and selling of merchandise in the house of God, why do so many churches, especially WOF churches? Should we not emulate the characteristics of Jesus? What exactly is supposed to be done in the church? We are supposed to *teach the people the law* and *preach the word* of God.

Teach The Law And *Preach* The Word!

Listen to the Bible teachings below and ask yourself why anything other than the Word is preached at any church. For example, why is a social message preached from a mainline church pulpit instead of God's Word? Exactly how much can anyone learn about God's Word in a short 10-minute sermon in a short hour-long service? Given the clear last days implications of Bible prophecy, is the Christian church preparing its congregations of people for Heaven or Hell with such limited instruction from God's Word?

> **God said: "For the lips of a priest should keep knowledge, and people should seek the Law from his mouth; for he is the messenger of the LORD of hosts." Malachi 2:7 NKJV**

> **Jesus said: "Do not think that I have come to abolish the Law or the Prophets; I have not come to abolish them but to fulfill them." Matthew 5:17 NIV**

> **Paul said: "Preach the Word; be prepared in season and out of season; correct, rebuke and encourage—with great patience and careful instruction." 2 Tim. 4:2 NIV**

God gave instructions that the *Law* should proceed from the mouth of the priest. Jesus made it clear that he did not abolish the *Law*. Paul taught Timothy to *preach the Word [Law]*. If you can understand these three Bible verses, you can understand what Jesus means by the term *lawlessness*!

Copyright 2005 Edward G. Palmer, All Rights Reserved.

Book of Edward—Chapter 16

Myth—God Owns Solid Rock

On a given Bible study in our small assembly, we would spend at least two solid hours studying God's Word. That is a minimum of 120 minutes per week in contrast to 10-minutes in many churches. Let's run the numbers and calculate what you may be getting taught in your one-hour service. If the sermon is only 10-minutes in length, in a 52-week year, you receive 520 minutes or 8.7 hours of instruction on God's word. Odds are strong that in this same time, the weekly sermons would be less than 50% concentrated on the actual word of God. Therefore, our little assembly would cover more Scripture in two weeks than the average mainline church covers in an entire year. Don't think just because you lug your Bible to a WOF church and spend 4-6 hours in an emotional service it is much better. I have carefully tracked many of the messages of these churches and they recycle the same stuff most of the time. Therefore, if you are a member of a WOF church, there is no doubt you are clocking more "in-church" hours. However, there is serious doubt if you are being taught anything more substantive from the Holy Bible than if you spent only one-hour a week in a mainline church.

This brings up the importance of getting into a solid Bible based church and also getting into a small Bible study group. One thing your family can do is to start reading a chapter a night at the dinner table. In an age when biblical knowledge may make a difference in your eternal soul, can you understand why you need to be reading the Bible? God makes it very clear that our faith is built up by hearing His Word.

"So then faith comes by hearing, and hearing by the word of God." Romans 10:17 NKJV

This isn't rocket science. How do you learn and master any subject? You study it. Reading instead of listening provides an estimated 75% of our knowledge. Therefore, if you never read your Bible, good luck. Jesus may say that you were lawless because you were mentally clueless about Bible teachings. Let me add another caveat. You might spend as much as 12-20 hours a week in a WOF church through various services like I did and still get very little Bible teaching. Why? It's because their mainstay of health and wealth messages constantly recycle the same verses. Start writing dates alongside Bible verses taught and you will get a rude awakening.

Copyright 2005 Edward G. Palmer, All Rights Reserved.

Myth—God Owns Solid Rock

The surprise you will get is how very little of the Bible you are being exposed to. If you are in a WOF church, you know Malachi 3:8 by heart. However, has the pastor ever taught you Malachi 3:16? How about Deuteronomy 14:22-29? The first is why it is good for God's people to discuss His Word just like we are doing here. The second is the actual Tithe Law and instructions from God. The tithe is the subject of the next chapter. For now you should understand it is not how many hours in church you are that matter, it is how many hours in God's Word that matters. Sitting in the church will not provide eternal life. Yet God's Word sinking deep into the bowels of your soul where your heart resides will.

In the naïve mind of Bible ignorant church attendees, all churches and or denominations might appear on the surface like they are equal. Their perception of the many different types of churches in Christianity might look something like this graphic. Again, using my church path as an example. On balance all of these churches are equal in their Bible ignorant eyes and no church is closer to God than any other. Such is the bliss of ignorance. Is there a single church that would steer you wrong? Hello. Anyone home?

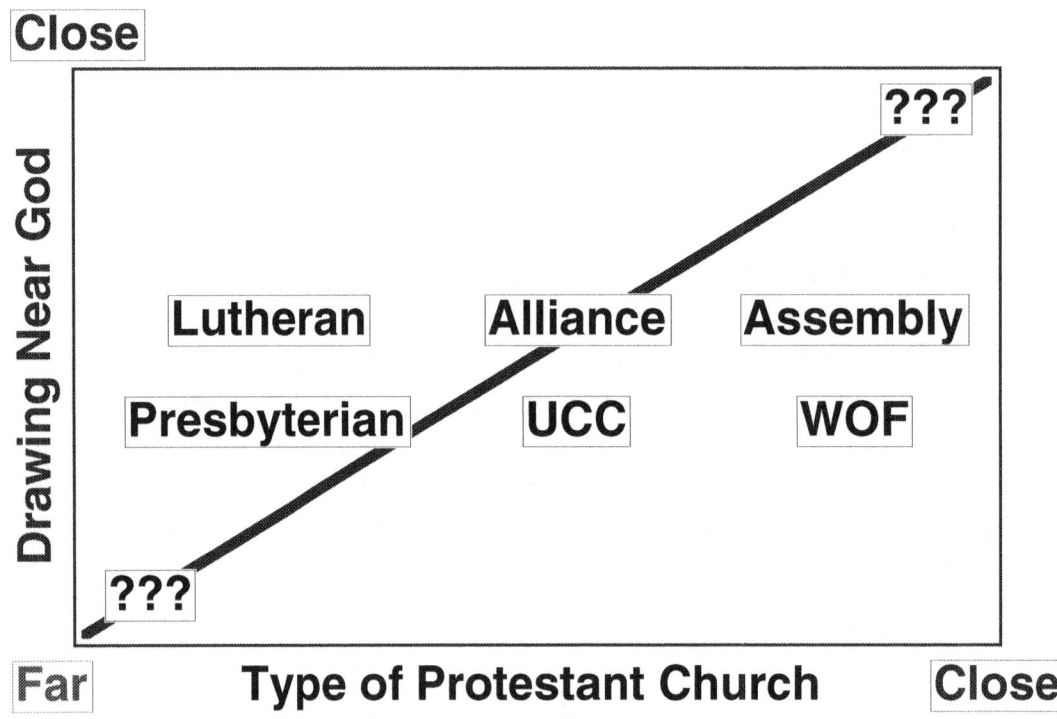

Copyright 2005 Edward G. Palmer, All Rights Reserved.

Book of Edward—Chapter 16

Myth—God Owns Solid Rock

You might not understand that you are sitting in a lair of Satan by just listening to the pulpit message. Remember, Satan's servants are supposed to appear and sound righteous. However, you should get out fast when the focus of the ministry is on things other than God's Word. I am telling you to not just listen to what the pastor says. I am telling you to take a close look at what is going on and the focus of the ministry. It is very important that you also look behind the scenes and into the hierarchy of the church and its leaders. Christ said: "You will know them by their fruits." It means you will know them by what they are doing and the focus of their ministry.

Again, to be fair to all Christian denominations, you never know for sure which church is of God unless you are already on the inside observing what is being taught and what the focus of the church is. From the outside appearance, all churches might be in Zone 2 in our three-zone analogy. God will sort out what churches are in Zone 1 and Zone 3 during the time Christ comes back. Who is really closer to God and who is closer to Satan will also be sorted out. In the interim, be aware again that you will not be collectively judged with everyone else who is inside the church that you attend. Instead, you will be judged individually as God has ordained.

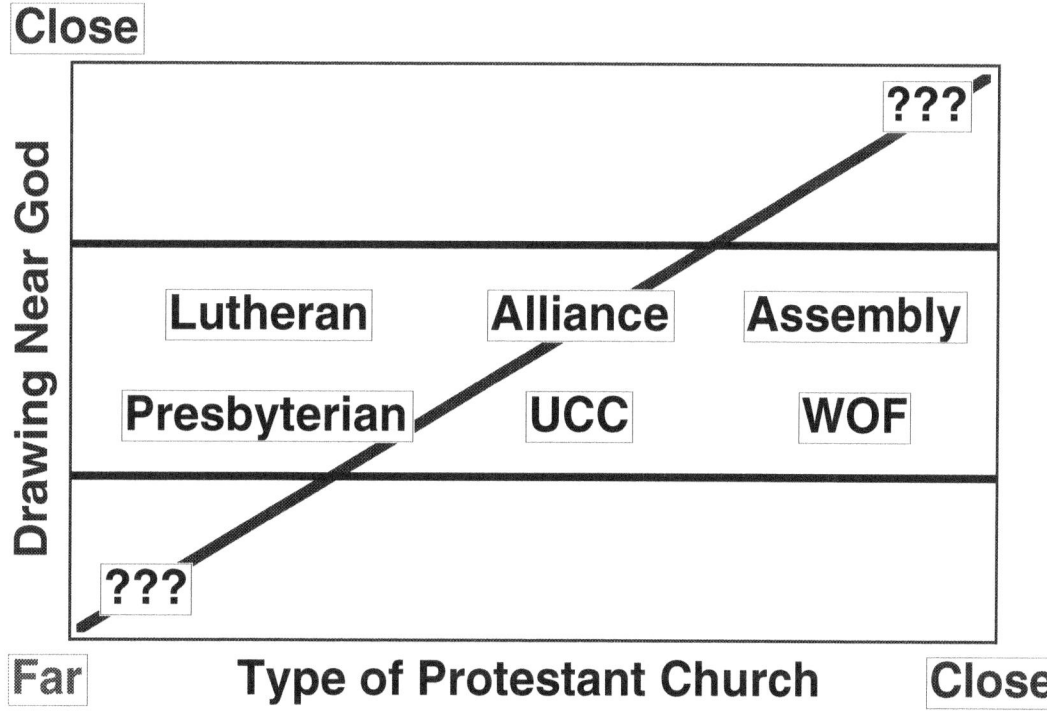

Myth—God Owns Solid Rock

Seven Signs Of A Satanic Church!

1. Church is unfaithful to God's Word.
2. Church does not preach God's Word.
3. Church preaches social messages v. Word.
4. Church gives lip service to God's Word.
5. Church focuses on the things of men.
6. Church focuses on things of the world.
7. Church has merchants inside or outside.

There are many warnings God has given the Christian church. To fully understand the different churches and God's warnings to them, you need to study Revelation chapters 1-3. You will find instructions for every church that now exists from God and HIS Son. You will find a church guide.

"Yet you have a few people in Sardis who have not soiled their clothes. They will walk with me ... he who overcomes will, like them, be dressed in white. I will never blot out his name from the *Book of Life*, but will acknowledge his name before my FATHER and HIS angels." Rev. 3:4-5 NIV

Go ahead and locate your own church in Revelation chapters 1-3 and find its strengths and weaknesses. In the message to the church at Sardis, Christ states that some people within the church are already dressed in white and listed in his *Book of Life*. Christ then makes note that there is still time for others in the church to join them. Maybe you? Hence the instruction "If you overcome *like those already dressed in white*." It is obvious that the congregation of the Sardis church is not condemned as a group. God has some people in that church as HE has in all the others. Therefore, God will deal with us on an individual basis. The truth of who is closer to God or Satan actually looks like the graphic below. Those closer to God will have HIS knowledge and a deep love for HIM in a passionately loyal heart.

Copyright 2005 Edward G. Palmer, All Rights Reserved.

Book of Edward—Chapter 16

Myth—God Owns Solid Rock

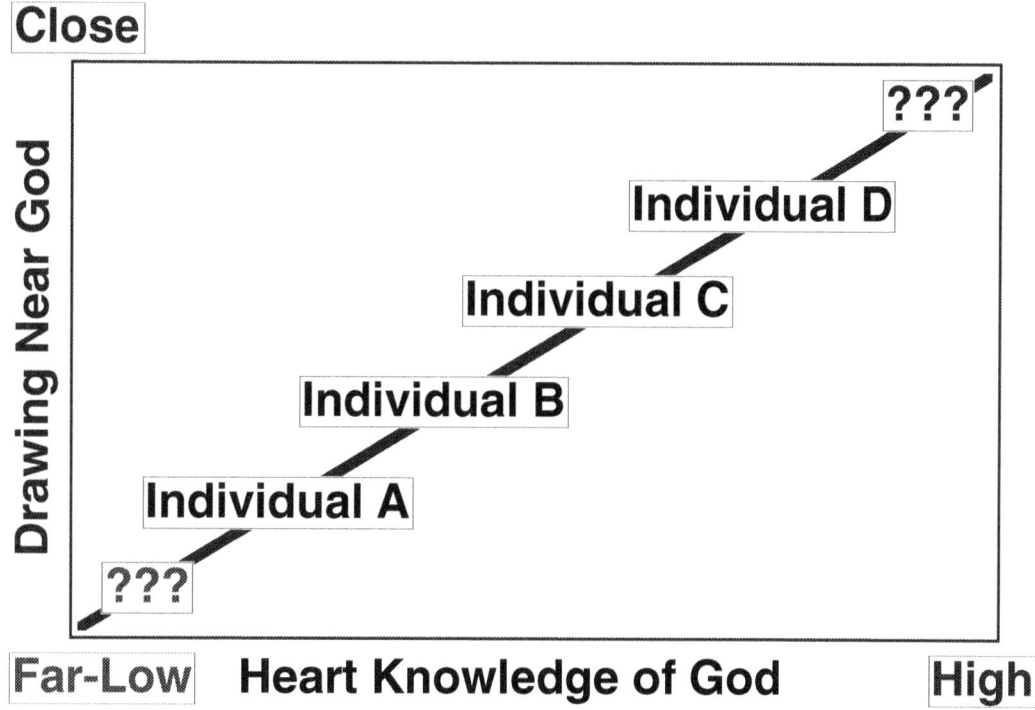

Note this warning in Revelation 2:4 to the church of Ephesus.

"Yet I hold this against you: You have forsaken your first love. Remember the height from which you have fallen! Repent and do the things you did at first. If you do not repent, I will come to you and remove your lampstand from its place." Rev. 2:4-5 NIV

Exactly whom is the "first love" talked about in this warning to the church at Ephesus? Can there be any first love other than that of Yahweh [God]? No, there cannot be any other. And, that includes God's human begotten Son Jesus Christ. There are many Christians today who have forsaken the first love of God Almighty. They are so focused on Christ; they forget that Christ came to bring us back to our first love, which is God. What is the penalty for failing to return to our first love? It is the taking away of our lampstand. In plain English, it is the erasing of our name from the *Book of Life*. It gets back to the first commandment. Thou shall have no other gods before me; I am a jealous God, etc.; this includes Jesus.

Myth—God Owns Solid Rock

Verily I say that you need to listen carefully now. "Every Christian who substitutes Jesus Christ in the place of Yahweh [God] does not truly understand the relationship of Jesus to Yahweh [God] and has forsaken their first love." There can only be ONE first love and that is God Almighty. It is the person whom Jesus called the FATHER. Even in the book of Revelation, the relationship between Christ and God is very clear. Yahweh is Christ's God and they are not one and the same. Example, see Revelation 3:12.

> *WARNING: Do not pray and worship to Jesus Christ as your God. Pray and worship to Yahweh his FATHER like Jesus taught you to do. Indeed, you pray to the FATHER in Jesus' name to honor God's Son. However, do not think you can alter the relationship that God has established and substitute Jesus Christ as your God. This doesn't mean you cannot pray to Jesus as God's Son. You can. However, here again the words of Jesus tell you not to ask of him anymore, but instead to ask of the FATHER, our God. There are serious consequences and it is Christ speaking in Revelation 2 that makes this point clear. It is not I. Go back and study the False Trinity Doctrine chapter if you are still confused about who is our God. Failure to take heed to this warning may affect your eternal life. Your own personal lampstand may be taken away if you cannot get this straight and repent unto God. Jesus is not God Almighty!*

Many in Christendom seem to be just like the storybook character Pinocchio. Remember the story of this marionette made of wood that comes to life? Geppetto names his wooden marionette Pinocchio after a whole family named Pinocchio, because they *were all lucky*. Geppetto asserts the "name will make his fortune." Pinocchio sets off for one of his adventures and is greeted by a Fox who asks: "Do you want to double your gold pieces?" "What do you mean?" "Do you want one hundred, a thousand, two thousand gold pieces for your miserable five?" "Yes, but how?" "The way is easy. Instead of returning home, come with us." They start walking towards the city of simple Simons. Along the path, Pinocchio encounters a talking Cricket who says: "I want to give you a few words of good advice. Return home and give the four gold pieces you have left to your poor father

Myth—God Owns Solid Rock

who is weeping because he has not seen you for many a day." Pinocchio responds, "Tomorrow my father will be a rich man, for these four gold pieces will become two thousand." The Cricket cautions with the following: "Don't listen to those who promise you wealth overnight, my boy. As a rule they are either fools or swindlers! Listen to me and go home." The talking Cricket knows that bad and evil company will corrupt good character. It makes him smarter than many Christians who fellowship with such people.

> **"Do not be misled: Bad company corrupts good character."**
> **1 Corinthians 15:33 NIV**

Isn't the wealth pitch to Pinocchio similar to that from a preacher who says your offering will get you a 30, 60 or 100 fold return from God? That is a very good return on investment at a time when a bank savings account deposit might only bring you 1-2% annual interest. We all know the trouble Pinocchio got into by believing in a path to easy wealth and riches. Verily I say to you that many Christians are just as clueless on a similar fake path.

> **"[There are] men of corrupt mind[s], who have been robbed of the truth and who think that godliness is a means to financial gain." 1 Timothy 6:3-5 NIV**

I witnessed the same delusion of the storybook character Pinocchio in Christians who attended *Word of Faith* churches. Zone 3 churches *also* feed men and women exactly what their itching ears want to hear. What could be more enticing to itching ears than the promise of easy wealth and riches? William Neal Matthews once taught: "Who knows which offering God will bless this day? You need to give something into every offering." I placed money into four separate offerings that day at Solid Rock Church. Indeed, I was programmed to respond in the manner this pastor wanted me to. Are you also programmed in a similar manner with Zone 3 mythology?

After I gave my heart to God, I left an apostate church that was not faithful to the word of God. I traveled through Bible based orthodox trinity churches and ended up in a *Word of Faith* trinity church. The WOF church fed my emotions and cleverly hid its apostate messages. Such was the path of my church travels as I attempted to get closer and closer to my God.

Copyright 2005 Edward G. Palmer, All Rights Reserved.

Myth—God Owns Solid Rock

In the final analysis, I ended up exactly where Satan had hoped I would remain. I was grounded in biblical truth while in Zone 2 churches. I believed that Zone 3 churches provided a deeper worship experience without compromising the Word. I didn't realize Bible teachings were corrupted in very subtle ways and that evil was actively taking place behind the scenes.

Satan thought he found a permanent home for me in a Zone 3 WOF church that was designed to feed "itching Christian ears." However, he did not realize that my heart was loyal to God. He also did not realize it is truth that motivates me. When it comes to your soul, there is nothing of value on this earth. Now ask yourself this question. Exactly where is the loyalty of your own heart? Are you a member of a church that belongs to Satan and is designed to feed your itching ears with whatever your own social group will find acceptable? Or are you truly in a house of God that feeds you His Holy Word? Are you easily led astray by Bible ignorance like a ringed-nose cow? Or, is your mind continually fed and sharpened by the two-edged sword of God's Word? No one leads a mind focused on the Word astray from God.

> **Jesus Said: "Feed my sheep!"**
> **Jesus Said: "Feed my sheep!"**
> **Jesus Said: "Feed my sheep!"**

"The third time [Jesus] said to him, 'Simon son of John, do you love me?' Peter was hurt because Jesus asked him the third time, 'Do you love me?' He said, 'Lord, you know all things; you know that I love you.' Jesus said, 'Feed my sheep.' " John 21:17 NIV

What do you think Jesus wanted Peter to feed us? Is it not the bread of eternal life contained in God's Holy Word Jesus wants us to consume? Jesus gave us the answer to this critical church question in Matthew.

Jesus said: "It is written: 'Man does not live on bread alone, but on every word that comes from the mouth of God.' "
Matthew 4:4 NIV

Myth—God Owns Solid Rock

Let me repeat the teaching of Jesus and let it sink deep into your soul. Jesus taught that every single word from the mouth of God was important to you. That is what you are to live on! Therefore, any church that does not give you the words of God Almighty is an apostate church of Satan. This includes God's Word in Malachi 2:7, where HE tells you to seek out the Law from the mouth of the priest. Jesus repeatedly teaches us that the Law does matter in spite of what orthodox Christian Church doctrine espouses.

We Are To <u>Live</u> On *Every* Word From God's Mouth!

Living on God's words can determine the destination of your soul. For the truth is only found in God's Word. What Jesus gave to us while on earth was simple instructions to get us back into God's Word. He didn't change anything of God like many churches teach. Therefore, the only real church of Jesus today is the church that will staunchly defend all of God's Word unaltered by manmade doctrines like the trinity concept. If it is not plainly spoken in the Word, it should not be taught or endorsed by the church. The big lesson in this chapter is that churches will alter the Word in subtle ways to feed Christians exactly what they want to hear from a social and economic perspective. It is almost always different than what the Bible says about any subject. Why? One is a focus on the things of men and the other the things of God. Stick to the Word and find an assembly of believers that will reinforce one another with God's Word. It can save your family.

There are only two more issues to talk about here to bring me spiritual satisfaction from God on this chapter. First, we need to go back and discuss the subject of naming names and why evildoers need to be fully and publicly exposed. You need to understand spiritually why it is that this is a sound biblical teaching. Those doing evil do not have to live life in their evil by covering over their sins. They can stop hiding their sins and make amends. They would receive mercy if they came clean.

> **"People who cover over their sins will not prosper. But if they confess and forsake them, they will receive mercy."**
> **Proverbs 28:13 NLT**

Copyright 2005 Edward G. Palmer, All Rights Reserved.

Myth—God Owns Solid Rock

You were already taught on page 547 some key aspects of what the Bible teaches about naming evildoers. Paul writes in Ephesians chapter five, "it is shameful even to mention what the disobedient do in secret." Paul is talking about "the fruitless deeds of darkness" and he admonishes us to "expose these evil deeds." Some churches teach us to "hide" the evil so that the Church will not be embarrassed. Yet this is not biblically correct. Here are some additional Bible verses you need to be aware of so that you do not support church evil by turning your back and ignoring sin in the Church. If you talk about evil in private, you are engaged in gossip. Also, the sin will not get addressed when only a few people know about it. Think of how many priest molestations could have been prevented if the first molestation was made extremely public. When you can understand this simple fact, you will understand Paul's teaching to Timothy below. Going completely public is a warning to others not to sin. Give evildoers no hidden sanctuary.

Rebuke Publicly So Others Take Warning!

"Do not entertain an accusation against an elder [or pastor] unless it is brought by two or three witnesses [or is obvious and documented in publicly available records]. Those who sin are to be rebuked publicly, so that the others [senior church officials] may take warning." 1 Tim. 5:19-20 NIV

In the above teaching, it is obvious that a strong public witness needs to be made against any church official that is guilty of serious sin [evil]. I have added the comment that the verse obviously is meant to include any pastor who is guilty and also where obvious records exist that document the evil activity. In the case of William Neal Matthews, Minnesota state records document his theft of Solid Rock Church in Elk River, MN and the matter is not open to whether or not he did it. There are those who know the details of the theft and those who don't. I will explain how he stole the church in a moment. Christians who refuse to go public are actually supporters of evil. Everyone who hid a priest's molestation enabled that priest to continue it. If you think it is evil to expose such evil, you are ignorant of the Bible. It is not evil to simply obey what the word of God tells us to do. It is righteous.

Myth—God Owns Solid Rock

I identified and located about 100 adults that witnessed the corporate meetings conducted by Matthews in the process of his theft. Literally about 86% of these professing "spirit-filled" believers would not stand on the truth of what they witnessed. The most repeated statement I heard was: "I do not want to get involved." Another interesting statement was: "I will pray about it." Does anyone need to pray about telling the truth? This is someone who obviously is programmed and headed in the wrong spiritual direction. Run these numbers and you will find that only 14% of this group of believers in a *Word of Faith* church would stand tall for God as HIS witness to the truth.

"Now get up and stand on your feet. I have appeared to you to appoint you as a servant and as a witness of what you have seen of me and what I will show you." Acts 26:16 NIV

If God or HIS Son shows you evil in the church, will you be a witness for them? If not, you will surely be one of those whom Jesus says: "I never knew you." I thought I had reached the zenith of believers who had strong faith and would stand firm for God. I thought I was at the top of all church groups and had gotten as close to God as any church would allow. Surely telling the truth in a court of law would not be a big deal to those who shared with me and also witnessed the events of this church theft. Yet it was.

I wonder what those in every church I ever attended would do under similar circumstances if I found 100 believers in each one of them. I have come to the belief that my Lutheran brothers would make a better showing. It's because I do not believe they have been programmed to ignore evil and "just let God deal with it." I believe this is a specialty teaching in *Word of Faith* and *Pentecostal* churches. Certainly it exists in the Catholic Church given all the priest scandals. What would your own church do? Would more than 14% of your church membership tell the truth in a courtroom?

Now I have to ask you this question. How many in the 100 would lie under oath to cover up the sin of the pastor or elder? Don't tell me that no one would, as I do not believe it. In fact, I believe at least 7 of 100 would step up to the plate in a courtroom to misstate facts, lie or in some other way back up the sinners Paul is talking about in his letter to Timothy.

Myth—God Owns Solid Rock

The Confused Church Is Dressed For Satan!

I've got good reason to think that many believers would be active on Satan's behalf even though they are in the church. After all, Judas was one of twelve original apostles and his evil alone represents 8%. The church of Christ is so confused today that it is "literally dressed for Satan" instead of being dressed for the "bridegroom" who is Christ. Only those who obey God's Word are dressed in white robes awaiting the bridegroom [Christ]. The list below is observations of the many faces of evil in the church. The list includes the actions of Senior Pastor William Neal Matthews and others.

How A Confused Church Supported Evil!

1. Pastor intimidated people with spiritual power plays.
2. Pastor intimidated people with threats of lawsuits.
3. Pastor intimidated board into signing unseen documents.
4. Pastor intimidated staff members into moving out of town.
5. Pastor stood up in front of congregation and outright lied.
6. Pastor manipulated the corporate meetings of the congregation.
7. Pastor filed fraudulent Articles of Incorporation changes.
8. Pastor asked others to ignore the law.
9. Pastor hid material information from members of congregation.
10. Pastor systematically eliminated all opposition within church.
11. Pastor literally kicked opposing people out of the church.
12. Pastor violated various By-Law provisions of corporation.
13. Pastor violated various Articles provisions of corporation.
14. Members loved the pastor more than they loved God's Word.
15. Members loved the pastor over the truth of the evil that he did.
16. Members refused to get involve when they knew the truth.
17. Members refused to come forward unless they were subpoenaed.
18. Members turned their backs and simply left the church.
19. Members turned their backs because they signed documents.
20. Members denied their own first hand knowledge & involvement.
21. Members took the pastor's side and would not examine the facts.

Copyright 2005 Edward G. Palmer, All Rights Reserved.

Book of Edward—Chapter 16

Myth—God Owns Solid Rock

You get the picture in the items above, but the list is not a complete list by any means. The shock that many in the church would not stand up for God and tell the truth about the theft of Solid Rock Church was one surprise. Yet it did not come close to the shock I received from civil authorities and outsiders that could help, but also chose to ignore the crime.

To understand why civil authorities would also turn their backs, I have to go back to a meeting I had with an IRS manager. I was summoned to the IRS to tell them everything I knew about Solid Rock Church. The church was in trouble with some taxes and I do not know how it came to be that they called me in. I was struck by the comment of an IRS manager who told me that if you wanted to be a thief, the best thing to do was to start a church. Yes, that's right. He went on to explain that in order for them to take action against a church, they have to first go before a judge and prove their entire case. Of course, this gets to be a Catch 22 since they are denied access to the information they need right off the bat. Very interesting. Huh?

When I informed the state attorney general's office, they refused to take action because of "budget constraints." A swindler steals a church and its property worth an estimated $6 million [or more] and the state has budget concerns? That doesn't say much for public officials charged with dealing with crime. I received the same reactions from other civil authorities that would prefer the matter just go away. My guess is that Matthews knew of these kinds of church and public reactions from his prior experiences. That is why I think he believed he could actually get away with his theft. Yet, again I ask, has he really gotten away with his crime? Stealing from God?

"For such men are false apostles, deceitful workmen, masquerading as apostles of Christ. And no wonder, for Satan himself masquerades as an angel of light. It is not surprising, then, if his servants masquerade as servants of righteousness. Their end will be what their actions deserve." 2 Cor. 11:13-15 NIV

In The End They Get What Their Actions Deserve!

Myth—God Owns Solid Rock

Nothing will escape the end time review of your life's actions at the time of judgment if you are evil. Paul reminds us those deceitful workmen like William Neal Matthews will in the end get a payback regardless of whether or not it occurs on this earth. Here is a list of some reactions from people who could have done something about this crime but chose not to.

How Community Players Supported Evil!

1. Local newspaper refused to run ads under threat of lawsuit.
2. Local newspaper refused to assist in informing community.
3. Large chunk of membership simply formed a new church.
4. State Attorney General ignored two written theft complaints.
5. City Police Chief ignored a written theft complaint.
6. County Sheriff ignored a written theft complaint.
7. County Attorney blew off a written theft complaint.
8. Large Minneapolis law firm compromised a righteous judge.
9. An unrighteous judge threw out a civil case on a technicality.
10. District Assembly of God sold out the congregation for money.

If you steal an automobile, the county attorney won't hesitate to prosecute you. However, steal a church and that is very a different matter. You can see that people had the opportunity to do their job or at least be a righteous person and help where they could. Yet in many instances, the theft of a church is a hot potato. Those charged with criminal prosecution will pass it off as a civil litigation issue. Once done, you need deep pockets to litigate any solution. Wow. Someone can steal a church and when the beans are spilled on how it happened no one cares. Should I? Such is the depth of the confusion over righteousness in the church and society at large today.

> **"I wrote to the church, but Diotrephes, who loves to be first, will have nothing to do with us. So if I come, I will call attention to what he is doing, gossiping maliciously about us. Not satisfied with that, he refuses to welcome the brothers. He also stops those who want to do so and puts them out of the church." 3 John 1:9-10 NIV**

Copyright 2005 Edward G. Palmer, All Rights Reserved.

Book of Edward—Chapter 16

Myth—God Owns Solid Rock

> "Everyone who does evil hates the light, and will not come into the light for fear that his deeds will be exposed."
>
> John 3:20 NIV

> "I do not want you to be participants with demons."
>
> 1 Corinthians 10:20 NIV

> "What do righteousness and wickedness have in common? Or what fellowship can light have with darkness?"
>
> 2 Corinthians 6:14 NIV

> "Among them are Hymenaeus and Alexander, whom I have handed over to Satan to be taught not to blaspheme."
>
> 1 Timothy 1:20 NIV

> "Their teaching will spread like gangrene. Among them are Hymenaeus and Philetus, who have wandered away from the truth. They say that the resurrection has already taken place, and they destroy the faith of some."
>
> 2 Timothy 2:17-18 NIV

> "Alexander the metalworker did me a great deal of harm. The Lord will repay him for what he has done."
>
> 2 Timothy 4:14 NIV

> "By their fruit you will recognize them. Do people pick grapes from thornbushes, or figs from thistles?"
>
> Matthew 7:16 NIV

Clearly Christ's original apostles were not reluctant to tell the people the names of those who did evil. Jesus Christ taught us that we would know them by their fruit. He was teaching us to make a clear distinction between recognizing evil or "making a judgment" and "passing judgment." When you make a judgment, you are exercising spiritual discernment about what is happening around you. When you are passing judgment, you are acting as executioner and God has said that vengeance belongs to HIM.

Myth—God Owns Solid Rock

Making A Judgment Is Not Passing Judgment!

"Do not judge, and you will not be judged. Do not condemn, and you will not be condemned. Forgive, and you will be forgiven." Luke 6:37 NIV

"Stop judging by mere appearances, and make a right judgment." John 7:24 NIV

"For rulers hold no terror for those who do right, but for those who do wrong. Do you want to be free from fear of the one in authority? Then do what is right and he will commend you." Romans 13:3 NIV

Indeed the authorities are no threat to those who do right. Paul makes that clear in Romans 13. He also makes it clear you are to do what is right. If you hide crime, you are an accomplice to crime. Paul also makes it clear that we are to judge those within the church and kick out those who do evil. We are not to worry about those outside the church, remember?

"What business is it of mine to judge those outside the Church? Are you not to judge those inside [the Church]? God will judge those outside. Expel the wicked man from among you [inside the Church]." 1 Cor. 5:12-13 NIV

The instructions from God remain the same in the Old Testament and the New Testament. God's people are not to tolerate evil in their midst. We are to purge these evildoers and kick them out of the Church. The world itself will still be a pit of evildoers. Yet, if the Church is not any different to those evildoers, how will they be saved? One man wrote to me a while back and told me to hide all the information on Matthews' church theft because it made Christianity look bad. Christianity already looks bad and hypocritical for the very reason that it does hide evil in the Church and puts on a false front. It gets people into a church, but mentally sound people will leave the house of hypocrisy. They know God doesn't sanction or hide evil.

Copyright 2005 Edward G. Palmer, All Rights Reserved.

Book of Edward—Chapter 16

Myth—God Owns Solid Rock

Therefore, the new church attendee that protests to his friends, "they are just a bunch of hypocrites inside that church" — after being exposed to a church that hides sin and evil has every right to do so. In the first place, he or she is exercising discernment like Paul taught by "judging those inside the church." If they find evil being supported, it doesn't take much mental power to conclude that it is not a house of God, even if it professes to be. The true house of God does not condone or hide evil. Secondly, they can get all the evil they want on the streets. Why go to a church and pay offerings to get their form of evil? Besides being hypocritical in nature, it is also sheer stupidity. The church that does not stand for truth and righteousness is a house of Satan and the average Joe is smart enough to realize that fact. Why? God has placed that much inside his heart and mind. Thirdly, when they inform all whom they know, they keep them from unsuspectingly being taken advantage of by evil. This means they do what the apostles did even if the Church at large doesn't get the truth that we should "expose the evil."

I doubt if anyone ever regretted exposing church evil. However, I suspect that many lose much sleep by hiding it. This is especially true when the knowledge of evil they have hid has resulted in the perpetuation of evil onto another family or child. When you step into a church you have a right to expect God's people to be there. When you hide the evil, you fail to let people know that there are Satan's people inside that church.

I had started attending Solid Rock Church in the summer of 1992. My spiritually adopted daughter Karen and her family attended the church and I usually just sat with their family. I had become accustomed to writing dates alongside Bible verses taught by the pastor. I had done this for many years to help me see the breadth of my Bible studies. I also marked the margins up with notes and the name of the pastor who taught the lesson. I even put a date by my individual study verses so I could see how often I returned to the verse. Therefore, my Bibles have become quite colorful and dense with study notes over many years. One advantage of this note keeping is that I have a fairly good historical record of what has been taught at the church I attend. For example, William Neal Matthews was installed as Senior Pastor of the Elk River Assembly of God Church on December 13, 1992 and he taught the first four verses in Jeremiah 23 on righteousness.

Myth—God Owns Solid Rock

How do I know that is fact? I wrote it in my Bible and put a line next to the verses that were taught. What did this church want to hear about after suffering through a sex scandal with a prior pastor? Why, righteousness of course. It was sweet music to our itching ears and Matthews knew it would be so. In this thoroughly decimated church, those "elect" who remained in the assembly welcomed this teaching with open arms. Why not?

The Branch Of Righteousness!

" 'Woe to the shepherds who are destroying and scattering the sheep of MY pasture!' declares the LORD. Therefore this is what the LORD, the God of Israel, says to the shepherds who tend MY people: 'because you have scattered MY flock and driven them away and have not bestowed care on them, I will bestow punishment on you for the evil you have done,' declares the LORD. 'I MYSELF will gather the remnant of MY flock out of all the countries where I have driven them and will bring them back to their pasture, where they will be fruitful and increase in number. I will place shepherds over them who will tend them, and they will no longer be afraid or terrified, nor will any be missing,' declares the LORD." Jeremiah 23:1-4 NIV

I remember how wonderful that message was to the wearied ears of the congregation. But listen. It was not Hoogenboom who scattered the flock of this church. He was knocked off his perch by Satan and after his fall, most of the flock simply left on their own because they did not want to be associated with the evil that the church represented. Instead, I tell you that it was William Neal Matthews who scattered the flock of this church. He systematically drove away the people of this church. The lesson is a strange one. Whatever you think might be going on is probably opposite of what is actually going on. That is Satan's strategy today. It is Matthews who will answer to God for his own lack of righteousness and the scattering of the flock. "I will bestow punishment on you for the evil you have done" declares the LORD. Matthews' first lesson was the stuff of *Orwell's 1984*! [2]

Myth—God Owns Solid Rock

A good swindler executes various events in such manner that they do not seem to be connected in any way to one another. The swindler would do this over a long enough period of time so as not to draw any attention to the con he was working. The longer the time the more obtuse and difficult it is to understand the various events and their connection to one another. In other words, the dots [events] become more difficult to connect over time or to associate with each other. If the swindler is very successful, those being swindled with never become aware of the con. If the swindler is somewhat successful no one will know until it is too late to do anything about the con. In many cases, the con artist leaves town before the con becomes exposed.

The average person being swindled only sees a bunch of disconnected dots like those in the graphic below. They may be multiple colors and not obviously related to one another. Each dot represents a key event that needs to be executed by the con artist for the swindle to become successful.

You Only See Isolated Events

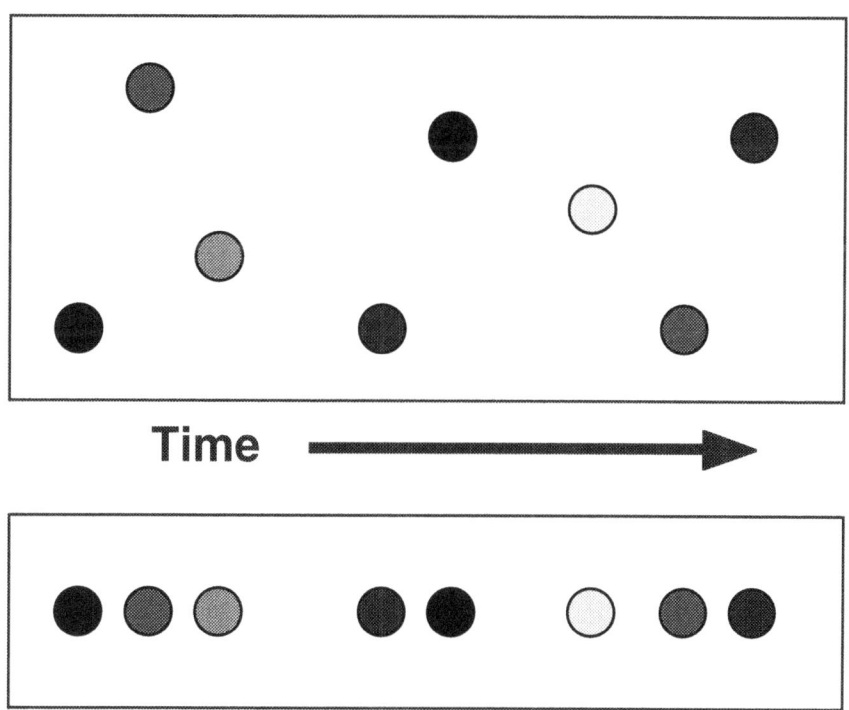

Time ⟶

But, The Swindler Sees Linear Events

Myth—God Owns Solid Rock

When the con gets exposed, all the dots become connected and everyone can then understand what has happened. Usually a sleuth will connect the dots for others to clearly see what took place. This assumes that someone got a clue to the swindle at some point in time.

Exposed Con Reveals Connections

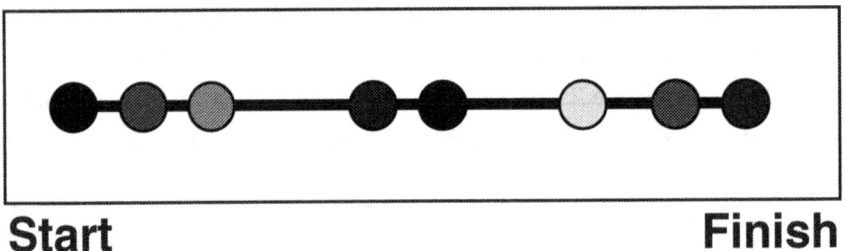

Start Finish

Eight Seemingly Isolated Solid Rock Events!

1. 1991 – Hoogenboom sex scandal rocks Elk River AG Church
2. 1992 – Matthews candidates for senior pastor (September)
3. 1992 – Matthews installed as senior pastor (December)
4. 1993 – Matthews instructs membership classes (May)
5. 1993 – Matthews requests name change (July)
6. 1993 – Matthews files first false Article changes (July)
7. 1995 – Matthews requests change to AFCM Church (July)
8. 1995 – Matthews files final false Article changes (October)

The theft of Solid Rock Church took place over a period of four years. The events listed above appear totally unconnected with one another. They remained that way for ~1 1/2 years after I left the church on November 20, 1996. It was not until April 3, 1998, when I got the Article filings from the Minnesota Secretary of State's Office that I began to piece together the nature of the church swindle that Matthews had pulled off.

God had planted me into that church for a specific reason. I studied corporate law for my own corporations for over thirty years. I understood Articles of Incorporation and By-Laws. Indeed I had created them.

Copyright 2005 Edward G. Palmer, All Rights Reserved.

Book of Edward—Chapter 16

Myth—God Owns Solid Rock

Here is the context of Matthews' **SWINDLE START**: The Elk River Assembly of God Church was doing some great things in the City of Elk River. Then Pastor Hoogenboom's sexual sins were made public. The church became decimated and only a few elect people remained in the assembly. A temporary pastor was there when I began to visit and the church was actively seeking a new pastor. Inside the church, Matthews had family members who were recommending him for the position.

Matthews was a licensed Assembly of God minister and was the pastor of a church in Chelsea, Michigan. He was raised near Elk River in Buffalo, Minnesota and was interested in moving back. The Elk River church was a congregational church established under Minnesota's Non-Profit Corporation Act, Chapter 317A. The By-Laws provided that every member had an equal vote in all matters. They also established criteria for members and directors. The church was incorporated in October 1977 and until July 1993 virtually no changes to the Articles of Incorporation were made. I was attending the church services every week albeit I did not have a clue as to what was happening behind the scenes.

Matthews presented himself as a candidate for senior pastor in September 1992, was voted in and installed in December. I was present from his beginning message until the time I left and I missed very few services. I was not present for the vote on his candidacy since I was not a member. God was pressing me to join the church. So in May 1993, I attended the eight weeks of required membership classes, which Matthews taught. These meetings occurred just prior to the change of name business meeting. According to By-Laws, all Article changes had to be posted on the wall of the church for four consecutive weeks and formal notice had to be mailed to all voting members. Both of these were done. The only change that Matthews requested the members make was the Article I name change.

I remember debating whether or not I should go to the meeting and observe. Like I had a choice. I didn't. God told me to go. I didn't want to get stuck and since I wasn't a member, I sat way in the back next to a door for an easy escape if I got bored. The discussion over the name change was coming to an end. Should I tell the members what God had told me earlier?

Myth—God Owns Solid Rock

I concluded that I would just keep my mouth shut. However, when asked if there was anyone else who wanted to speak, I experienced one of those weird moments with God. The last call to speak sounded like an auctioneer in slow motion to me. Does anyone else want to speak, going once, going twice, anyone? Just then I was unexpectedly and physically ejected out of my pew seat. It felt like two angels had grabbed me by my arms. As they lifted me up, one raised my right hand high up into the air. Before I could figure out what was happening, I heard Matthews say that I wanted to speak. I did? I looked around, but I was alone. The nearest body was at least thirty feet away. I went down to speak after it obviously looked like I had volunteered. I did explain why the name should be changed and what God had told me. However, what took place in the pew that night was so weird I immediately wrote down the following note in my diary about the event. I just could not believe it. God had manifested something physical in my life. It would not be the last time.

> **Notepad:**
> 7/1 Push out of my seat with my hand forced in the air? It sure felt like it as God had me stand witness to the church vote on a name change and get up and speak to the members about it. We are now the "Solid Rock Church". Praise you Lord!

I didn't realize the significance of that moment. However, God had made a mental and physical record of the meeting that night in my mind and in my diary. Alongside the memo I wrote above, I attached a copy of the only article change the church authorized that day. The members only voted to change the name and God wanted to give me a strong record of the event. I have a daily diary that goes back almost three decades. I track daily events, create a record of actions and make notes in my combination diary and planner. Sometimes I look back and cannot decipher my handwriting, but the note above is crystal clear to me.

I became a member of the church two weeks after the name change. I also gave away ownership of everything I owned at that time. It was a spiritual milestone in my life. I chose stewardship over ownership.

Myth—God Owns Solid Rock

One item that I gave to Solid Rock was 545,000 shares of common stock in the small technology company I started. I wanted to help rebuild this church. As a member, I felt that I could help move the church forward from the devastation caused by Hoogenboom's scandal. I was very excited by what I perceived as a righteous and honest minister who seemed sincere in trying to right the wrongs that had been committed. I joined the ushers and was one of the leaders. It was my job to recruit and schedule ushers. As time progressed I nestled into worshipping God in a deeper way.

I had no clue as to what was transpiring behind the scenes. I didn't know that as I was joining the church, Matthews was preparing false Article of Incorporation changes to file with the Minnesota Secretary of State. It would be the first of several perjuries he was prepared to make as part of his church swindle. Matthews had been the senior pastor of this church for less than eight months and was now prepared to commit fraud to steal the church from its denomination first and then from its members second.

The filing Matthews made with the Secretary of State implemented wholesale changes to the Articles that were not authorized by the members. Matthews was testing the waters with a proverbial sucker punch at an early point in his ministry. Who would find out? Who would object? When the board asked to see the entire document they were signing, he intimidated them into signing a signature page without presenting the entire filing to them. The board failed in its duty to catch the start of Matthews' swindle. For the time being, everything was unfolding as Matthews had planned.

I sat in the sanctuary and read my Bible even while Matthews spoke. I read front and back of what he taught. I was on the lookout for any type of apostasy. There were some quirky teachings, but nothing out in the open from an apostasy perspective. I stepped into deep worship many times for that is what God told me to do. Many times I would go out in the spirit and get lost with God. I experienced healing at the altar in prayer. I also became a worshipper who would unabashedly worship God in praise and worship. I told God that if no other person went to that altar to raise his or her hands in dance, praise and worship — that I would. Many times I would write in my diary — Wow! The level of my worship experience reached new heights.

Myth—God Owns Solid Rock

If you ask: "Did I enjoy myself?" In terms of praise and worship of God, the answer is a resounding yes. I learned to step into the Holy of Holies anytime I wanted to and that spiritual gift is still with me to this day. I reached a deeper level of worshipping God. I also reached a much closer walk and fellowship with HIM. I didn't have to know why I was at Solid Rock because God had told me to go and observe. For me, that was enough. Yet let me ask this question of you. If you were at a friend's party and you very much enjoyed yourself and yet the friend picked your pocketbook by lying to you, would you have reason to be concerned about that individual? What if that friend was supposed to be a righteous minister who took over a ministry devastated by a previously unrighteous man? Concerned? Do you think that you and your other friends might have been seriously duped? Do you think this might represent the epitome of evil?

Indeed, the sheer level of deception that was unleashed on this Assembly of God congregation and its denomination leaders is only rivaled by what Judas Iscariot did to Jesus Christ when he betrayed our Lord. It was a betrayal unimaginable in the house of God. Who thinks of this stuff except Satan and his servants? Certainly a man of God does not lie to members of his church, his deacons, denomination overseers, the State of Minnesota, and the Courts in Minnesota. That is why I can tell you in all confidence that William Neal Matthews is an unrepentant servant of Satan. There are many who serve with Matthews in his evil actions that I do not know by name. I do know that God sees virtually everyone involved and knows exactly what each individual has done in the theft of HIS property. By the way, if you are intent on stealing something, where is the common sense in stealing from God Almighty unless you do not really believe in HIM?

No one found out about Matthews' false Article of Incorporation filing in 1993 and from the outside everything appeared righteous just like Apostle Paul taught it could be in 2 Corinthians 11. People continually disappeared from the congregation without any notice. That should have been a clue, but things moved fairly fast from week to week. Matthews did not give the congregation time to think and he held services on many nights during the week and every holiday demanding people attend. I brought Jackie to a few services, but she saw right through Matthews' character.

Copyright 2005 Edward G. Palmer, All Rights Reserved.

Book of Edward—Chapter 16

Myth—God Owns Solid Rock

At first I thought maybe she was one of those people who Matthews said, "Had problems with spiritual authority." However, Jackie was always insightful into the character of people. She could sense who was a rotten apple and who was a good person. I admit that I could get taken advantage of before I would know half of what she instantly knew in terms of character issues. In the end, her assessment of William Neal Matthews was right. And, I did get duped like many others in the congregation whose tendency like mine is to simply trust and operate in faith. Matthews knew that in this house of God, most people were like me and would give him the benefit of the doubt even as he secretly stabbed us in the back, one by one. I need 3-4 years before I can really get to know someone. If there is deception, I need a clue that triggers a concern so I can reflect on my experience. Otherwise there has to be something obvious thrown in front of my face. I do not have the character perceptions of my beloved wife Jackie. I miss her inputs.

Time traveled fast and before long we were into mid 1995. Other Assembly of God churches were criticizing Matthews' ministry as out of step with Assembly teachings. Actually, the church had evolved away from being an Assembly church and into being a *Word of Faith* church and this was by design. It was Matthews' setup phase of the swindle and it had been successfully executed. Matthews had orchestrated other Article changes after the name change. One of the changes deleted the Assembly of God denomination out of the Articles. They had a provision to settle property disputes should a division of the church occur. I remember how Matthews phrased that change request. He told us that the District Office was getting ready to take the church away from us and that we needed to make the change to save the ministry. Really? I doubt it.

As a result of deleting them out of the Articles, the Minnesota District Assembly of God initiated a lawsuit against Solid Rock Church and its board of directors. Eventually, the District Office settled the lawsuit behind the scenes and sold out the congregation of the church for four plots of land worth at least $90,000. Many of the members wanted to remain within the Assembly. In the Assembly lawsuit, they identified the right Article changes as being a cause of legal action. However, they did not know that Matthews had falsified the Articles and that members did not vote in those changes.

Myth—God Owns Solid Rock

The congregation was asked to make a minor change, but Matthews made wholesale changes to the Articles of Incorporation. He filed the falsified Articles with the Secretary of State under sworn oath that they were actions of the members of the corporation. The District Office realized that the Article changes disenfranchised the denomination that built this church. Matthews isolated the District from the congregation through his lawyers. The District Office thought the congregation had voted in the changes. The congregation didn't even know about most of the changes. We just believed Matthews when he told us the District was trying to take away our church. What a setup! Matthews' con duped the Minnesota District Assembly of God Office and the congregation simultaneously. When the District Office settled the lawsuit it was all about money, because it was going to cost a small fortune in legal fees to continue with the lawsuit. The District Office did not know that their settlement was also based on Matthews' fraud. He had lied about the Articles changes; the congregation did not authorize them as the District Office had been led to believe. The swindle was succeeding.

The next event of the con was a denomination switch. A meeting was held in July of 1995. Matthews' pitch was to change from an Assembly of God Church (AG) to an Association of Faith Churches and Ministers Church (AFCM).[3] The AFCM is a ministry of Jim Kaseman in Branson, Missouri. The local District authority was Mac Hammond[4] of Living Word Ministries in Brooklyn Park, Minnesota. Matthews taught that the Assembly of God wanted to stifle the *move of God*, which was in our church. At the business meeting, he discussed a critical report that was sent to Assembly churches concerning *Word of Faith* churches and what seemed "counterfeit miracles, signs and wonders." You know, the stuff of 2 Thessalonians 2:9-12. It was a warning to Assembly churches that was endorsed by the District.

Matthews did not provide copies of the report at the business meeting, which was hastily called to discuss his concerns. There were no Article changes even proposed at the meeting. A resolution was approved to check out the changes required to Articles and By-laws to become an AFCM church. A committee was to report back to the congregation on the changes needed, but this never happened. Instead, in October 1995, Matthews' filed another final set of fraudulent wholesale Article changes.

Myth—God Owns Solid Rock

This time, Matthews disenfranchised the entire membership of their voting rights. He vested all voting rights into himself and his board, which coincidentally was now out of the congregation's control and was starting to shrink. Read Article IV that Matthews filed below and ask if any reasonable congregation would knowingly vote to give away its member voting rights. Matthews' used another ruse as an excuse to file additional lies with the Minnesota Secretary of State. Yet, no one knew he was making these false Article of Incorporation changes. The members knew nothing of these changes and did not vote for any of them. This evil was taking place behind the scenes. Church members only saw Matthews' angelic face and smile as he cleverly worked his swindle from an "appearance of righteousness."

Falsified October 1995 Article IV Filing!

To assure the corporation of its sovereignty and independence and to perpetually protect the church, all ecclesiastical and legal power and authority relative to the corporation shall be exercised by and in accordance with the New Testament Church pattern. Thus under the leadership of the Holy Spirit the Board of Trustees shall conduct all the business of the corporation (church) and shall be the only voting members of the corporation (church). The number of Trustees, and their qualifications shall be established in the Bylaws of this corporation. The qualifications of members and the manner of their admission shall be fully provided in the Bylaws.

Matthews never informed the church that Jim Kaseman's AFCM[5] church requirements stated that the members could not have voting rights. Therefore, the AFCM denomination shift was also a part of Matthews' ruse. In a later lawsuit, Matthews' attorneys claimed that the congregation waived its rights to any changes Matthews chose to make. However, legally, one cannot waive any rights they are not informed they are waiving. Existing Articles and Bylaws stated clearly that all Article changes had to be posted for four weeks and formal notice supplied to voting members. But why should that stop a swindler? Therefore, Matthews succeeded in keeping both the Assembly of God and the congregation in the dark about his con activities including his fraudulent filings with the Secretary of State.

Myth—God Owns Solid Rock

Everything seemed to be unfolding in the swindle as Matthews had planned, but the AG lawsuit was soaking up money. So in September 1996, Matthews relented to the Minnesota District Assembly of God and allowed them to talk to the congregation. They would have their say and we would then vote as to whether or not we still wanted to change affiliations. Not a single member at large like myself had any clue that Matthews had already falsified the changes he needed with the Minnesota Secretary of State. His fraudulent Articles filing already disenfranchised the entire membership. Now, Matthews asked us to vote again. It worked for us, since none of us knew we had no voting rights under Matthews' new falsified Articles.

The District Office presented their case to the members, but Matthews refused to allow any discussion to take place. Of course, we voted again to leave the Assembly of God denomination. However, the entire vote was all based on misleading information and the withholding of material facts. We were like a ringed-nosed cow easily led in any direction Matthews wanted. The membership had relied on its board. However, Satan's "righteous appearing" servant deceived the board, church members and denomination.

We were never told anything else about the denomination switch. So in October of 1996 I asked Matthews the big question: "Are we now an AFCM Church?" I was told yes. Yet, virtually not a word had ever been said about changes to the Bylaws or Articles. There had been no posting of changes as required in existing Bylaws and Articles. Therefore, none of the members knew Matthews had relegated us to second-class citizens and taken away our voting rights under the guise of the New Testament church.

At a Wednesday, November 20, 1996 service, only two days before a Harvest Dinner meeting, Matthews abandoned God's Word in a clear and distinct way; he finally slipped. I caught the apostasy. Matthews hoped to raise $100,000 from his congregation on Friday. To do so, he would openly lie about the word of God. I left the church and other than meeting once with Matthews to discuss his apostasy I never returned. Yet there existed many unanswered questions in my mind. As a truth seeker, I eventually started to investigate the church. I knew something smelled afoul. One big question was, what exactly is on file with the Secretary of State's Office?

Copyright 2005 Edward G. Palmer, All Rights Reserved.

Book of Edward—Chapter 16

Myth—God Owns Solid Rock

As a businessman myself, I had made several filings with the state. It was only a matter of making a request and sending a small payment and I could obtain a copy of all of the church filings. It was April 3, 1998 when I examined Matthews' Article filings. The depth of his swindle was obvious and breathtaking. I had attended every one of the business meetings and all I saw in the state filings were one lie after another sworn under oath to state officials with the penalty of perjury. God knew the evil that Matthews had planned so HE planted an apostle into the church as a witness. I had no idea when God sent me to the Elk River Assembly of God Church that this is where it would all end. I was the only church member who understood what Bylaws and Articles were about and how they impacted governance of the church. Suddenly I became a sleuth.

I asked AFCM if Solid Rock Church was affiliated with them. They faxed back this resolution from William Neal Matthews' dated 11/7/96.

CORPORATE RESOLUTION

At a meeting of SOLID ROCK CHURCH, INC. Elk River, Minnesota, held on November 7, 1996, a motion was made and carried that SOLID ROCK CHURCH, INC. disaffiliate from ASSOCIATION OF FAITH CHURCHES AND MINISTERS, INC. (AFCM).

Date 11/7/96

President (Pastor)

So, on September 12, 1996, members vote to change from Assembly of God affiliation to AFCM affiliation. I ask Matthews in October if we were an AFCM Church. He says yes. Then on November 7, 1996 he files a resolution with the AFCM to "disaffiliate." That means eight weeks after the members voted to affiliate, he sent a resolution to disaffiliate. I can tell you that a business meeting was not held on November 7, 1996 except perhaps with Matthews and his cronies. Why should there be? It was a full year earlier that he took the voting rights away from the congregation even if none of us knew it. Think it can't get more interesting? You're wrong.

Myth—God Owns Solid Rock

I sent a packet of information to Mac Hammond at Living Word in Brooklyn Center. Church officials requested a meeting with me. One of my friends warned me that I should take someone with me so I took my friend Dean. At the time I was called into the meeting, they tried to prevent Dean from joining me. I said there was nothing to talk about if Dean couldn't attend. They relented and let him in. Then for the next half hour proceeded to educate me on my spiritual ignorance and why I needed to drop this issue. Yes, that is right, Living Word Church as the District overseer of AFCM Ministries was not interested in righteousness when it came to this theft. They like civil authorities wanted to bury the entire issue. "Let God deal with it." Hello. Anyone home? If you are truly called into ministry, do you not think that righteousness should matter to you? Jim Kaseman sent me a letter and said: "I would appreciate it if you would not use my name or the name of AFCM." Well Jim, you and the AFCM are a part of Matthews' lie.

In late 1998, a foreclosure notice appeared in the Sherburne County Citizen paper. It was the AG District Office foreclosing on Matthews.

NOTICE OF MORTGAGE FORECLOSURE SALE

NOTICE IS HEREBY GIVEN, that default has occurred in the conditions of that certain Mortgage, dated the 1st day of November, 1996, executed by Solid Rock Church, a Minnesota non-profit corporation, as Mortgagor, to the Minnesota District Council of the Assemblies of God, a Minnesota religious corporation, as Mortgagee, filed for record in the Office of the County Recorder in and for the County of Sherburne, State of Minnesota, on the 4th day of December, 1996, at 4:53 p.m., and recorded as Document No. 336443.
That the original principal amount secured by said Mortgage is $90,000.00.

MINNESOTA DISTRICT COUNCIL ASSEMBLIES OF GOD, MORTGAGEE

EASTLUND, SOLSTAD & HUTCHINSON, LTD.
Dale J. Moe
Attorneys For Mortgagee
1702 Midwest Plaza Building
801 Nicollet Mall
Minneapolis, MN 55402-2585
(612) 339-8931

(Published in the *Sherburne County Citizen* 10/03/98; 10/10/98; 10/17/98; 10/24/98; 10/31/98; 11/07/98)

Matthews settled with the Minnesota District Assembly of God Office for $90,000 on November 1, 1996. He didn't have money so he backed the debt with property adjacent to the church. Matthews couldn't pay up so the District Office foreclosed on the property Matthews used as security.

Myth—God Owns Solid Rock

After scoring a settlement with the Assembly of God, the next week Matthews dumped the AFCM. Everything took place without anyone the wiser until I obtained a copy the falsified Article filings from the Secretary of State. More details are on the Internet at http://www.james417.org. The James 417 Association website is a virtual archive of the Solid Rock Church theft. It will serve as a warning of Satan's Zone 3 church. Remember, Satan will feed your itching ears exactly what they want to hear. Don't accept any apostasy! Do you think the $100,000 Matthews sought to raise November 22, 1996 at the Harvest Dinner might be used to pay off the AG District?

So what about the New Testament church? Three clearly NT church characteristics are 1) submitting to Christ, 2) appointing of elders and 3) meeting in homes, all of which describes my church. Study Acts 14:23, Romans 16:5, 1 Cor. 16:19, Ephes. 5:24 and Col. 4:15. Should you vest all voting power into one person and his or her board? You decide, is it right that one person own all church property, planes, expensive cars, etc.— when Christ told his apostles to go out without a moneybag? Again, Satan's zone giveaway is the focus on the things of men, not of God. Paul taught Titus.

> **"The reason I left you [was to] ... Appoint elders in every town [church], as I directed you." Titus 1:5 NIV**

> **"[Elders] must ... encourage others by sound doctrine and refute those who oppose it. For there are many rebellious people, mere talkers and deceivers ... They must be silenced, because they are ruining whole households by teaching things they ought not to teach—and that for the sake of dishonest gain [money]." Titus 1:9-11 NIV**

> **"They claim to know God, but by their actions they deny HIM. They are detestable, disobedient and unfit for doing anything good." Titus 1:16 NIV**

**"They are disqualified for every good work!"
Titus 1:16 NKJV**

Copyright 2005 Edward G. Palmer, All Rights Reserved.

I wonder. Could I have ever written this book without first having traveled through all of the churches on my path towards getting closer to God? I doubt it. Likewise, had I not spent an enormous amount of time in a *Word of Faith* church observing, I could not appreciate how clever Satan has gotten inside the different churches. Certainly, this book is part of God's plan to frustrate the ways of the wicked. Be glad, God searches for the heart of your soul. HE is a patient God, but time is getting shorter. Take heed.

"The LORD watches over the alien and sustains the fatherless and the widow, but HE frustrates the ways of the wicked." Psalm 146:9 NIV

PRAYER. O LORD GOD, bless the people who are reading this chapter and book. Open up their hearts and minds. I pray that worldwide YOU will open the eyes of YOUR people to the simple truth contained in YOUR Holy Bible. I pray that YOUR people will grow strong in YOUR Word and that they will not be led astray. FATHER, give them a sincere heart that loves YOUR truth. The truth of YOUR Word is being ignored en masse in today's Christian Church. FATHER, let everyone who will stand firm and tall for YOUR truth find a fellowship that respects that truth. There are no gray areas or situational moral dynamics acceptable in YOUR Holy Word. Somehow the Church of YOUR Son Jesus Christ has become lost in a sea of wickedness and Bible ignorance. Help our poor souls return to you God.

"When you observe how much time you and your family spend in God's Word instead of the church building, your faith will start to get strong. When you get strong in the Word, you will not be led astray by teachings designed to feed your itching ears the things of men." The Apostle Edward

If God's Spirit Dwells In Your Heart, Your Spirit-Soul Knows That It's A …

Myth—God Owns Solid Rock

Copyright 2005 Edward G. Palmer, All Rights Reserved.

Book of Edward

Chapter Seventeen
Myth—Giving 10% Is A Tithe

The Tithe Law
Deuteronomy 14:22-29

[22] "You shall surely tithe all the yield of your seed produced by your field each year.

[23] And you shall eat before the LORD your God in the place in which HE will cause HIS name [and presence] to dwell the tithe (tenth) of your grain, your new wine, your oil, and the firstlings of your herd and your flock, that you may learn [reverently] to fear the LORD your God always.

[24] And if the distance is too long for you to carry your tithe, or the place where the LORD your God chooses to set HIS name [and presence] is too far away for you, when the LORD your God has blessed you.

[25] Then you shall turn it into money, and bind up the money in your hand, and you shall go to the place [of worship] which the LORD your God has chosen.

[26] And you may spend that money for whatever your appetite craves, for oxen, or sheep, or new wine or stronger drink, or whatever you desire; and you shall eat there before the LORD your God and you shall rejoice, you and your household.

[27] And you shall not forsake or neglect the Levite [God's minister] in your towns, for he has been given no share or inheritance with you.

Myth—Giving 10% Is A Tithe

[28] At the end of every three years you shall bring forth all the tithe of your increase the same year and lay it up within your towns.

[29] And the Levite [because he has no part or inheritance with you] and the stranger or temporary resident, and the fatherless and the widow who are in your towns shall come and eat and be satisfied, so that the LORD your God may bless you in all the work of your hands that you do." Deuteronomy 14:22-29 AMP

Jesus' Tithe Instructions

Jesus said: "Woe to you, scribes and Pharisees, pretenders (hypocrites)! For you give a tenth of your mint and dill and cummin, and have neglected and omitted the weightier (more important) matters of the Law—right and justice and mercy and fidelity. These you ought [particularly] to have done, without neglecting the others." Matthew 23:23 AMP

Take some time and reflect on what God's Word actually says about the tithe in the above Bible verses. Pay attention to the fact that instead of turning over your tithe to God's minister, you are supposed to only "share" a portion of your tithe "food" with him. This is a big contrast to the Word of Faith Church teachings. I used the Amplified Bible in the above citations. Both the bracketed and parenthesized words are how the Amplified Bible presents these verses. The small caps "LORD" is my own clarification to indicate it is Yahweh [God] that is referred to and not Jesus. One Amplified Bible goal is to bring a more robust understanding of both the Hebrew and Greek into the translated English text. This is the reason for the use of bracketed and parenthesized words. In the last chapter I used the NIV or New International Version for most Bible verses to illustrate that it doesn't matter, which Bible you use. Some Bibles express a verse better than others and multiple translations clear up errors. I use the Amplified Bible in this chapter, because it is popular in *Word of Faith* (AFCM) churches.

Myth—Giving 10% Is A Tithe

As you might expect, I do have a couple of final thoughts from God on the last chapter before I proceed with our tithing discussion. If you have been the victim of a fraud by any ministry, you should know that all states have fraud laws. The statute of limitations for fraud is usually six years from the actual date you discover the fraud and not from the date the fraud is committed. Thus state fraud laws explicitly recognize the game of the con artist is to deceive and conceal their swindle. Some people may not find out about a fraud for twenty years. When they do discover the fraud, the statute of limitations is usually six years from that date. In the case of Solid Rock Church, the fraud that was worked on the Minnesota District Assembly of God in its settlement with Matthews may be open to litigation for six years after the Minnesota AG District finally discovers that they were hoodwinked by Matthews' lies about corporate Article changes. Matthews had carried his deception (fraud) into settlement talks and misled the AG District Office about the underlying factual basis of all corporate Article changes.

Ministries like Solid Rock Church in Elk River, Minnesota are often very *spiritually abusive* to people. They can and will destroy entire families, wrecking marriages and scattering God's people in all directions. I bear witness for God of such evil. If you are wondering if spiritual abuse is taking place in your own church, there is a wonderful book titled: *The Subtle Power of Spiritual Abuse,* by Authors David Johnson & Jeff VanVonderen, (Bethany House Publishers, 1991)[1]. I highly recommend this book, as it helped me understand what was going on at Solid Rock Church. Remember, if you can reason with God, you should be able to with church leaders.

All right, hang on to your hat. This is going to be a very interesting chapter and not at all what I had originally thought, again. God gave me so much input today on this chapter that I am myself wowed over things HE has shown me. It is Saturday, January 3, 2004. If you have been programmed to "tithe" ten-percent (10%) of your gross annual income to your church, I am willing to make a substantial bet that your preacher has not taught you either of the two citations I opened this chapter with. Why? Within both of those citations lies the truth of the tithe; neither bodes well for the apostate church.

Myth—Giving 10% Is A Tithe

If you do actually give your church ten-percent of your gross income as a tithe, you have been programmed with the Christian mythology of a Zone 3 church of Satan, which I talked about in the last chapter. That is a harsh statement I know, but God has made it very clear to this apostle what an abomination the modern day tithe teaching is. Furthermore, there is no need to get offended, embarrassed or to even feel stupid about your Bible ignorance. I used to be programmed with the tithe mythology just like you may be. I have studied the tithe many times in depth and over the years. Yet, today, God showed me things that I never saw before in His Word.

Your pastor wouldn't lie to you about money, would he? Yes, indeed he would! What you now need to learn is the simple truth about the tithe. It was not designed to make you rich. Nor was it designed as a curse for those who fail to tithe. It was designed as a form of worshipping God and to teach you to reverently fear Him. Yes, I said the tithe was designed so you could learn to fear God. Remember my earlier teaching that perfect love casts out all fear. Fear of God evolves into perfect love, but godly fear is always with you to keep you safe in His loving arms. Move away from God once you know Him like I do and you will feel a sense of fear. Stay close to Him like I do and all you can feel is a sense of His overwhelming love. It is a huge contrast and somewhat of a conundrum in and of itself. Until you learn to actually "fear" God, you will never learn how to step into a "perfect love" of God. A healthy fear of God comes from a full understanding that He does exist, but every preacher who teaches the apostasy of the modern tithe has virtually no fear of Him. They also do not know God or else they would not engage in such a modern abomination of the Word. Where is His truth?

Now the first thing you should do with your apostate preacher is to ask him to explain the "Tithe Law" in Deuteronomy 14:22-29 and also the fact that Jesus makes it clear that the tithe is part of the Law in Matthew 23:23. Most, if not all, preachers who tell you to bring your tithe money to the church also tell you that you are not under the Law. So, which is it? If you are under the Law, the tithe applies! If you are not under the Law, why should you tithe? This subject is most certain to get interesting, because Jesus also taught that we should do the things of the Law, didn't he? Huh? Is it possible we are subject to the Law in ways not heretofore explained?

Myth—Giving 10% Is A Tithe

Before we look at some of the apostasy being taught by the culprits in the pulpits in order to grab your money, let's take a close look at what the tithe is actually supposed to be as given to us in the word of God. I will talk about the modern tithe teachings that lead so many astray in a short while.

Do you remember we learned that no one could lead you astray when you possess first hand knowledge of God's Word? Well, brother or sister, what you will learn in this chapter is a good illustration of how you can be led around like a ringed-nose cow because of your lack of such first hand knowledge. You will also learn just how easy it is for the preacher to empty your pocketbook when you are ignorant of scripture. Perhaps the biggest question that should now arise in your mind is this: "If the pastor would lie about the tithe to get your money, what else is he or she willing to lie about?" Sexual intimacy with your spouse? Pastoral adultery? Church theft? Healing? True faith? The Law? Homosexuality? Etc.?

Look, if your pastor does not understand what the Bible *really* teaches about the tithe in the above citations, you are listening to someone that is spiritually blind to God's Word; get out of Satan's den! Yes, if you were thinking it was about time to exit a church focused on the things of men, the truth of God's tithe should be all you need to leave and find a new church. That is, assuming that you do not accept any false teachings from the word of God from those who claim to be "anointed." Look, if one is anointed of God, he or she does not speak against the Word! Such people are ministers of Satan "appearing righteous." My guess is that many people will remain in their apostate ministry even when they do learn of the truth. That is what many did at Solid Rock. Yet, verily I say unto you, God will still hold you accountable to HIS truth regardless of what you believe.

Once you know the truth, to continue on supporting a ministry that lies is not going to win you points with God. To know the truth and then support lies is *to be lawless*. It puts you into the group that Jesus said he would reject. Remember the second prophecy? "They perish because they did not love the truth!" Take heed. Let's look closer now at what the "Tithe Law" in the Word says we should *really* do to tithe. The instructions from God are not open to modern manipulation and I will explain to you why.

Myth—Giving 10% Is A Tithe

Tithing Instructions From God & His Son*!

Just by studying the opening verses, you learn the following facts about the tithe instructions from God and His Son*. *Note: Bible citation remains the same for each item below until the next citation is provided.*

1. You shall surely tithe each year. [Deut. 14:22]
2. You tithe from the produce of your field.
3. You tithe the YIELD [increase] of the seed produced by your field.
4. You ought to obey these matters of the Law*. [Matt. 23:23]
5. You shall eat the tithe before God. [Deut. 14:23]
6. You shall eat the tithe in the place God chooses.
7. You shall eat the grain, wine, oil, and firstlings.
8. You shall eat the tithe to learn to reverently fear God.
9. If the distance is too far, convert the tithe to money. [Deut. 14:24]
10. Then carry the money to God's place of worship. [Deut. 14:25]
11. Then spend the money on your heart's desires. [Deut. 14:26]
12. Throw a celebration and rejoice with your family.
13. If you want, get some strong drink too.
14. Consume the tithe and rejoice before the LORD.
15. Don't forget the minister at your tithe party. [Deut. 14:27]
16. Ministers have no inheritance [property].
17. Consume your tithe before God two of three years. [Deut. 14:28]
18. The third year, use the tithe to stock the food shelves.
19. Feed and satisfy the Levites from the food shelf. [Deut. 14:29]
20. Feed and satisfy the stranger from the food shelf.
21. Feed and satisfy the temporary resident from the food shelf.
22. Feed and satisfy the fatherless from the food shelf.
23. Feed and satisfy the widow from the food shelf.
24. Take care of people and God will bless your work.
25. You ought to tithe as part of the Law*. [Matt. 23:23]
26. You ought to do right as part of the Law*.
27. You ought to have justice as part of the Law*.
28. You ought to have mercy as part of the Law*.
29. You ought to have fidelity as part of the Law*.

Copyright 2005 Edward G. Palmer, All Rights Reserved.

Book of Edward—Chapter 17

Myth—Giving 10% Is A Tithe

God has thrown another issue at me for this chapter. That is the issue of the Law. Many teachers say we are not under the Law anymore. A lot of times, these are the same *Word of Faith* teachers that tell you to "obey the Law" by tithing. Yet, Jesus says in Matthew 23:23 that we "ought to have tithed *without* neglecting the other weightier matters of the Law." Thus, isn't Jesus *really* telling us that we need to obey the Law to some degree; at least certain aspects of it? How then can this teaching of Jesus be reconciled with the common *Word of Faith* teaching that Apostle Paul says we are no longer under the Law? Is Jesus giving us a clue as to which Christians he will tell: "I never knew you, get away from me you who are lawless?"

Think about this teaching of Jesus for a moment and ask yourself this question. If we do not have to obey the Law like *Word of Faith* ministers and others preach, does that exclude us from Jesus' statement that the Law requires us to *also* do what is right, ensure justice, have mercy and have fidelity? Verily I say to you that Christianity has misrepresented the words of Christ concerning the Law and its teachings. How else could you explain Christ's statement about these Law requirements? Do what is right! Ensure Justice! Have mercy! And, have fidelity! Fidelity is simply a loyal heart for God. Ignoring the tithe issue for the moment, let me ask you this, which of these other four requirements of the Law do you think no longer matter to God and His Son? Are these four, matters of faith, or matters of legalism?

Yes, God dumped all of that on me this morning and I am wearied eyed tonight. It's about 5:15 p.m. I will take a break; catch my breath and resume another day. I need to think about this Law stuff that God is asking me to discuss with you. It's pretty heady stuff, isn't it? Before I get back, you too should take some time and think about what God's instructions are telling you about the tithe. It is obvious that most ministers like item ten in the above list when it comes to the tithe, "Bring the tithe money to worship!" Likewise, it is clear that they ignore item eleven, "Spend the tithe money on your heart's desire and *then* worship God." Exactly where is the instruction to give the minister the tithe money and what about the other twenty-seven items? They all reflect on the tithe, don't they, especially Jesus' instructions on the Law in Matthew 23:23? It is now January 6, 2004 and I am back to write for God. Translating Moses instructions into a graphic looks like this.

Myth—Giving 10% Is A Tithe

Three Year Tithe Law Instructions

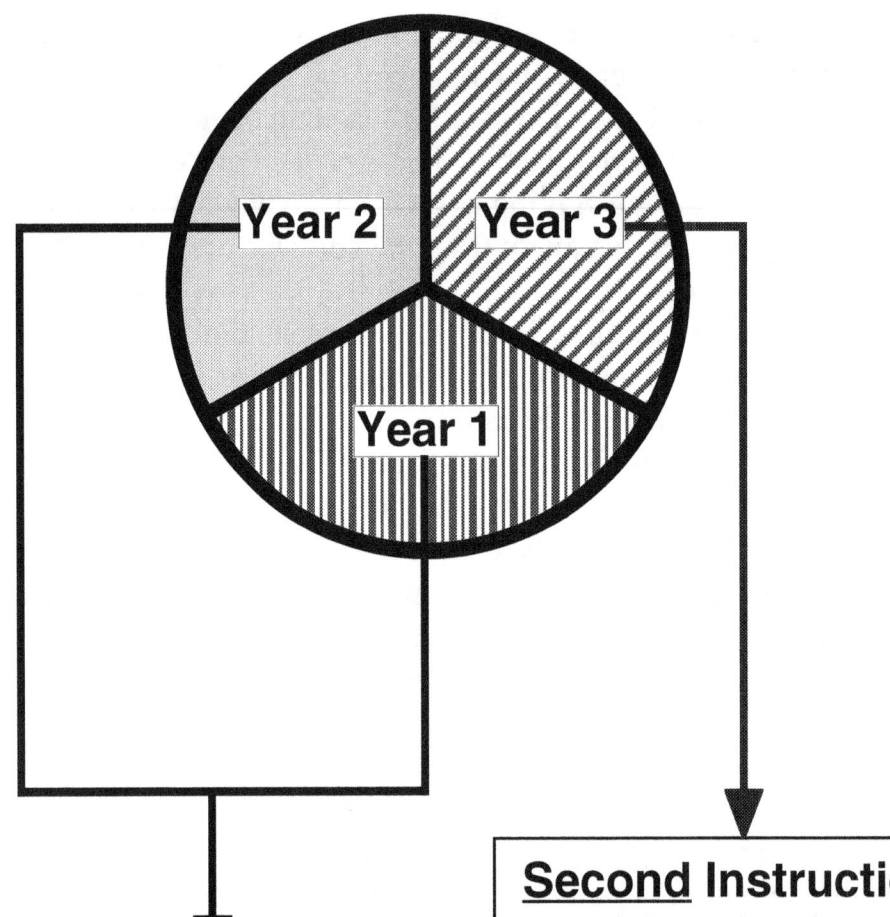

First Instruction

Household consumes tithe in a celebration to teach the fear of the LORD our God. Don't forget to bring the minister with you.
[Deuteronomy 14:22-27]

Second Instruction

Bring the tithe to the local food shelf and store it up to feed the following people:
a) Minister
b) Stranger
c) Temporary Resident
d) Fatherless
e) Widow
   [Deuteronomy 14:27-28]

Copyright 2005 Edward G. Palmer, All Rights Reserved.

Book of Edward—Chapter 17

Myth—Giving 10% Is A Tithe

You've got to admit that the picture in the preceding graphic is far different than the picture the tithe preacher peddles, isn't it? Before I get into some specific false tithe teachings, let me give you another illustration, which astounded me when God revealed it to me. What I want you to see is that God's intention for the tithe as taught in Deuteronomy 14:22-29 had two basic elements to it. First was the fear and worship of the LORD. Moses makes it clear that you showed your fear of the LORD by consuming your tithe and rejoicing before the LORD for two out of every three years. The second element is taking care of the destitute or those in need like the local ministers who served God. Moses makes it clear that you accomplished this by bringing your tithe to the food shelf (storehouse) in the third year.

Tithe & Lawlessness Connection

O.T. Tithe Law	N.T. Lawlessness
A) Fear God	A) Obey Law
B) Take Care of People	B) Take Care of People

Forget about the "money" the preacher wants for the moment. I will discuss it further in a while. For now I want you to mentally compare the essence of the "Tithe Law" as contained in Deuteronomy 14:22-29 to the groups of people who Jesus will say: "I never knew you." Remember that the first group is cited in Matthew 7:21-23 and Jesus says that they were "lawless." This is just another way of saying they did not obey the Law! But, which Laws? Well, for starters, what about the Law requirement to do what is right; ensure justice; execute mercy; and, fidelity (or faithfulness) to the LORD? Can we sweep these Law requirements under the carpet, even if we can sweep the tithe under the carpet? Then there is the issue of caring.

Myth—Giving 10% Is A Tithe

Do you remember the words of Jesus in Matthew 25:35-46 from the last chapter? Jesus rejects those who failed to feed the hungry, give drink to the thirsty, take in strangers, clothe the naked, visit and care for the sick, and visit and pray for those in prison. Remember I also told you that God told me that these were also spiritual needs and not just physical needs? When we fear God, we keep HIS commandments regardless of what you have been taught. Part of those commandments is to care for people. Thus, the Tithe Law's two elements and the two groups of people Jesus rejects seem to be similar. Does this mean we need to tithe? The answer comes shortly.

For now, let me take another stab at explaining the conundrum of the issue of the Law that Jesus lays upon our hearts. It is true that Jesus spoke to the scribes and Pharisees when he said "they" should tithe and do all the other aspects, especially "the more weightier issues of the Law." Therefore, you could argue that we are not of this group and further that the covenant of Christ's blood altered the Law equation. What else does the Word teach?

> **Jesus said: "Go and learn what this means: 'I desire mercy [that is, readiness to help those in trouble] and not sacrifice and sacrificial victims.' For I came not to call and invite [to repentance] the righteous (those who are upright and in right standing with God), but sinners (the erring ones and all those not free from sin." Matthew 9:13 AMP**

> **God said: "For I desire and delight in dutiful steadfast love and goodness, not sacrifice, and the knowledge of and acquaintance with God more than burnt offerings."**
> **Hosea 6:6 AMP**

Both verses illustrate and contrast the issue of being either "in faith" or "in the Law." If you are "in the Law," you are concerned and focused on fulfilling the Law's instructions about sacrifices. Success is then based on ability to "keep the letter of the Law." But, in doing so, one can overlook the spirit of the Law and the matter of simple faith and trust in God. If you understand the distinction made in the above verses, you will gain insight on the laws and commandments of God.

Myth—Giving 10% Is A Tithe

Think about this for a moment. When the tithe preacher insists that you need to tithe or you'll be cursed, is he or she teaching you faith? Or, are they teaching you to "obey the Law?" Matters of the Law are legalistic in nature; matters of faith are by nature of our heart and soul. While both deal with issues of obedience, one is focused on the flesh and the other the spirit. If you think they are teaching you faith by tithing, you are wrong. They are trying to teach you that you need to be focused on the "sacrifice" of your money, which they claim is "required" of you. Instead of sacrifice, what?

Has your preacher once told you that the tithe is actually a part of the Law? Jesus clearly taught us that much in Matthew 23:23. However, tithing is not just a part of the Law per se [if you think of the Law as the first five books of the Bible], it is a part of the "ceremonial laws" as given by Moses and written in the *Book of the Law*. If you tithe, you submit to a ceremonial law or ritual, which you are not supposed to do under the new covenant of Christ. It also means you are cursed unless you obey all of the ceremonial laws. Why? It is because those are the requirements of the old covenant. Those who choose to live under the old covenant [by tithing, etc.] must also obey all requirements in Moses' *Book of the Law*.

> **"And all who depend on the Law [who are seeking to be justified by obedience to the Law of rituals]** (**this includes any tithing under the ceremonial laws*) **are under a curse and doomed to disappointment and destruction, for it is written in the Scriptures, cursed (accursed, devoted to destruction, doomed to eternal punishment) be everyone who does not continue to abide (live and remain) by all the precepts and commands written in the *Book of the Law* and to practice them." Galatians 3:10 AMP** **Apostle Edward's comments*

> **"Cursed is he who does not support and give assent to the words of this law to do them [as the rule of his life]. All the people shall say, Amen." Deuteronomy 27:26 AMP**

God Holds Us Accountable To Obey Laws—Which?

Myth—Giving 10% Is A Tithe

The Amplified Bible's expanded translation of Greek in Galatians 3:10 provides us with one answer to a fundamental Law question. Did Paul negate the teachings of Jesus on the Law? The Amplified Bible explains that the Law controversy *really* pertains to, "[Those] who are seeking to be justified by obedience to the law of rituals." These are the "ceremonial laws" and you will find them in Deuteronomy 12:1–16:17. What we need to sort out here is exactly what Jesus is referring to when he rejects all those who were "lawless." Obviously, Jesus claims they did not obey the Law. But, which law or laws? Remember that Jesus said there were "weightier" matters of the Law? Therefore, this is one clear distinction to be made for all Christians who seek to summarily dismiss the first five books of the Bible including God's Ten Commandments. Let's go back to Galatians.

> **"Yet we know that a man is justified or reckoned righteous and in right standing with God not by works of the Law, but [only] through faith and [absolute] reliance on and adherence to and trust in Jesus Christ (the Messiah, the Anointed One). [Therefore] even we [ourselves] have believed on Christ Jesus, in order to be justified by faith in Christ and not by works of the Law [for we cannot be justified by any observance of the ritual of the Law given by Moses], because by keeping legal rituals and by works no human can ever be justified (declared righteous and put in right standing with God)." Galatians 2:16 AMP**

Rituals In Moses' Law Cannot Justify Us!

> **"And enter not into judgment with YOUR servant, for in YOUR sight no man living is [in himself] righteous or justified." Psalm 143:2 AMP**

Thus in and of ourselves we cannot obtain righteousness. However, Luke made it clear that "Zacharias and Elizabeth were both righteous in the sight of God, walking blamelessly in all the commandments and requirements of the LORD." [See Luke 1:6]

Copyright 2005 Edward G. Palmer, All Rights Reserved.

Myth—Giving 10% Is A Tithe

Therefore, obedience to God leads to being righteous in HIS eyes even if keeping the rituals of Moses' laws does not. Note that Luke speaks of the "commandments" and "requirements" of God vs. the "ritual Laws." We also know that "whoever does what is right is righteous like Christ Jesus."

On the other hand, if you are "in faith," you recognize that there are weightier matters of the Law that should have priority in your thinking. You understand that God gave us the Law, but expects us to operate in faith. You understand the difference between the "weightier matters of the Law" and the "ritual matters of the Law." When eternal life is granted or refused, it will be granted for those who are "in faith" with God and refused to those who are "in the Law." Yet don't we need a clearer picture to avoid getting dismissed by Jesus as being lawless? Part of that clearer picture can be seen in Psalm 19, where King David makes four distinctions about the "Law."

> **"The <u>law</u> of the LORD is perfect, reviving the soul. The <u>decrees</u> of the LORD are trustworthy, making wise the simple. The <u>commandments</u> of the LORD are right, bringing joy to the heart. The <u>commands</u> of the LORD are clear, giving insight to life." Psalm 19:7-8 NLT**

David makes four distinctions about the instructions of God contained in the Bible's first five books, which *collectively* are called the "Law."

1. The **Law** of the LORD.
2. The **Decrees** of the LORD.
3. The **Commandments** of the LORD.
4. The **Commands** of the LORD.

Now consider the following distinctions in the Book of Deuteronomy.

1. **Commandments** of the Covenant — 5:6-21
2. **Commands** — 6:1-11:32
3. **Ceremonial Laws** — 12:1-16:17
4. **Civil Laws** — 16:18-20:20
5. **Social Laws** — 21:1-26:19

Copyright 2005 Edward G. Palmer, All Rights Reserved.

Myth—Giving 10% Is A Tithe

Tithing Is Living Under The Ceremonial Laws!

The Amplified translation of Galatians makes it clear that we are no longer governed by the ritual or "ceremonial laws." The "tithe law" is a part of these "ceremonial laws." Therefore, the answer to the question of whether or not you should tithe is clearly *no*! You should not tithe as God's Word makes it clear that those choosing to live under this section of laws are cursed. Here is a list of the *ceremonial laws* and verses in Deuteronomy.

1. Law of the Central Sanctuary   12:1-28
2. Law of Idolatry   12:29-13:18
3. Law of Food   14:1-21
4. Law of Tithes   14:22-29
5. Law of Debts   15:1-11
6. Law of Slaves   15:12-18
7. Law of Firstborn   15:19-23
8. Law of Feasts   16:1-17
    a. Passover
    b. Feast of Weeks
    c. Feast of Tabernacles
    d. Feast of Unleavened Bread

Indeed, those who tithe are in violation of Apostle Paul's instructions in Galatians 3:10. They are actually living under the ceremonial laws in disobedience to the word of God. Instead of being blessed as the *Word of Faith* preacher teaches, ironically they are actually under the Law's curse.

> **"Therefore let no one sit in judgment on you in matters of food and drink, or with regard to a feast day or a New Moon or a Sabbath. Such [things] are only the shadow of things that are to come, and they have only a symbolic value. But the reality (the substance, the solid fact of what is foreshadowed, the body of it) belongs to Christ."**
>   **Colossians 2:16-17 AMP**

Copyright 2005 Edward G. Palmer, All Rights Reserved.

Book of Edward—Chapter 17

Myth—Giving 10% Is A Tithe

Tithe Preachers Teach Things of This World!

Instead of teaching you that you no longer belong to this world and its systems, the *Word of Faith* preacher teaches you that you are a king or queen in this world. They lie about the tithe because they know it will feed your itching Christian ears that desire more of worldly things. Instead of teaching you to be an enemy of the world, they make you an enemy of God by their own greed that drags you deeper into the things of the world, the things of men. The lure of easy money "by tithing" is a good hook for those ignorant of the Word, because in the next breath following Malachi 3:8-10 out of the preacher's mouth are the words "some hundredfold, some sixty, some thirty" [Mt. 13:8]. Yet only Satan and his "righteous appearing" servants will teach that it is biblical to conform to this world and its ideas of personal health, wealth, and family success. God's Word doesn't teach conformity to the world's [men's] ideas! Consider the teachings of the word of God.

> **"Do not be conformed to this world (this age), [fashioned after and adapted to its external, superficial customs], but be transformed (changed) by the [entire] renewal of your mind [by its new ideals and its new attitude], so that you may prove [for yourselves] what is the good and acceptable and perfect will of God, even the thing which is good and acceptable and perfect [in His sight for you]."**
> **Romans 12:2 AMP**

> **"That I may in that same way come to know the power outflowing from his resurrection [which it exerts over believers], and that I may so share his sufferings as to be continually transformed [in spirit into his likeness even] to his death, [in the hope]." Philippians 3:10 AMP**

> **"Who will transform and fashion anew the body of our humiliation to conform to and be like the body of his glory and majesty, by exerting that power which enables him even to subject everything to himself." Philip. 3:21 AMP**

Myth—Giving 10% Is A Tithe

> Paul said: "But he is a Jew who is one inwardly, and [true] circumcision is of the heart, a spiritual and not a literal [matter]. His praise is not from men but from God."
> **Romans 2:29 AMP**

> "You [are like] unfaithful wives [having illicit love affairs with the world and breaking your marriage vow to God]! Do you not know that being the world's friend is being God's enemy? So whoever chooses to be a friend of the world takes his stand as an enemy of God. Or do you suppose that the Scripture is speaking to no purpose that says, the Spirit whom He has caused to dwell in us yearns over us and He yearns for the Spirit [to be welcomed] with a jealous love?" **James 4:4-5 AMP**

> Paul said: "For [as far as this world is concerned] you have died, and your [new, real] life is hidden with Christ in God." **Colossians 3:3 AMP**

In contrast to the wealth promised by the tithe preachers, the Word tells you to be transformed in a different way. Instead of being the next wealthy individual on the block owning expensive homes, cars, planes and other things—the Word teaches a new and different focus for true believers.

1. Don't be conformed to the world.
2. Be conformed to Christ's sufferings.
3. Be conformed to Christ's death.
4. Be a jealous lover of God's indwelling Spirit.
5. Be conformed to Christ's promise of a glorious eternal body.

Remember we learned that the "giveaway" of a Zone 3 church is its focus on worldly things? Well, you can see from the above verses exactly how dangerous such a focus is. Therefore, in addition to placing you under the curse of the Law, the tithe preacher also makes you an enemy of God. I'm sorry, the diamonds don't belong to believers, they belong to God and He will distribute them as He deems is in His best interest, not yours.

Myth—Giving 10% Is A Tithe

Let's return to the issue of which Laws we need to be concerned with. The fact Jesus rejects Christians, who are lawless to some extent, means that we must comply with some part of the "Law." It also means that we cannot summarily just dismiss the first five books of the Bible written by Moses. We get another clue from Paul's writings to the church at Ephesus.

> **"By abolishing in his [own crucified] flesh the enmity [caused by] the Law with its decrees and ordinances [which he annulled]; that HE from the two might create in HIMSELF one new man [one new quality of humanity out of the two], so making peace." Ephesians 2:15 AMP**

NOTICE: I have for sake of clarity and distinction in this book made an attempt to change all capitals on words obviously pertaining to Jesus so it will be clear we are talking about Jesus instead of his God [Yahweh] in the Bible verse. Hence in the above verse it reads "in his [own crucified]" vs. "in His [own crucified]" which is as it appears in the Amplified translation. I will try to be consistent in this method throughout the book where the use or lack of use of the capital letter is obvious in the context. The use of capitals referring to both Jesus and God do not reflect the truth of the relationship between the FATHER and HIS begotten Son. I am satisfied in the spirit that this is useful for all the discussions in this book.

I believe a correct interpretation of the above verse, with Galatians 3:10 in mind, would read "some decrees and ordinances in the Law have been annulled." Yet certainly this does not indicate that commandments and commands are annulled? Jesus must be thinking of something specific with his lawless comment. Consider these statements of Jesus.

> **Jesus said: "I assure you, most solemnly I tell you, if anyone steadfastly believes in me, he will himself be able to do the things that I do; and he will do even greater than these, because I go to the FATHER." John 14:12 AMP**

> **Jesus said: "If you [really] love me, you will keep (obey) my commands." John 14:15 AMP**

Myth—Giving 10% Is A Tithe

There is certainly a firm statement from Jesus in John 14:12 that those who "steadfastly believe" will be able to do the things he did, even greater things. When you reflect on this teaching of Jesus, do you think he obeyed God's Ten Commandments, all of them? What about the Sabbath? What about the rest of the Law contained in the first five books of the Bible? Since we are told that steadfast believers will "be able to do the things Jesus did" — we have another clue. I cannot believe that Jesus ignored God's laws as he came to us representing God in voice and deed. Furthermore, Jesus said he came to fulfill the Law and not to do away with it. Yet Paul in Ephesians 2:15 indicates "decrees and ordinances" of the Law are annulled. Again the big question looms, which ones? And exactly what should we be concerned about to prevent Jesus from rejecting us because we "practice lawlessness?"

There are two places where the words "practice lawlessness" shows up in the New King James Bible. The first is in Matthew 7:23 where Jesus rejects people because they "practiced" lawlessness. Note that this implies you don't have to be perfect, which I already discussed in an earlier chapter. The second place is Matthew 13:41 where Jesus sends his angels to gather out everything "that offends" and all of those who "practice lawlessness."

In Matthew 5:19 (AMP), Jesus gave the following instruction.

"He who practices *(the commandments*)* **and teaches others to do so shall be called great in the kingdom of Heaven."**

In Matthew 19:17-18 (AMP), Jesus gave the following instruction.

"If you would enter into the Life, you must continually keep the commandments. *[Which ones?]* **You shall not kill, you shall not commit adultery, you shall not steal, and you shall not bear false witness.** *[Others - v19] The Apostle Edward**

In Matthew 22:40 (AMP), Jesus gave the following instruction.

"These two commandments sum up and upon them depend all the Law and the Prophets."

The Summation Of The Law And The Prophets!

"You shall love the LORD your God with all your heart and with all your soul and with all your mind (intellect). This is the great (most important, principal) and first commandment. And a second is like it: You shall love your neighbor as [you do] yourself." Matthew 22:37-39 AMP

Now in your consideration of which laws to obey and not to obey, where does this teaching of Jesus fit in? Would you ignore the great first command or the second? If so, why? Within this teaching of Jesus lies the key to truly understanding all people of faith and what really drives them. That includes myself. I don't have to give much thought to the Law other than these two commands and I am assured of eternal life. The entire Bible stands on these two commandments. The person who earnestly takes them into the bowels of their soul will turn on the automatic pilot of their spirit with God. Think about these commands, I will come back to them later.

In John 14:21 (AMP), Jesus gave the following instruction.

"The person who has my commandments and keeps them is the one who [really] loves me; and whoever [really] loves me will be loved by my FATHER, and I (too) will love him and will show (reveal, manifest) myself to him [I will let myself be clearly seen by him and make myself real to him.]"

In John 14:23 (AMP), Jesus gave this clarification of verse 21.

"If a person [really] loves me, he will keep my word [obey my teaching]; and my FATHER will love him, and WE will come to him and make OUR home (abode, special dwelling place) with him."

I am a living testimony to the veracity of Jesus' teachings since both he and the FATHER dwell within me. They are both *REAL* to me!

Myth—Giving 10% Is A Tithe

They have both manifested themselves to me in a way that I know they are real. Have they made themselves "real" to you yet? If not, then maybe its because you "do not have their commandments" inside of you or maybe its because "you do not keep their commandments." Clearly the two issues of keeping the commandments and obeying what Jesus taught would be paramount in his determination of who practiced lawlessness. In his eyes, anyone who is disobedient to what he taught is lawless. Makes sense doesn't it? Isn't that why he said: "Why do you call me Lord and do not do what I say?" The connection between his followers and their obedience to what he said to do is clear. *Disobey Jesus Christ and you are lawless!*

Commandments & Commands Matter!

The commandments clearly matter, don't they? What about the issue of commands? Hear again, Jesus makes it clear that "commands" will be taken into consideration at the time of judgment. Listen to the clarity of these easy to understand verses.

> "I know His [Yahweh's] command is everlasting life. Therefore, whatever I speak, just as the FATHER has told me, so I speak." John 12:50 NKJV

> "I know that HIS commandments is (means) eternal life." AMP

> "You are my friends if you keep on doing the things which I command you to do." John 15:14 AMP

> "This is what I command you; that you love one another."
> John 15:17 AMP

Obedience Matters!

> "Then Peter and the apostles replied. We must obey God rather than men." Acts 5:29 AMP

Myth—Giving 10% Is A Tithe

> **"The Holy Spirit is bestowed on those who obey HIM (God)."**
> **Acts 5:32 AMP**

> **"He became the author and source of eternal salvation to all those who give heed and obey HIM." Hebrews 5:9 AMP**

> **"For the time [has arrived] for judgment to begin with the household of God; and if it begins with us, what will [be] the end of those who do not respect or believe or obey the good news (the Gospel) of God?" 1 Peter 4:17 AMP**

You can find more information about specific commands of God in Deuteronomy chapters six through eleven. If you read that section of the Bible, you will observe these interesting commands from God in the midst of some others. Question, which of the following four commands would no longer be important to God or HIS Son? Would any of these be part of a list that Jesus might have on the subject of those who "practice lawlessness?" Reflecting on the two great commandments above, one would think so. I do.

1. The command to teach the Law.
2. The command to remember the LORD.
3. The command to love God.
4. The command to study and obey the commands.

The Law Does Not Void Abraham's Covenant!

Let's consider a few more issues concerning the Law, starting with Apostle Paul's letter to the Galatians. I will then try to tie all the Law stuff together in a meaningful way for you. My desire is that you understand fully that the tithe is a part of the ceremonial laws that are now done away with, but the commandments, commands and some other laws still need to be obeyed. All of us need to understand exactly what Jesus means when he uses the phrase "you who practice lawlessness." If we don't understand it, it may be to our eternal damnation. Turn in your Bible to Galatians 3:15-29 for Paul's argument that the Law does not void out Abraham's covenant.

Copyright 2005 Edward G. Palmer, All Rights Reserved.

Myth—Giving 10% Is A Tithe

Galatians 3:15-29 AMP

[15] "To speak in terms of human relations, brethren, [if] even a man makes a last will and testament (a merely human covenant), no one sets it aside or makes it void or adds to it when once it has been drawn up and signed (ratified, confirmed).

[16] Now the promises (covenants, agreements) were decreed and made to Abraham and his seed (his offspring, his heir). HE [God] does not say, and to seeds (descendants, heirs), as if referring to many persons, but, and to your seed (your descendant, your heir), obviously referring to one individual, who is [none other than] Christ (the Messiah).

[17] This is my argument: The Law, which began 430 years after the covenant [concerning the coming Messiah], does not and cannot annul the covenant previously established (ratified) by God, so as to abolish the promise and make it void.

[18] For if the inheritance [of the promise depends on observing] the Law [as these false teachers would like you to believe], it no longer [depends] on the promise; however, God gave it to Abraham [as a free gift solely] by virtue of HIS promise.

[19] What then was the purpose of the Law? It was added [later on, after the promise, to disclose and expose to men their guilt] because of transgressions and [to make men more conscious of the sinfulness] of sin; and it was intended to be in effect until the seed (the descendant, the heir) should come, to and concerning whom the promise had been made. And it [the Law] was arranged and ordained and appointed through the instrumentality of angels [and was given] by the hand (in the person) of a go-between [Moses, an intermediary person between God and man].

Myth—Giving 10% Is A Tithe

[20] Now a go-between (intermediary) has to do with and implies more than one party [there can be no mediation with just one person]. Yet God is [only] one Person [and HE was the sole party in giving that promise to Abraham. But the Law was a contract between two, God and Israel; its validity was dependent on both].

[21] Is the Law then contrary and opposed to the promises of God? Of course not! For if a Law had been given which could confer [spiritual] life, then righteousness and right standing with God would certainly have come by Law.

[22] But the Scriptures [picture all mankind as sinners] shut up and imprisoned by sin, so that [the inheritance, blessing] which was promised through faith in Jesus Christ (the Messiah) might be given (released, delivered, and committed) to [all] those who believe [who adhere to and trust and rely on HIM].

[23] Now before the faith came, we were perpetually guarded under the Law, kept in custody in preparation for the faith that was destined to be revealed (unveiled, disclosed),

[24] So that the Law served [to us Jews] as our trainer [our guardian, our guide to Christ, to lead us] until Christ [came], that we might be justified (declared righteous, put in right standing with God) by and through faith.

[25] But now that the faith has come, we are no longer under a trainer (the guardian of our childhood).

[26] For in Christ Jesus you are all sons of God through faith.

[27] For as many [of you] as were baptized into Christ [into a spiritual union and communion with Christ, the Anointed one, the Messiah] have put on (clothed yourselves with) Christ.

Myth—Giving 10% Is A Tithe

[28] There is [now no distinction] neither Jew nor Greek, there is neither slave nor free, there is not male and female; for you are all one in Christ Jesus.

[29] And if you belong to Christ [are in him who is Abraham's seed], then you are Abraham's offspring and [spiritual] heirs according to promise." Galatians 3: 15:29 AMP

Abraham showed God a quality of sincere faith from within his heart. That kind of faith is missing in most of humanity. The reward of Abraham's covenant is for those who have similar faith. Such heart faith leads to trust, obedience and the solid belief that God is real. These qualities in your heart lead to righteous behavior or to doing what is right in God's eyes.

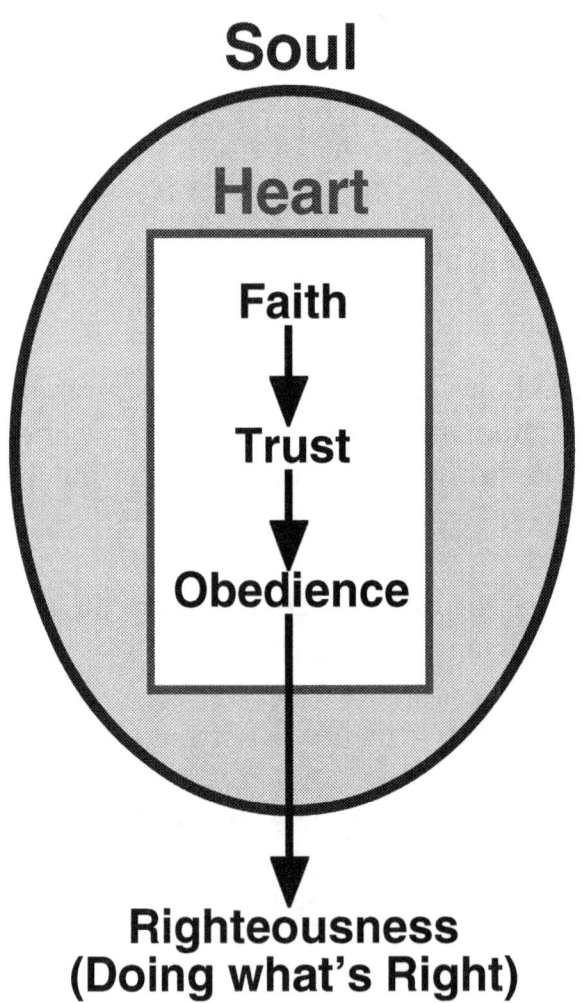

Copyright 2005 Edward G. Palmer, All Rights Reserved.

Book of Edward—Chapter 17

Myth—Giving 10% Is A Tithe

Paul teaches the Law was given to Moses 430 years after God made the covenant with Abraham. How did Abraham come to such faith? It was a decision of his heart, in the bowels of his soul, that God was real. God had already promised to multiply Abraham's descendents through an heir of Isaac. Abraham reasoned that if God could produce a son in his old age, HE was in control and could restore Isaac if he was killed. Abraham trusted God and ultimately that is what real faith is all about. His trust allowed him to do what was right in God's eyes, not his own eyes or the eyes of mankind. Abraham took God's two great commandments into his heart knowledge, even though those commandments had not yet been written.

It is not good enough to "claim you are in Christ" without actually being able to demonstrate the outcome of that belief. There is not a person alive truly in Christ, which can teach a distorted message of what the Word says. Your belief in Jesus Christ has to be translated into obedience to God. An apostate tithe message comes from someone who does not have a sincere and true belief like Abraham. People of God do not misrepresent God.

Faith is a decision of the heart. It leads to trust and then to obedience. Faith, trust and obedience are resident inside the heart of all true believers. When these attributes reside in your heart, it leads to a strong desire on your soul to always "do what is right." Doing what is right is being righteous, just like Jesus Christ. What starts as a decision of the heart, is ultimately manifested by the righteous behavior of our actions. Do you remember that this is one of the weightier matters of the Law that Jesus talked about in Matthew 23:23? The requirement to "do right."

If you can understand that the outcome of *real* faith is righteousness, you can understand why Apostle James taught you that faith without works is dead. James is simply stating that those who really have faith [know God] will demonstrate that faith and knowledge of God by doing the right thing. It also explains why Apostle Paul taught that those who *really* believed in their hearts would do so "unto righteousness." Therefore, true faith leads to righteous behavior even if it does not lead to perfection. The contrast is simple; keeping the Law won't lead you to righteousness. Righteousness is the outcome of true faith in our hearts for God and HIS Son.

Copyright 2005 Edward G. Palmer, All Rights Reserved.

Book of Edward—Chapter 17

Myth—Giving 10% Is A Tithe

Law Is A Contract Between God And Israel!

Apostle Paul also teaches in Galatians 3:20 that the Law is a contract between "God and Israel." It is not between God and the Americans, the British, the French, the Italians, etc. Nor is the Law a contract between God and Christians. Where then is the righteousness in misappropriating the word of God for self serving mammon purposes? So in addition to the tithe teacher placing you under a curse and making you an enemy of God, the tithe preacher robs God by trying to interfere in contractual matters, which he or she has no business being involved in. Listen, the minister is supposed to teach the word of God [and the Law], not pervert it!

Getting back to a couple of other nuances to consider. We know that we are not supposed to "live under" the ceremonial laws [of which tithing is a part], but what about the civil and social laws? Examining a couple of verses will answer this question for us. If you turn to Deuteronomy 17 and start reading about the administration of judges, you will quickly again find the use of sacrifices [rituals]. Therefore, civil laws appear to be in the same category of ceremonial laws. If you turn to Deuteronomy 21 and read about the rebellious son, you will find that social laws also fall in the same category; they "stoned" rebellious sons. It is clear that all the Laws involving rituals no longer apply to any true believer in Christ Jesus. To live under such ritual laws is to insult God's grace and the sacrifice of His Son.

Now I want to make sure you understand an important aspect of the Law in regards to these various decrees and statutes, especially the ones we no longer have to observe. To illustrate the point I want to make, go and study the "law of marriage" in Deuteronomy 22 and you will find the punishment for "not being a virgin" for a woman who has just been married, but exhibits no evidence of her virginity.

> **"But if it is true that the evidences of virginity were not found in the young woman, then they shall bring her to the door of her father's house and the men of her city shall stone her to death." Deuteronomy 22:20-21 AMP**

Copyright 2005 Edward G. Palmer, All Rights Reserved.

Myth—Giving 10% Is A Tithe

This was a great insult to any family in Israel at the time. It was also an act of grave danger to Israel itself as the Bible continues by saying that "She has wrought criminal folly in Israel by playing the harlot in her father's house. So you shall put away the evil from among you." God gave warning to Israel against sin and in many cases it might have resulted in a collective punishment or a curse upon the entire country. Sin was a very serious issue.

The concern about a daughter's virginity is very different today. At one end is the very loose moral construct that "kids will be kids" and you just can't stop teenagers from having sex. Some parents now think they should offer teenagers their own bedroom so sex can be experienced in a safer environment. How depraved is that? At the other end are serious concerns about AIDS and other sexually transmitted diseases. Few moral considerations from God's perspective enter mainstream parental decision making today, like it did back in Old Testament Israel.

The thought of exclusion from eternal salvation usually does not enter into parental consideration. I want you to realize a simple fact. Even though some biblical laws no longer apply to our daily lives, the requirement of God that we do what is right under any given circumstance still applies to our life. God's Word states that "fornicators" will not enter Heaven. One result of true belief in God is that we teach our children God's marriage and sex rules along with the eternal consequences of having loose morals. Even without explicit instructions from God, parents inherently know what is right and wrong. God will hold us accountable to HIS Word and for doing the right thing under any circumstance. Jesus will look for any "lawlessness."

This presents another conundrum, doesn't it? The Law might not directly apply, but the human issues expressed in the Law have not gone away. We are confronted with the same civil and social issues the Israelites were confronted with. Therefore, even though obedience to a Law might not be required, God will still hold us to a catchall standard of always doing the right thing. It eliminates most of the Law and further explains James 4:17.

"So any person who knows what is right to do but does not do it, to him it is sin." James 4:17 AMP

Myth—Giving 10% Is A Tithe

Paul also makes it clear that the Law is not for the righteous, but for the unrighteous. We can't be righteous? Wrong! Remember Luke 1:5-6?

"Knowing and understanding this: that the Law is not enacted for the righteous (the upright and just, who are in right standing with God), but for the lawless and unruly, for the ungodly and sinful, for the irreverent and profane, for those who strike and beat and [even] murder fathers and strike and beat and [even] murder mothers, for manslayers, [For] impure and immoral persons, those who abuse themselves with men, kidnapers, liars, perjurers—and whatever else is opposed to wholesome teaching and sound doctrine." 1 Timothy 1:9-10 AMP

Now, do you remember that I told you if you could truly understand the importance of the two great commandments, you could understand every person of faith like myself? That you would know what drives them? That if you could take these two commandments to the bowels of your soul and into your heart that you would be on automatic pilot with your spirit? Well, here is how it works.

The first commandment is to "Love God" — with *all your heart.* In other words, you need to take God into the bowels of your soul and into your very heart where every other person you deeply love finds true fellowship with your spirit. Where do you think my love for my beloved wife Jackie resided, in my mind? No, my love for her was in the bowels of my soul and in the very heart of my entire earthly being. Do you think I ever wanted to intentionally treat Jackie poorly? Do you think I even wanted to displease her? Do you think I wanted to disobey her desires for me when I knew it would hurt her spirit? Do you think I wanted to love her with every fiber of my earthly existence? Do you think I made mistakes during our thirty-nine year life together? The answers should be obvious to you. If you can fully understand the answers to these questions, it will resolve the conundrum of the *faith vs. law* debate in Christianity today. Virtually every strong feeling of love that ever emanated out of your physical being came from within your true heart. It's the heart inside your soul, not your physical heart organ.

Copyright 2005 Edward G. Palmer, All Rights Reserved.

Book of Edward—Chapter 17

Myth—Giving 10% Is A Tithe

The result of a true faith like that of Abraham's is a true love for God Almighty. What we feel inside of us for everyone we deeply love, we now feel that same power in our soul-spirit for God. We understand that His love is and will always be "our first love." This isn't a chronological first love; this is a prioritized "first love." Indeed, my love for Jackie was first in my heart chronologically, but it took second place in my heart when I found true faith and love for God. This didn't mean that I started to love Jackie any less. In fact, I became more in love with her. God doesn't take away a drop of love from your heart. Instead, He fills you and becomes your resource for an unlimited quantity of quality love. When God gets into your heart, your heart plugs into an unlimited love energy source just like a light plugs in an unlimited electric energy source when you plug its socket into a wall outlet.

When you get God into your heart, He will give you an unlimited love for others in your heart. That will allow you to execute the second great command of loving your neighbor "as you love yourself." God will show you how to love yourself and others once He gets inside your heart. All this love stuff doesn't make you a patsy anymore than it does God. True love executes discipline when it is required. True love is a tough love. All God wants is what the Apostle James taught. He yearns for His Spirit to be welcomed into your heart with a jealous love from the bowels of your soul.

Indeed, once God has a home inside of your heart, your soul will desire to get truly acquainted with Him and His perspective on human life. You will study all His Law. You will learn what pleases and displeases Him. While you no longer have to obey the ritual Laws, you certainly want to do what is right in God's eyes to the best of your human ability. Your jealous love for God's indwelling Spirit will drive your righteous behavior. The conundrum is then solved, isn't it? Once He is truly in your heart, the Law becomes irrelevant. It is because you have become the new person that Paul talks about in Ephesians 2:15. You have morphed into a person of faith and are no longer conformed to the things of this world or the things of men; you are conformed to the things of God and of His Son. Yes, we do make mistakes and even sin, but God knows that our heart of faith always tries to do right even if we botch it. That's when you will truly feel forgiveness. Do you get it? Faith starts with the simple decision of your heart to love God!

Copyright 2005 Edward G. Palmer, All Rights Reserved.

Book of Edward—Chapter 17

Myth—Giving 10% Is A Tithe

Bible Is Clear—Some "Law" Still Active!

As convenient as it is for many to take a broad brush and sweep all of the Law [first five books of Bible] under the carpet, Paul and John's writings confirm some of the Law still applies to our lives, even if the ceremonial laws and others do not. Read carefully who is excluded from an eternal life in Heaven and ask yourself where the criterion comes from.

> **"For God's [holy] wrath and indignation are revealed from Heaven against all ungodliness and unrighteousness of men, who in their wickedness repress and hinder the truth and make it inoperative." Romans 1:18 AMP**

> **"Do you not know that the unrighteous and the wrongdoers will not inherit or have any share in the kingdom of God? Do not be deceived (misled); neither the impure and immoral, nor idolaters, nor adulterers, nor those who participate in homosexuality, nor cheats (swindlers and thieves), nor greedy graspers, nor drunkards, nor foulmouthed revilers and slanderers, nor extortioners and robbers will inherit or have any share in the kingdom of God." 1 Corinthians 6:9-10 AMP**

> **"But as for the cowards and the ignoble and the contemptible and the cravenly lacking in courage and the cowardly submissive, and as for the unbelieving and the faithless, and as for the depraved and defiled with abominations, and as for murderers and the lewd and adulterous and the practicers of magic arts and the idolaters (those who give supreme devotion to anyone or anything other than God) and all liars (those who knowingly convey untruth by word or deed)—[all of these shall have] their part in the lake that blazes with fire and brimstone. This is the second death." Revelation 21:8 AMP**

Myth—Giving 10% Is A Tithe

> "[But] without *(outside Heaven*)* **are the dogs and those who practice sorceries (magic arts) and impurity [the lewd, adulterers] and the murderers and idolaters and everyone who loves and deals in falsehood (untruth, error, deception, cheating)." Revelation 22:15 AMP** *The Apostle Edward**
>
> **"Then I will draw near to you for judgment; I will be a swift witness against the sorcerers, against the adulterers, against the false swearers, and against those who oppress the hireling in his wages, the widow and the fatherless, and who turn aside the temporary resident from his right and fear not ME, says the LORD of hosts." Malachi 3:5 AMP**
>
> **"Blessed are those who do HIS commandments, that they may have the right to the tree of life and may enter through the gates into the city." Revelation 22:14 NKJV**

Yes, Paul states that the ceremonial laws and others no longer apply, but he also confirms that the "laws of sexual sins" contained in Leviticus 18 must apply as do the penalties contained in Leviticus 20. Consider Paul's writing that homosexuals will not get into Heaven. Then consider Leviticus 20:13 in which the penalty for homosexuality is death. In the end, are these not the same result from God? It is obvious that our personal behavior still matters to God, even if we do not have to obey some laws.

Remember that these verses do not apply to the righteous because they operate in faith with God seeking to please HIM. They simply do not commit the evil that invokes the rejection of Christ. If they do engage in such evil, they are simply not saved. They are only pretenders and will be confronted by Jesus as he says to them: "I never knew you."

Did you observe part of the Ten Commandments in the above verses? Thou shall not murder? Thou shall not commit idolatry? Thou shall not commit adultery? Thou shall not steal? Thou shall not bear false witness? These are familiar Bible teachings, aren't they? They are commandments, which still remain active behavioral standards with other parts of the Law.

Copyright 2005 Edward G. Palmer, All Rights Reserved.

Myth—Giving 10% Is A Tithe

In Exodus 20 you will find the contract between God and Israel, which contains all of the "Ten Commandments." In Exodus 21, you will find the "Rights of Persons." In Exodus 21:33, you will find "Rights of Property." In Exodus 22:16, you will find God's idea of "Proper Conduct." In Exodus 23, you will find God's idea of "Proper Justice."

Church & Sabbath Laws No Longer Apply!

In Exodus 31:13, you learn that as part of the contract, the "Sabbath is a sign" between God and Israel. Do you remember that Paul taught us in Colossians 2:16-17 not to be judged by anyone concerning the "Sabbath?" What Paul means is that the Sabbath Law with its ceremonial and behavioral rules no longer apply to the Christian. Take a deep breath for a moment now and let me fully explain what Paul is teaching us about the "Sabbath."

FACT: Jesus Christ destroyed the church and its hierarchal structure. Communication with God before Christ looked something like this graphic.

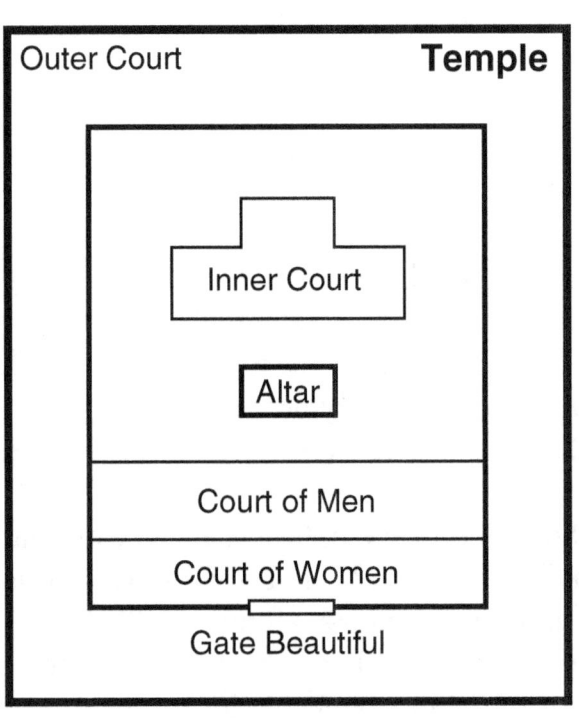

Copyright 2005 Edward G. Palmer, All Rights Reserved.

Book of Edward—Chapter 17

Myth—Giving 10% Is A Tithe

Before Christ, communication with God was very complicated and had to be done in accordance with specific rules. Failure to follow the rules could literally result in the death of a priest or even the high priest. There were rules for the priesthood and who could be a member. There were rules for the priest to follow in the temple. There were rules for the high priest to follow in the temple. Daily, weekly, monthly and special occasion sacrifices had to be prepared according to specific rules and formulas set down in the Law. There were rules for the outer court, the inner court, the altar, etc. Get the picture? Communication with God was highly structured and not really available to the average person. God communicated with few people in a direct way. In between the average person and God was a heavy [church] bureaucracy with many statutes [laws] and rules. There were many rules for how the Sabbath was to be observed *to keep it holy*.

When Christ gave his life as a sacrifice for our sins, it altered the existing hierarchal structure and established a new-direct communications model [environment], which looks like this graphic. Now it is up to you to talk directly with God. If you need help, Christ is available as a mediator. There is no intermediary between you and God Almighty.

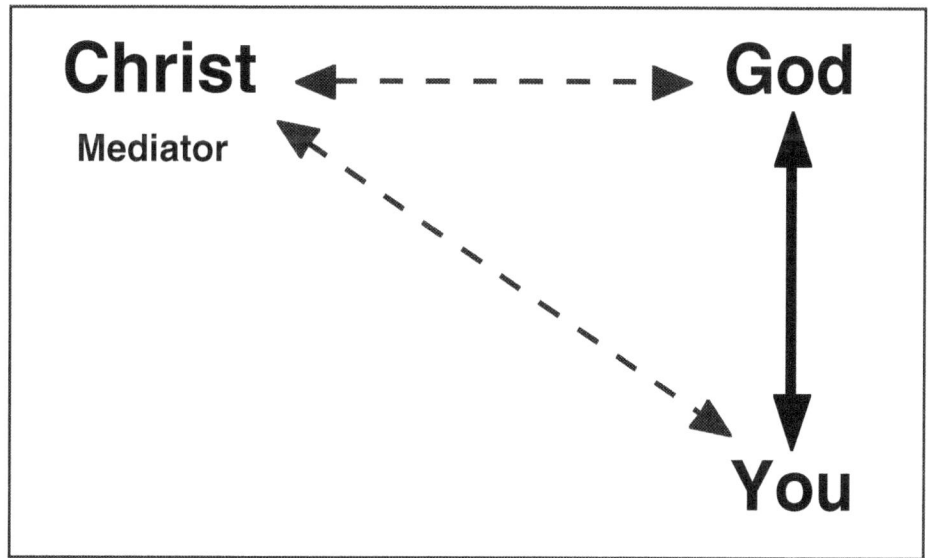

Christ Created A New Communications Model

Myth—Giving 10% Is A Tithe

Go Directly To The FATHER And Ask HIM!

Jesus said: "At that time you won't need to ask me for anything. *The truth is, you can go directly to the FATHER and ask HIM,* **and HE will grant your request because you use my name. You haven't done this before. Ask, using my name, and you will receive, and you will have abundant joy." John 16:23-24 NLT**

If you truly understand what Christ is saying to you about directly communicating with God, you will realize that the modern day church has tried to reinsert itself between you and God. Yet the Bible makes it clear that no one stands between you and God. Not even Christ, your mediator. By nature Christ is there to help you as needed. He is your one and only mediator with God. This does not make him a go between you and God or else Christ would not have told you to "go directly to the FATHER." In stark contrast, Moses was an intermediary between the Israelites and God. The people of Israel did not talk directly with God like you and I can as a result of "being in Christ." Get used to it and understand what Christ has done.

The veil of the temple has been ripped in two and the temple building is now completely destroyed. Today, there is a new and different temple that God wants to dwell in. It is the temple of your body built of flesh and not a temple structure built of brick, wood and mortar.

> **"For there [is only] one God, and [only] one mediator between God and men, the man Christ Jesus."**
> **1 Timothy 2:5 AMP**

FACT: Your body is *now* the temple God seeks to dwell in.

> **"Do you not know that your body is the temple (the very sanctuary) of the Holy Spirit who lives within you, whom you have received [as a gift] from God? You are not your own." 1 Corinthians 6:19 AMP**

FACT: Common people could not enter the *old* Holy of Holies.

"And the Holy Spirit uses all this to point out to us that under the old system the common people could not go into the Holy of Holies as long as the outer room and the entire system it represents were still in use." Hebrews 9:8 LIV

FACT: We can *now* enter the *new* Holy of Holies at any time.

"And so, dear brothers, now we may walk right into the very Holy of Holies, where God is, because of the blood of Jesus." Hebrews 10:19 LIV

If you think that God wants you to sit in your pew on Sunday morning and just get apostasy dumped on you in a one-way verbal transaction, you are wrong. HE wants a two-way communication and a direct fellowship with you. Yet, it is impossible for you to fully participate with God unless you appreciate the fact that Christ destroyed the old Temple and Sabbath laws. HE did this to give us a better covenant. If you tithe and observe other ritual Old Testament laws, you are not under the new covenant of Christ. If you are shallow in God's Word, you cannot engage God in deeper conversation.

FACT: Jesus Christ annulled all of the Sabbath laws and rules related to personal and Temple rituals. Read carefully the Sabbath commandment and the accompanying rules to implement it given by God to "keep it holy" in HIS eyes. Remember, we are not talking about worshipping God on a Saturday or Sunday, we are talking about how to obey the "instructions that accompanied" the fourth commandment of God, which was given to man as part of the contract between God and Israel.

The Sabbath Commandment

FOURTH COMMANDMENT: "Observe the Sabbath day, to keep it holy, as the LORD your God [has] commanded you."
                                            Deuteronomy 5:12 NKJV

Myth—Giving 10% Is A Tithe

The fourth commandment explicitly tells the Israelites to observe the Sabbath—*"As the LORD your God commanded you."* Therefore, unlike the nine other commandments, which are very clear on their face, the Sabbath commandment came with detailed instructions and ceremonies to follow. A penalty of death came to those who failed to follow some of the instructions.

Sabbath Instructions

1. Don't cook on the Sabbath day. Prepare all your food the day before. [Exodus 16:23]
2. Do not gather food from the field on the Sabbath. [Exodus 16:25-26]
3. God gives bread for two days on the sixth day. [Exodus 16:29]
4. Do not work on the Sabbath. Your son, daughter, servants, cattle, and stranger shall not work on the Sabbath. [Exodus 20:10-11]
5. Whoever does *any* work on the Sabbath day shall surely be put to death. [Exodus 31:15; 35:2]
6. The Sabbath shall be a sign between God and Israel. [Ex. 31:17]
7. Israel shall keep the Sabbath throughout their generations as a perpetual covenant. [Exodus 31:16]
8. You shall kindle no fires in your dwellings on the Sabbath. [Exodus 35:3]
9. The Sabbath is a statute [law] forever. [Leviticus 16:31]
10. In the seventh month, first day, you shall have a Sabbath-rest, a memorial of blowing of trumpets. [Leviticus 23:34]
11. On the fifteenth day of the seventh month, when you have gathered in the fruit of the land, you shall kept the feast of the LORD ... and on the first day there shall be a Sabbath-rest. [Leviticus 23:39]
12. Every Sabbath you shall put the showbread and frankincense in proper order as a memorial ...taken continually from the children of Israel by an "everlasting covenant." [Leviticus 24:5-8]
13. Aaron and his sons shall eat it in a holy place. [Leviticus 24:9]
14. The land shall keep a Sabbath to the LORD. [Leviticus 25:2]
15. The LORD said to Moses, "the man [who gathered sticks on the Sabbath] must be put to death; all the congregation shall stone him to death outside the camp." [Numbers 15:33-36]

Copyright 2005 Edward G. Palmer, All Rights Reserved.

Book of Edward—Chapter 17

Myth—Giving 10% Is A Tithe

The above list is just a sampling of the various Sabbath instructions found in the Bible. I could write an entire book of the detailed instructions telling you how God wants you to keep the Sabbath day holy. That is how many instructions there are in the Bible. I didn't even get into the various sacrifices and the preparation of those sacrifices for the Sabbath.

Now don't try to tell me that you want to keep the Sabbath day holy in accordance with biblical instructions. You don't. In fact, you cannot comply with the Sabbath commandment, because you cannot comply with the instructions that are attached to that commandment. It's the same with the tithe law, because Christ's new covenant altered the Law. That doesn't mean you can't worship God on Sunday. More about worship shortly.

Indeed, Jesus Christ destroyed the structure of the church and there is no longer a need to observe the ceremonies associated within the church itself or for the Sabbath day. Listen carefully here. I am not telling you to stop the worship of God on a regular basis. I am telling you that the communications model with God has changed and that the Sabbath laws were a ceremonial aspect of the Law like the tithe law. Both the Sabbath and tithe law no longer apply under the new covenant with Christ.

Some of my friends, seeking to get close to God agonize whether the Sabbath should be observed on Saturday or Sunday. Let me be clear here. I agree that the Sabbath in the Bible was held on a Saturday as celebrated by modern day Jews. However, the Sabbath law and its rules no longer apply.

There is no intermediary *between* you and God like the church and its hierarchy. Jesus Christ told us to go *directly* to God with our petitions, as we learned earlier. It is you direct to God. Period. Need help? Christ will be there for you as a mediator. If you can understand that the Sabbath was part of the ceremonial aspects of the Law, you no longer need to worry about which day of the week you should worship God.

Then there is the usual proverbial question. What would Jesus do? The answer is clear in the Bible. Jesus and his disciples did not follow the ritual laws of the Sabbath as observed by the Pharisees. Listen to the Word.

Copyright 2005 Edward G. Palmer, All Rights Reserved.

Book of Edward—Chapter 17

Myth—Giving 10% Is A Tithe

When Jesus and his disciples went through a grain field on a Sabbath day they were hungry. As a result, the disciples picked heads of grain to eat. The instruction in Exodus 16:25-26 from God is clear. "Do not gather food from the field on the Sabbath." God had already commanded that a man be stoned to death for simply gathering "sticks." See # 2 & 15 in the above list. In the eyes of the Pharisees, what the disciples did was worthy of death. It was written in the Law to put men to death for such behavior. Now Christ was on the scene offering a new "Sabbath" and "mercy" perspective.

FACT: God altered the Sabbath laws with Christ's sacrifice.

"And when the Pharisees saw it, they said to him, see there! Your disciples are doing what is unlawful and not permitted on the Sabbath." Matthew 12:2 AMP

Jesus replied that when David was hungry, he and those with him went into the house of God and "ate the loaves of the showbread—which was not lawful for him or those with him to eat." Jesus continues on with the following dialogue.

"But I tell you, something greater and more exalted and more majestic than the temple is here! And if you had only known what this saying means, 'I desire mercy [readiness to help, to spare, to forgive] rather than sacrifice and sacrificial victims,' you would not have condemned the guiltless." Matthew 12:6-7 AMP

"For the Son of Man is Lord [even] of the Sabbath."
Matthew 12:8 AMP

FACT: Jesus did not observe all the ritual laws of the Sabbath.

"Then some of the Pharisees said, 'This man [Jesus] is not from God, because he does not observe the Sabbath.' But others said, 'How can a man who is a sinner (a bad man) do such signs and miracles?' " John 9:16 AMP

Copyright 2005 Edward G. Palmer, All Rights Reserved.

Myth—Giving 10% Is A Tithe

FACT: Jesus revealed new things about the Sabbath.

Jesus said: "So it is lawful and allowable to do good on the Sabbath days." Matthew 12:12 AMP

It was the custom of Jesus to teach in the synagogue on the Sabbath day. [Luke 4:16] What do you think he taught about, the social matters of the day or Scripture? It is clear that "teaching the Word" is the pattern to be followed in the New Testament church [and Synagogue]. This was reading verbatim from Scripture. Jesus would not condone an apostate doctrine like the modern tithe teaching. If you think Jesus would, you do not know him. Listen—the New Testament pattern *is very clear*; stick to the word of God.

"The voices of the Prophets ... are read every Sabbath."
Acts 13:27 NKJV

"The next Sabbath almost the entire city gathered together to hear the word of God [concerning the attainment through Christ of salvation in the kingdom of God]."
Acts 13:44 AMP

The Sabbath was a day in which people gathered together to hear the word of God. Today, when they gather together for a 10-minute sermon, how much of God's Word do they get? When they gather in an emotionally charged *Word of Faith* meeting for 4-6 hours, how much of God's Word do they get? The answer to both questions is very little. Instead, the culprits in the pulpits most often will feed itching Christian ears exactly what they want. It will be apostasy. It will not be sound doctrine from God's Word.

God has one *main* requirement of believers: To accept Christ in our hearts in a way that leads us to righteous behavior [true faith in God]. This leads to getting baptized by immersion as a testimony to others that *we do have a personal relationship with God [who dwells in our heart]*. All other church rules are voluntary. There is no need to worry if you worship God on the right day. When you are in faith, a daily worship song will rise out of your heart unto God Almighty. You will know that HE dwells inside you.

Copyright 2005 Edward G. Palmer, All Rights Reserved.

The Sabbath Lord Dwells Inside People of Faith!

If God is in your heart like HE is in mine, everyday will be a Sabbath day and there will be nothing special about any day of the week. That is because I am in a constant state of fellowship, prayer and worship day and night with God. Every moment I am alive is spiritually special to me and I cannot stop thinking about or talking with God. Isn't that what Paul meant when he said we should pray without ceasing? Yes, it is possible to live continually in God's Spirit. Those who are in faith know what that means. And the more you walk with God, the deeper HE will take your faith.

If you grasp the truth of these Sabbath statements, you may be able understand the following teaching found in the Gnostic Gospel of Truth.[2]

> "He labored even on the Sabbath for the sheep which he found fallen into the pit. He saved the life of that sheep bringing it up from the pit in order that you may understand fully what that Sabbath is, you who possess full understanding."

> "It is a day in which it is not fitting that salvation be idle, so that you may speak of that heavenly day which has no night and of the sun which does not set because it is perfect. Say then in your heart that you are this perfect day and that in you the light which does not fail dwells."

Verily I say to you that the Sabbath is indeed within me day and night because the Lord of the Sabbath dwells inside of me. Therefore, there is no longer a need for a ceremonial day for me to worship God. Every day is a day of worship for me. And I am free, as Paul has taught, from the physical aspects of the Sabbath. This does not mean I do not need fellowship. The issue of denying corporate fellowship, however, does not necessarily mean assembling in a church building. It has more to do with "watching over one another" through the godly support of Bible believing friends. Together in the Lord, we uphold one another as we each progress in our faith and evolve to the point where the Sabbath is indeed a "perfect day in each one of us."

Myth—Giving 10% Is A Tithe

The teaching in the Gospel of Truth about the Sabbath truly resonates within my own spirit and understanding of God. As you learned earlier, do not waste a lot of time on the Gnostic Gospels[3]. However there are a few books with interesting teachings like the one above, which I cited earlier in chapter 14. See page 479. I am aware that some might think I could not be of God since I have referenced a Gnostic Gospel. However, truth seekers will search for truth without preconceived notions about what is useful to read or not read without first examining the content under question. There is enough canonical support in the Gnostic books I cited as useful to convince me they are reasonable to study. Of course, then there is the spiritual insight God has given me as comfort. It is HIS apostolic calling and the reason this book even exists. To those who condemn me and say I am wrong, I invite you to write your rebuttal and I will surely read it carefully and respond.

If you choose to join a large church, you also need to join a small group of believers to fellowship with and study Scripture. A small group of 7-12 people will allow each of you to deepen your understanding of God's Word. That is because in a small group you can give each other feedback and uphold each other in your faith and studies. Don't expect anything from a big church except a one-way dump of what most likely will be an apostate message. Only a rare pastor would allow a two-way discussion with his congregation. It's sad, since our God allows such an opportunity for you. Who should you mainly fellowship with? It is God and HIS Son. You won't find any church in this verse.

"And [this] fellowship that we have [which is a distinguishing mark of Christians] is with the FATHER and with HIS Son Jesus Christ (the Messiah)." 1 John 1:3 AMP

There are many reasons to join a large church, but make sure it is firmly focused on the word of God and not man made or denominational doctrines. You might join a church for its adult Bible study classes or even for children or teenage fellowship groups for your kids. Whatever the reason you join, you are voluntarily accepting the churches criteria. Don't fall for the apostate message that "you are planted here" and "have no right to leave." You are only planted where your spirit feels at home.

Myth—Giving 10% Is A Tithe

Do Not Forsake Or Neglect To Assemble Together!

You'll find home churches in the New Testament. They provide the kind of give and take that allows you to grow in HIS Word. As the apostasy of the church at large becomes more visible, there are an increasing number of these small church cells popping up around the world. Biblical truth should reign. If you join a small group and there is no give and take in the discussion, but only a one-way dump—get out! It is another place of Satan again waiting for you. Godly reason is the hallmark for the small Bible cell. It is a true place of God and a wonderful spiritual place to learn the truth of God's Word. It is exemplified by the ability to reason with one another over the meaning of all scripture. When you join your mental reasoning with others and multiple Bible translations, you will truly find God's presence.

> **"And let us consider and give attentive, continuous care to watching over one another, studying how we may stir up (stimulate and incite) to love and helpful deeds and noble activities, not forsaking or neglecting to assemble together [as believers], as is the habit of some people, but admonishing (warning, urging, and encouraging) one another, and all the more faithfully as you see the day approaching."**
> **Hebrews 10:24-25 AMP**

I am aware that many people have left the church. They have been scattered by the hypocrisy and apostasy in the pulpit and assembly. Some have forsaken and neglected to get together with other believers. Let me make it clear, it is not important for you to belong to a large church, but it is important to have the support and regular fellowship of real believers. Our faith is built up by knowledge of the Word and by fellowship with believers.

> **"But without faith, it is impossible to please and be satisfactory to HIM. For whoever would come near to God must [necessarily] believe that God exists and that HE is the rewarder of those who earnestly and diligently seek HIM [out]." Hebrews 11:6 AMP**

Copyright 2005 Edward G. Palmer, All Rights Reserved.

Book of Edward—Chapter 17

Myth—Giving 10% Is A Tithe

Now as you reflect on all this law teaching and the fact that the Sabbath commandment has strings attached to it, listen to the summation of this issue from Apostle Paul.

"Everything is permissible (allowable and lawful) for me; but not all things are helpful (good for me to do, expedient and profitable when considered with other things). Everything is lawful for me, but I will not become a slave of anything or be brought under its power." 1 Corinthians 6:12 AMP

Verily I say to you that "the day is approaching" fast now. If you can understand the teachings in this chapter, you will no longer be hung up with the issues of the Law such as tithing and Sunday services. Paul wasn't and neither was Jesus. Yet you will be hung up on learning as much as you can about God as you too seek to get acquainted with HIM before it is too late.

One could envision a laundry list of what laws, commandments, commands, etc. to obey. If such a clear list existed, you would not run up against Jesus saying you "practiced lawlessness"—would you? My guess is that you would, since you would not be operating in faith. The big list of rules did not help the Israelites. Why would another list help us now? Such a list only reinforces a losing legalistic mentality.

What you need to do is activate your faith. Therefore, I tell you to give your heart completely to God just like Abraham did and obey HIS commandments. Then read the Law so you can get a perspective of how God feels about our human civil and social issues. You will learn obvious common sense things like HE wants obedient and respectful children. When you fully appreciate HIS perspectives, you can teach them to your family and your friends. Only by understanding God's perspective can we realize what is right and what is wrong. When Jesus says to do what is right, he means we should do what is right in God's eyes. This comes natural to those with a heart for God. Remember, they are on automatic pilot with their soul-spirit. However, it does not come natural to those who "appear to be righteous," but have not taken the leap of faith. Another way of expressing that leap of faith is a total 100% surrender of everything in your life to God.

Copyright 2005 Edward G. Palmer, All Rights Reserved.

Book of Edward—Chapter 17

Myth—Giving 10% Is A Tithe

Let's see if I can draw another picture for you of some signs of being lawless or in faith. There are thirty signs in each list below. As for the tithe and Sabbath laws, you can include them in the lawlessness column, because people who practice them are cursed according to the Word!

Signs of Lawlessness and Faith

Lawlessness
- Ungodliness
- Faithless
- Unbelieving
- Unrighteousness
- Wickedness
- Truth Repressors
- Truth Hinderers
- Liars
- Wrongdoers
- Impure
- Immoral
- Idolaters
- Adulterers
- Fornicators
- Homosexuality
- Lesbianism
- Cheats
- Swindlers
- Thieves
- Robbers
- Greedy graspers
- Extortioners
- Slanderers
- Drunkards
- Foulmouthed
- Revilers
- Depraved
- Murderers
- Sorcerers
- Lewd

Faith
- Indwelling Spirit of God
- Indwelling Spirit of Christ
- Indwelling Spirit of Truth
- Other Spirits of God
- Obey Commandments
- Obey Commands
- Obey Sexual Laws
- Obey God
- Obey Jesus Christ
- Trust
- Obedience
- Faithfulness
- Believing
- Fidelity
- Justice
- Mercy
- Truth
- Honesty
- Right
- Righteousness
- Doing What is Right
- Truth Supporters
- Good Works
- Brave
- Noble
- Courage
- Moral
- New Covenant
- One God
- One Mediator-Christ

Copyright 2005 Edward G. Palmer, All Rights Reserved.

Myth—Giving 10% Is A Tithe

To eliminate any confusion about the sections of the Law that I have talked about in this chapter, I offer this final graphic on the issue. This is not some catchall list. The only way to fully please God is to operate in faith as discussed in Hebrews 11:6. Please note the following important issue. I did not show the Holy Spirit on the new communications model nor is the Spirit shown in the below graphic. What you need to understand is that the Holy Spirit is the Spirit of truth and it is one of *seven* Spirits that belong to God Almighty. When you obey the Holy Spirit, you obey God HIMSELF. This is not a "third" person as the trinity doctrine claims. Go back and study the *False Trinity Doctrine* if this is not clear in your mind.

The "Law" To Those "In Christ"

Lawlessness
- Ignores all of the "Law"
- Says no "Law" Applies
- Disobeys Commandments
- Disobeys Commands
- Disobeys Sexual Laws
- Distorts Word for Money
- Are Friends of the World

Cursed Observe
- Ritual Laws
- Ceremonial Laws
- Tithe Laws
- Law of Feasts
- Civil Laws
- Social Laws
- Sabbath Laws

Faith
- Obeys God
- Obeys Christ
- Obeys Commandments
- Obeys Commands
- Obeys Sexual Laws
- Does not observe Tithe Law
- Does not observe Ritual Law

Now make note of the matrix structure [dotted lines] of Christ's new communications model. While we go direct to God, we are still answerable to Christ. Therefore, those in faith obey God *and* Christ who is the head of the church. All true believers [the real church] answer to Christ as spiritual supervisor in [the boss] God's organization structure. Christ reports to God.

Myth—Giving 10% Is A Tithe

You can observe from this discussion that you cannot summarily dismiss the Law if you define it as the first five books of the Bible written by Moses. Likewise, you cannot simply say that all of the Law still needs to be obeyed. I know of many well-intentioned Christians who tithe and others who even observe the laws of the festivals, etc. They are seriously lacking in understanding and as a result they are living under a curse according to the Word. I have observed much destruction in families who have attempted to tithe for riches. It doesn't work. Only when you give from your heart, will God honor your gift. *Word of Faith* churches teach a "give to get" message and it is an outright abomination to God. HE will surely repay those who lie about HIS Word and use the Old Testament tithe law as a means of making themselves rich.

We are taught in the New Testament that much of the "Law" is still active from a behavioral standpoint. However, we are also taught that both tithing and Sabbath laws no longer apply, as do the other ceremonial or ritual laws. Only when you understand the Law and what is still active can you understand what an abomination the modern tithe teaching is to God.

A friend of mine asked me last week if it really mattered. "After all, aren't we all headed toward the same goal?" The question that all believers should really ask is this: "Does the truth really matter to God?" We are not called to go around the world and beat people into submitting to Christ or to teach them to tithe. God will make sure that all whom HE calls makes it to their heavenly home. Instead of multi-million dollar ministries proselytizing the world with apostate messages, a simple and humble missionary starting up a local Bible study group is the proper way to dispense the Word in areas of the world that do not know the gospel. This is especially true in the poor areas of the world where God's truth is really needed.

The "tithe" money in *Word of Faith* churches is used by Satan to spread a distorted and apostate message. The underlying message is to go out and get others to tithe so the minister can fly his plane, drive expensive cars and live in his palatial estate. Hello. Virtually none of this is biblical. Not the message or the use of the money. It is time for Christians who unwittingly support such apostasy to wake up to the truth of God's Word.

Copyright 2005 Edward G. Palmer, All Rights Reserved.

Book of Edward—Chapter 17

Myth—Giving 10% Is A Tithe

The tithe was a method in Old Testament Israel to fear God and take care of people. Nowhere in the Bible is it used to make ministers rich. If you tithe, you live under a curse.

You might not realize that fact [you live under a curse] until Jesus Christ tells you someday to be gone "you who practiced lawlessness." It is another way of telling you that you never did live in faith and therefore could not please God. No, you chose to live under an old covenant and not Christ's new covenant. Guess what? You failed to keep "all of the Law" as instructed for those who live under it.

Instead of making your pastor a multi-millionaire by giving 10% of your income, you would be better off giving directly to God and His Son as I discussed earlier. That would be at least get you close to what the tithe was intended to accomplish. It would show your fear of God, your obedience to Him and your willingness to care for others—even if it was no guarantee of personal health, wealth and success.

There is very good little booklet called "The Tithing Dilemma" [4] written by Ernest L. Martin, Ph D, a biblical scholar who is now passed away. You may want to get a copy for additional tithing study. Here are some notable excerpts worthy of being mentioned in this chapter.

Christ Was A Poor Man!

P33[5] — "Christ did not concentrate on getting money. While he was preaching he admitted he was so poor that 'the Son of man hath not where to lay his head' (Matt. 8:20). Throughout his ministry he was in poverty. 'Though he was rich, yet for your sakes he became poor, that ye through his poverty might be rich' (II Cor. 8:9). And poor he was! He did not have enough money to pay the half shekel for the upkeep of the temple (Matt. 17:24-27). The Bible shows he never had an over abundance of financial support ... P34— Both he and Peter were so 'broke' that a fish had to fetch a Shekel in order for them to meet their financial obligations to support the temple."

Myth—Giving 10% Is A Tithe

Jewish Rabbis Know Better!

P7[6]— "Jewish rabbis know better [than to say you should tithe]. They realize that it is biblically improper (actually, it is a blatant disobedience to the laws of the Bible) for anyone to pay or to receive the biblical tithe today. And any minister or ecclesiastical leader who uses the biblical tithe today is an outright *sinner* in the eyes of God." *Jews do not tithe today!*

Free Will Offerings Built The Temple!

P13[7]— "The old covenant society which Moses established at Mount Sinai, whether religious or secular, was supported (at first) simply by free will contributions. This is precisely the way the Christian Church was financed at first … there was no law of tithing that was being applied in the building of the holy sanctuary. Tithing was not seen as a necessary thing by Moses until almost a year later (Lev. 27:30-33)."

Only Two Types Of Income Tithed!

P14[8]— "There were only two types of income that were tithable: One was from agricultural production. 'All the tithe of the land, whether of the seed of the land, or of the fruit of the tree, is the LORD'S' (Lev. 27:30). This meant that a tenth of all agricultural produce of the land of Israel, whether fruits or vegetables, had to be tithed. The second type of tithable income was the increase of animals. 'All the tithe of the herd or flock, whatsoever passeth under the rod, the tenth shall be holy unto the LORD' (verse 32). Only these two specific income producers were subject to the tithe. … Only owners of farms and flocks were required to tithe." *Who did not tithe? All other occupations and sources of income such as fishermen, mining industries, weaving, handicraft sales, trades, any form of manufacturing and professional services were not tithable under the tithe law. No tithe was required of priests.*

Levites Provided Society's Services!

P25[9]— "Now look at what [the tithe] meant for the people of Israel. While the ordinary Israelite gave his tithe every third and sixth year to the Levites (and the destitute), notice the services he got besides the management of the temple. Israel got [Levite] teachers for their children, physicians for their ills, scribes, musicians, singers, judges and law enforcement officers. A part of the tithe paid by the Israelites even went to support a type of social security service every third and sixth year of a sabbatical period for taking care of the destitute. This shows that the **one tithe**, which was distributed evenly over a seven-year period, was not simply intended for religious purposes (as is the case with most Christian churches today). The tithe was something similar to our taxes that support our educational institutions, our government hospitals, our law enforcement agencies, our cultural societies, etc. When one sees the true picture of the tithing system, the early Israelites didn't get too bad of a deal in their giving of tithe."

Malachi 3:10 Applied To Palestine Jews!

P26[10]— [Who does Malachi refer to?] "The answer is plain. It was the ancient Jewish nation that existed in the time of Malachi. This is what the context shows. Verse 8: 'Will a man rob God? Yet ye have robbed me, but ye say, wherein have we robbed thee? In tithes and offerings.' And who were these 'robbers?' They were the people of Judah who lived in Palestine. They were not giving their tithe or proper animal sacrifices. For their lapse they were being 'cursed with a curse: for ye have robbed me, even this whole nation' (verse 9). Malachi was scolding the Jews who lived around Jerusalem in the early part of the fourth century before Christ. He was not talking about the modern United States. ... [Malachi's] was a message solely and exclusively to the nation of Judah in the fourth century B.C. That is what the Bible says."

Myth—Giving 10% Is A Tithe

Christ's Death Cancelled Tithe!

P32[11]— "The carnal regulations became redundant. They were simply 'meats and drinks, and divers washings, and carnal ordinances, imposed on them until the time of reformation' (Heb. 9:10). Since the time of Christ's death and resurrection, all the physical ordinances of the Old Covenant (including tithing) were done away (II Cor. 3:6-18)." *Note: All of Martin's references are from the King James Bible.*

Martin goes on to explain that Christ did not create money absorbing church structures. These would be huge ministry business operations that are virtually black holes for money. In other words, they are money pits and some cost $100,000 or more per week just to keep the doors open and pay for the operating costs of staff, including the pilots for the private planes, etc. When Christ sent out the seventy, he sent them without "purse, nor scrip, nor shoes" [Luke 10:3-16] and told them to eat and drink whatever they were given in the house in which they were received. Thus, Christ's ministry operated on freewill offerings and not tithes. Furthermore, the tithe could only be given to Levites. Christ was from the tribe of Judah and like his twelve disciples, was not entitled to receive tithes under the Law.

Paul financed his own ministry by working as a tent maker. He did this so as not to be a burden. The message from Christ and Paul were the same: "Freely you have received, freely you should give."

There are many ways to finance ministries. However, the tithe is not one of them. You could, if you wanted to make a donation, give 10% of your income to the ministry. Likewise, you can give 90% of your income. That they would love. But to think for a moment you are tithing like the Law in the Old Testament required is to embrace a boldface lie. What was the second prophesy I opened this book with? It was the Word indicating that those who did not love the truth would perish. Therefore, if you love God and His Holy Word, you will no longer accept apostate teachings like the modern day tithe doctrine of men. To do so, places you under the curse of the Law and threatens your own eternal salvation as someone lawless.

Copyright 2005 Edward G. Palmer, All Rights Reserved.

Book of Edward—Chapter 17

Myth—Giving 10% Is A Tithe

Malachi Is Basis Of The Apostate Tithe Doctrine!

For four years I sat patiently in the congregation at Solid Rock Church listening to various tithe messages from William Neal Matthews, which could run 30-60 minutes and were centered on Malachi 3:8-10. You know, "Will a man rob God?" Here is the entire section in the Amplified Bible.

> "Will a man rob or defraud God? Yet you rob and defraud ME. But you say, in what way do we rob or defraud YOU? [You have withheld your] tithes and offerings. You are cursed with the curse, for you are robbing ME, even this whole nation. Bring all the tithes (the whole tenth of your income) into the storehouse, that there may be food in MY house, and prove ME now by it, says the LORD of hosts, if I will not open the windows of Heaven for you and pour you out a blessing, that there shall not be room enough to receive it. And I will rebuke the devourer [insects and plagues] for your sakes and he shall not destroy the fruits of your ground, neither shall your vine drop its fruit before the time in the field, says the LORD of hosts. And all nations shall call you blessed, for you shall be a land of delight, says the LORD of hosts." Malachi 3:8-12 AMP

Before I continue, check out Malachi 3:16. Has your preacher ever taken you this far in his or her tithe teaching? It is only four verses farther. God makes it clear that those who actually fear HIM and talk to one another are written in HIS book of remembrance. Pretty cool, huh?

> "Then those who feared the LORD talked often one to another; and the LORD listened and heard it, and a book of remembrance was written before HIM of those who reverenced and worshipfully feared the LORD and who thought on HIS name. And they shall be MINE."
>   Malachi 3:16-17

Myth—Giving 10% Is A Tithe

I already told you that there were some odd teachings from Matthews albeit not obviously apostate. For four years I listened to his message of "testing or proving" God. In other words, Matthews taught that when you give God your tithe, God would open the windows of Heaven and pour out such a blessing that you would not be able to contain it. However, on one fateful day in November 1996, he changed the message. I now know that he had successfully completed his church theft and was very confident that he could say whatever he wanted to about God and money, which is hindsight. As Matthews taught the tithe that day, these were the some of his words.

> *"I taught you tithing, tithing, tithing, tithing, tithing, tithing. Now, if you tithe and that's all you do is tithe—you will never have the abundant lifestyle that God wants you to have in being in the land of more than enough. Because the tithe is not yours. It's not yours! It's God's already. It's already HIS! So you're not giving HIM anything except you're being a good steward of what HE'S given you. So you can't give the tithe and say now: 'God bless me.' " Pastor William Neal Matthews (11/20/96)*

He repeated himself at least three times and every time he talked I stared at God's Word. For four years he gave the message that God would bless tithers with overflowing blessings, but now the tithe blessing no longer existed. Furthermore, the tithe wasn't good enough. I still remember sitting in the pew and having God ask me to confront Matthews about his apostasy. I did and the details are in the last chapter.

No More Compromise On God's Word!

I realize now that God was almost done training me inside the church and was giving me one final lesson about HIS Word. The message to me was clear, "Edward, never under any circumstance accept another message that does not fully line up with MY Holy Word." It was also a message that it was time to leave. My assignment to worship and witness at Solid Rock Church was coming to an end. It was over four weeks later. I've already taught you how I got here. Now think carefully about what Malachi says.

Myth—Giving 10% Is A Tithe

Malachi Only Teaches Tithing Food!

What is wrong with the apostles of tithing is their misrepresentation of Malachi 3. It is rather obvious that God's Word concerning the tithe in Malachi only revolves around the issue of food. Where is the slightest hint about giving money to the minister in these tithe instructions? The only place money is talked about is where Moses teaches you to temporarily convert the tithe into money when you have a long journey. Then you are to immediately convert it back into [your heart's desire of] food and drink and to consume it. Just an amusing aside note: Do you think the old adage that "Charity begins at home" might have something to do with consuming the tithe with family, friends and ministers for two of three years? Interesting.

These five aspects of food only are present in Malachi 3:8-12.

1. Food to feed people out of the temple food shelf (storehouse).
2. A full tithe of the yield produced from the land, herds & flocks.
3. A full tithe of the yield produced from the trees of the land.
4. Rebuking the devouring meant keeping insects from eating crops.
5. A land of delight meant a land that produced abundant crops.

The curse that God talked about was the curse of "crop failure." Is the United States, which now feeds most of the world under a crop failure curse by not tithing? No, it's because the tithe does not apply today and this place is not the land of Israel. The tithe only pertained to the land within Israel. Without question all of Malachi's teachings were about obtaining the tithe food to continue to feed God's people. More specifically, the temple food shelf was seriously depleted and the Levites and those in need were not being properly taken care of [fed]. Therefore, the tithe storehouse was only about storing "food" for the people. It was never about fulfilling the worldly desires of the minister and his family nor was it about any "world outreach."

> "And all the tithe of the land, whether of the seed of the land or of the fruit of the tree, is the LORD'S. It is holy to the LORD." Leviticus 27:30 NKJV

Myth—Giving 10% Is A Tithe

Who Robbed God Of Offerings?

You already learned from Martin that it was the nation of Judah living around Jerusalem that was not bringing in the tithes of "the seed of the land" and "the fruit of the tree" to the temple. But who is it that was robbing God of offerings? If you only listen to apostate tithe preachers and teachers like William Neal Matthews, they will tell you that it is you who are not only robbing God of the tithes, but *also* robbing God by not giving offerings in addition to the tithe. Yet this is also a lie and not biblical. We learn in Numbers 18:21-32 further instructions from God and find the basic elements of the tithe and offerings that Malachi speaks about.

> **God says: "Behold, I have given the children of Levi all the tithes in Israel as an inheritance in return for the work which they perform ... For the tithes of the children of Israel, which they offer up as a heave offering to the LORD, I have given to the Levites as an inheritance ... When you take from the children of Israel the tithes which I have given you from them as your inheritance, then you shall offer up a heave offering of it to the LORD, a tenth of the tithe." Numbers 18:21-26 NKJV**

Therefore, the following simple facts exist about who made the tithes and who made the offerings and why both are cited as missing by Malachi.

Fact: The tithe was 10% of the produce of the land, herds & flocks.
Fact: The people gave the tithe to the Levites as an inheritance.
Fact: The Levites were required to give 10% of the tithe to God.
Fact: The Levites tithe was called a "heave offering" to distinguish it.
Fact: The priests ate the heave offering in the temple.

When Malachi says God is robbed of tithes and offerings, he is saying that the people are not tithing to the Levites and because of that, the Levites do not give their heave offerings. Verily I say unto to, it was not the people who *"also"* robbed God of offerings like some tithe teachers claim.

Copyright 2005 Edward G. Palmer, All Rights Reserved.

Book of Edward—Chapter 17

Myth—Giving 10% Is A Tithe

The reason the Levites tithe was called a heave offering is because it was aimed at God above in Heaven. It was "a lifting up" offering to God. The same could be said about the tithe, but God makes a Temple distinction between the "tithe" of the Israelites and the "offering" of the Levites.

A Gross Blessing Or A Gross Lie?

At the top of the tithe apostasy is the assertion that you owe the tithe on your gross income. After all, the tithe preacher will rant, "Do you want a gross blessing or a net blessing?" This is yet another example of someone who truly delights in lies and the misrepresenting of God's truth. Listen up. God made it clear that only the YIELD of the land should be tithed. The simple formula to find the yield of the land is as follows:

Yield Equals Output <u>Minus</u> Input!

Suppose a farmer started his crop year by planting 10 bushels of corn seed and after looking at the harvest, the farmer thinks he will wind up with 20 bushes of corn seed. How much should he tithe? Two bushels would scream Matthews. And it must be the first two bushels picked! Well if that was so, how would the farmer know his true bushel yield? Suppose he is under pressure from Matthews the tithe apostle and decides to just do what he says. The farmer picks one bushel at a time and tithes 10% of that bushel and every bushel picked thereafter. That is tithe formula Matthews insisted that he follow. The farmer continues to do the same, pick and tithe, but after the tenth bushel there was no more corn in the field to pick. At the end of the harvest, the farmer only gets back 9/10th of the seed that he started with. Now what? The apostate tithe preacher got want he wanted, didn't he?

The farmer tithed one bushel and wound up with less than he started with [nine]. He never obtained a yield and disobeyed God's command to only tithe of the yield. Ten bushels *out* minus ten *in* equals a *zero yield*. Guess what? No tithe was due from the farmer. Who robbed God? Yes, it was the apostate tithe teacher who *extorted* a bushel of seed from the farmer when God had said under such conditions he was not supposed to tithe.

Copyright 2005 Edward G. Palmer, All Rights Reserved.

Book of Edward—Chapter 17

Myth—Giving 10% Is A Tithe

If It Can't Meet Your Need, Give It As Seed?

How was the farmer supposed to feed his family if he only wound up with nine bushels of planting seed back? If his family ate the planting seed, there would be no seed to plant for the next crop. Not to worry, under such terrible no-yield conditions, the Temple food shelf could be used to help carry the farmer and his family over to the next planting season. Still, there *is* a robber within this scenario, isn't there? Yes, it's the tithe preacher.

The preacher's next audacious statement is, "If you don't have enough to meet your need; you should give it to my ministry as seed!" Think about that apostate teaching for a moment. You don't have enough money to buy food or pay bills, yet the preacher tells you to give him whatever you have as seed for his ministry? In other words you should give out of your necessity, which the Bible teaches against. Here again is just another example of the extortion techniques of modern day tithe preachers. Listen to the Word.

"So let each one give as he purposes in his heart, *not* **grudgingly or** *of necessity***; for God loves a cheerful giver."**
2 Cor. 9:7 NKJV

The Business Gross Lie!

You could apply the same yield analysis to a small business. Say a small manufacturer makes a $100 sale. In Matthews' tithe mentality, the business owner needs to give him $10 because he is a modern day Levite [which is another Bible lie]. But this is the businessman's gross sale, not his gross or even his net profit. Say the businessman has $70 in cost of goods against that $100 *gross* sale. That means his actual gross profit is only $30. The businessman could easily have operating and overhead expenses of $20 against that $30 of gross profit. Therefore, his actual net profit or yield is only $10. How much would be tithable? It is $10 in Matthews' mind, but $0 [zero] in God's mind. *Remember, there were only two types of income tithable under the tithe law; both were food from the yield of Israel's land.*

Copyright 2005 Edward G. Palmer, All Rights Reserved.

Book of Edward—Chapter 17

Myth—Giving 10% Is A Tithe

Still, and for discussion sake, suppose the businessman listened to Matthews since he did not have time to study God's Word. Eventually he went broke and never understood why. Well for starters, he gave the tithe preacher $10 and his net profit was only $10. Therefore, he never made any profit to sustain his business operations. Who then robbed God? It wasn't the businessman. It was the tithe preacher. Such is the nature of the tithe today. Instead of people robbing God, it is the tithe preacher who robs God and has taught people to disobey what HIS Word teaches.

The Salaried Gross Lie!

Maybe you are a salaried person. Say your gross income is $3,000 per month. However, after taxes, social security, medical insurance and the cost of getting back and forth to work are factored in, you wind up with about $1200 per month for your family to live on. Subtract your $800 house payment and you now have only $400 to work with. How much does the tithe preacher want from you? Of course, he wants $300 or literally 75% of what you actually wind up with in your hands. Does this sound familiar to you? Who is robbing God? It is the tithe preacher. He is an extortioner and his extortion causes great pain in many families who sincerely do want to give to God and to do what is right in HIS eyes.

No One Can Out Give God?

There is this *true* statement: "I've never seen anyone out give God." However, if you tithe, you are not giving to God. HE has told you not to tithe. Therefore, the use of that statement with tithing is flawed. I have seen families live on the local food shelves because they tithed to the church. I have seen families lose their homes. I have even seen businessmen go bankrupt tithing to the church. What makes the difference between a gift of faith to God and the tithe? The tithe is based on lies and the misrepresenting of the word of God. Many who tithe do so because they are fearful of being cursed. What an irony. They are fearful of being cursed by not tithing and yet that is exactly what happens when they do tithe. What a satanic twist!

Copyright 2005 Edward G. Palmer, All Rights Reserved.

Book of Edward—Chapter 17

Myth—Giving 10% Is A Tithe

Do you suppose all such people who have suffered under the misery of the tithe preacher are unhappy? Not really. The tithe preacher just tells them about the area in the Word concerning suffering. You see there is no end to the twisting of scripture to make their corrupt arguments. The only clue you have is from your first hand knowledge of the Word. It helps if you can read. Look into Malachi scriptures and all you see is food. Look into the tithe laws and all you see is food. But if you never look, you just get led around like a ringed-nosed cow.

The tithe preacher isn't afraid of your intellect as he or she can feed you reasonably sounding answers. It is only your knowledge of the Bible that the tithe preacher fears. When Satan tried to persuade Jesus during his temptations, he quoted from the Bible. I should say he twisted the Word. In response, Jesus corrected him by saying "it is written."

I suppose you are now wondering about what you should do to give to God? You shouldn't. I have already itemized direct ways of giving to God and His Son. What about a general giving principle, is there one? You should give from a willing heart as God gives you peace over the matter. You can give anything. Jesus told the rich young ruler to give all that he had to the poor and follow him [go penniless]. Armand Hammer the great oil magnate was said to give 90% of his income away. You decide what it is from within your heart and through a prayerful talk with God. It is biblical to support any church you attend by giving gifts or making a pledge. However, you should not give out of any need, because we are told not to. Then there is the lesson of the widow who gave two mites in the offering. It was all she had. She gave out of her poverty. Meditate on this teaching of Jesus. If you put your trust in God, you will not be concerned about money.

> **"Then one poor widow came and threw in two mites, which make a quadrans. So he called his disciples [to him] and said to them, 'Assuredly, I say to you that this poor widow has put in more than all those who have given to the treasury; for they all put in out of their abundance, but she out of her poverty put in all that she had, her whole livelihood.'"**
> **Mark 12:42-44 NKJV**

Copyright 2005 Edward G. Palmer, All Rights Reserved.

Book of Edward—Chapter 17

Myth—Giving 10% Is A Tithe

If you are wondering what a mite was worth, it comes from the Greek word *lepta* and was a small copper coin worth a fraction of a penny. The widow in the New Testament gave everything she had. It is an interesting perspective for those who do it. When you give everything, God knows that your heart is where it belongs. Indeed, HE will take care of you. So another lesson of the widow is that of a sacrifice. In a way it is similar to the thought of blessing those who curse you; turning the other cheek; loving those who hate you; etc. How can the world see Christ in you if you are not different from other people? They simply can't. This then is what it means to not be friends with the world. Do not be concerned about money like the tithe preacher is whose path leads to eternal damnation and for all who follow.

Extortioners & Practitioners of Lies!

Woe to you preachers and teachers of the tithe. For you extort money from God's people by distorting HIS Word for your personal gain. You are a lover and practitioner of lies and you lead people astray from God. You also place people under the curse of the Law in the guise of being cursed if they do not obey what you tell them. You lie about the truth of God's tithe law and all of its instructions. In so doing, you condemn your own self to a fiery death. Repent and get right with God. Get out of the ministry if you cannot teach the word of God in a straight and honest way.

> **"And if you have not been faithful in what is another man's, who will give you what is your own?" Luke 16:12 NKJV**
>
> **Jesus said: "For what is a man profited if he gains the whole world, and loses his own soul? Or what will a man give in exchange for his soul?" Matthew 16:26 NKJV**
>
> **"And there is no creature hidden from HIS sight, but all things are naked and open to the eyes of HIM to whom we must give account." Hebrews 4:13 NKJV**

Myth—Giving 10% Is A Tithe

MEMO: If you do join a church, make sure you read its constitution and by-laws along with its statement of faith. This should include their Articles of Incorporation and whether or not they submit to government censorship as an IRS 501(c) (3) tax-deductible corp.[12] Such entities are restricted from telling you the truth about political candidates and parties. In exchange for tax-deductible gifts, they have agreed to keep silent on issues important to believers. If you are going to accept their membership criteria, you should know what the church stands for. I know of one very large ministry that has no membership criteria according to their website. Just show up with your tithe money. Yet verily I say unto you, if you only show up with your money and don't ask questions, you might find yourself in a satanic church. If you don't think they have some criteria, you will find out differently when you ask to see their Articles and By-Laws. You may even find out that you do not have true voting rights. You might also be shown the door because you ask too many questions. What would that tell you?

True believers really want to do what is right in God's eyes. The illustration earlier about the angst some Christians feel over whether we should be worshipping God on a Saturday vs. Sunday is a good example. We can get close enough to God to really desire to do what is right in HIS eyes even if we don't fully understand what is needed. That is why we will rely upon the shepherd of the church we are in. It is also the reason why God makes it clear that many of these shepherds are devils in disguise. HE will deal with them in HIS time. Verily I say to you that payback is coming.

The issue of tithing is no different. I remember vividly a distressed young wife who raced into the office where I and other ushers were counting the money given in the offering that morning. She was in tears and stated that she had the check for the tithe in her hand, but if she gave the money to us the family would not be able to pay their bills. Her husband might even leave her if she "gave away their bill payment money." Here was a believer who just wanted to do what was right. I remember praying with her that God would lead her to the right decision. Yet the anxiety she felt over the tithe and the family's inability to pay bills is felt in many homes across the country. For every one of these extortions, God will repay the teacher.

Copyright 2005 Edward G. Palmer, All Rights Reserved.

Book of Edward—Chapter 17

Myth—Giving 10% Is A Tithe

God Doesn't Need Your Money!

God doesn't need your money to accomplish His goals and that is why Christ taught us to travel light and to accept free will offerings. The modern day church has forgotten that Christ made it clear that no one comes to him unless the FATHER calls. It is God's responsibility to get the Word out into the hearts of His people. He can do that with true believers who will travel light according to His Word.

When my family got back from California in late 1985 and returned to Nowthen Alliance Church, we experience hard times. I remember groceries turning up at our doorstep at one point. I also remember how humbling that experience was because I knew that God was making a way where there was no way. He was teaching us to just trust in Him. Then another Sunday soon came along in which I only had twenty dollars to my name. At the time, we were still a family of five. After some serious prayer, I decided to give the twenty dollars in the offering that morning. It emptied my pocket and I told God specifically that it could do more for Him than it could for my family.

When we got ready to leave the church and shook hands with Pastor Paul Frederick and his wife Lois, Paul handed me an unmarked envelope. He said that someone in the church had given him the envelope and told him to pass it along as God directed. I still remember Paul telling me, "I believe God is telling me that I am suppose to give you this envelope." Paul did not know what was in that envelope that day nor did he know what I had done in prayer during offering time. To this day, I have never told him the rest of the story, which now brings tears to my eyes once again over its memory.

After Jackie and I left the church, I opened the envelope and found another twenty-dollar bill. I will never forget the message that God gave me that day. "Edward, I do not need your money to accomplish My will, I need your faith. I need you to do what I ask of you. I will care for your family." God has never failed to care for my family through our hard times. I tell you this because the tithe was a way to provide food for the needy and those who were destitute in Old Testament times. *The tithe was always about food!*

Copyright 2005 Edward G. Palmer, All Rights Reserved.

Myth—Giving 10% Is A Tithe

Listen to what Timothy taught us about the Word. Then, ask yourself which parts of God's Word (Scripture) you do not want to hear about. If you don't like all of God's Word, you should find a church of Satan to feed your itching ears. Otherwise, you should take heed to the prophecy of God and learn to love the truth of [all] His Holy Word. You simply cannot have it both ways. No amount of mouthing Jesus as your Lord will offset your failure to love the truth. A minister that teaches giving a tithe is required of you is an outright liar and in the end, he or she will get exactly what they deserve. According to Revelation, liars will not enter the kingdom of God. Ask your minister to repent and get straight with God or leave the ministry.

> **"Every Scripture is God breathed (given by His inspiration) and profitable for instruction, for reproof and conviction of sin, for correction of error and discipline in obedience, [and] for training in righteousness (in holy living, in conformity to God's will in thought, purpose, and action). So that the man of God may be complete and proficient, well fitted and thoroughly equipped for every good work."**
> **2 Timothy 3:16-17 AMP**

> **"Blessed (happy and to be envied) are those who cleanse their garments, that they may have the authority and right to [approach] the tree of life and to enter through the gates into the city. [But] without are the dogs and those who practice sorceries (magic arts) and impurity [the lewd, adulterers] and the murderers and idolaters and everyone who loves and deals in falsehood (untruth, error, deception, cheating)." Rev. 22:14-15 AMP**

Clearly the teaching in Revelation 22 pertains directly to the false tithe teaching of the church. Ministers do actually "love and deal" in the "falsehood of the tithe." Listen, just because your minister or prophet of God may have a multi-million dollar ministry, do you honesty think that it matters to God? What matters is the truth and who will obey it. If you think that the multi-million dollar ministry pulpit should take priority over God's Word, you are one of those whom Jesus will say: "I never knew you." Trust me, he will also tell the same thing to the false teacher that you serve.

WARNING. If you are a minister that teaches the modern day tithe apostasy, set your house in order with God. If you are a believer in the modern day tithe apostasy, set your house in order with God. Both of you should cease to spread these lies about God's Holy Word. Verily I say unto you, it is believers in the truth that shall see God's salvation for it is written, "They did not welcome the truth but refused to love it that they might be saved." [2 Thess. 2:10 AMP]

"Therefore God sends upon them a misleading influence, a working of error and a strong delusion to make them believe what is false. In order that all may be judged and condemned who did not believe in [who refused to adhere to, trust in, and rely on] the truth, but [instead] took pleasure in unrighteousness." 2 Thess. 2: 11-12 AMP

PRAYER. O LORD GOD, free YOUR people from the apostasy that is rampant in the Christian Church today. Surely, if a minister cannot teach the truth about money, they cannot be trusted to teach anything from YOUR Word. They are indeed unfit for anything good and should cease their ministry activities. What should stand true for all concerned is that these false teachers "will perish because they were not lovers of the truth!" Lovers of the truth do not pervert YOUR Word for anything. Amen.

"The tithe message in *Word of Faith* and other churches is an apostate teaching of Satan. Indeed, it is an abomination unto God. What was a form of worship, an acknowledgement of our fear of God, and food for people has been turned into a money-grabbing doctrine of men." The Apostle Edward

If God's Spirit Dwells In Your Heart, Your Spirit-Soul Knows That It's A ...

Myth—Giving 10% Is A Tithe

Book of Edward

Chapter Eighteen
Myth—Abortion Doesn't Matter

"When people who are fighting injure a pregnant woman *so that there is a miscarriage*, and *yet no further harm follows*, the one responsible shall be fined what the woman's husband demands, paying as much as the judges determine. If any harm follows, then you shall give life for life, eye for eye, tooth for tooth, hand for hand, foot for foot, burn for burn, wound for wound, stripe for stripe." Exodus 21:22-25 NRSV

"An hour is coming when those who kill you will think that by doing so they are offering worship to God." John 16:2 NRSV

"Love is patient; love is kind; love is not envious or boastful or arrogant or rude. It does not insist on its own way; it is not irritable or resentful; it does not rejoice in wrongdoing, but rejoices in the truth. It bears all things, believes all things, hopes all things, endures all things. Love never ends. But as for prophecies, they will come to an end; as for tongues, they will cease; as for knowledge, it will come to an end. For we know only in part, and we prophesy only in part; but when the complete comes, the partial will come to an end. When I was a child, I spoke like a child, I thought like a child, I reasoned like a child; when I became an adult, I put an end to childish ways. … And now faith, hope, and love abide, these three; and the greatest of these is love." 1 Cor. 13:4-13 NRSV

Apostle Paul taught: "Love does no wrong to anyone. That's why it fully satisfies all of God's requirements. It is the only law you need." Romans 13:10 LIV

Myth—Abortion Doesn't Matter

It is almost February and as I have reflected upon the last chapter, two spiritual thoughts remain stuck in my mind. The first is the issue of all the ceremonies. If you compare Christianity, Judaism and Islam, you will find a variety of ceremonies used in these religions to allow an expression of faith. However, God's Word makes it abundantly clear that we are no longer under any requirement to observe further rituals, the religious rules and mandates. Jesus said: "Go directly to the FATHER with your [sincere heart and righteous] petitions." Therefore, what really matters to God is the spiritual intent inside of your heart. If your heart is truly with God, you won't have any difficultly understanding why abortion is such an abomination to HIM.

The second issue that stuck in my mind is that of the rationalization of mankind, which now comes to bear on the issue of abortion. I felt like I was choking [spiritually] as I read the many rationalizations of Christian pastors, ministers and others who assert that the Bible actually supports abortion.

I was not prepared for the sorrow and pain I felt over this last week just reading and studying those rationalizations. Verses in the Bible are contorted to rationalize abortion. Some claim abortion is of service to God.

> **Jesus said: "What do you think? A man had two sons; he went to the first and said, 'Son, go and work in the vineyard today.' He answered, 'I will not'; but later he changed his mind and went. The father [then] went to the second and said the same; and he answered, 'I go, sir'; but he did not go. Which of the two did the will of his father?" They said, "The first."**
>
> **Jesus said to them, "Truly I tell you, the tax collectors and the prostitutes are going into the kingdom of God ahead of you. For John came to you in the way of righteousness and you did not believe him, but the tax collectors and the prostitutes believed him [and turned to righteousness]; and even after you saw it, you [still] did not change your minds and believe him [by turning yourselves to righteousness]."**
> **Matthew 21:28-32 NRSV**

Myth—Abortion Doesn't Matter

The Heart vs. The Intellect!

This chapter might be an emotional one for many people. I am not an exception. Therefore, forgive me in advance if I present you with something that gets you emotionally upset. Above all, I want you to hang in there with me so you can truly understand God's view of the abortion issue. Before I get too far, we need to revisit the heart and the intellect. You know, the mind vs. what is in the bowels of your spirit-soul, which I talked of earlier?

If you are just tuning into the book by reading this chapter, you will miss important material that is relevant to your full understanding of the abortion issue. The first nine chapters are especially critical to a reasonable and full understanding of this chapter. God has given this material to me in a specific sequence. Much of the material preceding each chapter is actually precedential in nature. Therefore, go back and at least read the first nine chapters [if not all chapters] before going on if you have not already done so. It would be best if you do read this book sequentially from front to back. Only then will you get all of what God wants you to experience.

I don't think there is a better illustration of the difference between the heart and the intellect than the subject of abortion. As I have read many writings on the subject, they all either fall within the side of the heart or the side of the intellect. The heart sees the true meanings of the word of God. On the other hand, the intellect analyzes and parses sentences and even seeks to read into different Bible verses spiritual facts that are non-existent.

Remember back in chapter 2 on page 24 when I asked the important question of you: "Are they [the apostles] writing mail to you?" The Bible is written directly to those with a heart for God and you will not understand Scripture if your heart is not fully with God. HE gives understanding to the heart so that you can properly understand the nuances of Scripture. Don't tell me that the Bible can be properly interpreted with just your intellect. It can't and I won't buy such an assertion. I have been talking with God for almost three decades on the issue and I know better. The big question now is whether or not you are reading someone else's mail? Are you?

Myth—Abortion Doesn't Matter

Let me remind you that this book is written for those who claim to be Christians. It is not written for the general population. At one abortion web site, they claim that there are only "two types of abortion supporters." One group is those people who are ignorant of abortion facts and the reality of abortion. The second group is those who profit from the abortion industry. It is indeed a huge industry.

I estimate the abortion industry at $1 billion dollars or more annually. Assume there is 1,500,000 annual abortions in the United States and each one cost an average of $700. Its simple math —1,500,000 times $700 each equals $1.050 Billion. I just recently paid about $350 to have a single tooth extracted. Surely killing a baby by abortion methods is a little more costly than a single tooth extraction. But the industry doesn't stop there. Another aspect of the abortion mill is the market for baby parts. That's right, there is a market for eyes, livers, spleens, brains, etc. That market can range anywhere from $700-$2000 for the separated body parts of each baby [1].

Therefore, Christian mothers, if you kill your baby by abortion, it doesn't stop there. The parts from the baby may find a final home in a trash dumpster, an incinerator or even for use in other bodies or medical research. Collectively speaking, the abortion industry in the United States can be easily estimated in the $1-2 billion dollar range given the above assumptions. This is just my own humble marketing analysis. Go ask your local abortion doctor what he charges and run your own numbers on market size. Looking at market size and what is going on, it is easy enough to understand why two groups of people are said to exist. So-called Christians would be found in both of the above groups. Even in the industry itself.

Yet there is the matter of the heart and its dedication to God Almighty. Verily I say unto you that if you have not fully given God your heart and all that you are in this life to God, you will not be able to fully understand HIS view on abortion. You will, like many people who read the Bible, simply be reading someone else's mail. Consider for the moment the issue of communications between two people deeply in love with each other. This could be you and God. Or, it could be you and your spouse. Hey, what about your grandma and grandpa?

Copyright 2005 Edward G. Palmer, All Rights Reserved.

Myth—Abortion Doesn't Matter

Go up into the attic of your grandma and grandpa who have passed away and you might find some love letters that were written between the two of them during a time of war. That is what is hidden inside my attic, love letters between Jackie and I during the Vietnam War in the 1960's. Some statements in those letters are perfectly clear. You know. Statements like — "I love you" — do not need any interpretation. Yet some other statements will leave you with question marks about what the lovers are talking about.

Perhaps some important context is missing? The things that are equally understood by both lovers do not need to be fully explained in the letters, do they? They are taken for granted, aren't they? Now, years later, you want to understand the full story. How do you go about that? The easiest way is to get to know all you can about the life of your grandparents, the values they held, the events that drove their lives, etc. In other words, the more you learn about them, the easier it is to understand what they have written to one another in their love letters.

I just watched an interesting movie called Possession (2002) [2] that took this concept to the theater. Some interesting things written between two lovers drove another couple on a path of discovery to find out what they were really talking about. It was a very interesting movie, which is relevant. Understanding emerges in the story, as the true content of each lover's heart becomes revealed in the full context and synergy of both individual lives.

That is the way it is with understanding God. When you discover HIS heart's contents, you discover the meaning of what HE is telling us in the love letters HE has sent us. You will understand what is written in the Bible, when you realize the Holy Bible is a collection of love letters from God to each of us. Yet, if you only approach those love letters with your intellect, you are left with many gaps in understanding. When you seek the heart of the writer and HIS perspective, you gain true understanding of HIS meaning.

Is there really a difference in behavior when a person uses his or her mind versa his or her heart? Yes, there is. All you have to do is to meditate on the words of Jesus in Matthew 21:28-32 as shown above. Note: I will use the NRSV for the most part in this chapter, because that is what God told me to use. The reason will become apparent shortly.

Copyright 2005 Edward G. Palmer, All Rights Reserved.

Myth—Abortion Doesn't Matter

Two sons are given the instruction from their father to go and work in his vineyard. One rebels with his mouth and says "No!" But after a little thought, he gives in to his heart and obeys his father. The other uses his mind and intellect to deceive his father. He knows that the father probably won't go out and check up on him in the vineyard. So, he says: "Yes!" But, he does not go. Here is a clear example of how the intellect and heart work. Verily I say unto you, it is those whose heart is with God that will obey HIM. Those who operate solely off of their intellect will deceive themselves even as they think they are deceiving God. Only ignorant people think they can deceive God with such pretenses. God HIMSELF knows our heart's intent.

Now go back to the opening verse in this chapter. Exodus 21:22-25 is cited from the New Revised Standard Version. Meditate on this verse and translation for a moment. Does the Bible state that the fetus' life is worth less than the mother's life? Certainly seems that way, doesn't it? In fact, that is exactly what many would argue using the NRSV Bible translation. However, if your heart is with God, something doesn't add up with the translation. Why? All you have to do is to consider love. The Living Bible says "love does no wrong to anyone." Look at and carefully consider the "love" chapter in 1 Corinthians 13 for a moment. What exactly are the characteristics of love as defined in the Bible?

LOVE IS
1. Patient
2. Kind
3. Not envious, boastful, arrogant or rude
4. Does not insist on its own way
5. Is not irritable or resentful
6. Does not rejoice in wrongdoing
7. Rejoices in truth
8. Bears all things, believes all things
9. Hopes all things, endures all things

I submit to you a simple fact. If you take the position that the NRSV translation of Exodus 21:22-25 is true and that there is a different value placed on the life of the fetus and the mother—you do not know God! Just look at the love instructions and ask yourself this question. "Isn't there a

Myth—Abortion Doesn't Matter

conflict between what God has taught us on love and such an interpretation of Exodus 21?" Yes, there is a conflict. How do we resolve it? We go get some other translations. Let go directly to the Hebrew Bible. After all, it is their language, isn't it? Wouldn't they have the most accurate translation?

> **"And if men strive together, and hurt a woman with child, so that her fruit depart, and yet no harm follow, he shall be surely fined, according as the woman's husband shall lay upon him; and he shall pay as the judges determine. But if any harm follow, then thou shalt give life for life, eye for eye, tooth for tooth, hand for hand, foot for foot, burning for burning, wound for wound, stripe for stripe."**
> **Exodus 21:22-25 HEB**

Memo — I've been away from the book for over 5 Months.

It seems like I just wrote the above material, but that was all done at the end of January. It is now July 18, 2004 and I am just coming back to the book with the intent to finish it. I'll come back to a further discussion of Exodus 21 shortly. For now, you should reflect on the differences between the NRSV translation and the Hebrew Bible shown above.

So, what has happened in the last five months? I have had several issues to deal with. Remember that one room I promised Jackie I would paint? Well, I kept my promise to her. It took me an entire week of labor and I certainly have a higher appreciation for her wallpaper removal skills now that I've had to accomplish the task myself. I also took time to write her a final 20-page goodbye letter. Sorry, I can't share that one with you.

I also met and spent a few hours with an interesting woman that God told me to talk to. I'll share some of what God told me to say in the next chapter. You'll find it very interesting as I discuss sexuality in the context of a God ordained love between a man and a woman. Of course, I'll also discuss all the sexual perversions that mankind has dreamt up. Stay tuned, as you won't want to miss God's view of our human sexuality.

Copyright 2005 Edward G. Palmer, All Rights Reserved.

Book of Edward—Chapter 18

Myth—Abortion Doesn't Matter

However, perhaps the biggest diversion over the last five months has been a second attempt at seeking justice in the theft and fraud of Solid Rock Church. I did what God asked me to do. That was to file a second civil complaint and get it in front of a second judge for consideration. That goal was accomplished last Thursday morning.

However, I suffered a rather rapid and stunning legal defeat as the second judge opted for a procedurally based summary judgment choosing to ignore the fraud that was fully documented before her. Simply put, the fraud documentation now available in public records was ignored for a second time by the Minnesota Tenth District Court. Why? I do not know except that it appears that court "rules" trumps "justice."

There used to be a time in the United States when the courts dispensed justice and made every attempt to secure it. This should not be assumed in our country's courts anymore. Justice is now bought and sold in the court by who has the most expensive and experienced lawyers. It is a game of big guns. That is what the law has been reduced to. And, those big guns do not argue truth; they argue rules of court procedure. Advocate the right court procedural rules and guess what? Yes, the truth will be ignored and can even get buried in piles of legal documents and case law arguments. Ultimately, those who ignore the truth do so at their own eternal risk with God who warns us —

"They did not *welcome* the truth but refused to love it that they might be saved." [2 Thess. 2:10 AMP]

I will talk more about this case, the process and its outcome, along with my spiritual observations and U.S. justice in the upcoming chapter on politics. God has some things to say about justice. Stay tuned.

Right now, it also appears that I am going to receive a stiff civil fine [court sanction] of some dollar amount to be determined by the judge. This could be thousands of dollars. God has warned me to be prepared to take a hit for HIS righteousness' sake. I am at peace over the matter since I did exactly what HE asked of me. An interesting question to ask is whether or not this will be a bad thing for me. The answer is I really do not know.

> "HE restores my soul; HE leads me in the paths of righteousness for HIS name's sake." Psalm 23:3 NKJV

HE is leading you into paths of righteousness for HIS name's sake! Therefore, always do what God wants you to do and remember that HIS view is usually opposite of man's view in this earthly life. What man thinks is right is often wrong with God. In the end, if you are obedient, everything will work out fine. Even if that end is your eternal heavenly reward. And remember what Jesus taught concerning our eternal end. We should always consider Jesus' words and keep them at the front of our conscious minds.

> Jesus said: "Do not fear those who kill the body but cannot kill the soul; rather fear HIM who can destroy both soul and body in Hell." Matthew 10:28 NRSV

Sometimes What Seems Bad Is Good And Vice Versa!

There are many statements that are obvious in God's Word. It might be a biblical verse that says: "God hates this or that." If you engage in the pursuit of something that God hates, I can tell you that HE will repay you for those activities. Remember this verse from chapter 11, page 374?

> "Now the end has come for you, and I will send MY anger against you. I will judge you for the way you have lived, and I will make you pay for all your actions that I hate. I will have no pity on you; I will not hold back punishment from you. Instead, I will make you pay for the way you have lived and for your actions that I hate. Then you will know that I am the LORD." Ezekiel 7:3-4 NCV

When we engage in activities that God hates, we demonstrate a hatred for God and HIS ways. This is true whether or not we will recognize and acknowledge it as a spiritual fact. However, when seemingly bad or evil things or events happen to an individual, it is not always so clear a bad thing. For every action, there is a reaction and often an unintended consequence

Myth—Abortion Doesn't Matter

and even a series of unintended events that unfolds without any ability on our part to foresee or predict. You've already learned that we only see part of the picture right now and that God sees the entire picture. You've also learned that in *God's Eternal Character*, HIS bigger picture is always filled with items we do not have a clue about on this earth. If you don't remember the "big picture" discussion, go back and study chapter 11.

The Chinese Grandfather Story

The issue of what is really good or bad reminds me of the story of an old man in a small remote Chinese mountain village far away from any big city. A relative came to visit the old man one afternoon and asked: "How is it going?" The old man reported that his grandson had fallen off a horse while riding a few days ago and broke his leg in two places.

The relative said: "That's very bad!"

The old man replied: "Actually, no, it was good. That very afternoon, the Chinese army came to our small village and conscripted every young man the age of my grandson. They would not take him since he had broken his leg."

The relative said: "That's very good!"

The old man replied: "Actually, no, it was bad. The next day after the accident, my grandson developed a very bad leg infection that threatened to take his life. If the army had just taken him, my grandson would have gotten some immediate medical care that would have prevented this life threatening leg infection."

The relative said: "That's very bad!"

The old man replied: "Actually, no, it was good. That next day …"

And so the story of the old man and his grandson unfolds and every time the relative thinks something is bad, it turns out good and vice versa. In this story, it is difficult to foretell what is really good or bad until the next

Copyright 2005 Edward G. Palmer, All Rights Reserved.

Myth—Abortion Doesn't Matter

event or all the events in life actually unfold. Some strange things can occur that no one can predict. Even when something seemingly bad occurs in life, it can actually turn into something good. And sometimes there are many unintended consequences hard to predict.

Unintended Political Consequences Of Roe v. Wade!

Take the Roe v. Wade decision of 1973. Today, over 40 million babies have been aborted. As horrific as this statistic is, I just read some interesting statistics in a political study [3] of who is actually getting aborted. Children generally pick up and adopt the politics of their parents. Strangely enough, democrats or liberals are more apt, by one third, to abort their babies than republicans or conservatives are to abort theirs. Given known statistical data of abortions by year, who is getting abortions and what their political affiliation is, it can be accurately predicted who is being politically affected by the aborting [killing] of their own children. As it turns out, there are now millions of more missing liberal voters than conservative voters. Who could anticipate that the killing of babies by abortion would actually wind up giving an edge to one political party over the other?

[3] Table 1: Abortions in the U.S., 1973-1990

Years	Abortions	Aggregated	Election Affected
1973-74	1,643,200	1,643,200	1992
1975-78	4,939,800	6,583,000	1996
1979-82	6,202,800	12,785,800	2000
1983-86	6,314,800	19,100,600	2004
1987-90	6,325,400	25,426,000	2008

The Larry L. Eastland [3] study presents some interesting conclusions:

1. Six out of 10 Americans call themselves conservatives. Only a quarter of them are having abortions.

Myth—Abortion Doesn't Matter

2. A little more than one-third of Americans call themselves liberals. More than four in 10 are having abortions.
3. This means that liberals are having one third more abortions than conservatives.
4. There are 19,748,000 Democrats who are not with us today (49.37 percent of 40 million).
5. There are 13,900,000 Republicans who are not with us today (34.75 percent of 40 million).
6. By comparison, then, the Democrats have lost 5,848,000 more voters than the Republicans have.
7. In the 2000 election, there were 6,033,097 missing voters.

Eastland breaks down the missing voters by state. In Florida during 2000 there were 153,163 missing Democratic voters that had been aborted. Had these voters been alive, Eastland predicts that Florida would have voted for Al Gore by a 44,827-vote margin. The net result of the abortion industry is a cumulative gain for conservatives each new election cycle. It is growing and permanent in nature. It is also changing presidential election dynamics in a way that favors conservatives. In 2000, the aborted democratic babies would have swung the election to Democrat Al Gore instead of Republican George W. Bush. Yes, even abortion has unintended consequences. Get a copy of Eastland's entire study and educated on this aspect of the political ramifications of abortion. I can't fathom the evil that 40 million abortions represent. However, sometimes good comes out of evil by God's design.

Sometimes Evil Is Used By God For Good!

Last Thursday I felt a little like Joseph getting dumped into a deep well by his brothers who hated him and the special relationship that he had with his father. To say the least, it was lonely, dark and a little scary for me. It certainly seemed like a bad event was happening to me and it was filled with uncertainty over what life would bring next. I imagine that Joseph felt the exact same things I did and even more. You can understand why some con artist might want to keep you from telling the truth by throwing you into a deep well. But brothers are supposed to love you. Having said this, often God will use evil for good and we do not see God's complete plans and objectives until HE shows them to us or they unfold before our eyes.

Myth—Abortion Doesn't Matter

Joseph had a lot of time to think about what his brothers had done to him by selling him into Egyptian slavery. He was also in a position to execute vengeance against his brothers if he wanted to. Yet, Joseph knew that God had called him to walk the path he was on, even if that path brought times of grief and suffering. Joseph chose to take his hits for God's sake and to keep moving closer to the LORD. It doesn't matter if you can understand what is happening to you when bad things happen; it only matters if you keep your faith in God. In the end, your trust in God will eventually unfold into your reward as God HIMSELF chooses for you the life HE wants you to lead. Joseph said: "Do not be distressed … for God sent me [on this path]."

**"Then Joseph said to his brothers, 'Come closer to me.'
And they came closer. He said, 'I am your brother, Joseph,
whom you sold into Egypt. And now do not be distressed,
or angry with yourselves, because you sold me here; for
God sent me before you to preserve life.' "**
                                                            Genesis 45:4-5 NRSV

Our part of the equation is to obey God and do what HE tells us to do. Even if that causes earthly consequences for us. I did that much. Now, time will tell the rest of the story of the fraud that took place at Solid Rock Church in Elk River, Minnesota. The final outcome is in God's hands.

No one in society should rejoice when a judge ignores the truth and allows injustice to become manifest. The experience God took me through relates to these writings and even to this chapter. If I take a hit for HIS righteousness' sake, so be it; "THY will be done O LORD!" Let YOUR will reign in my life. One clear message for you is this: "Do what God asks you to do, even if you do not understand why on this good earth HE would ask that of you." It's because HE is not asking of you purely earthly things!

If you are knowledgeable in HIS Word; and,
If you are tuned into HIS Spirit; and,
If you are focused on HIS heavenly goal —

Only then, can you do what God will ask of you. Because only then will you know that your earthly life is just a small part of HIS bigger picture.

Book of Edward—Chapter 18

Myth—Abortion Doesn't Matter

This chapter deals with three perspectives of the abortion debate that God wants you to consider, which few people want to talk about. They are:

A) Love from HIS perspective.
B) Hate from HIS perspective.
C) Doing what HE wants you to do, instead of what you want to do.

Unlike the many arguments pro and con about abortion, I believe that these three perspectives from God's Word are what HE would have me teach you. You should love what God loves. You should hate what God hates. And, you should do what God wants you to do, even if it has consequences.

In the courtroom, I was painted as a hateful man who would wrongly accuse a local pastor. I have also had a self-described theologian tell me that the www.james417.org Internet site, which documents the church theft, is a "hateful" site. So, should Christians engage in hate? I can almost read your mind, as this question would seem like the antithesis of what it means to be a Christian. Well, if you think you should not engage in any hate, you are wrong again and simply programmed with false Christian dogma.

Before getting back to an exegesis of Exodus 21:22-25, let's discuss how and what every Christian should hate. That's right. Christians are supposed to hate certain things, because God does! If you've choked out all the hate inside of you, because your pastor tells you it is simply un-Christian like behavior—it may explain why you can support the legalized killing of babies through abortion. You've been programmed with forgiveness and love. At the same time, you've been denied important teachings on the many other attributes of God Almighty, such as hate.

So much of the pro-abortion argument is framed in the language of love. "If you love her, you'll let her have the abortion. Having a baby now will ruin her life. They can't afford a baby now. Who will take care of that baby? Etc." Even worse, perhaps over 70% of all abortions are framed by a question like this from a family member close to the pregnant woman: "If you really love your family, you'll have the abortion." Yes, families use "love" to pressure women into having abortions and killing their babies. But if this is love from the family, what exactly is hate?

Myth—Abortion Doesn't Matter

The Fear Of The LORD Is Hatred Of Evil!

"The fear of the LORD is hatred of evil. Pride and arrogance and the way of evil and perverted speech I hate."
Proverbs 8:13 NRSV

Those who fear the LORD have gained wisdom and understanding. God is a friend of those who fear HIM. HIS eyes are on those who fear HIM. The LORD has compassion on those who fear HIM. In fact, unless you have a sincere fear of God, you do not have any relationship with HIM. I have discussed this issue earlier and how it relates to "perfect love" which casts out all fear. Wisdom and understanding begins when you have an earnest fear of God. It is the kind of fear that gives you a healthy respect and concern for actually obeying God's laws and HIS rules. That is the fear of God that Jesus is talking about in Matthew 10:28. That is the reality of a true repentance of the heart, because it is a belief within the heart unto righteousness based on the fear of God. In other words, you truly believe God is real and you understand in your heart there are eternal consequences for bad earthly behavior. This is, in essence, what actually gives you reason to behave yourself in a godly manner while on this earth. Think about it.

"The fear of the LORD is the beginning of wisdom; all those who practice it have a good understanding."
Psalm 111:10 NRSV

"The friendship of the LORD is for those who fear HIM, and HE makes HIS covenant known to them."
Psalm 25:14 NRSV

"Truly the eye of the LORD is on those who fear HIM, on those who hope in HIS steadfast love." Psalm 33:18 NRSV

"As a father has compassion for his children, so the LORD has compassion for those who fear HIM."
Psalm 103:13 NRSV

Myth—Abortion Doesn't Matter

God Hates & You Should Hate Like HE Hates!

Merriam-Webster's 11th Collegiate Dictionary [4] contains the following definitions regarding hate and hateful.

Hate [noun]   **1 a:** intense hostility and aversion usually deriving from fear, anger, or sense of injury **b:** extreme dislike or antipathy: LOATHING <had a great hate of hard work> **2:** an object of hatred <a generation whose finest *hate* had been big business — F. L. Paxson>.

Hate [transitive verb]   **1:** to feel extreme enmity toward <hates his country's enemies> **2:** to have a strong aversion to: find very distasteful <hated to have to meet strangers> <hate hypocrisy> *intransitive verb:* to express or feel extreme enmity or active hostility.

Hater *noun.*

Hate one's guts: to hate someone with great intensity.

Synonyms   HATE, DETEST, ABHOR, ABOMINATE, LOATH mean to feel strong aversion or intense dislike for. HATE implies an emotional aversion often coupled with enmity or malice <hated the enemy with a passion>. DETEST suggests violent antipathy <detests cowards>. ABHOR implies a deep often shuddering repugnance <a crime abhorred by all>. ABOMINATE suggests strong detestation and often moral condemnation <abominates all forms of violence>. LOATHE implies utter disgust and intolerance <loathed the mere sight of them>.

Hateful *adjective*   **1:** full of hate: MALICIOUS **2:** deserving of or arousing hate.

Hatefully *adverb.*   **Hatefulness** *noun.*

Myth—Abortion Doesn't Matter

Hating what God hates does not mean that you hate people in your heart. It does not mean you are intrinsically *only* a hateful person. But, it does mean that hate is intrinsically part of you when you walk with God. That is because hate is an intrinsic part of God Almighty HIMSELF. Having the capacity to hate means, that like Christ, you too adopt the FATHER'S ways. To think simply because you hate what is evil means you are "hateful" per se is the stuff of Christian mythology.

This is the nuance many Christians fail to understand. Indeed, God has the capacity to forgive those who do hateful things in HIS eyes when they truly repent from inside their hearts. Again, this type of repentance is from the depths and bowels of their spirit-soul where the heart resides. We should adopt God's reasons, methods and strategies to hate what HE hates.

"You shall not hate in your heart anyone of your kin [family]; you shall reprove your neighbor, or you will incur guilt yourself." Leviticus 19:17 NRSV

There are a couple of important aspects in the above verse. First is the issue of where hate resides. Is it in the mind as the result of knowledge of God's Word? Or is it inside the heart, where permanency lies and action springs forth from? It makes a difference to God. When you hate someone in your heart, it is difficult to forgive. Therefore, God specifically would have you contain hate within your mind and intellect and not in your heart.

A second and equally important aspect of the above verse is that each of us has the duty to reprove or rebuke our neighbor when they commit sin. This means to gently or kindly scold them for wrongdoing and to get them to take godly action and make amends. There is a penalty from God for those who fail to reprove their neighbor when evil or improper action has taken place and you bear witness. Failure to reprove your neighbor means that you will incur guilt yourself.

Failure To Reprove Means You Incur Guilt!

Today, people want the ability to do anything they feel like doing. "If it feels good, do it." And, "what I feel like doing is none of your business!"

Myth—Abortion Doesn't Matter

In addition to those two facts, people want society and the government to sanction what they "feel" like doing as being "mainstream." In other words, they want morality taken out of challenging and influencing their behavior. Many would have you believe that evil actions are on a par with good actions. They would argue that what is bad for you is good for them. That is not God's ways and it wasn't always that way in the United States. I'll come back to this point in a moment. For now, consider the graphic below and the difference between mental thoughts flowing into and out of our mind vs. what resides in our heart and springs forth out of our heart.

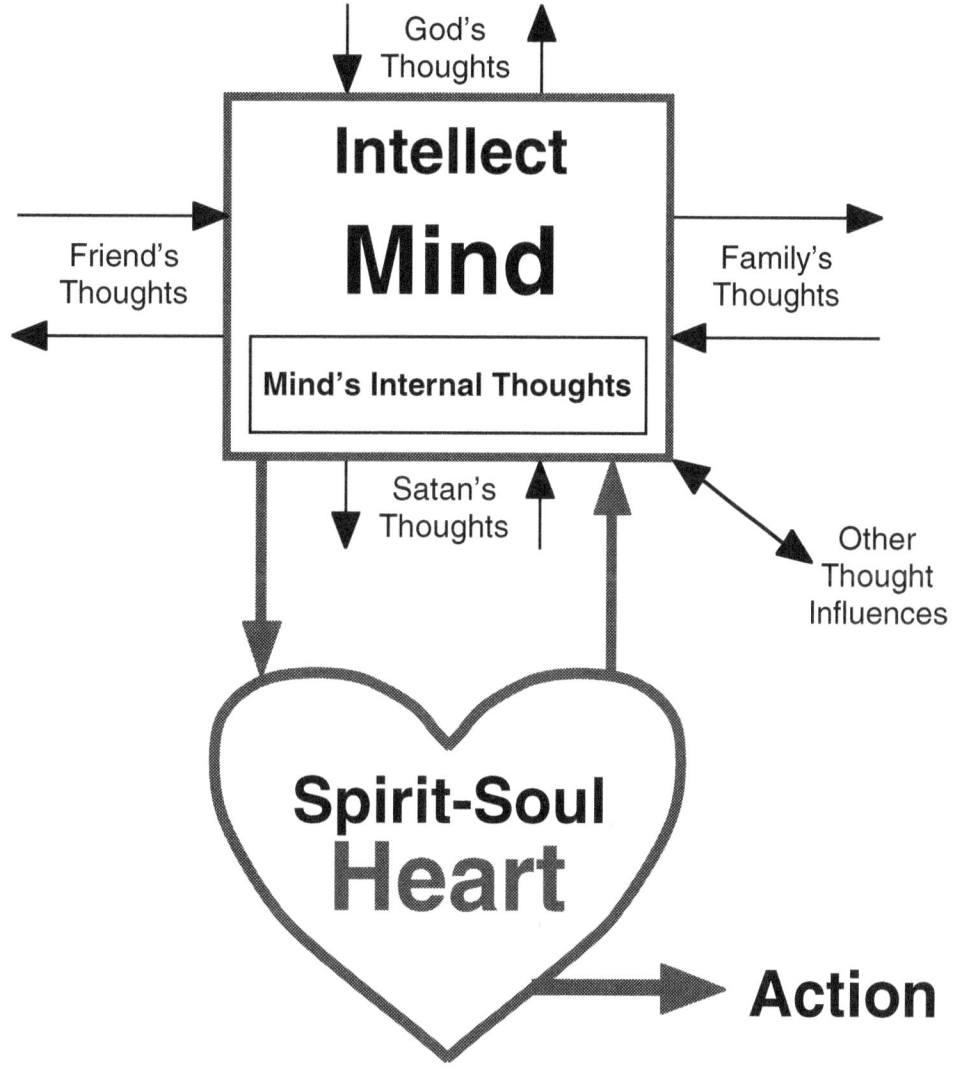

Myth—Abortion Doesn't Matter

God's Word teaches you to hate certain things, which HE considers to be evil. However, all of our hate should reside in our intellect and mind and not in our heart. When God says: "Do not hate your family in your heart," it means you should not put hate in a place of permanency. That is what the heart represents to us. In contrast, the mind is a place of temporary storage. We can alter our memory banks with new memories. We can erase hate and replace it with joy. That is what God does when a sinner repents and turns away from the "practice of sin."

If us mere humans were condemned for having a wrongful thought in our mind, there is not one human being that would be saved. Thoughts come and go into our minds from a variety of thought sources. They come from God and we send them to God. Likewise thoughts from Satan, family, friends along with thoughts from countless other sources enter our minds. When you watch a movie, thoughts flow into your mind. When you surf the Internet on your computer, thoughts flow into your mind.

When you accept a single news source as representing the truth of the situation or issue, thoughts not only flow into your mind but can even flow down into your heart, where permanency will take place. Make sure you do not put hate into your heart, because the heart is a welcome home for all sorts of evil that God despises. Remember, you are to guard your heart.

> **Jesus said: "For it is from within, from the human heart, that evil intentions come: fornication, theft, murder, adultery, avarice, wickedness, deceit, licentiousness, envy, slander, pride, folly. All these evil things come from within, and they defile a person." Mark 7:21-23 NRSV**

Sometimes, a flat out evil thought will enter your mind and you will wonder where it came from. That is because you will immediately disavow having originated it. The best explanation for that phenomenon is that thoughts travel through the air and our brains are receivers for thoughts [5] just like radios receive radio waves. In that scenario, at any given moment, you could receive thoughts from countless unknown sources. If an evil thought surfaces, just reject it immediately in "the name of Jesus" and move on.

Therefore, if you worried about the evil or mean spirited thought that occasionally surfaced in your mind, you could literally go nuts. Take responsibility for your own mental thoughts, but do not believe for a moment that only your thoughts will enter your head.

I've heard many public speakers assert that mankind is inherently good. I would basically agree since we are created in God's image. However, God makes it clear that the human heart is "inclined" towards evil from youth. Jesus already taught you evil intentions [action] springs forth out of what is in the heart of man [Mark 7:21-23].

Inclination Of The Human Heart Is Evil!

"And when the LORD smelled the pleasing odor, the LORD said in HIS heart, 'I will never again curse the ground because of humankind, for the inclination of the human heart is evil from youth; nor will I ever again destroy every living creature as I have done.' " Genesis 8:21 NRSV

When the Founding Fathers of the United States formed the U.S. Constitution they took into account this very biblical fact. They knew of man's inclination towards evil and especially when given "political power." I'll talk more about the issue of politics in chapter 20.

Now since God has made it clear our hearts are inclined towards evil, is it any wonder why HE would want to hold you accountable to reprove your sinful neighbor, friend or family member? God knows we needed the help of everyone around us to keep us on a godly path in our life. That is why tight knit communities and families work well. That is the way it was when I roamed Plymouth Avenue in Minneapolis as a budding teenager in 1959. Any young person who thought of getting into mischief was a target of the reprove of any observing adult in the vicinity in those days. We did not live in a society that simply "let you do your own thing" when what you were doing was wrong or evil. Today, if a reprove takes place to correct a child's bad behavior, the reprover might then become the target of a lawsuit.

Myth—Abortion Doesn't Matter

Society in the United States has changed for the worse and even towards outright evil since to take away the reproving of bad or immoral behavior results in a societal blind eye towards evil. Yet, verily I say unto you, God will still hold you accountable for failing to reprove and you will still incur guilt in HIS eyes. I've told you before, HE does not change.

If you understand that man and woman's heart has an inclination towards evil, you will understand why we need a collective and community wide oversight. This general failure to reprove bad or immoral behavior is now augmented by Court rulings that focus on granting minorities special rights at the expense of society's moral health. When the Supreme Court ruled in Roe v. Wade, they stripped away the stigma of "willful" abortion. In its place, an air of legitimacy to the idea of "willful" abortion was created. The Supreme Court started off by catering to a few women that wanted the right to abort their babies. However, this has turned into an industry that now murders an estimated 1,500,000 babies annually in the United States. It is estimated that worldwide abortion deaths is ten times as great a number.

That is exactly what happens when society fails to follow God's guidance. Instead of purging evil out of our midst as commanded, we now sanction evil conduct. Once that evil conduct is sanctioned, evil only escalates because people soon forget that it is evil. Taking God's morality out of society allows evil activities to be advocated as on a par with good. That is what has happened with abortion. Yet, has God changed HIS mind?

Since the Founding Fathers anticipated morality as a necessity in the formation of our Constitution, it is interesting to note exactly how many people now advocate that abortion is a right guaranteed by that Constitution. Our Founding Fathers would roll over in their graves if they knew how our society is interpreting their "moral" document. If you think our Founding Fathers granted a right to abortion in the Constitution they created, you are simply ignorant of history. The United States needs to get back to the moral ideals embedded in the foundation of our country. That means getting back to God's moral ways, which is what the U.S. Constitution is based upon.

U.S. Constitution Grants No Abortion Rights!

Copyright 2005 Edward G. Palmer, All Rights Reserved.

Myth—Abortion Doesn't Matter

Signers of U.S. Constitution—39

Instruction: Place a check mark next to every person who signed the U.S. Constitution[6] or who is identified as a founding father that did not sign the document that you think granted a woman abortion rights.

✔	U.S. Constitution Signer	✔	U.S. Constitution Signer
	Baldwin, Abraham		Morris, Robert
	Bassett, Richard		Paterson, William
	Bedford, Gunning Jr.		Pinckney, Charles Cotesworth
	Blair, John		Pinckney, Charles
	Blount, William		Read, George
	Brearly, David		Rutledge, John
	Broom, Jacob		Sherman, Roger
	Butler, Pierce		Spaight, Richard D.
	Carroll, Daniel		Washington, George
	Clymer, George		Williamson, Hugh
	Dayton, Jonathon		Wilson, James
	Dickinson, John		*Other Founding Fathers—16*
	Few, William		*Davie, William R.*
	Fitzsimons, Thomas		*Ellsworth, Oliver*
	Franklin, Benjamin		*Gerry, Elbridge*
	Gilman, Nicholas		*Houston, William C.*
	Gorham, Nathaniel		*Houstoun, William*
	Hamilton, Alexander		*Lansing, John Jr.*
	Ingersoll, Jarod		*Martin, Alexander*
	Jenifer, Daniel of St. Thomas		*Martin, Luther*
	Johnson, William S.		*Mason, George*
	King, Rufus		*McClurg, James*
	Langdon, John		*Mercer, John F.*
	Livingston, William		*Pierce, William L.*
	Madison, James Jr.		*Randolph, Edmund J.*
	McHenry, James		*Strong, Caleb*
	Mifflin, Thomas		*Wythe, George*
	Morris, Gouverneur		*Yates, Robert*

Copyright 2005 Edward G. Palmer, All Rights Reserved.

Book of Edward—Chapter 18

Myth—Abortion Doesn't Matter

If you were able to check anyone of the thirty-nine signers of our Constitution or the sixteen other Founders who did not sign the Constitution, as a supporter of abortion, send me a letter and explain your basis for what I would consider as the actions of a person ignorant of history. Honestly, on July 4, 1776 when the Declaration of Independence was signed, do you think these Founders were thinking about granting women the right to kill their babies as they started to draft the U.S. Constitution?

Our Founders wrote: "We hold these truths to be self-evident, that all men are created equal, that they are endowed by their CREATOR with certain unalienable rights, that among these are life, liberty and the pursuit of happiness." The United States Founding Fathers believed our CREATOR God created us with certain rights. Among those rights is the *right to life*! Yet, many ignorant people now argue that the child in the womb has no right to life, unless the *mother* grants it? Hello. Women are trying to usurp God's authority! Our Founding Fathers *knew* the CREATOR and would be appalled at how society is trying to eliminate the Constitution's moral foundation.

Eleven years after that bold declaration, the U.S. Constitution was signed on September 17, 1787. At least one author [7] has written a book that argues our Founding Fathers created a "secular" Constitution fashioned after the Virginia Constitution [8]. That our Constitution is a secular document cannot be disputed. However, that does not mean it was based on an immoral or amoral Virginia Constitution. A simple review of the Virginia Constitution dated June 29, 1776 reveals the following in Section 16.

> "SEC. 16. That religion, or the duty which we owe to our CREATOR, and the manner of discharging it, can be directed only by reason and conviction, not by force or violence; and therefore all men are equally entitled to the free exercise of religion, according to the dictates of conscience; and that it is the mutual duty of all to practice Christian forbearance, love and charity towards each other."

The U.S. is based on Christianity and God's morality! Our Founders knew God gave us a free will and required a choice from our heart. It means evil people, but it does not mean an evil society. They knew the difference!

Myth—Abortion Doesn't Matter

Not only did the Founders know the difference between evil people and an evil nation, the Constitution that they created made every attempt to ensure that the evil inclination of man's heart would not wind up perverting the nation's laws and moral foundation. These Founders also did not engage in politically correct (PC) speech such as *Pro Choice* which euphemistically now describes a woman's right to kill her baby.

Those who say they are "pro choice" are actually "pro murder." The Founding Fathers declared an unalienable "right to life." The denial of that *right* is not a "choice" — it is murder. God knows the difference and those who founded the United States of America knew the difference.

I am now writing on Monday, July 26, 2004. It is the eve of the Democratic national convention, which will nominate John F. Kerry as its presidential candidate for the upcoming election. While people play games with the "PC" language, there is no denying which major political party now stands for unlimited abortion on demand. It is the Democratic Party!

Democrat John F. Kerry states he is a Catholic and does not believe in abortion personally, but cannot force his personal beliefs upon the people. Verily I say unto you that God will hold the Catholic Church responsible for failing to teach HIS people the truth. Exactly what is that truth? It is that we are to be doers of the Word and not just hearers. Those who profess belief in God's Word, but fail to act upon that belief only deceive themselves. That is exactly what every person who stands with Kerry in his apostate Christian reasoning does. They deceive themselves. But they do not deceive God.

> **"But be doers of the Word, and not merely hearers who deceive themselves. For if any are hearers of the Word and not doers, they are like those who look at themselves in a mirror; for they look at themselves and, on going away, immediately forget what they were like. But those who look into the perfect law, the law of liberty, and persevere, being not hearers who forget but doers who act — they will be blessed in their doing." James 1:22-25 NRSV**

Sincere Belief Translates Into Action — Not PC Talk!

Copyright 2005 Edward G. Palmer, All Rights Reserved.

Book of Edward—Chapter 18

Myth—Abortion Doesn't Matter

The Nation's Founding Fathers are the benchmark for true patriotism and belief. Many of them died for their belief in God. Indeed, they were "doers of the Word." Now, take a moment and go back to the list of signers of the Constitution and other Founding Fathers. Place a check mark against every person you think would take the political position on abortion that Democrat John F. Kerry has taken. If you placed a single checkmark, you do not understand history. Our Founding Fathers were men of integrity who argued by reason, not by deception and politically correct speech.

Instead of doing what Kerry purports to be doing, he is actually a doer of his true belief. Simply put, Kerry does seek to impose his belief on the nation and that belief is the "right to murder." There is no way you can square what our Founding Fathers believed in and the beliefs of the present Democratic Party in the United States concerning abortion. If you are a committed Democrat, you should ask what John F. Kennedy believed in. Was it abortion on demand? Don't be ridiculous. The current Democratic Party has long since dropped its ties to the Founders of our country and to the party of JFK [the real JFK]. Instead, the present Democratic Party stands for every perversion that mankind can think up. Instead of God's morality, they hope to supplant a "morality of rights" upon our country. In the end, society decays and falls into an abyss because the moral underpinning which gave us our success gets shredded by evil people intent on creating an evil society. Too strong of language you say? Not in the eyes of God.

In the process of creating the U.S. Constitution, the framers looked into every civilization in detail and examined what made them collapse. A salient point that should not go unnoticed is that major civilizations decayed and fell apart when morality was set aside and decadence was prevalent. The U.S. is in decline because of moral decay. Is it too late to stop it?

"All deeds are right in the sight of the doer, but the LORD weighs the heart." Proverbs 21:2 NRSV

Abortion is not new to society since Roe v. Wade. But, the illusion that a woman can abort her baby and then simply choose at a later date to have one *is* new. Many believe they can have a baby whenever they choose.

Myth—Abortion Doesn't Matter

Jackie and I lost our first son Glen after only four short weeks of life. It was devastating to us and we were only 18 and 19 respectively at the time. We never forgot that trauma throughout our life. Jackie is with God now, but I will never forget Glen. It was 1965 and a baby's life was valued a lot more in those days. It didn't mean that a young unwed woman did not get pregnant. They did. However, if marriage was not an option, the woman most likely carried the baby and put it up for adoption. Jackie and I had friends who did just that. They put their baby into the hands of a capable mother and father who promised to love and raise that baby as their own.

Many people cannot have children. It is estimated that there are over 2 million people waiting to adopt a baby. Therefore, the "PC" statement of "no unwanted child" is a specious argument. Any woman who chooses to carry her baby to full term and then put that baby up for adoption will find a loving home for that baby. That includes handicapped babies as well.

No doubt there were the so-called "coat hanger" abortions in those days, but let me ask you this question. If abortion was illegal today, do you suppose there would <u>then</u> again be "coat hanger" abortions? This is also a specious argument, because abortion chemical technology has gotten well defined given the over 40 million abortions that have now occurred. Given modern methods, doctors don't need coat hangers. In my research, I have failed to turn up any significant quantity of women who had died from a "coat-hanger" abortion. Perhaps the most would be 50 women I suspect. However, today, it is estimated that as many as 300 women die each year from legal abortions. Why? It is a major health event by any stretch of the imagination and the danger to women is real. Why is the information about the dangers of abortion being withheld from women seeking abortions? The industry makes money killing babies and selling baby parts — not from counseling women of the dangers of abortion and the benefits of adoption.

Democrats and militant women now fight vigorously to maintain the right to a partial birth abortion. Lawsuits have been filed in three states and the courts have granted some clinics the right to continue what can only be described as a hideous procedure to kill a partially delivered baby. Why would any *good* people defend this procedure? It is the epitome of evil.

Copyright 2005 Edward G. Palmer, All Rights Reserved.

Book of Edward—Chapter 18

Myth—Abortion Doesn't Matter

Consider now what the partial birth procedure entails. The baby is delivered feet first. When the head is visible, the baby is stabbed with a sharp instrument in the back of the head and its brains are sucked out with a vacuum instrument. This collapses the head structure and the baby is pulled out of the uterus the rest of the way. No anesthesia is given to the baby during this procedure, which is available to the mother up to the day before the baby is delivered naturally.

Many people do not realize that a mother can abort her baby up to the day before it delivers naturally. Most states have laws that give the mother the right to abort the baby a full nine months. This is the right that abortion supporters are fighting for when they fight for partial birth abortion. While many people do not realize this, young teenage pregnancies often have had terrible consequences. Teenage mothers have been documented delivering their babies in a bathroom and then simply throwing them into a trashcan. Once discovered, these young ignorant mothers are then prosecuted for murder. What they failed to understand was that it is okay to kill the baby the day before it is born. Once born, however, the same act a mere 24 hours later or less becomes an act of murder in the eyes of the law. Yet, when society teaches a young woman it is okay to kill her baby, how is she supposed to understand it is murder if her timing is late a few hours?

After Glen died, it took Jackie and I almost three years before our daughter Paula was born. During that time, Jackie suffered miscarriages twice. These natural female body abortions will often occur spontaneously without warning. There is no guarantee that once you are pregnant that you will in fact carry that baby to term and even that the baby will be delivered in good health. Any number of things can go awry and those who support abortion rights mistakenly believe a woman can conceive anytime she wants to and then have that baby after carrying it 9-months. Indeed, many people are now ignorant on the sheer miracle of human life.

I have watched two good documentaries on the subjects of abortion and the miracle of human life. One was entitled *Eclipse of Reason* [9]. This is an abortion documentary and features a doctor who had performed many thousands of abortions. In the video, a 5-month gestated boy is aborted.

Book of Edward—Chapter 18

Myth—Abortion Doesn't Matter

Doctor Bernard Nathanson who produced *Eclipse of Reason* estimates that in 1993 over 400 late term abortions were performed daily. No doubt a much larger number exists in 2004. He stated, at the time, that women have experienced 7,500 serious complications from abortions each year. In some of the abortion complications, a dilation and curettage (D&C) procedure is needed. The procedure can cause damage to the lining of the uterus. Jackie suffered from the consequences of a D&C procedure after the last natural miscarriage she suffered circa 1966. According to her doctor in San Diego, California, the D&C had perforated her uterus. Had she gone to the wrong doctor, we were told she would have been unable to have any children. Only by the grace of God did we then have children. Thank you LORD!

In the video, Doctor Nathanson showed the instruments he used in performing routine abortions and then described how a baby boy 5-months old is systematically torn apart limb by limb. After the baby is torn apart and removed from the uterus, it is reassembled on a nearby table to ensure that all of the baby's body parts have been successfully removed. At that point, a D&C may be needed to further scrape and clean the woman's uterus.

After 20-weeks of gestation, a woman can feel her baby move. Do you think this movement represents something that is not living inside her womb? Below, *an abortion clinic* reveals the facts of fetal development.

Fetal Development Facts From An Abortion Clinic!

Week 2 — The fertilized egg implants itself onto the wall of the uterus and the embryo is about $1/100^{th}$ of an inch at this time [10]. Note: Week 2 of fetal development is defined as occurring 4 weeks after the first day of the last normal menstrual period. This is the gestational age calculation.

Week 4 — The embryo is about 1/6 inch long and has developed a head and a trunk. Structures that will become arms and legs, called limb buds, begin to appear. Blood is beginning to be pumped through fetal circulation. Heartbeat is visible by ultrasound.

Myth—Abortion Doesn't Matter

Week 6 — The embryo is about 1/2 inch and has a four chambered heart and nostrils. Fingers and toes begin to form. Reflex activity begins with the development of the brain and nervous system.

Week 8 — The fetus, until now called an embryo, is about 1 1/4 inches long with the head making up about half this size and weighs less than 1/2 ounce. The beginnings of all key body parts are present, although they are not completely positioned in their final locations. Structures that will form eyes, ears, arms and legs are identifiable.

Week 10 — The fetus is about 1 1/2 inches from head to rump, weighing about 1 1/2 ounces. Fingers and toes are distinct and have nails. The fetus begins small, random movements, too slight to be felt. The fetal heartbeat can be detected with a Doppler or heart monitor.

Week 12 — The fetus is about 3 1/2 inches from head to rump and weighs about 2 ounces. The fetus begins to swallow, the kidneys make urine, and blood begins to form in the bone marrow. Joints and muscles allow full body movement.

Week 14 — The fetus is about 4 3/4 inches from head to rump and weighs 4 ounces. The head is erect and the arms and legs are developed.

Week 16 — The fetus is about 5 inches from head to rump and weighs about 6 ounces. The skin is pink and transparent and the ears stick out from the head.

Week 18 — The fetus is about 6 1/4 inches from head to rump, weighing about 10 ounces. All organs and structures have been formed, and a period of simple growth begins. Respiratory movements occur, but the lungs have not developed enough to permit survival outside the uterus. By this time the woman may feel the fetus moving.

Week 20 — The fetus is about 7 1/2 inches from head to rump, has fingerprints and perhaps some head and body hair, weighing about one pound (16 ounces). There is little chance before this time that a baby could

Myth—Abortion Doesn't Matter

survive outside the woman's body. Fetal heartbeat can be heard with a stethoscope.

Week 22 — The fetus is about 8 1/4 inches from head to rump and weighs about 1 1/4 pounds. Changes are occurring in lung development so that some babies are able to survive (with intensive care services.)

Week 24 — The fetus is about 9 inches from head to rump and weighs about 2 pounds. The fetus can respond to sound. About 4 out of 10 babies born may now survive (with intensive care services).

Week 26 — The fetus is about 10 inches from head to rump and weighs about 2 1/2 pounds. The eyes are partially open and can perceive light. About 9 out of 10 babies born now will survive (with intensive care services).

Week 28 — The fetus is about 10 1/2 inches from head to rump and weighs almost 3 pounds. The fetus has lungs that are capable of breathing air, although medical help may be needed. The fetus can open and close its eyes, suck its thumb and respond to sound. Nearly all babies born now will survive (with intensive care services).

Week 30 — The fetus is about 11 inches from head to rump and weighs more than 3 pounds. Skin is thicker and pinker. Nearly all babies born now will live (with intensive care services).

Week 32 — The fetus is about 11 3/4 inches from head to rump and weighs about 4 1/2 pounds. Ears begin to hold shape. Almost all babies born now will live (with intensive care services).

Week 34 — The fetus is about 12 1/2 inches from head to rump and weighs about 5 1/2 pounds. Scalp hair is silky and lies against the head. Almost all babies born now will live.

Week 36 — The fetus is about 13 1/2 inches from head to rump and weighs about 6 1/2 pounds. Lungs are usually mature. The fetus can grasp firmly. Almost all babies born now will live.

Copyright 2005 Edward G. Palmer, All Rights Reserved.

Myth—Abortion Doesn't Matter

Week 38 — The fetus is about 14 inches from head to rump, may be more than 20 inches overall, and may weigh from 6 1/2 to 10 pounds. The baby is full-term and ready to be born. Note: Week 38 is 40 weeks after the first day of the last menstrual period, which is the gestational age.

The above fetal development facts were found online accompanied by ultrasound images of each fetal stage. This above information is presented by an abortion clinic in Kansas to comply with K.S.A. 65-6701, known as the "Women's Right to Know Act." Women seeking abortion services in Kansas are provided the above and other information at least 24 hours prior to an abortion procedure. This particular clinic claimed to be a "Specialist in 2nd Trimester Elective and 2nd/3rd Trimester Therapeutic Abortion Care" according to the information on their Internet site [9]. Therefore, you can also find descriptions of all available abortion methods that are used online. You should read this information and study the stated medical complications of abortion that clinics are now forced to disclose. If you do, it will educate you away from thinking that abortion is simply a benign procedure.

Having provided a woman with the above facts on fetal development, you might wonder, like I do, why any women would then still seek to have an abortion. You might also wonder why a clinic would specialize in late term abortions given the information they provide that the baby could live outside the womb after 20 weeks. Here is a medical clinic that on one hand tells you your baby can live if born early and then tells you how they can kill it for you. That's if you are a mother who wants to exercise a life *choice*!

Minnesota had a struggle passing a similar law, which was vetoed twice by a governor that felt it was a burden on women seeking to have an abortion. It took nine years to get a law to inform women of their health risks and fetal facts. How can the facts of fetal development, the abortion methods used and the medical risks involved be a burden on women? Too many women operate off of ignorance when it comes to having an abortion. They need to get educated, if not for their baby's sake, for their own health's sake. Does your state have a "Women's Right To Know Law?" If not, it probably speaks very loud to the power of the abortion industry and its politics over your state legislators *or* your governor.

Copyright 2005 Edward G. Palmer, All Rights Reserved.

Book of Edward—Chapter 18

Myth—Abortion Doesn't Matter

AbortionFacts.Com

It's only fair if I give you fetal development facts from an abortion clinic site that I provide you with some alternatives. There is an incredible wealth of information located online [11]. If you are serious about educating yourself on abortion facts, you'll certainly learn the truth. Some quick facts from abortionfacts.com are:

1. Heartbeat begins between eighteenth and twenty-fifth day.
2. Electrical brain waves have been recorded as early as forty days.
3. A baby can survive outside the womb as early as twenty weeks.
4. Pregnancy from rape is extremely rare.

You will find answers to a lot of the social questions surrounding the abortion debate at the above site as well as statistics and various help menus. In fact, the site's mission statement says: "We have brought together quality information on the abortion debate from many different sources and made it available to the world in one abortion mega site." I agree that there is a tremendous wealth of information at this site.

AbortionTV.Com

Another site to view is the abortiontv.com site [12]. This is another abortion mega site, but with a different focus. You'll find some online tests that will challenge your knowledge. One that I found interesting challenges your thinking about aborting a fetus that may be deformed. The answer is on the next page. Don't peek. **What would you do in the following situation?** *A woman has tuberculosis and the father has syphilis. Together they had four children and she is now pregnant with their fifth child.*

1. Their first child was born blind.
2. Their second child was stillborn.
3. Their third child was deaf & dumb.
4. Their fourth child was born with tuberculosis.

Would you recommend that they abort their upcoming fifth child?

Myth—Abortion Doesn't Matter

If you chose to recommend abortion, you recommended aborting Beethoven's life. If you chose against abortion, you saved Beethoven's life. The test concludes: "Every baby won't grow up to be a Beethoven, but doesn't every human deserve the chance to make the most of their life?"

Ultrasound images have gotten so sophisticated that you can literally see the baby's developing organs emerge. I recently viewed some 3D ultrasound images at BBC News [13]. These ultrasound images captured babies wanting to move forward [walk] in the womb when held in an upright position, laughing in the womb, yawning in the womb, sucking on their thumbs in the womb, etc. What these scans by Professor Stuart Campbell at London's Create Health Clinic showed is amazing. Is not science and technology now validating what God has taught us in His Word?

1. At 8 weeks, a fetus is able to kick and straighten their legs, turn around and move their arms up and down.
2. At 10 weeks, a fetus can move their arms and legs with a range of movements that are fluid and supple.
3. At 18 weeks, a fetus can open their eyes although most doctors thought eyelids were fused until 26 weeks.
4. At 22 weeks, babies are capable of fine hand and finger movements. In a short space of time, one baby is observed scratching, rubbing and patting his cheeks before doing the same thing to his nose.
5. At 24 weeks, when retinal development is complete, babies open and close their eyes intermittently. This helps the baby to perfect the blinking reflex, which will protect his eyes when born.
6. From 26 weeks, babies appear to exhibit a whole range of typical baby behavior and moods, including scratching, smiling, crying, hiccoughing, and sucking.
7. Observed in the womb, a baby's brain development is sufficient to enable them to apparently sense the other parts of their body. They can bring their fingertips together so they touch. They can feel.
8. Although grasping begins early on, it becomes better established during the last trimester. Babies grasp hands, feet, fingers, toes *and, most commonly, their umbilical cords.*

Myth—Abortion Doesn't Matter

In the NOVA documentary entitled *Miracle of Life,* [14] WGBH in Boston presents the "first filmed record of human conception." It shows the millions of male sperm and how they attempt to impregnate a single female egg. An Amazon.com review states: "The viewer follows an egg from its follicular development in an ovary, through the delicate, flowery fallopian tube for fertilization, and on to the uterus for development and eventual birth. Likewise, we follow the shorter journey of millions of sperm as they develop and strive mightily to reach the egg." A health teacher in a middle school comments: "There is no doubt left by the video about when life begins—the moment of conception is the beginning of life." Indeed, one concludes after watching this documentary that human life is indeed a miracle to behold with wonder and awe. It is what our God has created.

A Mother's Womb Should Protect New Life!

"When the LORD saw that Leah was unloved, he opened her womb; but Rachel was barren." Genesis 29:31 NRSV

"Then God remembered Rachel, and God heeded her and opened her womb." Genesis 30:22 NRSV

"Did not HE who made me in the womb make them? And did not ONE fashion us in the womb?" Job 31:15 NRSV

"Thus says the LORD, your Redeemer, who formed you in the womb: I am the LORD, who made all things, who alone stretched out the heavens, who by MYSELF spread out the earth." Isaiah 44:24 NRSV

"Can a woman forget her nursing child, or show no compassion for the child of her womb?" Isaiah 49:15 NRSV

Wouldn't the Prophet Isaiah be shocked to learn that millions of women now show "no compassion for the child of their womb?" Society has trained women to ignore the compassion, which is a God given part of their nurturing nature. Since God fashions us in the womb, women having abortions show no compassion on the most innocent of God's creation.

Copyright 2005 Edward G. Palmer, All Rights Reserved.

Book of Edward—Chapter 18

Myth—Abortion Doesn't Matter

Elizabeth tells Mary: "For as soon as I heard the sound of your greeting, the child in my womb [John the Baptist] leaped for joy." Luke 1:44 NRSV

"For YOU alone exist, and we are a work of YOUR hands, as YOU have declared. And because YOU give life to the body that is now fashioned in the womb, and furnish it with members, what YOU have created is preserved amid fire and water, and for nine months the womb endures YOUR creature that has been created in it. But that which keeps and that which is kept shall both be kept by YOUR keeping. And when the womb gives up again what has been created in it, YOU have commanded that from the members themselves (that is, from the breasts) milk, the fruit of the breasts, should be supplied, so that what has been fashioned may be nourished for a time; and afterwards YOU will still guide it in your mercy." 2 Esdras 8:7-11 NRSV

There is a DESIGNER behind human life and HE gave instructions for the way life is to be nurtured inside and outside of the womb. No man or woman has a right to interfere with what God has wrought by HIS hands.

"For it was YOU who formed my inward parts; YOU knit me together in my mother's womb. I praise YOU, for I am fearfully and wonderfully made. Wonderful are YOUR works; that I know very well. My frame was not hidden from YOU, when I was being made in secret, intricately woven in the depths of the earth. YOUR eyes beheld my unformed substance. In YOUR book were written all the days that were formed for me, when none of them as yet existed." Psalm 139:13-16 NRSV

David knew God had created him. It wasn't a lucky sperm mating with an egg. It was *the* sperm mating with *the* egg ordained by God for the creation of David. Every fetus has unique DNA and fingerprints, which is different from everyone else in all humanity. David knew how precious his human life was and that God created it with predestination and purpose.

Copyright 2005 Edward G. Palmer, All Rights Reserved.

Book of Edward—Chapter 18

Myth—Abortion Doesn't Matter

The Female's Egg "Selects" The Right Sperm!

This idea of biblical predestination is confirmed by the fact that the female's oocyte [egg] actually demonstrates a selection process is in play during conception. In other words, God has given the oocyte or egg the intelligence to select just the right sperm to mate with and not just any sperm that might arrive. Millions of sperm start the trek towards the egg, but only a few sperm actually arrive at the egg. When they get there, all of those sperm cycle around the egg attempting to gain entry. However, the oocyte has to take action to enable a sperm to enter and it picks just the right one out of the many that have arrived to mate. The union of the oocyte [egg] and sperm create a zygote cell and human life begins to unfold. The zygote is the point of conception and there is observable intelligence within the process. Yes, it is God that has fashioned HIS creation in the womb.

There Is Life In Human Blood!

The zygote or fertilized egg has intelligence from God to then attach itself to the uterus and create its own unique blood and circulation system. It is not the woman's blood that flows through the fetus; it is the fetus' blood! When my son Brian was born in 1972, he developed Rh-positive blood, but Jackie's own blood was opposite. It was Rh-negative. As a result, her body started to create antibodies that then attacked Brian's "foreign" blood. I'm happy to report he's healthy at age 32. However, he had to have a complete blood transfusion in the hospital after he was born to clear out the harmful antibodies. When Jackie and I had children, the Rh risk factor for serious complications increased after each additional birth. After Brian's near death, we stopped having children as the inherent risks in our procreation became too great. Modern medicine can now give Rh shots to a woman who has a different Rh factor than her husband. There is life in the blood and God does not want anyone to shed innocent blood. Shedding innocent blood terminates innocent life. That is God's perspective!

> "Therefore I have said to the people of Israel ... the life of every creature is its blood." Leviticus 17:14 NRSV

Myth—Abortion Doesn't Matter

> **"For your own lifeblood I will surely require a reckoning: from every animal I will require it and from human beings, each one for the blood of another, I will require a reckoning for human life. Whoever sheds the blood of a human, by a human shall that person's blood be shed; for in His own image God made humankind." Genesis 9:5-6 NRSV**

> **"So that the blood of an innocent person may not be shed in the land that the LORD your God is giving you as an inheritance, thereby bringing bloodguilt upon you."**
> **Deut. 19:10 NRSV**

> **"From oppression and violence HE redeems their life; and precious is their blood in HIS sight." Psalm 72:14 NRSV**

Does all of this information on fetal development sound like some mass of tissue is in the womb awaiting a breath of air from God to establish actual life? Not hardly. A few years ago, I lost my grandson Dylan who was taken by c-section stillborn at seven months. The cause of death was a twisted umbilical cord. It would appear that he played and twisted the cord too much, eventually cutting off his supply of life sustaining nutrients.

Dylan would have been my daughter Patty's second boy. We were all looking forward to his birth, when suddenly he stopped moving. In the hospital I had the opportunity to hold Dylan and I can tell you he was perfectly developed. At six pounds, he would have made it outside the womb if an accident had forced a premature birth before he died. Dylan's fully formed and perfect body changed hearts on the issue of legal abortion.

If you choose to abort your baby, you should realize that is exactly what you are doing. You are not dealing with a glob of tissue that has no life. You are killing a living and breathing baby at some stage of their development. What can their lungs breathe in the womb? They can take in amniotic fluid inside the uterus. That is what protects them and flows into their lungs when they open their mouths. The idea that there is no life until they breathe air is just another specious argument. God has provided the

Myth—Abortion Doesn't Matter

baby in the womb with life and survival until he is born. It is the mother's charge from God to protect that baby inside her womb from any harm. It is the mother and father's charge from God to then protect that baby after he or she is born and for as long as that child needs nurturing and care.

In the early 1970's when the abortion debate raged, I supported the idea of a woman's right to choose. I was wrong. It wasn't the first time and it won't be the last. It wasn't until 1978-79 after I read the Bible that I realized just how wrong I was. You too can change your position when you realize God's perspective. That is why I changed. I came to know HIM.

The doctor in the *Eclipse of Reason* stopped performing abortions because of what the ultrasound images disclosed to him. He could literally watch the baby take evasive action in the womb attempting to avoid being killed by his instruments. This doctor witnessed and documented that there was human intelligence observable in the baby and at work in the womb.

Contrary to popular mythology, life does exist in the womb. This doctor states that ultrasound images document that a first, second or third trimester abortion is no different than infanticide. It is just murder at a different stage of the baby's development.

The idea that a baby is not a viable human being until it leaves the womb is just another specious argument. If a mother does what God charges her to do and protects her baby in the womb, the baby can become a viable human being. It won't occur at birth neither just because it breathes air. At what point could you just walk away from any child and expect it to live by taking care of itself? One year? Two years? Three years? Get real. The idea that a baby has to first emerge to become "viable" is just another evil argument. As our level of technology continues to expand, life will be pushed back to the very point of conception. That is when human life truly begins.

The simple proof of the fact that human life begins at conception *is the fact* that a fertilized egg [zygote] can be transplanted and placed into any woman's womb that will protect her baby. That "womb" protected baby will then come to full term barring any complications in the pregnancy.

Myth—Abortion Doesn't Matter

Neonatologists specialize in keeping babies alive. The technologies they use have pushed the survivability of babies delivered prematurely down to a weight of only 1-2 pounds. Consider the wonder of the Internet picture [15] shown below. If you walked away from a 1-2 pound baby, it would die within a few hours. However, neonatology can help these babies to survive. It is well known now that a baby prematurely born at 5 months can live. Had the 5-month gestated boy aborted in the documentary *Eclipse of Reason* been born prematurely instead, he would be alive today. That is something every woman should consider carefully. After all, it's now *her* choice?

Taking care of the fetus has advanced to the point where surgery on the fetus can take place inside the mother's womb. In the picture [16] on the next page, baby Samuel is undergoing spina bifida surgery at 23 weeks of gestation. In a very emotional picture of human life in the womb, the baby is shown holding the surgeon's finger. You don't think that there is a human baby with intelligence in the womb? Get educated and if you call yourself a Christian, get right with God on human life. Every baby inside a womb is God's creation in spite of whose female egg or male sperm may be involved. That is what God's Word teaches us.

Doctor's Hands Hold Tiny Baby!

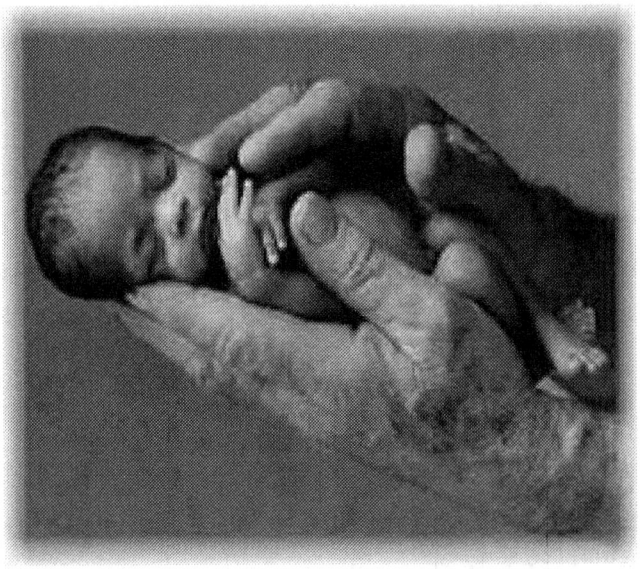

Myth—Abortion Doesn't Matter

Doctor Performs Spina Bifida Surgery On Fetus!

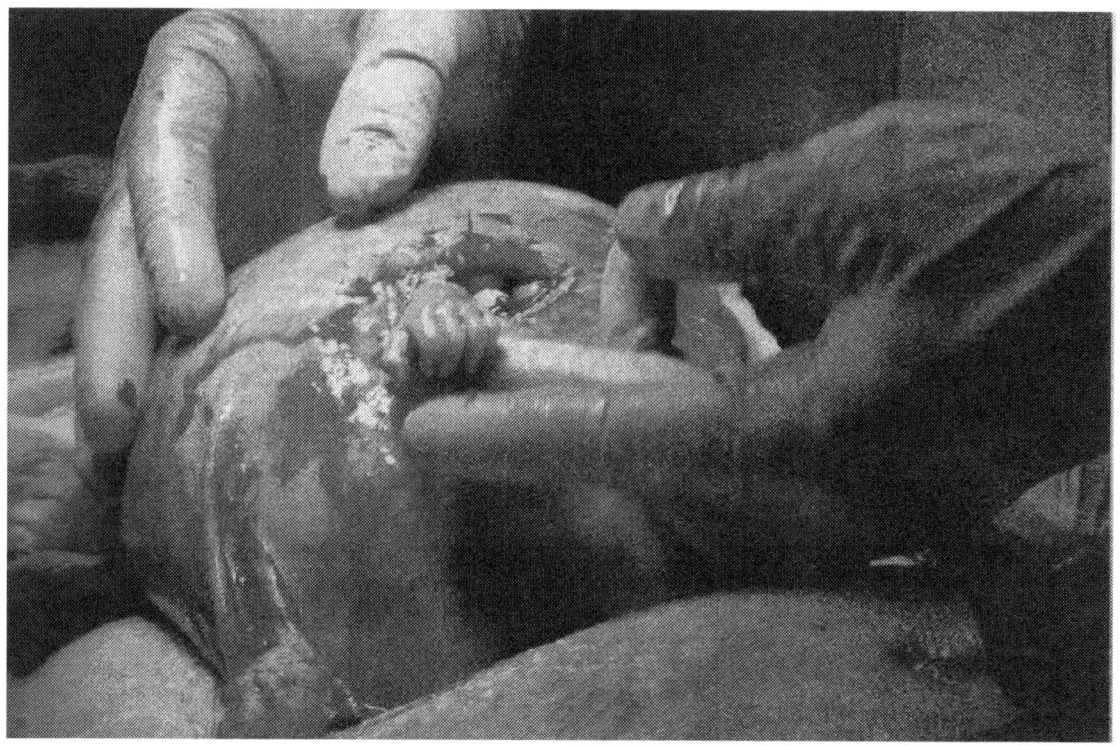

The baby shown in the first photo is only as big as the loving hands that hold it. Perhaps that baby only weighed 1-2 pounds? I remember when my daughter Patty was born. She wasn't much bigger than this. She could literally fit in a small shoebox. Of course it didn't take long for her to grow.

More amazing to me is that Jackie's father Archie was born and only weighed an estimated 1-2 pounds. In the early 1900's they didn't have incubators, but the mothers had compassion for their babies and would fight tooth and nail to help them survive. They had compassion for their babies while in the womb or out of the womb. In the case of Jackie's father, Archie was placed in a small box on an oven door that was used to keep him warm. He eventually grew strong enough to take off of the oven door and away from what had to be a wood or coal based heat source. That is Archie's story as best I can recall. Yet, what if there had been no compassion in the heart of Archie's mother? What then?

Myth—Abortion Doesn't Matter

Only God Knows Your Future Descendants!

The consequences of "aborting" Archie are staggering to me. I would never have met my beloved Jackie and enjoyed our 39-year marriage. We would not have three adult children alive today and seven going on eight grandchildren. Think about the future generations that are enabled as the result of the compassion of Archie's mother for a child of her womb. Those who abort a baby have no idea of what was supposed to come about as a result of that baby's life. These people play God, but are ignorant of the future generations that will unfold. Perhaps they are aborting another Beethoven? Perhaps a future president of the United States, artist, inventor, humanitarian, etc is being aborted. Who can tell the "predestination and purpose" of a newborn baby except our God? Archie's family tree unfolds.

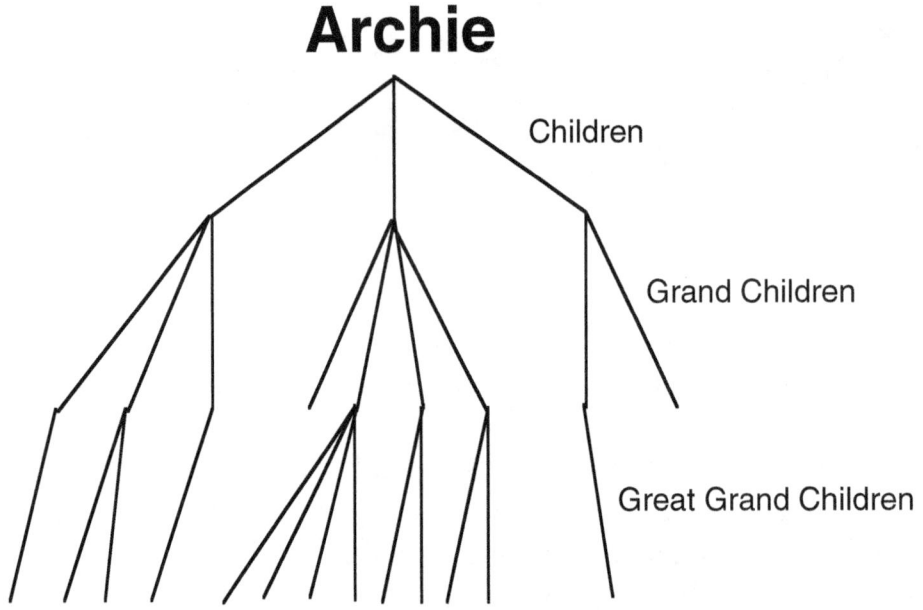

This family tree is only three generations. What would 41 generations look like? Thousands of lives would emerge because of one. I lost my own father when I was 13. Archie was a father to me for over 30 years. I loved him as my own dad during that time and I'm crying just thinking of the love he brought into my life and what that love has meant to me. Where there is love, there must be compassion. Where there is compassion, there is mercy.

Copyright 2005 Edward G. Palmer, All Rights Reserved.

Book of Edward—Chapter 18

Myth—Abortion Doesn't Matter

There Is A Time For Compassion!

Compassion is a good thing. You can tell that by all the politicians that seek to offer compassion to the families of the 932+ soldiers now lost in the Iraq during the War on Terrorism. I spent 7.5 years in the U.S. Navy and three tours off Vietnam. My heart too goes out to those lost in war fighting for our freedom. A good deal of that fight for freedom is for your "right to life." It is for that very ideal imbedded in our Declaration of Independence. Yet many of those who have compassion for the loss of our soldiers have no compassion for the loss of 4,000+ innocent unborn babies aborted each day.

Some of those who advocate abortion on demand express compassion and mercy over the loss of various animal and sea creatures. Substantive campaigns from abortion supporters have been waged to save from death the spotted owl, dolphins, whales, eagles and various other creatures. But these same people worshipping at the altar of "woman's choice" offer the creature that God created in HIS own image no compassion or mercy. Then there is PETA [17] — an organization using violence to protest unfair and inhumane treatment of animals. Where is their compassion and mercy for unfair and inhuman treatment of human babies? It's the height of hypocrisy when they'll go nuts over the way chickens are killed at a poultry plant but won't utter a word about the way humans babies are killed in the womb?

A key biblical question to ask is this. Exactly when is an abortion sanctioned in God's Word? The biblical answer is that it isn't except in the case of a natural miscarriage uninfluenced by human causation.

Lifestyle Choice Abortions

When should we give compassion and mercy to a woman to allow her a lifestyle choice abortion, since having her baby would be inconvenient? The biblical answer is never. God's *fashioned human life* should not be the subject of the capriciousness of any woman's lifestyle *choice*. Life in the womb should be honored and respected, not tampered with. However, given man's intervention by artificial insemination, the issue has become more complicated for women. We have intruded onto God's sacred ground.

Copyright 2005 Edward G. Palmer, All Rights Reserved.

Myth—Abortion Doesn't Matter

What about the case where a woman is artificially inseminated with 10 embryos with the hope that one takes, but they all do? Should the woman be expected to carry all of them to term? No, it would put her life in danger. Whenever man has intruded onto God's sacred ground, he has created many such problems. Here is a novel question. If a woman cannot conceive, what makes her think she was supposed to? Cruel question? Maybe. But I am mindful of Scripture where God has closed and opened wombs without the benefit of doctors, sperm banks and artificial insemination technology. Who knows the reasons why some women have no children, some have one child and others have many. This is where true faith comes into play. There are always reasons why these things occur, but today we grow impatient and we want what we want when we want it. That certainly pertains to children.

The ultimate lifestyle abortion recently occurred in New York by a 34-year old woman [18] who found herself pregnant with three babies. In this case she had not seen a fertility expert, but had simply gone off birth control pills. She had a set of twins in her womb and a third baby estimated to be three days older than the twins. She decided it was her *choice* to engage in a practice called *selective reduction*. Since she only wanted one, she aborted the twins and carried the third to full term. To abort the twins, the doctor injected a shot of potassium chloride into the hearts of those two babies.

In her own words, Miss Richards says: "Peter asked, 'Shouldn't we consider having triplets?' And I had this adverse reaction: 'this is why they say it's the woman's choice, because you think I could just carry triplets. That's easy for you to say, but I'd have to give up my life.' Not only would I have to be on bed rest at 20 weeks, I wouldn't be able to fly after 15. I was already at eight weeks. When I found out about the triplets, I felt like: It's not the back of a pickup at 16, but now I'm going to have to move to Staten Island [from Manhattan]. I'll never leave my house because I'll have to care for these children. I'll have to start shopping at Costco and buying big jars of mayonnaise. Even in my moments of thinking about having three, I don't think I was ever considering it."

This is the epitome of the lifestyle choice abortion and it is happening all too often now because many women believe its okay to kill their babies.

Copyright 2005 Edward G. Palmer, All Rights Reserved.

Book of Edward—Chapter 18

Myth—Abortion Doesn't Matter

Rape Abortions

Merriam-Webster's [4] *rape* definition is: "*Unlawful sexual activity and usually sexual intercourse carried out forcibly or under threat of injury against the will usually of a female or with a person who is beneath a certain age or incapable of valid consent.*"

So what about rape? This is a specious argument in the abortion debate since it is almost non-existent in abortion statistics. While we should have compassion and mercy on a rape victim, it should occur as the rape perpetrator is sufficiently punished by either castration or death.

"But if the man meets the engaged woman in the open country, and the man seizes her and lies with her, then only the man who lay with her shall die. You shall do nothing to the young woman; the young woman has not committed an offense punishable by death, because this case is like that of someone who attacks and murders a neighbor. Since he found her in the open country, the engaged woman may have cried for help, but there was no one to rescue her."
Deut. 22:25-27 NRSV

When a promised [committed] woman was raped in biblical times, she was expected to cry out for help, but this was not always possible. The punishment for such rape was "death" for the man. If we don't have the courage to kill the rapist, we should at least castrate him. That is my own humble opinion. On the other hand, the raped woman was not to be harmed. This also pertained to any child in her womb, which might be caused by the rape. I'm sorry to inform you, but killing babies wasn't an option in those days for victims of rape. It wasn't the baby's crime!

If a woman was able to cry out for help, which was nearby but did not do so, her penalty was also death. The two biblical points to consider are: First, every woman was required to cry out for help. Second, everyone was required to come to the rape victim's aide. How many needless rapes have occurred because people, who could have helped the victim, refused to get

Myth—Abortion Doesn't Matter

involved? God still expects us all to "reprove" evil. *Jackie's advice to a rape victim would be to try to vomit, get sick and otherwise be a big turn off.*

Then there is the nuance of the rape of a non-committed woman in which case the man was forced into marriage for life and had to pay her father a stiff fine for taking his daughter's virginity. However, once again, killing the baby was not an option justified by the rape. That is because everyone knew that life was *still* a precious gift from God in spite of rape!

Incest Abortions

> Merriam-Webster's [4] *incest* definition is: *"Sexual intercourse between persons so closely related that they are forbidden by law to marry; also: the statutory crime of such a relationship."*

So what about incest? This is also a specious argument since it too is almost non-existent in abortion statistics. While we should have compassion and mercy on an incest victim, it should occur as the incest perpetrator is sufficiently punished by either castration or death. This of course assumes an act of incest rape has occurred, which will be discussed shortly. A study has been conducted on rape and incest victims. According to the authors of *Victims and Victors,* [19] "Many women in our sample aborted only because they were pressured to do so, and most reported that the abortion only increased their experience of grief and trauma." In addition to this unexpected reality, post-abortion research discloses women having abortions experience many harmful physical and psychological complications [20].

Two central biblical questions concerning rape and incest are: "What crime has the baby committed? And, who has authority to sit in judgment over the execution of the baby in the womb except God HIMSELF?"

Now if you profess to be a Christian, you should know that incest was part of the genealogy of Jesus Christ. Yes, that is right. If every incest baby were killed by abortion since time immemorial, Jesus Christ would not have been born because when you abort Perez you delete Jesus. Is this not God's way of teaching us not to kill the baby if incest or rape occurs? Study carefully now the genealogy of Christ as explained in Matthew 1:1-17. Note there are 41 generations from Abraham to Jesus Christ.

Myth—Abortion Doesn't Matter

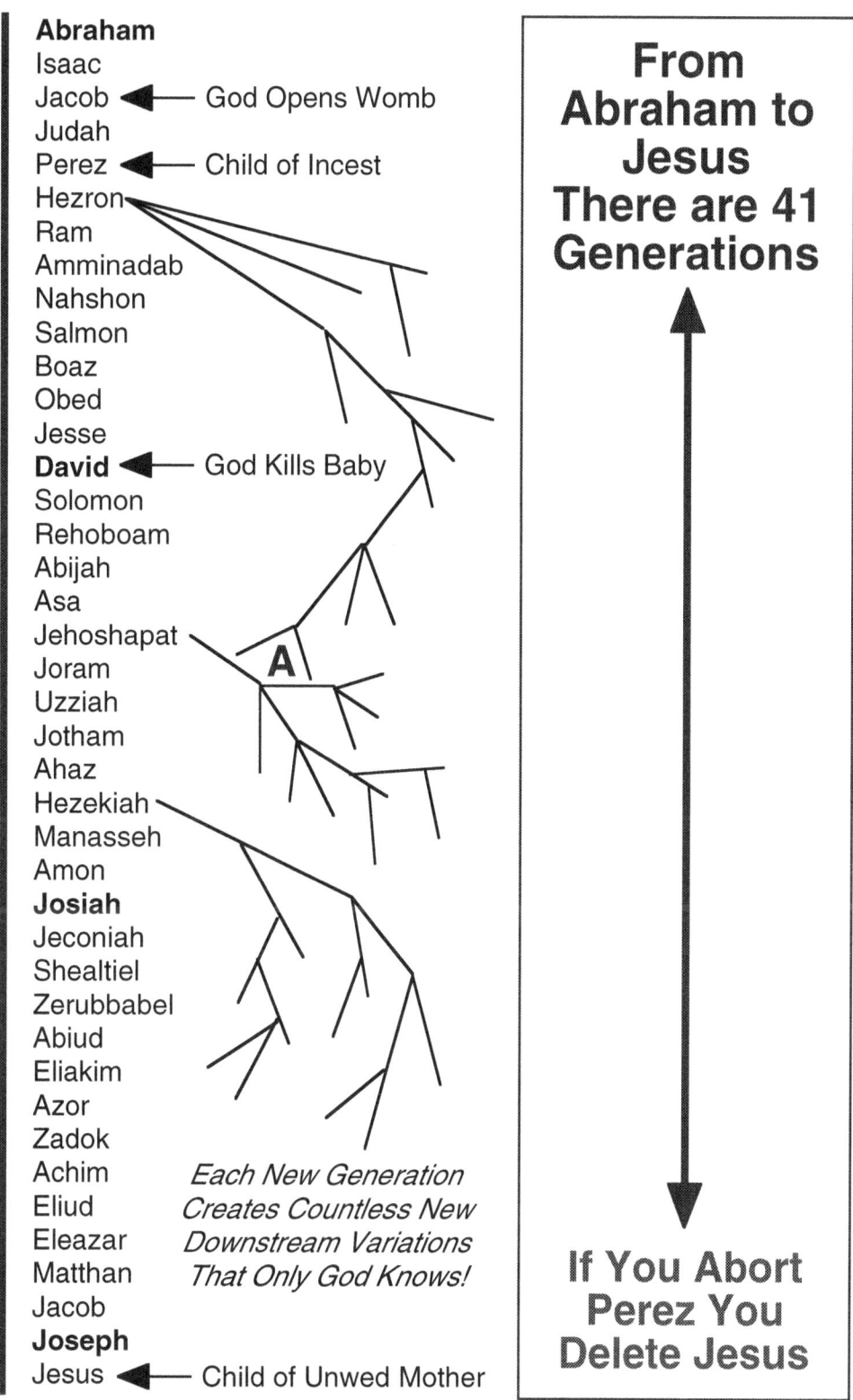

Book of Edward—Chapter 18

Myth—Abortion Doesn't Matter

The family trees represented in the above graphic are for illustration purposes, but the prior family tree of Archie was exact. Archie to his third generation has already engendered 25 human lives. His descendants in the 41st generation might add up into the thousands, since growth is geometric in nature. Archie's descendants are also reflective of a period in society that socially stigmatized large families.

When Jackie and I had three children walking with us, many looked down upon us as having too many children and being irresponsible. That is the way attitudes were in the 1970's. Today, men and women marry later in life and have even fewer children. However, that is not how it was in the time of Jacob, when he fathered twelve children. Jackie had wanted a dozen children, but fate required us to stop at the fourth live birth. Who except God knows what lies in the future of a baby? It is possible that descendants down stream generations later can actually cross one another's path leading to countless variations in humanity. This is represented by point "A" in the above graphic illustrating family trees. You are a descendant of all your ancestors' efforts. Any one of their abortions would have deleted you.

In this real sense, aborting a baby commits genocide on that baby's God given line of descendants. Doesn't God tell us this much in Deut. 30:19 and isn't *life* a choice of the heart as discussed previously in chapter seven? Listen and consider HIS Holy Word again as it may be clearer in the context of abortion. "Choose *life* so that you *and* your *descendants* may live!"

> **"I call Heaven and earth to witness against you today that I have set before you life and death, blessings and curses. Choose life so that you <u>and</u> your <u>descendants</u> may live."**
> **Deut. 30:19 NRSV**

The above graphic illustrates several important issues in the abortion debate. First consider that God opened the womb of Leah allowing her to conceive. Later HE opened the womb of Rachel.

> **"When the LORD saw that Leah was unloved, he opened her womb; but Rachel was barren." Genesis 29:31 NRSV**

Myth—Abortion Doesn't Matter

Rachel was distressed that Leah was having children and that she was not. That is when she told Jacob that if he [Jacob] didn't give her children she would die. Jacob's angry response was, "Do you think that I am God?"

"When Rachel saw that she bore Jacob no children, she envied her sister; and she said to Jacob, 'Give me children, or I shall die!' Jacob became very angry with Rachel and said, 'Am I in the place of God, who has withheld from you the fruit of the womb?'" Genesis 30:1-2 NRSV

There wasn't a fertility clinic to attend or artificial insemination to obtain and certainly no doctor's *selective reduction* practice to limit the quantity of naturally occurring fetuses in the womb. God was in control and only HIS gift of life was needed. This was obtained through earnest prayer and a sincere heart. Yes, women actually prayed to God to have children and even today many continue with this practice.

The issue of incest comes into play when Jacob's descendant Judah [one of Leah's sons] unwittingly has sex with his pledged daughter in law who tricks him. This is a very interesting story that unfolds in Genesis 38 and is worthy of your careful study.

Judah took [selected] a wife named Tamar for his firstborn son Er. But Er was wicked in the sight of God who soon killed him. Judah's second son Onan was then required by tradition to take Tamar as his own wife providing his brother with an heir. Assuming Tamar could conceive, that child would then become Er's descendant. Onan knew this fact and rather than provide semen for Tamar to conceive, he "spilled it on the ground."

"But since Onan knew that the offspring would not be his, he spilled his semen on the ground whenever he went in to his brother's wife, so that he would not give offspring to his brother." Genesis 38:9 NRSV

The fact that he would not honor his brother with an heir angered God who then also killed him.

Myth—Abortion Doesn't Matter

> **"What he did was displeasing in the sight of the LORD, and [so] HE put him [Onan] to death also." Genesis 38:10 NRSV**

At this point, it was the duty of Judah's third son Shelah to take up Tamar as his wife and provide her with an heir for his brother Er. However, Shelah was too young so Judah sent Tamar to her father's house until he got older. It seems that Judah then decided not to take a chance with Shelah so he basically ignored Tamar's rights under family custom and Jewish law.

After Judah's wife died, he took a trip to Timnah to his sheepshearers. Tamar knew about the trip and posed as a harlot along the road. Judah then unwittingly had sex [incest] with his daughter in law. She obtained a pledge of Judah's signet, cord and staff until he later delivered a "young goat" he promised for her sexual services. Of course, when the goat was sent, the harlot Judah thought he had sex with and his pledge were never located.

Later Tamar is discovered with child and Judah is forced to deal with the fact he had withheld Shelah and was unrighteous in the matter towards Tamar. He also had to deal with the fact it was Tamar, his own daughter in law, whom he had sex with and not some harlot practicing along the road. Out of this unknown act of incest, Judah's semen gave Tamar twins whose names were Perez and Zerah. Perez is the fourth generation from Abraham in the lineage of Jesus Christ.

If Perez would have been aborted, 36 successive generations would not have followed and Jesus would not have been raised as Joseph's son as God designed. But you say, Edward, God would still have had Jesus born! If you think that, you miss the point of generational genocide when a baby is aborted. Substitute your own family here. Now remove your father's life from the equation. Where does that leave you? It deletes you! The point here is that only God knows the future of our descendants. When you mess with human life, you mess with God's perfect design for the future.

God can open the womb and even sanction a baby's birth that was the result of an act of incest. God can also kill a baby HE doesn't want to live. That is what happened to King David with the first child born of Bathsheba

Copyright 2005 Edward G. Palmer, All Rights Reserved.

Book of Edward—Chapter 18

Myth—Abortion Doesn't Matter

through his act of adultery. Murder and adultery were a part of David's sin with Bathsheba. The story is found in 2 Samuel 11. David repents and has another child with Bathsheba. Solomon is the second child of Bathsheba by David's semen and Solomon takes his place as the 14th generation from Abraham in the lineage of Jesus Christ.

Perhaps the ultimate message of love and life from God is of Mary herself as an unwed mother. This unwed mother was not deprived of her child in an age when a woman pregnant out of wedlock would be stoned to death. God ensured that a loving man with a caring heart would protect Mary. That is what my father did when he married my mother. She was an unwed mother with my sister Barbara. I can tell you that in all the years of my father's life, Barb and I had no clue that we did not have the same father. All we both knew was my father's love. That is what real love does. That is what God would ask of you and I concerning all children of the womb.

From the cross itself, Jesus Christ taught us to open up our hearts to love others. It doesn't matter if a child is related. You can love all children and they can love you back. All you need is a heart that is open to love.

"When Jesus saw his mother and the disciple whom he loved standing beside her, he said to his mother, 'Woman, here is your son.' Then he said to the disciple, 'Here is your mother.' And from that hour the disciple took her into his own home." John 19:26-27 NRSV

I'm back into tears again as I reflect on how Christ's message has played a role in the life of Jackie and I. Many times we have opened our hearts to an unrelated person. We have offered them love and have received love. Our lives have been enriched because of that willingness to even love others as our own children. We can love the rape victim, the incest victim and even the mother whose life is endangered by childbirth. Yet we would not just love the mother. We would also love the child of her womb. That is what God wants all of us do. HE wants us to choose love *and* life!

The act of incest between Judah and Tamar was not a forced rape nor did Judah who was deceived willingly do it. There are other such acts of

Myth—Abortion Doesn't Matter

deception in the Bible when it comes to incest. Study what Lot's daughters did when they got him drunk in Genesis 19. Not all acts of incest are by unwilling partners or by partners who are both willingly entering into the act. Yet any act of incest that fits within the same definition of forced rape or statutory rape should be dealt with on the same terms.

The perpetrator of incest rape should be killed or castrated or put away in prison for a very long time, as any rapist should. Incest is clearly defined as sex between closely related individuals. But it even applies to those in close proximity with your family such as adopted children or guests. You wouldn't expect an adopted child or a guest to take advantage of your young daughter sexually. This also fits the definition of incest and rape.

The headline [21] reads: *"Teen Gets 50 Years For Sexually Assaulting Girl, 10."* In a recent story, a teenage boy who was taken in to live with a Florida family was convicted of sexually abusing their young daughter on a regular basis starting at the age of 8. He was 19 when he was convicted and she was only 10. This is incest. In the biblical sense, incest involves people who are considered too close of a kin or relation. When this young man was accepted into the love of this family, he became a big brother in God's eyes and had no business sexually assaulting the parent's young daughter. While the judge did not sentence this 19-year old to death or castration, the 50-year prison sentence should send a strong message out into society. I would have preferred that he be sent back to his CREATOR because we are to *purge* evil!

The story doesn't end yet; this 10-year old got pregnant. She and her parents did not know that she was pregnant when she went into the hospital with stomach pains. In the hospital, she delivered a 1 pound 12 ounce boy. When the baby was ready, the girl and her parents took him home. They showed the love, compassion and mercy that God wants all of us to have for all babies. Rape and incest *are* terrible, but willfully killing the child in the victim's womb is an even worse thing in God's eyes. There should be love, compassion and mercy for the victim and for the child in her womb. If the victim is unable to raise the child, only a little love, compassion and mercy are needed to carry *her* baby to term. If she can give the child that much, God will provide her baby with a loving family to take over the rest of the job of raising the child. In this way, her baby's descendants can then live.

Copyright 2005 Edward G. Palmer, All Rights Reserved.

Book of Edward—Chapter 18

Myth—Abortion Doesn't Matter

Life of Mother Abortions

We don't know who will be a future descendant and that is why we should not abort any baby for any reason other than as needed to save the life of the mother. And guess what? It is not a given that this would be every mother's choice, because many mothers would sacrifice their own life in a heartbeat so that their baby could live. There is a strong connection and spiritual bond between a child and its mother. It is the kind that allows a mother to offer her own life to save her child's life. Why? Her spirit can transcend the nature of our earthly journey and look down the line towards the future descendants of her child. She recognizes that her role as an ancestor is already fixed, but her child's descendants is not. Such a decision is a choice of love and it surely carries with it God's eternal perspective.

> **"No one has greater love than this, to lay down one's life for one's friends." John 15:13 NRSV**

Of course, Jesus was talking about the life he was getting ready to lay down for his disciples, but the principle is universal when it comes to great love. Isn't it easier for a parent to sacrifice their life for their child's? I believe that where there is true love, this is an instinctive characteristic and not something that a parent has to think much about. Great love makes great sacrifices and such love can be found throughout humanity among those who do not insist on their own way. It fulfills God's teaching in 1 Cor. 13.

> **"Love is patient; love is kind; love is not envious or boastful or arrogant or rude. It does not insist on its own way; it is not irritable or resentful; it does not rejoice in wrongdoing, but rejoices in the truth. It bears all things, believes all things, hopes all things, [and] endures all things."**
> **1 Cor. 13:4-7 NRSV**

Love Does Not Insist On Its Own Way!

The New Living Translation states: "Love does not demand its own way." Yet isn't that exactly what the 34-year old Manhattan woman did?

Myth—Abortion Doesn't Matter

Isn't that exactly what many women do when they abort their baby? Whatever the excuse, it all boils down to that fact, which demonstrably shows a lack of love in God Almighty's eyes. Therefore, every Christian woman should study carefully what God teaches about love. Aside from not demanding one's own way, love bears all things, believes all things, hopes all things and endures all things. There is not a woman alive that cannot bear carrying her baby, cannot believe in the best for her baby, cannot hope for the best of all things for her baby and cannot endure the 9-months it will take to carry that baby to term. God has never taught us that life would always go our way. Sometimes the unexpected happens. When Jackie was with child, we had the attitude that she was "pregnant with possibilities."

Indeed every woman with child is pregnant with the possibilities of countless successive generations, which belong to that child. If you abort the child, you delete the child's descendants. Genocide? I think so.

Yet the baby's life would most likely be safe in all but the rarest of circumstances since *the life of the mother* argument is just another specious argument without merit and almost totally non-existent. No one argues not saving the life of the mother! Given 20-week babies can also survive, it is likely both mother and child would survive a crisis. That assumes of course that [the mother's and other's] "love doesn't demand its [their] own way!"

Embryonic Stem Cell Research

Abortion knows no limits when it comes to human life. That fact is illustrated by lab-created human embryos, which are destroyed or aborted as stem cells are harvested. The promise of stem cell research is for a cure to a variety of diseases and even a veritable treasure chest of human spare parts. Need a new kidney? Stem cell research offers the promise of growing you a new one that won't be rejected by your body. Theoretically, every body part can be grown again if the stem cell can be properly activated and directed to do each task. However, this is human life and those engaged in embryonic research will eventually answer to God. Let no one be confused about stem cells either. As of this date, adult stem cells offer equal or more promise and do not involve the creation and destruction of human life in its embryonic stage, which we know leads to a fully grown human baby in a willing womb.

Myth—Abortion Doesn't Matter

Life Belongs To God And Not Mankind!

Isn't embryonic research just another Frankensteinian science project? It might not involve the digging up of graves as in Mary W. Shelley's novel *Frankenstein* [4] and its numerous movie incarnations, but the scientific goals in regards to the "creation of life" are nonetheless similar. Frankenstein's willful destruction of human life to gain body parts is a relevant story idea. The scientific arguments for humanity's benefits are no doubt also similar. But life belongs to God and not mankind. Society should collectively get back to respecting human life from the moment of our conception until the moment of our natural death. Science should not be involved in the willful creation of human life *or* the willful destruction of human life in the guise of benefiting human life. If you support *any* embryonic research, you do not respect God; you profane His Holy name. Further, you do not know God!

"Know that all lives are MINE; the life of the parent as well as the life of the child is MINE." Ezekiel 18:4 NRSV

Not only does all human life belong to God, but also there is life in the human blood, and that blood-life belongs to the soul. We learn this soul fact in Genesis 9:4-7 by reading *The Stone Edition of the Tanach* and its Hebrew rendering [22] of Torah Scripture. Its commentary reinforces WHO owns life.

[4] "But flesh; with its soul its blood you shall not eat. [5] However, your blood which belongs to your souls I will demand, of every beast will I demand it; but of man, of every man for that of his brother I will demand the soul of man. [6] Whoever sheds the blood of man, by man shall his blood be shed; for in the image of God HE made man. [7] And you, be fruitful and multiply; teem on the earth and multiply on it." Genesis 9:4-7 TAN

The *Stone Tanach* commentary [23] on Genesis 9:1 reads: "The words '*Be fruitful and multiply*' will be repeated in verse 7. Here it is a blessing that the human race would be prolific; there it is a command to beget children (*Rashi*)."

Copyright 2005 Edward G. Palmer, All Rights Reserved.

Book of Edward—Chapter 18

Myth—Abortion Doesn't Matter

The *Stone* commentary [24] of Genesis 9:5 reads: "The Torah places another limitation on man's right to take a life: God will demand an accounting from one who spills his *own* blood, for a human being's life belongs not to him but to God."

The *Jewish Study Bible*, [25] adds the following commentary: "Genesis 9:5-6: By man in v. 6 may be more accurately rendered as 'in compensation for a human being.' Human life is sharply distinguished from animal life; the idea that human beings are created in the image of God (Gen. 1:26-27) requires a higher degree of respect for human life. In the Talmud [26], v. 5 is interpreted as a prohibition of killing oneself (*b. B.K. 91b*), and v. 6 is cited in support of the prohibition of abortion (*b. Sanh. 57b*). Jewish law strictly forbids suicide and allows abortion only in extreme situations and never for the purpose of birth control."

Get the blood-life-soul picture?

1. All life belongs to God.
    a. Life of the parent belongs to God.
    b. Life of the child belongs to God.
2. Every human's blood has a life force contained in it.
3. The blood-life-force belongs to each human's soul.
4. God requires an accounting of any shed human blood.
5. Any man who sheds blood will have his own blood shed.
6. God will demand the soul of the human who sheds human blood.
7. God created man in HIS image.
8. God commanded man to beget children.

If you can understand that our soul owns our blood's life force, maybe you can then understand why God had the following dialogue with Cain.

> **And the LORD said, "What have you done? Listen, your brother's blood is crying out to ME from the ground!"**
> **Genesis 4:10 NRSV**

Blood Is Crying Out To ME From The Ground!

Myth—Abortion Doesn't Matter

We know that a 4-week old embryo has its own blood circulation. Do not the souls of aborted embryos and fetuses scream out from the ground to God? If the blood of Cain screamed out to God, surely the blood of millions of innocent fetuses will. *Christian, your brother and sister's blood is crying out to GOD from the ground. Can you hear? If not, why? I can hear them!*

I don't believe there is one scientist who will stand before God and proclaim that a human embryo is not innocent blood in HIS eyes. Even at the stage of conception in a petri dish in a science lab, life belongs to HIM. And who will be held accountable to God for the shed innocent blood of those human embryos and the estimated 40 million+ aborted babies since 1973? I believe that every single human that supports abortion will be held accountable to God. Woe to everyone who fails to reprove such evil.

God's Word Prohibits Abortion!

In an email letter to my dear friend Dean, Reverend Paul Schenck, the Executive Director of www.gospeloflife.com and www.faithandaction.org explains this blood life Scripture even further from his Hebrew perspective. Paul was born and raised a Jew along with his twin brother Rob in a New York Jewish family. Both Paul and his brother converted to Christianity and both of them are Christian ministers. Therefore, when Paul cites additional supporting Hebrew and Rabbinic text, you should listen carefully.

Rev. Paul Schenck writes [27]:

Dear Dean:

May God bless you and keep you today and everyday!

The text I referred to was the Hebrew version of Genesis (what we call "B'reshith" in the Hebrew) 9:6. This passage is the object of the oldest gloss on a scriptural text that we have from Rabbinic Judaism.

The Rabbis read the Hebrew as -- shefech dam ha'adam b'adam damu y'shafecha key b'etzelem elohim asah et-hadam – "He who sheds the blood of the human who is in the human, by a human shall his blood be shed."

Myth—Abortion Doesn't Matter

The ancient Rabbis said this is the prohibition of abortion; the "human (adam) within the human (b'adam)" is the child in the womb. So, this prohibits the taking of a life in the womb. In addition, the Rabbis state that to kill the child in the womb is equivalent to killing all the generations that would have come from that child - so it is morally equivalent to genocide.

The Rabbis point out that this proscription comes within the context of what are called the "Noachides" or commandments of Noah. Even before the Ten Commandments were given at Sinai, there were certain laws, according to the Rabbis, that were given through Noah and were binding on all men. Among them, no man may take an innocent life even if this is the only way to save his own.

This is what the prohibition against abortion was based upon. This was also directly connected to the duty to have children: Gen 9:1,7 "Be fruitful and increase."

This puts the lie to the oft-repeated fallacy that while Christianity is mostly pro-life, Judaism is mostly pro-choice. Even in modern Judaism, abortion is permitted only if there is a direct threat to the life of the mother by carrying the unborn child to term or through the act of childbirth. In such a circumstance, the baby is considered 'a rodef', a pursuer after the mother with the intent to kill her. Nevertheless, as explained in the Mishna (Oholos 7:6), if it would be possible to save the mother by any other means, including amputation of a limb, abortion would be absolutely forbidden.

Reverend Paul Chaim Benedicta Schenck

God Commands: "Do Not Sacrifice Your Offspring!"

"You shall not give any of your offspring to sacrifice them to Molech, and so profane the name of your God: I am the LORD." Leviticus 18:21 NRSV

Myth—Abortion Doesn't Matter

Molech: *"(Moloch)* [28] *(has the same consonants as the Semitic word for king). The name of the national god of the Ammonites, to whom children were sacrificed by fire. He was the consuming and destroying and also at the same time, the purifying fire."*

YAHWEH warned HIS people not to follow the evil ways of the Ammonites by sacrificing their sons and daughters. In fact, HE taught them not to intermarry, because they would then become corrupt and just as evil. Despite God's repeated warnings and instructions, HIS people intermixed in marriage and soon engaged in the same evil act of sacrificing their own offspring by fire to the idol Molech. Solomon even built a place of worship for Molech for the Ammonite wives he had married. God taught HIS people "right from wrong, but they would not listen or obey." Sacrificing children is an abomination and incredibly evil in God's eyes. Do you respect God?

In God's Perspective: "What An Incredible Evil!"

"The sins of Israel and Judah-the sins of the people of Jerusalem, the kings, the officials, the priests, and the prophets-stir up MY anger. MY people have turned their backs on ME and have refused to return. Day after day, year after year, I taught them right from wrong, but they would not listen or obey. They have set up their abominable idols right in MY own Temple, defiling it. They have built pagan shrines to Baal in the valley of the son of Hinnom, and there they sacrifice their sons and daughters to Molech. I have never commanded such a horrible deed; it never even crossed MY mind to command such a thing. What an incredible evil, causing Judah to sin so greatly!" Jeremiah 32:32-35 NLT

Isn't abortion just society's *new* way to sacrifice an offspring? What makes Abortionites any different than the Ammonites? Verily I say unto you, abortion *is* the willful sacrifice of our children and it is an even worse abomination and act of evil in God's eyes. Is there a difference to God in aborting a baby in the womb or taking a 1-2 year old and putting him or her on a pile of fire to sacrifice to Molech? What about a 12-year old sacrifice?

Myth—Abortion Doesn't Matter

Fallen Angel Teaches Man To Kill Embryo!

It would seem to me that the sheer volume of sacrificed offspring of the Abortionites makes their evil worse in God's eyes than the sacrifices of the Ammonites offspring to Molech. Abortionites now sacrifice over 4,000+ offspring each day. In their wildest imagination, the Ammonites didn't even scratch the surface of that abominable evil. If you think that abortion is a modern method of killing an embryo, think again. It has ancient roots! The only thing new today is the efficient methods abortionists have found to "smite" the human life in the womb. In fact, we read in the Book of Enoch that it was one of the fallen angels that taught mankind to kill the embryo.

> **"And the fifth [angel] was named Kasyade; this is he who showed the children of men all the wicked smiting of spirits and demons, and the smiting of the embryo in the womb."**
> **Project Timothy Online — Book of Enoch 69:12** [29]

> **"The name of the fifth [angel] is Kasyade: he discovered to the children of men every wicked stroke of spirits and of demons: The stroke [smite] of the embryo in the womb [is] to diminish [kill] it." ENO 68:18** [30]

Perhaps you think that all of the above-mentioned Scripture represents some nice stories and simplistic blood-life-soul metaphors? Maybe. But no one can deny that ancient documents tell the story of the killing of babies in the womb and also of child sacrifice to idols. No one can deny that God has indicated in the Christian Holy Bible how evil this is in HIS eyes. Therefore, intellectually, one returns to a salient point made earlier in the book. That is: "You either believe in God's Word or you don't." If you think you can lift salvation via Christ out of Scripture and just ignore these life facts from God, guess again. Such a person *will* hear Jesus say: "I never knew you!"

Beyond actual Scripture, there is the issue of the character of God. Study HIS character and you will come to the conclusion that the Hebrew interpretation is correct. "He who sheds the blood of the human who is in the human [womb], by a human shall his blood be shed."

Copyright 2005 Edward G. Palmer, All Rights Reserved.

Book of Edward—Chapter 18

Myth—Abortion Doesn't Matter

Genesis 9:6 should not engender some kind of debate. God created us in His image. God told us to 'beget' children. God told us not to shed any innocent blood. God told us not to sacrifice children. Listen carefully! Perk up, as the next question is critical. Are not these simple teachings from God His eternal characteristics? Doesn't abortion run counter to His commands? He has not changed. It is human rationalization that tries to alter His Word.

A Perspective On Love, Compassion & Mercy!

The picture [31] at the right is of a 6-week old fetus. You can observe the head, eyes, hands and tiny fingers in this 1/2 inch 1/2 ounce baby. If you go back to page 706, you will again learn that this baby already has a four chambered heart and nostrils. That beside fingers, toes are now forming and reflex activity has begun with the development of the brain and nervous system. Electrical brain waves have been recorded around this point in development. Do you still think this is just a glob of tissue suitable to be sucked out of the woman's womb with a vacuum device?

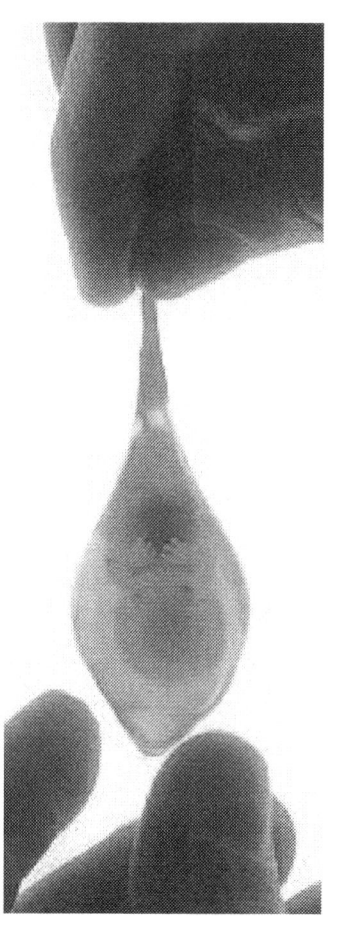

Most women will not even realize that they are pregnant and "with child" until after the baby has become at least this age and is well on its way to full development. However, most abortions occur after this point and it is clearly the murder of human life at the altar of "woman's choice." If you offer compassion and mercy in this life, God will give you compassion and mercy.

> **"But the woman whose son was alive said to the king — because compassion for her son burned within her — 'Please, my lord, give her the living boy; certainly do not kill him!'" 1 Kings 3:26 NRSV**

Myth—Abortion Doesn't Matter

God's illustration in 1 Kings 3 shows a woman who would rather give up her child to another woman than see that child be killed. Solomon demonstrates wisdom by offering to cut this baby into two pieces and give each woman who claims the baby one-half. However, the true mother then steps forward and offers to give the child to the other woman rather than see that child be killed. God's Word says: "Compassion for her son [baby] burned within her." Don't sacrifice your baby!

Last week a headline [32] read: *"Doctors Struggle To Help Tiny Baby."* In yet another illustration of life from God, an 11-ounce baby boy was born very prematurely at 23 weeks. "Born in Hutchinson, a team from Children's Hospital and Clinics was there to help keep Gabriel alive." He weighed less than a 12-ounce can of Pepsi or Coke and was physically smaller in size, yet after five weeks and 1 pound 9 ounces he has almost doubled his weight. Gabriel's mother says: "Oh my God, he's so little. I was trying to think of an angel, so I picked the name Gabriel because it means messenger of God. He's here for a reason, he's got a point to make and so far we've been lucky and grateful with Gabriel and he's been doing well." Minnesota's Gabriel is taking Neonatology to another new level because of his 11-ounce birth.

The joy I observed in Gabriel's mother's eyes while watching the news story is the joy I saw in Jackie's eyes after she gave birth to our own children. Even with the trauma of an early birth, one can observe the love in a mother's eyes for her baby. It is the God given mother's love that we are witnessing. It bears all things, believes all things, hopes all things and endures all things for her baby. We shouldn't question the joy of a woman who has just given birth even under traumatic conditions for her joy is God given and normal. Instead, we should question why any woman would give up her baby without the fight of her life. That is an abnormal response. It is not a God given response; it is a manmade-programmed lifestyle response. It is not God friendly; it is worldly.

> **"When a woman is in labor, she has pain, because her hour has come. But when her child is born, she no longer remembers the anguish because of the joy of having brought a human being into the world." John 16:21 NRSV**

Myth—Abortion Doesn't Matter

If you want a simple message of life from the Bible, it is Apostle John's teaching that bringing your baby into the world will bring you joy. You don't have to have everything just right before you give birth. I don't recall anyplace in the Bible where you should first get established with a home, a car, a savings account, a college fund for each prospective child, etc before you and your spouse have a baby. The only thing you need is love in your heart for that child. Children raised in abject poverty can still rise to untold heights of achievement. It happens all the time and the Horatio Alger stories are a testament to this reality.

I remember living in the projects of north Minneapolis in 1959. The family next door had six kids and the mother was pregnant once again. We were all living in poverty so I asked the mother, "How can you have another child given your financial situation?" Her response to me was: "If there is room in the heart, there will be room in our family." She is right. It's all about the heart and who has room [love] in it and who doesn't. Got love?

Tiny Gabriel's message from God is simple for anyone to understand. Compassion and mercy must be given to the most defenseless members of society to protect their lives. There is no human in need of more protection than a tiny baby inside a mother's womb. The reason baby parts are more valuable [1] when "processed" v. "unprocessed" is because of the tiny [almost microscopic] nature of those baby parts at an early age. See above photo. If you abort a baby, its tiny body will be dissected at the cellular level and used in countless evil experiments. This is *not* love, compassion or mercy!

> **"As a father has compassion for his children, so the LORD has compassion for those who fear HIM." Psalm 103:13 NRSV**

> **"The LORD is good to all, and HIS compassion is over all that HE has made." Psalm 145:9 NRSV**

> **"The compassion of human beings is for their neighbors, but the compassion of the LORD is for every living thing."**
> **Sirach 18:13 NRSV**

Myth—Abortion Doesn't Matter

Want Mercy? Then Proclaim Mercy!

"Embrace your children until I come, and proclaim mercy to them; because M\ysprings run over, and M\y grace will not fail." 2 Esdras 2:32 NRSV

"But if you had known what this means, 'I desire mercy and not sacrifice,' you would not have condemned the guiltless."
Matthew 12:7 NRSV

"Blessed are the merciful, for they will receive mercy."
Matthew 5:7 NRSV

"Thus says the L\ord of hosts: Render true judgments, show kindness and mercy to one another." Zech. 7:9 NRSV

"Woe to you … for you … have neglected … justice and mercy and faith." Matthew 23:23 NRSV

"For judgment will be without mercy to anyone who has shown no mercy; mercy triumphs over judgment."
James 2:13 NRSV

"H\e makes room for every act of mercy; everyone receives in accordance with one's deeds." Sirach 16:14 NRSV

"If one has no mercy toward another like himself, can he then seek pardon for his own sins?" Sirach 28:4 NRSV

"Because you have forsaken M\e, I also will forsake you. When you beg mercy of M\e, I will show you no mercy."
2 Esdras 1:25 NRSV

"If you, then, will rule over your minds and discipline your hearts, you shall be kept alive, and after death you shall obtain mercy." 2 Esdras 14:34 NRSV

Copyright 2005 Edward G. Palmer, All Rights Reserved.

Book of Edward—Chapter 18

Myth—Abortion Doesn't Matter

God Helps In Human Procreation!

"Now the man knew his wife Eve, and she conceived and bore Cain, saying, 'I have produced a man with the help of the LORD.'" Genesis 4:1 NRSV

Eve, who bore the first human child, acknowledged that her child "was produced with the help of the LORD!" This is the truth of procreation and a woman does not have a child "on her own." She also does not have a child when it is actually born and delivered out of the womb. A woman "is with child" from her time of conception. That is God's perspective as HE has fashioned that child in the womb because HE loves children.

Abortionites Are Lovers Of Themselves!

Abortion fulfills some "last days" prophecy in that it is a documented act of a woman's self-love over her God-love by those who Timothy says are "*lovers of themselves.*" Apostle Timothy speaks directly to women who take their baby's life via abortion. Yes, some Abortionites are "captivated silly women, overwhelmed by their sins and swayed by all kinds of desires, who are always being instructed and can never arrive at a knowledge of the truth." They look inward instead of to God. I didn't say it, Timothy did.

"You must understand this, that in the last days distressing times will come. For people will be lovers of themselves, lovers of money, boasters, arrogant, abusive, disobedient to their parents, ungrateful, unholy, inhuman, implacable, slanderers, profligates, brutes, haters of good, treacherous, reckless, swollen with conceit, lovers of pleasure rather than lovers of God, holding to the outward form of godliness but denying its power. Avoid them! For among them are those who make their way into households and captivate silly women, overwhelmed by their sins and swayed by all kinds of desires, who are always being instructed and can never arrive at a knowledge of the truth." 2 Tim. 3:1-7 NRSV

Copyright 2005 Edward G. Palmer, All Rights Reserved.

Book of Edward—Chapter 18

Myth—Abortion Doesn't Matter

God Loves Children!

"Behold, children are a gift of the LORD; the fruit of the womb is a reward." Psalm 127:3 NASB

"YOU created my inmost self, knit me together in my mother's womb. For so many marvels I thank YOU; a wonder am I, and all YOUR works are wonders. YOU knew me through and through, my being held no secrets from YOU, when I was being formed in secret, textured in the depths of the earth. YOUR eyes could see my embryo. In YOUR book all my days were inscribed, every one that was fixed is there." Psalm 139:13-16 NJB

"Upon THEE I was cast from birth; THOU hast been my God from my mother's womb." Psalm 22:10 NASB

"Thus says the LORD: For three transgressions of the Ammonites, and for four, I will not revoke the punishment; because they have ripped open pregnant women in Gilead in order to enlarge their territory." Amos 1:13 NRSV

"Then they made their sons and their daughters pass through the fire ... and sold themselves to do evil in the sight of the LORD, provoking HIM. ... And the LORD rejected all the descendants of Israel and afflicted them and gave them into the hand of plunderers, until HE had cast them out of HIS sight." 2 Kings 17:17-20 NASB [33]

"The sin of child-sacrifice, in fact, is mentioned as one of the major reasons that the kingdom of Israel was destroyed by the Assyrians and the people taken into exile. Notice that this practice was a religious ritual. Not even for 'religious freedom' can the killing of children be tolerated." [33]

" 'Who are these with you?' ... [They are] 'The children whom God has graciously given [to] your servant.' "
Genesis 33:5 NASB

Myth—Abortion Doesn't Matter

There Is A Time To Hate! Eccles. 3:8

Fast forward 18 years from now and ask yourself how the child of the 34-year old Manhattan woman who aborted his twin siblings will feel when he finds out the truth of her actions. Will he feel that his mother truly loved him or that he was just the lucky fetus? What if his mother had wanted two? Would she have chosen the twins over him? Now think about a child whose mother carried to term and then gave up to adoption. He was told his mother chose to give him life because of her love, but was unable to raise him as her own child. Perhaps these young men will meet in college and compare their mother's love someday. Who will say their mother had the *greatest* love? The selfish interests of one woman were interrupted by the reality of three babies and a future lifestyle different than what she had planned. She hated the idea of a life focused on motherhood and three children.

Childbirth is not the time for anyone to hate; it is a time to rejoice over "the children whom God has graciously given." However, there is a time to hate and God's Word makes that fact abundantly clear. You should hate what God hates. HE hates the shedding of innocent blood and the killing of children either in the womb or out of the womb. No one can deny the clear Bible references that prohibit abortion unless they are among those who Jesus does not know. Do you know God's Son? If you do, you should also know God and that HE expects us to hate all forms of evil.

My friend Dean said: "It's a paradox. You are actually loving when you hate what God hates." Indeed, love should be genuine and part of that genuine love is to hate what is evil and to hold fast to what is good.

"Let love be genuine; hate what is evil, hold fast to what is good." Romans 12:9 NRSV

The "A" exegesis graphic below takes into account the character of God. Many doctrines are limited to the *Biblical and Historical* context "B." Because that approach fails to take into account what God loves and hates, it yields false doctrines such as claiming the Bible supports abortion or trying to say that the Bible is silent on the subject. Model "C" places "B" into the context of "A." Only with this model can you discern God's truth.

Copyright 2005 Edward G. Palmer, All Rights Reserved.

Book of Edward—Chapter 18

Myth—Abortion Doesn't Matter

God's Character
Context of what He Loves and Hates!

A

Theology Consistent With God's Character

B

| Biblical & Historical Context |
| Theology In Context | Theology Out of Context |

C

God's Character
Context of what He Loves and Hates!

| Biblical & Historical Context |
| Theology In Context | Theology Out of Context |

Theology Consistent With God's Character

Myth—Abortion Doesn't Matter

If You Can't Hate, You Don't Know God!	

God hates these seven abominable things.
  1. A proud look
  2. A lying tongue
  3. Hands that shed innocent blood
  4. A heart that devises wicked plans
  5. Feet that are swift in running to evil
  6. A false witness who speaks lies
  7. One who sows discord in a family
	Proverbs 6:16
	
	All table verses are from NRSV. Note: This is not a full or complete study of what God hates.

God hates all evildoers.	Psalm 5:5
God abhors the bloodthirsty and deceitful.	Psalm 5:6
God hates wickedness.	Psalm 45:7
God hates robbery and wrongdoing.	Isaiah 61:8
God hates evil in hearts and false oaths.	Zechariah 8:17
God hates divorce.	Malachi 2:16
Hate every false way; Hate the double-minded.	Psalm 119:104; 113
Hate those who hate the LORD.	Psalm 139:21
Hate intensely what God abhors.	Sirach 17:26

"There is a time to hate!" Eccles. 3:8 NRSV
"The LORD loves those who hate evil." Psalm 97:10 NRSV

Exodus 21:22-25 Exegesis!

This brings us back to an exegesis of Exodus 21:22-25 and whether God places a different value on the life of the mother and the fetus [baby] in her womb. Some modern translations give that exact impression by using a "miscarriage" metaphor. The NRSV translation is not alone and even a Hebrew translation [34] makes the same mistake. These interpretations fail to consider the bigger context of God's eternal character. Therefore, they are myopic in their interpretation of Exodus 21:22-25. This doesn't make them useless translations since most Bibles do contain some vagaries. However, the NKJV is one modern translation that does get Exodus 21 right. The NKJV wording parallels the KJV translation, but with updated English.

Copyright 2005 Edward G. Palmer, All Rights Reserved.

Book of Edward—Chapter 18

Myth—Abortion Doesn't Matter

[22] "If men fight, and hurt a woman with child, so that she gives birth prematurely, yet no harm follows, he shall surely be punished accordingly as the woman's husband imposes on him; and he shall pay as the judges determine. [23] But if any harm follows, then you shall give life for life, [24] eye for eye, tooth for tooth, hand for hand, foot for foot, [25] burn for burn, wound for wound, stripe for stripe."
Exodus 21:22-25 NKJV

"Some common errors in the translation of these verses [35]*:*

I) 'With the result that her child comes out' is often translated, 'so that she has a miscarriage' (ex. NASB, NRSV). This is impossible because:

 a) The Hebrew text (page 684) says literally, 'so that her fruit goes out.' The verb that translates 'goes out' is the word, which refers to the ordinary birth of a child, not a miscarriage. Also, the noun that translates 'fruit' is the ordinary word for a child or offspring [birth], not a stillbirth. (See Gen. 25:24-26, 38:28-29; Job 1:21; 3:11, Eccles. 5:15; Jer. 1:5, 20:18)

 b) In Hebrew, a miscarriage or stillbirth is indicated in only two ways. 1. By the description of the child (ex. Numbers 12:12) or 2. By the Hebrew word for 'miscarrying' whether with humans (ex. Ex. 23:26; Hosea 9:14) or animals (ex. Gen. 31:38; Job 21:10) or land and plants (ex. II Kings 2:19, 21; Malachi 3:11).

II) Another common error of translation is the addition of words, which are simply not in the Hebrew text as God has given it to us. For example, in the NASB, the middle of verse 22 is translated, 'yet there is no <u>further</u> injury.' (NRSV states '<u>if any harm follows</u>') Likewise in verse 23 they write, 'But if there is <u>any further</u> injury.' These words give the impression that 1) verse 22 refers to a miscarriage and 2) that the <u>death</u> of the unborn baby isn't worth as much as even the *slight injury* to the mother. This couldn't be farther from the truth."

Myth—Abortion Doesn't Matter

"Therefore, these verses tell us that if some irresponsible person causes a premature birth with no injury to mother or child, the irresponsible person still must be punished simply because of the danger it caused both mother and especially to the child. Furthermore, if any injury is done, the guilty person suffers equally, and the list begins by emphasizing that if the baby dies, the guilty one is to be killed also, as a murderer. Verse 23 applies specifically to the unborn baby because the 'life for life etc.' principle applies to a woman, even if she is not pregnant. So the unborn child is considered fully human. To kill an unborn child is murder (life for life) punishable by death. [35]

Other verses from the Bible show that God considers the unborn child fully human: Psalm 139:13-15; Job 3:11 (we are already whole persons at birth); Jer. 1:5; Luke 1:39-44. Psalm 127:3-5 speaks for itself." [35]

Continue reading in Exodus 21:26 and you'll find that if a servant is struck by its master and loses an eye, the servant will be set free "for the sake of that eye." In Exodus 21:27 you'll find out that if a servant loses a tooth, the servant will be set free "for the sake of that tooth." Now consider that it is the master's wife who is with child and whose baby is prematurely killed. Do you honestly expect that only a fine would be given for the death of the master's child when freedom is given for the simple loss of a tooth to a servant? Woe to all who fails to take into accounts the character of God in their exegesis. HE will repay you for such evil and especially the church, which teaches HIS Word. I am not exempt. Abortion is evil!

What if you've had an abortion, supported an abortion or failed to reprove an abortion? What then?

It is never too late to repent to God for having an abortion, supporting abortion or failing to reprove an abortion. True repentance involves a changed heart. It means that you recognize the truth of God's perspective on the issues of human life and turn away from self-serving, self-loving ways. True repentance is observable by your reproving of all abortion activity. If you would not hesitate to make a public reprove of abortion, you have truly repented in your heart. God corrected my sin of supporting abortion in the 1970's and I repented. *"For whom the LORD loves HE corrects, just as a father the son in whom he delights." Proverbs 3:12 NKJV*

Copyright 2005 Edward G. Palmer, All Rights Reserved.

WARNING. If you are a minister that teaches that abortion rights are okay, set your house in order with God. If you are a believer in abortion rights, set your house in order with God. Both of you should cease to spread these lies about God's Holy Word. Verily I say unto you, it is believers in the truth that shall see God's salvation for it is written, "They did not welcome the truth but refused to love it that they might be saved." [2 Thess. 2:10 AMP]

"Therefore God sends upon them a misleading influence, a working of error and a strong delusion to make them believe what is false. In order that all may be judged and condemned who did not believe in [who refused to adhere to, trust in, and rely on] the truth, but [instead] took pleasure in unrighteousness." 2 Thess. 2: 11-12 AMP

PRAYER. O LORD GOD, free YOUR people from the apostasy that is rampant in the Christian Church today. Surely, if a minister cannot teach the truth about how precious human life is, they cannot be trusted to teach anything from YOUR Word. They are indeed unfit for anything good and should cease their ministry activities. What should stand true for all concerned is that these false teachers "will perish because they were not lovers of the truth!" Lovers of the truth do not pervert YOUR Word for anything. Amen.

"The social idea that abortion is somehow authorized, condoned, or okay with God and that it really doesn't matter to HIM is sheer mythology. Those who believe abortion is okay do not have God and HIS Son dwelling inside their hearts. True love does no harm!" The Apostle Edward

If God's Spirit Dwells In Your Heart, Your Spirit-Soul Knows That It's A ...

Myth—Abortion Doesn't Matter

Book of Edward

Chapter Nineteen
Myth—Sexuality Doesn't Matter

"The LORD respected Abel and his offering, but HE did not respect Cain and his offering. And Cain was very angry, and his countenance fell. So the LORD said to Cain, 'Why are you angry? And why has your countenance fallen? If you do well, will you not be accepted? *And if you do not do well, sin lies at the door [of your heart]. And [sin's] desire is for you, but you [yourself] should rule over [sin].*' " Genesis 4:4-7

"The mouth of an *immoral* woman is a deep pit; he who is abhorred by the LORD will fall there." Proverbs 22:14

"I wrote to you … not to keep company with … anyone named a brother, who is *sexually immoral* … " 1 Cor. 5:9-11

"But the … *sexually immoral* … shall have their part in the lake which burns with fire and brimstone, which is the second death." Rev. 21:8

"But outside are dogs and sorcerers and *sexually immoral* and murderers and idolaters, and whoever loves and practices a lie."
Rev. 22:15

"Come, let us make our father [Lot] drink wine, and we will lie [and both have sex] with him, that we may [get pregnant and] preserve the lineage of our father." Genesis 19:32

[The homosexual men said], "Bring out the man who came to your house, that we may know him carnally!" Judges 19:22

Myth—Sexuality Doesn't Matter

WARNING: *This is a sexually explicit chapter designed for mature readers and students of the Holy Bible. Having said that, I am writing this chapter with my grandchildren in mind who now range in ages 1-16. God, in HIS divine wisdom, is sexually explicit in the Holy Bible. The reason for that is HIS desire that we should be informed of all sexual matters from HIS perspective. If you are old enough to understand this paragraph, you are old enough to read this chapter. If you do not fully understand what I am saying right now, go get your parent or guardian to assist you before continuing on. For too long, Christians have not had a substantive teaching about God's perspective on human sexuality.*

God has said that those who are "sexually immoral" are excluded from Heaven and are even destined for "the lake of fire and a second death." Therefore, every Christian should learn God's truth and HIS perspective on our human sexuality. These might be *the* end times! In this chapter, I will attempt to clarify what God considers sexually *moral v. immoral* in HIS Holy Bible. While it is true that the Bible does not speak directly to some sexual subjects like oral sex or masturbation, God's Word still provides guidance to us on those subjects. Just like the subject of abortion, if you consider HIS character and relevant Bible verses, God will give your heart understanding of human sexuality. This assumes you've given your heart to God.

The last chapter considered the *heart v. intellect* in obeying God. This chapter considers the issue of you exerting control over your own sin. God expects you to exert control over sin! Given the physical pleasure in sex, it has to be the biggest test of our human spirit's ability to demonstrate control. Many fail to exert *any* control over their sexual sins. Others simply ignore sexual sins claiming that Jesus Christ has forgiven them and its now okay to be a "willful sinner." Yet God *does* reject sexually immoral people.

God Says To <u>Rule</u> Over <u>Your</u> Sin!

"**If you do well, will you not be accepted? And if you do not do well, sin lies at the door [of your heart]. And its desire is for you, but you should rule over it.**" Genesis 4:7 NKJV

Copyright 2005 Edward G. Palmer, All Rights Reserved.

Book of Edward—Chapter 19

Myth—Sexuality Doesn't Matter

> "You will be accepted if you respond in the right way. But if you refuse to respond correctly, then watch out! Sin is waiting to attack and destroy you, and you must subdue it."
> **Genesis 4:7 NLT**

> "If you do well, will you not be accepted? And if you do not do well, sin is lurking at the door; its desire is for you, but you must master it." **Genesis 4:7 NRSV**

> "If you do well, you hold your head up; if not, sin is a demon crouching at the door; it will desire you, and you will be mastered by it." **Genesis 4:7 REB**

> "If you are doing right, surely you ought to hold your head high! But if you are not doing right, sin is crouching at the door hungry to get you. You can still master him."
> **Genesis 4:7 NJB**

Is there a demon called sin crouching at the door of your heart seeking to master you and make you a slave to do its bidding? God's Word makes it clear that it is up to you to exercise control and "rule over that sin demon." The Revised English Bible says that the "demon" called sin seeks to master you. However, the New Jerusalem Bible says, "You *can* master [the demon] sin!" Consider the instructions from God to rule over and master *your* sin.

1. Sin desires to rule over you.
2. You must subdue sin.
3. You must master sin.
4. If you don't master sin, it will master you.
5. Sin is a *demon* crouched at your door and its desire is for you.
6. Even though sin is hungry to get you — *you can still master* sin!

The spiritual irony is that you cannot control sin when you don't even know what sin is. You can't know sin unless you know God and submit or surrender to HIS will. I was thinking about this issue and how difficult and complicated it can be to just change a bad habit. Control over sin?

Myth—Sexuality Doesn't Matter

Really? Exert control over our sin? For a moment, it seemed like a totally ridiculous idea to me a few nights ago. I have struggled to change many habits over my life. While I have succeeded for the most part, not one habit change has ever been easy for me. Now, here I am presenting the issue perhaps for you of having to face changing a sexual habit with eternal and mortal soul consequences that you have been engaged in for a very long time. This could be homosexuality, lesbianism, fornication, adultery, etc. Before I got too far in my thoughts, God reminded me of HIS Word in 4th Maccabees of which I wrote to you about earlier. You can go back to that discussion if you've forgotten [p219]. The essence of HIS teaching is that we *can* exert control over sin by first knowing HIM and what HE calls sin.

Reason, being the ultimate virtue of wisdom, will allow you to rule over your emotions. In order to obtain this skill, you first have to surrender to God. Go back to the discussion on "How to exercise control over sin with *reason*" if you need to review the teaching [p231]. It's as simple as ABCD.

#	Attribute	Spiritual Translation and Meaning
A	Salvation	Surrender of 100% of your heart to God Almighty.
B	Surrender	Respect for God and HIS righteousness and laws.
C	Respect	Wisdom or the fear of God unto true obedience.
D	Wisdom	Control by *reason* over sin crouched at your door.

Another spiritual irony is that you cannot control sin unless you first obtain wisdom from God since *reason* is the tool you will use to control sin and it is the highest virtue of wisdom [4 Maccabees 1]. Control over sin is the result of giving your heart to HIM. Don't expect to *exert* control over sin without getting to know HIM. You can't control what you do not know. And many don't care about sin, because they simply don't care about HIM.

Yet people can exert some control over sin and most routinely do! Remember, God has placed in our minds and hearts HIS laws. People who just listen to the Spirit inside them are a law unto themselves in God's eyes, but many people ignore what God has put inside of us. Yet, a full surrender of the heart leads to practical if not complete control over *all* willful sin.

Myth—Sexuality Doesn't Matter

> "For when Gentiles, who do not have the law, by nature do the things in the law, these, although not having the law, are a law to themselves, who show the work of the law written in their hearts, their conscience also bearing witness, and between themselves their thoughts accusing or else excusing them." Romans 2:14-15

It's <u>Your</u> Job To Control <u>Your</u> Sin!

The above discussion might challenge your thinking as someone who is "named" a Christian. How many times have you been taught you cannot help yourself and that is why you need Jesus? It's Christian mythology. God HIMSELF teaches you that *you* are responsible for ruling over *your* sin and not letting sin rule over you. That is what Hebrews 10:26 imparts as it teaches you salvation does not exist for those who choose to be willful sinners. Christ is supposed to bring you back to the FATHER. Your return to HIM is demonstrated by your heart's righteous behavior & actions.

Everyone who has "surrendered" knows that he or she can then exert control over sin and can certainly stop being a willful sinner. This doesn't make you perfect, but it does mean that you have chosen God's righteous side. Go back and read chapter 5, *Practice from the Heart,* if you do not fully understand that a behavioral transformation takes place in every true [sincere] believer's heart. Why should you exert control over your human sexuality? It means eternal life or a second death; that's why!

Guard Your Heart With Wisdom's *Reason*!

I provided a graphic of the communications model between the mind and heart in the last chapter. HIS Word states our intentions and actions in life flow out of what is in our heart. That is why God says to guard our heart carefully. WISDOM'S REASON *is* the guard that protects your heart.

> "Above all else, *guard your heart*, for it is the wellspring of life." Proverbs 4:23 NIV

Myth—Sexuality Doesn't Matter

"Above all else, *guard your heart*, for it affects everything you do." Proverbs 4:23 NLT

"*Guard your heart* more than anything else because the source of your life flows from it." Proverbs 4:23 GW

"With closest custody, *guard your heart*, for in it are the sources of life." Proverbs 4:23 NAB

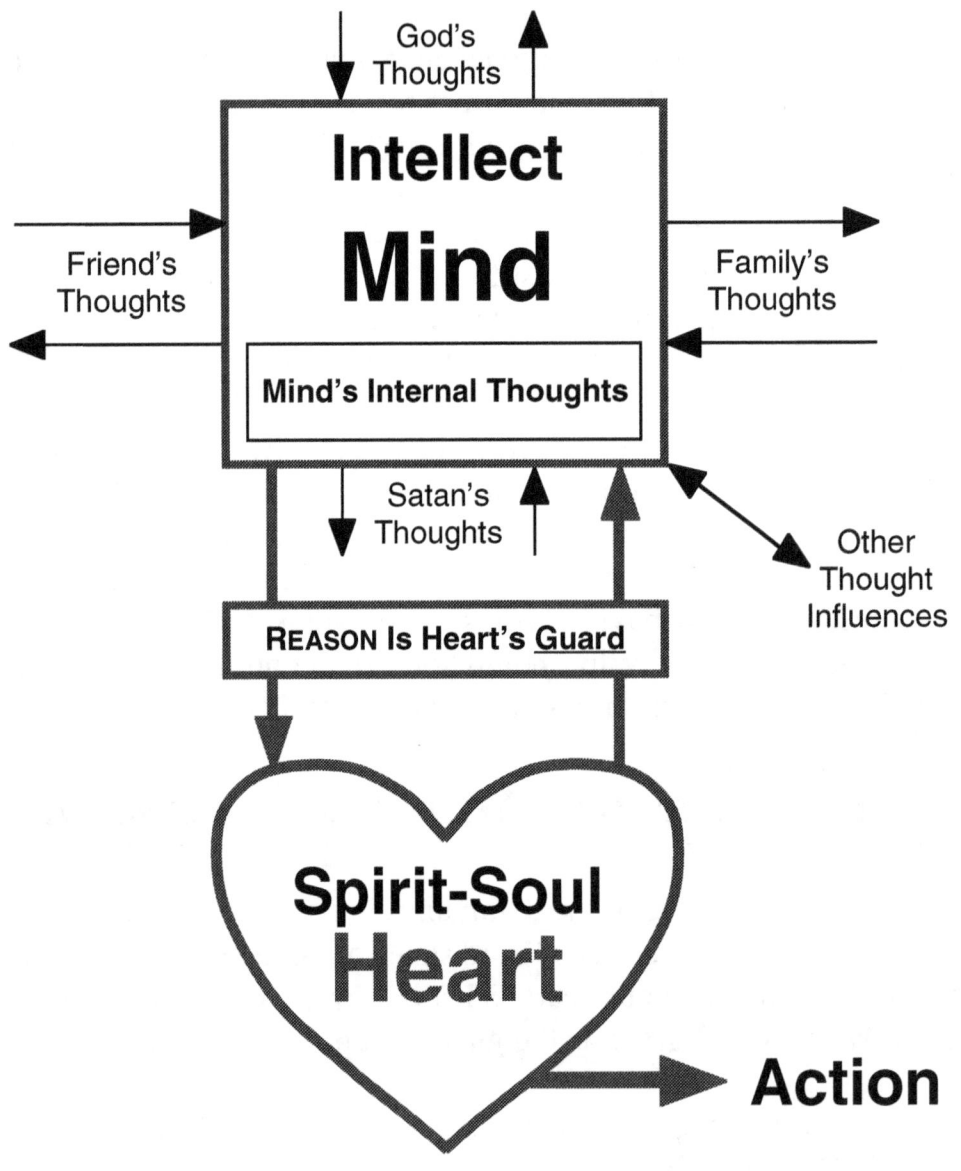

Myth—Sexuality Doesn't Matter

What will keep you safely in the path of sexual morality with God? It is the top virtue of wisdom called *reason*. Go back and study chapter 9 until you understand why godly *reason* is important to your eternal life. You cannot be rational on this earth without God and this attribute, which is possessed by those who love and fear HIM. Without this spiritual quality, you reason from a secular and morally debased position ignoring the fact that God does exist. This won't help you from an eternal perspective even though it may sooth your mind over the sexual immorality you are engaged in. But when you have God's wisdom, *reason* becomes sovereign over your emotions causing you to obey what God has commanded. Then you can understand what I've written concerning rational judgment on p238.

"When you exercise rational judgment, your reason will put into check your emotions. Then, your reason is sovereign over your emotions. With understanding and wisdom from God, you reason that God's Law:

1. Prevails even over the affection for parents, so that virtue is not abandoned for their sakes. 4 Mac 2:10
2. Is superior to love for one's wife, so that one rebukes her when she breaks the law. 4 Mac 2:11
3. Takes precedence over love for children, so that one punishes them for misdeeds. 4 Mac 2:12
4. Is sovereign over the relationship of friends, so that one rebukes friends when they act wickedly. 4 Mac 2:13" *And, God's Law*
5. Is sovereign over human sexual behavior unless one chooses to be *"sexually immoral"* and by such behavior the lake of fire and its second death as judgment. Rev. 21:8, 22:15

Reason is the gatekeeper to your heart. It only allows in what is truly in the core of your soul and being. If that is sexual immorality, then sexual immorality, which is evil, will reign in your heart. If your *reason* is that of God's wisdom, then it stops sexual immorality and other evil from going in and out of your heart. It is the guard that says no to anything that will cause you to sin. It functions that way because HIS Spirit informs you when sin is present or will be forthcoming. It is a spiritual *gift of fear* that God imparts to all who walk with HIM to remind us of our eternal life or death.

Book of Edward—Chapter 19

Myth—Sexuality Doesn't Matter

Mind Controls Wisdom's *Reason* Gatekeeper!

"Wisdom is with aged men, and with length of days, [comes a better human and spiritual] understanding." Job 12:12

God has imparted to me the gravity of this chapter for Christendom. I don't believe, however, that the seriousness of these writings will be limited to this chapter. This entire book should be earth shaking to a sleepy Church that has for too long simply ignored or altered His Word. And, for too long has also ignored the sexual nature and attributes of His human body design. Unlike Apostle Paul who was single and most likely tried to live a celibate life, I have spent most of my life as a sexually active male. That includes the sharing of a faithful, passionate and at times a very vigorous sex life with my wife of almost four decades. I have watched our marital interests in sex wax and wane and wax again over these many decades.

Sexuality has always been on my mind to varying degrees and I have studied and reflected on this matter to great extent over the years, both in His Word and in my discussions of the heart with Him. In addition, I have studied sexuality from a secular perspective and at one time I even had a library of books on sex that was fairly comprehensive in all respects. For reasons of mental sanity I disposed of that library section. Now, of course, I have access to a virtual sex library on the Internet. I've just spent 40-hours doing sex research on the Internet. I conclude that, while as parents or other family, we might want to hide sex information or not fully discuss sex with our children — that nothing is hidden regarding human sexuality and all of its imports good and evil to the student with unfettered online access.

I have carefully considered sexuality in terms of Scripture, my life's experiences and God's human body design. I believe God has given me the wisdom and understanding with the length of my days and the experiences of my own sexuality to provide you with this detailed discussion on sex.

"And to man He said, 'Behold, the *fear* of the Lord, that is *wisdom*, and to depart from evil is *understanding*.'"
Job 28:28

Copyright 2005 Edward G. Palmer, All Rights Reserved.

Book of Edward—Chapter 19

Myth—Sexuality Doesn't Matter

> **"Who has put *wisdom* in the mind? Or who has given *understanding* to the heart?" Job 38:36**

If you've ever wanted to identify a controversial Bible verse in terms of varied translations, Job 38:36 is an interesting choice and the diversity of translations is mind boggling to me. For example, the NIV and NRSV have "understanding" in the mind. The NIV has "wisdom" in the heart and the NRSV has "wisdom" in the inward parts. The NLT refers to "intuition and instinct." Other translations like the NJB use a bird analogy, "Who endowed the ibis [long slender bird related to the herons] with wisdom and gave the cock his intelligence?" Where did that come from? The meaning of the Hebrew appears somewhat unclear, but *The Stone Edition Tanach* [1] reads:

> **"[Do you know] who placed wisdom in the innards? Or who imbued the heart with understanding?" Job 38:36 TAN**

You might have thought that this Hebrew translation would settle the issue of where *"understanding"* resides, but the *Jewish Study Bible* reads:

> **"Who put wisdom in the hidden parts? Who gave understanding to the mind?" Job 38:36 JSB**

Is it important to know where *wisdom* and *understanding* reside? Yes, because God is questioning Job about his human intelligence and what he understands. You should be aware of these translation nuances. I'll use the NKJV for several reasons. First, it is a known fact that true understanding never occurs unless an issue actually leaves our mind and gets down into our heart. The heart is where our true belief [understanding] resides and that is why the old adage "take it to heart" gets its common sense meaning.

The NKJV translation is spiritually consistent with Apostle Paul's teaching on salvation to "Believe in your heart *unto* righteousness." Paul knew if you were saved, your actions would change because of a changed understanding in your heart. The NKJV is also consistent with God's teaching that the heart is "inclined" [action oriented] towards evil from its youth and Jesus' teaching that evil [action] comes from within our heart.

Myth—Sexuality Doesn't Matter

In contrast, wisdom connotes a depth of intellectual knowledge and mental discernment that only comes from the length of one's days, studies, experiences and God's input into the spirit-soul-mind. Therefore, wisdom and its "chief virtue" called *reason* is a faculty of the mind and its intellect while understanding is a faculty of the heart. Thoughts occur in the mind, the heart and in the "gatekeeper" of *reason*. Expressing these three internal primary thought sources yields the following graphics model.

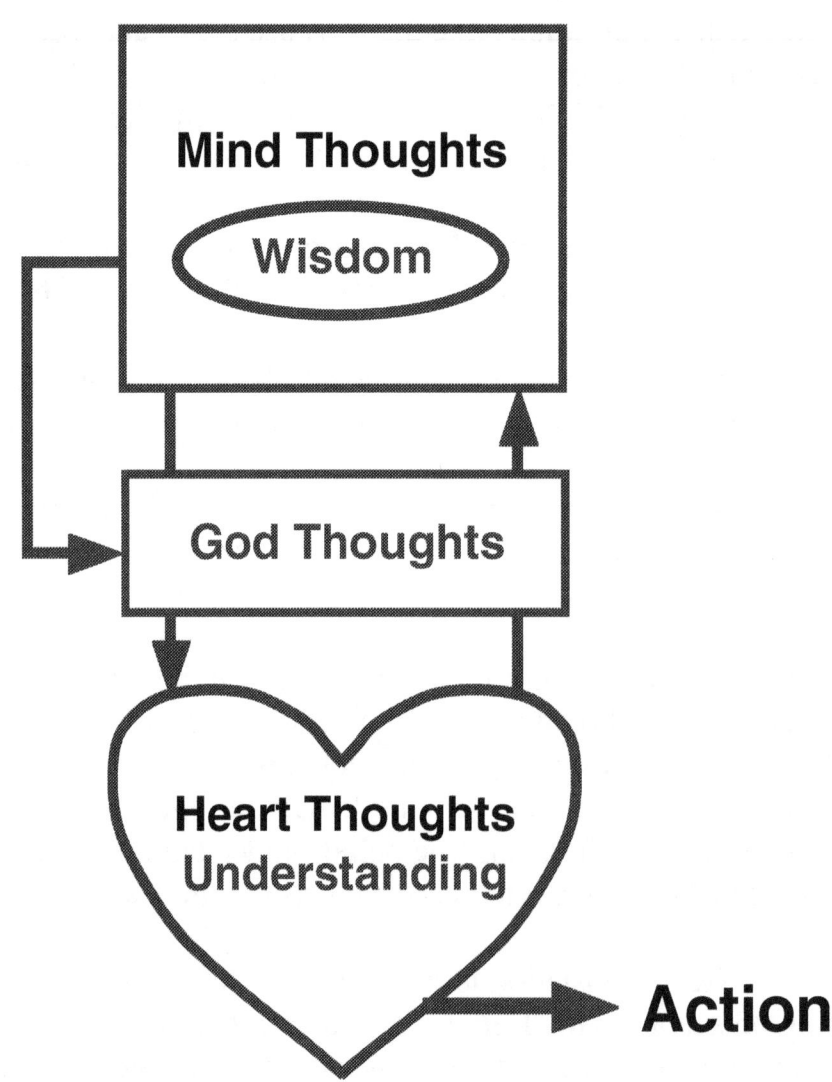

Three Primary Thought Sources "With God"

Myth—Sexuality Doesn't Matter

Those who "walk in the spirit" exhibit three primary sources of thought energy: A) mental thoughts from our mind, B) heart thoughts from our soul and C) thoughts of God from our spirit. The Spirit uses wisdom's *reason* as a gatekeeper to help us exert control over sexual immorality and other sins. The gatekeeper raises God's spiritual thoughts and inputs regarding every internal thought that flows back and forth from our mind to our heart. Visualize the gatekeeper as a simple light switch. If you get a *GO* signal from God, the light is turned *ON* guiding your path and confirming the action you plan is okay. If you get a *NO* signal from God, the light is turned *OFF* confirming the action you plan is not okay with HIM. Without God, only two primary thought sources normally come into consideration.

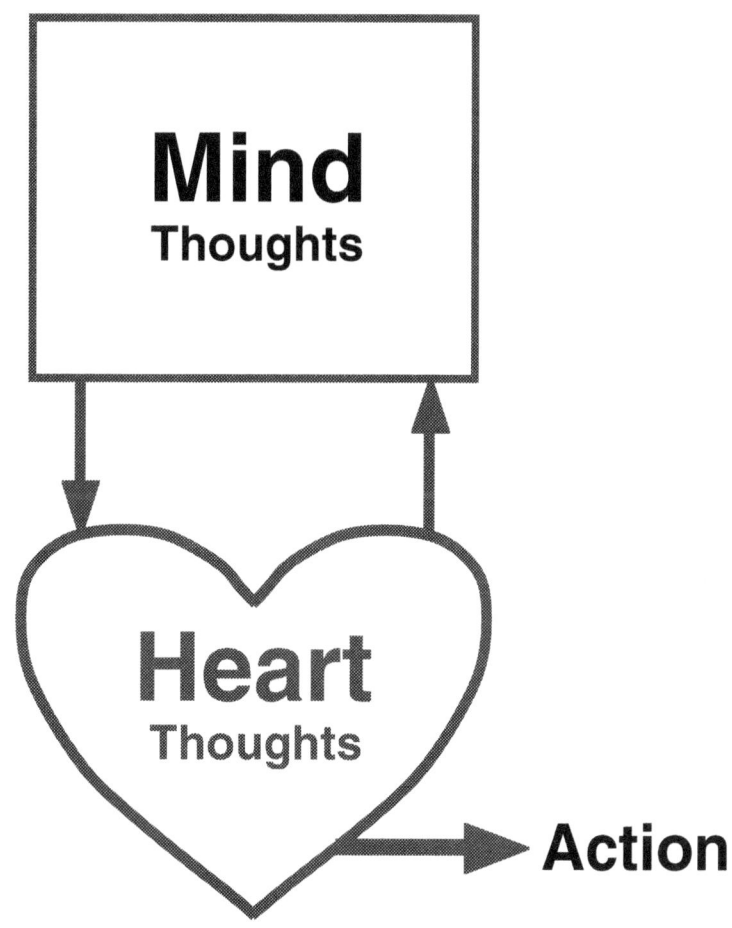

Two Primary Thought Sources "Without God"

Myth—Sexuality Doesn't Matter

In the simplest of explanations, without God, man thinks thoughts of what he wants to do in his mind and thoughts of what he thinks will feel good in his heart. Ergo, "If I want to do it and it feels good, I can do it!"

However, President Abraham Lincoln said [2], "When I do good, I feel good; when I do bad, I feel bad. That's my religion." The maxim holds true for all who walk with God, because they know what is good and what is bad. It would also hold true for those using only two primary thought sources that give deference to God by listening to HIS "internal" Law, which HE has written on our mind and heart. Paul taught that those who do listen to God's soft inner voice are saved, because "Their conscience bears witness, and between themselves their thoughts accuse or else excuse them." Indeed, those who obey God's inner voice are saved no matter what Christianity has to say about salvation. What a wonderful feedback mechanism God has given us. Good feelings set in when we do well. Bad feelings and remorse set in when we do badly or engage in sin. We get HIS feedback into our conscience as a soft inner voice regardless of whether we will listen to it.

A large body of sinners believes that "If it feels good, just do it!" And that is why they engage in acts of sexual immorality. In the three-thought model, it shows that God will actively engage our spirit telling us that even if it feels good physically, we are not to engage in evil. Remorse still sets in after immoral sex in a two-thought source person. However, this remorse is often compartmentalized mentally [set aside in the mind] and then denied. That is how President Bill Clinton dealt with his sexual immorality and adulterous acts with Monica Lewinsky in the White House. Can you see the contrast in the personal beliefs of these two presidents? Lincoln believed, "When I do good, I feel good." Clinton, who was then sexually immoral, simplistically believed "If it feels good, just do it." Clinton explained that, "I did it because I knew I could?" What about control? Are we animals?

Back in Genesis 4:7 God said to Cain, "If you do well, will you not be accepted?" It was another way of saying, "When you do good, you'll feel good and when you do bad, you'll feel bad." This is part of the internal ability to control sin that God built inside us. All any of us really has to do is listen to God's soft inner voice of conscience. Cain did not seek God's

Myth—Sexuality Doesn't Matter

heart. Nevertheless, God taught Cain [and us] that he [we] could control his [our] sin. However, no one can control sexual sins if their mode of thinking is "If it feels good, just do it." We have to *actually* do what *is* good! God is the ONE that defines what is good sexually and HE wants moral sex inside and outside of the marriage! This begs the question of whether there is such a thing as moral sex outside of the confines of marriage. Is there? If we are going to consider such intimate acts as fondling of our lover's breasts and joint fondling of each other's genitals even with clothes on [intense petting] and outside of marriage—this question needs to be properly addressed. Is the act of touching genitals and breasts a mortal sin? If it is, few of us can escape God's wrath. Exactly where is the line that godly *fear* should set in?

Clinton's sexually immoral actions were based on human feelings and not on considered thoughtfulness. As such, Clinton demonstrated he was a two-thought source person who *could* ignore God's soft inner voice. God was subservient to Clinton's desires. That is why he pronounced to our society that he couldn't find "oral sex" anywhere in the Bible. Ergo, he felt "oral sex" did not fit into the *legal* definition of sexual relations. What about the *moral* definition? There was time when lawyers did not formulate lies by parsing words in the English language. That is what Clinton did when he used his "oral sex" excuse and also when he parsed the word "is" in Federal Court to obfuscate the truth. Are these the actions of a Christian? No!

Lincoln based his actions on wisdom and the intellectual ideals of a God given morality as detailed in the Holy Bible, which should always be obeyed. His was a full thought process from a person living with three primary thought sources guiding his considerations. In Lincoln's moral and simpler time, all actions boiled down to simply doing what was good and *moral in God's eyes*. Most people understood God's morality in those days, which is not true in the year 2004. This moral decay includes all Islamic countries that rationalize the beheading of innocent people in the name of Allah. However, God's morality is different. HE hates the shedding of innocent blood. The general lack of morality in the world's population is therefore not limited to the United States; it is a worldwide evil.

> # Thoughts, <u>Then</u> Actions, And <u>Then</u> Emotions!

Myth—Sexuality Doesn't Matter

Do a good deed and you'll feel good. Do a bad deed and you'll feel bad. Our emotions will always follow our actions. Our actions will always follow thoughts. Feeling bad? Then take some action that is good and you'll feel good again. You can literally change your emotions and present feelings in life simply by changing your thoughts. Changed thoughts result in changed actions, which result in changed emotions. God has built inside of us a unique human feedback process, which convicts us of evil and sin whether or not we "actively" walk with God. That is what the soft inner voice of conscience is all about. It is God tugging on every heart to change our lifestyle while we still can. A normal thought-action process is simple.

A. Normal Thought-Action Process

Thoughts, leads to **Actions**, which lead to **Feelings**

B. Sexually Immoral Action-Thought Process

Feelings, leads to **Actions**, which lead to **Thoughts**

C. Spiritually Enhanced Thought-Action Process

Spirit influenced **Thoughts**, leads to **Actions,** which lead to **Feelings**

God's feedback also emerges in the feelings that we encounter after any action we take. Do we feel good about what we have done? Or, do we feel bad? God meant for a Spirit-led active thought process to guide our actions and prevent sin. Sexually immoral people have bought a debauched feel-good philosophy, which turns off God's soft inner voice of conscience that could spare them much misery in this earthly life. However, they can't turn off HIS feedback by way of our emotions. God will make sure we get HIS input one way or another even if it's an after action emotion that makes us feel bad. Those who embrace God and walk with HIM as I have done will find that HIS Spirit will actively influence their thoughts. They'll also adjust to God's life plan instead of their own life plan, as I certainly have done.

Myth—Sexuality Doesn't Matter

Therefore, our thoughts normally lead to external actions that may or may not have an impact on others. Those actions also may or may not be sinful *in God's eyes*. However, another model exists for the celibate priest, monk, eunuch or otherwise self-contained person who is physically isolated from external sexual influences for a variety of reasons. These people cut off or limit sexual inputs in the hopes of maintaining some degree of control over this area of their minds, hearts and bodies. A two-thought model is presented albeit the individuals cited are likely using a three-thought model.

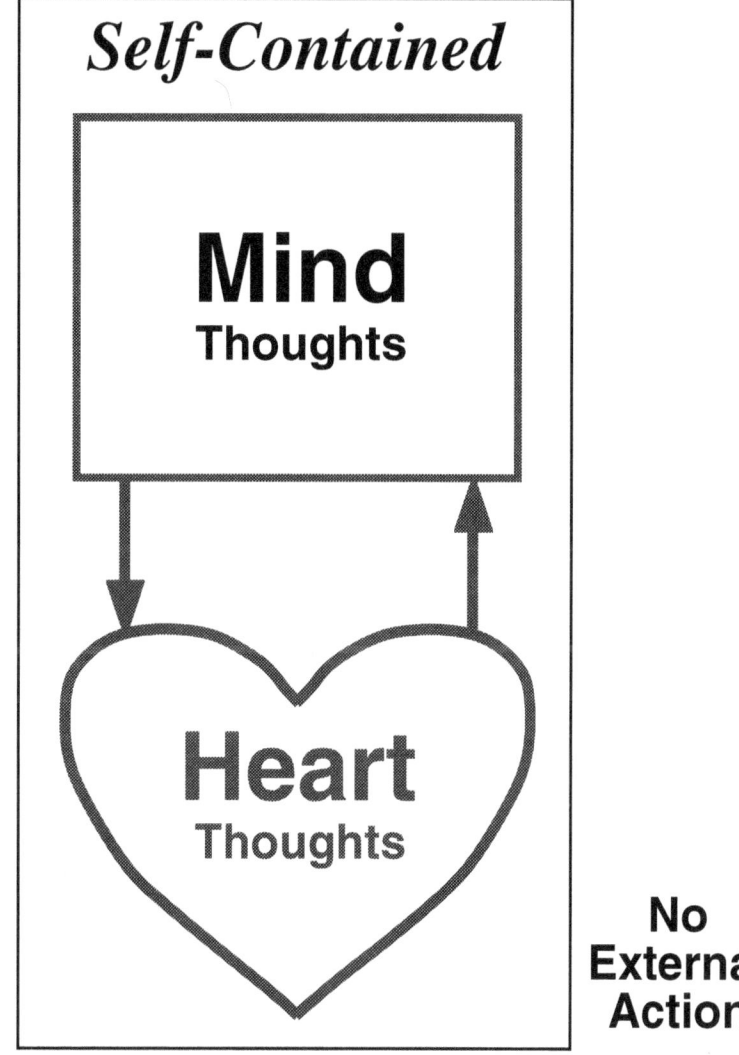

Two Thought Self-Contained Action/Sin Model

Myth—Sexuality Doesn't Matter

The above model reflects on individual sexual acts that have no impact on another individual and may have been done in privacy by one's self. For example, the solitary act of masturbation either male or female is raised by the implications of the model. If such an act is done in private and alone without impacting others—is it still an act of sexual immorality? Is it the "impure" sexual thought that condemns such an individual, as many Christians would assert? Is it the physical stroking of the penis or vagina and clitoris that is sexually immoral? And is the mere touching or looking at one's genitalia sufficient to get us into trouble with God? These are some of the sexual questions that Christian parents and others would like answers to.

Certainly by HIS design of the human body, HE made sex good and very pleasurable to engage in. The Church, however, has historically gone out of its way trying to convince everyone that sex is not supposed to make us feel good. Yet anyone who has actually experienced sex will recognize this teaching as a lie that is inconsistent with God's *pleasure* design of the human body. This has led to great confusion and I might add considerable mental agony over all sexual activities including those in the sanctity of the marriage bed. Ergo, if it feels good and is moral sex, why can't I feel good about enjoying it? There should be morality and also honesty about the human body in Church sexual teachings. Should a teenage boy be led to feel guilt because of a nocturnal emission of semen? Or that if he touches his penis while urinating that he might experience a sensation of arousal even though sex is not on his mind? Thus, a huge disparity exists between body realities and Church teachings in many quarters.

The three levels of sexual immorality shown on page 766 take us away from what might be innocent and normal sexual thoughts in our mind to engaging in *actions* that God *will* deem "sexually immoral." If thoughts leave the mind and get into the heart unchecked or unfiltered, they then have the possibility of leaving our being in the form of some *action* influencing or impacting others. If a thought is self-contained and does not leave our being, it does not usually impact others. I do not believe self-contained sexual thoughts are considered by God to be "sexually immoral" unless they impact others. Some external *action* must occur before we cross that line. For example the idea of "lust in the heart" that Jesus said was equivalent to adultery carries with it the definition [3] of having "*the strong desire to have*

Myth—Sexuality Doesn't Matter

sex with somebody, usually without associated feelings of love or affection." You can't be guilty of lust for simply thinking a sexual thought. Many men, including myself, might look admirably upon a physically endowed and shapely woman. This is not lust or immorality in God's perspective. That doesn't mean various churches would not condemn it. Consider carefully the words of Jesus, *because sin happens when heart action takes place*!

> **Jesus said: "But I say to you that whoever looks at a woman to lust for her has already committed adultery with her in his heart." Matthew 5:28** — *The heart's action is "to lust."*

The meaning of Jesus' words is, *"lusting for her in your heart!"* If you are walking with God, the gatekeeper stops all lustful thoughts from entering the heart. If you are not walking with God, most likely the thoughts still do not go down into the heart. It takes a lot of sexual energy to get from the mind to the heart. The mass majority of men can ogle a woman without getting lustful for her in their heart. Even if the act of ogling a woman is in itself a suggestive act. Exactly how do you think that male and females begin any relationship except by carefully eyeing one another first? I'm sorry, but ogling does not rise to the level of a mortal sin. In fact, it is questionable as to whether it even rises to the level of a sin albeit it could.

The mere visual or even mental thought that a woman is beautiful and physically looks good also does not rise to the level of mortal sin. Nor does the instant thought that it might be nice to have sex with her, since that is not a matter of the heart unless some action actually accompanies it. Mental thoughts in this sense are not a sin. If they were, 100% of all people would be doomed to the lake of fire. Instead, it is quite a normal activity to check out the opposite sex. In fact, we are all equipped to do so by design.

That doesn't mean that mental thoughts cannot doom a person to a life of sexual immorality, as they can. But those thoughts have to get lodged in the heart and not just the mind. Consider this Bible verse.

> **"For as he thinks in his heart, so is he. 'Eat and drink!' he says to you, but his heart is not with you." Proverbs 23:7**

Myth—Sexuality Doesn't Matter

Indeed, the *Strangest Secret* according to Earl Nightingale [4] is the fact that "we do become what we think about in our heart." Guard your heart as it is the where actions emerge from. Still, you get the picture. Thoughts are at several levels and those leading to sexual immorality are of the heart and not of the mind. That means you can carry on an unabashed sexual dialogue with God unafraid. It is not a sin to talk about any aspect of your sexuality directly with God. So go ahead and get sex answers for yourself in a direct dialogue. God *is* your friend. If sexual immorality resides in your heart, it *will* emerge as human sexual activity on three different levels. All three levels, if unrepented and practiced, will take you to the lake of fire.

Level I - Lewdness

Preoccupied and obsessing over sex.

Level II - Lasciviousness

Engaging in sexually enticing behavior.

Level III - Licentiousness

Engaging in sexual activities without God's moral considerations.

Myth—Sexuality Doesn't Matter

If you want to really meet a scary person, find someone without any sense of conscience, about good and evil. I met a young woman once who was exactly like this. She was an acquaintance of my son many years ago who I had met briefly while picking up my son. She had crashed her car and called my insurance agent pretending to be my daughter. She placed her car on my family auto insurance policy and then filed an accident claim.

I never would have known had I not seen the monthly insurance bill requiring a payment for a car I did not own. When I eventually confronted her about what she had done, I was dismayed to learn she had virtually no conscience about good or evil. Ultimately isn't that what the conscience attempts to impart, a sense of right and wrong, good and evil? Both Jackie and I concluded that she was the scariest person we had ever met, because there was no sense or mental consideration about what is good and evil in her mind, only considerations of what she wanted to do or what she felt might feel good. It didn't matter that she committed a crime against me or any other another person. She had no remorse or emotional feedback.

I believe this woman suffered from fetal alcohol syndrome but I am not sure. In any case, there are human beings walking the street totally devoid of any sense of right and wrong or good and evil. I'm sure they are mentally ill people for the most part. God in HIS infinite mercy will take our mental and physical problems into consideration during our judgment. That is what HIS mercy and grace are for; HE does not condemn the mentally ill. Yet, where is the excuse for those who do know better? There isn't any.

Part of the problem in conveying a sense of what is sexually immoral from a biblical perspective is the inconsistency of word use in the various translations and the use of some rather archaic terms. For simplicity, I have reduced sexual immorality down to three basic levels. In a very real sense, once you enter Level-I of sexual immorality, which is lewdness, sexual sins can continue taking you deeper and to a point of no return with God unless you can quickly put a spiritual reality check into play. Level-I is the point where a real sense of *the fear of God* should set in. Being "preoccupied and obsessing" over sexual things isn't just thinking sexual "mind" thoughts; it is getting into trouble from sexual "heart" thoughts.

Book of Edward—Chapter 19

Myth—Sexuality Doesn't Matter

A simple test for lewdness is this: "Are your sexual 'preoccupations and obsessions' of the heart beginning to interfere with your daily life?" For example, are you routinely showing up late for work because of your sexual activities? When sexual activities start interfering with normal day-day life activities and the responsibilities that you have to your family and work, it is a sign that you are becoming a *lewd* person. This is the time when a spiritual reality check should take place and a healthy fear of God should set in.

Jesus said: "For from within, *out of the heart* of men, *proceed* evil thoughts, adulteries, fornications, murders, thefts, covetousness, wickedness, deceit, *lewdness*, an evil eye, blasphemy, pride, foolishness. *All these evil things come from within and defile a man*." Mark 7:21-23

Paul taught: "Let us walk properly, as in the day, not in revelry and drunkenness, *not in lewdness and lust*, not in strife and envy." Romans 13:13

"Lest, when I come again, my God will humble me among you, and I shall mourn for many who have sinned before and have not repented of the uncleanness, fornication, and *lewdness* which they have *practiced*." 2 Cor. 12:21

Jesus taught that lewdness was an evil action from the heart, which defiles us in God's eyes. Paul taught that those who have "put on the new man" are no longer *practitioners* of lewdness. Paul laments that he expects to be humbled by God for so-called Christians who never did repent of their lewdness in spite of his teachings and their presumed belief. In Paul's eyes they were "insincere" believers who did not take his teachings to heart. It isn't an act of lewdness that gets us in trouble with God. It is the continued practicing of such evil or the practicing of any evil activity. God expects us to return to righteousness if we want eternal life. This doesn't mean we are no longer sexual beings. To deny our human sexuality is to deny God's wonderful and creative design for the male and female body and for much of Christianity that is what the Church does, either implicitly or explicitly in spite of graphic biblical teachings on sex. The Church is scared of sex talk!

Copyright 2005 Edward G. Palmer, All Rights Reserved.

Book of Edward—Chapter 19

Myth—Sexuality Doesn't Matter

Depending upon translation, you can expect to find an intermingling of the words, *lewdness*, *lasciviousness*, *licentiousness* and *debauchery*. They are often used interchangeably as references to sexual immorality. The word *lewd* shows up three times in the King James Bible. It is used in the context of *lewd acts*, *lewd women* and *lewd fellows* [men]. Guess that covers all the bases, but it doesn't give us clarity to the term itself. To get a better feel for the issue of being *lewd*, you will need to examine the word *lewdness*. An examination of how different Bible translations treat the word *lewdness* in Judges 20:6 is interesting. We'll use the King James as a base translation.

Lewdness – Judges 20:6 KJV

KJV	"lewdness"
NKJV	"lewdness"
NAB	"monstrous crime"
NAS	"a lewd and disgraceful act"
NJB	"a shameful act"
NIV	"this lewd and disgraceful act"
NRSV	"a vile outrage"
LIV	"a terrible crime"
NLT	"a terrible and shameful crime"
GW	"did this perverted and godless thing"

I'll talk further about the subject of Judges 20:6 shortly. However, one cannot help but notice the disparity in the descriptive words used from being *lewd* to being a *vile outrage* or even a *terrible crime*. These words and even the word *lewdness*, fails to convey the message that the perpetrators are headed for the lake of fire, because they are engaged in sexual immorality. In short, this verse like many others fails to convey the complete message that you need to hear concerning sexual immorality. I'll have to admit, I doubt if you will get a *complete* picture here in this chapter as well. The best I can hope to do for you is to sound a warning alarm if you call yourself a Christian. God has expectations concerning our sexuality. Perhaps I will spur you on to your own Bible study on the subject of sex. Unlike the word *lewd*, you won't find the word *lascivious* in the KJV. You'll have to search on *lasciviousness*, which provides the following comparison.

Myth—Sexuality Doesn't Matter

Lasciviousness – Jude 1:4 KJV

KJV	"lasciviousness"
NKJV	"lewdness"
NAB	"licentiousness"
NAS	"licentiousness"
NJB	"debauchery"
NIV	"license for immorality [licentiousness]"
NRSV	"licentiousness"
LIV	"we can do what we like without fear"
NLT	"God's forgiveness allows us to live immoral lives"
GW	"excuse for sexual freedom"

To locate *licentious*, we can use the New American Bible translation and 2 Timothy 3:3 for a comparison of these different translations. The word *licentious* does not appear in the KJV. Neither does *licentiousness*, but this word can be found in other Bible translations as indicated above.

Licentious – 2 Timothy 3:3 NAB

KJV	"incontinent"
NKJV	"without self control"
NAB	"licentious"
NAS	"without self control"
NJB	"profligates"
NIV	"without self control"
NRSV	"profligates"
LIV	"think nothing of immorality"
NLT	"no self control"
GW	"lack self control"

I suspect that the reason you'll find these three archaic words defining sexual immorality used almost interchangeably is that they all get down to the singular issue of a lack of self-control. Even the King James Version's use of the word *incontinent* means a lack of self-control in the 1611 King's English. Isn't that where we started in this chapter? God commands us to exert self-control over our human sexuality. If we don't, we are immoral!

Myth—Sexuality Doesn't Matter

Gavin de Becker wrote the book titled, *The Gift of Fear* [5]. Mr. de Becker's first chapter is titled: "In the Presence of Danger." As a violence assessment specialist, de Becker's clients read like a list of who's who in the upper crust of society. The question he poses is exactly when should we listen to our fears? When should we really be concerned about danger? He concludes that when we actually do feel a sense of fear, that it is a gift we have built inside of us. We can get into some complex situations where we do sense some danger, but often we cannot put our finger exactly on the source of our danger feelings or on why we may be apprehensive.

De Becker points out that our subconscious is constantly assessing our surroundings and is constantly taking in sensory inputs of our environment. If our consciousness is raised to sense danger, it is because our subconscious and even our spirit are performing internal calculations at a subconscious level before alerting us. What we usually get is just a sense of uneasiness. Ever been in a place where you could easily sense danger? Maybe even some outright evil presence? When should we be concerned? Obviously, before we are seriously injured or even killed, before harm comes our way!

What if someone threatened your life? At what point should you get concerned? De Becker concludes that there are always "precursors" to look for. If someone is threatening your life, what have they done so far? Have they just sent you a scary letter? Have they done this to others before you? Have they taken it to the next action level? I.E. Have they stalked you, tried to shoot you? Etc.? The threats to take serious come from people that will always take it to the next action level. While many people will be satisfied scaring you with a life-threatening letter, others will not stop at that point. Those are the ones to be concerned with. De Becker teaches to look for precursors to the next possible action. In other words, if the writer is serious about killing you [or your soul], what is the next action they might take and are they now engaged in getting ready for that action? Are there precursors?

This *gift of fear* is also something that every Christian who possesses godly wisdom carries with them. When they get off onto an immoral path, these people will feel the fear of God just like I do. It's because our internal spirit is always assessing God's perspective on our behavior. Our heart's

Myth—Sexuality Doesn't Matter

gatekeeper also informs us when we get off base with one of HIS threatening statements from the Holy Bible. "Thus sayeth the LORD...!"

The question is are we listening? Do we take HIM seriously? The Bible teaches us: "Has HE said and will HE not do?" When HE says that our sexual immorality will lead to our destruction, will HE carry through on HIS threat? Has HE already done this before? Is that HIS character? Listen, take a journey and read the Bible's stories of sexual immorality and see that God means exactly what HE says. You can start with Noah and the story of why the flood occurred. There are many examples of the destruction of people for sexual immorality. Trust me, you can take God at HIS Word.

We enter into sexual immorality at the beginning of our sexual heart "obsessions" [lewdness]. They cause a "preoccupation" with sex and before we realize it we are engaging in sexually enticing behavior of the kind that God condemns [lasciviousness]. The next Level III finds us engrossed in unrestrained wanton acts of sex with total disregard for all morality in God's perspective [licentiousness]. In all levels, we are sexually out of control and headed for the lake of fire. Yet even in our acts of sexual immorality there are many precursors; spiritual warning signs all along our immoral pathway.

Think about Clinton's White House adultery. Now work backwards from his impeachment trial. Before impeachment occurred, he had lied to a Federal Court under oath. *Note: Many people think Clinton was impeached because of illicit sex in the Oval office, but this is not the case.* Clinton was impeached because as our chief law enforcer, he lied under oath in Federal Court [liar]. And, before that what? He did engage in an illicit sexual affair with Monica Lewinsky [licentiousness]. At some prior point, he engaged in sexually flirtatious behavior with the intern [lasciviousness]. And before that, came his obsession with having "immoral sex" [lewdness]. Should we have been surprised? No. We shouldn't have been surprised because as Governor of Arkansas, Clinton had exhibited licentious behavior over many years with many women. Elect a sexually immoral person president and you still have a sexually immoral person. If you think morality is irrelevant to the U.S. presidency, you are a spiritually ignorant person. At the very least, we deserve the right to elect a moral president to guide our country and not a liar who would destroy people to cover up his illicit sexual affairs.

Myth—Sexuality Doesn't Matter

That is what Clinton did to the many women he was lewd, lascivious and licentious with. He sought to personally destroy these women's lives and reputations for telling the truth and their side of their sexual encounter. Americans were duped into believing moral character didn't matter in the highest office of our land, but we were wrong. Clinton took our society and culture down a morally debased path that will reverberate for many years. His "oral sex" comments reached our youth and we now find ourselves with "girls as young as twelve years old performing oral sex on boys" [6] because Clinton wrongly taught this generation that "oral sex" wasn't actually sex. Aside from his immorality with Monica Lewinsky, Clinton's "oral sex" teachings to our youth will be his lasting legacy. Clinton was an immoral president and all of the citizens in America should be ashamed that we were collectively gullible enough to vote him into office. Yet this is just one illustration of sexual immorality and the precursors that accompany it.

Think about the issue of a homosexual relationship [licentiousness]. What do you think might be some precursors to this sexual immorality? The fact that various churches are now teaching that homosexuality is okay with God can certainly be a precursor. Woe to any church that teaches that the licentiousness of homosexuality or lesbianism is okay with God. Before any Gay relationship starts, there had to be a Gay encounter where individual lewdness was converted into lascivious behavior. This could be a meeting at a Gay bar or event. Before going to the Gay bar, perhaps the individuals picked up a flyer for a Gay event designed for Gays to meet one another. A businessperson had to create the flyer to "entice" lewd people to the event. That would have been an act of lascivious behavior. Woe to anyone who causes another to commit sexual immorality. Perhaps a childhood event caused a young male or female to get confused over their sexuality. If a young male's penis is stroked, it gets erect. A teenage boy could be led to believe that if his penis gets erect when stroked by another male, that it is a confirmation of homosexuality. Get real. Anything rubbing a penis is likely to invoke the male body's autonomic response mechanism and *force* an erection. There is no doubt in my mind that the Gay community on this very issue has led astray many young males. Teenagers with their hormones raging and not developed mentally, sexually and spiritually can be easily swayed into believing such a sexual lie. That might be the *first* precursor!

Copyright 2005 Edward G. Palmer, All Rights Reserved.

Myth—Sexuality Doesn't Matter

Then there is the recent story of Jimmy Swaggart apologizing for a remark he made about Gays [7]. Remember Swaggart? According to the article: "Swaggart was a popular television evangelist during the 1980's until a 1987 sex scandal involving a prostitute that he met in a seedy New Orleans motel. Swaggart never confessed to anything more than an unspecified sin. A few years later, he was stopped by police while driving in California with a suspected prostitute in his car." Think about all the precursors that were ignored by Swaggart along his own immoral pathway. Before he wound up with a prostitute engaging in licentious and lascivious behavior, he had engaged in lewdness in his heart. Did he ignore spiritual caution flags or is he *abhorred* by the LORD as taught in Proverbs 22:14?

All three illustrations demonstrate a lack of moral clarity and sexual self-control. Moral clarity in the United States has been under attack all of my life. Satan seeks to confuse mankind about what is sexually okay in God's eyes. Yet, HIS Word has not changed and HE will still hold us accountable for *all* sexual immorality. How is it that the people can be duped into electing an immoral president who calls himself a Christian? How is it that teenagers are easily confused about their God given sexuality? And how is it that immorality in the house of God can stand as if it didn't matter? You can trace this immorality to the Christian orthodox teaching of the trinity doctrine. Intellectually, it is a logical conclusion of the mind that licentiousness is a valid lifestyle if our sins no longer matter. Ergo, if Jesus forgave *all* of my sins, even my future acts of sexual immorality no longer matter. If you believe this apostate spiritual reasoning, you are destined to hear Jesus say, "I never knew you." Go back and study chapters 1-14 for the truth about sin. Sin does matter to God, especially once you proclaim Jesus Christ as your Lord and savior. Sexually immoral sins lead only to the lake of fire and a second death. I didn't make the rule, God did!

God gave us a strong mind. It enables us to understand HIS Word in all of its intellectual, spiritual and emotional respects. However, without the wisdom's gatekeeper, we can fall prey to the false security of a forgiveness theology that is replete with apostasy and wickedness. Indeed, the continued willful sin in the name of Jesus Christ is wicked and the ultimate blasphemy before a holy God who sacrificed HIS only begotten *human* Son Jesus!

Myth—Sexuality Doesn't Matter

Once saved, your sins are washed white as snow and your heart is also supposed to be cleansed of all of its wickedness. Do you remember that God stated our heart was inclined towards evil from its youth? Do you think that salvation is an actual reality if the heart is not transformed from its proclivity towards wickedness to that of being a slave unto righteousness? Yet if you continue to practice sexual immorality, you only delude yourself. You testify that your heart is not cleansed unto righteousness through *true* belief. In the end you deceive yourself because you are not a doer of the Word. The *gift of fear* is a part of wisdom's *reason*! And yet if you practice sexual immorality, it also demonstrates that you have no fear of God.

> **"Behold, the fear of the LORD, that is wisdom, and to depart from evil is understanding." Job 28:28**

> **"For God has not given us a spirit of fear, but of power and of love and of a sound mind." 2 Tim. 1:7**

> **"But without faith it is impossible to please HIM, for he who comes to God must believe that HE is, and that HE is a rewarder of those who diligently seek HIM." Hebrews 11:6**

Paul Teaches *"Slave To Righteousness,"* **Not** Perfection!

> **Jesus answered them, "Most assuredly, I say to you, whoever commits sin is a slave of sin. And a slave [of sin] does not abide in the house forever, but a son [slave of righteousness] abides forever." John 8:34-35**

> **"And because you are sons, God has sent forth the spirit of HIS Son into your hearts, crying out, 'Abba, FATHER!' Therefore you are no longer a slave [to sin] but a son, and if a son, then an heir of God through Christ." Galatians 4:6-7**

> **"No slave can serve two masters ... you cannot serve [both] God and [sin]." Luke 16:13 NRSV** *[Choose your master!]*

Myth—Sexuality Doesn't Matter

> "And having been set free from sin, you became slaves of righteousness. I speak in human terms because of the weakness of your flesh. For just as you presented your members as slaves of uncleanness, and of lawlessness leading to more lawlessness, so now present your members as slaves of righteousness for holiness. For when you were slaves of sin, you were free in regard to righteousness."
>
> **Romans 6:18-20**

> "I find then a law, that evil is present with me, the one who wills to do good. For I delight in the law of God according to the inward man. But I see another law in my members, warring against the law of my mind, and bringing me into captivity to the law of sin, which is in my members [flesh]."
>
> **Romans 7:21-23**

Apostle Paul knew that perfection on his own strength would not be possible in this earthly life, but that he could still be a slave to righteousness. What does this mean? It means that we have obtained the gatekeeper from God and/or we have acknowledged HIS internal laws written on our hearts and minds. It means that we now strive to live and abide by HIS laws and that we do not *practice* sin. We *were* a slave to our flesh and sin, but *now* we are slaves to righteousness. This doesn't mean our flesh can't rule at times, as it can. It means that as we walk in HIS Spirit, we can deny the natural inclinations of our heart and flesh towards evil. God gave up HIS expectations for our human perfection when HE gave us HIS Son.

In the practical sense, you can consider the homosexual who has come clean with God and ceased *practicing* his homosexuality. But then soon is confronted with a relapse on a night when his spirit was weak and his flesh was strong. This will not get him into trouble with God, because the blood of Christ has him covered. Yet, in contrast, is the homosexual who simply ignores all of the precursors. He knows that if he goes to a Gay bar that he will "hook up" for the night. The *fear of God* should set in at that point! This is different than a bad *event* "in the flesh." God knows we can't be perfect, but HE expects us to walk "in the Spirit" and not the flesh.

Myth—Sexuality Doesn't Matter

> **Jesus said, "Therefore you shall be perfect, just as your FATHER in Heaven is perfect." Matthew 5:48**
>
> **Jesus said to him, "If you want to be perfect, go, sell what you have and give to the poor, and you will have treasure in Heaven; and come, follow me." Matthew 19:21**
>
> **Jesus said, "I in them, and YOU in me [Jesus]; that they may be made perfect in One, and that the world may know that YOU have sent me [Jesus], and have loved them as YOU have loved me [Jesus]." John 17:23**
>
> **Paul taught, "[Jesus] we preach, warning every man and teaching every man in all wisdom, that we may present every man perfect [to God] in Christ Jesus." Col. 1:28**

Therefore, Paul made it clear that our flesh will control us at various times, but that we are *still* — to constantly exert control over the flesh [sin] by walking in the Spirit. Paul knew that perfection in terms of 100% control over all our sin, outside of Christ, was not possible. All who seek perfection before God will only find it in obedience to God's Word, as they walk in the Spirit, and not by their flesh. Obedience is what it means to be "in Christ." Paul's teaching on this subject is consistent with God's instructions to Cain to "rule over sin." God did not expect Cain to be free of sin. HE expected Cain to exert control and to rule over the sin that sought to master him.

God's Spirit right now is telling me that the doctrine of our human "perfection" is a vile teaching in some parts of the Church. It is vile for the very reason that it misrepresents the gift that God gave us in HIS Son. If you think that, after accepting Christ, you will never sin again — you are very delusional and do not understand Scripture. The doctrine that sin no longer matters is an even more vile teaching in some parts of the Church. If you think that continued "willful sinning" or a lifestyle of licentiousness is sanctioned, after accepting Christ, you are also very delusional. God expects us to try with all of our heart and HE understands that we'll drop the ball on occasion. Ergo, "Every man [presented] perfect [to God] in Christ Jesus."

Myth—Sexuality Doesn't Matter

The Debased Cannot Engage In Critical Thinking!

God speaks to me in many ways. One of those ways is HE simply throws stuff in my face in a timely manner. In a way I just cannot ignore. It's weird, but I love HIS inputs. This could be a personal conversation, a relevant experience, a book, a news article, a radio or television program, etc. Each chapter is written with HIS Spirit guiding me. I have no outline and rely completely upon HIM and HIS Word for content. In a way, each chapter is a puzzle and God supplies me with each specific piece that I need in a timely manner. God supplies each page's content at the time I actually need it and not before. Faith requires that I trust HIM. Since I sincerely believe that HE is [exists] and that HE is a rewarder of those who diligently [with their whole heart] seek HIM, everything works out fine. Not as I suppose it should be in life, but as HE desires it to be.

The spiritual irony here is that one cannot perceive the *entire* truth and reality of life unless he or she possesses godly knowledge and spirituality. You can't get to this place in your life until you literally jump into the river [of God's life] so to speak and experience HIS reality. It is, I suspect, the ultimate Catch 22 for humanity. Until you believe that God exists and you surrender your heart to HIM, you'll just be another clueless human about the total reality of our earthly existence.

I experienced God's timely input the other night as I was going to bed. Suddenly I found my spirit leading me to turn on the television at 11:50 p.m. I tuned into the Tavis Smiley [8] show on public television in Minneapolis. Tavis was interviewing left wing comedian and satirist Bill Maher. To say that Maher is morally debased is an understatement. One only has to listen to his diatribe and ridicule towards people of faith to grasp that fact.

What bemused me was a couple of statements that Bill Maher made. First, he said, "People of faith are not critical thinkers." Then, in a response to Vice President Dick Cheney's comments about Gay civil unions, he said, "When it's close to you, Republicans understand and have compassion." He was referring to Cheney's lesbian daughter and his different stance on the issue of Gay civil unions or marriage to that of President George W. Bush.

Copyright 2005 Edward G. Palmer, All Rights Reserved.

Book of Edward—Chapter 19

Myth—Sexuality Doesn't Matter

Both statements reflect Bill Maher's spiritual ignorance and lack of knowledge about God and what true faith is about. Maher mocks God, but fails to understand that people of faith are the real critical thinkers. They are critical thinkers because they understand God's perspective. People of faith are three-dimensional people. People like Maher are two-dimension people. It gets back to having three primary sources of thought input or only having two primary thoughts. Maher, like Clinton, thinks with his mind and heart, but lacks any capacity to think with his soul.

One thing is for sure. It *is* harder to live up to your faith in God when sin reigns close to your heart as in the illustration of Dick Cheney and his lesbian daughter. However, if any parent has true love and compassion, they will reprove their children for everyone's eternal sake. That will be more meaningful to their adult child than the temporary satisfaction of any lesbian or other sexually immoral relationship.

People like Bill Maher, devoid of God, are simply debased of any spiritual discernment ability. They simply cannot understand truth because the truth is not in them. As a result, they are stuck in a two-thought mode and can only belittle what they cannot possibly comprehend. The real issue, which Maher fails to grasp, is not whether sin will occur in our family or society, but whether a morally true love would still stand tall to teach our family and society that immorality costs us all too much. Past generations of Americans had such morally based love. Like the unpredictable genocide that occurs with abortion, sexual immorality takes an unpredictable toll on not just the sinner, but on those who love them and want to do their best to support them. It also takes a collective toll on society changing it from a moral one to an immoral one. God turns HIS back on immoral societies!

Would the sexually immoral person be so inclined to sin if they knew it was equivalent to tying a spiritual boat anchor around the neck of those who love them? Family that fails to reprove sexual immorality can wind up in the same eternal boat, because God says that they will bear sin-guilt by not reproving sin. Woe unto all families and our society if we continue to succumb to the pressures of immorality. All of this is too complicated for a simple two-dimensional, two-thought source person to fully comprehend.

Book of Edward—Chapter 19

Myth—Sexuality Doesn't Matter

God Created Us Naked, Sexual & Holy!

"And they were both naked, the man and his wife, and were not ashamed." Genesis 2:25

In the beginning we stood before God naked without shame. In fact, our nakedness did not interfere with our holiness. Only after Eve's sin did we feel shame. The shame came from the evil side of human sexuality and not from the good side. We were designed as naked, sexual and holy beings. Even today, with our clothes on, we still stand before God naked!

"And there is no creature hidden from HIS sight, but all things are naked and open to the eyes of HIM to whom we must give account." Hebrews 4:13

How wonderfully free it must have been in the beginning for Adam and Eve. Having been created naked, sexual and holy — I conclude that there is nothing sinful about our naked body per se. For example, it was not a sin for Adam to look at Eve's naked body and vice versa. Note that being totally naked that every physical aspect of the human body was exposed for examination and curiosity without any concern about sin. However, God later established some rules, which defined the nakedness of kin as it relates to sexual immorality. Consider HIS rules on uncovering nakedness of kin.

Don't Uncover The Nakedness Of Kin!

"None of you shall approach anyone who is near of kin to him, to uncover his [or her] nakedness: I am the LORD.

[7] The nakedness of your father or the nakedness of your mother you shall not uncover. She is your mother; you shall not uncover her nakedness.

[8] The nakedness of your father's wife you shall not uncover; it is your father's nakedness.

Copyright 2005 Edward G. Palmer, All Rights Reserved.

Book of Edward—Chapter 19

Myth—Sexuality Doesn't Matter

[9] The nakedness of your sister, the daughter of your father, or the daughter of your mother, whether born at home or elsewhere, their nakedness you shall not uncover.

[10] The nakedness of your son's daughter or your daughter's daughter, their nakedness you shall not uncover; for theirs is your own nakedness.

[11] The nakedness of your father's wife's daughter, begotten by your father—she is your sister—you shall not uncover her nakedness.

[12] You shall not uncover the nakedness of your father's sister; she is near of kin to your father.

[13] You shall not uncover the nakedness of your mother's sister, for she is near of kin to your mother.

[14] You shall not uncover the nakedness of your father's brother. You shall not approach his wife; she is your aunt.

[15] You shall not uncover the nakedness of your daughter-in-law—she is your son's wife—you shall not uncover her nakedness.

[16] You shall not uncover the nakedness of your brother's wife; it is your brother's nakedness.

[17] You shall not uncover the nakedness of a woman and her daughter, nor shall you take her son's daughter or her daughter's daughter, to uncover her nakedness. They are near of kin to her. **It is wickedness**.

[18] Nor shall you take a woman, as a rival to her sister, to uncover her nakedness while the other is alive.

Myth—Sexuality Doesn't Matter

[19] Also you shall not approach a woman to uncover her nakedness as long as she is in her customary impurity [menstrual cycle or period]." Leviticus 18:6-19

"The man who lies with his father's wife has uncovered his father's nakedness; both of them shall surely be put to death. Their blood shall be upon them." Leviticus 20:11

"If a man takes his sister, his father's daughter or his mother's daughter, and sees her nakedness and she sees his nakedness, **it is a wicked thing**. And they shall be cut off in the sight of their people. He has uncovered his sister's nakedness. He shall bear his guilt." Leviticus 20:17

"If a man lies with a woman during her sickness [menstrual cycle or period] and uncovers her nakedness, he has exposed her flow, and she has uncovered the flow of her blood. Both of them shall be cut off from their people." Leviticus 20:18

God makes it clear that we are to abstain from sexual intercourse during a woman's menstrual cycle. It was a serious act that led to social isolation. I'm wondering how anyone found out, but then some men just can't keep their mouths shut or even like to brag. God doesn't explain why we should abstain from sex at this time of the month, but it is logical to assume that this is a special time for a woman's health and for whose body is shedding its uterine lining. Blood flowing out of her body is not to be contaminated by intercourse [penis or semen].

Curiously, there may even be some protective aspect for the male penis in HIS command. Who knows? Therefore, men should change their love making desires for the sake of their wife's health, as there is always a reason why God asks us to do something. Nakedness of your wife during her menstrual cycle is related directly to vaginal intercourse. This does not necessarily mean that a husband and wife cannot use alternative methods of making love or simply just making out. That includes men simply holding their wives and forgoing direct *sexual* activity during this time of month.

Myth—Sexuality Doesn't Matter

I'll plead guilty to violating this sex rule a number of times when I was a young man and my hormones raged. If a male doesn't get sex, he might even believe he'll die or his penis will even fall off. Humorous as it is, that is how intense the male sex drive can get at times. I remember some very intense internal and physical sexual pressures *from my body* in which there was little thought possible other than "I've got to have sex—now!" Most males can attest to such intense physical pressures to have sex at some time in their life. I'll admit that I was totally ignorant of spiritual things at the time and of how God will protect our human bodies by commands in which HE provides no explanations. I was also ignorant of the spiritual aspect of sexuality that is invoked by simply holding your wife in a loving way without any expectation of her having to physically "put out." Learning to adoringly caress your wife without sexual physical expectation can be an incredible spiritual foreplay for a later more gratifying time of making love.

Most of God's nakedness rules relates to the possibility of incestuous relationships. God wants us to maintain a sexual distance when it comes to those in our immediate family or "near of kin." That includes stepsisters, stepbrothers, aunts, and uncles, etc. Even adopted sons and daughters count as immediate family and "near of kin." God's expectation is that only a husband and wife will get naked together. Nakedness does lead to sexual activity and sexual immorality is directly implied in the above "near of kin" relationships. God specifically says it is "wicked" for a man to see both a woman and her daughter naked. Why, if not for the certainty of sex? It is also "wicked" if a brother and sister lie together. And in the case of a son lying with his father's wife, that they should be put to death [son and wife].

As a parents raise their children, they bathe and care for them up to the age they are able to do so on their own. Prior to puberty, parents must teach their children to bathe themselves. It is wicked for a mother to see her son, who is past puberty, naked. Likewise, it is wicked for a father to see his daughter, who is past puberty, naked. This is also simple common sense and decency! Where disability occurs or death is imminent, for a child, it alters God's concerns. During Jackie's dying process, when she was no longer able to care for herself, it was her sister that primarily cared for her and saw her [Jackie's] nakedness. If not her sister, then it was I. Jackie inherently knew that it was wrong for her son or two daughters to see her nakedness.

Myth—Sexuality Doesn't Matter

Summary Of God's Nakedness Rules!

Instructions: Pick out who you are in the left hand column and then observe whom you should not be seeing naked in the right hand column.

Who You Are!	Do Not Uncover Kin's Nakedness!
Everyone	Anyone near of kin to you. Near of kin does not include your spouse.
Husband and Wife (Married Couple)	Protect wife's nakedness [and blood flow] during her menstrual cycle.
Mother or Father	*Children after puberty, unless dying.*
Man (Husband)	Son's daughter or daughter's daughter; daughter in law; brother's wife; woman and her daughter; woman's daughter's daughter; woman and her sister; and, a woman during her menstrual cycle.
Woman (Wife)	Woman's son; *son's son or daughter's son; sister's husband; son in law; husband during her menstrual cycle; a man and his son or son's son, etc.*
Son	Father; mother; father's wife; your sister; father or mother's daughter; father's wife's daughter; father or mother's sister; *father's brother* or his brother's wife; *your brother, etc.*
Daughter	Father; *mother; father's wife; father or mother's son; father's wife's son; father or mother's brother; father's sister or his sister's husband; your sister, etc.*

Step & adopted family members are also near of kin!

Copyright 2005 Edward G. Palmer, All Rights Reserved.

Book of Edward—Chapter 19

Myth—Sexuality Doesn't Matter

If at all possible, even during death, the above nakedness rules should be followed to honor God's instructions. HE has mercy and grace for those who find themselves caring for a family member in which these rules are violated out of perforce.

Not all nakedness relationships were disclosed, because in the days when the rules were dictated, there was little sexual immorality on the part of wives and females in general. Most of the problems were on the part of males. You can't make such a general statement today with the emphasis on legalizing Gay and lesbian relationships and the drive to make them morally equivalent to those of heterosexuals. This apostolic and *interpretive* fact is reflected in the italic relationships shown in the table rows. Note: This is not an attempt to provide a complete table of forbidden nakedness relationships, but only to illustrate the types of relationships that you should be concerned about regarding seeing someone naked. Again, if it doesn't feel, seem or look right, it just isn't spiritually right and it is the Spirit that speaks to your conscience. Common sense and decency guides most people on nakedness.

Note that God does not say you could not examine and look at your own body. In fact, in Clifford and Joyce Penner's book *The Gift of Sex*, [9] this is exactly what they suggest you do. Get to know your own body. Then get to know the body of your lover also, who should be the spouse you are married to. This is a book on sex written by Christian authors and with a biblical perspective. It is an excellent read and I highly recommend it for all Christian couples to understand their sexuality and God's *gift of sex*.

Sexual fantasies float around the human mind on a seemingly regular basis if not an occasional one. Anything can trip and ignite a sexual thought or fantasy. Men are very visually stimulated and a shapely woman passing by a man's eyes are sometimes all it takes to evoke an automatic physical response. Many times a young man will experience an erect penis [boner] involuntarily simply because an unintended visual stimulation enters his eyes. Other times there are intentional visual stimulations such as when a man opens up and views a sexually explicit magazine of nude women, etc. However, at this point in time, everything is still located in the mind, not the heart. It hasn't gotten down to the heart where action occurs until our

Myth—Sexuality Doesn't Matter

gatekeeper opens up the heart's door. Again, this is to say that there is a distinct difference between what is in our mind, goes in and out of our mind, and what is in our heart or goes in and out of our heart. The heart betrays the essence of our soul and who we are to God. So, don't start going nuts over occasional perverse mental thoughts. Listen, we all get them! Go nuts when you start taking actions from your heart on those perverse thoughts.

I talked about this issue of random mental thoughts in the last chapter [p695-696]. Our minds do not get us into immediate trouble with God. It is what we allow into and out of our hearts that actually *results in sin*. Ergo, "guard your heart!" Yet, we *should* also guard our minds as well. One can become mentally obsessed with sexuality and this *will* most likely then lead to sexual immorality. In that sense, it is *a focused sexually oriented mind* that leads to sexual immorality, not the random sexual thoughts of the mind. Guarding our thoughts is why Paul taught us the following:

> **"Finally, brethren, whatsoever things are true, whatsoever things are honest, whatsoever things are just, whatsoever things are pure, whatsoever things are lovely, whatsoever things are of good report; if there be any virtue, and if there be any praise, think on these things." Philip. 4:8 KJV**

Train your mind to think on these positive things. A mind focused primarily on sexual thoughts is a lewd mind. If sex is your top priority in life, you will likely exhibit lewdness and get in trouble with God regarding sexual immorality. We are created as sexual beings and two attributes of our sexuality are rather obvious. They are procreation and pleasure. The pleasure aspect of our sexuality no doubt enhances procreation. God meant for us to "beget" children <u>and</u> to enjoy sex. Mankind, however, has from time immemorial perverted the nature of our God given human sexuality with all kinds of lewd, lascivious and licentious behavior.

There is no more obvious spot to observe sexually immoral behavior than in the movies. I'm talking about the movies that are shown in theaters; I'm not talking about the pornography flicks that now invade our society. The sexual immorality shown in the average movie theater is enough to boggle your mind. As a movie aficionado, I am speaking from experience.

Myth—Sexuality Doesn't Matter

At last count, I had rated 1291 movies at a university [10] movie-rating site. Only 10% of them reached the level of what I would call a "must see" movie or that I would recommend to just any person. The majority of movies *today* are junk films with questionable morality. That includes fake documentaries like the "Fahrenheit 9/11" from left-wing ideologue Michael Moore. Lies, propaganda, sexuality and immorality seem to be the favorite scripts for Hollywood filmmakers. Couple "theater" movies and their sexual perversions with all the sales pitches that *use* "sex" to sell products, and its easy to get overwhelmed with "random sexual thoughts in the mind."

Now add the porn industry into the equation. I am told that people viewing porn movies or videos in their home on DVD, VCR, cable, satellite or on computer connections to the Internet have now reached a level that exceed the number of people that watch sports. In trips during the last four years, pornography was offered at virtually every hotel and motel I stayed at. Most locations also offered movie channels such as Showtime, Cinemax, and HBO, which are themselves a convenient source of soft core porn at various times throughout the day.

I once visited my sister during a time when she subscribed to all the movie channels the cable offered. I remember turning on the TV only to find one man and two women naked together on a bed engaged in sex. Woe to subscribers of satellite, cable or Internet channels that provide sexually immoral content. They *will* be affronted with lewdness and licentiousness along with the very substance of what God deems lascivious. Yes, I know that parental controls are available to limit the exposure of children. Who manages the adults? If the lascivious [sexually enticing] adult shows are available, every human male will eventually be tempted to turn the blocking controls off at some point and "take a look-see." Myself included.

Such channels are immoral precursors and if watched, it is immoral behavior. I've tried the movie channels. My male flesh liked the sexually enticing shows and *all* males are of the same design, even if there are greater levels of individual control. To think otherwise about the flesh is to deny its power to engage us all in sexual sin or it is ignorance of human sexuality. The solution is to unplug the smut and find some better entertainment!

Book of Edward—Chapter 19

Myth—Sexuality Doesn't Matter

Most cable and satellite operators package and sell their filth with the good stuff. In fact, one usually cannot subscribe to just the Disney channel or some other wholesome channel without getting one or more objectionable channels. The solution is to unsubscribe to your cable or satellite and tell them when you can just subscribe to the moral channels you want, you'll reconsider. Does it make sense to subscribe to a few good channels when your family gets subjected to sexual immorality on many other channels? While you may be able to program around some channels, let me ask you this question. Why should you have to even allow sexually immoral content into the privacy of your home? Such programming brought into your home is a sexually immoral precursor. Verily I say unto you that it will present a moral conflict to those in your home. It will cause some people to sin!

God has some clear ways to identify sinners and exclude them from an eternal life. One of those is stated in James 4:17, which is a catchall definition of sin. "If you know what is right to do, but you do not do it, then to *you* it is sin." God *will* hold you responsible for what you know and do, not what others know and do. I taught on Leviticus 19:17 in the last chapter, which is God's command that you "reprove" your neighbor's sin [those in your gates, family or close to you] *or else you will bear their guilt*. So we are obligated to God to do what is right and not to give sin an easy "pass" or allow sin to go unchallenged in our family, neighborhood, or society. A third warning from God is that we are not to be a cause or an enabler of sin.

> **Jesus said, "But whoever causes one of these little ones who believe in me [or the FATHER] to sin, it would be better for him if a millstone were hung around his neck, and he were drowned in the depth of the sea. Woe to the world [society] because of offenses! For offenses must come, but woe to *that* man by whom the offense comes!" Matthew 18:6-7**

Woe to any person by whom the offense comes! Allowing sexually immoral content into your home *will* cause or enable sin. If you subscribe to "adult" channels, you are inviting sexually immoral content into your home. The word "adult" is a euphemism for an immoral pornographic sex show. The solution is to unsubscribe & unplug the "sexually immoral" precursor!

Copyright 2005 Edward G. Palmer, All Rights Reserved.

Book of Edward—Chapter 19

Myth—Sexuality Doesn't Matter

God has just reminded me of a key aspect to this discussion that is often ignored for sake of convenience. Assume for a moment that you could actually order only the moral channels that you wanted for your own home, but to do so, you would have to obtain those "moral" channels from a purveyor of "immoral" channels. I.E. You select 50 moral channels out of the purveyor's 130 total channels of which remain several quasi-moral if not outright immoral channels. Now what? Are you falling into the category of causing or enabling others to sin simply by engaging in commerce with what is presumably only a moral offering to your house? The answer is yes, you are. If you support a business that offers part of his services in support of immorality, you are supporting that immorality. The solution is to only do business with those who do not engage in providing any immoral or evil services. I admit, in 2004, that this could be a challenge. Yet, it is possible to take a stand for morality even if it means having to alter your plans.

It's now October 7th and for the last few days God has given me more insight on the minimum righteousness requirement that Jesus spoke about. Do you remember my teaching on this subject in chapter 6? If not, you can review the discussion starting on page 104. For now, God wants me to refresh your memory in the current context of sexuality. HE does not expect perfection out of your life, but there is a minimum righteousness standard.

> **Jesus said, "For assuredly, I say to you, till Heaven and earth pass away, one jot or one tittle will by no means pass from the Law till all is fulfilled. Whoever therefore breaks one of the least of these commandments, and teaches men so, shall be called least in the kingdom of Heaven; but whoever does and teaches them, he shall be called great in the kingdom of Heaven. For I say to you, that unless your righteousness exceeds the righteousness of the scribes and Pharisees, you will by no means enter the kingdom of Heaven." Matthew 5:18-20**

I want you to observe that in these verses Jesus states that those who break the commandments and teach others to do so will be called the least in Heaven. Jesus is talking about the Law, which he says is still active.

Myth—Sexuality Doesn't Matter

Jesus says the Law will not pass away until Heaven and earth pass away if you take him literally. Note that breakers of the commandments *will still* get into Heaven! And those who teach such apostasy will be *"called the least* in the kingdom of Heaven." Therefore, God does not have the idea you need to be perfect in HIS eyes. As I stated before, you are perfect in Christ. At least those who are sincerely "in Christ." Yet immediately following that statement of not requiring perfection to get into Heaven, Jesus states that there is, nonetheless, a minimum righteousness standard. What is it? *Your own righteousness has to exceed that of the scribes and Pharisees!*

Jesus is saying that you should be better at righteousness than the leaders of your church. For sure, you should be better than those leaders who fall into the category of a scribe or Pharisee. These people followed the letter of the Law, but not the spirit. They also insisted on strictly following their oral traditions or doctrines, even if there was no biblical foundation. I liken them to modern day preachers who do not teach God's Word, but teach their own doctrines and interpretations of Scripture. Preachers of today's tithe doctrine are scribes and Pharisees, because they pervert God's Word and impose the strictness of *their own doctrine* on the people. For a detailed discussion of why the tithe doctrine is false, go back to chapter 17.

Jesus is saying that many of the people you think are godly are really hypocrites and behind the scenes they are unrighteous people. Ergo, you had better be more righteous than those people. Scary? Well, God told me that it's not difficult to get beyond HIS minimum righteousness standard. The three social norms listed below and discussed above were in common use during my youth, but they have almost faded out of everyday societal practice. Think carefully and you'll realize that Jesus doesn't eliminate your own personal responsibilities to God. Jesus only helps you in your *gap*!

Do the Right Thing!
Or, it means you willfully sin!   *James 4:17*

Reprove and Rebuke Sin!
Or, it means you bear the guilt of sin!   *Leviticus 19:17*

Don't Cause Another to Sin!
Or, it means a terrible woe will come to you!   *Matthew 18:6-7*

Copyright 2005 Edward G. Palmer, All Rights Reserved.

Book of Edward—Chapter 19

Myth—Sexuality Doesn't Matter

Now when I say, "do the right thing"— I am telling you not to sin and to do what God will say is right. This "right thing" is given to us in His Word and in our soft inner voice of conscience. It is always good and not evil. It is not what your neighbor, friend, family or society might believe is right. Regardless of your knowledge of the Bible or overall education, God imparts to everyone's spirit a sense of what is really right in any given situation. That is the essence of James 4:17. You can be right with God by simply listening to what your conscience tells you to do. If you are ignorant of the Word, you can get into trouble with God by condoning, causing or enabling what He calls sin. How can you effectively *eternalize* yourself in these regards if you are ignorant of His Word? While you study and learn, listen carefully to His righteous laws written on your heart and mind.

My discussion with God didn't stop at just how to get beyond the minimum standard. It continued into all the *woes* of the Bible. Isaiah 30:1 states, "Woe to the rebellious children ... that they may add sin to sin." *They continue to sin!* Isaiah 45:9 states, "Woe to him who strives with his [her] Maker!" *They argue with God!* Jeremiah 23:1 states, "Woe to the [false] shepherds who destroy and scatter the sheep of My pasture." Ezekiel 13:3 states, "Woe to the foolish prophets who follow their own spirit and have seen nothing!" Ezekiel 34:2 states, "Woe to the shepherds ... who feed themselves [and not My flock]!" And, Matthew 23:14 states, "Woe to you, scribes and Pharisees, hypocrites!" Guess what? All of the unrighteous preachers and teachers cloak secrets, but they are all naked in God's eyes!

> **"Woe to you who desire the day of the Lord! For what good is the day of the Lord to you? It will be darkness, and not light. It will be as though a man fled from a lion, and a bear met him! Or as though he went into the house, leaned his hand on the wall, and a serpent bit him! Is not the day of the Lord darkness, and not light? Is it not very dark, with no brightness in it?" Amos 5:18-20**

> **"Woe to him [her] who gives drink to his [her] neighbor [friend, family, etc.], pressing him [her] to your bottle, even to make him [her] drunk that you may look on his [her] nakedness [and have sex with them]!" Habakkuk 2:15**

Myth—Sexuality Doesn't Matter

We entered into the discussion of *woes* when Jesus taught us that it applied to *everyone* who causes another person to sin. If you study the word in Scripture, you will find these attributes apply to biblical *woes*: pain, grief, misery, trouble, death and darkness. All of the above *woe* warnings are pertinent to today's churches. Many [11] *will* try to convince you that sexually immoral behavior has no downside to those who claim Christ as their savior. They are wrong. There are simply too many warnings from God HIMSELF to the contrary. It is about time the *entire* Church woke up and took notice.

The so-called, Episcopal Church "*spirit-led*" ordination of V. Gene Robinson, a practicing homosexual, as bishop is an example of which the Prophet Amos is speaking to in Amos 5:18-20. Churches that sanction homosexuality in the name of God are like many apostate churches happily waiting for the "Day of the LORD." Jumping up and down in aisles to the cadence of an emotional music concert, I can hear their voices, at the top of their lungs, singing "Come Lord Jesus Come!" Come indeed, God says to these immoral people. The *woe* warning of Amos is a warning to delusional congregations who have been led to believe that their personal behaviors have no consequences. It challenges the Christian dogma that "Jesus saves me from all my sin!" Does he indeed? A righteous God responds with this question: "For what good is the day of the LORD to you?"

This is relevant to our present discussion because God has told me that the minimum righteousness criterion trumps the mouthing of, "Jesus is my Lord!" Put another way. Do you think God rejects those who meet HIS minimum righteousness standard but never heard of Christ? Or do you think God accepts those who claim Christ but do not meet HIS minimum standard? Hello, it's not my word; it's HIS! God's Word teaches us that *those who are sexually immoral are not even in the* "minimum righteousness game." HIS instructions for the "sexually immoral" trump Christ's salvation! Salvation does have responsibilities and I'm *still* talking about *practitioners* of sin.

> **"But the cowardly, unbelieving, abominable, murderers, *sexually immoral*, sorcerers, idolaters, and all liars shall have their part in the lake which burns with fire and brimstone, which is the second death." Rev. 21:8**

Myth—Sexuality Doesn't Matter

The Sexually Immoral Do Not Meet God's Minimum Righteousness Criteria!

If you fall into any of the above categories of Rev. 21:8, it leads to a second death. Your destination is eternal damnation *unless you change your ways* and nothing that you can mouth about Jesus Christ will keep you out of the "lake, which burns with fire and brimstone, which is the second death." Wake up to the Word! These *are* sins that *will* lead to the death of our soul. These are not sins that Christ can eliminate for you *unless* you have ceased them and as illustrated earlier merely had a relapse. Christ will fill the gap for every person who ceases such acts of evil and sincerely moves beyond the minimum righteousness standard. Jesus will not wash your *continued* evil, wicked and *sinful* lifestyle clean and white for God. It is an insult to God for you to believe such apostasy, much less teach such evil! It insults HIS Spirit of grace. Therefore, breaking a commandment is one thing, but living a life of wickedness is something altogether different to God.

If you think it is okay to engage in pornographic movies as a husband and wife together, you are wrong. If this is what it takes to turn one or more partners on to sex, you have already entered the realm of lewdness and of sexual immorality in God's eyes. Furthermore, how right in God's eyes is it for one partner to get "heated up" sexually by watching a porn video only to expect the other partner to then satisfy his or her pent up sexual urges? You decide, but I know God's perspective. This is not the way God expects any man to treat his wife and men, no doubt, are the main abusers of porn.

Some months ago, I found myself looking in the corner of a video store I frequented. It had a private "adult" section walled off with "cameras" monitoring the area. Suddenly, I decided it was time I took a look at what was in that area. Actually I felt the Spirit telling me I needed to check the area out. I did and even rented what I felt might be the most innocuous movie of the lurid stuff I saw on the shelves. *Hot Showers #7* [12] turned out to be a visual instructional video for prospective lesbians. I was shocked and cancelled my membership citing the "adult" movie section that I found morally wrong and evil. Don't support stores that sell pornographic goods!

Copyright 2005 Edward G. Palmer, All Rights Reserved.

Myth—Sexuality Doesn't Matter

You should be aware if your teenager is sexually active or is confused about his or her gender. Especially if they hold a belief that they may be a homosexual or lesbian. Any sexually confused teen will find a huge library of porn videos available to teach them how to make love and have sex with a person of the same gender.

There is no doubt in my mind that the homosexual and lesbian communities are very grateful for such porn videos and regularly use them to indoctrinate sexually confused teenagers into their immoral communities. These teens won't have to go to a storefront to rent such a video. They can rent it on the Internet in the privacy of any home or office. I am equally convinced that the teen's prospective sex partner will have a library of such videos handy along with popcorn and candy for the teen's first same gender sex party or experiment. Their prospective partner may even have some alcohol or drugs available, which usage has a high correlation to teen sexual activity. Remember the *woe* warning of God in Habakkuk 2:15 above about seeking to influence another's behavior with the bottle. *The bottle* is any substance such as alcohol or drugs that is used to loosen the inherent moral constraints of an individual. Such behavior is wicked and evil.

Do some research and mentally tune into in every aspect of your teenager's life. Do not take anything for granted. Parents should be mentors to their teens, but above all else, they should first be parents. There will be time to be friends later when they actually reach adulthood.

I started checking out the shelves of some so-called "family" video stores. Without exception, these video stores had soft-core porn movies on their shelves. I know, because I rented some of them. I was caught off guard by a Meg Ryan movie I rented. It was titled *"In the Cut"* [13] and I was shocked to find myself watching Meg Ryan totally nude in a soft-core porn movie. What is the difference between soft-core and hard-core porn? Hard core pornography is unabashed lurid sex between men and women, men and men, women and women or multiple mixed sex partners. Not to mention the possible use of sex toys, machines or other objects in the act of sex. There is no movie plot and it is simply sex being performed in a variety of lurid and sexually immoral ways.

Myth—Sexuality Doesn't Matter

However, soft-core porn, which is "softer" and not so "obvious," is being introduced to the family video store in a surreptitious way. Soft-core porn uses actors that have name recognition like Meg Ryan. It incorporates these recognized "stars" along with pornography into a quasi movie setting so that you think you may be watching a movie. You aren't, you are just watching sexually immoral pornography packaged for the masses in a less obvious and offensive way. That's so you can say you watched a [Meg Ryan, etc.] movie instead of that you watched pornography. You can also call it "lite porn" if you want, but it doesn't matter. It is still porn and it is still unacceptable in God's eyes. And, it still fits His description of what is considered sexually immoral leading to the lake of fire.

Meg Ryan is the romantic sweetheart who starred with Tom Hanks in such movies as "*Sleepless in Seattle*" and "*You've Got Mail.*" I rented the movie because I had generally enjoyed movies with Meg Ryan. However, I found myself watching an unadulterated porn video. Meg Ryan had moved from being America's sweetheart to becoming a porn star. How could that have happened? I later read a comment from her where she said: "I'm not the person whom people think I am." No kidding! But shouldn't there be a general announcement of the big porn switch so we can *forget* about such people? Isn't it evil when someone establishes a following based upon generally clean, virtuous or morally acceptable movies and then switches to a genre of unabashed sexually immoral pornography? Yes, it is evil and there is no doubt that such a change is designed to corrupt another audience of innocent people and confuse them about what is morally acceptable. The solution is to write these people off. Do not have anything to do with them since they've revealed their true stripes. That includes renting or viewing any other movie of theirs. If they engage in evil, they are not on God's side. Don't support them in any way. Once again think about what Paul taught.

> **"But now I have written to you not to keep company with anyone named a brother, who is sexually immoral ... not even to eat with such a person." 1 Cor. 5:11**

> **"And have no fellowship with the unfruitful [evil] works of darkness, but rather expose them." Ephesians 5:11**

Copyright 2005 Edward G. Palmer, All Rights Reserved.

Book of Edward—Chapter 19

Myth—Sexuality Doesn't Matter

Sexual Immorality Insults God's Grace! Heb 10:29

Note that Paul indicates that you cannot call yourself a brother or sister in the Lord Jesus Christ when you are a sexually immoral person. You could have certainly been a sexually immoral person in the past. And you might even still experience a relapse at times. But, to actively live in the flesh in a lifestyle of sexual immorality means that you never received the Gospel of Christ. Not the one Jesus preached! Not the one Paul preached! And, not the one that I preach! Otherwise a transformation in your life away from such a lifestyle "of the flesh" would have taken place. *A new person!*

"And those who are Christ's have crucified the flesh with its passions and desires. If we live in the Spirit, let us also walk in the Spirit." Galatians 5:24-25

"Therefore put to death your members, which are on the earth: fornication, uncleanness, passion, evil desire, and covetousness, which is idolatry. Because of these things the wrath of God is coming upon the sons of disobedience, in *which you yourselves once walked* **when you lived in them."**
Col. 3:5-7

"Brethren, if a man is overtaken in any trespass, you who are spiritual restore such a one in a spirit of gentleness, considering yourself lest you also be tempted." Gal. 6:1

Our conversion to Christianity does not do away with our human sexuality. It just does away with our immoral sexuality. The latter is of the flesh while the former is still part of the Spirit and our human body design. As we shed the old man and put on the new man, we shed immoral sex and put on moral sex. If we deny our human sexuality, we deny the wonderment of God's body design for the man and woman HE brings together in a holy marriage with a sanctified married bed. Sexuality and sexual immorality is not the same thing even if the Church is confused in various quarters on the differences. Our sexuality is good, but sexual immorality is bad.

Copyright 2005 Edward G. Palmer, All Rights Reserved.

Book of Edward—Chapter 19

Myth—Sexuality Doesn't Matter

Memo: Woe to the Islamists [14] who *murder* people in the name of God for they will *also* find a home in "the lake of fire, which burns with brimstone, which is the second death." Is God a liar? No, it is the Islamic terrorists who lie about God. Nothing in the Qur'an will save them from the condemnation of God found in Revelations 21:8. Woe to the many Islamic clerics who keep their mouths shut about the vile evil of these Islamists who claim to be doing what the Qur'an tells them to do for God. Nothing in the Qur'an will save them from the *Woe* pronounced by Jesus Christ in Matthew 18:6-7. Indeed, the silence of clerics and mullahs who claim to represent Islam places their behavior on the side of causing people to sin and of actually supporting evil in God's eyes. Verily I say unto you, the God of the Jews, Christians and Muslims will repay these silent Islamic leaders. Verily I say unto you, HE will repay all who engage in evil or support evil by their silence and failure to reprove what they *should* know is evil! *End Memo.*

Some people believe there is sanctuary and even secrecy among a larger group for their individual evil behavior. They believe their individual responsibility will get lost in the crowd. Is that why evil people often want to get a crowd involved? Is there cover for sin in the large group? Who gets blamed in a crowd? Verily I say unto you that every individual is still naked before God and cannot hide their individual behavior or the true nature of their heart by following the crowd or siding with the majority on any issue. God commands you to speak the truth and not to be swayed by a majority opinion. Don't be a follower. God now holds us individually responsible!

> **"You shall not follow a crowd to do evil; nor shall you testify in a dispute so as to turn aside after many to pervert justice." Exodus 23:2**

> **"Do not join a crowd that intends to do evil. When you are on the witness stand, do not be swayed in your testimony by the opinion of the majority." Exodus 23:2 NLT**

This is another issue that is opposite with God and the world. You *can* get lost in the crowd from a worldly perspective and if the majority believed like you did, who would fault you? God, who looks at the heart!

Myth—Sexuality Doesn't Matter

It's October 8th at 7:45 p.m. and I just got back from dinner. While I was studying uptown at the restaurant, God reminded me of the importance of this "crowd mentality." It relates to the *individual* issue of being "faithful even unto our death." Verily I say unto you that it is better to die telling God's truth than to be silent and live. Every silent Islamic leader should consider that maxim. Listen, any committee you serve on won't matter to God. And the corporate management you serve and report to won't matter to God. And the church you attend won't matter to God. And what your pastor taught won't matter to God. At the time of *your* judgment, it will only be *you* explaining your actions to God and HIS Son. Will Christ be your advocate if you didn't meet the "minimum righteousness standard" that he taught? I doubt it. What you can expect to hear from Jesus is the words "I never knew you" coupled with the fearful expectation of some "terrible woe" you are headed towards. Is that *woe* the lake of fire? Probably.

I confronted the *corporate* manager where I rented "*In the Cut*" and asked him this question. "If I told you that you had pornography on the shelf of your video section, would you be concerned?" He said: "It depends upon what you call pornography." I replied: "Female masturbation, full frontal nudity and onscreen sex that did not leave anything to imagination?" He took down the name of the movie, but months later it still remains on the shelf of this so-called "family" oriented grocery store with a video section. The manager is reported to be a Christian. Do you think he can hide behind the corporate management staff? It doesn't work that way with God.

Meg, if you are reading this discussion, you should be ashamed of yourself. You should also look online for your nude photos and comments about your pornographic movie. You should be ashamed of those comments as well. They are a testimony to the many people who have been subjected to the evil in which you have participated. In the online archives of Internet porn sites, you'll find Meg Ryan's nude images, which are now propagated throughout the world electronically from server to server. In one online review, a male commented, "She should have done the movie when she was young." He referred to Meg Ryan's lack of youthful looking breasts. Such stuff is now common on the Internet. It wasn't the first time that my family was morally betrayed by an established artist or writer that we liked.

Copyright 2005 Edward G. Palmer, All Rights Reserved.

Book of Edward—Chapter 19

Myth—Sexuality Doesn't Matter

I recall when my daughter Patty was in fourth grade around the age of ten. Patty was a voracious reader and found a children's author named Judy Blume she liked. Such books, as "*Are You There God? It's Me, Margaret*" were popular and might even have been a little controversial in 1980. Patty tells me this book dealt with a young girl experiencing her first period. In any case the author was quite prolific in terms of children's books and then one day Patty came home toting a Judy Blume book called "*Wifey*." Of course, the name immediately caught my eye since it did not seem like the name of a fourth grader's book. I took the book and examined it. After that I confiscated it and wanted to know where she got it. It came from the library in our small town. Judy Blume established herself as a beloved writer of children's books and then just decided she wanted to write a porn novel. I remember feeling how wrong this was for a writer to establish a following of young girls on what was morally acceptable and generally good books only to switch sides and offer something inherently evil. *Wifey* fits the bill of what God refers to as lascivious or sexually enticing material.

You can go to Amazon.com [15] on the Internet and read the first five pages of *Wifey*. They are accessible online when you search under Blume. Then, ask yourself why a popular children's book writer would write such an adult porn novel. She could have published her adult porn novel under a different name. Yet that wouldn't take advantage of her established child audience for her adult trash, would it? Same thing with Meg Ryan who established a wholesome image in films only to then turn to pornography. Of course, once people like this show such evil do not support them in any way. Why should you let your young daughter read children novels from a writer who also writes adult smut? Hello, isn't it also supporting evil to buy good books from people engaged in selling immoral books? Yes, it is.

I'm sure the corporate person who ordered "*In the Cut*" for the video store did so on the strength of Meg Ryan's name. She was a renowned star with a strong following and favorable reputation. It is highly doubtful that this person ever viewed the video. I'm also sure that the librarian who ordered "*Wifey*" did so on the strength of Judy Blume's name. She too was a renowned book author with a strong following and favorable reputation. Likewise, it is highly doubtful that the librarian read this porn novel. These are just two of countless examples of what had *appeared* righteous was really lawless. Don't get duped by outside appearance; consider the inside.

> **"Even so you also outwardly appear righteous to men, but inside you are full of hypocrisy and lawlessness." Matt. 23:28**

The lesson is simple. You cannot drop your guard down just because something appears wholesome on the surface. And, once you realize you've been duped, you must move on and not continue to support such evil. In fact, as I taught in chapter 16, evil people who disguise themselves as good people are now abundant in the Church. Satan has had 2,000 years to infiltrate the Church with his servants and there are now many in disguise.

> **"And this occurred because of false brethren secretly brought in (who came in by stealth to spy out our liberty which we have in Christ Jesus, that they might bring us [back] into bondage)." Galatians 2:4**

> **"For certain men have crept in unnoticed, who long ago were marked out for this condemnation, ungodly men, who turn the grace of our God into lewdness and deny the only Lord God and [His Son] our Lord Jesus Christ." Jude 1:4**

> **"Beware of false prophets who come disguised as harmless sheep, but are really wolves [evil people] that will tear you apart." Matthew 7:15 NLT**

A huge issue involved in this "switching sides" is Satan's strategy of confusing us and blurring the lines of distinction between what is good and evil. Would something originating from [or starring] a person who you've grown to like, because of their prior works, be part of evil? Yes, they could be. That is one of the strategies of Satan today. Hence, there are people throughout society that proffer what appears to be good. You had better get accustomed to looking a little deeper into everything they peddle and get ready to stop sin at any time. Satan is building up what *appears* to be good people waiting for the day to bring more evil into our lives. This is a time to be vigilant about all forms of sin. Don't follow a modern day piper of sin.

Myth—Sexuality Doesn't Matter

When I was a teenager, the cool thing for young males to do was to get our hands on a Playboy magazine and look at the nude photos. They were exciting and of course lascivious in nature. My how the times have changed! Go and perform an online "image search" using *Google's* [16] renowned search engines with their safe search feature turned off. Type in the word "nude" and you'll be presented with literally hundreds of offensive nude photos that would put Playboy's 1960 vintage magazines to shame as being too puritan and old style. What male needs a Playboy magazine today? The answer is none. They just need an online connection.

Can it get worse? Yes, you can select the country of your desire and search on "Japanese nude" etc. Try the plural word "nudes" and you'll get another volume of offensive and sexually lascivious photos. There is no password feature [17] to the *Google Search Engine* so parents beware. Every parent should do this exercise to learn the true nature of the Internet when it comes to sexually immoral materials. The Internet can lead your children down a path towards the lake of fire if you are not supervising them. If you have a high speed Internet connection to a kid's computer, you have given him or her a virtual sex library and any attempt to control its use will be fruitless. Save for you looking over their shoulder and having means to unplug and lock up the connection. Who knows more about the Internet and computer, you or your teenager? You should eliminate Internet privacy, police the connection, or any other way to prevent giving your children what amounts to an unabashed lewd, lascivious and licentious sex library.

One of the things I found most disturbing was what the Internet is now doing with pop culture icons. Pick any female star and search on her name. With Google's safe search feature off, you will find many nude photos. Often, the nude photo of the star is actually a fake. Porn sites in Germany and other foreign countries that operate beyond U.S. laws have taken almost every female star and have placed her head on some other woman's naked body. In some instances, this is not needed since stars like Meg Ryan have provided enough nude photos on their own. Still, the porn sites like to get creative with computer programs like Adobe Photoshop and Illustrator by making improvements on the star's body shape in creative nude illustrations. Ergo, no sagging breasts in porn illustrations.

Myth—Sexuality Doesn't Matter

Then there are pop icons like Paris Hilton whose now infamous oral sex video finds a pervasive home on Internet porn sites. You start off, with an innocent search for a star's picture and quickly without effort wind up at a graphic porn site that boggles the mind. This is the nature of the Internet today in terms of lewdness, lasciviousness and licentiousness. The question Americans should ask themselves is this: "Are we now meant to deteriorate into a debased and sexually immoral society, because our U.S. government cannot control the sexually immoral smut that now pervades our lives and culture?" *I remember the time when porn was isolated and constrained!*

There are ways to isolate and filter electronic porn and I often wonder why it is not done? One method is to assign blocks of I.P. addresses in which all adult sites must relocate to. The I.P. [Internet Protocol] address is similar to your home's address and that is how your computer finds a site. It is a number with the format "255.255.255.255." All web sites have such an address. When you type in a site name like www.apostleministry.org, your computer will first contact a local DNS or Domain Name Server who may already have the actual address. If not, that server contacts a top-level server to get the numeric address. In this case, it contacts the ORG name server, which will then return the actual address so your computer can connect.

The reason the DNS process exists is because few people could remember an actual digital numeric address. Therefore, the domain name servers transparently translate easy to remember names into digital addresses for Internet users. If a block of I.P. numbers were used for all "adult" sites, it would be a simple matter to then electronically filter out all of the smut.

Requiring "adult" sites to use a domain suffice like "*xxx*" does the same thing [I.E. www.thepornsite.xxx]. These two solutions eliminate the smut problem by providing effective filtering means. I know, because I am a Webmaster and I have placed thousands of pages on the Internet. I also own and operate web and mail servers. I know how the Internet works! So, with at least two methods available to eliminate smut, what are we waiting for? Why isn't one of these two methods or some other method used to stop the onslaught of sexual immorality throughout our society? Could it be because large corporations are financially benefiting from pornography? Is this why the problem of porn is getting so big?

Copyright 2005 Edward G. Palmer, All Rights Reserved.

Book of Edward—Chapter 19

Myth—Sexuality Doesn't Matter

Blue-Chip Corporations Profit From Porn Industry!

According to a recent article [18], "The porn industry earns between ten and fourteen billion dollars a year in the United States — and some of America's blue-chip corporations are sharing in those enormous profits." The term "blue-chip" refers to America's most respected corporations. Are the very top echelons of America's large corporations involved in peddling pornography? The article cites a report from the *Concerned Women of America* "CWA," which lists the following blue-chip corporations that are now profiting from selling pornography.

AT&T	MCI	Time-Warner	Comcast
Echostar	DirecTV	Hilton	Marriott
Sheraton	Radisson	VISA	MasterCard
		America Express	

Are you shocked? You should be. Most people do business with at least one of these blue-chip corporations. With such heavyweights in the corporate world promoting pornography, is there any reason not to expect that it would proliferate throughout our society and pervade our lives? In other words, some of these corporations are basic to our everyday way of life from supplying our telephone and cable service to providing financial services to us. They use profits from our moral transactions to fuel their immoral business activities. Do we wind up supporting evil through our ignorance of their business practices? Yes! Is it time for a boycott? Yes!

According to the CWA report, "AT&T and MCI made one billion dollars last year from dial-a-porn calls. AT&T made over $300 million from its cable and satellite porn channels. Echostar and DirecTV made over $200 million each. And hotel corporations made over $200 million each from porn movie rentals." CWA spokesperson Jan LaRue says it is a sad situation, "We spend hundreds of millions of dollars of federal tax money trying to convince the public of 'safe sex' and yet we've got a $12 billion industry promoting unsafe sex." *Woe to every corporate executive who has played a role in enabling and promoting pornography. Verily I say unto you that you will be naked before God unable to hide behind a corporate excuse.*

Book of Edward—Chapter 19

Myth—Sexuality Doesn't Matter

But you say, Edward, this is a privacy issue. Not with God it isn't and it seems like it isn't with established U.S. laws concerning the distribution of pornography. The courts have ruled that pornography in the privacy of your home is protected, but not the distribution of pornography. In an article titled *"It's Not a Privacy Issue,"* [19] established U.S. laws are discussed. The author writes, "Forty percent of all hotels and motels in the U.S., fall within legal guidelines," to be prosecuted for the distribution of pornography. He sites the Cincinnati Marriott Northeast, as well as 23 of the top 25 largest hotels in the greater Cincinnati area as being distributors of pornography. Is it any wonder when you travel nowadays that you are constantly affronted with pornography in places that used to be a family place for rest and sleep? *Woe to everyone who seeks to use the law to cloak evil. God will repay.*

A group called "Citizens for Community Values" (CCV) [20] is active in the greater Cincinnati area and they have surveyed 174 Tristate hotels. They found 98 of 174 or 56% who did not offer adult pay-per-view movies. The group plans to survey hotels in every other major city. Currently they are providing a list to prosecutors of hotels that offer adult movies, because they believe it violates existing laws on the distribution of porn. They are also sponsoring a new web site [21] to list "clean" hotels that do not offer porn. The power of the Internet to do good, should also be acknowledged. I personally use the Internet for many tasks. Without question, if I could locate a hotel that did not offer porn when I traveled, I would do so. Such a site would allow me to spot precursors to sexual immorality. But without such a resource, it is difficult to make porn free hotel travel plans.

Now I want you to fully get the gist of what I am teaching you. You need to eliminate the precursors to sexual immorality in your life. If you have a stack of pornographic movies, burn them. Don't give them away and enable or cause another to sin. Destroy them. Get them out of your life and other lives. Do the same thing with everything that falls into the category of being lewd, lascivious or licentious. These things are stepping-stones into the realm of sexual immorality. Got a phone book of Gay bars? Get rid of it. Got a phone list of Gay or lesbian partners? Get rid of it and change your phone number; make it unlisted. Find some new acquaintances that will help keep you straight. Stop seeing people who want you to participate in

Myth—Sexuality Doesn't Matter

what they think is fun, but what God declares is sexually immoral. Choose to eternalize your life in the here and now. You'll enjoy the earthly ride a lot more knowing you have a heavenly destination.

My friend Dean has hammered home a central theme on Hollywood actors that he has declared evil people. His strategy is not to support them in any manner. Once an actor gets on Dean's list, he will never again spend a dime on anything they do. He won't watch their new movies in a theater and he won't rent any video in which they take part. He won't even listen to anything they have to say. In short, he won't have anything to do with them. I told him he might quickly run out of movies to watch since most of what Hollywood offers seems to have something of a tinge of evil to it these days. Brother Dean is also a movie aficionado like me, but a very selective one. Still, I really get Dean's message! Do you? Isn't it the same message of Jesus Christ in Matthew 18:6-7? Woe to you who cause another to sin? If you pull your support, you reprove such evil. Even if they don't know what you've done, God knows. If you don't reprove, you bear their sin-guilt!

Dean's strategy can be deployed to all aspects of evil in our society. Why should you stay at a hotel that profits from porn? Why should you invest in the stock of corporations that profit from porn? Why should you support movie stars that act in porn? Why should you support authors who write porn novels? Why should you support any evil? Why support …

_____

_____ *[Name the evil]*?

As a final note on hotel porn, it is interesting to observe that when checkout time occurs, you won't find any "porn" itemized on the hotel bill. The purveyors of porn will do everything they can to eliminate any external knowledge of pornography use and protect your secrecy. That is so you'll come back knowing that they will "cloak" your porn use and seemingly protect your privacy. One does wonder, however, what their "internal" porn database on viewing habits would disclose. There is no doubt that they keep one from my business perspective. Wouldn't it be interesting if the internal computer records of hotel porn use ever got into the public domain?

Copyright 2005 Edward G. Palmer, All Rights Reserved.

Book of Edward—Chapter 19

Myth—Sexuality Doesn't Matter

Jan LaRue, CWA [18] spokesperson, sums up the corporate peddlers of porn this way. "How strange it is that these mainstream corporations would market a product that they dare not show at their annual Christmas party or at their shareholder's convention. They cannot allow it on corporate premises or at corporate activities because they know they would risk losing millions of dollars to claimants for sexual harassment or hostile work environment claims — and yet they're profiting from it by putting it out there in American homes and hotels." *Woe to the corporate hypocrites!*

The headline read *"China Offers Rewards for Reporting Porn"* [22] and seemed strange to me on this Columbus Day. China is now aggressively pursuing policies to eliminate online pornography *in their country* and even offers rewards of up to $240 to individuals who report pornographic web sites. Strange, isn't it? I was born in a country founded on the morality of Judeo Christian Scripture and yet it is a communist country that sees the evil and immorality in pornography. They shut it down and we, in the United States, fail to inasmuch pass simple laws to keep it isolated to a "warehouse" district like it was in my Minneapolis youth. Yes, the smut was still present in the 1960's, but it was physically isolated to certain junk parts of town. It did not pervade society in the metaphorical sense it now does electronically. The perverts were the only ones who showed up at the smut businesses in those days. Now strangely the perverts cloak their behavior and the entire society [rest of us] is under the onslaught of porn at every turn of the head. *Woe to every politician that does not take action to shut down this porn!*

Lewd Is Sexual Immorality & Wickedness!

Another perspective on the three levels of sexual immorality comes from Strong'S Concordance [23] and the modern dictionary [24]. Strong'S defines *lewd and lewdness* as "wickedness" and assigns these characteristics to it in its Bible study list: Shameful, sexual, youthful, adulterous, filthiness and folly. Strong'S defines *lasciviousness* as "unbridled lust" and provides the following Bible study list and characteristics:

Myth—Sexuality Doesn't Matter

Strong'S Concordance: Lasciviousness = Unbridled Lust!

Flows from the heart	Mark 7:20-23
Seen in the flesh	Gal. 5:19
Characterizes the old life	1 Pet. 4:3
Found among Gentiles	Eph. 4:19, 20
Sign of apostasy	Jude 1:4
Among Christians, lamentable	2 Cor. 12:21
To be cast away ("wantonness")	Rom. 13:13

I've already mentioned that the word *licentious or licentiousness* is not used in the King James Version and that is the text used for Strong'S Concordance. Also, that other translations use these words instead of lewd or lewdness. It is useful to reflect on Strong'S because it takes you back to a more innocent time when the language was not twisted to deceive people.

The Merriam-Webster [24] dictionary definition of *lewd* is *"sexually unchaste or licentious."* This modern dictionary therefore confirms the interchangeability of the words *lewd* and *licentious*. Unchaste is defined as lacking in chastity, which is defined as abstaining from unlawful sexual intercourse. Chastity also means having purity in heart or intent [in regards to sexual activity]. *Licentious* means the lacking of any moral restraint or disregarding restraints when it comes to sexual behavior. The anything goes and free sex mentality that emerged in the late 1960's and early 1970's in the United States typifies what it is to be lewd in God's eyes. Apostle Paul makes it clear that those who are *lewd* do not inherit the kingdom of God. Therefore, the words *lewd* and *licentious* both define part of what God terms "sexually immoral," which qualifies for the lake of fire and second death.

> **"Now the works of the flesh are evident, which are: adultery, fornication, uncleanness, *lewdness*, idolatry, sorcery, hatred, contentions, jealousies, outbursts of wrath, selfish ambitions, dissensions, heresies, envy, murders, drunkenness, revelries, and the like; of which I tell you beforehand, just as I also told you in time past, *that those who practice such things* will not inherit the kingdom of God." Galatians 5:19-21**

Myth—Sexuality Doesn't Matter

Again, it is not having been lewd that crosses a line with God. It is those who continue to practice lewdness. God forgives the homosexual or lesbian after accepting Christ, because their true and sincere repentance results in a cessation of lewdness. However, to continue to live in such a "work of the flesh" condemns one in God's eyes no matter how much one can utter the words "Jesus in my Lord." It is "lawlessness" in God's eyes and one reason why Jesus says: "I never knew you."

Sex Choices And Vessels Of Honor & Dishonor!

It's October 16th and during last Wednesday's third presidential debate the question arose: "Do you think that homosexuality is a choice?" Bush answered that he didn't know and Kerry answered that he didn't think so. Kerry said, "These people were just being who they were; no one chooses to be Gay." I'm going to talk more on this subject in a moment. For now, let me say that all love is a choice from the heart and that all sex is also a choice from the heart. No human is ever forced to love another or to engage in any act of sex. To argue otherwise places the human being on the same level of creation as that of animals. We know that this is not God's design. It also denies the command from God that we "control" sin. Again, this is where we started and it is the central theme of this chapter. God created two!

> **"So God created man in HIS own image; in the image of God HE created him; male and female HE created them."**
> **Genesis 1:27**

God did not create several variations of the human species from a sexual perspective. HE only created the male and the female, just two human sexual identities. HE meant for these two sexual beings to be joined together and to become one flesh. For a man to choose another man or a woman to choose another woman, as a mate, is to make a choice no matter how else it is portrayed in society. So, three fundamental facts are: A) All love is a choice; B) All sex is a choice; and, C) There are only males and females that make those choices. In addition, there is the issue of a *vessel of honor* or a *vessel of dishonor*. God has created human vessels of dishonor!

Myth—Sexuality Doesn't Matter

> **Jesus said, "No one, when he has lit a lamp, covers it with a vessel or puts it under a bed, but sets it on a lampstand, that those who enter may see the light." Luke 8:16**
>
> **"Does not the potter have power over the clay, from the same lump to make one vessel for honor and another for dishonor?" Romans 9:21**
>
> **" 'The LORD knows those who are HIS,' and, 'Let everyone who names the name of Christ depart from iniquity.' But in a great house there are not only vessels of gold and silver, but also of wood and clay, some for honor and some for dishonor. Therefore if anyone cleanses himself from the latter, he will be a vessel for honor, sanctified and useful for the Master, prepared for every good work." 2 Tim. 2:19-21**

It would be wrong to presume that since God has created a vessel of dishonor that it infers that homosexuals are created that way. No, there is no such thing as a "created" homosexual except in the homosexual community. Active homosexuals and lesbians are indeed "vessels of dishonor" and to the extent they exist in this world, they exist to lead all righteous people astray from their God given human sexuality. I've heard that modern day pollution is responsible for modifying the genes of some people and turning them Gay. That is a specious argument, because 2,000 years ago and from time immemorial mankind has engaged in the same sexual perversions. Ergo, long before our modern industrial society, the same sexual perversions were recorded. To claim otherwise is to engage in lies and deception. Indeed, the active Gay community and other ungodly people are engaged in turning God's grace into licentiousness. It's simply not new. Study Romans 1-2.

The Ungodly Turn God's Grace Into Licentiousness!

The trinity doctrine has produced many Gay and other apostate ministries that promote the false idea that Christ forgives "all" of your sins in a way that allows you to continue with a lewd or licentious lifestyle.

Myth—Sexuality Doesn't Matter

One example of a primarily Gay congregation is the Metropolitan Community Church [25] in Huntsville, Alabama according to a local news article on WHNT-TV. The pastor supporting homosexuality took issue with the pastor of the St. Luke Missionary Baptist Church, who's nearby sign read: "Homosexuality is a sin that God hates." In a predictable response from the apostate church, the pastor said: "It's very sad for any church to use their sign to promote hate. It goes against the Bible. God is a god of love!" This is not a new teaching. It existed 2,000 years ago. Apostle Paul taught in Romans 1-2 that Gays preached the same false message to their brethren in biblical times, even though they knew it was evil and led to eternal damnation in the lake of fire and a second death.

> **"And even as they did not like to retain [or obey] God in their knowledge, God gave them [homosexuals and lesbians] over to a debased mind [as vessels of dishonor in this world], to do those things which are not fitting; being filled with all unrighteousness, sexual immorality, wickedness, covetousness, maliciousness; full of envy, murder, strife, deceit, evil-mindedness; they are whisperers, backbiters, haters of God, violent, proud, boasters, inventors of evil things, disobedient to parents, undiscerning, untrustworthy, unloving, unforgiving, unmerciful;** *who, knowing the righteous judgment of God, that those who practice such things are deserving of death, not only do the same but also approve of those who practice them."* **Romans 1:28-32**

> **"For certain men [and women] have crept in [to the Church] unnoticed, who long ago were marked out for this condemnation, ungodly men [and women], who turn the grace of our God into lewdness and deny the only LORD God and [HIS Son] our Lord Jesus Christ." Jude 1:4**

> **"For when they speak great swelling words of emptiness, they allure through the lusts of the flesh, through lewdness, the ones who have actually escaped from those who live in error." 2 Peter 2:18**

Copyright 2005 Edward G. Palmer, All Rights Reserved.

Book of Edward—Chapter 19

Myth—Sexuality Doesn't Matter

Note that Paul makes it clear that these homosexuals and lesbians actually did know what God expected of them. Nevertheless, they still practiced their sexual abominations and taught others from their pulpits to also practice them. No doubt Gays think there is comfort in numbers. The big push to get society's recognition of Gay perversions today is in part their erroneous belief that there is comfort in society's approval. *Woe to the society that approves homosexuality as a mainstream lifestyle comparable to that of heterosexuality for surely God will abandon such a debased place.*

"But we know that the judgment of God is according to truth against those who practice such things. And do you think this, O man, you who judge those practicing such things, and doing the same, that you will escape the judgment of God?" Romans 2:2-3

Paul also taught that many people were hypocrites in that they railed against the abomination of homosexuality and lesbianism, but in secret they practiced such things. Paul makes it clear that *all* who practiced such sexually immoral things will not escape the judgment of God.

Satan's strategy is to negate God's Word. And if Satan could figure out how to confiscate the tens of millions of Bibles out in the world, he would have an easier task. As it is, too many people have the Word and it is clear. God does *hate* homosexuality! If you missed the discussion in the last chapter on why you should hate what God hates, this would be a good time to go back and review it. Yes, the Christian Church should teach people to hate — to hate all evil in any form. It doesn't get more evil and wicked in my mind than when a church denies the written word of God and teaches lies seeking to turn God's grace into licentiousness.

Woe to the apostate preacher, teacher or church that adds or subtracts to and from God's Word; denies God's Word; lies about God's Word; and or, turns God's grace into licentiousness! Surely there should be a fearful expectation of judgment and fiery indignation from God.

Myth—Sexuality Doesn't Matter

The Sexually Confused Need Medical Help!

Men may choose to have sex with other men. Women may choose to have sex with other women. In the case of men with men, they can engage in anal sex pretending it is a woman's vagina. In the case of women with women, they can obtain an attachable dildo, strap it on one partner and pretend that one is the male. In both instances, they can swap positions when one partner is finished and the other one wants to be satisfied. Both homosexuals and lesbians are also capable of engaging in simultaneous oral sex and masturbation with one another. I suspect there are also countless variations on what is physically possible with same gendered sex activities. Does all this sound too clinical? Well, I suppose it is since it describes the physical act of sex but it does not describe the spiritual act of "making love."

In the physical sense, the male penis and female vagina produce lubricants for each other during sexual mating. In the healthy male and female engaged in heterosexual sex, both of the partners not only produce lubricants, but they are also capable of reaching a simultaneous orgasm with one another. This simultaneous orgasm transcends the limited act of penile ejaculation in the male because it involves many other organs. This is to say that there is sex that involves ejaculation for the male and that there is sex that involves a male orgasm in which ejaculation is just a part of the male's whole experience. In sharp contrast, neither the anus nor the dildo is capable of performing for one's partner what God has designed into the human body of the heterosexual's partner to do naturally. And while "getting it off" together might occur in a homosexual or lesbian couple, it would be simple minded to compare it to a heterosexual couple's simultaneous orgasm.

The heterosexual's orgasm can involve the spirituality of the oneness of flesh. This can take the heterosexual couple connected to God to a higher experience during orgasm, which cannot occur in the homosexual or lesbian act of sex. This is God's spiritual aspect of sex. Don't expect God to show up during same gender sex. In contrast, the heterosexual couple that is open to the Spirit will find a sexual freedom that can only exist for those who are truly connected with one another and their God. Those couple's that have experienced this heightened climax will know what I am talking about.

Copyright 2005 Edward G. Palmer, All Rights Reserved.

Book of Edward—Chapter 19

Myth—Sexuality Doesn't Matter

In heterosexual, homosexual or lesbian acts of sex, both oral sex and masturbation of each other's partner can occur. *The Gift of Sex* discusses both of these issues in detail. Concerning oral sex, it states that "the male and female sex organs are generally clean and free from disease producing microorganisms and the urinary tract system is a sterile system." However, and in contrast, "The rectal area and mouth are contaminated with disease-producing microorganisms. Therefore, if the body is cleanly washed and there are no infections present, contamination of the mouth from the genitals is impossible. If contamination takes place because of infection, it will usually be communicated from the mouth to the genitals rather than from the genitals to the mouth." [26]

The Penner's continue, "It is important to keep in mind that just because something is not clearly wrong or dirty or unnatural, does not necessarily make it right, natural, or necessary for you."

We'll talk more on the subjects of masturbation and oral sex shortly. For now, consider that the anus is the body's opening to discharge human waste. In other words, the human body digests its nutrients and discharges excrement or feces as solid waste. Everything unfit for the health of our human body is eliminated and discharged from our anus during regular bowel movements. That includes disease and infections fought off by the body. In other words, there is more than just routine body waste coming out of our "poop shoot." Yes, there are disease-causing microorganisms. When a man shoves his penis into an anus, it is the same thing as crawling up a sewer pipe naked and exposing your body to God knows what. The anus has the same types of microorganisms found in sewer pipes, because human waste is found there. Thus, it is a ready source of potential disease for sex partners. It is like playing Russian roulette with a pistol.

When the genitals are exposed to anal discharge, an infection can occur. This fact is confirmed by the necessity of females to wipe them selves from the front to the back after a bowel movement to prevent infection from occurring. Microorganisms found in anal discharges can just as easily infect the male penis. The anus is also an absorber and can be infected by a man's penis. You can literally deliver medicines via the anus.

Myth—Sexuality Doesn't Matter

All of this information is more than you want to hear. I know. The bottom line is this. God did not create the anus for use with the male penis. All anal sex is wicked, evil and sexually immoral in God's eyes. That includes male on female anal sex. Anyone who engages in anal sex has crossed the line with God in terms of sexual immorality.

In movies and television shows, you might get the impression that many people are now actively engaging in anal sex. It is a popular sexual presentation to show a male having sex with a woman from the rear. Of course, the Hollywood crowd would like you to believe that this is anal sex between a male and female. Ergo, if anal sex between a male and female is okay, it is okay between a male and another male. Well, despite this popular sexual scene, all anal sex is bad. God summed this up with a condemnation of the sodomites in 1 Corinthians 6. These were people who allowed their anus to be used for sex by homosexuals; sodomites are male prostitutes.

> **"Do you not know that the unrighteous will not inherit the kingdom of God? Do not be deceived. Neither fornicators, nor idolaters, nor adulterers, nor homosexuals, nor sodomites [male prostitutes]." 1 Cor. 6:9**

> **"Don't you know that those who do wrong will have no share in the kingdom of God? Don't fool yourselves. Those who indulge in sexual sin, who are idol worshipers, adulterers, male prostitutes, homosexuals [will not inherit the kingdom of God]." 1 Cor. 6:9 NLT**

Of course this is a part of the Gay numbers game. Ergo, let's get more heterosexuals engaging in anal sex and they won't object to our male on male sex. Intellectually, one might then extend such anal sex to animals. Ergo, if anal sex is okay, bestiality is okay. Such is the sexually immoral logic of those who don't get it. These are sexually confused people who need some medical help to sort out their true sexuality. Then there is the so-called transsexual. The man who feels he is really a woman or the woman who feels she is really a man. Should anyone have a sex change operation? What about people with characteristics of both genders? Know any?

Copyright 2005 Edward G. Palmer, All Rights Reserved.

Book of Edward—Chapter 19

Myth—Sexuality Doesn't Matter

I remember seeing an interview with what appeared to be a gorgeous woman many years ago. She was the type that could win the Miss Universe contest in a heartbeat. She was the proverbial "knock out" to use some male vernacular with meaning. She was not only beautiful she was physically almost a perfect specimen for the female sex. The only problem was, she used to be a he. I was fascinated by her story. Here was a case of a female trapped in a male body? Ever wonder how that could happen?

As it turns out, a small segment of the baby population is born with dual genitalia having characteristics of both male and female. In the past, apparently the doctor just made a decision at birth and "decided the sex." I understand that today, if such an event occurs, they would watch the child for a while to make a more educated sex decision. However, I would say that getting the sex mixed up is a rare occurrence. Nevertheless, in the tens of thousands of people I have seen during my life, I remember a handful with such odd characteristics. I remember looking at a shapely body from the rear view thinking "this girl looks hot" only to find out that it was a he instead of a she. I also remember seeing what looked like a husky looking man only to find out it was a she instead of a he. Yet in all my life, I could count such instances on one hand. They are rare and not the norm!

I once saw a documentary on males having sex change operations and who and why they were having them. Unlike the "knock out" I mentioned above, every one of the documentary males changing to females were ugly and had no obvious feminine characteristics such as a female shaped body. How do they change a male into a female? They hollow out his penis, cut a cavity into his body where a vagina would be and invert the penis' skin for a pretend vagina. Then, they put the man on female hormone therapy to alter other male features. He then dresses and experiences life as a woman???

In a recent study [27], 1% of the surveyed group stated that they were asexual and "have never felt sexually attracted to anyone at all." They lead a life without sex and have no concerns about this lack of sexual interest. In fact, there is now "The Asexual Visibility and Education Network" with an online store that supports "asexuality." In addition to a 1% asexual group, the study cites only a limited 3% homosexual population.

Myth—Sexuality Doesn't Matter

The Gays would like you to believe that one out of ten or 10% of the population is homosexual or lesbian. This is a lie that is oft repeated to an uninformed general population. During the Gay marriage fiasco in San Francisco, the mayor of the city cited such a statistic. You can run your own numbers using the population of San Francisco and the number of Gay marriages that have occurred there and elsewhere. I did some number crunching and struggled to find a 1.5% Gay and lesbian population based on their aggressive Gay marriage campaign. When you get down to the actual facts, this is a limited population on the fringe of the mainstream. Don't believe for the moment that it is pervasive throughout society. In fact, you'll also find that homosexuals and lesbians are clustered in a few select areas. San Francisco, Minneapolis and New York City all have sizable Gay populations. Those sections of these cities with the Gay concentrations are the modern day Sodom's of the world. Yet if you run their numbers against the populations of those cities, you'll struggle to find even a 1% Gay and lesbian population in those cities.

There is justification to be concerned about a person who is confused about his or her sexuality and God's gender design. This is especially true for young teens that are being aggressively influenced and pursued by the peddlers of the Gay agenda. You know, the people who want to teach your Kindergarten student it is okay for Johnny to have two daddies or Mary to have two mommies. Sexually confused people should get some medical [28] help. For example, they can now get a complete body scan. Go ahead and get one if you are confused. Get a complete blood work up and physical. Determine for yourself whether you are more male or more female. If you think you are a woman trapped in a man's body and your doctor and family agrees, go ahead and get a sex change operation. Maybe you are one of those unfortunates in which the doctor did make a wrong choice at birth.

Once you determine if you are a male or a female, then live that life in holiness to God. Don't think for one moment you can be a male engaging with another male in sex. Don't think for one moment you can be a woman engaging another women in sex. All such people are sexually immoral in God's eyes. *Woe to all sexual perverts for they are condemned to the lake of fire and a second death.*

Myth—Sexuality Doesn't Matter

Do you think it is a cruel thing or mean for me to remind you of God's Holy Word? You shouldn't if you really call yourself a Christian. And let me remind you that this is whom the book is written for.

"You shall not lie with a male as with a woman. It is an abomination [to God]." Leviticus 18:22

"If a man lies with a male as he lies with a woman, both of them have committed an abomination [before God]. They shall surely be put to death. Their blood shall be upon them." Leviticus 20:13

Verily I say unto you that a woman shall not lie with another woman as with a man. It is an abomination unto God. Verily I say unto you that if a woman does lie with another woman as with a man, that they shall both be surely put to death in the lake of fire, which awaits the sexually immoral of this earthly plane of existence. Indeed, their blood shall also be upon their own heads. They too will have only themselves to blame.

"For this reason God gave them up to vile passions. For even their women exchanged the natural use for what is against nature." Romans 1:26

The human history written in ancient manuscripts belie the argument that homosexuals, lesbians and transsexuals are victims of "gene" pollution. The same kind of sexual perversions have existed from time immemorial, as long as man has been on this earth. Therefore, the only intellectually sound conclusions that can be drawn is that such people are either sexually confused, in need of help, or have simply made a choice of behavior that is unacceptable to God. Those who are confused or in need of help can find it when they seek it. Instead of seeking help to alter your physiology, why not seek help that will reinforce the genitalia you are already equipped with? Why not reinforce your God given body design? If you are a man, reinforce your manhood. If you are a woman, reinforce your womanhood. Eliminate any precursors to your sexual confusion. If you've made the wrong choice, repent and become a vessel of honor unto God. Listen to HIM!

Myth—Sexuality Doesn't Matter

Sexual Pleasure Is A Part of God's Design!

Perhaps the most confusing church teaching either direct or implied is that our God given *gift of sex* is somehow bad for us. Secondly, that if we do experience sexual pleasure, it must certainly be sinful. Therefore, at the opposite end of immoral sex and the teaching that all sexual pleasures are good is the idea that all sexual pleasures are problematic with God. So, let's examine this area for a while. Is all sexual pleasure bad for us? Should sex be limited to strictly the area of procreation? How did the church and Christianity reach some of its conclusions?

I was musing about the bases of church sexual teachings and found that it isn't hard to understand why the church is often confused. Consider for a moment some of the ground that we've already covered. First, since sex feels good, all sex must be good for us. That I suspect is the basis of the licentious theology, which incorporates the thoughts that all love is of God and that all sins are truly forgiven. Ergo, for a man to love another man or a woman to love another woman sexually is okay in God's eyes, because it is of love first of all and secondly, sins no longer matter to those who accept Christ. Thus, it is easy to understand the sexually perverted apostate church and its sexual freedom logic. However, it has to ignore a lot of God's Word. In fact, it has to add and subtract and lie about God's Word as well.

Then there is Lot who was so drunk he didn't realize he was having sex with his two daughters on two different nights. I can understand how this is possible from a human perspective having spent 7 1/2 years in the U.S. Navy. I remember several sailors commenting about having a rude awakening. That is, waking up with someone ugly in bed that they had no memory about meeting and hooking up with. It wasn't a good story in most cases. That is what alcohol, drugs and other substances can do. They can alter the mind and our human behavior to the point where we no longer are in control. From this illustration, you can imagine all kinds of precursors that the church would find objectionable. I suspect that is why some teach against dancing albeit "there is a time to dance" [Eccles. 3:4]. Ergo, if you don't go to the party [dance] you won't get drunk and lose control.

Copyright 2005 Edward G. Palmer, All Rights Reserved.

Book of Edward—Chapter 19

Myth—Sexuality Doesn't Matter

Then there is Onan who refused to climax and ejaculate into Tamar's vagina to impregnate her. The Word says that every time he was with Tamar that "he spilled his seed [semen] on the ground" and that God killed him for this behavior. Several church teachings could easily have emerged from just this one story. I.E. Sex is strictly for procreation [begetting] because we are not meant to enjoy it. Sex is a duty to procreate and it is a sin to practice any form of birth control. And, of course, masturbation [which is an often presumed behavior of Onan] is bad for you. We've already discussed this story and what made God mad was that Onan did not honor his brother with a child. That was the custom of the time under Jewish law when a brother died. The story has nothing to do with sexual pleasure, birth control or masturbation.

The church might even ponder Onan's willful destruction of his semen [seed] and then conclude this fact alone is a good cause to condemn masturbation. The Catholic Church claims masturbation is a "gravely disordered action" [29]. A "grave sin" can become a mortal sin in Catholicism by being accompanied with a) deliberate action, and b) knowing it is not what God wants and still ignoring that fact. Therefore, in Catholicism, masturbation can be either a "venial" or "mortal" sin depending upon conditions. The Bible states, "There is sin that leads to death and sin that doesn't" (1 John 5:16). However, I know of no qualifications to the sins that God itemizes and states *will* lead to the lake of fire and a second death. The question then becomes whether masturbation is sexually immoral falling in the same category that God has put homosexuality and lesbianism. The same basic question can be asked of oral sex. Is it sexually immoral?

Therefore, the sound mind that God has given us takes such a theology to task. First of all, just in the act of mating, literally hundreds of millions of sperm will die each month with only one lucky sperm actually mating with an egg on one day [to survive sex]. Yet even this sperm does not maintain its identity; it becomes one-half of the zygote's beginning. See *Miracle of Life* section in the last chapter for further discussion. Secondly is the fact that the testes in the male are a "sperm factory" that never shuts down throughout the male's life. Thus, in every ejaculation whether in a vagina or out of a vagina, the male produces hundreds of millions of sperm of which 99.9999999% will be destroyed during every male's life.

Myth—Sexuality Doesn't Matter

While the term *masturbation* has negative connotations in the act of solitary sex, does that really define everything about masturbation? Here again, the sound mind has to look deeper. Exactly what is masturbation other than the stroking of the penis or the vagina-clitoris? And while this may be the solitary act of a self-contained person, exactly what do you think occurs in every marriage bed between almost every husband and wife? Yes, it is the joint stroking of each other's genitals. Isn't this also masturbation? Yes, of course it is. Isn't this a sin? I highly doubt it. For two lovers to stroke one another's genitals is to offer pleasure to each other as foreplay prior to actual sexual intercourse.

Therefore, besides the issue of destroyed sperm being specious, the fact that lovers masturbate one another's genitals during the act of sex also belies the theology that masturbation is a "grave sin." Intellectually the question can be posed like this. Is our God so capricious that it is okay for the wife to masturbate the husband's penis, but condemns the husband to the lake of fire if he does so himself? Likewise, is our God so capricious that it is okay for the husband to masturbate his wife's vagina-clitoris, but condemns the wife to the lake of fire if she does so herself? The answer is no, because our God is a god of order and not of confusion. Clearly the issue of masturbation does not rise by itself to the level of sexual immorality in either of these two contexts. That, however, does not mean that the act of masturbation cannot become a precursor to actual sexual immorality.

What about when one of the married lovers rubs his or her genitals against the thigh of the other to obtain the pleasure of this erotic act during lovemaking? Isn't that also masturbation? Yes, it is. Is it sinful? No, it is not. The marriage bed is sanctified in God's eyes for the pleasure of the two lovers. Aside from anal sex, bestiality or dragging a third party into the bed, it is hard to understand how these lovers can sin with only their own mutually acceptable and beneficial love making pleasures.

The same reality occurs when considering oral sex. Is this not simply the act of masturbation in a different form? Yes it is. Therefore, oral sex would be condemned if God condemned masturbation. Yet because God says the marriage bed is sanctified, both of these are also in that context.

Myth—Sexuality Doesn't Matter

To think otherwise poses an interesting dilemma in itself. Are lovers not supposed to touch one another? Are they not supposed to feel the erotic pleasures of their skin touching and rubbing against each other? To caress and love one another with all that their body offers in terms of God's gift of human sexuality? Is a man allowed to touch, caress, kiss, lick and suck on his wife's breast, but not also allowed to do so with her entire naked body? Anyone who has ever made passionate love to his or her lover would laugh at such an outrageous proposition, because it only demonstrates a thorough lack of understanding human sexuality. It also demonstrates a lack of God's *gift of sex* and someone who has never experienced the gift's pleasures.

To be enraptured [filled with delight] by your wife's love is a biblical instruction. Also, we are to let the breasts of the wife of our youth satisfy us *at all times*. Yes, female breasts sag with age and as children are born, the female body gets changed from its youthful form. God says to let the breasts of the love of our youth sustain us throughout our life.

> **"Let your fountain be blessed, and rejoice with the wife of your youth. As a loving deer and a graceful doe, let her breasts satisfy you at all times; and always be enraptured with her love." Proverbs 5:18-19**

Let me translate this for you. Jackie and I were 17 and 18 when we got married. She was 56 when she died. In the 39 years we were married, I was always enraptured by her love. And her breasts always satisfied me. This is an instruction to be faithful to one another even into old age and despite the shifting form of the body. It is also an instruction to be sexually passionate regardless of how long you have been married. You are never too old for sex; Abraham and Sarah proved that point.

Sexual intercourse is another form of masturbation. Does not the penis stroke the vagina-clitoris and vice versa? How are all these forms of masturbation different to God when the end result of ejaculation or climax in the marriage bed is the same? God says sex is good when it is in a marriage. That is why the marriage bed is sanctified and fornication or sex outside of marriage is condemned and termed sexually immoral.

Myth—Sexuality Doesn't Matter

The male body creates internal sexual pressures and for most men there is nothing that can be done short of getting castrated. For example, during sleep and about every 90 minutes, the body forces blood to flow into the male penis to cause an erection. Often that erect penis will then rub against the sheets, shorts, wife, etc. and lead to sexual intercourse or maybe just a nocturnal emission. The male may be dreaming and without any awareness find his penis being stimulated and leading to an emission. Yet isn't this also just another variation of masturbation? Yes it is. And, it explains why so much sex takes place in the middle of the night in young couples. Fortunately for the male, the pressures decrease with age, but do not entirely go away. This presents the intellectual conclusion that God's body design for the male is of one that requires ejaculation. In other words, if the male does not have sex or masturbate to relieve the body's sexual pressures, the body itself will find a way to relieve its sexual pressures.

An article posted on NewScientist.com [30] references an Australian study conducted on masturbation. "A team in Australia led by Graham Giles of The Cancer Council Victoria in Melbourne asked 1079 men with prostrate cancer to fill in a questionnaire detailing their sexual habits, and compared their responses with those of 1259 healthy men of the same age. The team concludes that the more men ejaculate between the ages of 20 and 50, the less likely they are to develop prostrate cancer." There is increasing scientific evidence that supports God's male body design.

> **"And the LORD God said, 'it is not good that man should be alone; I will make him a helper [and sex mate] comparable to him.' " Genesis 2:18**

"It's a prostatic stagnation hypothesis," says Giles. "The more you flush the ducts out, the less there is to hang around and damage the cells that line them." Intellectually it is clear that male ejaculation has physical health ramifications for the prostrate.

> **"So God blessed Noah and his sons, and said to them: 'Be fruitful and multiply, and fill the earth.' " Genesis 9:1**

Myth—Sexuality Doesn't Matter

Clearly God has commanded us to have sex in a moral way. That is evidenced in many verses. So, it is clear that males in general were meant to mate with a female and that sex was to be a regular part of their lives. I used to joke with Jackie and tell her that on the days we had sex, I felt my life was extended by one day and on the days we did not have sex, I felt my life was shortened by two days. Something inherently in my body has always told me and confirmed that sex was good. The pleasurable aspects of human sexuality cannot be denied by theologies that ignore God's body designs.

"So husbands ought to love their own wives as their own bodies; he who loves his wife loves himself." Ephes. 5:28

"Nevertheless, because of sexual immorality, let each man have his own wife, and let each woman have her own husband. Let the husband render to his wife the affection due her, and likewise also the wife to her husband. The wife does not have authority over her own body, but the husband does. And likewise the husband does not have authority over his own body, but the wife does. Do not deprive one another except with consent for a time that you may give yourselves to fasting and prayer; and come together again so that Satan does not tempt you because of your lack of self-control." 1 Cor. 7:2-5

There would be a whole lot more sexual activity if married couples realized they had authority over each other's body. If they realized there were health benefits to married sex, they would not get so easily dissuaded from their *duty* to have sex with one another by the pressures of life. Paul also teaches that having sex is part of the *control* of sin. If married sex falls in this category of *sin control* — masturbation must also fall there.

"No temptation has overtaken you except such as is common to man; but God is faithful, who will not allow you to be tempted beyond what you are able, but with the temptation will also make the way of escape, that you may be able to bear it." 1 Cor. 10:13

Myth—Sexuality Doesn't Matter

Are you gasping for air yet? Hold on, there is a lot more ground to cover. Consider that sex therapists [31] like Sue Johanson of Canada also advise the use of masturbation to level out the sexual needs of married couples. Maybe the husband wants sex seven times a week and the wife two times, then what? I'd say, let's take the average. But others say work out a compromise and if needed the other person can masturbate in between sex encounters. Sounds clinical I know, but it is a solution if both partners agree. Jackie and I were watching a show where the wife was upset that her husband would have sex and then masturbate later on the same day. Jackie's feeling was that his body belonged to his wife. This is biblical. Therefore, any such solution to different sex needs should be mutually agreed upon. This is especially true because this is the level of intimacy that will enable marriage to survive. If you can't talk about sex needs with one another, it is not a good long-term sign. Get to know one another's body and needs in a very intimate way. As your marriage progresses, children and other life forces will take away the spontaneity that was present in the early years. If you want to continue with an active sex life, you'll have to start planning it.

Masturbation cannot take the place of vaginal sex for the male or female. It is inferior in major ways. For the male, masturbation leads to ejaculation, but this is not the same as having an orgasm. When the male penis is inside the female's vagina and they are face to face, their entire bodies become involved as chests, breasts, legs, thighs, lips, eyes, etc. touch each other. When an orgasm occurs, it transcends masturbation, because it involves many other organs than just the genitals. It also involves the spirit side of the relationship, which heightens the sexual drama. Yet, clearly the act of masturbation plays a role in all married sex to some degree.

Therefore, while masturbation is a "dirty" word, the reality is that most people engage in some form of it either with their lover or by themselves. I won't even bother citing statistics from sex studies, because you can find those on your own. Can masturbation be a problem? Yes, it can. When it interferes with the normal sexual relationship of the married couple, it can pose a problem. Likewise, it can be an aide to marital sex when the male has a hard time "holding on" and experiences a premature ejaculation.

Myth—Sexuality Doesn't Matter

Masturbation before sex can often relieve the pent up sexual pressure in the male. Regular active married sex would also alleviate the male's body pressure. Does the female experience similar sexual pressures? I can't say for sure, but I would have to believe she does. Therefore, one can conclude intellectually that couples engage in masturbation of each other during foreplay, masturbation is useful in alleviating premature ejaculation and it is harmful when it interferes with the couple's sexual relationship. In *The Gift of Sex*, a complete discussion of the subject is available. [32]

Give your children some perspective on masturbation and its broader role in married sex. If you do not teach your children these things, they will learn them on the Internet at sites that teach both male masturbation [33] and female masturbation [34]. If you don't talk about oral sex, your children may learn the full details on the Internet at Sue Johanson's web site [31].

You can contrast the male sperm factory with the female's stockpile of eggs, which are emitted one at a time each month throughout her life until menopause at which time there are no more eggs. Note that the egg stock not only depletes, but can also become of questionable quality after age thirty-five. As the female egg stock dries up and peri-menopause sets in, the woman's vagina may stop producing the level of lubricant that it used to, which can complicate sexual intercourse. With some K-Y Jelly or other lubricant, however, sexual enjoyment can continue on indefinitely for the female's clitoris does not stop producing sexual enjoyment for her. These aspects of God's male and female body design pose an interesting question: If we are only to have sex for purposes of procreation, why is it we can still physically enjoy sex long after the possibility of procreation has gone away?

If just *begetting* children was the only reason for moral sex, it yields several idiotic results. If sex is only to beget children, then sex after the wife is pregnant is a sin. How logical is that? Some of the greatest sex a married couple can have is during pregnancy albeit within reasonable physical limits. The issue of rear-entry vaginal sex came up when Jackie asked her nurse how we could enjoy sex in the later months of one of our pregnancies. As it seems, God has made a provision for moral sex that allows the penis to enter the vagina from the posterior or buttocks area of the body.

Myth—Sexuality Doesn't Matter

Rear-entry vaginal sex is possible during pregnancy and at other times. What is amazing is that the penis is inclined to slope upwards towards the clitoris during face-face or missionary sex, but the vagina is also equipped with two sensitive areas on the opposite side of its opening. From a rear-entry vaginal sex position, the penis would engage those sensitive areas of the vagina by the male's upward sloping penis. According to *The Gift of Sex*, "These [4 and 8 o'clock positions of the open face-face vagina] are often more highly sensitive areas in the vagina." [35]

Thus the female and male body is both capable of sex throughout pregnancy. What about the issue of menopause? If sex were just for procreation, then sex after menopause would be a sin. Aside from the fact that our bodies do not stop enjoying sexual pleasures just because of menopause, there is the clarion example of Abraham and Sarah. Sarah had already passed menopause and her womb was dry according to the account in Genesis 18:11. Yet this did not daunt God who told them to keep up the sex and she would get pregnant according to HIS timeline. I note that it took awhile and that Sarah was 90 and Abraham was 100. Do you think they enjoyed sex while trying to make a baby? I did and I am sure that their bodies were better off than those of a comparable age today. Abraham remarried after Sarah's death and had other children around the age of 137. One can only intellectually conclude that sex *also* exists for the pleasure of the human race and not just for the limited and sole purpose of procreation.

The issue of male or female body discharge is also brought forth in the Bible and no doubt confuses the church. God says to stay away from those who are "unclean" for different periods of time. Consider HIS Word.

Bodily discharges meant people were unclean!

"If any man has an emission of semen, then he shall wash all his body in water, and be unclean until evening. And any garment and any leather on which there is semen, it shall be washed with water, and be unclean until evening. Also, when a woman lies with a man, and there is an emission of semen, they shall bathe in water, and be unclean until evening." Leviticus 15:16-18

Myth—Sexuality Doesn't Matter

> "If a woman has a discharge, and the discharge from her body is blood, she shall be set apart seven days; and whoever touches her shall be unclean until evening."
> **Leviticus 15:19**

When you consider the teachings on the issue of being unclean in God's eyes, it is easy to understand a variety of church teachings against even the idea of sex. However, all of our uncleanness has passed in God's eyes through His Son's sacrifice. Consider the Word.

Those in Christ are washed clean spiritually!

> "Now where there is remission of these, there is no longer an offering for sin. Therefore, brethren, having boldness to enter the Holiest [Holy of Holies] by the blood of Jesus, by a new and living way which he consecrated for us, through the veil, that is, his flesh, and having a High Priest [in Christ Jesus] over the house of God, let us draw near with a true heart in full assurance of faith, having our hearts sprinkled from an evil conscience and our bodies washed with pure water." **Hebrews 10:18-22**

You should understand that those who are sincerely "in Christ" are not unclean or inhibited in any way from freely entering the Holy of Holies! I've heard it said often that you truly are not with God until He has gotten into your pocket book. Listen, this is real truth. Until you surrender your human sexuality to God, you are not fully surrendered to Him. Money? He doesn't care about your money and He certainly doesn't need your money! Remember, Jesus sent his apostles out into the field without a money purse and they never lacked anything! He cares about your heart and your obedience! When you surrender your sexuality to God, then you've truly surrendered. Long before I did that I had already surrendered my pocketbook. We humans like to hold out from a total surrender. We like to have some control and sexuality is the last hold out in my opinion. Yet if you do surrender your sexuality, you can find God in every aspect of your life. That includes while you are engaged in the spiritual act of making love.

Copyright 2005 Edward G. Palmer, All Rights Reserved.

Book of Edward—Chapter 19

Myth—Sexuality Doesn't Matter

Both Jackie and I met God during our sexual intercourse. I remember distinctly hearing her call out to God at times. "O God!" We never did talk about this so I am unsure about all that she talked to God about during sex. Maybe it was just a praise statement of thanks. Sounded like that to me. I can tell you that we had both invited HIM into our bedroom and into our sex lives. We never regretted the sexual freedom God gave us to experience and we fully enjoyed HIS *gift of sex*. The act of making love is different than the worldly act of having sex. The first is a spiritually based experience of mutually enjoying each other's bodies and of giving and receiving pleasure to one another. The latter is getting f#~~#d to use today's sexual vernacular. It might describe the physical aspect of sex, but it leaves God out of the picture. Forty years ago, everyone used the spiritual language of "making love" to fully describe marital sex. Today? Marriage is left out of the talk.

The Penner's pointed out the Song of Solomon in a discussion of oral sex in their book [36]. I will quote briefly from their book.

"There is a great deal of interest in and at the same time a great deal of doubt regarding this activity [oral sex]. Solomon in the Song of Solomon refers continually to enjoying the delights of his lover's body. He speaks of feeding among the lilies (4:5). His partner says, 'Awake, north wind, and come, south wind! Blow on my garden that its fragrance may spread abroad. Let my lover come into his garden and taste its choice fruits' (4:16). In the following verse King Solomon says, "I have come into my garden. ... I gather my myrrh with my spices. I have eaten my honeycomb and my honey; I have drunk my wine and my milk" (5:1). His love responds, 'Eat, O friends, and drink; drink your fill, O lovers.' Many references speak of the oral delights of one's lover and the enjoyment of her full body. Every part is talked about: hair, lips, neck, breasts, stomach, legs, and feet. The lovers usually refer to the genitals as 'the garden of spices.' The book speaks of total body involvement."

Indeed, in the Song of Solomon, we find the passion of lovers who would use their mouth, their lips and their tongue on their lover's body. They would engage all of their senses including hearing, taste, smell and touch. Yet to discuss such lovemaking would only be in spiritual terms.

Copyright 2005 Edward G. Palmer, All Rights Reserved.

Myth—Sexuality Doesn't Matter

In the process of foreplay during love making, erotic pleasures are evoked in both lovers by the use of their entire bodies. This includes skin touching skin along the entire length of the body, the use of our hands and of course the use of our mouths, lips and tongues. The act of oral sex between passionate lovers may seem as natural to some as any other aspect of their sexuality. Still, to others, it may seem incredibly repulsive. The spiritual guidance here is simple. One should not be forced into doing something that doesn't feel right to them. Therefore, what is acceptable for one lover may not be for the other lover.

The Penner's summarize: "The Scriptures are not clear on the matter of oral sex, and so it is one of those gray areas where various biblical teachings will come into play. The principle of what is loving and caring for the other person must be addressed. On the other hand, the teaching that our bodies are each other's to enjoy must also be incorporated." [37] I highly recommend their book for a more complete discussion of oral sex.

Do I personally believe that masturbation and oral sex are okay for the Christian? Yes, I do, but only in the context of marriage and only in the context of what feels natural for both lovers. This is not something that can be forced on either partner. It either comes naturally as it does to many married couples or it doesn't. In all cases, care must be given to the act of sex from a cleanliness perspective. In this respect, I agree with Solomon that the ability to enjoy the fullness of our lover's body is a wonderful gift from God. Now I realize that I have just taken a position that is opposite of many in the Church. It certainly isn't the first. However, I was a young sailor passionately in love with my wife and our love knew no limits for one another. That existed for a full fourteen years before I gave my heart to God. Now, twenty-five years after that surrender to God, nothing has changed in my views of making love in a God sanctioned marriage bed.

Pleasure is a part of our sexuality! To deny that pleasure or diminish those who feel pleasure with guilt teachings on the "immorality of pleasure" per se is what truly leads to unchecked sexual immorality. When the church denies the reality of our bodies, it demonstrates ignorance of sex. This fails to then make the critical distinction that sexual pleasure in marriage is okay.

Myth—Sexuality Doesn't Matter

Then there is Judah who unwittingly has sex with Tamar only to later find out it was his daughter in law. What's that all about? Did Tamar have her face hidden? If so, then Judah was only having sex and was certainly not into "making love." One might erroneously conclude that we are not supposed to "make love" and that sex is again just a duty to "beget." Still, Judah thought he was engaging a prostitute and "getting it off" is all that mattered in such instances.

The same thing could not be said about Jacob and Leah. Jacob went into his tent thinking he would be "making love" to Rachel. Laban, his father in law, substituted Leah. Yet, Jacob did not know until the next day when he woke up? What's that all about? Was Jacob drunk? It is hard to imagine not having a face-to-face meeting in the bed. What about Leah's voice and even her body size? Jacob had spent seven years of labor to earn the right to Rachel. One might erroneously conclude once again that we are not supposed to "make love" and that sex is again just a duty to "beget."

God Designed Women to Enjoy Sex!

If sex was just a duty to beget, then there is a serious discrepancy in the design of the female body. For one, there is the female clitoris, which is a source of intense pleasure to women. So much so that some African tribes are given to the idea of circumcising women by cutting off the clitoris. The reasoning is simple; women should not have sexual pleasure. How twisted is that logic? And the fact that such an evil practice exists is a testimony to the fact that God designed the female body to experience sexual pleasure.

Sex is not a sin unless it crosses the defined lines drawn by God HIMSELF. The church cannot impose its "sex" sanctions on pleasure simply out of the thought that if it feels good it must be sinful. God designed our bodies to enjoy sexual pleasures knowing it would "feel good." Yet the enjoyment of our sexual pleasures can only be in the context of marriage. It is outside of this limited framework that God condemns the sexually immoral. In the case of solitary sex, which is self contained, it is moral until it enters the heart and begins to function as a precursor of external sexual activity, which will lead to lewdness, lasciviousness and licentiousness.

Copyright 2005 Edward G. Palmer, All Rights Reserved.

Myth—Sexuality Doesn't Matter

Married Sex Is God's Safe Sex Solution!

Listen. Wives do not give up your sexy nightclothes, as it is okay to be sexually enticing to your own husbands. Remember, the marriage bed is sanctified in God's eyes and married moral sex is a blessing from God.

I suspect that many Bible verses have led to a sexual crisis in some Christian minds that fear that they do not know where to draw the line. To practice safe sex in God's eyes, restrain sex to the marriage bed and limit it to one man and one woman in the spiritual state of being one flesh. Any sex out of these simple boundaries can get you into trouble with God. Yet there is more to the idea of married sex, there is married "moral" sex.

"Marriage is honorable among all, and the [marriage] bed [is] undefiled; but fornicators and adulterers God will judge." Hebrews 13:4

"Let marriage be held in honor by all, and let the marriage bed be kept undefiled; for God will judge fornicators and adulterers." Hebrews 13:4 NRSV

"Marriage should be honored by all, and the marriage bed kept pure, for God will judge the adulterer and all the sexually immoral." Hebrews 13:4 NIV

Would you drag an animal in the marriage bed and practice bestiality because you think that the marriage bed is somehow sanctified? No. Sexual immorality can occur in the marriage bed as well. What God is telling us is sexuality in the context of marriage between a man and woman is sanctified in HIS eyes and that *their marriage bed* [wherever they sleep together] is undefiled unless they engage in lewd and sexually immoral conduct.

From a mental standpoint, a husband and wife should not worry about how many times per day they are having sex. However often they have sex is still sanctified in God's eyes unless it is immoral sex. A married couple

Myth—Sexuality Doesn't Matter

would not be considered lewd just for thinking about sex morning, noon or night. That is not abnormal for a husband and wife passionately in love.

Therefore, the idea of being lewd goes much further than just normal sex between a husband and wife and takes on the thought of being engrossed by sex. This is to say that a husband and wife can get overly engrossed in sex. When sex starts to take on dimensions outside of the *privacy* of the marriage bed, it becomes lewd in God's eyes. Maybe you think it would be exciting to have sex on a bench in Central Park in downtown Manhattan? Of course, you reason that you might not get caught at 2 a.m. in the morning. Watch out, this is taking on an attribute of lewdness in God's eyes.

Any form of public exposure of the genitals would be considered a violation of lewd laws in most states. It would also be considered lewd in God's eyes. In a recent news article, a couple was arrested for having sex at the Alamo [38] in San Antonio, Texas at 5:30 p.m. They were charged with "public lewdness." In another article [39], a high school senior streaked his commencement ceremony in Pennsylvania after being denied the right to walk with his classmates. He was arrested and the judge sentenced him to six months to two years in prison for his "nakedness" in front of the many young children. Many, even I, would argue that the punishment does not fit the crime. Yet, court tolerance of such lewd behavior is no longer a given, especially when the lewd exposure is in front of little children. In another article, a Republican congressman [40] is being confronted with a 1974 picture of his streaking prank back when he was an 18-year old college student. With modern computers, you should understand that your public immorality will exist forever and will haunt you all the days of your life.

The propensity of young people towards exhibiting themselves nude in public is striking. Today, it is not rare for young women to simply strip their blouses and bras off in displays of public nudity. This can even extend to taking off their bikini bottoms. Then there is the issue of almost walking around nude to begin with on beaches with thongs that bare almost all there is to see. In a quasi documentary [41] of the college spring break in Cancun, Mexico, young women and men engage in morally loose behavior that bares all and leaves little to the imagination. Such behavior transcends being lewd and lascivious. It is in the realm of licentiousness devoid of morality.

Myth—Sexuality Doesn't Matter

When you've got godly *reason* as the guard to your heart, it will warn you whenever you are crossing a sexually immoral line with God. You only have to listen to the soft voice that raises the spiritual caution flag. If it feels uncomfortable, don't do it. If it seems perverse, don't do it. If it involves public exhibitionism, don't do it. Most of this is simple common sense when you realize sanctified sex occurs in the privacy of a married couple's bedroom. Again, this is husband and wife wherever they sleep.

Having sex with someone you love in the context of the traditional marriage bed can take you beyond the mere physical aspects of sex and into the spirituality of oneness of flesh. This oneness of flesh can also take you and your lover [spouse] into a place of oneness with God. I lost track of the number of times both Jackie and I were taken to a place of wonder during sex that only a true oneness of flesh can take you with God. Those who have experienced this know what I am talking about. You don't get that kind of heightened *spiritually based* sexual experience with a cheap date on a one-night stand in some sleazy hotel room. This is a spiritual experience!

Reason is the guard that keeps your heart straight. In 1959, I was prowling the streets of Minneapolis hunting for a sweetheart. I was only 13 years of age. In those days, a guy would have to date a girl for months if not a couple years before he could get to first base [petting]. If you were able to get anywhere with a girl faster and in a matter of only a few dates, that girl was said to be easy [a slut]. All the boys wanted to date a promiscuous girl, but none wanted to marry her. I've observed the same male behavior all my life. Many women don't really get this male irony. In the age of women's lib, many simply move in with a man and give him all the sex he wants.

Women often then find out that marriage becomes the last thing on their man's mind. Many articles and books have been written on the subject of living together, which document the problems associated with couples in cohabitation. This includes a substantially greater chance of divorce should a cohabitating couple decide to later get married [42]. Common sense suggests that a lack of 100% commitment at the start of living together would lead to a less than 100% commitment after marriage at a later date. Go search the Internet and study up on this issue.

Myth—Sexuality Doesn't Matter

Don't live together unless you have no intention of a successful long-term marital relationship. Also, don't live together just because your friends believe it is okay. A huge population of today's youth is now programmed to believe that it is okay to live together, but peer pressure is a stupid reason to commit a mortal sin with God.

Still, cohabitation is the popular thing to do today among many young couples, isn't it? According to the *Second Edition of Should We Live Together* [43], "No positive contribution of cohabitation to marriage has ever been found." And, "Virtually all research on the topic has determined that the chances of divorce ending a marriage preceded by cohabitation are significantly greater than for a marriage not preceded by cohabitation." Of course, these facts run counter intuitive to a naïve couple, which thinks that cohabitation will "test out their compatibility with each other." Quite frankly, *without making a commitment of marriage to each other*, they've already flunked the one true compatibility test. Yes, they've flunked! If you and your lover are not committed for eternity, why are you planning to live together? True sexual joy and oneness *only* flows from *committed* hearts.

When did the secular trend of cohabitation start? I'm unsure, but I remember one day about ten years ago when my daughter Patty informed me that her and her fiancé were planning to buy a house. While their scheduled wedding date wasn't far off, I insisted that they plan the wedding before the house. Furthermore, "Don't expect me to walk you down a wedding aisle if you choose to move in together as it won't happen." Patty and Jon were raised as Christians and chose to get married first. They finalized their house purchase after their marriage. She has told me several times that they were glad I insisted they get married first. Listen, parents, all of you have a role to play in spiritually guiding your adult children in righteousness.

The message for every parent is simple. If you fail to reprove the sin of your children in these regards, God will hold you accountable for their sin. You will bear their guilt in HIS eyes. And if you sincerely love your children, why on earth would you allow them to engage in what God calls a mortal sin? A mortal sin is a sin that leads to our *eternal* death. In this case it is the sin of fornication or unmarried [uncommitted] sex. You might think

Myth—Sexuality Doesn't Matter

taking such a parental position is being old fashioned, but has God changed? No, I've taught you repeatedly that this is not the case and we will all face HIM at some point. Verily I say unto you, the promiscuous nature of today's youth is attributable to a failure of their parents and also of society at large.

I've got family members who are now cohabitating with a lover. I'm sure they know where I stand on this issue, yet they are uncommitted to their partner or maybe it is the other way around. To the handsome young man I would say, "Why have you not asked the beautiful woman you are now living with to marry you? Exactly what are you afraid of when it comes to marriage? Don't you love and cherish this woman enough to want to spend your life and grow old with her? If not, send her away and find a woman you do want to spend your life with. If you love her, then get off your duff and marry her!" You two are engaged in a mortal sin in God's eyes, even if it is a popular thing to do in today's secular culture. Don't you realize this? To the beautiful young woman, I would say: "Doesn't the man you live with love you enough to make you an honest woman in the eyes of the God you profess to believe in? Wake up to God's perspective on human sex and *eternalize* your life and your lover's life!"

Men have a conquering mentality. If a woman gives him everything he wants, he has accomplished his primary goal. So, why *then* get married? Listen, women, do yourself a favor and start being a little hard to get into the sack. Make the next sexual encounter a biblical marriage event and you'll be surprised at the results you'll get with your man. I would ask this simple question. If a man doesn't love you enough to marry you, why would you want to have sex with him? In the biblical sense, you are then engaging in sexual immorality that has eternal consequences. In the simple human physical sense, the issue of sexually transmitted disease and even a possible death-causing sexually transmitted disease is a very real possibility today.

Let's take a moment now to review God's Word on the topic of living together [cohabitation] and the issue of fornication. Cohabitation in this sense means two people living and sleeping together having sex as a man and woman, however, they are legally unmarried and at the moment are uncommitted for eternity in God's eyes.

Myth—Sexuality Doesn't Matter

These are self-centered fornicators who maintain and reserve the option of exiting their live-in relationship at any point either partner might consider it's in their individual best interest. Children may or may not be involved in the relationship as well as adultery.

Fornication [44]: Consensual sexual intercourse between two persons [who are] not married to each other. *Note: This could be sex between a man and woman, who both are unmarried or it could be sex between a married man or woman and an unmarried partner. The Bible condemns both fornicators and adulterers in the marriage bed. Thus, the adulterer is also a fornicator in God's eyes. See Hebrews 13:4.*

"For this you know, that no *fornicator*, unclean person, nor covetous man, who is an idolater, has any inheritance in the kingdom of Christ and God." Ephes. 5:5

"When I come again, my God will humble me among you, and I shall mourn for many who have sinned before and have not repented of the uncleanness, *fornication*, and lewdness which they have practiced." 2 Cor. 12:21

"Now the works of the flesh are evident, which are: *adultery*, *fornication*, uncleanness, lewdness, idolatry, sorcery, hatred, contentions, jealousies, outbursts of wrath, selfish ambitions, dissensions, heresies, envy, murders, drunkenness, revelries, and the like; of which I tell you beforehand, just as I also told you in time past, that *those who practice such things will not inherit the kingdom of God*." Galatians 5:19-21

"Therefore put to death ... *fornication*, uncleanness, passion, evil desire, and covetousness, which is idolatry. Because of these things the wrath of God is coming upon the sons of disobedience, in which you yourselves once walked when you lived in them." Col. 3:5-7

Myth—Sexuality Doesn't Matter

WARNING: Verily I say unto you that living together as a man and woman [as described above] without the commitment of holy matrimony is a mortal sin in God's eyes and it will lead to a second death in the lake of fire for both of your souls. Once again, I did not make the rule; it is God that made it! Take heed unless you do not care about the eternal consequences of your actions on this earth. If you are a parent, it is time to rethink your sanctioning of such immoral behavior on the part of your adult children. I remind you that you do not have to carp on your children about their sins, but you will be held accountable for failure to *reprove* your children and in all of the ways that you support their sins. God and HIS Son will interpret your silence on the issue of your children's sin as your sanctioning of sin.

A Godly Relationship Has Committed Hearts!

I was reflecting again about Adam and Eve who were totally naked in the Garden of Eden and obviously without a marriage license. However, that does not mean that they weren't married in God's eyes. It also doesn't mean that they weren't committed to each other in their relationship. The word of God says:

> **"So then, they are no longer two but one flesh. Therefore what God has joined together, let not man separate."**
> **Matthew 19:6**

> **"Therefore a man shall leave his father and mother and be joined to his wife, and they shall become one flesh. And they were both naked, the man [Adam] and his wife [Eve], and [they] were not ashamed." Genesis 2:24-25**

It was God that joined Adam and Eve together. They didn't need a piece of paper called a marriage certificate to legitimize their marriage. Part of being joined together today by God is the natural characteristic and desire of each person's heart for a commitment to their prospective partner. It is that "natural commitment" of the heart for one another, which results in a godly marriage.

Myth—Sexuality Doesn't Matter

Where there is no such heart commitment, I believe there is no calling by God to get together or to get married. This is just another test of the start of a life-long relationship in God's eyes. If your prospective partner's heart needs convincing, you are barking up the wrong tree. If you've got to twist your partner's arm or even repeat the request more than twice for a marriage commitment, walk away from the relationship. It is just not of God.

Likewise, do not rush out to get a marriage certificate just because I've reminded you that you are headed towards Hell in such a relationship. If your heart is not right with God, no legal paper will mean anything to your soul's eternal outcome. If you are living together now, I suggest you first repent to God and then separate for a period of not less than 90 days from each other. Why 90 days? To give both of you some space, time and distance to clear your minds and to think clearly about what you really want in life. Start to date again and reconsider your relationship with one another in the perspective of an eternal life. If you find that your hearts *then* want to spend the rest of their lives together, feel free to *then* get married. Only *when you are married* will it be safe to resume sexual activities. Of course, we are then talking about the marriage bed and your first wedding night. They are fun and possess sexual freedom in God's eyes for true lovers.

Millions of people are now dying of AIDS, which is preventable in all but the most rare cases. When you have casual sex with anyone, you are literally having sex with everyone your partner has ever had sex with. If ever there was a time to return to old fashioned courting rituals between a man and woman, it is today. Get to know your prospective lover before you get married. Then, in the marriage bed, you *will* find the freedom to let loose and enjoy what God has given us in terms of true sexual pleasures.

God Defines Mortal Sin, Not the Church!

Now lets add some clarity to the issue of mortal sin. The Church has distorted this subject and I will now remind all Christians that it is God Almighty and HIS Word that defines what constitutes a mortal sin and not the Church.

Myth—Sexuality Doesn't Matter

All mortal sin by H<small>IS</small> definition is the type of sin that keeps you out of Heaven, gets you throne into the lake of fire and ultimately results in your second death. That *second death* is the death of your soul. Therefore, the idea that mortal sin is a "qualified or conditioned" type of "grave sin" and the idea of "venial sin" per se is simply wrong. Go back and study Lev. 18:22, 20:13; John 8:34-35; Romans 1:26-32; Romans 2:2-3; 1 Cor. 6:9; 2 Cor. 12:21; Col. 3:5-7; 2 Peter 2:18; Jude 1:4; and, Revelations 21:8, 22:15 along with others and show me any qualification from God. Those who do what God says will result in the lake of fire and second death will actually find them self there and no church theology will prevent Christ from fully executing God's will in this regards. To teach otherwise is apostasy.

My sixteen year old grandson Christopher and I had a conversation a few weeks ago and I was trying to illustrate the issue of exactly how *reason* works in the area of male sexuality. I told him I remembered what it was like when I was sixteen back in 1962. My hormones raged and my young male body was on autopilot. Young men don't have to think much about sex to experience a spontaneous erection. This erection fact of the male sexual makeup takes place even into the mid 30's or longer. Just seeing a beautiful woman, whether I even thought about her breasts or other body parts was irrelevant. It just happened, even in some rather embarrassing situations. If a young man actually thinks about sex, he is liable to go nuts. Instead, to counter this autonomic physical response, a young man thinks about fixing a car engine or any other mental thought that might take his mind off the idea of sex. This aspect of a young male body continues on for quite some time. Even in marriage, thinking of sex while having sex can lead to premature ejaculation in an inexperienced male. It is an attribute of male sexuality.

Between Christopher and I is my son Brian who is now 32 years old. I remember when Brian was 13 years old. It was 1985 and it seemed like female liberation was unfolding in terms of sexual freedom. A young girl 15 years old was trying to bag Brian in the sack, which is to say have sex with him. My first male thought was: "Darn, I should have been so lucky back in 1959." That thought quickly gave way to yikes! Jackie and I had a few talks with Brian about sexuality to say the least.

Copyright 2005 Edward G. Palmer, All Rights Reserved.

Myth—Sexuality Doesn't Matter

Today, female behavior is even worse. Many women will go out for sex with a guy on the first date without any compunction. I am encouraged by some statistics I saw that indicate this trend might be changing. It would be best if young women took on some biblical righteousness and started to protect their virginity until marriage.

Given the fact that many women and young girls are morally loose, I told Christopher to be spiritually prepared for unexpected sexual encounters. I would certainly say that this statement about moral looseness applies to many young women and girls even in the Church today. I told Christopher to imagine what it would be like to be in a private room and alone with a young woman. Suddenly she just takes all her clothes off. Now what?

I can tell you what most sixteen-year old male bodies will want to do. Being on autonomic autopilot, they would want to jump her bones and have sex. I know that is what my sixteen-year old body would have wanted to do. What will you do? If you don't have God's wisdom inside of you, you will probably have sex. However, if you have wisdom's *reason*, you will be able to ignore the fact that you might then have a spontaneous erection due to her body's naked visual stimulation. *Reason* will allow you to tell the gal to put her clothes back on. If you truly love her, tell her that you want to save sex for your wedding night. Here's a novel question. If a girl would put out for you on your first date or have sex without much work on your part, wouldn't she do the same for other males she is interested in? Isn't she a proverbial slut, because she is easy?

Girls, think about this proven fact of the male psyche. No matter how much your boyfriend begs or coerces you to have sex, he will no longer think about you in the same way once you do *put out* and have sex with him. In fact, you might lose his true affections altogether. This is a strange attribute of the male psyche that is incontrovertible. A man thinks of a woman differently *after* they have sex. If a man *conquers* your sexuality too fast, it will mess his mind over and he might just conclude, "you are easy."

The male autonomic erection response is turned off at age 58. If a woman suddenly just took off her clothes for me, I just might actually start laughing. There would be no spontaneous penile erection, because at this age, a man *has* to actually think about sex. Therefore, as a man ages, his sexual mindset does a 180-degree turn on him. While sexual *enjoyment* in his youth was once dangerous to think about in terms of causing a premature ejaculation, an older man can think about enjoying sex and in many cases he must intently think about sex to even have sex. This freaks a lot of males out as they think their equipment or maleness has failed them. It hasn't. It only has changed in terms of a different operating mode. This change can lead to longer and more satisfying sex later in life. There is no question that age changes the male and female body. Both male and female must adjust to the changes brought on by age. If done properly, our human sexuality can be enjoyed throughout old age. Once again, consider Abraham and Sarah.

"But MY covenant I will establish with Isaac, whom Sarah shall bear to you at this set time next year." Genesis 17:21

Sarah was 90 years old and Abraham 100 when Isaac was born. God explains Abraham's heir in Genesis 18:14 by reassuring him that it will happen. God said, "Is anything too hard for the LORD?" The story doesn't end there. Sarah died at age 127 [Gen. 23:1]. At age 137, Abraham married Keturah, one of his concubines, who gave him six more sons [Gen. 25:1-2]. There is no need to fear a loss of sexuality with old age, but there is a need to adapt to our older body and maybe make some changes in nutrition. If you are a male experiencing issues with maintaining an erection, you might try 2,000-3,000 mg of L-Arginine and L-Carnitine daily. [45] The male body uses these essential amino acids [nutrients] to maintain the nitric oxide levels essential to penile erection. There are other nutrients. Search the Internet for these nutraceuticals and don't fear sex in your old age.

My message to Christopher was to be spiritually prepared for any unexpected sexual encounter. Without such preparation, a young man's body will be on autonomic autopilot and sex an easy decision. However, those whom the LORD loves, HE will protect. Those whom HE abhors will fall at the lips of the immoral woman. That is something to think about.

"The mouth of an *immoral* woman is a deep pit; he who is abhorred by the LORD will fall there." Proverbs 22:14

Myth—Sexuality Doesn't Matter

If a woman saves her virginity for marriage, she has something that is truly sacred and precious to offer her prospective husband. If she adopts the idea of casual sex as being okay, there is nothing special that she has to offer her partner. She has given up all that she had to offer. In a crude sense, how is free sex any different to your man than that of an ordinary prostitute's? Except for the fact he doesn't pay for it? Of course, no man is going to treat you like a prostitute in an outright open way, but why then does marriage become such a difficult subject to talk about to the lover you cohabitate with? Would you have sex and live together if you knew it might destroy any possibility of marriage and a true long-term loving relationship as a husband and wife? Yet that is exactly what is happening in our society today in a world that cheapens sexuality and the institution of marriage. [43]

Cohabitation and living together is a mortal sin in God's eyes when sex is a part of the picture. It is fornication. And even if sex is not an initial consideration, it can quickly become part of the picture when a male and female live together, because "maximum privacy *will* lead to maximum intimacy." This is an incontrovertible fact of male-female relationships. A male and female should not delude themselves that sex can be restrained or denied while living together for other "compatibility testing" reasons. Cohabitation is on the rise today. Yet, it is only a small part of the sexually immoral practices currently going on. The big picture looks like this.

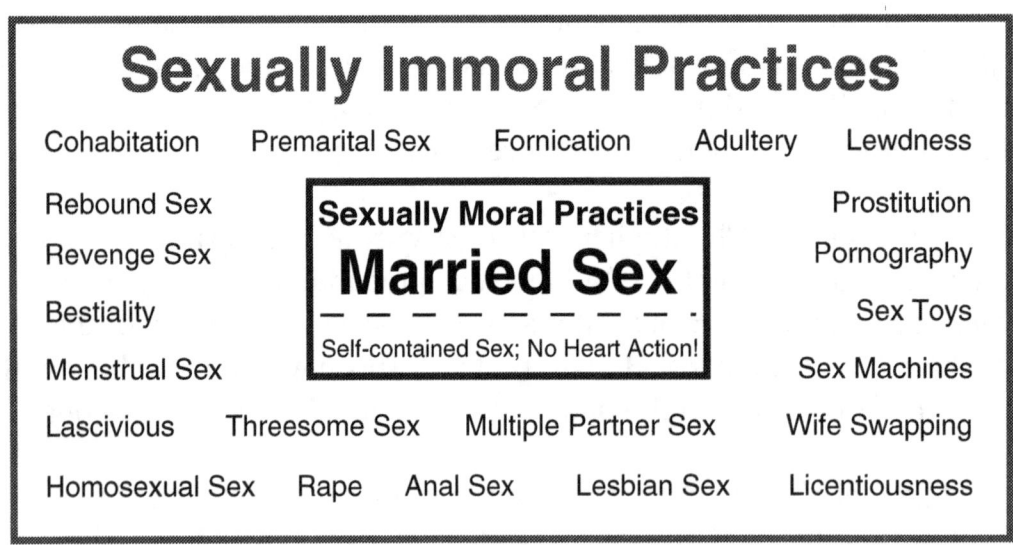

Copyright 2005 Edward G. Palmer, All Rights Reserved.

Myth—Sexuality Doesn't Matter

In the big picture, there are many more immoral kinds of sex activity than there are moral kinds of sex activity. That is demonstrated in the above graphic by the limited size of the box labeled "Sexually Moral Practices." Moral sex is primarily limited to sex between a married man and his wife. This is the essence of Hebrews 13:4 and many other biblical verses. The item labeled "Self-contained Sex; No Heart Action!" identifies solitary sex, which does not involve external activity. This is masturbation and would certainly not involve other people or sexual objects and toys. I believe that Matthew 5:30, 1 Cor. 10:13, and Romans 1:26-27 are relevant to the issue of masturbation.

> **"And if your right hand causes you to sin, cut it off and cast it from you; for it is more profitable for you that one of your members perish, than for your whole body to be cast into Hell." Matthew 5:30**

> **"No temptation has overtaken you except such as is common to man; but God is faithful, who will not allow you to be tempted beyond what you are able, but with the temptation will also make the way of escape, that you may be able to bear it." 1 Cor. 10:13**

> **"For even their women exchanged the natural use for what is against nature. Likewise also the men, [left] the natural use of the woman." Romans 1:26-27**

God designed the male body to ejaculate in nocturnal emissions when sexual pressures build up too much. It is not unnatural for the penis to be masturbated. This occurs in a variety of ways as mentioned earlier. Is it a sound theology to teach a male to ignore the sexual pressures that build up and to go literally crazy mentally? Or is it a more valid theology to teach the male not to waste any energy on the sexual pressures and if needed, go take care of the issue in a matter of a few minutes? Therefore, one theology can result in males obsessing over internally generated sexual pressures all day long. In the other, the pressure is dealt with and not allowed to consume any excessive amount of time in the male's mind. Which is more biblical?

Myth—Sexuality Doesn't Matter

The latter fits clearly in God's command to control our sin, while the former allows sexual pressures to accumulate unabated, which is definitely a lack of exerting any control over the issue. The latter also keeps a door open to an external sinful solution rather than a self-contained moral solution. This is a male issue, but no doubt similar issues are in play in the female body. A woman's vagina is also flooded with blood and swells up during REM sleep and no doubt this fact creates similar urges in her body. It's a fact that 1 Cor. 10:13 seems to fit the scenario in that God "will also make the way to escape [the temptation of sex], that you may be able to bear it."

The use of the human hand is natural and the same as married couples use on each other. In contrast, sex machines, dildos, vibrators, large plastic dolls and other objects used to masturbate with or on have crossed the line and are externally oriented and lewd behaviors. These behaviors are in the heart and have resulted in "external" actions. They are not self-contained within one's self. You say, but Edward, what's the difference? In one case, it is natural and the mind is exerting some control preventing excess and keeping things self-contained. In the other case, clearly the issue is in the heart, has resulted in external actions to obtain objects and is unnatural.

While Paul teaches on the natural use of the woman in Rom. 1:26-27, it applies broadly on the use of the sex organs per se and other body parts. The male and female genitals were meant to engage each another. That is what is natural. It is also natural for couple's to use their hands and touch one another's genitals. Therefore, it is not immoral to touch one's genitals or even to masturbate one's partner. Yet it would be immoral to stick a foreign object into the vagina. Likewise, sticking the penis into any foreign object is also immoral. This deals with the issue of being natural and exerting some control over our sexuality in a way that "allows us to escape and to bear the sexual temptations." However, Matthew 5:30 presents another perspective from Jesus.

I've already talked about this teaching at least once. If a limb offends you, cut it off and that is exactly what Jesus is teaching you. "For it is more profitable for you that one of your members perish, than for your whole body to be cast into Hell." This is one solution to an "out of control" body.

Myth—Sexuality Doesn't Matter

Once you've entered the heart and are engaged in masturbation with objects, toys, and machines — it is a short distance to the prostitute and other areas God has clearly condemned as being "sexually immoral." Jesus is teaching that if we cannot control a body part, we should cut it off. For the male it might mean getting castrated or other things. However, God has reminded me that even in the case of castration, that it will not eliminate immoral sex in the true pervert. Such a person still has other body parts such as his mouth, lips, tongue, hands, feet, etc. and while the penis would not be then able to engage in sexual immorality — many other body parts would still be available. Ergo, God's command to control sin and not to allow sin to control you. Masturbation can be an effective means of controlling sin and limiting sex to the area of marriage or to one's self.

When I reflect on the issue of my male experiences, I remember the physical pressures involved in most men while overseas in the Navy on long extended tours of duty. The male body "generates" internal sexual pressures and there are ways men deal with these pressures. My observations is that: a) men are kept on exhausting schedules and this diminishes the libido; b) men will masturbate to eliminate the pressures; c) men will obsess over having sex and drive themselves nuts; d) men will seek out prostitutes and pay for sex; e) men will engage in other sexually immoral behaviors; and, d) many will blame the loss of their libido on the idea the military is slipping them saltpeter. This latter item has been proven to be a myth. Saltpeter is potassium nitrate and it can cause several harmful effects to the human body and has not been demonstrated to decrease male sex drives. Yet, we all believed this as fact when I was in the military. I understand that even today, the saltpeter myth permeates military and other male establishments. Ejaculation is consistent with God's male body design. It will happen one way or another in males. Ergo, self-contained masturbation is consistent with the body design and God's command to control sin.

> **"Now Samson went to Gaza and saw a harlot [prostitute] there, and went in to her." Judges 16:1**
>
> **"For the men [of Israel] themselves go apart with harlots [prostitutes]." Hosea 4:14**

Myth—Sexuality Doesn't Matter

Marriage Is Between One Man And One Woman!

Marriage is the God ordained union of one man and one woman. It is not between two men or two women or any combination of one man and two or more women or one woman and two or more men. All such thoughts are sexually deviant and lewd. That doesn't mean that men in the Bible did not have multiple legal wives and even multiple concubines, which is defined as a " 'wife' who is not a legal wife." [46]

Remember our discussion of Jacob who fathered twelve sons from four women? Two were legal wives and two were maidservants or concubines given to Jacob by his two legal wives. Or what about Solomon who had 700 wives and 300 concubines? Doesn't that make Solomon a fornicator? For the moment, you'll have to consider that Solomon had a commitment from those women to only him for sex and that all of them including the concubines were considered as wives. I wonder who made up those rules? I also wonder what a nut Solomon had to be. Wisdom? To love one woman her whole life is enough of a challenge to me.

I have read where ancient Jewish law permitted up to four wives assuming you could keep them fed, clothed and otherwise satisfied up until one Rabbi altered the law with a ruling that one wife should be enough. Yet if God intended for us to have multiple sexual partners, why didn't HE provide Adam with multiple wives? Surely HE knew the sexual drive of the male would not be satisfied with just one wife? Surely HE knew that the sexual drive of the male might even want a male partner? Get real and think about these scriptures when it comes to the sacrament of marriage.

> **"And the LORD God caused a deep sleep to fall on Adam, and he slept; and HE took one of his ribs, and closed up the flesh in its place. Then the rib, which the LORD God had taken from man HE made into a woman, and HE brought her to the man. And Adam said: 'This is now bone of my bones and flesh of my flesh; she shall be called Woman, because she was taken out of Man.' " Genesis 2:21-23**

Myth—Sexuality Doesn't Matter

> "So God created man in H<small>IS</small> own image; in the image of God H<small>E</small> created him; male and female H<small>E</small> created them."
>
> **Genesis 1:27**

> "H<small>E</small> created them male and female, and blessed them and called them Mankind in the day they were created."
>
> **Genesis 5:2**

> Jesus said, "Have you not read that H<small>E</small> who made them at the beginning 'made them male and female?'"
>
> **Matthew 19:4**

> Jesus continued and said, "For this reason a man shall leave his father and mother and be joined to his wife, and the two shall become one flesh? So then, they are no longer two but one flesh. Therefore what God has joined together, let not man separate." **Matthew 19:5-6**

So the penetrating question of God's human creation is why not multiple partners or same-sex partners? Sound like a facetious question? Maybe it would 2000 years ago, but in 2004 AD when Gay marriage and civil unions are being politically advocated for even by factions of the Church, it is a very serious moral issue. The answer is that God created us male and female to become one flesh in a unique spiritual union designed to bring us sexual pleasure and the joy of birth. The sexual organs, that God gave man and woman were meant for each other in the union of marriage.

God did not create multiple partners. God did not create a man and then a male helpmate. God did not create a woman and a female helpmate. All of these are serious perversions for the reasons already discussed. But verily I say unto you, every Christian should heed the words of God and "let not man separate" what God H<small>IMSELF</small> has joined together. H<small>E</small> has joined a man and a woman together! That is the institution of marriage. H<small>E</small> created marriage, man didn't! Political attempts to alter what is marriage are direct attacks on God's institution. Those who advocate altering marriage put themselves in direct conflict with God. Verily I say to you, H<small>E</small> will repay.

Copyright 2005 Edward G. Palmer, All Rights Reserved.

Book of Edward—Chapter 19

Myth—Sexuality Doesn't Matter

Extricating God Shows A Lack Of Wisdom!

Extricating God out of the decision-making process leaves us without the ability to fully reason [to be 100% rational], since it leaves us devoid of wisdom. Wisdom is only contained in the context of knowledge of both the world and of God. Read chapter 9 again, *Rationalization of Mankind*, if you don't get the full impact of this biblical truth and understand that it is a fact.

The Bible teaches humans they cannot be 100% rational without also knowledge of God and HIS truth [see page 219]. Therefore, a common element in all of the myths that are presented in this book is the fact that mankind and Christianity have extricated knowledge of God and HIS eternal character out of their decision-making processes. As a result, many of the decisions are unwise, lacking wisdom, which God defined and provides.

This certainly pertains to the issue of abortion and to the issue of our sexuality. In the case of abortion, God clearly indicates that HE will pay us back for doing what HE hates. In the case of those who are sexually immoral, God goes further and teaches us they "shall have their part in the lake of fire" [Rev. 21:8] and "are outside of Heaven" [Rev. 22:15]. Given these clear teachings, it is important to understand what God is talking about. Our eternal salvation depends upon understanding God and Christ is no excuse for those who are sexually immoral. He will simply tell them: "Depart from me you who are lawless" and "I never knew you!"

If you search the Holy Bible, you'll find five verses with the term "sexually immoral" in it and no verses with the phrase "sexually moral" in them. All of the references to *sexually immoral* are contained in the New Testament and that should be a clear warning to those who seek to use Christ as a covering for "continued" sin. One thing is clear, if there is *immoral sex* defined in the Bible, then *moral sex* must also exist. In HIS image, humans are created as sexual beings. So what is sexually moral in God's eyes if not exactly what I have already taught you? I welcome your input and verse citations. If you want to debate these teachings, put your thesis together and again I say I will surely read, study and respond to it.

Copyright 2005 Edward G. Palmer, All Rights Reserved.

Book of Edward—Chapter 19

Myth—Sexuality Doesn't Matter

Homosexuality And Lesbianism Are Mortal Sins!

The headline [47] read, "Rosie To Marry Girlfriend." If you listen to Rosie O'Donnell, you'd get the impression that Gay marriage was a right for all citizens of the United States. You'd also get the impression that this immorality will still be getting a ticket to Heaven. At least that is what she told a news reporter on one of the daily shows I happened to catch. She claimed to be saved through Jesus and fully expected to get a home in Heaven. I'm sorry to be the one to have to inform you Rosie, but you are engaged in a mortal sin that God says warrants a place in the lake of fire and a second death. It's time to dust off that Bible in your closet and take a closer look at what is written about your behavior.

Then there was the rampant abuse of civil law that took place in several cities and city officials took it upon them self to grant licenses and marry homosexual and lesbian couples. Rosie said, "I think the actions of the president are, in my opinion, the most vile and hateful words ever spoken by a sitting president." Note: Bush called for a constitutional amendment to ban Gay marriage. Rosie continued, "I am stunned and horrified. I find this proposed amendment very, very, very, very shocking and immoral. And, you know, if civil disobedience is the way to go about change, then I think a lot of people will be going to San Francisco. And I hope they put more people on the steps to marry as many people as show up. And I hope everyone shows up."

Rosie stated she planned to marry her girlfriend Kelli Carpenter and in fact at the height of the Gay marriage frenzy in San Francisco they were married in a civil ceremony. The California Supreme Court as a violation of civil law annulled Rosie and Kelli's marriage and all the others. That hasn't stopped the Gay activists from aggressively promoting their marriage and other political agendas. Neither has it stopped them from claiming 10% of all adults are Gay. As I mentioned earlier, the San Francisco mayor was one of those promoting that number. By the way, Rosie O'Donnell was one of those people who hid her true evil colors while building up a following as a daytime talk show host.

Myth—Sexuality Doesn't Matter

Instead of the whopping 10% claimed by the Gay community, the U.S. Census Bureau reports [48] the following statistics: Total households in the U.S. are 105.5 Million. Same sex households were 594,000. Do the math and you'll find out that Gay households represent .00563 of the total or roughly a little over 1/2 of 1%. But that is not all. Assuming that there are 2 Gays per household, there would be 1,188,000 total Gay people not including those single and still at home or living alone. However, as of July 1, 2003 there were 290,809,777 people in the United States. Therefore, Gays living together as a percent of the total population are .00408 or less than 1/2 of 1% of the U.S. population. You can be generous and say there are an equal number of people not living together and you still wouldn't come up with 1% of the U.S. population. The Gay community is engaged in deception, which should not surprise anyone. *Meredith's Book of Bible Lists* [49] has a list of thirty statements about homosexuals from the Bible.

1. God gives homosexuals up to uncleanness (Rom. 1:24)
2. Homosexuals dishonor their own bodies between themselves (Rom. 1:24).
3. Homosexuals corrupt the word of God by changing HIS truth to a lie (Rom. 1:25).
4. Homosexuals worship and serve the creature more than the CREATOR (Rom. 1:25).
5. God gives homosexuals up to their vile affections (Rom. 1:26).
6. God gives homosexuals over to a reprobate mind (Rom. 1:28).
7. Homosexuals are filled with all unrighteousness (Rom. 1:29).
8. Homosexuals end up being motivated to do things that are not convenient (Rom. 1:28).
9. Homosexuals are filled with fornication (Rom. 1:29).
10. Homosexuals are filled with wickedness (Rom. 1:29).
11. Homosexuals are filled with covetousness (Rom. 1:29).
12. Homosexuals are filled with maliciousness (Rom. 1:29)
13. Homosexuals are filled with envy (Rom. 1:29).
14. Homosexuals are filled with murder (Rom. 1:29).
15. Homosexuals are filled with debate (Rom. 1:29).
16. Homosexuals are filled with deceit (Rom. 1:29).
17. Homosexuals are filled with malignity (Rom. 1:29).

Myth—Sexuality Doesn't Matter

18. Homosexuals are whisperers (Rom. 1:29).
19. Homosexuals are backbiters (Rom. 1:30).
20. Homosexuals are haters of God (Rom. 1:30).
21. Homosexuals are despiteful (Rom. 1:30).
22. Homosexuals are proud (Rom. 1:30).
23. Homosexuals are boasters (Rom. 1:30).
24. Homosexuals are inventors of evil things (Rom. 1:30).
25. Homosexuals are disobedient to parents (Rom. 1:30).
26. Homosexuals are covenant breakers (Rom. 1:31).
27. Homosexuals are without natural affection (Rom. 1:31).
28. Homosexuals are unmerciful (Rom. 1:31).
29. Homosexuals are implacable (Rom. 1:31).
30. Homosexuals are without understanding (Rom. 1:31).

Take a moment and compare the statements of Rosie O'Donnell and other Gay activists to the above list. The statement that the president of the United States is immoral fits several items on the list. The Census Bureau also reports the following top ten Gay cities. Four of these are in California, which obviously is the #1 state for Gays. Note that these hot beds of sexual immorality peak at 2.7% of households in San Francisco. Yet, this is not a percent of population. Using Minneapolis, same sex households total 2,622 or roughly 5,244 people in a city with a population of 337,000. Therefore, Gays as a percent of the Minneapolis population [50] are about 1.5%.

#	City	Percent of Gay Households
1	San Francisco, CA	2.7
2	Fort Lauderdale, FL	2.1
3	Seattle, WA	1.9
4	Oakland, CA	1.8
5	Berkeley, CA	1.8
6	Atlanta, GA	1.7
7	Minneapolis, MN	1.6
8	Washington, DC	1.5
9	Long Beach, CA	1.4
10	Portland, OR	1.3

Myth—Sexuality Doesn't Matter

Factoring in the entire population of Minnesota yields a maximum Gay population of somewhere between .5 to 1%. I believe the same would be true for all the other states listed. When the entire United States population is factored in, clustered Gay populations are diluted. I personally believe that the real Gay population would fall to a level between .4 to .6 % or very close to the level of populated Gay households. To reach .6 % would grant a 50% increase in the Gay population over that located in Gay households. This is to say that yet another uncoupled 594,000 Gays are living somewhere else other than in a Gay household. Since it is a proven fact that Gay clusters exist, this type of argument appears specious. Gays are not evenly distributed in a normal distribution pattern statistically across the United States. That is part of the Gay deception. For example, just because Minneapolis is a hotbed of Gay activity, doesn't mean that St. Paul or Rochester are. Then think about the voluminous small communities and towns across the country. They would be expected to max out at .1% or less Gay population. Yes, $1/10^{th}$ of 1% would be the most you would find in 80-90% of all small communities.

Yet to get to 1% of the U.S. population requires an extra population of Gays of 1,720,097 or roughly 150% or 1.5 times the Census Bureau data on the Gay household population. Where are these Gays located? Therefore, despite Gay claims to the contrary, the real Gay population consisting of both homosexuals and lesbians is certainly less than 1% of the total population of the United States. Yes, Gays believe that strength lies in numbers and that is why they gather in clusters. God commands us not to follow the crowd mentality, but to use righteous judgment at all times.

Now, ask yourself this question. Are homosexuals in the mainstream of society or do they represent a perverted sexual fringe element of society? Should the 99% normal citizens of the United States alter their marriage criteria for the 1% immoral Gay population when it comes to marriage? No! *Woe to the society that does alter the institution that God HIMSELF ordained.*

Should we allow the Massachusetts' Supreme Court to dictate what is now considered marriage? If you factor in the population that approved the Massachusetts' and the U.S. Constitution, you could not come up with a more dishonest intellectual conclusion about the framers intentions!

Myth—Sexuality Doesn't Matter

Signers of U.S. Constitution—39

Instruction: Place a check mark next to every person who signed the U.S. Constitution[51] or who is identified as a founding father that did not sign the document that you think granted homosexuals the right to marry.

✔	U.S. Constitution Signer	✔	U.S. Constitution Signer
	Baldwin, Abraham		Morris, Robert
	Bassett, Richard		Paterson, William
	Bedford, Gunning Jr.		Pinckney, Charles Cotesworth
	Blair, John		Pinckney, Charles
	Blount, William		Read, George
	Brearly, David		Rutledge, John
	Broom, Jacob		Sherman, Roger
	Butler, Pierce		Spaight, Richard D.
	Carroll, Daniel		Washington, George
	Clymer, George		Williamson, Hugh
	Dayton, Jonathon		Wilson, James
	Dickinson, John		*Other Founding Fathers—16*
	Few, William		*Davie, William R.*
	Fitzsimons, Thomas		*Ellsworth, Oliver*
	Franklin, Benjamin		*Gerry, Elbridge*
	Gilman, Nicholas		*Houston, William C.*
	Gorham, Nathaniel		*Houstoun, William*
	Hamilton, Alexander		*Lansing, John Jr.*
	Ingersoll, Jarod		*Martin, Alexander*
	Jenifer, Daniel of St. Thomas		*Martin, Luther*
	Johnson, William S.		*Mason, George*
	King, Rufus		*McClurg, James*
	Langdon, John		*Mercer, John F.*
	Livingston, William		*Pierce, William L.*
	Madison, James Jr.		*Randolph, Edmund J.*
	McHenry, James		*Strong, Caleb*
	Mifflin, Thomas		*Wythe, George*
	Morris, Gouverneur		*Yates, Robert*

Myth—Sexuality Doesn't Matter

If you've checked a single person above, you are ignorant of history. The same type of chart could be put together for virtually every state in the union in regards to their constitution. Virtually none of the framers of the states in our great nation granted homosexuals the right to marriage or civil unions. To think otherwise is to deny the Judeo Christian heritage of this nation. There is no doubt an additional population of sexually confused people, but you'd be hard pressed to come up with some number that is meaningful. Gays frame the debate in terms of civil rights and compare their cause to women suffrage, slavery and black civil rights.

In a recent ABC News Primetime Sex Survey [52], fifty-five percent of the adults stated "homosexuality is OK for some people." However, sixty-five percent of young adults said the same thing and seventy-one percent felt premarital sex was okay. These stats are a testament to the power of the Gay public relations effort and a testament to the failure of the Church in terms of teaching morality to young people. As the debate shifts from morality in the biblical sense to the so-called "morality of rights" in the civil or legal sense, I conclude that our society is increasingly becoming debased. At some point God will abandon the United States, as sexual immorality has consequences on this earth and in Heaven.

Sexually Immoral Behavior Has Consequences!

I've already mentioned a few consequences of sexually immoral behavior. A congressman finds his college streaking-prank thrown into his face 30 years later while facing reelection. A high school streaker gets sent to jail for six months to two years. A young couple gets arrested for having sex at the Alamo late in the afternoon. Some are very serious consequences.

The headline read: "For Teens, Sex & Drugs Go Together." [53] The "Columbia center study did not ask teens about their own sexual activity, but asked them to estimate how many of their friends were sexually active." It produced statistics correlating sex to substance abuse. Twenty-five percent of the teenagers surveyed reported that at least half of their friends were sexually active [group one]. In group two, forty percent of the teenagers reported that none are. The following table compares the two groups.

Myth—Sexuality Doesn't Matter

More Likely To Have Tried	Group 1	Group 2
Alcohol	66%	10%
Cigarettes	45%	8%
Marijuana	45%	2%
Gotten drunk in last month	31%	1%

The study also found a correlation to time spent with friends. The more time spent with friends, the more likely teens are to smoke, drink and use drugs. Sexual immorality has consequences in areas of substance abuse.

If you remember the discussion about rape in the last chapter, this headline might surprise you. "Girl, 12, Blamed by Judge for Sex Act." [54] "A judge freed a man who had sex with a girl of 12 – and said it was her fault they ended up in bed." The man "met the girl in an Internet chat room and later twice had sex with her at her parent's home when he was 18." The girl's parents allowed the man to stay at their house and apparently she went into his bedroom. The judge said she was a "willing participant" and had instigated sex when she went into his bedroom. The judge seems to have a boys will be boys attitude recognizing the automatic penile response, but seems to lack the common sense that a 12-year old should not be making sex decisions and an adult should be held to adult standards of behavior. Of course, many people are upset with this judge over his sex rulings. One wonders what kind of mindset allowed the girl's parents to authorize an 18-year old to spend the night as a potential boyfriend of their 12-year old daughter. Sexual immorality has consequences in the courtroom and in society's perception of what is a sexual decision for a 12 and 18-year old.

Breastfeeding has become a subject of debate and a recent headline read: "On Breastfeeding, Rights and Good Manners." [55] You wouldn't think that forty states have breastfeeding legislation, would you? "Some, like California, give women the right to breastfeed 'in any location, public or private, except the private home … of another;' the mother may sue if breastfeeding is denied." What's with this? The issue of lewdness. Listen, a nicely shaped breast with a baby suckling can be an erotic lascivious visual stimulation for some men. What about common sense and modesty?

Myth—Sexuality Doesn't Matter

Common sense and modesty would resolve a lot of the concerns about breastfeeding. Yet the objections to public breastfeeding are paradoxical given the degree to which we are inundated with sex these days. Perhaps there is a "public" backlash, because people are trying to find some place of sexual safety where their senses are not assaulted. That would explain the hoopla over a two-year old girl in a public pool without a shirt. Several people were sexually offended that the mother took her shirt off. Hello. Sexual immorality has consequences in areas of public behavior. Even to the point of being immodest on one hand, because of perceived rights and of being ridiculous on the other hand because there is getting so much offense.

The issue of birth control relates to sexual immorality. Birth control is immoral except when used within a marriage or for some medical reason. After Brian was born, Jackie had a tubal ligation, which was a permanent method of birth control. There is nothing wrong with birth control in the institution of marriage. However, all forms of birth control outside of the marriage are precursors to sexual immorality. If, for example, there were not the "pill" or other means of birth control, people would be more careful about their sexual habits. At least they were before the "pill" came along and I am old enough to remember. Readily available methods of birth control have contributed significantly to the epidemic of sexual immorality in our world and the ultimate birth control women use is the act of abortion. The use of abortion in any instance except to save the life of the mother is immoral and evil. If it is used as a birth control method, it is also wicked in God's eyes. Sexual immorality has traumatic life consequences.

The headline read: "Aborted Baby's Head Left Inside Woman." [56] A British woman sick with autoimmune hepatitis, a disease eating away her liver, was diagnosed 12-weeks pregnant during her treatment. She already had three children and was depressed taking six pills a day according to her own words. She "reluctantly" decided to have an abortion. Davina, age 29, in her own words states, "When I woke up on the ward, they said that I had three scans and everything was fine." But once she returned home, an unseemly problem began to make itself known. "At midnight, my ex-partner knocked on the door to check if I was all right ... I went to the bathroom and as I was sitting there, I just felt something slip out of me as if I

Myth—Sexuality Doesn't Matter

had just given birth. I looked in the toilet and saw this lump that seemed to have a bone in it. So I showed it to my partner." The article said, "The couple realized they were looking at the face of their unborn child, seeing the eyes, nose, mouth and ears. The tiny head measured no more than four centimeters" or about 1 5/8 inches.

Davina said, "We just broke down and cried at what we were seeing. We couldn't believe it." Indeed, in the photos of the mother and baby, one could easily see the resemblance. Davina continues, "I feel as if I'm going insane now; I can't just let this happen to me." What if abortion was only used as a last resort to save her life and not as a first medical option? Would she still have had to endure such a sordid experience? Sex has consequences when it relies upon abortion to eliminate pregnancy issues.

The fallout from the Episcopal Church ordination of V. Gene Robinson as bishop of New Hampshire is still unfolding. The headline reads: "Bishop: Anglican Church may be beyond repair." [57] "The global Anglican Communion is 'broken' and may be beyond repair, the most influential Anglican leader in Africa said today." When the church itself engages in trying to make sexual immoral conduct acceptable, it has wide ranging consequences.

The consequences of the Episcopalian's abominable action began to take shape in the headline, "Anglican Panel Blasts Episcopal Church for Gay Stance." [58] "An Anglican Church commission sharply criticized the U.S. Episcopal Church on Monday for consecrating a Gay bishop and called on the church to apologize and refrain from promoting any other clergy living in a same-sex union." The commission stated, "Until there is an apology, those who took part in consecrating Robinson — which would include presiding Bishop Frank Griswold — should consider whether to withdraw themselves from functions of the Anglican Communion." Verily I say unto you, the fallout in the Anglican Church is just beginning. Inviting sexual immorality inside the church and trying to sanction it with the word of God has serious consequences. *Woe to all who do not condemn this action in the Anglican Church for verily I say unto you that God will repay these church leaders for the blaspheme that they fail to rebuke and what the Robinson action represents in causing others to sin.*

Myth—Sexuality Doesn't Matter

The news headline read, "Housewives Too Hot for Advertisers." [59] Referring to the new ABC Sunday night series "Desperate Housewives" — the article indicates that advertisers are yanking their spots due to the racy content. "A spokesman for Tyson told the magazine that the show is 'not consistent with our core values.' No need to worry about ABC. It has doubled the price of a 30-second ad from $156,000 to $300,000." Here is an example of feeding racy content to a willing public. Yet it is also an example that moral people and businesses with core principles do not have to support immorality in any form that it takes. Sexual immorality takes many forms today and even racy television shows have consequences.

The headline read, "Sexually Transmitted Infections [STIs] continue to increase during 2003 in UK." *Medical News Today* reports the following stats on sexual disease in the UK. [60]

1. Chlamydia increased by 9%
2. Syphilis increased by 28%
3. Gonorrhea decreased by 3%
4. Genital warts increased by 2%
5. Genital herpes decreased by 2%

The chairman of the Health Protection Agency said, "These are all preventable infections and it is a cause of considerable concern that we are still seeing increases in new diagnoses of STIs across the UK and unsafe sex is undoubtedly a main contributor to this." Maybe it is, but what about the issue of sexual immorality? That has to be the precursor to unsafe sex. Yes, sexual immorality can wreak havoc on our body and has consequences.

If you don't think such stuff applies to rich American communities, you are wrong. The headline read, "Not a simple answer for desert's syphilis problem." [61] It is subtitled, "Epidemic puts rate of Palm Springs cases of disease higher than any city in U.S." Yes, we are talking about syphilis epidemic in Palm Springs, California where the rich and famous gather. "Despite a year of education and testing efforts, Palm Springs alone has a syphilis rate of 81.8 per 100,000 people in 2003, twice the rate of the nation's No. 1 city for syphilis, San Francisco."

Myth—Sexuality Doesn't Matter

"The disease, health officials say, is being spread in the desert almost exclusively by Gay men, many of whom are also HIV-positive." The article also states, "Today, health officials say there is a syphilis problem in several American cities with substantial Gay populations – San Francisco, New York and Atlanta." Verily I say unto you that sexual immorality has many earthly consequences in addition to eternal ones. You can put your mind at ease over all of the sexually transmitted infections and disease by just stopping your sexually immoral behaviors. *Woe to those who do not stop!*

The last illustrative headline read, "Google vs. Evil." [62] "The world's biggest, best-loved search engine owes its success to supreme technology and a simple rule: Don't be evil. Now the geek icon is finding that moral compromise is just the cost of doing business." The article estimates that 80% of current Internet searches are done at Google. I've talked about them during the discussion on pornography. Google's founders established the corporate core value of "Don't be evil." It is a good slogan. However, if your technology provides access to unlimited online pornography, evil is exactly what you are being. Remember that Jesus taught us not to cause anyone else to sin? Well, despite lofty ideals on not being evil, Google has crossed the line with God into sexual immorality.

The way it works is simple. I've talked about precursors to some length already and you'll have to admit, Google can be a precursor to sin. Going to Google can be a precursor to sin. It fits those roles just knowing that it is a portal that allows access to unlimited pornography, lewdness, lasciviousness and licentiousness. Yet in God's eyes, it is also an enabler of sin and plays a causation role in regards to sin. Think about it this way. If Google's technology allowed a search on only morally based content, could it then be used to locate porn? For our purpose, let's say that eliminating all adult content sites leaves only "morally based content." This thought shows the importance of proper identification of adult sites in regards to either I.P. addresses or domain name suffices. The end result would be a business that was more in tune to its "Don't be evil" core value. Remember the China discussion on page 806 and how they are working to eliminate porn? China shut down access to Google's search engine, but later agreed to turn it back on when Google modified its search engine for China. Why not for all?

Myth—Sexuality Doesn't Matter

Sergey Brin, the Google founder that oversees the "Don't be evil" corporate policy says he finds himself "choosing the path of usefulness over a righteous crusade." Well, Sergey, if its useful to filter out pornography for China, why not for the United States? Unfortunately, I've never read any discussion of how "usefulness" can supersede "righteousness" in the Bible. Stick to the core value and start filtering out adult sites. Corporations that engage in pornography, promote pornography or enable pornography are all the same to God. They cause others to sin. Verily I say unto you that the sexually immoral actions of all businesses will have consequences with God.

It doesn't take a lot of brainpower to understand the moral decline in the United States and the rest of the world. Just open your eyes to the daily onslaught of headlines that document the vile, evil, wicked, and the sexually immoral acts in society. I know that one can get turned off to such news, but before you turn off, you'd better turn on to sexual morality and how it can benefit your family today and for eternity. While such headlines represent a micro view of the planet's sexual health, God also has a larger view in the Bible. Consider the sin of Lot's two daughters in Genesis 19:32 and its consequences. The Bible records the following:

"Thus both the daughters of Lot were with child by their father. The firstborn bore a son and called his name Moab, he is the father of the Moabites to this day. And the younger, she also bore a son and called his name Ben-Ammi; he is the father of the people of Ammon to this day [Ammonites]." Genesis 19:36-38

Do you recall the Ammonites from the last chapter? They worshipped their god Molech [also called Milcom] by sacrificing their children with a "consuming" fire. The incest of Lot's younger daughter fathered Ammon, the founder of the Ammonites, which held a hatred for the people of Israel.

"The prophets predicted fearful judgments against the Ammonites because of their hostility to Israel (Jer. 49:1-6; Ezek. 25:1-5, 10; Amos 1:13-15; Zeph. 2:8)." [63]

Myth—Sexuality Doesn't Matter

Solomon married Ammonite wives and other foreigners, eventually building "a high place" for their idol worship, which actually included child sacrifices. This was an abomination to God who became angry with him.

"For it was so, when Solomon was old, that his wives turned his heart after other gods; and his heart was not loyal to the LORD his God, as was the heart of his father David. For Solomon went after Ashtoreth the goddess of the Sidonians, and after Milcom the abomination of the Ammonites. Solomon did evil in the sight of the LORD, and did not fully follow the LORD, as did his father David. Then Solomon built a high place for Chemosh the abomination of Moab, on the hill that is east of Jerusalem, and for Molech the abomination of the people of Ammon. And he did likewise for all his foreign wives, who burned incense and sacrificed to their gods.

So the LORD became angry with Solomon, because his heart had turned from the LORD God of Israel, who had appeared to him twice, and had commanded him concerning this thing, that he should not go after other gods; but he did not keep what the LORD had commanded. Therefore the LORD said to Solomon, 'Because you have done this, and have not kept MY covenant and MY statutes, which I have commanded you, I will surely tear the kingdom away from you and give it to your servant.' " 1 Kings 11:4-11

Lot's oldest daughter fathered Moab, the founder of the Moabites who often participated with the Ammonites in their evil against the Israelites. These people had their own brand of idolatry that angered the LORD.

"The Moabites maintained hostile relations with the Israelites and frequently moved against them in war (Judg. 3:12-30; 1 Sam. 14)." [64]

Myth—Sexuality Doesn't Matter

Yes, sexual immorality has consequences and long before the modern day Abortionites learned to sacrifice their babies at the altar of "choice" — the Ammonites and Moabites were busy burning children alive by fire. I wonder, is it better to be ripped apart by medical instruments limb by limb or burned alive by fire? Perhaps some Abortionite will provide an answer to that question? And, in our modern day, would we be killing 4,000 babies per day if there weren't so much sexual immorality in the United States?

Consider the sin of the homosexuals in the Benjamin city of Gibeah.

"As [the Levite and his concubine] were enjoying themselves [as guests of an old man in the city of Gibeah], suddenly certain [homosexual] men of the city, perverted men, surrounded the house and beat on the [old man's] door. They spoke to the master of the house, the old man, saying, 'Bring out the man [Levite] who came to your house, that we may [have sex with him and then] know him carnally!' " Judges 19:22

The story begins in Judges 19:1 when a Levite "took a concubine from Bethlehem in Judah." However, "his concubine played the harlot against him, and went away to her father's house at Bethlehem in Judah, and was there four whole months." Eventually the Levite went to pick her up and found himself detained somewhat by his father-in-law over many days. Finally, the Levite refused to stay any longer and left with his concubine wife late one afternoon. As they are traveling it is getting late and they decide to head to Gibeah, because it was "of the children of Israel." But when they got there, no one would give them lodging.

It was too late to go on and it appeared that they would be forced to stay in the "open square" that night. However, a concerned citizen offers to put them up, but only "do not spend the night in the open square." We find that they are enjoying themselves when homosexuals demand the old man give up the Levite so they could have anal sex with him and force him to do unspeakable things against his will. Verse 23 continues.

Myth—Sexuality Doesn't Matter

> "But the man, the master of the house, went out to them and said to them, 'No, my brethren! I beg you, do not act so wickedly! Seeing this man has come into my house, do not commit this outrage. Look, here is my virgin daughter and the man's concubine; let me bring them out now. Humble them, and do with them as you please; but to this man do not do such a vile thing!' But the men would not heed him. So the man took his concubine and brought her out to them. And they knew her and abused her all night until morning; and when the day began to break, they let her go."
>
> Judges 19:23-25

These homosexual perverts ganged raped the Levite's concubine all night long and let her go in the morning. She only made it to the doorstep where she died. The following summary of the incident is found in *Meredith's Book of Bible Lists* [65].

"A Levite's concubine played the part of a harlot and went home to her father (Judges 19:1, 2). This indirectly led to a situation in Gibeah where the concubine was forcibly and continuously raped until it caused her death (Judges 19:22-28). The Levite cut up the body of the concubine and sent the twelve pieces throughout the tribes of Israel. This led to a war, which nearly wiped out the Benjamites and created a scarcity of wives for [the remainder of] that tribe. This led to the slaughter of all the inhabitants of Jabesh-gilead except for the female virgins. This provided 400 virgin wives for the Benjamites. An additional 200 virgins were required, and thus was initiated a sanctioned kidnapping of women from among the daughters of Shiloh to provide wives for the Benjamites (Judges 21)."

Sexual immorality has far reaching consequences just like the genocide of abortion. It is hard to predict the fallout from the sexual immorality you engage in today. Does it lead to the destruction of a baby? How do you know that baby was to be destroyed? It could have been another Perez leading to another Jesus forty-one generations later.

If the concubine wife had not played the harlot, who knows what the outcome would be. It was her harlotry that led indirectly to the situation in Gibeah. Likewise, the Levite trusted his brethren in Israel and had no idea such evil, like that of Sodom, was present in the tribe of Benjamin. The sheer audacity of the homosexuals led to over 25,000 deaths and almost wiped out the tribe of Benjamin. Today, there is a kindler and gentler Gay community. They only want the right to teach our Kindergarten children that they can choose the Gay lifestyle. To teach them that it's morally the same as a heterosexuals'? Yet is this not just as vile a thing as relentlessly raping the concubine? To me it is. It is the relentless raping of a young child's mind by a satanically false programming against their God given human sexuality. It is very evil and there is no doubt about it.

The Biggest Consequence: God Abandons Us!

The biggest consequence of all is that God will abandon an evil or wicked nation and HE will curse the land and its people. If the United States continues on its path towards becoming an immoral society, surely God will walk away and curse the nation and its people that our founders created to honor HIM. Yet, would this be anything different than what happened in the state of ancient Israel? Did they not already take the path that the United States is on from a morality standpoint? Do we honor God by killing babies in the name of civil choice and by sanctioning homosexual marriage in the name of civil rights? Only an immoral evil society thinks that way. These are just a couple of the many wicked activities that will cause the United States to lose the hand of God and HIS blessings. Consider HIS Word!

> **"Then the anger of the LORD was aroused against this land, to bring on it every curse that is written in this book."**
> **Deut. 29:27**

> **"The curse of the LORD is on the house [nation] of the wicked, but HE blesses the home [nation] of the just."**
> **Proverbs 3:33**

> **"But those who rebuke the wicked will have delight, and a good blessing will come upon them." Proverbs 24:25**

Myth—Sexuality Doesn't Matter

> "For the land is full of adulterers; for because of a curse the land mourns. The pleasant places of the wilderness are dried up. Their course of life is evil, and their might is not right." Jeremiah 23:10

> "So the LORD could no longer bear it, because of the evil of your doings and because of the abominations which you committed. Therefore your land is a desolation, an astonishment, a curse, and without an inhabitant, as it is this day." Jeremiah 44:22

> " 'I will send out the curse,' says the LORD of hosts; 'It shall enter the house of the thief and the house of the one who swears falsely by MY name. It shall remain in the midst of his house and consume it, with its timber and stones.' "
> Zech. 5:4

> " 'If you will not hear, and if you will not take it to heart, to give glory to MY name,' says the LORD of hosts, 'I will send a curse upon you, and I will curse your blessings. Yes, I have cursed them already, because you do not take it to heart.' " Malachi 2:2

Do you get the picture? Sexual immorality has consequences too broad to fully comprehend. God visits the iniquity "[parents put] *on their children* to the third and fourth generations" [Exodus 20:5]. I.E. Children raised by Gays support sexual immorality. They are raised in iniquity and naturally lack God's morality. Yet, God has made it very clear that those "who practice sexual immorality" are eternally condemned.

It's October 25th and five days ago my ninth grandchild, Bronson Jack Palmer was born. He weighed in at 10 lbs 11 oz and my son Brian and his wife Brandee exhibited the joy of the choices they have made. They have chosen to love each other and their two boys. Is love as simple as making a choice? Yes, and I believe love and sex are both choices. For example, I had an interesting talk with God about this subject months ago, when HE told me to contact a special woman I didn't know. More in a moment …

Myth—Sexuality Doesn't Matter

Love And Sex Are Both Choices Of The Heart!

Even if you think you're programmed for same gender sex, no one forces you to love or to have sex. It is always a choice that you make. Yet, sexual choices are often a "gateway" choice towards either Heaven or Hell.

↑ **Heaven Bound Sex** ↑

Ecstasy

Walk in Spirit

Connected Flesh

Marriage

Moral Sex Gate

Heart Choice

Immoral Sex Gate

Pseudo Marriage

Unconnected Flesh

Walk in Flesh

Pseudo Ecstasy

↓ **Hell Bound Sex** ↓

Copyright 2005 Edward G. Palmer, All Rights Reserved.

Book of Edward—Chapter 19

Myth—Sexuality Doesn't Matter

There is a moral sex gate that has a path leading to Heaven and an immoral sex gate with a path that leads to Hell. Once we've entered the immoral sex gate, it is like turning your car down a one-way street. It is not easy to just turn around and then retake the right path you should have taken. Yes, both paths are equated as equally valid, but astute readers of the Bible will recognize such teachings as satanic lies. Habits build up fast in the area of sex and those around us often reinforce our sexual belief system. If that belief system sanctions sexual immorality, it will be very difficult for anyone to make a change to morality without an awful lot of energy. This is true for any major habit, but habit change takes on tougher dimensions in the area of sex due to its bodily pleasures. Yet the Bible reminds us that we can control sin. We do not have to live with a bad choice; we can change habits!

The differences between the two sexual gateways are remarkable. The moral sex choice leads to marriage, a connected flesh, walking in the Spirit and the God given ecstasy that comes only through the sexual freedom that is found in the marriage bed. In contrast, an immoral sex choice leads to a pseudo marriage [I.E. Gay marriage or civil unions], unconnected flesh, walking in the flesh and only a pseudo ecstasy that falls far short of what God had intended. There is no sexual freedom from God on this pathway to Hell. Verily I say unto you that those who have entered the immoral sex gate headed towards Hell will have to expend an enormous energy to reverse the eternal destination that they have wittingly or unwittingly chosen. Yet it can be done, because at the foundation of love and sex lies the moment-to-moment choices we make "to love" or "to engage in sex." We can make a new and different choice the moment we can get our head straight and then our heart straight. Remember, our heart *choice* can be as simple as a "light switch" being turned ON or OFF [see chapter 7 and page 383].

Now, back to that special woman. It's almost seventeen months since Jackie has been gone. I've often wondered how I have survived save for her dog Annie I've had to care for along with this book that God has me writing. Aside from them, it has been a struggle to find the zest I once had for life's adventure. I do believe that I will find it again some day. God will restore me completely in HIS time, not mine. For many months after Jackie's death, the name of a particular woman appeared in my prayers while speaking in tongues. Quite frankly I hadn't realized that fact for a full nine months.

Copyright 2005 Edward G. Palmer, All Rights Reserved.

Book of Edward—Chapter 19

Myth—Sexuality Doesn't Matter

In my prayers I asked God to send me another wife who was as righteous as Jackie. You see the same prophecy that had Jackie leaving me so early also had me remarried by age 60. It's hard to believe, but since the first part of the prophecy actually came true I am now inclined to think the second part might also. However, I do not know for sure who this woman will be and there are now only 14 months remaining until that birthday. This should make life a little more interesting, yet there are many unanswered questions are in my mind. The only thing I am confident about these days is God's command to finish this book. In fact, nothing major will happen in my life until this book is completed. God has made that fact clear to me.

In my prayers, I asked God for the following four qualities in a wife.

1. Righteousness
2. Spirituality
3. Passion
4. Humility

I slowly began to understand that one of the words I spoke in tongues was actually the not-so-obvious name of a woman I had briefly met years earlier. She was the daughter of a dear friend of mine and she fit all four of the criteria in my prayers. Once I realized these facts I started to dialogue with God about her and I believe God told me to get a hold of her and talk. I also came to the belief that God was telling me she would be my next wife and that we would live a long life together. "Go talk to her about this Edward!" That's the message I think I got from God.

Let's see if I have the instructions right LORD. YOU want me to talk to this woman who I've known less than 15 minutes and whom I met only briefly about four years ago? Then YOU want me to tell her that we should get together, maybe date, because YOU told me we are meant to be together for the rest of our lives? Hello. Anything sound weird about this? Maybe I am just a lonely middle-aged fool? Yet God persisted with me for months and I eventually relented and was able to spend three hours with the woman who happened to be single and lived a 1,000 miles away. You have to have a sense of humor when God asks you to do something. I asked my friend to bring her to our Bible study the next time she came to visit. It happened.

Myth—Sexuality Doesn't Matter

I remember when I first laid eyes on this woman at our Bible study. As I went to open the door, the first thought that ran through my mind was: "God what are you getting me into?" Her physical attributes were different than the diminutive wife I had known for four decades. To say I was a little apprehensive about her is an understatement. Yet as we spent time in the Bible study, God's Spirit systematically melted my heart in a way that astonished me. God gave this woman favor with me in a way that I had never before experienced. I literally felt my resistance wane as I listened to her talk and observed her beauty. Where on first sight I was thinking, "I'll have to pass on that proposed meeting LORD" — I soon found myself asking her out to dinner to have the talk that God wanted me to have with her. She declined the dinner offer, but agreed to get together at a coffee shop with me in a few days after I told her God wanted me to talk to her about something. When she asked what, I said it would have to wait. What had happened?

The truth that Jesus is not God and that you cannot simply "mouth" Jesus as Lord and expect to get to Heaven without a minimum amount of righteousness are teachings opposite of trinitarian orthodoxy. God has challenged Christianity's apostate teachings, reminding Christians that their beliefs hold little validity in HIS Word today and that their "Jesus" salvation doctrine was like a sieve that would lead many to Hell instead of Heaven. Well, the fact God has me opposing orthodoxy has not passed over my head by any means. I speculated that maybe one person in 10,000 or more might have studied HIS Word diligently enough to understand these biblical facts. The first thing that happened was I found out that this woman did understand these facts. I asked her father if he'd been teaching her the stuff we've been studying. He said no, but that she had learned the truth herself. If that didn't astonish me enough, I found that she could quote the Bible back to me almost as well as I could quote it to her. Then was the fact she had read the King James Bible from front to back and was quoting from that version. Even I could never get past Genesis in the King's English of 1611. Yes, she was impressive. After the Bible study I found myself pondering the odds. What are the odds she had actually read the King James Bible from front to back? What are the odds she had studied it enough to be fluid in Scripture understanding and able to quote it with ease? What are the odds she would come to the same biblical truths as God had led me to? Wow!

Copyright 2005 Edward G. Palmer, All Rights Reserved.

Myth—Sexuality Doesn't Matter

I remember thinking, "Okay God, now YOU'VE got my attention!" As an ex-quality control engineer and manufacturing executive, my statistical background had me astonished that God would ask me to talk to a woman that actually could be compatible with what HE was asking me to do. What is that? It is to teach Christians the truth of HIS Word and to ask them to stop their apostate teachings about the Bible, salvation, Christ and about God HIMSELF. It is to give Christianity the message that many Christians will be going to Hell, because they are practitioners of lawlessness in God's eyes. That Jesus will be telling them "I never knew you." This book is the message God has given me to explain which Christians Jesus is talking to.

Suddenly I began to wonder where God was leading me with this particular woman. There is no doubt that without a good wife as a helpmate that I am not whole. The moment Jackie began to die, I could feel part of my own flesh being ripped out of my chest. I am incomplete and both God and I know that I will remain incomplete until HE brings a new helpmate worthy of the task HE has called me to do. That's to say my next wife would also have to be worthy and willing to support such a ministry. I've never had any exposure to an arranged marriage especially any kind of spiritual one. In fact, the whole idea seemed strange to me so I immediately clicked off a mental list of criteria that my next wife would "absolutely" have to have. "So, I guess LORD, that in addition to the four character attributes I already asked for, I *will need* the following other attributes."

1. She'd have to love children.
2. She'd have to love shopping.
3. She'd have to be excited about life.
4. She'd have to want to live a long life.
5. She'd have to be a strong woman.
6. She'd have to be an independent thinker.
7. She'd have to be knowledgeable of the Bible.
8. She'd have to be supportive of the ministry.
9. She'd have to be spiritually compatible.
10. She'd have to be sexually compatible.
11. She'd have to be willing to follow my spiritual lead.
12. She'd have to not want to start a new family.

Myth—Sexuality Doesn't Matter

I remember reading an employment agency maxim once that said if you listed seven "must haves" on any job description, that you would never find anyone to fill the position. Perhaps I was getting a little carried away? I admit I asked my daughters what attributes they'd like to see in my next wife. Loving children and shopping were their top choices. As I mentally reflected on the list I had created, I realized that this woman was most likely batting in the ninety-percentile range. Still, she was nine years younger and although in her late forties was never married and never had kids. I had found out quite fast that she just loved kids. Now I wondered.

What if I did marry a 50-year old and she came up to me and asked if we could make a baby? Well, I know myself and would actually say yes to such a request, after we assessed the risks to her health. If I loved a woman enough to choose to spend my life with her, I would love her enough to honor her request. Yet, I personally do not want to start a new family, because I do not want to be an 80-year old at my kid's H.S. graduation. In my mind this was almost an instant and easy way to eliminate anyone from my internal dating criteria. Also in my mental lists were no smoking and no drinking alcohol, etc. I would not date any woman who was into these substances. She had passed all the easy screens, but then came the meeting.

We met at Panera Bread in Anoka one afternoon about 6 p.m. She beat me there and was having dinner. Independence observed. I told her at some point I was not into independence per se. I was into interdependence. That is what it means when a husband and wife rely upon each other as best friends and also rely upon their God. Yet, to get to interdependence, you've got to at least become independent. Only independent people can choose to be mutually interdependent upon one another. Those who are dependent upon God do not take action alone. Those who are interdependent with God understand that HE will guide their path so they can take independent action. It explains why so many people think that God will take care of everything and don't understand that God calls us all to action. Same thing occurs in long-term marriages. Each interdependent partner knows they can take independent action, because both have committed hearts to each other and the decisions they make work towards the good of both lovers. Or, they simply do not matter in the context of their committed hearts.

Myth—Sexuality Doesn't Matter

I purchased dinner and sat down. We began to talk. She was easy for me to have a conversation with and time passed too quickly. Before we noticed, no one else was in the restaurant and they were mopping the floor. She asked the worker if they were trying to close. Over three hours had passed and it seemed like fifteen minutes to me. We left and parted ways. I gave her the first seventeen chapters of the book to read and give me feedback. I had noticed that she had the same type of personality that I have and might even scare a few men. For me, however, it was very attractive.

During our meeting, I marveled at her beauty both external and internal and listened intently as she spoke. God allowed me to look deep into her soul and heart. The warm fuzzy that God had given me at our Bible study had blossomed into an incredibly deep spiritual understanding. I began to say yes to whatever God was planning. I offered my friendship and told her I would be there if she needed me. Eventually I broke the news telling her that I felt the two of us were meant to spend our lives together, because of what God told me. Of course, she was flabbergasted. Anyone would be, wouldn't they? Still, we continued to talk and I believe we could have talked all night long. It was something I only experienced with Jackie and I knew that whatever the outcome, this was a special woman in my eyes.

Quite early along in the conversation, she confessed that due to medical problems she had a hysterectomy. Without knowing it, I was struck by her candor and wondered if God had nudged her conversation. What was the number one concern on my mind suddenly no longer existed. As we continued to talk, I found out that she was systematically getting rid of things and simplifying her life. She was giving a lot of things away and admitted when her dog died that she wouldn't get another. I had come to the same conclusion since dog ownership would hinder traveling. Both of us expressed a love for our old "puppies" and a desire to care for them until God takes them to their next life. I asked her why she was doing what she was doing. She said she didn't know why, but only that God had asked her to get ready. Get ready for what? She didn't know. At some point she said she had no plans to come back to Minnesota, but then quickly added that if God asked her to "I'd do it in a heartbeat." I left that night in awe and wondering what might happen in the future for both of us.

Myth—Sexuality Doesn't Matter

Of course, I also somewhat felt stupid. I laughed as I told my sister in law Candy and her husband Al. "What a pickup line, huh? God wants us to be together? I'll bet that's the first time you've heard that line." Candy said no and indicated that Al had once told her the same thing. Still, it was both a funny and to my intellectual side stupid conversation. So I asked God why HE would have me tell her that. Here is the substance of HIS answer and part of the email letter that I later sent to her.

Dear _____,

It didn't take long after our meeting last Thursday evening for me to ask God exactly why HE would have me tell you that we are meant to be together for the rest of our lives. It isn't the first time God has asked me to do something I personally think borders as the actions of a fool or even some spiritual fruitcake. Trust me, I've met many of them.

So, God ... Why?

The answer God gave me is this. "Ed, love flows from the committed heart. Not from the human flesh. Isn't that how it was when you chose to love ME?" Of course, it is true. I first chose to love God and THEN love flowed freely from my heart AFTER I made the choice of my heart. HE made it clear to me that it pertained to our human love also. First comes the choice. For me, it becomes a choice of the love that God has chosen for me. I know that only she could be a perfect love. The kind that lasts a lifetime and the kind that Jackie and I had.

I began to reflect back on the event when God gave me the "I know" inside of me concerning Jackie Bowers. I knew her at the time even less than I know you. I knew even less about her than I know about you. As I chased her around the proverbial dining room table, she asked: "Why me?" I told her I just know it is you that I am supposed to be with. She also said: "I've done some things in my past" — But, I stopped her before she could continue on and said: "I do not care about whatever occurred in your past. I only care about making a new life together with you." Any choice of the heart always begins with a lot of uncertainty.

Myth—Sexuality Doesn't Matter

Teri DeSario and K.C. had a 1970's vintage love song called "Yes, I'm Ready" which expressed the uncertainty of our love choice and all of the possibilities associated with it. The song also speaks to the mystery of our heart's love choice. The unknowing aspects of one's love for another are mentally set aside, when the heart makes the choice to love. The lyrics state, "I am ready to fall in love" and "I'm willing to learn." Part of the lyrics is an admission that we remain ignorant of how to love our lover, how to hold his or her hand and the lovers ask one another, "Are you ready?" Both of the lovers respond, "Yes I'm ready. Ready to love you, hold you, kiss you, want you, squeeze you, and need you. O, I'm ready. Yes, I'm ready."

When I chose Jackie in my heart, I basically told her "I am ready to fall in love." When I chose God, same thing. "I'm ready to fall in love." That is what I feel in my heart, soul and spirit towards you.

God is right. First comes the choice of the heart in terms of its commitment. Then comes the statement from our heart: "I'm ready to fall in love." Out of the heart's commitment flows true love. It is the kind of love that can laugh its way through life. It is the kind of love that can also see the humor in God's response to a very non-specific prayer. Reflecting back, you know HE answered the prayer in HIS humorous way and not in the way you wanted. It is the kind of love that sees the humor in God's directions even when they challenge your earthly perspectives on foolishness. Ed

There was a lot more that I wrote to this special woman. For the moment we've decided to just be friends. You've already learned that any commitment of the heart must be from both individuals. That is how you know that God is involved. My prayer is that God will tell this woman what HE has told me. We'll see where it all winds up. However, perhaps the only reason HE put me through this exercise is so I could write to you that love is indeed a choice. And once love is activated, marriage is the next choice. And after marriage, sex becomes a choice. If the heart is committed to each other, your sexuality will work itself out in the freedom of the marriage bed. Love is not like magnets with polar opposites clinging together. All love is a heart choice and a willingness to learn to love another to the fullest possible human ability. This "fullness" only takes place in the sanctity of marriage.

Myth—Sexuality Doesn't Matter

After reflecting upon who this woman was, our meeting and the talk we had and all of her attributes, I was stunned by exactly how perfect she was in my eyes. Yet then, why wouldn't she be? God had sent me to her. I could have dated 10,000 women and never found one that was such a perfect match. Well God, if this is my next wife, you'll have to tell her at least as much as you've told me. If not, guide me into the arms of who ever she is. We'll see what the future brings in the next 14 months. The future? I give it fully over to God. I know HE has the real plan. For now, you should realize these important facts about the choice of love, marriage and sex.

1. Love is a choice.
2. Marriage is a choice.
3. Sex is a choice.
4. Sexual freedom and true ecstasy is found in a marriage choice.
5. The choice to love is an ongoing choice every day of our lives.
6. The moment we choose to stop loving, the relationship ends.
7. The choice to love exists even if we temporarily dislike someone.
8. The love of God manifests itself in our obedience and respect.
9. The love of a spouse manifests itself in mutual love and respect.

In the four decades that Jackie and I were married, there were plenty of days when we didn't particularly like each other. There were also times when we didn't particularly like the decision of the other person. Yet, there was never a single moment of time when we did not love each other. Love is a choice even during times when you might not like someone. Isn't that what God does while HE waits for someone to change their sexually immoral behavior? Yes, HE chooses to love you up to the time of judgment, even if HE dislikes or hates the evil you are now engaged in on earth.

Those who have long lasting marriages understand that every day is a day to choose to love. It's the same thing with God. Every day I choose to love HIM and to walk in HIS Spirit. When your love takes on the import of its daily choices, you will find yourself moving close to godlike behavior and you will find the freedom of married sex and the true ecstasy it offers.

Myth—Sexuality Doesn't Matter

The Freedom Of Married Sex!

My friend Robert once taught me the maxim: "You make the choices and then the choices drive your life." It is true that actions flow *after* you've made the choice. Remember it is thoughts [choices], then actions, and then emotions: that's our normal process. When you choose only moral sex and marriage, your choices lead to the sexual freedom found only in married love; it is devoid of the guilt and destruction found in all immoral sex.

"When a man has taken a new wife, he shall not go out to war or be charged with any business; he shall be free at home one year, and bring happiness to his wife whom he has taken." Deut. 24:5

"If a man is newly married, he must not join the army, nor must he be pestered at home; he must be left at home, free of all obligations for one year, to make his new wife happy."
Deut. 24:5 NJB

I certainly like the idea of bringing happiness to a new wife and not having to worry about anything else for a year. Don't you? Of course, this isn't all about sex, but sex is a good part of it. During the first year of marriage, the old adage is to put a penny in the jar every time you have sex. Then, after the first year, take a penny out. The speculation is that you'll never remove all the pennies put in during the first year. I can't say if this is true. It may be for some couples. Yet it does raise some sex questions.

How much sex is the right amount? A lot depends upon the couple, but it is not unusual for a newly married couple to engage in sex more than once a day and every day during the first year. A lot relates to the passion of the two lovers and whether they have found God's sexual freedom in their marriage. Sexual freedom relates to the idea of being able to "let your body do what it naturally wants to do." That statement should intrigue you. I've already talked about the autonomic and automatic penile response in males, but when it comes to the couple making love, there is more to know.

Myth—Sexuality Doesn't Matter

The Gift of Sex [66] explains our autonomic and automatic body responses. "Look at the overall effects of our body systems as they interact with each other. ... The endocrine glands produce hormones (including sex hormones), which stimulate the nerves to carry messages to the brain. The brain then sends messages back via the nervous system to our muscular and vascular (blood vessel) systems. This process produces sexual arousal and response. In turn, this response stimulates the glands to produce more hormones, which again send messages to the brain via the nerves, and thus the cycle tends to be self-perpetuating. Because of the building nature of our body's interaction, the more sexual arousal and satisfaction, the more drive."

The Penner's describe the physical process singer Barry White [67] describes in his hit love song "Can't Get Enough of Your Love, Babe." In the third stanza, the lyrics state, "It's like the more you give, the more I want. And baby, that's no lie, oh, no, babe ... what is this love you're giving me?" The lyrics capture part of the mystery of God's gift of sex. HE has provided our bodies with a unique feedback mechanism. The more sex we have with our lover, the more sex our bodies will want to have with our lovers. The less sex we have with our lovers, the less sex our bodies will want to have with our lovers. Does this make sense to you? I've lived the truth of this reality in marriage. Indeed it is a strange fact.

During that first year that we are all over each other's body in marriage, it seems like sex is an all-consuming activity. Life changes when the first child arrives. Our time is now no longer dedicated just to our lover. Often this produces a dramatic effect and it is a fact that many divorces occur after the first child arrives. This is usually a male that cannot face having sex with a "mother." Assuming the couple gets past this sexual hurdle, they will soon find that sexual spontaneity is no longer possible or is steadily disappearing. When the second child arrives, the spontaneity is almost impossible as the demands of raising two children strip away the energies of both lovers. A combination of physical and emotional stress either sets in or both lovers are just flat worn out by the time they hit the sack. Is this the end of marital sex? It can certainly seem like the end and what is happening to our sex lives that used to be so vigorous, robust and spontaneous? The Penner's continue with the explanation.

Myth—Sexuality Doesn't Matter

"On the contrary, when one of the body systems interferes with or inhibits this natural building cycle, arousal and/or response may be difficult. As a rule, emotional barriers are what get in the way of the sexual response cycle." Take the following Scripture for illustration and its implications.

> **"I beseech you therefore, brethren, by the mercies of God, that you present your bodies a living sacrifice, holy, acceptable to God, which is your reasonable service."**
> **Romans 12:1**

Some Christians might interpret this verse to mean we are not to engage in sex. If so, they have the ultimate emotional barrier to sex. But, let's get real here. God has created our bodies to have and enjoy sex and therefore, such an interpretation would be spiritually ignorant. Remember that Paul also told married couples it was their duty to one another to have sex. A more accurate interpretation would be the following two actions:

1. Force your body to engage only in moral sex.
2. Force your body to be a slave unto righteousness.

Anyone who eliminates sexual immorality and is a slave to God's righteousness will find that they have offered their bodies as a "living sacrifice, holy and acceptable to God." These two items alone will make you friendly to God but an enemy of the world. Yet, they do not deny your God given gift of sex. Nor did Paul ever teach you to deny your sexuality.

"Within this arousal cycle we need to differentiate between the two branches of our nervous system and their effects during the sexual process. The autonomic or involuntary nervous system has two branches: the sympathetic nervous system (S.N.S.) and the parasympathetic nervous system (P.N.S.). These function without our willing them or even being conscious of them. They affect our bodies' responses in exactly opposite ways. Thus, together they can either increase or decrease the activity of our body organs. The P.N.S. has an up building effect on the body. It is in action when we are relaxed and more passive. The S.N.S. is our 'fight or flight,' that is, our energy system. It goes into action when we are anxious or intensely aroused emotionally."

Myth—Sexuality Doesn't Matter

"According to Helen Singer Kaplan [68], sexual excitement or arousal is controlled by the P.N.S. When we are aroused, the genitals rush full of blood and fluid producing the erection in the male and vaginal lubrication and swelling in the female. This is an involuntary response. We cannot decide to try to be aroused. Arousal is a response our bodies make that can occur only as we are relaxed and allow our bodies to receive pleasurable sexual stimuli. Soaking in the positive stimulation will trigger the P.N.S. and set our complicated brain-nervous system and vascular system in motion."

Ergo, human sexuality functions as an autonomic automatic system when we get our brains out of the way and just let our bodies do what they were designed to do and what they naturally want to do. In fact, maximum sexual enjoyment occurs as we simple "lose control" sexually in the freedom of the marriage bed. That losing control is letting our bodies do what comes naturally in the process of making love. I've often thought that Christian women can be more sexually responsive because they've already given up control to God. If a Christian enters the Holy of Holies, they may also find themselves slain in the spirit and on the floor. To get to that spirit realm, you've got to give up total control and allow your body to do what is natural in the spirit. It is allowing yourself to diminish as an entity and allowing God to engulf you with His Spirit. The same kind of process occurs in the sexual realm as we get our brains out of the way of enjoying sex.

Another songwriter named Eric Carmen [69] wrote a love song in 1988 entitled "Make Me Lose Control." It captures the essence of this moment with the lyrics "So, take me over the edge, make me lose control." Listen.

> (Turn) turn the radio up for that sweet sound
> Hold me close never let me go
> (Keep) keep this feelin' alive
> Make me lose control
> Baby, baby
>
> (When) when I look in your eyes, I go crazy
> Fever's high with the lights down low
> (So take) take me over the edge
> Make me lose control

Myth—Sexuality Doesn't Matter

It's paradoxical that God calls on us to control our sin and to make our bodies a living sacrifice while at the same time building something inside of us that requires us to actually "give up and lose control." The riddle is solved when you realize that God is only asking you to lose control in the moral setting of the marriage bed and of His Holy Spirit. You get maximum benefits from God in the spiritual realm after you give up total control to Him. You get maximum benefits in sex after you give up total control to your lover and your body responses. In both cases, you'll have to get your brain out of the way as it will stop you from fully entering these two realms.

The Penner's continued: "In contrast, anxiety or effort will act as an inhibitor by triggering the S.N.S., shutting off the parasympathetic and, thus, blocking the natural, building sexual cycle we previously described. Thus, when we allow ourselves to 'soak in' sexual pleasure through what we touch or hear or see, our P.N.S. will automatically cause us to become sexually aroused. This involuntary arousal will cause a man's penis to become erect and a woman's vagina to swell and lubricate."

"Neither of these responses will occur if a man or woman is trying to get aroused or watching themselves to see if arousal is occurring."

"When we are trying, our brain or head is in control, and, again, interferes with the involuntary control of the P.N.S. We have found it helpful for some men and women with arousal problems to think of 'getting with' their parasympathetic or getting out of their heads and into their penises or vaginas — going with the sensation of the moment. Or another way of saying this is that we have to let our bodies respond without letting our brains get in the way." You'll find a detailed discussion of the above facts in the Penner's book, *The Gift of Sex*, chapter 7. Again, I highly recommend their book for all Christian couples.

Do You Want God's Gift of Sexual Ecstasy?

Then, let go, lose control and let your body enjoy sex!

Copyright 2005 Edward G. Palmer, All Rights Reserved.

Myth—Sexuality Doesn't Matter

The process is the same if you want spiritual ecstasy. I've been to both of these places many times. Verily I say unto you, these are the two places I have found myself in God's presence. Yes, when I was physically coupled with my wife in a state of sexual ecstasy, I found myself close to God. Yes, when I offered myself spiritually to God and was slain in the spirit falling onto the floor, I found myself in God's presence. Yet in both cases, I was in a state of being beyond reason and self-control. That is what it means to be in a state of ecstasy.

Ecstasy[70] 1: a state of being beyond reason and self-control
2: a state of overwhelming emotion; especially [a] Rapturous delight.
3: TRANCE, especially: a mystic or prophetic trance.

Therefore, God has given us two methods of entering a state of ecstasy or "rapturous delight." One is in the physical act of making love in the context of moral sex and the marriage bed. One man, one woman, HIS design and with sex is both the physical and the spiritual realm. The second takes place in the act of intense worship. One human heart to God, giving up all pretense of any physical control and entering into only HIS control as you diminish yourself and your thoughts and allow HIM to engulf you with HIS control and HIS thoughts. Both are states of ecstasy on earth. Try them.

The headline read, "Asia lags behind Europe in sex, reveals Durex Survey [71]." The article states, "People around the world slip between the sheets on an average of 103 times per year, compared to 127 times in the previous year's poll, according to figures published by condom manufacturer Durex. Asians are the least sexually active, the survey says. Japanese have just 46 rolls in the hay per year, followed by Hong Kong, and Singaporeans with 79, Taiwanese with 80, Indians with 82 and 90 for Chinese, the survey said. By contrast, the top 11 nationalities in the sex stakes were European, with the French topping the charts with 137 sexual encounters per year, followed closely by Greece, Serbia-Montenegro and Hungary." Well, how do you feel about your own sexual frequency now? Depressed? How low can sexual frequency go in marriage? Marriages can become sexless, that is how low it can go.

Myth—Sexuality Doesn't Matter

An article [72] titled, "We're Not In The Mood" states, "Psychologists estimate that 15 to 20 percent of couples have sex no more than 10 times a year, which is how the experts define sexless marriage." But former U.S. Labor Secretary Robert Reich "jokes about the pressure couples are under in speeches he gives on overworked Americans. Have you heard of DINS, he asks his audience? It stands for dual income, no sex."

According to a 2002 study [73] by the respected National Opinion Research Center at the University of Chicago, "Married couples say they have sex 68.5 times a year, or slight more than once a week." NORC says, "The numbers haven't changed much over the past 10 years."

The pressures on the modern marriage can all but wipe out sex. As I reflect back on my experiences, I realize how much my entrepreneurial endeavors took me away from a more robust sexual life. If the business activity did not wear me out physically, it often left my brain wracked. I now can appreciate just how much those brain thoughts, including worry, interfered with our sexual ecstasy by inhibiting my P.N.S.

If you are raising a family, start setting aside a time during the week for a date between lovers. Do not let anything interfere with your date night. Secondly, start planning for sex. Don't wait for spontaneity to return as you might find yourself very old. Put the kids to bed EARLY every night and make time for one another. Keep them on a schedule and don't take them to activities every night of the week. Limit chasing during the evenings to one night. If you've got three kids and every kid gets his night, plus Wednesday night and Sunday are for church, you've just planned away five nights of seven. You should be planning "to be a family." Turn the television off and plan each evening to have dinner together and talk about life.

Put some excitement into your sex life. Should a married couple limit sex to the bedroom? What about sex in the other rooms of the house? What about sex on the floor, on different furniture, in a tent, in your car, etc? A married couple is free to have sex in any "private" location where they won't be disturbed. That includes behind a curtain in a one-room apartment in a third world country with kids on other side disciplined not to disturb.

Copyright 2005 Edward G. Palmer, All Rights Reserved.

Book of Edward—Chapter 19

Myth—Sexuality Doesn't Matter

Eliminate alcohol and tobacco from your life. Alcohol dampens the sexual response of the body and will ruin sex at some point in a marriage. In fact, as little as two drinks can affect your sexual prowess. Tobacco causes short-term memory loss and a laundry list of other problems all of which will dampen your sex life at some point. I speak from experience in these matters having been both a drinker and a smoker. Plan to engage your lover with a clear mind, whole body and 100% of your heart. To state another way, go to your lover with your full wits about you. That is when you can relax, get your brain out of play and allow your P.N.S. to take over. That is when ecstasy is possible. Isn't that also what God wants from you, a clear mind, whole body and a fully committed heart?

If married sex is not up to where you want it to be, it is a matter of intimacy for the most part. This is to say the lovers are not being as intimate as they need to be. Little things creep into a marriage and before you realize it, a wedge is between the partners and often sex is even used as a weapon of sorts. Remember Paul's admonishment to come together. Don't give Satan a foothold in your marriage by using sex as a negotiating tool. Instead, use sex as an intimacy tool to enhance your relationship. There is help forming a deeper level of intimacy. Lana Holstein, M.D. [74] has written a book entitled "How To Have Magnificent Sex: The 7 Dimensions of a Vital Sexual Connection." The book deals with the levels of sexual intimacy. I haven't read the book, but I saw her PBS television special and highly recommend her instructions to take your sexual intimacy to a higher level.

There is also Dr. John Gray and his "Men are from MARS & Women are from Venus" [75] materials. He has a great audio program along with other resources to enhance your sex life and increase the intimacy in your marriage. You don't have to settle for a dissatisfying sex life. In fact, if you do, it is indicative of intimacy problems and I suspect a marriage that might lead to divorce. Intimacy means good communications. This leads to good sex. Poor sex is a reflection of communications and intimacy issues in a marriage. It is also a sign of a wavering heart, financial problems or other things such as worry that dampen or destroy intimacy. This kind of stuff needs to be dealt with out in the open between the lovers if the marriage is to continue on. But at the heart of all marriages lies a singular Bible verse.

Myth—Sexuality Doesn't Matter

Husbands Love Wives — Wives Respect Husbands!

"Nevertheless let each one of you in particular so love his own wife as himself, and let the wife see that she respects her husband." Ephes. 5:33

When all else is said, marriage doesn't get much simpler than this Bible verse. Women need to know that their husbands love and cherish them. Men need to know that their wives respect them. A woman who does not feel loved will eventually want a divorce. A man that does not feel respected will eventually want a divorce. I have witnessed many marriages over the years and I can attest to the validity of these simple instructions from Apostle Paul. Study the entire context of Paul's instructions.

"Wives, submit to your own husbands, as to the Lord. For the husband is head of the wife, as also Christ is head of the church; and he is the savior of the body. Therefore, just as the church is subject to Christ, so let the wives be to their own husbands in everything. Husbands, love your wives, just as Christ also loved the church and gave himself for her, that he might sanctify and cleanse her with the washing of water by the word, that he might present her to himself a glorious church, not having spot or wrinkle or any such thing, but that she should be holy and without blemish. So husbands ought to love their own wives as their own bodies; he who loves his wife loves himself. For no one ever hated his own flesh, but nourishes and cherishes it, just as the Lord does the church. — Nevertheless let each one of you in particular so love his own wife as himself, and let the wife see that she respects her husband." Ephes. 5:22-33

If you want a long marriage filled with joy, this is the formula. Which comes first? Does a wife respect a husband who loves her? Does a husband love a wife who respects him? There can be interaction between these two characteristics. However, if both husband and wife do their own duty, you'll find that intimacy, sex and joy will flourish in the marriage.

Copyright 2005 Edward G. Palmer, All Rights Reserved.

Book of Edward—Chapter 19

Myth—Sexuality Doesn't Matter

A long time ago I listened to an interview of Elke Sommer, the famed movie star. When she was asked what caused her divorce, she stated: "My passion turned into compassion." I've thought about her statement a lot over the years. It was the poignant confession that while love still remained, her passion for her lover dissipated. Put another way, what was once her sexual passion became the ordinary caring compassion of any human companion or friend. As a husband and wife drift away from their sexual joy, it is a sign that something is amiss in the relationship. Sex is to marriage as the Canary is to the coal mine. It is a marital life sign that needs some attention. This is especially true in a young marriage where health issues do not interfere with sex. The cruelest thing that can happen in a marriage is for a lover's passion to turn into compassion, because this is a very slow process and indicative of a sexless marriage.

Sex Falls Into God's <u>And</u> Satan's Zones!

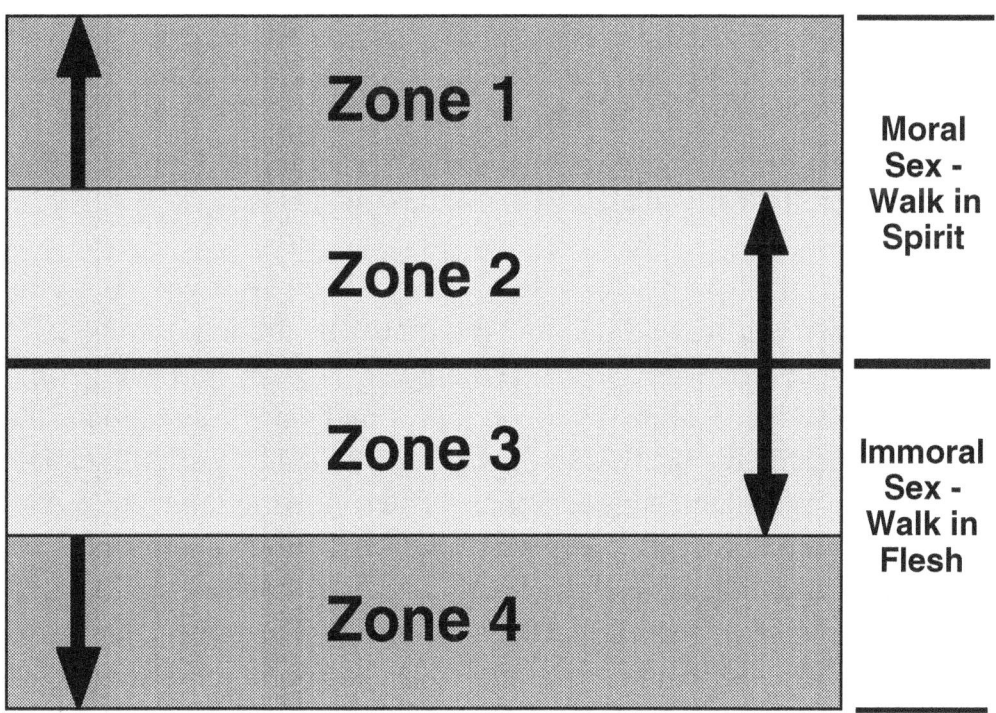

Myth—Sexuality Doesn't Matter

The four-zone graphic shown above is the same model I have used to illustrate the choices of our hearts and whether they are aimed at God or Satan. Go back to chapter 7, page 164 and review the material if you did not read *Choices from the Heart*. Zones 1-2 are righteous zones, belonging to God. Zones 3-4 are unrighteous zones, belonging to Satan. Righteousness is the centerline dividing zones 2-3. Those who walk a narrow path live in zones 1-2 and belong to God.

Those who walk the wide path alternate between zones 2-3 and want to play on both sides of the spiritual fence. Jesus says you cannot walk the wide path and get to Heaven. Those in zone 4 clearly belong to Satan. The minimum righteousness line is somewhere in zones 1–2. I have speculated that it may be at the dividing line, but I do not know for sure where it is. It may even vary for different individuals, since James 4:17 carries with it that kind of implication. I.E. God raises the bar for those more informed.

Those in zone 1 are really close to God. This is where I like to be. The closer to the top of zone 1 you get, the nearer to God you are and the less you are concerned about anything physical on this earth. That includes human sexuality and marriage. This is where the holiest of people live and it explains Paul's instructions why all should join him in this state of wonder and to avoid the *distraction* of marriage [1 Cor. 7:35]. Yet, verily I say unto you that you can enjoy a second state of wonder in a moral marriage and there is no doubt that God created us for that purpose also.

Those in zone 4 are really close to Satan. The closer you get to the bottom, the closer you are to Satan and the more you are into sexual immorality and perverted sex. This is where very wicked and evil people live. There are no fence sitters in either zone 1 and 4 as these humans have chosen and dedicated themselves to either God or Satan. Various sexual practices can be associated with all zones. The following table analyzes which zone you are in regards to a given sexual practice. Therefore, our sexual practices are indicative of the heart choices we've made and whether our heart choice is aiming towards Heaven or Hell. The table is arranged in alphabetical order by sexual practice and while it is comprehensive, it is not meant to be all-inclusive.

Myth—Sexuality Doesn't Matter

Item #	Sexual Practice	Mortal	Zone Map
1	Abstinence	†	1, 2
2	Adultery [B]	✖	4
3	Artificial Insemination [C]	✍	1, 2, 3, 4
4	Anal Sex	✖	4
5	Bestiality	✖	4
6	Birth Control	✍	1, 2, 3, 4
7	Cohabitation	▼	3, 4
8	Confused Gender Sex	▼	2, 3
9	Fornication	✖	4
10	Homosexuality	✖	4
11	Immoral Sex	✖	3, 4
12	Incest	✖	4
13	Lasciviousness	▼	2, 3, 4
14	Lesbianism	✖	4
15	Lewdness	✖	2, 3, 4
16	Licentiousness	✖	3, 4
17	Married Moral Sex [B]	†	1, 2
18	Masturbation [D]	✍	1, 2, 3, 4
19	Menstrual Sex	▼	2, 3
20	Mental or Physically Sick Sex	▼	2, 3, 4
21	Moral Sex	†	1, 2
22	Multiple Sex Partners	✖	4
23	No Sex	†	1, 2
24	Nocturnal Emissions	†	1, 2
25	Nude Photos [E]	✍	1, 2, 3, 4
26	Oral Sex [D]	✍	1, 2, 3, 4
27	Petting, Fondling Breasts, etc.	✍	1, 2, 3, 4
28	Pornography	✖	3, 4
29	Premarital Sex	✖	3, 4
30	Prostitution	✖	3, 4

Book of Edward—Chapter 19

Myth—Sexuality Doesn't Matter

31	Rape	✘	4
32	Rebound Sex	▼	2, 3
33	Revenge Sex	▼	2, 3
34	Self-Contained Sex [D]	†	1, 2
35	Sex Toys	✘	3, 4
36	Sex Machines	✘	3, 4
37	Sexual Thoughts	✍	1, 2, 3, 4
38	Solitary Sex [F]	✍	1, 2, 3, 4
39	Spiritually Confused Sex	▼	2, 3, 4
40	Threesome Sex	✘	4
41	Transexuality	✘	3, 4
42	Walk in Flesh	▼	3, 4
43	Walk in Spirit	†	1, 2
44	Wife Swapping	✘	4

Notes

a) Mortal Column Key
   1. † Safe sex practice or involuntary body function.
   2. ✘ Sexually immoral mortal sin.
   3. ▼ Precursor that can lead to mortal sin.
   4. ✍ Context causes practice to be immoral or moral.

b) Married sex can also be immoral.

c) Just because science can create babies, does not mean it is supposed to. Artificial insemination is playing god and carries with it the same risk that Sarah did by offering her maidservant to Abraham. It can create another Ishmael. Sarah had a "work around" when she really just needed faith. When a woman surrenders her womb to God, she can then accept God's answer. Care should be taken and the use of multiple eggs avoided when it may result in the selective reduction abortion procedure talked about earlier. A baby can be a blessing, but there are many wonders in this life, including adoption, and a couple should be cautious if using artificial insemination is just a means of circumventing what God has naturally given them. Or, if it means they will later be engaged in abortion. Both are faithless acts.

Myth—Sexuality Doesn't Matter

d) All sex is diminished or non-existent in the upper part of Zone 1 with those who live in a constant state of holiness to God. The most holy state we can enter sheds the flesh and encompasses a spiritual state of being ONE with God. We cannot live in this state constantly since our human body functions cannot go totally ignored indefinitely. Yet, in this deep state of the spirit, one does not care about the flesh or sex.

e) There is nothing inherently evil about nude photos and they must be distinguished from pornographic images. They must also be separated from the nakedness of the next of kin issue. Many nude photos reflect the beauty of our God given body design. Pornographic photos exhibit acts of sex in a variety of ways. And a nude photo of a woman next to a sex toy or machine is in itself pornographic. Sex poses that expose genitals inherently tend to be pornographic in nature.

f) Solitary sex is not necessarily moral self-contained sex.

Note: In addition to what zone a sexual activity may fall in, it is useful to also consider some examples of what is lewd, lascivious or licentious. This table only offers examples; it is not meant to be complete.

Lewd	<ul><li>Soft core porn movies</li><li>Flashing breasts</li><li>Baring buttocks or mooning</li><li>Sexually provocative dancing, hands on breasts</li><li>Female buttocks rubbing a male's crotch dancing</li></ul>
Lascivious	<ul><li>Streaking</li><li>Nakedness</li><li>Sexually flirtatious behavior; single to married</li><li>Women engaging in sexually provocative poses</li><li>Skimpy clothing, which is sexually suggestive</li></ul>
Licentious	<ul><li>Adultery</li><li>Fornication</li><li>Homosexuality</li><li>Lesbianism</li><li>Anal Sex</li><li>Prostitution</li><li>Pornographic nude photos, movies, etc.</li></ul>

Myth—Sexuality Doesn't Matter

Will You Tell God You Could Not Control Yourself?

Before I wrote the last chapter, I imagined what the idea of controlling sin might feel like when standing before God. Jesus said we would not have any excuses for our sin, so imagine that you are standing before Christ and his FATHER, our God. You are asked the question of why you supported abortion. You protest that you never supported abortion, yet God tells you that you still bear the guilt of others because you failed to reprove abortion, which you knew was evil. How would a moment like that feel?

Would it feel a little life threatening? It should. Perhaps you are one of those who are "named" a brother or sister in the Lord Jesus Christ who claims the Bible is silent on the issue of abortion, teaches abortion is okay because the life of the fetus is of less value than the mother, or that you took the word of your pastor that abortion was okay. How will you explain to God that you supported the following evil in HIS eyes?

1. You supported the shedding of innocent blood.
2. You supported the sacrifice of children.
3. You supported the idea of "love" as being self-centered.
4. You supported apostate verse translations of HIS Word.
5. You denied HIS eternal character in your decisions.
6. You denied what HE placed in your heart and mind.
7. You chose to be friendly to the world instead of to God.
8. You failed to hate what God HIMSELF considers evil.

Real peace of mind comes from true repentance and this means making a change of behavior. It means you stop doing what God abhors and you start doing what HE loves. Remember, HE has said clearly that HE will "make every person pay for doing what HE hates" [Ezekiel 7:3-4]. Listen, this is a simple thing to understand. If you engage in sexual immorality, you will be thrown into the lake of fire and suffer the second death. It's HIS Word! And, your protests about trusting in the name of Jesus will do you no good, since he will simply say: "I never knew you, be gone you who practiced lawlessness." Remember Jesus said: "Why do you call me Lord and do not do what I say to do?" Why?

Copyright 2005 Edward G. Palmer, All Rights Reserved.

Book of Edward—Chapter 19

Myth—Sexuality Doesn't Matter

> **Jesus said: "But why do you call me 'Lord, Lord,' and do not do the things which I say?" Luke 6:46**

> **"For whoever does the will of my FATHER in Heaven is my brother and sister and mother." Matthew 12:50**

Therefore, when it comes to eternal salvation, your obedience and actions will declare to God and HIS Son whom you really are and where your heart really lies. Do you have a righteous heart or an immoral one?

If you think Jesus will welcome you with open arms after a lifestyle of sexual immorality *at your end*, without the sincere repentance of the heart, you've been deceived like many others by Christian mythology. This is simply not true. Go back and read the prior chapters until you understand this spiritual reality. You cannot continue on with a lifestyle of willful sin doing what God hates and consider yourself a Christian. The truth of salvation lies in two separate groups of people.

God shows no partiality to those who fear HIM, because it shows that they are wise of heart. The second group HE somewhat ignores until they give HIM their heart and enter into the first group. These two types of people are the righteous and ungodly as taught in Psalm 1.

> **"Therefore men fear HIM; HE shows no partiality to any who are wise of heart [who rely upon HIM]." Job 37:24**

> **"For the LORD knows the way of the righteous, but the way of the ungodly shall perish." Psalm 1:6**

> **"They will be condemned at the time of judgment. Sinners will have no place among the godly." Psalm 1:5 NLT**

> **"You can be sure of this, the LORD has set apart the godly for HIMSELF. The LORD will answer when I call to HIM."**
> **Psalm 4:3 NLT**

Myth—Sexuality Doesn't Matter

If you find yourself gasping for air because the verses are challenging your idea of salvation, it indicates that you've just started reading the book with this chapter. Go back and read *The False Trinity Doctrine* and *The False Salvation Doctrine*. They will explain the Christian myth that we can sin with impunity by mouthing Jesus as our Lord. That myth runs rampant and deep within the Church today.

You could have led a very hideous life right up until the day of your death. Even on your deathbed, you could then have shown God a true repentance from your heart. HE will know as HE sees the truth of your heart. But, if this action is only on your deathbed, you may not have had any time or opportunity to demonstrate your faith to God by *works of faith* as Apostle James taught us to do. Another spiritual irony is if true repentance does occur [even on your deathbed], God would treat you just like Moses or any other servant of HIS, because HE impartially loves all who fear HIM.

I was just discussing this characteristic of God in a recent Bible study. A dear friend of mine has three sons who do not know the LORD. In our studies, God confirmed that even though he [their dad] has walked about 40 years with HIM, his three sons would find God's love for them identical to that for their father the moment they give HIM their sincerely repentant hearts. Someone can walk 80 years or more with God and the next person one minute and that second person would be loved by God just as much as the first person who walked 80+ years. This is God's way, not man's way.

The difference is the lost time of fellowship. The longer you wait to repent, the more years you lose without HIM. I lost 32 years of my life before I connected. Several times tears have come to my eyes just thinking of those lost years. What could have my first 32 years been like *with* HIM? I'll never know. You will receive eternal life and HIS impartial love the moment you surrender your heart 100% to God. However, you will miss HIS companionship every moment you delay. Delay long enough and you lose out for eternity. You'll never know how wonderful it is with HIM until you actually jump into the "spiritual river that flows from HIS throne."

"But many who are first will be last, and the last first."
                                                    Matthew 19:30

Copyright 2005 Edward G. Palmer, All Rights Reserved.

Myth—Sexuality Doesn't Matter

> **"And he showed me a pure river of water of life, clear as crystal, proceeding from the throne of God and of the Lamb." Rev. 22:1**

On the other hand, if you bought into the myth that you can simply utter the words "Jesus is my Lord" without making a change in the bowels of your soul where your heart resides, guess what? Yes, it's the lake of fire and second death for you. It is also the merciless words of Jesus you will hear as he says: "I never knew you."

Do you want to take the chance on your deathbed to get "real" with God and Jesus? If you've already spent your life "named" a Christian, what makes you think you can change anything on your deathbed? You've had days, weeks, months and even years to demonstrate a true repentance. Yet, you have demonstrated no repentance from your heart and have walked a life of sexual immorality. Therefore, even though you might have felt good emotionally and satisfied mentally by apostate teachings that supported your sins, you failed to gain eternal life at the end. Instead, you've only garnered eternal damnation. Why? You never got HIS truth on human sexuality.

> **"Therefore, my beloved, as you have always obeyed, not as in my presence only, but now much more in my absence, work out your own salvation with fear and trembling."**
> **Philip. 2:12**

In late August my daughter Paula and her four kids left to return to Colorado. We shared two wonderful weeks together. Christopher, my oldest grandson, arrived a couple weeks earlier by plane. Their visit brought some life back into my house, which has seemed too quiet since my beloved wife Jackie got her wings.

Soon after her arrival, Paula told me: "I actually saw a crumb falling from the table while the kids were eating. I think I felt mom's spiritual presence." Imagine food crumbs falling in slow motion from the table to the carpet in what can seem like minutes, yet just fractions of a second. I think that is what Paula saw with her eyes.

Myth—Sexuality Doesn't Matter

That is a perfect illustration of what happens when a person's spirit is with you. Paula knew that her mother kept an immaculate house and could always spot any crumbs on the carpet. In fact, her eyes were able to see dirt that I could not see. For me, everything is out of focus at five feet. I think Jackie was blessed with 20/10-vision. Paula found herself in her mother's kitchen cooking and feeding the grand kids at her mother's table. Suddenly she began to see things as her mother's eyes would see them. She took on Jackie's perspective and found herself wanting to live up and fulfill her mother's expectations. Paula wanted to please her mom even though she is with the LORD and HIS only human begotten Son, our Lord Jesus Christ.

I've found myself doing the same thing. In 39-years of marriage, I learned a lot about Jackie's expectations; what she loved and hated. I find I want to please those I love, even when they are no longer with me. This is the way Christ's spirit works. When it is inside us, it has us wanting to please God Almighty.

I've talked about this stuff before. This phenomenon occurs with those who are truly "in Christ." Once your heart has made the transition to righteousness, Christ's spirit inside of you causes you to see things from God's perspective. Suddenly you want to know what HE loves and hates. You then want to please God so you get your act straight and obey what HE tells you to do. Jesus said that those who are his brother and sister do the will of his FATHER. We know what that will is, because God pours HIS Spirit out upon all who are "in Christ" in abundance.

If you do not find yourself actively wanting to please God Almighty and obey HIM, at all times, it only means that you are not truly saved. You do need God as a part of your decision-making processes. If you don't take into consideration HIS perspective, HIS character, what HE loves and what HE hates — you most certainly lack wisdom. And it is obvious you do not have wisdom's *reason* controlling the actions of your heart. In fact, your body impulses are not bridled by *reason,* as they should be in those who claim to know God.

Copyright 2005 Edward G. Palmer, All Rights Reserved.

Myth—Sexuality Doesn't Matter

Reason Does Bridle All Of Our Body's Impulses!

"For the emotions of the appetites are restrained, checked by the temperate mind [having a knowledge of God], and all the impulses of the body are bridled by *reason*."

"And why is it amazing that the desires of the mind for the enjoyment of beauty are rendered powerless? It is for this *reason*, certainly, that the temperate Joseph is praised, because by mental effort he overcame sexual desire. For when he was young and in his prime for intercourse, by his *reason* he nullified the frenzy of the passions. Not only is *reason* proved to rule over the frenzied urge of sexual desire, but also over every desire." 4 Macc. 1:35-2:4

The Pharaoh's wife demanded Joseph have sex with her. However, in the 4th Book of Maccabees, the Bible teaches us that by mental effort Joseph "overcame sexual desire" even though he was in his "prime for intercourse." Clearly *reason* rules whenever we engage our brains. Ironically, when we engage our brains, we also engage the sympathetic nervous system, which opposes the autonomic parasympathetic system that stimulates our arousal cycle. In other words, sexual immorality becomes impossible for anyone who "mentally" considers God as part of his or her thought processes.

Engage Your Brain To Stop Sexual Immorality!

Do you want to stop your sexual immorality? Then just start using your brain. It might be that easy. And we know that a brain equipped with the word of God and HIS wisdom — will surely get the job done. The lesson of Joseph and the Pharaoh's wife is proof positive from the Bible that we do not have to succumb to base body instincts. God's body design with its P.N.S. and S.N.S. involuntary functions correlates perfectly with this Bible teaching. If God's will is considered, the brain just shuts down the sexual urge and arousal cycle with the S.N.S. Only when you ignore God can your P.N.S. then take over. <u>Think</u> about it!

Copyright 2005 Edward G. Palmer, All Rights Reserved.

> *WARNING. If you are a minister, teacher or a named Christian that teaches homosexuality, lesbianism and other acts of sexual immorality are okay, set your house in order with God. All of you should cease to spread these lies about God's Holy Word. Verily I say unto you, it is believers in the truth that shall see God's salvation for it is written, "They did not welcome the truth but refused to love it that they might be saved."*
> 2 Thess. 2:10 AMP

> **"Therefore, whether you eat or drink, or whatever you do, [including sex] do all to the glory of God." 1 Cor. 10:31**

> **"I have found … a man after MY own heart, who will [actually] do all [of] MY will." Acts 13:22**

> *PRAYER. O LORD GOD, free YOUR people from the apostasy that is rampant in the Christian Church today. Surely, if a minister cannot teach the truth about human sexuality, they cannot be trusted to teach anything from YOUR Word. They are indeed unfit for anything good and should cease their ministry activities. What should stand true for all concerned is that these false teachers "will perish because they were not lovers of the truth!" Amen.*

"The social idea that homosexuality, lesbianism and other acts of sexual immorality are somehow authorized, condoned, or okay with God and that it really doesn't matter to HIM is sheer mythology. Those who believe such stuff do not have God and HIS Son dwelling inside their hearts. Verily I say that they lack the ability to *reason*!" The Apostle Edward

If God's Spirit Dwells In Your Heart, Your Spirit-Soul Knows That It's A …

Myth—Sexuality Doesn't Matter

Book of Edward

Chapter Twenty
Myth—Politics Doesn't Matter

"HE is the ROCK, HIS work is perfect; for all HIS ways are justice, a God of truth and without injustice; righteous and upright is HE." Deut. 32:4

"Surely God will not listen to empty talk, nor will the Almighty regard it. Although you say you do not see HIM, yet justice is before HIM, and you must wait for HIM." Job 35:13-14

"The fear of the LORD is the beginning of knowledge, but fools despise wisdom and instruction." Proverbs 1:7

"Better is a little with righteousness, than vast revenues without justice." Proverbs 16:8

"What is desired in a man is kindness, and a poor man is better than a liar." Proverbs 19:22

"A lying mouth destroys the soul." Wisdom 1:11 NRSV

"But there shall by no means enter it [Heaven] anything that defiles, or causes an abomination or a lie, but only those who are written in the Lamb's *Book of Life*." Rev. 21:27

"But outside [of Heaven] are dogs and sorcerers and [the] sexually immoral and murderers and idolaters, and *whoever loves and practices a lie*." Rev. 22:15

"Those who hate the righteous shall be condemned."
Psalm 34:21

Myth—Politics Doesn't Matter

It's November 6th and our citizens of the United States have re-elected President George W. Bush. The number one reason cited by voters in the election was "Moral Values." [1] The United States has been teetering on the precipice of a moral abyss with God and HE has been getting ready to turn HIS back on this great nation.

However, with the 2004 elections, we've managed to take a moral step back from the abyss. Are we now safe with God? Or, is there more that this great nation needs to do? This chapter exposes the Christian myth that politics doesn't matter. It begins by examining the Abortionite admonition to the moral voter that he or she "needs to consider the bigger picture." Or as one person recently opined [2] in the Minneapolis StarTribune:

> *"I am a Christian Kerry supporter who awoke Wednesday to the sobering fact that George W. Bush would most likely be our president for four more years. I was heartbroken, but this was nothing compared to how my coworkers' gloating made me feel. One person looked me in the eye and with manic gleam stated, 'This is a win for all faith-based people.' As a 'faith-based person,' I look to a statement Hubert Humphrey made to help make political decisions: 'The moral test of government is how that government treats those in the dawn of life, the children; those in the twilight of life, the elderly; and those in the shadows of life, the sick, the needy and the handicapped.'"*
> *Cindy, Bloomington MN*

I agree the issue of "seeing the big picture" is what *every* Christian needs to consider. But, Cindy, come on, wouldn't Hubert spin in his grave if he thought your quoting him suggested that the slaughter of millions of tiny babies via abortion didn't fit his criteria? I think Hubert would believe that abortion does mistreat "those in the dawn of life, the children." If we cannot protect these babies, the weakest members of the human family, indeed the government has failed its moral test. The majority of citizens saw that Kerry and his party did not offer godly morality. They only offered a return to the destructive policies that almost destroyed our society's moral underpinning. Indeed, it is a "bigger picture" that *Cindy and others* need to understand.

Myth—Politics Doesn't Matter

Can Abortionites and half of those who call themselves Christian sacrifice godly morals for a feeding spot at the public trough? To put it another way, are those who call themselves Christian able to vote against God's interests and in favor of their own or party's interests with impunity? Here is a Bible clue that contrasts the issues of poverty and integrity.

"Better is the poor who walks in his integrity than one perverse in his ways, though he be rich." Proverbs 28:6

"It is better to be poor and honest than rich and crooked."
Proverbs 28:6 NLT

"Better someone poor living an honest life than someone of devious ways however rich." Proverbs 28:6 NJB

You can think of integrity as it applies to standing tall and firm for the word of God. Those who sincerely believe in the Word, have no problem standing on its *truths* in this limited earthly life. They understand that life doesn't end when we shed our earthly vessel, this human body.

Integrity [3]
1: firm adherence to a code of especially moral or artistic values: INCORRUPTIBILITY
2: an unimpaired condition: SOUNDNESS
3: the quality or state of being complete or undivided: COMPLETENESS. Synonyms see HONESTY

Before I continue, the LORD gave me a postscript to the last chapter. The day after I finished writing it, I found myself in excruciating pain in the back of my left leg centered behind the knee. I took a five-mile walk the day before, yet I perceived no problems with my leg at that time. When I awoke the next morning, I felt no pain. Yet sometime in that afternoon, I found myself engulfed in serious pain that had me limping on my left leg for two days. By the time it was all over, I experienced pain up and down my left leg from my ankle to my buttocks. To this day, I have no clue as to what had happened to me. Somehow I just wracked my left leg.

Myth—Politics Doesn't Matter

I asked God what had happened. HE said the leg pain was to remind me of how pain relates to sex. I was reminded of pain I suffered and how it and Jackie's pain had both affected our sex life. When a body is in pain, all of its systems work overtime just to deal with the pain; sex is not *then* an option. If you reflect on the sympathetic nervous system, it is normal that the body's S.N.S. will *then* dampen the sexual drive of the P.N.S.

All bets are off when it comes to sex when there is either physical pain or illness in one of the lovers. In the case of a spouse with a terminal disease, the other spouse's S.N.S. will inhibit their sex drive. For example, I personally could not imagine having sex and putting pressure on Jackie's cancerous pancreas. My desire was to get her healed and not to aggravate her pain, much less cause any accelerated pancreatic problem via sex.

God has built a sex "turn-on" and "turn-off" system into our bodies. Great sex presumes that a couple remains healthy, which is critical in old age. If one lover allows his or her body to degenerate into a dysfunctional state, or incurs a state of pain, illness or disease, sexual activities will decline fast even to a zero sex state. The healthy partner's passion might turn into compassion and eventually even divorce. Take care of your body and keep yourself sexually healthy. Quit smoking and other "body abusive" activities. This is also a good reason to avoid immoral sexual activities. Such behavior is a fast track towards a zero sex future and life of misery. I've now almost eliminated two decades of pain with the nutrients that I take. God reminded me of the pain-sex connection with the leg problem. I had almost forgot.

Sex is not a subject that is open to discussion for many individuals. In fact, subjects in human sexuality such as oral sex and masturbation are taboo topics considered too personal and private by most people. You should not discuss marital sex with friends as it belongs as a private matter between you and your spouse in the confines of your own marriage. Therefore, unless you need sex counseling, your sex life should remain private and between you, your spouse and God. I am thankful to God for HIS gift of sex and the joy it has brought to my life. It's my prayer that this sex information will be a blessing in your own careful study of God's perspective on sexuality.

Myth—Politics Doesn't Matter

I heard a political writer postulate that the voters in the "Red States" [4] were voting against their family's economic interests by voting Republican. He reasoned that poorer people would be better off with Kerry as president. Really? Incredulous as it might seem, maybe these poor people realize it is better to be "poor and honest" than "rich and dishonest." In the most basic analysis of the 2004 presidential election, I believe it really boiled down to this fundamental understanding of the majority of U.S. citizens. The elitists do not understand how anyone can vote against their economic interests. Yet those with God understand that HIS morality must come first, not last.

Another political writer [5] wrote: "Disappointed Democrats have had two weeks to argue about what went wrong for John Kerry on November 2. And they've had any number of plausible theories to choose from: Too many religious conservatives came out for President Bush; too few young people came out for Kerry; and so on. But none among the most commonly circulating postmortems has yet won an enthusiastic Democratic embrace.

Except, that is, for this one: George W. Bush won reelection because ... well, because there are just too many damn *dumb* people in this country, that's why." The article continues by illustrating how the elitists explain our collective stupidity, "Americans who persist in thinking well of their president are able to do so only because they 'suppress awareness of unsettling information' and instead 'cling so tightly to beliefs' that have otherwise been 'visibly refuted' by the media and rejected by 'the majority of people in the world.' "

Intellectually, if you really think about it, how dumb is the 51% of the electorate who refused to elect two lawyers from the Senate into the office of presidency? Even I could make a sound intellectual argument that it is the other 48% who voted for Kerry and Edwards, the two lawyers, which are the really clueless part of the electorate. And, listen, one of the lawyers was an experienced *trial* lawyer to boot. Still, despite all the political rhetoric, this election was about moral values, moral values, and moral values. Even if many of our citizens and half of those who call them self a Christian do not fully understand why, morality does matter to the soundness of our society. The majority of U.S. citizens historically knew this much in their hearts.

Myth—Politics Doesn't Matter

The Democratic hand wringing and name calling [dumb or stupid] fails to properly consider at least two voting blocks. Consider the black vote, which overwhelmingly went to Kerry. At 89% for Kerry in 2004 [6], the black vote was monolithic for the Democrats. Same thing occurred in the 2000 election [7], when 90% went to Al Gore. This monolithic "block" vote for Kerry meant that 89-90% of every black that called him or herself a Christian also voted for Kerry. Were these blacks "smart" or did they vote for their personal interests instead of voting for God's interests?

To the credit [or stupidity] of the black community depending upon your view, Bush received 11% of a black turnout of 13.2 million voters in 2004 [8]. This was up from 8% of about 10.5 million black voters in 2000. Do the math and Bush got 1,452,000 black votes in 2004 up from 840,000 in 2000. This is an increase of 612,000 votes over the 2000 vote. I would have to believe that this increase in black voters for Bush is directly attributable to the moral values issue. In other words, these additional 612,000 black voters decided to put God's morality ahead of traditional Democratic economic and social interests. However, black columnist Star Parker [8] writes that, "Black Christians still vote overwhelmingly Democratic!"

What do Democrats support and want from our government?

1. Unlimited abortion
2. Gay marriage
3. Government mandated wages
4. Embryonic stem cell research
5. Racial quotas for colleges
6. God out of the pledge of allegiance
7. God taken off of our money
8. Prayers taken out of our schools
9. Affirmative action quotas for jobs
10. Government jobs vs private jobs
11. Government control of health care
12. Government mandated health care
13. Ten Commandments out of schools
14. Total separation of Church and State

Myth—Politics Doesn't Matter

What are some things Democrats and Republicans both want?

1. Better health care
2. More affordable health care
3. A clean environment
4. Peace instead of war
5. Elimination of poverty
6. Elimination of discrimination
7. Fair and honest elections
8. Adult and umbilical cord stem cell research

A basic philosophical difference between the two parties is that the Democrats want the government to take charge and provide security for everyone from cradle to grave. Yet, when has a government delivered real security? Just look at Canada's national health care. I'm told you can wait five weeks for routine surgery. Take a priority number! And when I visited Canada a few years ago, government agencies were shut down two of their five-day weeks for lack of funds. Does a free money ride exist in society? No, ultimately, someone has to pay. The liberal soak the rich mentality is not a solution because the rich have investment income instead of wage or salary income. I remember the infamous 10% luxury tax a few years ago that the liberals passed to "soak" the rich who purchased yachts among other items. The result was that no one purchased new yachts and it almost eliminated 25,000 good paying industry jobs before the law was repealed.

Another flaw in the soak the rich mentality is that people change the way they do business. People do not live static lives that allow confiscatory taxation to take place. Once the government decides to punish anything with such taxation, people will change their lives accordingly, because everyone leads dynamic lives responding constantly to changing economic conditions. Ergo, "They didn't buy yachts!" The most progressive tax policy we could adopt as a society would be just a straight flat tax with no deductions except maybe mortgage interest and charitable contributions. In Russia's [9] move to democratic reforms, they adopted a flat tax rate of 13%. Of course, I believe a minimal amount should be exempt from all income taxes for the sake of family survival. No tax on the first $_____ of family income?

Myth—Politics Doesn't Matter

Another problematic policy idea is to tax corporations. The majority of corporations are simply small businesses. Many of these businesses are not flush with cash and the owners work long hours just for the privilege of working for themselves. As an entrepreneur with almost forty years of experience I can vouch for that. I was also the president of the Minnesota Entrepreneurs and I am well versed in these issues. The fundamental fact that belies the demagoguery on this issue is that corporations do not pay taxes — they simply collect taxes. Any tax levied against a corporation is just passed down and is reflected into the price of everything they sell or service. Therefore, in the most honest analysis, corporate taxes are simply hidden consumer taxes. Yes, consumers pay all corporate taxes one way or another. The most reasonable corporate tax would just cover government expenses of administering corporations from a legal perspective.

The Republicans want government out of our lives for the most part. They want to empower the individual as much as possible realizing that an empowered individual society is what has always made us a great people. The government should eliminate the obstacles holding back the people so that we can all have an equal opportunity to rise to the level of success that we choose. However, when the government tries to achieve equal results for people, they step on immoral ground. That is because to guarantee a better result for some people inherently means guaranteeing a worse result for other people. Affirmative action is a classic example where quotas and preferences are now having the effect of "reverse discrimination."

People might now view Republicans as a moral party and Democrats as an immoral party. Yet is it that simple? I saw what a third party would look like when Jesse Ventura was elected as governor of Minnesota. What Minnesotans got from the "Reform Party" was immoral social policies and moral fiscal policies, a compromise between the two major parties. Many are dissatisfied with compromises over values made in both of the major parties. That has led to the Reform, Green and Constitutional Party plus others. Fiscal hawks with loose morals are gathering in the Reform Party. Christian moral hawks are gathering in the Constitutional Party and radical environmentalists are gathering in the Green. People in both major parties are threatening to leave and support another party. So, even the political parties are constantly changing in the United States. Politics does matter!

Myth—Politics Doesn't Matter

The "Moral Values" issue is reflected in what the Democrats want for our society. As an exercise, put the numbers 1-14 on a piece of paper and go back to the prior list of fourteen items. Put a ✔ mark against any number on your paper that you think is a valid "moral values" issue. Now put a "✘" mark next to any number that you think would be a valid "moral values" issue with God using HIS perspective. Clearly God has a different opinion than a lot of Democrats. One perspective God has is about family support.

> **"But if anyone does not provide for his own, and especially for those of his household, he has denied the faith and is worse than an unbeliever." 1 Tim. 5:8**

> **"But if any provide not for his own, and specially for those of his own house, he hath denied the faith, and is worse than an infidel." 1 Tim. 5:8 KJV**

> **"But those who won't care for their own relatives, especially those living in the same household, have denied what we believe. Such people are worse than unbelievers."**
> **1 Tim. 5:8 NLT**

Yes, rugged individualism didn't just start with conservatives. It is fundamental biblical truth! What does this mean in practical terms for our society? It means we take care of our elderly parents and we do not just shove them off on government programs. Some liberal friends believe it is "moral" to siphon off parental assets and then shove their parents onto government Medicaid programs. It is immoral. When Jackie's mom entered the final four years of her life, it was Jackie and I that cared for her. We would not shove her off to a nursing home or attempt to hide her assets for personal gain. Yet to some liberals, this is their "moral" right.

Every able-bodied person in a household should be working to help support that family's needs in every respect. It means that pregnant unwed teenagers are supported at home and not shoved onto government welfare programs needlessly. It means if men father a child, they should take care of that child and its mother. It is their moral duty in God's eyes. It means that we are all "morally" obligated to take care of our own family members.

Myth—Politics Doesn't Matter

It is not the government's moral job to take care of family members! In God's eyes, government should be the last resort and not an easy tactic to gain a larger discretionary family budget at the expense of taxpayers. Listen to Paul's instruction on taking care of widows, as it is a clear example of widows with family and widows without family and how even grandchildren are responsible for taking care of their elderly grandparents in need. Pay attention now. If you are truly a Christian, then God's Word should be reflected in the public policies of your political party, the nation and in your election votes! Politics does matter.

> **"Honor widows who are really widows. But if any widow has children or grandchildren, let them first learn to show piety at home and to repay their parents; for this is good and acceptable before God." 1 Tim. 5:3-4**

Yes, some 2000 years ago people were also sponging off of others because families turned their backs on their moral obligation to care for one another. Piety in the simple sense of this Bible verse means having fidelity to the natural obligations of caring for parents and other family members.

Piety [3]   1: the quality or state of being pious: as
   a: fidelity to natural obligations (as to parents)
   b: dutifulness in religion: DEVOUTNESS

There are religious communities that do understand Paul's teaching. Mormons as a subset of Christianity, even with some theological issues I take exception to, clearly takes care of everyone within their society. Of course, they do not pay social security taxes and instead provide for their own with a ten percent tithe strategy and collective assistance to one another. It's a good family care strategy and tradeoff for them from a tax perspective. The point here, however, is that what they do in caring for families is what God wants all of us to do. Don't shove your family member onto welfare or Medicaid programs when you know that you could help them make a better life. Whose help will be more meaningful to family in the long run? It isn't the government's whose programs tend to enslave people rather than give them a helping hand that lifts them out of their problem.

Myth—Politics Doesn't Matter

A second monolithic voting block for the Democrats is the Jewish vote. Kerry [10] won 78% of the Jewish vote; Bush won 22%. Like the Black vote, the Jewish vote also increased for Bush. In 2000, he received 19%. Again, the increase was due to moral issues. In the analysis of the Jewish vote, one writer notes, "the bolstered Republican presence in the Senate and House of Representatives prompted concern among heads of Jewish organizations in New York."

"They predicted 'anticipated conflicts' between the Republican majority on Capitol Hill and the Jewish community on issues such as the separation of Church and State, abortion, Gay rights, and same-sex marriage issues, one Jewish community leader said Wednesday, on which 'the vast majority of the Jewish community disapproves of the Republicans' positions and views.' And yet it was Republican stances on these issues that mobilized the massive majority among New York's Orthodox community, especially in Brooklyn's ultra-Orthodox neighborhoods, that voted for Bush. According to unconfirmed results, Bush won 75 percent of Jewish votes in two large Brooklyn voting precincts that have a substantial concentration of Orthodox Jews." [10]

The article points out that Orthodox Jews do not exceed 10 percent of the Jewish community so their total voting impact would not be great. Ergo, 78% of Jews voted for Kerry. While a Black majority voted for economic interests in supporting the Democrats, Jews voted in the majority for social policies they supported. All four of the concerns expressed by the Jewish leader above are moral value issues. The comments made indicate a Jewish majority for immoral social policies. Likewise, the Orthodox vote appears clearly to support moral value positions. We can surmise that there is a lot of confusion in different communities. Both the Black and Jewish majority of voters understand politics. That much is also clear. Yet, like many other subgroups, these majorities lack a clear understanding of God Almighty.

There also appears to be a connection between different levels of faith in God and the positions that individuals take on political issues. Data from a Gallup survey [11] shows a direct correlation between church attendance and candidate. The more people attended church, the more they voted for Bush.

Myth—Politics Doesn't Matter

Gallup's Poll Shows Nation Morally Divided!

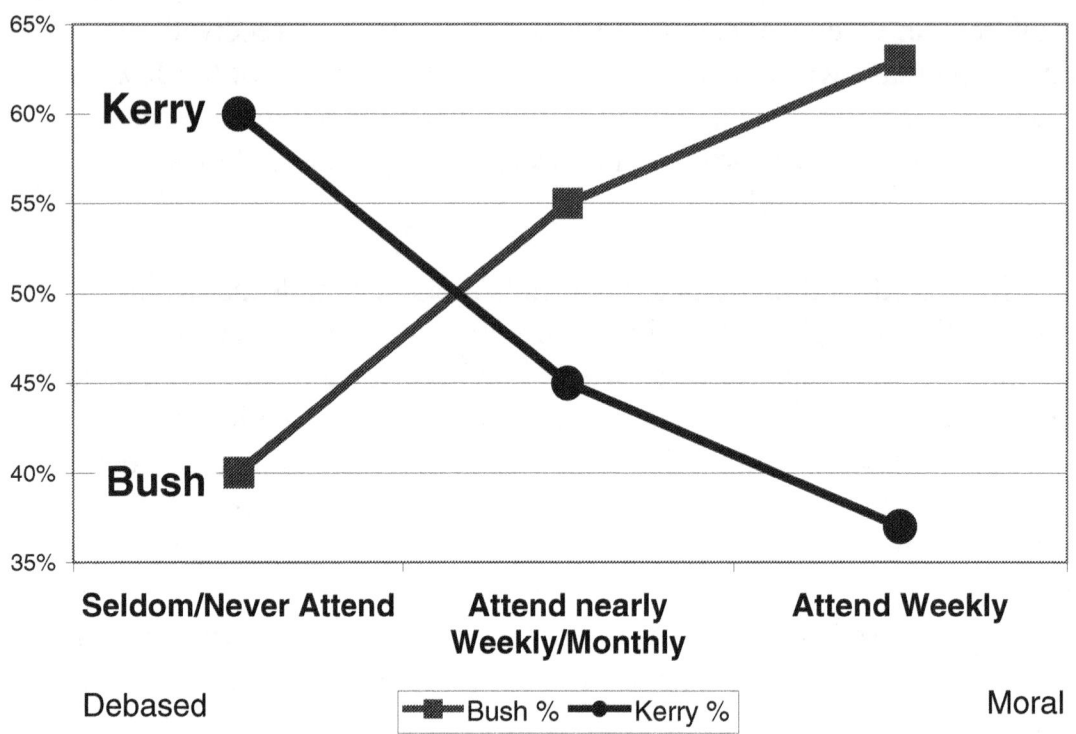

Debased ———Bush % ———Kerry ——— Moral

Tabular Data

Church Attendance	Voter %	Bush %	Kerry %
Seldom/Never Attend	40%	40%	60%
Attend nearly Weekly/Monthly	29%	55%	45%
Attend Weekly	31%	63%	37%

This chart shows the dramatic contrast and opposite directions of the voters during 2004. It is, in plain terms, the contrast between moral values derived from God and the "morality of rights" promoted by the Democrats. We started as a morally unified nation over 225 years ago. But, in 2004, the more a voter attended church, the more they voted for Bush. The opposite occurred for Kerry who garnered 60% of voters who seldom or never attend church. This graph should be a wake up call for all moral voters.

Book of Edward—Chapter 20

Myth—Politics Doesn't Matter

Consider the above data and realize that the 63% of the voters who attend church overwhelmingly voted for Bush. Yet 37% of those attending church weekly voted for Kerry and 45% of those attending weekly/monthly voted for Kerry. Christians themselves are now not united on the issue of moral values. Another way to view this information is that the less moral people were, the more they voted for John Kerry in 2004. Or, the more debased people were, the more they voted for Kerry. Clearly the election of 2004 was one based on moral values, yet it is still not as simple as it first appears when you consider the nation's voters who identify themselves as "evangelical Christians." Their vote breakdown [12] might surprise even you.

Religion & Ethics Newsweekly

Religious Groups and Voting Behavior
2004 and 2000 (two-party vote)

	Bush	Kerry	Bush	Gore
All white born again Protestants	78%	22	71%	29
Regular attending	81%	19	80%	20
Less regular attending	71%	29	54%	46
All white non-born again Protestants	52%	47	56%	44
Regular attending	54%	46	62%	38
Less regular attending	53%	47	52%	48
Mormons	80%	20	*	*
All Catholics	52%	48	49%	51
White Catholics	56%	44	53%	47
Regular attending	60%	40	59%	42
Less regular attending	53%	47	48%	52
Hispanic Catholics	42%	58	31%	69
Black Protestants	16%	83**	9%	91
Jews	25%	74	20%	80
Unaffiliated	30%	70	32%	68

*not asked in 2000
** more than weekly attenders were 22% for Bush and 78% for Kerry

Myth—Politics Doesn't Matter

The above table was part of an "Election 2004 Analysis" of the religious vote found on www.pbs.org [12]. Anchor Bob Abernathy as his introduction to a discussion of this issue said: "The religious vote was decisive in President Bush's reelection this week. Massive get-out-the-vote efforts among evangelical Protestants and conservative Catholics provided the margin of victory for the President. Despite the Democrats' attempts to reach out to people of faith, experts say an ongoing 'religion gap' in American politics was even more pronounced… Among all voters, 'moral values' edged out terrorism, the economy, and Iraq as the top issue of concern. This was particularly true for evangelicals. Many of them were galvanized by the issue of Gay marriage."

Anchor Abernathy asked Professor John Green, an expert in religious voting the following: "John, moral values means different things to different people. Is there any consensus about that?" Professor Green answered, "No, there really isn't. To conservative Christians the phrase 'moral values' tends to refer to sexual behavior and issues such as marriage and abortion. To more liberal Christians, secular people, Jews, and Muslims, that tends to oftentimes mean social justice questions — poverty, the environment, war and peace. We all think that morality is important, but we can't agree on what is moral." [12]

Religious People Can't Agree On Morality!

Why can't religious people agree on what is moral? What is going on in the culture that prevents Christians from a unified understanding of moral values? After all, our country was founded on the same moral values and those values held until the 1960's. If there is a moral concern from people of faith, there should be. There is a culture war going on and whether this will be a "moral" nation as defined by God in the Holy Bible is exactly what is up for grabs. Can 22% of "born-again evangelicals" vote against God's moral values with impunity? What about 47% of white Protestants? Can they vote against the mores in the Holy Bible they base their faith upon? Can social justice even take place in a society that does not adhere to God's moral values? I for one do not believe you can have justice if you don't have God's morality. HE defined morals, justice and injustice, didn't HE?

Myth—Politics Doesn't Matter

How morally right is a government policy that taxes moral people when those tax funds are then used for immoral purposes? Imbedded within such a policy is the distinct fact that it is unjust to the just. How right is a government policy that taxes moral people to support other people, which their own families refuse to support and which they themselves when able simply refuse to work? How just is it to tax people to support discretionary spending of other individuals and families? Imbedded within these types of government policies is an inherent injustice against moral and righteous people. Same injustice occurs with same sex marriage if you really think about it. There is an injustice imposed on those who *are* actually moral.

So, what about this question I have heard many times concerning Gay marriage? "How does Gay marriage affect my heterosexual marriage?" The question is usually followed by a quick assertion that "it doesn't." Well, let me tell you how it affects heterosexual marriage. If you are following along sequentially in this book, you've already learned that abortion is genocide and that we cannot predict what will happen generations later. You've also learned that sexual immorality can have a generational impact on society, which can even result in God abandoning a nation. And ...

A third generational impact on society began when single men and women were allowed to adopt children. Liberals ruled that the opposite sex supporting spouse was "not needed anymore" in single parent adoption. At this point, society abandoned a godly perspective on adoption and parenting. It became a "morality of rights" issue. It was an easy step to then allow two men or two women to adopt. Two Gay parents must be better than a single parent? Census estimates that 166,007 children are now being raised in Gay households [13]. Society has "created" Gay families by changing the basis of adoption from "morality" to the "morality of rights." The next logical step for Gay families is to gain same sex marriage. Yet, this type of policy thinking denies children the moral benefit of both a mother and a father. It is simpleminded to think children are raised equally well in a one-parent or same-sex coupled household from a societal health perspective. No fault divorce enhanced the adoption trend, as did the birth control "pill" and teen pregnancies. Liberals championed the "morality of rights" transformation and its attempted destruction of moral valves. The pill, adoption, limitless government supports, etc. were argued as societal "moral rights."

Myth—Politics Doesn't Matter

Biblical Morality = Assistance + Tough Love!

Throughout history there have been individuals who would not lift a finger to help themselves. They sponged off of society and played on the conscience of socially concerned people who confused "moral rights" with morality and compassion. True compassion is embedded in the words of Apostle Paul who clearly expected that those who could contribute would do so. The Bible combines tough love and help for those who sincerely need it with a policy of holding able bodied people accountable to contribute labor.

"For even when we were with you, we commanded you this: If anyone will not work, neither shall he eat." 2 Thess. 3:10

When people are unwilling to help themselves, tough love is required to deal with the situation. The government is best left out of these areas, as spiritual problems are the root cause. Ministries such as Sharing & Caring Hands, Gospel Mission, Salvation Army, etc. are best equipped to help such people. They understand tough love is the only way to lift such people out of their existing miserable life. That is why channeling funds to religious groups make sense. These foot soldiers know how to get the people saved, even from their own desire to destroy themselves. Would you give the homeless drunk money to buy a bottle of booze? No. If you have a guilty conscience, you should give to the charitable organizations shown above and refer people in misery to them and others like them. You can also give the homeless a car ride down to these places that can really help. Don't try to "buy" a clear conscience. Not even with tax dollars! Isn't that what social Christians do when they support liberal "morality of rights" programs?

Do "moral rights" become needed when a family does not want to take care of its own? What would God think of moral rights policies? HE would ask, "Why are you not taking care of your own family members?" The liberals have led us down a path of immoral policies, which are now threatening the very foundation of our great nation. Today the "morality of rights" is a euphemism masquerading as "morality." But morality is only found and derived from one place, the Bible. It is God's gift to mankind just like HE gave mankind the gift of sex and the gift of marriage. To quote Senate Majority Leader Bill Frist, "Moral values don't change!" [14]

Copyright 2005 Edward G. Palmer, All Rights Reserved.

Myth—Politics Doesn't Matter

The "morality of rights" is reflected in how many young people now believe that homosexuality and lesbianism are healthy for society. After all, it's their "right" to choose their own sexual preferences. While this is true in the privacy of anyone's immoral bedroom, what makes any voter think that the government has to support what Gays believe? As the children of single parents and Gays grow up, they will raise families of their own, straight or Gay, that will more easily support Gay marriage. Why? It is because to those adults, they never had the moral benefit of both a mother and father. A single parent or two same sex parents was the norm. Certainly God was left out of their upbringing. What's the impact to heterosexual marriage?

1. The first impact to heterosexual marriage is that it alters the definition of what a nuclear family is from the traditional model of God's design with a mother and a father raising children to the "any type of construct is a family" model of an ungodly society.

2. The second impact is the destruction of traditional family values and the supposition that single or Gay parenting is morally equivalent to God's family standard. It isn't. I bear witness for God to the attempt to destroy the family structure HE designed. Also, the result that the lack of a two-parent godly household has had on the development of children in the nation and the world.

3. The third impact to heterosexual marriage is that it alters what our children and grandchildren are taught in public schools about morals, sexuality, marriage and acceptable family relationships.

4. Fourth, when I don't believe that Gay marriage is moral, why is it that I should I have my family subjected to this forced Democratic "absolutist moral dogma?"

5. Fifth, why should the government financially support immorality?

6. Sixth, why should my family be taxed to support immorality?

You get the point, don't you? Gay marriage impacts heterosexual marriage in significant ways from morals, sexuality, marriage structure, family relationships, education, government support, private and public benefits and even personal income taxes imposed on the just. It's injustice!

Myth—Politics Doesn't Matter

To think that Gay marriage doesn't impact heterosexual families in these significant immoral ways is simpleminded thinking. Gay marriage helps further the destruction of what was once the common moral ground that our country stood firm on.

United States Was Founded As A Christian Nation!

Our nation was not founded as a multicultural nation with several distinctly different sets of mores. We began as a melting pot nation where all in the country accepted what was our common Judeo Christian heritage. Our Constitution forces no one to acknowledge or worship God, but make no mistake — this nation was created as a godly nation based on biblical morality. The Declaration of Independence and Constitution acknowledge this fact and it is reflected in our "moral" laws and legal framework. To think otherwise reflects an ignorance of United States history. Even this should not surprise moral people as liberals in the field of public education at all grades have perverted history. Yet our history remains unchanged. Anyone who wants to learn the truth can ascertain it.

Consider the words of Alexander Hamilton who authored the majority of the Federalist Papers and wrote in paper no. 2 the following. [15]

> *"With equal pleasure I have as often taken notice that Providence has been pleased to give this once connected country to one united people—a people descended from the same ancestors, speaking the same language, professing the same religion [Christianity], attached to the same principles of government, very similar in their manners and customs, and who, by their joint counsels, arms, and efforts, fighting side by side throughout a long and bloody war, have nobly established their general liberty and independence."*

> *"This country and this people seem to have been made for each other, and it appears as if it was the design of Providence that an inheritance so proper and convenient for a band of brethren, united to each other by the strongest ties, should never be split into a number of unsocial, jealous, and alien sovereignties."*

Myth—Politics Doesn't Matter

The Federalist Papers were published in newspapers under the name "Publius" as our great nation considered approving the Constitution. There was great opposition at the time to ratifying the Constitution in the State of New York. Thomas Jefferson and James Madison assisted Alexander Hamilton in making the Publius arguments to adopt our great Constitution. Our Founding Fathers were all people of great faith. They understood that you couldn't force people to acknowledge that God exists or to worship God. These are matters of the heart as I have previously taught you. The free will that God extends to humans was codified in our U.S. Constitution. Yet this was a Christian nation from the beginning with biblical morality right up until this moment in time when we find ourselves standing at the precipice of a moral abyss with God. Will this nation find its moral compass again and return to a godly society? *Woe to the United States if it doesn't.*

Few people would argue that we should invade the privacy of a Gay couple's bedroom and charge them with acts of sodomy. Yet at the other end, why should kindergarten children be taught that Gay sexuality is moral? Why should kindergarten children be taught it is morally equivalent if little Johnny has two daddies or two mommies instead of one of each? Such moral tripe is the "absolutist morality" being forced upon us by liberals. And, make no mistake about this either — the majority of the country now realizes that it is the liberal Democrats that have taken us to the edge of this moral abyss with their policies. In fact, it was fifty years of liberal moral leadership that led us to this point in time. Only by the shift towards a more conservative administration have we been able to "begin" to back away from immoral public policies.

Is it moral to create a class of citizens that are dependent upon the government for their livelihood? No, it is immoral. Is it moral to promise some members of the electorate "gifts" that come at the expense of other members of the electorate? No, it is immoral. Is it moral to try to convince the electorate that government should eliminate their economic suffering? No, it is immoral. Suffering is a part of this earthly life and no one argues that we should not mitigate it wherever and whenever possible. But to institutionalize the idea that government is the solution to family problems is to just create another myth primarily designed to keep elitists in power.

Myth—Politics Doesn't Matter

The real solution for families is to get the government off of our backs and get all of us off our duffs. Decades of liberal Democratic policies have created a dependency class of people. It will take decades to help them get a new life.

Eleven (11) States in 2004 overwhelmingly rejected the idea of Gay marriage and civil unions. They amended their state constitutions to reflect their decision. Already lawsuits have been started in the courts to try to over throw the decision of the people. Court challenges to this government "by the people" represents an in your face assault on the definition of marriage, which has existed for over 5,000 years. And, as you learned in the last chapter, man did not define marriage, God Almighty did. The repudiation of Gay marriage recognizes that people understand this "moral value" despite attempts by activist judges to redefine what marriage means. Only another amendment to the U.S. Constitution will prevent a continued legal assault on the institution of marriage. And when the people speak, the legislatures and courts should listen up. This is a government of the people, not the courts.

I bear witness to the liberal policies that have changed our nation because I was raised in the democratic stronghold of Minneapolis. As a lifelong Minnesotan, I saw first hand the morally destructive policies of the liberal left side of the political spectrum. I also had the unique privilege of seeing both sides of political issues from the two fathers in my life. My natural father died when I was only 13 years old. I was fatherless until 18 when I married Jackie. Her father then became my father for another 23 years until he died. My own father was an independent musician who wanted to decide where and when he worked. As the musician union took hold in the 1940's to 1950's, my father found himself increasingly being shut out from work, because he refused to join the union and kowtow to their demands. In contrast, my father in law was a common laborer all of his life and worked for one company over 40 years. He was a union man and if he had not been a union man, he would have suffered immensely as a laborer. His union experience was a positive one and kept his livelihood viable.

Throughout my life I have considered both sides of the political issues because of the influence of these two men. In Minnesota, for the most part,

Myth—Politics Doesn't Matter

if you didn't vote for the Democratic Party, you most likely threw your vote away for many decades. This is not the case today as the state is fairly evenly split. However, as I grew up, I watched the Democrats govern. It was a Democratic policy that decided to bus my children to three separate schools throughout their public education. As a result, we left the city of Minneapolis where my wife and I were raised and moved to a small rural town after our eldest daughter Paula finished first grade. It was Democratic policy that led to the tear down of low-income high-rise housing near the downtown area of Minneapolis that I used to play in. One of our childhood friends was living in one of those apartments as a poor young adult. The city never replaced that "poor" housing stock and basically threw these poor people on the streets to fend for them self.

It was a Democratic policy that led to the destruction of 40-year old low-income two story family apartments. They are now replacing them with higher income housing. My family used to live in one of those two story apartments in 1959 when they were first built and I was 13. Where do those poor families go? Again, they are out on the streets hunting I suspect. I also witnessed the mentally ill people get thrown out on the streets to fend for themselves. In part the law might have played a role. If it did, it was also under Democratic governance at both the state and federal levels. All my life I have heard how Democrats represent poor people. But in my first hand experience, I have witnessed mostly rhetoric. The policies of Democrats have usually been serving other powerful interests. The only thing for sure I could count on from the Democratic Party is higher taxes, poorer education, higher medical costs and a litany of legal abuses and injustice. In contrast, I have witnessed the Republicans try to help people get their lives together and even reduce their taxes. They have a distinctly different approach.

The policies of the Democrats seem to have good intentions. It is a good thing to help the poor, but it is immoral to create systems that enslave the poor. Everyone wants lower medical costs, but it is immoral to create an environment that leaves no accountability in the use of medical services and that allows trial lawyers to get rich with class action lawsuits. We humans make mistakes and that includes doctors, but if something isn't done soon to reform litigation — which doctors will deliver our babies? If you haven't noticed, these doctors are disappearing around the country.

Copyright 2005 Edward G. Palmer, All Rights Reserved.

Book of Edward—Chapter 20

Myth—Politics Doesn't Matter

What is the difference between large city voters in "Blue Counties" [16] and small city or rural voters in "Red Counties?" It is the simple difference between those who believe the government owes them something and the others who just want the government off of their backs. The latter group would rather be "poor and honest" than "rich and crooked."

What about that "Blue County" separation of Church and State issue? Shouldn't God be excised out of the government at all costs? If so, then consider these issues and the realities of such an immoral policy. [17]

1. We should stop naming public streets and roads after religious leaders and even change the names of those already so named.
2. We should eliminate the Martin Luther King holiday because it clearly is named after a religious leader.
3. It should be illegal to close down government offices on Sunday.
4. Good Friday, Easter, Thanksgiving, and Christmas Holidays should be eliminated in all government offices.
5. It should be illegal for government employees to belong to any religious organization.
6. It should be illegal for government employees to attend any private ceremony where references to God are made.
7. We need to change all of our money.
8. We need to change the façade on the front of the Supreme Court where a statute of Moses is holding the Ten Commandments.
9. We need to change all of the swearing in ceremonies.
10. It should be illegal for any government office to voice an opinion, interfere, rule, issue licenses, legislate, etc. on any religious sacrament including the act of marriage.
11. It should be illegal to hold religious services in the military.
12. Government employees with biblical names should not be hired.
13. The "Declaration of Independence" should be declared null and void since it refers to "Nature's God, Creator & Supreme Judge."
14. The "U.S. Constitution" should be declared null and void since it refers to the "Year of our Lord."

Myth—Politics Doesn't Matter

Christians lack a collective and common agreement on what is a moral value issue, so I have put together the following two tables. They provide a broad view of the issue and what I believe God wants you to consider. His moral values cut across many areas in society and not just abortion and Gay marriage. The election in 2004 was not lost because of the Gay marriage issue; it was lost because of 50 years of cultural decay that has chipped away at what was once our nation's common moral understanding. To eliminate confusion, God has guided me into defining the following items as either morally right or morally wrong in His eyes. If you think the Bible speaks differently on any of these items, please do send me your arguments and verse citations. I will surely study and respond to them.

God's Moral Values Table I

#	Moral Values Issue	Morally Right	Morally Wrong
1	Abortion		✔
2	ACLU Legal Assaults on God		✔
3	Adultery		✔
4	Boy Scouts Ostracized for Beliefs		✔
5	Causing People To Sin		✔
6	Causing a Lie		✔
7	Cloning Life		✔
8	Cohabitation or Living in Sin		✔
9	Cursing		✔
10	Demagoguery		✔
11	Disrespectful attitudes		✔
12	Divorce		✔
13	Elimination of Character Teachings		✔
14	Elimination of Morals in Schools		✔
15	Elimination of Prayer in Schools		✔
16	Elimination of God in Institutions		✔

Myth—Politics Doesn't Matter

17	Elimination of God in Pledge		✔
18	Elimination of God in Moral Values		✔
19	Embryonic Stem Cell Research		✔
20	Failure to Teach Children Morals		✔
21	Failure to Teach U.S. Moral History		✔
22	Gay Adoption		✔
23	Gay Marriage		✔
24	Gay Civil Unions		✔
25	Hate Speech		✔
26	Homosexuality		✔
27	IRS Approval of Church Donations		✔
28	Institutionalized Dependent Policies		✔
29	Institutionalized Poverty Policies		✔
30	Lesbianism		✔
31	Lies & Misleading statements		✔
32	Military Experiments on Servicemen		✔
33	Morality of Rights		✔
34	Multiculturalism		✔
35	News Defined As What's Perverse		✔
36	News Manufacturing		✔
37	News Manipulation		✔
38	Out of Wedlock Babies Socially OK		✔
39	Political Correct Speech Restrictions		✔
40	Pornography		✔
41	Prostitution		✔
42	Single Parenting as a Social Norm		✔
43	Slothfulness		✔
44	Uncivil Behavior		✔
45	Voting Party Interests over God's		✔

Copyright 2005 Edward G. Palmer, All Rights Reserved.

Myth—Politics Doesn't Matter

#	Moral Values Issue	Morally Right	Morally Wrong
46	Voting Self Interests over God's		✔
47	Voting State Interests over God's		✔
48	Vote Buying via Demagoguery		✔

God's Moral Values Table II

#	Moral Values Issue	Morally Right	Morally Wrong
1	Able Bodied People Contribute	✔	
2	Adult or Cord Stem Cell Research	✔	
3	Civil Discourse in Leaders	✔	
4	Clothing the Naked	✔	
5	Families of Widows Support Them	✔	
6	Feeding the Hungry	✔	
7	Giving Drink to the Thirsty	✔	
8	God's Morals in U.S. Presidents	✔	
9	Morals as defined by Holy Bible	✔	
10	Reproving the Sin Around Us	✔	
11	Respecting the Elderly in Society	✔	
12	Smoking Bans & Limitations	✔	
13	Supporting Moral Values on the Job	✔	
14	Taking in Strangers	✔	
15	Taking Care of Orphans	✔	
16	Taking Care of the Sick	✔	
17	Taking Care of Widows w/o Family	✔	
18	Telling the truth - Honesty	✔	
19	Visiting those in Prison	✔	
20	Voting to Support God's Morality	✔	
21	Women's Right to Know Laws	✔	

Myth—Politics Doesn't Matter

Aside from Hubert Humphrey's test of a moral government, we should also ask whether the proposed policy contains within it a "seed of injustice" against any segment of our population. Many government policies do exactly that. The idea of sanctioning the systematic slaughter of babies is injustice to 50% of the population. The idea of taxing moral people to pay for immoral policies is injustice to just as many. Whenever such injustice is found, factions of society have the right to rise up and fight a just cause. In fact, injustice is a basic cause of many wars. Don't expect a moral people to allow immorality to continue on indefinitely. As we look at this issue in our country, the big question is not whether immoral people will leave our nation and find "perceived refuge" in an immoral nation. The big question is whether as a nation we have the fortitude to stand for God's morality, not the manmade "morality of rights" eagerly promoted by immoral people.

Some liberals want to leave the U.S. for Canada. They have legalized Gay marriage [18], and abortion and they have even passed laws that put people in jail for reading aloud what the Bible says about homosexuality. It is now criminal to use a Bible to teach that homosexuality is immoral in Canada. [19] It is considered "hate speech" forbidden by Canadian law and subject to criminal penalties. Is that where the Gays want to take the United States? When I think of hate speech, I think of racial slurs, curses and threats along with other forms of communication such as burning crosses and painted swastikas aimed at demeaning people of ethnic groups and even political persuasions. The 2004 elections reached a high water mark in political hate speech when President Bush was equated with Hitler by liberal Democratic operatives. Such talk is evil in God's eyes, but the Founding Fathers of our nation believed that the voters would ultimately sift out the truth from the lies. They did. That is how free speech works in the eyes of our nation's founders. What would they think of modern communications?

I have no doubt that the above two tables are very controversial and might even provoke some anger. It is of little concern. Of more importance to me is that you gain a better perspective on how God's Word views these issues. I fully realize that 50% of the Christians reading this book are likely to care less what God's Word has to say. In fact, that is exactly what Jesus has prophesized. The "fifty-percent" factor is discussed in the next chapter. Still, I have hope that many Christian souls *will* be saved by these writings.

Copyright 2005 Edward G. Palmer, All Rights Reserved.

Myth—Politics Doesn't Matter

You might scoff at the notion that divorce is immoral, but God says that He "hates divorce." Why? The Word says it leads to ungodly children. In other words, single parenting leads to ungodly children. Think about His perspective and then reflect on proper public policy. Should there be "easy" divorce procedures like the so-called no fault divorce? Or, should there be a tougher stance forcing counseling to keep marriages together?

> **"But did He not make them one, having a remnant of the Spirit? And why one? He seeks godly offspring. Therefore take heed to your spirit, and let none deal treacherously with the wife of his youth. 'For the Lord God of Israel says that He hates divorce, for it covers one's garment with violence,' says the Lord of hosts. 'Therefore take heed to your spirit, that you do not deal treacherously.' " Malachi 2:15-16**

> **Jesus said to them, "Moses, because of the hardness of your hearts, permitted you to divorce your wives, but from the beginning it was not [to be] so. And I say to you, [that] whoever divorces his wife, except for sexual immorality, and marries another, commits adultery; and whoever marries her who is divorced commits adultery." Matthew 19:8-9**

> **Paul taught, "Now to the married I command, yet not I but the Lord: A wife is not to depart from her husband. But even if she does depart, let her remain unmarried or be reconciled to her husband. And a husband is not to divorce his wife." 1 Cor. 7:10-11**

Therefore, the Bible is clear that divorce should not be an option for God's people. It is also true that God gave man and woman the Oneness having a remnant of His Spirit for purposes of godly children. Remember the admonition in the last chapter about letting the "breasts of the wife of your youth satisfy you?" I know that many so-called Christians will go nuts over the above tables. That is why I offer these teachings on divorce to you. If you cannot get your heart wrapped around His teaching on divorce, don't bother to try to understand the other items; you don't have a pure heart!

Myth—Politics Doesn't Matter

The Pure In Heart Will See God!

"With the merciful YOU will show YOURSELF merciful; With a blameless man YOU will show YOURSELF blameless; With the pure YOU will show YOURSELF pure; And with the devious YOU will show YOURSELF shrewd. YOU will save the humble people; But YOUR eyes are on the haughty, that YOU may bring them down." 2 Samuel 22:26-28

"The words of the LORD are pure words, like silver tried in a furnace of earth, purified seven times. YOU shall keep them, O LORD, YOU shall preserve them from this generation forever." Psalm 12:6-7

"The statutes of the LORD are right, rejoicing the heart; The commandment of the LORD is pure, enlightening the eyes; The fear of the LORD is clean, enduring forever; The judgments of the LORD are true and righteous altogether."
Psalm 19:8-9

"All the ways of a man are pure in his own eyes, but the LORD weighs the spirits." Proverbs 16:2

"Even a child is known by his deeds, whether what he does is pure and right." Proverbs 20:11

"There is a generation that is pure in its own eyes, yet is not washed from its filthiness." Proverbs 30:12

Jesus said, "Blessed are the pure in heart, for they shall see God." Matthew 5:8

"Pure and undefiled religion before God the FATHER is this: to visit orphans and widows in their trouble, and to keep oneself unspotted from the world." James 1:27

"And everyone who has this hope in HIM purifies himself, just as HE is pure." 1 John 3:3

Copyright 2005 Edward G. Palmer, All Rights Reserved.

Book of Edward—Chapter 20

Myth—Politics Doesn't Matter

As I get closer to the end of this book, I am stunned by just how much is written in the Bible about what seems to be going on today in the United States. At times, it feels like I am actually living in biblical times. Just look around you and consider what is happening. Then carefully read God's Word, where you will find society's actions and God's reaction. It is very astonishing. I believe we are repeating every sin that Israel did as a nation and it will lead to one of two outcomes. Either we will repent and return to God's morality or HE will abandon us. This is evidenced by how the United States is nearly evenly split 50/50 on moral values. In the spiritual sense, I feel that God has us in the crosshairs of HIS wrath wondering what will be our "political choices." Can we return to being a moral society?

Will there be a payback for the immoral people of this earth? Yes, there will. And you can see by the verses above that purity of our hearts will matter. Only if we have a heart that is pure towards God can we understand why the items shown above as being morally wrong are wrong and the items shown above as being morally right are right in God's eyes. Today I am puzzled why so many Christians who claim Jesus as their savior would vote to support immoral policies in government. It's not only here; Canada is far ahead of us. Yet, those who are really with God are like-minded people, just like Christ was like-minded with God. They have the unity of HIS Spirit and a common understanding of all moral value issues. Like-mindedness and purity are precursors for the unity of the body. These are not just a spiritual force they are also a political force. Politics does matter to God.

Unity Means Pure Hearts And Like-Mindedness!

"And do not be conformed to this world, but be transformed by the renewing of your mind, that you may prove what is that good and acceptable and perfect will of God."
Romans 12:2

"Be of the same mind toward one another. Do not set your mind on high things, but associate with the humble. Do not be wise in your own opinion." Romans 12:16

Copyright 2005 Edward G. Palmer, All Rights Reserved.

Myth—Politics Doesn't Matter

> "Now may the God of patience and comfort grant you to be like-minded toward one another, according to Christ Jesus, that you may with one mind and one mouth glorify the God and FATHER of our Lord Jesus Christ." Romans 15:5-6

> "Finally, brethren, farewell. Become complete. Be of good comfort, be of one mind, live in peace; and the God of love and peace will be with you." 2 Cor. 13:11

> "Fulfill my joy by being like-minded, having the same love, being of one accord, of one mind." Philip. 2:2

> "Let this mind be in you which was also in Christ Jesus." Philip. 2:5

> "Whose end is destruction, whose god is their belly, and whose glory is in their shame — who set their mind on earthly things." Philip. 3:19

> "Set your mind on things above, not on things on the earth." Col. 3:2

> "These are of one mind, and they will give their power and authority to the beast." Rev. 17:13

God makes it clear that Christians are not the only group of people that may be like-minded. Evil people are also "of one mind" and part of that is by God's judgment day design. Study Revelation chapter 17 to explore how evil people will turn their political powers over to Satan. Evil people will parish despite the mythology that exists in Christian circles. Every Christian's choice is to be moral in God's eyes or in the world's eyes. With God, it's HIS morality; with the world, it's a "morality of rights" issue. As the political split continues to take shape in the United States, the real Christians are easily identifiable as those who adhere to the Word. This isn't rocket science and it gets back to those Christians who are "sincere" toward God. Many *are* named Christian, but many Christians exist in name only.

Myth—Politics Doesn't Matter

Warren Court's 1962 School Prayer Decision, In Engel v. Vitale, Started Nation's Moral Decline!

From the moment the U.S. Constitution was approved and for almost two full centuries our citizens had a unified understanding of moral values and morality. What was the milestone, event or turning point that destroyed that common moral understanding? The nation started its moral decline when the Warren Court ruled that prayer could not be said in public schools. The decision was made on June 25, 1962 and is recorded as U.S. Supreme Court, Engel v. Vitale, 370 U.S. 421 (1962). *Woe to these debased justices.*

"Almighty God, we acknowledge our dependence upon THEE, and we beg THY blessings upon us, our parents, our teachers, and our country."

That simple 22-word non-denominational prayer, which did not invoke a Catholic or even a Christian conception of God, was ruled as a violation of the separation of Church and State. For almost 200 years our nation's schools were free to engage in a daily prayer and society did not think it was evil or against our Constitution. What happened?

I remember in the 1950's as an elementary student leaving the school grounds at Seward Elementary in Minneapolis for an hour and marching up to a local church a few blocks away where we learned about God. I can't tell you want we learned, but I remember taking the trip. I also have no ill feelings about it. Suddenly in June 1962, Earl Warren's Supreme Court ruled that we could not speak God's name in public schools. Why? Perhaps it was Warren's liberal Scandinavian background that led to a belief that "God" doesn't belong in schools? I guess we'll never know for sure. However, there was a confluence of events that took place historically that we should all be aware of. Many events led us to this point in history.

The U.S. Constitution provides for the impeachment of justices that step out of line. Historically speaking, the Warren Court just had jumped off the moral cliff. Why wasn't there an outrage in Congress and the nation?

Book of Edward—Chapter 20

Myth—Politics Doesn't Matter

During 1962, both houses of Congress and the Presidency belonged to the Democrats in overwhelming numbers. Consider that the Senate was veto proof with 65 Democrats and only 35 Republicans. That means that the Democrats could do anything they wanted to in the Senate because they possessed such a large majority. Consider that the House of Representatives was also overwhelmingly Democratic and almost veto proof with 263 Democrats compared to 174 Republicans. John F. Kennedy was President and Lyndon B. Johnson Vice President. Democrats ruled our government!

House Has Power To Impeach Judges!

The Constitution grants the sole power of impeachment to the House of Representatives. It grants the sole power for trials of impeachment to the Senate. Had the Democrats exerted their power of impeaching the Supreme Court judges that "legislated" a ban on school prayer, they would have had their way. They didn't even raise a stink about it! Why? The Democratic Congress had it within their power to pass an amendment to the Constitution and pass it on to the States that proclaimed such an innocuous prayer for the general well being of the "students, parents, teachers and country" — was exactly what our Founding Fathers did approve. But, they took no action against the Court or to clear up the misunderstanding about our Constitution that the Court clearly had. Make no mistake about it; Democrats had a lock on the government reigns of power. Instead of being concerned about God, the Democratic Party had entered Kennedy's Era of the "Rights of Man."

Kennedy's Era Of "Rights of Man!"

In John Kennedy's acceptance speech for the Democratic nomination, we find the following statements. [21]

"I am grateful, too — I am grateful, too that you have provided us with such a strong platform to stand on and run on. Pledges, which are made so eloquently, are made to be kept. 'The Rights of Man' — the civil and economic rights essential to the human dignity of all men — are indeed our goal and are indeed our first principle. This is a Platform on which I can run with enthusiasm and with conviction."

Myth—Politics Doesn't Matter

"To uphold the Constitution and my oath of office, to reject any kind of religious pressure or obligation that might directly or indirectly interfere with my conduct of the Presidency in the national interest. My record of fourteen years in supporting education, supporting complete separation of Church and State and resisting pressure from sources of any kind should be clear by now to everyone."

Did Kennedy have a need to prove he supported "complete separation of Church and State?" Is that why his administration did not create an outcry and firestorm over the ban on school prayer? You'll find out shortly that there were many other crises going on simultaneously that had his attention. Yet those who had the constitutional power to address the activist Court clearly failed to do so. It was the House Democrats.

I've read and studied the Supreme Court's ruling and found it debased and incredibly flawed. Certain parts of it seem quite logical. However, the Court fails to point out who has suffered with an innocuous prayer designed primarily to promote an awareness of the God who our founders claim put our great nation together. The Court decision quotes James Madison, the author of the First Amendment saying "It is proper to take alarm at the first experiment on our liberties." Hello. For almost two hundred years no one thought a public "school prayer" to be a subject of contention. Therefore, it could hardly be thought a "first experiment on our liberties" as Madison had warned. Otherwise such a long history of the country would not have been possible without early litigation emerging. Likewise, it can hardly be thought of or viewed as the State imposition of a religion or as an assault on our liberties. After all, the prayer was nondenominational and voluntary. The Supreme Court rationalized their judicial activism to alter our society.

"In June 2004, the Supreme Court blocked a law designed to shield Web-surfing children from pornography, ruling that requiring adults to register or use access codes before viewing objectionable material would infringe on their rights." [22] Does the greater good of society no longer matter to the activist Court? Why is it that the safety of our children is ignored because the Court finds it inconvenient to adults? Does the Court now worship at the altar of individual rights over societal rights? In the process of upholding some individual rights, the Court stomps on others!

Myth—Politics Doesn't Matter

Woe to the United States people if its Congress does not reign in such judicial activism. Verily I say unto you that the Court cannot grant adult perverts such rights when they do engender sexual sin in our children. The Supreme Court in the United States is the direct cause of many people's sin by their consistently immoral rulings. God will repay. Another headline that read, "Combating Judicial Political Activism" [23] points out exactly how autonomous judges are. There are no checks on judges except impeachment and it is high time that all Legislatures create committees to oversee and reign in this "judicial legislative activism." It is their responsibility.

Supreme Court Justice Antonin Scalia recently commented in a lecture at the University of Arkansas in Little Rock. [24] "From abortion to the death penalty, the Supreme Court is being asked to determine moral issues that fall outside of the scope of strict constitutional interpretation. It is blindingly clear judges have no greater capacity than the rest of us to determine what is moral." This comment from a respected member of the U.S. Supreme Court begs some questions. First, if we are predisposed to moral error in the Court, why should we not be predisposed to error on the side of a "decent" society whereby the "moral rights" of the majority are protected and favored? Secondly, why doesn't the Court have a greater moral education than the rest of us? Thirdly, why hasn't the Constitution itself been amended with some basic "melting pot" mores? Today, it seems that "rights" have become the "morality of rights" or the "Rights of Man" — even when such rulings violate the rights of the mass majority of society. I.E. Why is it a "right" to teach children homosexuality is okay when it violates the "rights of 99% of society" that believe the exact opposite? Surely if the Court should *morally* error, it should be in favor of the latter.

Kennedy's "Rights of Man" dialogue was not just in his acceptance speech at the 1960 Democratic Convention. It is also found incorporated into the 1960 Democratic Platform [25], which states:

"In 1796, in America's first contested national election, our Party, under the leadership of Thomas Jefferson, campaigned on the principles of 'The Rights of Man.' Ever since, these four words have underscored our identity with the plain people of America and the world."

Myth—Politics Doesn't Matter

The 1960 Democratic Platform near its end states:

"When group interests conflict with the national interest, it will be the national interest which we serve. On its values and goals the quality of American life depends. Here above all our national interest and our devotion to the Rights of Man coincide. ... But man does not live by bread alone. A new Democratic Administration, like its predecessors, will once again look beyond material goals to the spiritual meaning of American society. ... The new Democratic Administration will help create a sense of national purpose and higher standards of public behavior. ... In this spirit, we hereby rededicate ourselves to the continuing service of the Rights of Man everywhere in America and everywhere else on God's earth."

When you understand what Kennedy stood for and that he was Bill Clinton's idol, you might understand why Clinton spent the first two weeks of his own presidency focusing on advancing the Gay rights agenda. After all, it was a "Rights of Man" issue in his eye. Clearly as we entered the fall of 1960, there was a renewed emphasis on individual rights. Given the racial tensions I witnessed, there should have been. Yet, I don't think that Jefferson was of the mind that the rights of a single man should rule over the rights of 99 other men when it came to such commonly understood moral values as teaching children in kindergarten that homosexuality is okay. Clearly each man has his speech protected by the Constitution as well as his liberty. As the 1960's began to unfold, morality would take a back seat to the "Rights of Man" and the "New Frontier" of space and technology.

For over 40 years, the Democratic Party was in solid control of the government of the United States. When school prayer was banned in 1962, the Democratic Party was in control of both chambers of Congress and the U.S. Presidency. When abortion was legalized in 1973, it was their party that was in control of both chambers of Congress. Only in the Presidency will you find more of a party balance over time. The following tables make it very clear where responsibility lies for the moral decline in the United States. It lies firmly as a legacy of the Democratic Party. Only they had the constitutional power to confront the activist Supreme Courts of Justice Warren's ban on school prayer and Justice Burger's legalization of abortion.

Myth—Politics Doesn't Matter

Control of House & Majority Leader

Congress	Years	DEMS	REPS	House Majority Leader
84th	1955-1957	■		D – Samuel T. Rayburn, TX
85th	1957-1959	■		D – Samuel T. Rayburn, TX
86th	1959-1961	■		D – Samuel T. Rayburn, TX
87th	1961-1963	■		D – John W. McCormack, MA
88th	1963-1965	■		D – John W. McCormack, MA
89th	1965-1967	■		D – John W. McCormack, MA
90th	1967-1969	■		D – John W. McCormack, MA
91st	1969-1971	■		D – John W. McCormack, MA
92nd	1971-1973	■		D – Carl Albert, OK
93rd	1973-1975	■		D – Carl Albert, OK
94th	1975-1977	■		D – Carl Albert, OK
95th	1977-1979	■		D – Tip O'Neill, MA
96th	1979-1981	■		D – Tip O'Neill, MA
97th	1981-1983	■		D – Tip O'Neill, MA
98th	1983-1985	■		D – Tip O'Neill, MA
99th	1985-1987	■		D – Tip O'Neill, MA
100th	1987-1989	■		D – Jim Wright, TX
101st	1989-1991	■		D – Thomas S. Foley, WA
102nd	1991-1993	■		D – Thomas S. Foley, WA
103rd	1993-1995	■		D – Thomas S. Foley, WA
104th	1995-1997		■	R – Newton L. Gingrich, GA
105th	1997-1999		■	R – Newton L. Gingrich, GA
106th	1999-2001		■	R – J. Dennis Hastert, IL
107th	2001-2003		■	R – J. Dennis Hastert, IL
108th	2003-2005		■	R – J. Dennis Hastert, IL

Note: I've used the phrase "for 40-50 years" the Democrats have had control. They had a lock on the House of Representatives for forty years non-stop. During this period, the United States began its moral decline and judges were allowed to legislate. During the period of time from 1995 to the present 2004, it has been a time of transition to a different party rule. It has been a slow turn to a moral basis of governing. We are not there yet.

Copyright 2005 Edward G. Palmer, All Rights Reserved.

Book of Edward—Chapter 20

Myth—Politics Doesn't Matter

Control of Senate & Majority Leader

Congress	Years	DEMS	REPS	Senate Majority Leader
84th	1955-1957	■		D – Lyndon B. Johnson, TX
85th	1957-1959	■		D – Lyndon B. Johnson, TX
86th	1959-1961	■		D – Lyndon B. Johnson, TX
87th	1961-1963	■		D – Mike Mansfield, MT
88th	1963-1965	■		D – Mike Mansfield, MT
89th	1965-1967	■		D – Mike Mansfield, MT
90th	1967-1969	■		D – Mike Mansfield, MT
91st	1969-1971	■		D – Mike Mansfield, MT
92nd	1971-1973	■		D – Mike Mansfield, MT
93rd	1973-1975	■		D – Mike Mansfield, MT
94th	1975-1977	■		D – Mike Mansfield, MT
95th	1977-1979	■		D – Robert C. Byrd, WV
96th	1979-1981	■		D – Robert C. Byrd, WV
97th	1981-1983		■	R – Howard H. Baker, Jr, TN
98th	1983-1985		■	R – Howard H. Baker, Jr, TN
99th	1985-1987		■	R – Robert Dole, KS
100th	1987-1989	■		D – Robert C. Byrd, WV
101st	1989-1991	■		D – George J. Mitchell, ME
102nd	1991-1993	■		D – George J. Mitchell, ME
103rd	1993-1995	■		D – George J. Mitchell, ME
104th	1995-1997		■	R – Dole & C. Trent Lott, MS
105th	1997-1999		■	R – C. Trent Lott, MS
106th	1999-2001		■	R – C. Trent Lott, MS
107th	2001-2003	■	Coup	D – Thomas A. Daschle, SD
108th	2003-2005		■	R – Bill Frist, TN

Note: Senate control by Democrats has prevented a full disclosure of what the Republican Party governance would actually be like. In addition, the Republicans in the Senate have never had the veto proof majority the Democrats enjoyed during their reign in power. As a result, a coup d'etat was pulled off in 2001 that allowed the Democrats to retake the Senate when Jeffers, a Republican switched party affiliation.

Copyright 2005 Edward G. Palmer, All Rights Reserved.

Myth—Politics Doesn't Matter

Control of U.S. Presidency

Number	Years	DEMS	REPS	President
34th	1955-1957		■	R – Dwight D. Eisenhower, TX
	1957-1959		■	R – Dwight D. Eisenhower, TX
	1959-1961		■	R – Dwight D. Eisenhower, TX
35th	1961-1963	■		D – John F. Kennedy, MA
36th	1963-1965	■		D – Lyndon B. Johnson, TX
	1965-1967	■		D – Lyndon B. Johnson, TX
	1967-1969	■		D – Lyndon B. Johnson, TX
37th	1969-1971		■	R – Richard M. Nixon, CA
	1971-1973		■	R – Richard M. Nixon, CA
	1973-1975		■	R – Richard M. Nixon, CA
38th	1975-1977		■	R – Gerald Ford, MI
39th	1977-1979	■		D – Jimmy Carter, GA
	1979-1981	■		D – Jimmy Carter, GA
40th	1981-1983		■	R – Ronald W. Reagan, CA
	1983-1985		■	R – Ronald W. Reagan, CA
	1985-1987		■	R – Ronald W. Reagan, CA
	1987-1989		■	R – Ronald W. Reagan, CA
41st	1989-1991		■	R – George H.W. Bush, TX
	1991-1993		■	R – George H.W. Bush, TX
42nd	1993-1995	■		D – Bill Clinton, AK
	1995-1997	■		D – Bill Clinton, AK
	1997-1999	■		D – Bill Clinton, AK
	1999-2001	■		D – Bill Clinton, AK
43rd	2001-2003		■	R – George W. Bush, TX
	2003-2005		■	R – George W. Bush, TX

The presidency is the most balanced in terms of party affiliation. This should not surprise us since the President has to reach across both party lines when seeking election. It is an irony that Eisenhower appointed Earl Warren and Nixon appointed Warren Burger to the Supreme Court. The Warren and Burger Courts were the most legislatively activist courts in history. Again, the impeachment solution rests solely with the House of Representatives!

Copyright 2005 Edward G. Palmer, All Rights Reserved.

Book of Edward—Chapter 20

Myth—Politics Doesn't Matter

The President does his best to nominate good judges to the Court. The Senate is charged with the duty of verifying that they are good judges. However, once they are in the job for life, only the House of Representatives has any power to do something about abusive Court behavior. And, the only things they can do are impeach, amend the law, or amend the Constitution.

We entered 1960 with a declaration from Pope John XXIII that Catholics had a duty to support moral candidates and parties. The penalty is ex-communication if they didn't. So what happened in 2004 when 48% of Catholics voted for Kerry and his party, which advocated immoral policies opposed by the church? Consider these events in 1960 for further context.

1960 — U.S. Elects Kennedy President, Platform: New Frontier & Rights of Man!

Year	Date	Event Headline in Chronicle of 20th Century [20]
1960	Jan 24	"Pope John XXIII inaugurated today the first synod on church discipline ... *Catholics would be liable to ex-communication if they join or vote for political parties or persons promoting heretical ideas or doctrines.*"
	Jan 31	JFK Announces bid for presidency
	Feb 13	French tests atomic device; becomes 4th nuclear nation
	Feb 7	More biblical texts uncovered in Israel
	Feb 27	Negro sit-ins integrate lunch counters
	May 7	Humphrey quits as Kennedy wins [easily] again
	May 23	Israel captures Eichmann, death camp chief
	July 8	Soviet Union indicts Gary Power U-2 spy plane pilot
	July 15	Kennedy named; Johnson takes 2nd place
	Aug 7	Castro nationalizes all American property
	Sep 26	Kennedy and Nixon meet in first TV debate
	Oct 12	Nikita bangs desk with shoe at U.N. session
	Nov 9	Kennedy elected by narrow margin [of 120,000 votes]
	Dec 1	Birth control pill to go on sale in U.S.

Myth—Politics Doesn't Matter

1961 — U.S.S.R & U.S. Arms Race, Cuba & Bay of Pigs Fiasco!

Year	Date	Event Headline in Chronicle of 20th Century [20]
1961	Jan 20	Youngest President [Kennedy] sworn in, urges service
	Feb 1	First U.S. solid fuel [Minuteman] missile launched
	Mar 21	Kennedy increasing aid to Southeast Asia
	Mar 30	X-15 reaches new speed (2,650 mph) & height (31 mi)
	Apr 2	Forty more [ancient] scrolls found in Palestine
	Apr 12	Soviet Union puts first man in space
	Apr 25	Bay of Pigs landing in Cuba is fiasco
	May 1	Castro makes Cuba Socialist; ends vote
	May 15	First American [Alan Shepherd] in space for 15 min
	May 28	U.S. helps Vietnam stop [Laotian] infiltration
	Jun 4	Soviet-American summit [reaches agreement on Laos]
	Jul 21	Gus Grissom follows Shepard into space
	Jul 25	U.S.S.R. and U.S. plan bigger defense
	Aug 7	Soviet cosmonaut orbits 17 times
	Aug 31	Berlin cut in two by Communist wall
	Oct 9	Maris exceeds the Babe's total [home runs] by one
	Oct 18	Chubby Checker has us all doing the twist [dance]
	Oct 28	American and Soviet tanks face each other [in Berlin]
	Nov 14	U.S. advisors in Vietnam raised to 16,000
	Dec 22	1st American slain by Viet Cong forces

    Did you notice the "birth control pill" on December 1, 1960? When you look at the events of 1960-1962 you see a new frontier in science. In April 1961, the "Bay of Pigs" was a huge embarrassment for Kennedy. In August, the Soviets were advancing into space faster than we were. Also in August, East-West Germany and the communist crisis are unfolding over Berlin. In November, Kennedy sends 16,000 "advisors" to Vietnam. The world was a dangerous place then and it still is. Yet, should U.S. external "worldly" interests over shadow U.S. internal "moral" interests?

Myth—Politics Doesn't Matter

1962 — Supreme Court Bans School Prayer, Cuban Missile Crisis Shakes World!

Year	Date	Event Headline in Chronicle of 20th Century [20]
1962	Jan 4	Saigon gets new aid; U.S. Army units added
	Feb 4	JFK orders total ban on Cuba imports
	Feb 26	Glenn is first American to orbit earth
	Feb 28	RFK says U.S. stays until Viet Cong beaten
	Apr 22	Charismatic Kennedy at popularity peak
	May 24	U.S. Carpenter orbits [earth], misses landing, rescued
	May 31	Israel hangs Eichmann for death camp acts
	June 25	Court bans official prayers in schools. *"The ruling builds the 'wall of separation' between church and state, that Thomas Jefferson referred to, higher and sturdier."* Note: Court activism ended school prayer.
	Jul 11	Satellite sends first worldwide TV show
	Aug 5	Marilyn, beautiful but damned, kills herself
	Aug 12	Soviet spacecraft orbit the earth in tandem
	Aug 17	First man is killed climbing the [Berlin] Wall
	Sep 30	Rioting erupts as Ole Miss admits Negro
	Oct 28	Cuban missile crisis: The week that shook the world
	Dec 14	Spacecraft sends close-up photos of Venus

John F. Kennedy got us into Vietnam. As 1962 began to unfold, we see that U.S. Army units are added to Vietnam; Cuban imports are banned; and, John Glenn is the first American to orbit the earth. In April, we read "Charismatic Kennedy at popularity peak." Two months later, the Supreme Court in an exercise of raw judicial "legislative" power bans school prayer. Where was Kennedy's concern? The Democratic Platform of 1960 referred to "God's earth!" What had occurred in society was simply the "granting" of special rights to individuals [atheists] under the guise of a Jeffersonian "Rights of Man" doctrine. Wouldn't Jefferson be surprised? The "Rights" he believed in were clearly stated in the Declaration of Independence as the "Unalienable Rights endowed by our CREATOR!" Eliminate God? Hello!

Myth—Politics Doesn't Matter

With prayer eliminated from schools and God taken out of our public education, society began to become increasingly debased. No doubt the sexual freedom offered by the "pill" aided and abetted a moral decline. For almost two centuries we enjoyed a common moral understanding among our people. Yet, in only a mere 10 years after prayer was taken out of schools, we find evidence of a disturbing moral decline. In September 1972, the saga of the Watergate break-ins begins to unfold. In October, sex therapy clinics are noted to have spread nationwide. In November, we learn of 500 secret sex change operations in the prior six years. Did the excise of God from our schools have any determinant effect on our moral decline? The answer is yes, whether you believe it or not. Without an awareness of God throughout society, cultures trend naturally towards debasement. The Court accelerated this debasement trend by legalizing the killing of babies in January 1973.

1972 — Nixon Reelected In Landslide, Different Morals & Watergate!

Year	Date	Event Headline in Chronicle of 20th Century [20]
1972	Jan 5	Washington: Nixon signs $5.5Bil bill for space shuttle
	Feb 28	Pres. Nixon visits China
	Mar 2	Spacecraft if launched to explore Jupiter
	Apr 30	North Vietnamese launch invasion of South
	May 13	Americans heavily bomb Hanoi, Haiphong
	May 16	Stalker shoots down Wallace during speech
	Jun 17	Five burglars caught in Watergate offices
	Sep 8	Arabs massacre 11 Israeli Olympians [in Munich]
	Sep 15	Seven in Watergate break-in are indicted
	Oct 1	Sex therapy clinics spread nationwide
	Oct 3	Nixon and Gromyko sign arms limit treaty
	Nov 1	500 Sex changes done in past 6 years
	Nov 7	U.S. B-52's set one-day bombing record
	Nov 8	It's Nixon by a landslide
	Dec 19	Last, longest Apollo moon visit ends
	Dec 30	Nixon orders an end to bombing in North [Vietnam]

Myth—Politics Doesn't Matter

1973 — Supreme Court Legalizes Baby Killing, Watergate Consumes Nixon Presidency!

Year	Date	Event Headline in Chronicle of 20th Century [20]
1973	Jan 21	State laws denying early abortions voided. "[The Supreme Court] by a 7-to-2 vote today, ruled states cannot prohibit or restrict a woman's right to abortion during her first three months of pregnancy ... On record President Nixon has opposed abortion. Three of his four Supreme Court appointees, however sided with the majority. ... *William Rehnquist and Byron White alone dissented. White wrote that he rejects a morality that values the 'convenience' of the pregnant mother more that the ... life or potential life which she carries.*"
	Jan 22	LBJ, a hard-driving man, driven no more [dies]
	Jan 27	U.S. agrees to stop fighting in Vietnam
	Jan 30	Liddy and McCord guilty at Watergate
	Feb 8	Watergate inquiry likely to continue
	Mar 28	Political element if Watergate laid bare
	Mar 29	United States ends war role in Vietnam
	Apr 30	Four top Nixon aides quit over Watergate
	May 17	Senate panel begins Watergate hearings
	Jun 21	Supreme Court sets obscenity standards
	Jun 25	Dean accuses Nixon and two chief aides
	Jul 30	All Nixon's official discussions on tape
	Aug 8	Agnew discloses he's under scrutiny [Nixon's V.P.]
	Oct 12	Agnew resigns; Ford is chosen to succeed
	Oct 22	Yom Kippur attack surprises Israel
	Oct 27	Nixon places troops on worldwide alert
	Nov 26	Nixon's secretary admits spoiling tape
	Dec 15	Psychiatrists say homosexuality not illness

Copyright 2005 Edward G. Palmer, All Rights Reserved.

Book of Edward—Chapter 20

Myth—Politics Doesn't Matter

On December 15, 1973, "The American Psychiatric Association ... approved a resolution calling for 'civil rights' legislation ... that would ensure homosexual citizens the same protections guaranteed to others."

At the end of 1973, the American Psychiatric Association approved a resolution calling for "Gay civil rights." You learned on p550 of chapter 16, that the church itself was actively engaged in promoting Gay and lesbian relationships by 1982. Immoral people seeking to rationalize their immoral behavior under the guise of the "morality of rights" or the "Rights of Man" Democratic political doctrines had permanently breached the mores that the United States was founded on. Can this moral breach be repaired?

In the midst of both the "prayer" and "abortion" Court decisions were worldwide calamities that threatened the massive destruction of mankind. Is it any different today? No. In fact, you can almost bet that throughout our lives that "wars and rumors of wars" along with their anxieties will plague humanity. It is meant to be. However, abandoning our moral foundation is a political option for U.S. society. We do not have to allow our society to degenerate into a totally debased society. Yet, morality is a political will that needs to be exercised to stop the decline. Politics does matter!

> **Jesus said: "You will hear of wars and rumors of wars. See that you are not troubled, for all these things must come to pass, but the end is not yet." Matthew 24:6**

Being faithful to God is not a matter of pretend public behavior. If we don't vote politically to support HIS will, we are unfaithful in the most naked sense before HIM. You can't expect Jesus to be your advocate before God Almighty if you secretly vote for immoral political parties and candidates. Your "public" persona will not stand HIS "heart test" at judgment time.

> **"He who is faithful in what is least is faithful also in much; and he who is unjust in what is least is unjust also in much. Therefore if you have not been faithful in the unrighteous mammon, who will commit to your trust the true riches? And if you have not been faithful in what is another man's, who will give you what is your own?" Luke 16:10-12**

Copyright 2005 Edward G. Palmer, All Rights Reserved.

Myth—Politics Doesn't Matter

> "But as God is faithful, our word to you was [certainly] not [duplicitous, meaning both] Yes and No." 2 Cor. 1:18

> "Be [even politically] faithful until [your] death, and I will give you the crown of life." Rev. 2:10

Our nation also needs to be faithful to God. We cannot be diverted from HIS moral concerns just because the world seems to be falling apart. Diverting our attention from God is a game that Satan plays. It is meant to take God out of our mental considerations. However, we need to FIRST be morally faithful to God. Then, HE will take us through the ugly trials of the world safely. Yet, can a nation with millions of moral hypocrites condoning evil — produce anything but evil? Paul's teaching on not saying "Yes and No" is instructive, because to do so means you *are* a duplicitous hypocrite, saying you believe one thing [in HIS Word] and doing the opposite [ignoring HIS Word]. In the end, this is an issue of being faithful in the small things even unto our death. "Real" Christians adhere to HIS Word and give thanks to God. This demonstrates an understanding of God; it isn't complicated.

> Jesus said, "Therefore do not worry, saying, 'What shall we eat?' or 'What shall we drink?' or 'What shall we wear?' For after all these things the Gentiles seek. For your heavenly FATHER knows that you need all these things. But seek first the kingdom of God and HIS righteousness, and all these things shall be added to you. Therefore do not worry about tomorrow, for tomorrow will worry about its own things. Sufficient for the day is its own trouble[s]."
> Matthew 6:31-34

Elitists think that you are not enlightened if you believe in God, yet the exact opposite is the truth. It is those who do not acknowledge God who are unenlightened. When you understand God, you understand why HE told David the following in 1 Kings 2:1-4, *"If your sons take heed to their way, to walk before ME in truth with all their heart and with all their soul, you shall not lack a man on the throne."* [Nor will such a godly nation lack MY protection]. The Founders of our nation understood these facts. Consider Washington's first Thanksgiving Proclamation. [26]

Myth—Politics Doesn't Matter

George Washington's 1789 Thanksgiving Day Proclamation

 WHEREAS it is the duty of all nations to acknowledge the providence of Almighty God, to obey HIS will, to be grateful for HIS benefits, and humbly to implore HIS protection and favor; and Whereas both Houses of Congress have, by their joint committee, requested me "to recommend to the people of the United States a DAY OF PUBLIC THANKSGIVING and PRAYER, to be observed by acknowledging with grateful hearts the many and signal favors of Almighty God, especially by affording them an opportunity peaceably to establish a form of government for their safety and happiness:"

 NOW THEREFORE, I do recommend and assign THURSDAY, the TWENTY-SIXTH DAY of NOVEMBER next, to be devoted by the people of these States to the service of that great and glorious BEING who is the beneficent author of all the good that was, that is, or that will be; that we may then all unite in rendering unto HIM our sincere and humble thanks for HIS kind care and protection of the people of this country previous to their becoming a nation; for the signal and manifold mercies and the favorable interpositions of HIS providence in the course and conclusion of the late war; for the great degree of tranquility, union, and plenty which we have since enjoyed; — for the peaceable and rational manner in which we have been enable to establish Constitutions of government for our safety and happiness, and particularly the national one now lately instituted; — for the civil and religious liberty with which we are blessed, and the means we have of acquiring and diffusing useful knowledge; — and, in general, for all the great and various favors which HE has been pleased to confer upon us.

 And also, that we may then unite in most humbly offering our prayers and supplications to the great LORD and Ruler of Nations and beseech HIM to pardon our national and other transgressions; — to enable us all, whether in public or private stations, to perform our several and relative duties properly and punctually; to render our National Government a blessing to all the people by constantly being a Government of wise, just, and constitutional laws, discreetly and faithfully executed and obeyed; to protect and guide all sovereigns and nations (especially such as have shewn kindness unto us); and to bless them with good governments, peace, and concord; to promote the knowledge and practice of true religion and virtue, and the increase of science among them and us; and, generally to grant unto all mankind such a degree of temporal prosperity as HE alone knows to be best.

GIVEN under my hand, at the city of New York, the third day of October, in the year of our LORD, one thousand seven hundred and eighty-nine.

(Signed) G. Washington

"Only do not rebel against the LORD, nor fear the people of [other nations], for they are [impotent]; their protection has departed from them, and the LORD is with us. Do not fear them. [The LORD, HE is our protection!]" Numbers 14:9

God is close to righteous people and that spiritual fact is something ungodly people will never understand. However, HE is also close to the righteous nation. When a nation places God first, HIS protection will be over that nation. When a nation denies God, that nation will not only lack HIS protection, but can even wind up with HIS curses. That is Israeli history from Abraham's faith. It is U.S. History from our Founding Father's faith. Our founders chose God and formed a Christian nation. They were united in their spiritual understanding. When our country was founded, it was not considered something strange to believe in God like it seems today. To the contrary, to not believe in God was strange and debased. If you want the enlightenment that our Founding Fathers had, start reading the Holy Bible and compare it to the historical writings of these great men.

Myth—Politics Doesn't Matter

Yesterday was November 25 and Thanksgiving 2004. Washington's message is one that characterizes our Nation's founding as firmly imbedded in Christianity and godly behavior. This proclamation should be taught throughout our schools and imbedded into the consciousness of our society. Yet we clearly have to then recognize our godly heritage. Today, there is a lot of revisionist history makers in society that seek to deny the United State's moral foundation. Verily I say unto you that the founders of our great nation were not hypocrites that feigned moral behavior with God, which is all too common today in the men and women of politics. The founders were genuine believers in God and HIS human Son Jesus Christ.

The lessons in Washington's Proclamation are many. Consider that both of the houses of Congress were moral and passed a joint resolution requesting the country's moral President take action. Consider the following statements of governmental doctrine from the first President of our country.

1. Nations have a duty to acknowledge the providence of God.
2. Nations have a duty to obey HIS will.
3. Nations have a duty to be grateful for HIS benefits.
4. Nations have a duty to humbly implore HIS protection and favor.
5. All people should observe Thanksgiving with a grateful heart for the many and signal favors of Almighty God.
6. All people should be especially grateful that God allowed us to establish peaceably a form of government for their safety and happiness.
7. Thanksgiving is a time for the people to thank God Almighty!

For two centuries our schools were free to teach the heritage of our great nation. Morality was automatically taught as our children learned U.S. history and the struggles of our Founding Fathers and the trust that they held in God. The U.S. Constitution, Declaration of Independence, Washington and other Presidential writings such as Lincoln's speeches were laced with respect and humility towards God. Eliminating God from public schools has created a debased society and one that is now heavily ignorant of the DIVINE Providence of our nation's beginning. Historical ignorance is so replete that many named Christians will also argue that the nation was not founded on Christianity and biblical morals. We *used to be* a nation of "godly" laws!

Copyright 2005 Edward G. Palmer, All Rights Reserved.

Myth—Politics Doesn't Matter

Promote Practice Of True Religion & Virtue!

The first President of the United States makes it clear that we as a nation [and other nations] are *"to promote the knowledge and practice of true religion and virtue."* Why the first Amendment? It is there to prevent the government from establishing its own "official" religion. That is what had happened in England; the government took away religious freedom. However, it's a long way from "establishing a religion of the government" and "taking God out of our public institutions." Everyone that is ignorant of U.S. history is politically complicit in the debasing of our society and will have a price to pay with God. *Woe to those who try to alter U.S. history and remove God. Woe to the ungodly activist judges. HE will repay both!*

U.S. History is a Testimonial of "People of Faith," "Biblical Morality," and "God's Providential Handiwork!"

There are many other references to God and lessons in Washington's first Thanksgiving Day Proclamation. However, the main point from all of this history is that we have a political duty to God to be a moral people first. From that moral foundation, God will indeed protect us. I know that many people will not believe what I have just said, but that is the teaching of the Holy Bible. God will protect and prosper HIS people when they adhere to HIS commandments and walk in HIS instructions. God will also forgive a repentant nation that turns its back on evil and returns to HIM.

"If MY people who are called by MY name will humble themselves, and pray and seek MY face, and turn from their wicked ways, then I will hear from Heaven, and will forgive their sin and heal their land." 2 Chron. 7:14

Have we gone too far? Maybe. But God makes it clear that the United States can return to HIM if it has the political will to set its house in moral order. In contrast, when a nation is immoral, God will curse that nation with HIS fury. From this perspective, I ask the question: "Are we now being cursed by God for killing 40+ million innocent babies?"

Myth—Politics Doesn't Matter

God Says: "Therefore Blood Shall Pursue You!"

Does God send terror to disobedient and evil people? Yes, HE does. Will the United States get any peace from the "blood" attacks until it ceases the shedding of innocent blood within its borders? No, there will be no peace in this country from terrorism until the abomination of abortion is legally stopped. Furthermore, just legalize Gay marriage or civil unions and see what else God sends our way! Verily I say unto you, God's providential hand does not protect evil nations that engage in abominations unto HIM.

> **"Their feet run to evil, and they make haste to shed innocent blood; their thoughts are thoughts of iniquity; wasting and destruction are in their paths." Isaiah 59:7**

> **"Now therefore, amend your ways and your doings, and obey the voice of the LORD your God; then the LORD will relent concerning the doom that HE has pronounced against you. As for me, here I am, in your hand; do with me as seems good and proper to you. But know for certain that if you put me to death, you will surely bring innocent blood on yourselves, on this city, and on its inhabitants; for truly the LORD has sent me to you to speak all these words in your hearing." Jeremiah 26:13-15** *Woe to the Abortionites!*

> **Thus says the LORD: "Execute judgment and righteousness, and deliver the plundered out of the hand of the oppressor. Do no wrong and do no violence to the stranger, the fatherless, or the widow, nor shed innocent blood in this place." Jeremiah 22:3** *Woe to the Islamic terrorists!*

> **"Because you have had an ancient hatred, and have shed the blood of the children ... therefore, as I live, says the LORD God, 'I will prepare you for blood, and blood shall pursue you; since you have not hated blood, therefore blood shall pursue you.' " Ezekiel 35:5-6** *Woe to those who shed the blood of children, for blood shall pursue them!*

Copyright 2005 Edward G. Palmer, All Rights Reserved.

Book of Edward—Chapter 20

Myth—Politics Doesn't Matter

> "Therefore I poured out MY fury on them for the blood they had shed on the land, and for their idols with which they had defiled it." Ezekiel 36:18

We have gone from a moral nation that taught the providence of God on our country and HIS morality to an immoral nation that slaughters babies in wholesale at the altar of a "woman's choice" and rationalizes sodomy as a "privacy" issue in the bedroom. In the process, we have gone from a nation blessed by God to a nation that has signs of HIS fury unfolding in the form of terror. How long will this nation keep its back turned on HIS morality? *Woe to all of us in the United States if we cannot repent as a nation!*

God Says: "I Will Even Appoint Terror Over You!"

> "But if you do not obey ME, and do not observe all these commandments, and if you despise MY statutes, or if your soul abhors MY judgments, so that you do not perform all MY commandments, but break MY covenant, I also will do this to you: *I will even appoint terror over you*, wasting disease and fever which shall consume the eyes and cause sorrow of heart. And you shall sow your seed in vain, for your enemies shall eat it. I will set MY face against you, and you shall be defeated by your enemies. Those who hate you shall reign over you, and you shall flee when no one pursues you." Leviticus 26:14-17

You will do well to study the entire chapter of Leviticus 26 as verily I say unto you it *all* applies to America as much as it applies to Israel. We too have made a covenant with Almighty God. We too have a responsibility to adhere as a nation to HIS statutes, judgments and commandments. God not only teaches that HE will send HIS terror and HIS fury, but also makes it clear that we can be defeated by our enemies and that those who hate us will rule over us. I believe that is exactly what is happening today in the United States. Terrorists are ruling over us. If you don't think so, consider how much our lives have been altered. How many new "rules" govern our lives? What is our national obsession, God or terrorism? Isn't it prophetic?

Myth—Politics Doesn't Matter

Commingling Values Corrupts Moral Unity!

When one thinks of commingling in business, it means the mixing of funds from private and business accounts. The use here refers to the mixing of our cultures. Our nation was safe for 200 years as we enforced the idea of the "melting pot." Immigrants were required to learn the English language and "melt" into our society. We did not teach public education in Spanish or any other language. The liberals' push for multiculturalism is also part of our nation's moral decay. Instead of "melting" into our Christian values and heritage, pagan values and foreign languages have been commingled. You can now travel to some parts of the United States and you will not be able to understand the local language because they do not speak English.

Multiculturalism is just another good sounding liberal policy that has had destructive effects on the morals of our nation. Instead of enforcing a common set of American values, Democratic policies have caused factions within our nation in the guise of heritage. There has never been a problem maintaining an immigrant population's heritage. Just ask the Italian and Irish immigrants you find in New Jersey and New York. Yet you won't find those populations behaving as if they were still in Italy or Ireland. They came for the American dream realizing that they would have to melt in and learn our culture to be successful. The biggest failure of multiculturalism is the failure to teach that immigrants can't be successful if they don't melt in. That is the reality of immigrating to the United States. Like it or not, the de facto language is English and one's ability to use it is critical to success in America. Every immigrant should be taught that fact, in English of course.

Today we are a nation of immigrants. To be an American means you are someone who has accepted the nation's mores and has melted in. My grandparents on my mother's side were full-blooded Germans and on my father's side French Canadians. I am a product of the their mixture. My wife had English and Norwegian backgrounds and our children are a product of an even greater mixture. Yet, never in my life have any of my or my wife's ancestors thought of them self as anything but American. They were proud to "melt" in and adopt the mores of a godly nation. There are many warnings from God not to adopt the cultures of ungodly people.

Myth—Politics Doesn't Matter

Do Not Be Yoked Together With Unbelievers!

"When you come into the land which the LORD your God is giving you, you shall not learn to follow the abominations of those nations." Deut. 18:9

"You shall not intermarry with them, nor they with you. Surely they will turn away your hearts after their gods."
1 Kings 11:2

Solomon did not follow God's instructions and eventually his heart was turned away from the LORD. In return, God removed HIS blessings on Solomon's government. This isn't complicated stuff. It is simply human nature. If a culture is raised to worship idols, it will take generations to alter and dilute that evil behavior. When America's emphasis was on being a godly nation and a melting pot, wherein immigrants adopted the basic mores of Christianity—we seemed to prosper. But the nation changed when the Supreme Court decided it was wrong to talk about God in public schools. Only an Amendment to the U.S. Constitution can repair the breach in morals of this country. We as a nation now find ourselves yoked together "within" to immoral people and even immoral Christians who feign an understanding of God. With our religious freedom, no immigrant is required to become a Christian. We do not have a national religion. However, the Holy Bible is the foundation of our nation's mores, legal system and also our government operations. Because the founders knew there were evil people, they knew we had to have a moral standard and the standard they chose was the Bible.

"Do not be unequally yoked together with unbelievers. For what fellowship has righteousness with lawlessness? And what communion has light with darkness?" 2 Cor. 6:14

Today it seems like everyone is doing his or her own thing. The national and common interests we have as a people of God are routinely dismissed in favor of selfish personal and even pagan interests. There is nothing new here as Paul chastised some followers for selfish and ungodly behavior.

Copyright 2005 Edward G. Palmer, All Rights Reserved.

Myth—Politics Doesn't Matter

> **"For first of all, when you come together as a church, I hear that there are divisions among you, and in part I believe it. For there must also be factions among you, that those who are approved may be recognized among you. Therefore when you come together in one place, it is not to eat the Lord's Supper. For in eating, each one takes his own supper ahead of others; and one is hungry and another is drunk." 1 Cor. 11:18-21**

Even in the holy sacrament of communion, Paul makes it clear that people engaged in self-serving behavior, which did not consider that their group's [or nation's] larger interests should rise above their own personal interests. Today, it is the same among many who call themselves Christian. They argue against God's morals for their own personal immoral interests.

> **"For I say, through the grace given to me, to everyone who is among you, not to think of himself more highly than he ought to think, but to think soberly, as God has dealt to each one a measure of faith." Romans 12:3**

A Nation Must Be United Spiritually!

> **Jesus said, "Every kingdom divided against itself is brought to desolation, and every city or house divided against itself will not stand." Matthew 12:25**

"Liberty cannot be preserved without a general knowledge among the people, who have a right, from the frame of their nature, to knowledge, as their great CREATOR, who does nothing in vain, has given them understandings, and a desire to know; but besides this, they have a right, and indisputable, unalienable, indefeasible, divine right to that most dreaded and envied kind of knowledge; I mean, of the characters and conduct of their rulers." John Adams, *Dissertation on Canon and Feudal Law*, 1765. [27]

"Children should be educated and instructed in the principles of freedom." John Adams, *Defense of the Constitution*, 1781.

Myth—Politics Doesn't Matter

"If there is a form of government, then, whose principle and foundation is *virtue*, will not every sober man acknowledge it better calculated to promote the general happiness than any other?" John Adams, *Thoughts of Government*, 1776.

"It is the duty of all men in society, publicly, and at stated seasons, to worship the SUPREME BEING, the great CREATOR and PRESERVER of the universe. And no subject shall be hurt, molested, or restrained, in his person, liberty, or estate, for worshipping God in the manner most agreeable to the dictates of his own conscience; or for his religious profession or sentiments; provided he doth not disturb the public peace; or obstruct others in their religious worship." John Adams, *Thoughts on Government*, 1776.

"Men must be ready, they must pride themselves and be happy to sacrifice their private pleasures, passions and interests, nay, their private friendships and dearest connections, when they stand in competition with the rights of society." John Adams, *letter to Mercy Warren*, April 17, 1776.

"National defense is one of the cardinal duties of a statesman." John Adams, *letter to James Lloyd*, January 1815.

"Public virtue cannot exist in a nation without private, and public virtue is the only foundation of republics. There must be a positive passion for the public good, the public interest, honor, power and glory, established in the minds of the people, or there can be no republican government, nor any real liberty; and this public passion must be superior to all private passions." John Adams, *letter to Mercy Warren*, April 16, 1776.

"Remember democracy never lasts long. It soon wastes, exhausts, and murders itself. There never was a democracy yet that did not commit suicide." John Adams, *letter to John Taylor*, April 15, 1814.

"The foundation of national morality must be laid in private families. How is it possible that Children can have any just Sense of the sacred Obligations of Morality or Religion if, from their earliest Infancy, they learn

Myth—Politics Doesn't Matter

their Mothers live in habitual Infidelity to the fathers, and their fathers in as constant Infidelity to their Mothers?" John Adams, *Diary*, June 2, 1778.

"The only foundation of a free Constitution, is pure Virtue, and if this cannot be inspired into our People, in a great Measure, than they have it now. They may change their Rulers, and the forms of Government, but they will not obtain a lasting liberty." John Adams, *letter to Zabdiel Adams*, June 21, 1776.

"We have no government armed with power capable of contending with human passions unbridled by morality and religion. Avarice, ambition, revenge, or gallantry, would break the strongest cords of our Constitution as a whale goes through a net. Our Constitution was made only for a moral and religious people. It is wholly inadequate to the government of any other." John Adams, *Address to the Military*, October 11, 1798.

"Democracy will soon degenerate into an anarchy, such an anarchy that every man will do what is right in his own eyes and no man's life or property or reputation or liberty will be secure, and every one of these will soon mould itself into a system of subordination of all the moral virtues and intellectual abilities, all the powers of wealthy, beauty, wit and science, to the wanton pleasures, the capricious will, and the execrable cruelty of one or a very few." John Adams, *An Essay on Man's Lust for Power*, August 29, 1763.

"Judges, therefore, should be always men of learning and experience in the laws, of exemplary morals, great patience, calmness, coolness, and attention. Their minds should not be distracted with jarring interests; they should not be dependant upon any man, or body of men." John Adams, *Thoughts on Government*, 1776.

"Our Constitution was made only for a moral and religious people. It is wholly inadequate to the government of any other." John Quincy Adams, 6th U.S. President, Democratic. [28]

"The first and almost the only Book deserving of universal attention is the Bible." John Quincy Adams [29]

Myth—Politics Doesn't Matter

"I speak as a man of the world to men of the world, and I say unto you, Search the Scriptures! The Bible is the book of all others, to be read at all ages, and in all conditions of human life." John Quincy Adams [29]

"From the day of the Declaration — they (the American people) were bound by the laws of God, which they all, and by the laws of the Gospel, which they nearly all, acknowledge as the rules of their conduct." John Quincy Adams [29]

Stop for a moment and before you proceed, go back over and study these quotes. If you examine the writings of our Founding Fathers, you will learn the basis of our great nation. That basis was the Holy Bible and Christianity. If there was a huge failure in the Constitution, it is the failure to state that moral basis plain and clear. The Founders knew that everyone did not agree on theology, but they failed to grasp the idea that 200 years later, an activist Supreme Court would alter the nation's moral foundation and cast it into a path of destruction. We do stand at a moral abyss that threatens to destroy our democracy and the writings of our founders knew that if we ever reached the point we are at — liberty could be destroyed. I see immorality in the courts that now routinely dispense injustice. Why? Our nation has failed to adhere to its founders' advice and only install moral judges. The choice before our nation is whether we will survive as a great nation or indeed devolve into the anarchy that John Adams predicted. We are at least 50% along a path of anarchy. And why should I or anyone else who is moral obey an immoral government? When Paul wrote in Romans 13 his instructions to obey the government, it is explicit that the government was godly and righteous. That is why Paul taught the following.

> **"For rulers are not a terror to good works, but to evil. Do you want to be unafraid of the authority? Do what is good, and you will have praise from the same. For he is God's minister to you for good. But if you do evil, be afraid; for he does not bear the sword in vain; for he is God's minister, an avenger to execute wrath on him who practices evil."**
> **Romans 13:3-4**

Myth—Politics Doesn't Matter

Verily I say unto you that no "real" Christian has any duty to obey an immoral government that sanctions abortions, Gay marriages and other forms of evil that are explicitly identified in the Holy Bible as abominations unto God. Instead, such people have the same moral duty that our Founders had. They are required to fight such evil and immorality with all the vigor that they have. Many Christians now find themselves in an immoral society much like Lot did in Sodom. Yet, this cannot stand for very long.

Politics Has Become The Art Of Lying!

Politics has become the "art of lying" and the number of examples is great. When Nixon lost to Kennedy it is commonly believed that Illinois and Texas were stolen at the ballot box. If so, these were lies from pubic officials. Nixon decided to forgo a recount believing "it would be bad for the nation." Then, when Nixon became president, he engaged in a variety of activities including lying. When his lies and complicity in the Watergate break-ins were confronted with impeachment, Nixon resigned believing "it would be bad for the nation to go through an impeachment trial."

Therefore, while Nixon may have been a victim of lies and himself engaging in lies to the nation, he ultimately thought of the greater good of our country. This was not the case when Clinton was confronted with impeachment for lying to a Federal Court. Here, the nation's highest official charged with enforcing our laws had lied to the nation and the court. Instead of stepping down and thinking of the greater good of our country, Clinton and the Democrats fought to maintain their power. Had Clinton resigned like Nixon, Gore would have become president. It is highly likely that Gore would have then been <u>reelected</u> instead of George W. Bush being elected president. Therefore, it is irony that Clinton's selfish ambitions fed back onto his Democratic Party and in effect helped to destroy its majority.

There is no greater example of the lies of politicians than the issue of Clinton's Impeachment. When it came to vote, the Democrats voted as a block in the Senate — Nay! John Adams pointed out that the most cherished knowledge our people could obtain would be the details of the character and conduct of our national rulers. Was lying institutionalized?

Myth—Politics Doesn't Matter

The moral decay in society is epitomized by the Democrats' actions in the Senate during impeachment. The institution charged with protecting our long-term constitutional interests now found that their own party interests were more important than national morality. In the end analysis, this was a complete moral failure on the part of the Democratic Party. When Clinton lied to the face of the nation's people and then to the Federal Court, why should the people have any faith in him? Furthermore, when the main effort of his party in the Senate was to cover up and obscure those lies, why should the people have any faith in the Democratic Party?

When Democratic Senators voted nay on Impeachment, they told the Nation that it is okay for the President and other politicians to lie. They tried to cover their decision under the guise of a personal moral failure, but that does not excuse the direct lies to the people of this country, to Clinton's own staff and to the Federal Court. Clinton should have resigned. For lack of that, Democrats should have forced him to step down for the good of the Nation. Our country cannot tolerate such lies in government. That is why Clinton falls behind Nixon in the rank of U.S. Presidents. At least Nixon had the decency to resign. Now what? Should a nation trust a political party that is documented to support the lies of its leaders? No, it shouldn't.

During the 2004 Presidential Campaign, Kerry repeatedly told the lies that the U.S. "had gone it alone" in Iraq and that "we didn't use diplomacy." Part of the reason this didn't stick with the American people is that they were both lies. The U.S. had worked with the United Nations for 12 years and 17 resolutions and nothing had been resolved with Iraq. That is hardly rushing to the use of force and bypassing diplomacy. The many countries and thousands of soldiers helping our nation in Iraq also belie the claim that we "had gone it alone." In fact, every time Kerry opened his mouth and repeated these lies, he insulted my intelligence and no doubt the intelligence of millions of other Americans. Words carry meanings and people have a right to hold politicians to the precise meaning of their words.

The Democratic Party playbook involves repeatedly dispensing lies. Repeat a lie long enough and people will believe it. That was the tactic of Hitler's public relations expert. In 2004, it was a tactic of the Democrats.

Myth—Politics Doesn't Matter

As Democratic operatives and politicians referred to Bush as Hitler or made some other vile lie, I heard Bush several times dismiss the vitriolic language as being "just politics." Aside from the outright lies of various groups, we even witnessed the CBS NEWS organization trying to fabricate a huge lie on the eve of the election with fraudulent documents. Now referred to as "Rathergate" — this mainstream news outlet has documented that it is okay to lie, as long as you can get away with it. In this case, Dan Rather didn't get away with it. What does it mean when leaders and journalists will willingly lie to the American people? It means we are at a moral abyss and that the truth and civility, which used to permeate American political life no longer does. For many, it is now about obtaining their personal goals at all costs, even if it means outright lying to and misleading the American people.

To add insult to injury in the Clinton Impeachment saga, the Clinton Library in Arkansas now represents his impeachment as the "politics of personal destruction." Clinton is still held in high respect by Democrats to this date and his wife may even run for the presidency herself. Yet, should the nation support her? When you piece together this picture, you find that the Democratic Party is a party that supports liars. That lying is a mode of operation in their political playbook, which seeks dominance and power over the American people. Yet, where is the morality in their lies? Where is the morality in allowing our children and successive generations to be duped by lies at a library designed to conceal the truth of Impeachment? Perhaps the saddest fact of the Democrats' behavior is that Clinton was not held morally accountable and now a party that still "believes his lies and rationalization" will foist his immorality on future generations via his presidential library.

Lying is a serious offense with God and those who practice lying, "shall have their part in the lake, which burns with fire and brimstone, which is the second death." Again I ask, "Do you believe God's Word?"

"A lying mouth destroys the soul." Wisdom 1:11 NRSV

"But … all liars shall have their part in the lake which burns with fire and brimstone, which is the second death."
                                                                Rev. 21:8

Myth—Politics Doesn't Matter

> "But there shall by no means enter [Heaven] anything that defiles, or causes an abomination or a lie, but only those who are written in the Lamb's *Book of Life*." Rev. 21:27

> "But outside [of Heaven] are dogs and sorcerers and [the] sexually immoral and murderers and idolaters, and *whoever loves and practices a lie*." Rev. 22:15

Can Justice Be Obtained In An Immoral Society?

An interesting question to ask is whether it is possible to obtain justice in an immoral American society. Is it? And, if we deny God's morality and His Bible basis of virtue and justice, exactly what is the basis of justice that we use? The *morality of rights* or the *Rights of Man*? The graphic below illustrates our current justice system. You are just as likely to experience injustice in U.S. courts, as you are justice. Why? Let me explain.

Myth—Politics Doesn't Matter

The U.S. justice system does not seek justice. Surprised? You shouldn't be with all the injustice that permeates our society. Instead, it is an advocacy system that seeks winners and losers. The justice system is nothing short of a rat maze as shown in the lower part of the above graphic. Once you enter the legal maze, you cannot exit except by a legal "rules" method. Judges are craftily guided by court rules instead of justice per se. As a result, those who lie and can hire the biggest guns for attorneys will often prevail, because their "rules" arguments and lies will force the Judge into giving them want they want.

If you've studied the above quotes of John Adams, you now realize that the Massachusetts' Supreme Court morally erred when it ruled that the State must marry Gays and lesbians. It is obvious that the justices were debased and did not take into consideration the morality built into the State's Constitution by its Founders. Secondly, they did not seek God's morality — they bought the *morality of rights* or the *Rights of Man* argument. They amplified the moral breach that exists within our justice system and it will result in nationwide litigation. There are many examples of injustice.

Consider that the Senate is the highest court in our land when it comes to impeachment. Did the Senate render justice? No, the Senate sanctioned immorality. The outcome of their immoral decision will reverberate in society for decades to come. What shall we now tell high school students? That they need to be honest? Why? They have observed with their own intellect that the President of the United States could lie, even under oath, with impunity. Yet, you know if the average man or woman in the United States lied to a Federal Court the way Clinton did and got caught, he or she would wind up in jail. There is a double standard in our legal system and justice is won or lost depending upon the legal resources you can afford.

And what if you cannot afford to hire a competent attorney? What if you've been charged with a criminal offense and must be assigned a public defender? Well, you had better pray a lot. I have observed that public defenders actually work for the County Attorney's Office and their job is to get you to cooperate with the State in its effort to prosecute you. They will even counsel you to lie to make it easier on yourself. Don't believe me? Then consider the case of Chuck Schuldt who was railroaded by the court.

Copyright 2005 Edward G. Palmer, All Rights Reserved.

Book of Edward—Chapter 20

Myth—Politics Doesn't Matter

Chuck and his wife Sharon attended Solid Rock Church in Elk River, Minnesota when I attended the church. After I left, they continued to attend. Chuck was old in the physical sense and 75 in the chronological sense. He suffered from diabetes and the effects of his disease almost made him blind. He literally could not see 3-5 feet in front of his face. Chuck and Sharon loved kids and would often baby sit for the teenage daughter of a woman named Gwen in the church. They lived in a dilapidated trailer in the city of Monticello about 20 miles from the church. Gwen and her family lived in the same trailer park. The church bus picked up Chuck, Sharon and other people in the trailer court each Sunday. Since Chuck and his wife did not drive and were poor, this was their only way to get to church.

Gwen stated she had been manic-depressive and on medication when she claimed to be healed by Pastor William Matthews' prayer. She stopped taking her meds. Chuck was soon charged with being a sexual pervert and said to have exposed himself to Gwen's daughter. Matthews openly referred to Chuck as a pervert in the church and made him sit in the back pews away from Gwen. At Matthews' counsel, without talking to Chuck, Gwen pressed charges. Chuck's life was destroyed by lies, which led to his death.

God told me to go talk to Chuck and find out what had happened. He also told me to advise him to stick to the truth at all costs. I knew he would be given a public defender that would ask him to lie to make it easier on himself in the court. That is exactly what was taking place. I asked Chuck if he had exposed himself to Gwen's daughter. He said no. When I asked what happened, he said he was taking a shower and had just come out of the bathtub when Gwen's daughter busted into the bathroom. His rickety old trailer didn't provide much security, so only a modest amount of pressure was required to force the warped bathroom door open. Gwen's daughter saw Chuck naked. It is unlikely Chuck saw clearly who had come into the bathroom. I had prayed over him earlier at church for his near blindness.

I then explained that he needed to stand for the truth in court. I also advised him that if he succumbed to the public defender's pressure to lie, that he would live to regret it. I counseled Chuck to stand tall for God's righteousness and that given his side of the story, it was not his fault that the girl had inadvertently or even forcibly came into the bathroom on him.

The church presumed he was guilty and never sought the actual facts. The church business manager and assistant pastor showed up at court and listened to a coerced false confession. Even though the public defender said it would be over fast for him without trouble, Chuck spent several weeks in jail and was abused by law enforcement officials as a sex pervert. He later died a broken man on the floor of his trailer having lost what little honor he had as a poor man. For a person that loved children, Chuck died a convicted sex offender in Minnesota because of a legal system that lies and a church that was unrighteous in its service to poor people.

"You shall do no injustice in judgment. You shall not be partial to the poor, nor honor the person of the mighty. In righteousness you shall judge your neighbor." Lev. 19:15

God commands us to be impartial and Pastor Matthews committed sin in God's eyes when he failed to consider Chuck's side of the story showing preference to Gwen. The most striking issue though with justice is the fact that the public defender asked Chuck to lie. He didn't just ask him to lie; he pressured him to lie to "take the easy path with the court and put the matter behind him." It was an easy case for the County Attorney and another notch on his prosecutorial belt. The big lesson is: Don't expect justice when you won't stand up for righteousness. Also, when the court's appointed public defender asks you to lie, make sure you tell the truth and tell the judge that you are being asked to lie by the court appointed attorney.

Injustice occurs because the system seeks winners and losers and not justice. Otherwise, you would not have public defenders advising their clients to lie so it would be easier on the County Attorney. In the case of the pastor, he'll get a chance to explain himself. That much I am sure. As will the business manager and assistant pastor who also ignored the truth.

The third example of injustice was my own experience in the court seeking a remedy to the theft of Solid Rock Church that I witnessed. This was a lesson in our justice system that I'll never forget. Do you remember where I left off in the story? I was expecting to be fined? You can get the theft details at the James417.org web site. For now, I'll just summarize the injustice that was wrought in the same District Court that railroaded Chuck.

Myth—Politics Doesn't Matter

Just like the Chuck, I too was poor. I had been living off of borrowed funds and did not have the finances to hire legal help after I realized how William Neal Matthews stole Solid Rock Church. When I sought legal help, the only firm who would take the case quoted $200,000 in estimated total costs and would not start without $100,000 in up front funds. It was out of the question. As I sought God in prayer, I came to the conclusion to file a private lawsuit seeking some stock returned. I, and over 300 others, had been duped into transferring assets into a corporation that was illegally altered without the consent of its non-profit voting members. In the civil sense, Matthews had successfully "converted" my personal property and that of others by lying. In the criminal sense, conversion is referred to as theft.

Court Round #1

There were two rounds of litigation in the court. In the first round I had no idea of what I had to do in terms of pro se litigation. That is when you file suit as an individual and litigate the matter by yourself. However, I knew I was a fast learner and a quick study. I filed discovery requests and a summary judgment motion. Some of my legal buddies gave me pointers. The church filed for a stay of discovery and for summary judgment. The initial document request had flushed out prima facie proof of the theft that took place at Solid Rock. That proof was in the form of the actual corporate meeting minutes as compared to the state filings that Matthews had made.

Matthews' first filing was supposed to be a corporate name change, but he made wholesale illegal articles filings with the Minnesota Secretary of State. Two years later at a meeting in which no changes were authorized, Matthews filed changes eliminating all voting rights except his own family. The second filing was proof of scienter, meaning that the filings had the full knowledge of Matthews and were aimed directly at stealing the church.

I got my chance in Court. The seasoned and righteous Judge I found myself in front of said he wanted to talk with both parties in his chambers before hearing any further arguments. As the Judge talked in his chambers, he told Matthews' attorneys that he would not grant their summary judgment motion and that unless they settled with me, we would both wind up in court arguing our cases. My mental reaction was — wow! The judge understands the nature of Matthews' clever church theft!

Myth—Politics Doesn't Matter

As we discussed the possible settlement terms, the church and Matthews' attorneys wanted me to sign an agreement that would muzzle any further discussion of the matter. I had already created the James417 web site and they wanted that shut down also. In return, they would give back the stock I had transferred. I refused because no amount of material gain on this earth is worth my soul. I also told them after the suit was settled I planned to give all the material to the Attorney General as I was convinced a huge crime had occurred. And, that I planned to write a book, which would contain a discussion of the church theft. The Judge told me that if I believed a crime had been committed, it was my duty to report it. We soon agreed before this first righteous judge to a settlement. They would return the stock and I would sign a limited non-disparagement agreement.

The opposing attorneys would draft a settlement agreement and get it back to me within a couple of weeks. Instead, they reneged on the Judge's mediated settlement and sent a letter demanding a payment of $100,000 to get the stock certificate back. I wrote a letter to the Judge asking what was up with this — didn't we have a settlement? He wrote back stating yes we did, but because they had done what they did, he would then have to recuse himself from the case. Cute legal trick huh? It was an introduction to the manipulation of the court, but I really didn't get the significance of it.

Nevertheless, a righteous judge who clearly saw the fraud that was wreaked on the church and my personal assets encouraged me. But now enters the much younger unrighteous judge, who is a stickler for "rules."

The second hearing was before Judge #2, who was not interested in hearing anything I had to say. In fact he told me to shut up. It seems the only pertinent matter in his Court was the defendants' summary judgment motion. They argued that I had failed to include the 11-essential elements of fraud in the *complaint* I filed. As such, the "rules" dictated the judge had to dismiss the case. I pointed out the corporate meeting minutes and the state filings, which showed a prima facie fraud had occurred and that I was a victim of that fraud. It didn't matter; the unrighteous judge ignored virtually all of the documentation of church fraud and ruled my *complaint* didn't have the requisite elements of fraud under the "rules." Dismissed!

Myth—Politics Doesn't Matter

I want you to understand this clearly. The documentation of fraud was in the court's hands. The first Judge saw it and served notice on the defendants attorneys. They compromised him and we wound up with a second judge that was not concerned with justice, but rules. Every District Court judge is granted significant authority when fraud is involved. The fraud was before the court, but the second judge granted summary judgment to the defendants and dismissed my case.

In court round #1, I was first introduced to a righteous judge and then to an unrighteous judge. I can certainly characterize the second judge as being unrighteous because, with documented proof of a massive church theft in his hands, he manifested injustice to hundreds of victims in the local community. Fraud *was* evidenced, but he chose to ignore the fraud.

Quite a contrast huh? A righteous judge mediates a settlement and an unrighteous judge sanctions fraud. Thus is the situation in District Courts. You should also know that the decisions of District Court judges carry heavy weight in Appeals Courts and are not easily overturned. Did I have money to wage an appeal? No. Did I have energy to wage an appeal? No. The unrighteous "rules-oriented" second judge, however, provided a five-page legal brief on what was wrong with the structure of the *complaint* I filed, in the strict legal rules sense. I studied the matter and took it to God in prayer. Now, not only had the church been successfully stolen but the court didn't even care. It was, by my estimate, a $6 million dollar theft. Not bad for a white-collar crime, if you believe that God isn't real.

I pondered the complexity of the legal system that exists in the U.S. and how the wealthy can buy justice that is denied to the poor. And, if you do not have finances in substantive civil matters, how the system locks you out from justice. I believed that my due process rights had been violated, because of some case law I had uncovered. If there was indication that fraud was involved, the District Court judge is granted great powers to prevent injustice from becoming manifested. Isn't that what took place? Later in a legal discussion, I learned that it is not unusual for a District Court judge to violate the law. The solution is to make an appeal. I have been told that the Appeals Court will uphold laws, which the District Court may ignore.

Myth—Politics Doesn't Matter

Take the matter to heart and be aware that if a District Court judge's ruling is overturned that there is no consequence to the overturned judge. Therefore, District Court judges have great legal authority to rule as they please and are basically unaccountable unless there is a public outcry over a case or perhaps some concerted impeachment effort. *Woe to the unrighteous court judges!*

Court Round #2

Almost two years had elapsed and I was approaching the statute of limitations for commencing any further legal action. In the research I had conducted, several lawyers advised I could refile if I could comply with the legal requirements of the *complaint*. The Minnesota Attorney General's Office even supplied me with a letter recommending I refile the *complaint*. Still, I wasn't sure I wanted to expend the tremendous effort involved. I took it to God in prayer over many months. The message I got was to get it in front of another judge. It made sense since the first judge saw clearly the church fraud. Maybe another judge would see clearly? Yet, I didn't know.

The amount of spiritual pressure I was feeling from God was great and I eventually caved in. After I filed a new and more detailed *complaint* encompassing all 11-fraud elements, I felt an incredible sense of relief. I knew then that I had done what God wanted me to do regardless of the outcome. The goal? It was simple. "Just get it in front of another judge." Of course, when I filed a discovery requests, I felt more peace.

Eventually I put together a summary judgment filing since I felt the documents obtained from the first court filing and the new complaint was proof positive that the fraud had been committed. Not only against my own personal assets but also against hundreds of other unsuspecting church victims. Some of these victims still go to this church and remain clueless that their pastor stole their church. When you think about, it sounds bizarre, doesn't it? Yet the public documents exist to prove it even if the courts want to ignore the fraud by playing "rules" games.

I did get the case before another judge. The third judge also turned out to be unrighteous. In the strangest moment of my life, I lost my voice.

Myth—Politics Doesn't Matter

I have long since relied upon God in terms of knowing what to say. However, suddenly I was speechless in the physical sense. I was unable to speak. When I opened my mouth, nothing came out. I had to take several glasses of water to begin a word and then it was difficult to speak anything. Perhaps it was the brazen evidence from the bench that this female judge could care less that a huge church fraud had occurred. For her, the only matter she was concerned with was whether I was entitled to be there in the first place. It was another "rules" argument that I was facing. Was I simply flabbergasted at the incredulity of the argument I was not allowed to refile a complaint because of the first court decision? I've heard being "speechless" comically talked about, but now I experienced it first hand. It wasn't funny. Perhaps God wanted me to just take whatever this court wanted to dump on me. In the end, that is what I did and exactly what happened.

Jesus said, "Now when they bring you to the synagogues and magistrates and authorities, do not worry about how or what you should answer, or what you should say. For the Holy Spirit will teach you in that very hour what you ought to say." Luke 12:11-12

There is a legal doctrine in the "rules" called "res judicata," which means that the matter has been fully settled. The second judge had dismissed the case in a way that gave rise to such an argument. The lawyers I talked to must have been ignorant or I was simply dumped on in violation of my rights, again. With 20-days to file an appeal, I just took the dump of this unrighteous female judge. This issue of fraud was now ignored by another court rule, which says that summary judgment, once granted, cannot be re-litigated. The first Court Order did not state "with prejudice" so every attorney I counseled with believed that I could refile. Go figure.

The third Judge dismissed the case "with prejudice" and ruled that I was harassing the church and Matthews' privies [other defendants] and awarded the defendants a total of $16,694.87 in costs and attorney fees to be paid of course by me. Imagine getting fined for standing up and reporting a $6 million dollar church theft. Now imagine that two of three judges turned their backs on the evidence of the fraud and used "rules" to dismiss the case.

Myth—Politics Doesn't Matter

You might say but Edward, aren't you obviously the one that is in error. If so, you'll have to explain the first righteous judge and also turn your backs on the public documents that now exist in this matter. Those documents can be accessed at James417.org and they do prove that Solid Rock Church was stolen. Do you think that this is the kind of government that Paul talked about in Romans 13? Is Paul talking about a government that punishes the righteous and rewards the wicked?

What is it that God would have me say to you? HE would have me tell you that the U.S. justice system is broke. That there are unrighteous judges throughout the country that no longer operates under HIS morality. HE would have me tell you that decades of righteous voting in our country will be required to set our courts back in moral order. *Woe to the judges that fine the innocent and reward the guilty for verily I say unto you that God will repay them!*

> **"To impose a fine on the innocent is not right, or to flog the noble for their integrity." Proverbs 17:26 NRSV**
>
> **"Justice is turned back, and righteousness stands afar off; for truth is fallen in the street, and equity cannot enter. So truth fails, and he who departs from evil makes himself a prey. Then the LORD saw it, and it displeased HIM that there was no justice." Isaiah 59:14-15**
>
> **"Therefore the law is powerless, and justice never goes forth. For the wicked surround the righteous; therefore perverse judgment proceeds." Habakkuk 1:4**
>
> **"They suppressed their consciences and turned away their eyes from looking to Heaven or remembering their duty to administer justice." Susanna 1:9** — *Woe to the unjust judge!*
>
> **"Do not add to HIS words, lest HE rebuke you, and you be found a liar." Proverbs 30:6**

Copyright 2005 Edward G. Palmer, All Rights Reserved.

Myth—Politics Doesn't Matter

> "They not only take away thankfulness from others, but, carried away by the boasts of those who know nothing of goodness, they even assume that they will escape the evil-hating justice of God, who always sees everything."
> Additions to Esther 16:4 NRSV

> "Therefore those who utter unrighteous things will not escape notice, and justice, when it punishes, will not pass them by." Wisdom 1:8 NRSV

> "If, then, it is evident that reason rules over those emotions that hinder self-control, namely, gluttony and lust, it is also clear that it masters the emotions that hinder one from justice, such as malice, and those that stand in the way of courage, namely anger, fear, and pain."
> 4 Macc. 1:3-4 NRSV

> "For reason does not rule its own emotions, but those that are opposed to justice, courage, and self-control; and it is not for the purpose of destroying them, but so that one may not give way to them." 4 Macc. 1:6 NRSV

> "Now the kinds of wisdom are rational judgment, justice, courage, and self-control." 4 Macc. 1:18 NRSV

> "You scoff at our philosophy as though living by it were irrational, but it teaches us self-control, so that we master all pleasures and desires, and it also trains us in courage, so that we endure any suffering willingly; it instructs us in justice, so that in all our dealings we act impartially, and it teaches us piety, so that with proper reverence we worship the only living God." 4 Macc. 5:22-24 NRSV

Injustice is rooted in lies and the lack of self-control. You learned in the last chapter that God expects you to exert self-control over your sins. That includes the sins of lies and bearing false witness, which are mortal in nature. Yet you must return to knowledge of God if you want safety.

Myth—Politics Doesn't Matter

A Biblical Message For America!

"Then it was not enough for them [the United States of America] to err about the knowledge of God [and of His only human begotten Son Jesus], but though living in great strife due to ignorance, they call such great evils peace."

"For whether they kill children in their initiations [abortions], or celebrate secret mysteries, or hold frenzied revels with strange customs, they no longer keep either their lives or their marriages pure, but they either treacherously kill one another, or grieve one another by adultery, and all is a raging riot of blood and murder, theft and deceit, corruption, faithlessness, tumult, perjury, confusion over what is good, forgetfulness of favors, defiling of souls, sexual perversion, disorder in marriages [Gay or lesbian marriage], adultery, and debauchery."

"For the worship of idols not to be named is the beginning and cause and end of every evil. For their worshipers either rave in exultation, or prophesy lies, or live unrighteously, or readily commit perjury [in the courts]; for because they trust in lifeless idols they swear wicked oaths and expect to suffer no harm [from Almighty God]."

"But just penalties will overtake them on two counts: because they thought wrongly about God in devoting themselves to idols, and because in deceit they swore unrighteously through contempt for holiness."

"For it is not the power of the things by which people swear, but *the just penalty* for those who sin, that *always pursues* the transgression of *the unrighteous*."

Wisdom 14:22-31 NRSV

"The Just Penalty Pursues The Unrighteous!"

Copyright 2005 Edward G. Palmer, All Rights Reserved.

Book of Edward—Chapter 20

Myth—Politics Doesn't Matter

I was born; raised, and lived most my life in the Democrat controlled State of Minnesota. During this same time, Democrats controlled the U.S. Congress. At age 58, only recently have I seen the country and my state begin to grapple with the immorality and evils that liberal policies have unleashed. Yes, I hold the Democrats spiritually accountable to God for the moral abyss we now find ourselves struggling with. Was John F. Kennedy the victim of Lee Harvey Oswald or did God take him out for removing prayer from public schools? It was Kennedy's watch and he failed God in a way that has led our nation to a moral abyss. If God took him out, it would not be the first time HE punished a morally failing leader.

Our country faces a new civil war; this time it is a moral war. Our nation cannot be just if it is not also moral and virtuous. It doesn't work. We cannot be a country based on the "morality of rights" or the "Rights of Man" because both lack eternal virtue. We must return to the country our founders created and recognize that our Constitution can only rule a moral and godly people. This new civil war involves tyranny from immoral judges that seek to legislate immoral laws. It is time for the people to reform our Constitution to make it clear we are a godly nation first and foremost and that we do not allow "activist" judges to "legislate" from the bench. Think about these seven societal changes in my life and tell me if they represent a positive impact on our culture and the mores our nation was founded on.

Democrat Societal Changes

1. Economic Slavery — Democrat policies required two incomes.
2. Tax Slavery — Democrat policies doubled family tax burdens.
3. No Fault Divorce — Democrat policies split families in two.
4. IRS Approval of Churches — Democrats made the law.
5. No Prayer in Schools — Democrats failed to stop activist judges.
6. Baby Killing — Democrats failed to stop activist judges.
7. Gay Marriage — Democrats appointed activist judges.

When Jackie and I were married, marriage was for life. There was no easy divorce. We did not need two incomes to support a family. No one killed babies for convenience and Gay marriage was unheard of. Who is responsible for such immoral policies? Liberal Democrats have led the way!

Myth—Politics Doesn't Matter

Democrats' Legacy Is A Moral Turpitude!

In 2004, the Democrats' political legacy is 40 plus years of policies that altered the common moral understanding our nation was founded on, allowing our country to drift into the depravity of a moral turpitude. We have become nothing short of a morally debased society as a result. This is true for an estimated 50% of U.S. citizens, which now think of morals as the "morality of rights" granted by some activist court's legislative efforts. These same people view the government as the protector of their immoral perverseness and the supporter of their slothfulness. Collectively, it seems we no longer agree about what morality means. It took 40 plus years for these Democratic policies to dig the immoral hole we now find ourselves in.

For the first time in generations, Republicans are in control of the Congress and the Presidency. They seek a morally based nation hoping to unwind some of the immoral policies of the Democrats. The only way our moral mess can be straightened out is to keep this party in control for the next 40-50 years. If the Republican Party does not stay on a moral course to return the nation to the moral moorings of our Founders, then those who are moral will have to find another political party to back. Our biggest moral problem is a runaway activist Court that feels compelled to order legislatures to pass immoral laws. Ergo, courts have "legislated" abortion on demand nationally and Gay marriage in Massachusetts. Historically, the prior House of Representatives, controlled by Democrats, failed to impeach the Justices that have led us to this state of moral turpitude. Can Republicans govern any differently? The Founding Fathers, when faced with a similar challenge involving morals provided their answer in the Declaration of Independence.

Our Founders Have Some *"Declaration"* Advice!

"Prudence, indeed, will dictate that Governments long established should not be changed for light and transient causes; and accordingly all experience has shewn that mankind are more disposed to suffer, while evils are sufferable, than to right themselves by abolishing the forms to which they are accustomed. But when a long train of abuses and usurpations,

Copyright 2005 Edward G. Palmer, All Rights Reserved.

pursuing invariably the same Object evinces a design to reduce them under absolute Despotism, it is their right, it is their duty, to throw off such Government, and to provide new Guards for their future security." [30]

[The Courts] have demonstrated "a history of repeated injuries and usurpations, all having in direct object the establishment of an absolute Tyranny over these States. To prove this, let Facts be submitted to a candid world. — [The Courts] have "refused [their] Assent to Laws, the most wholesome and necessary for the public good. [The Courts have] forbidden ... Governors to pass Laws of immediate and pressing importance, unless suspended in their operation till [their] Assent should be obtained."

We live in a society that whenever a moral law is passed or even a governmental policy is implemented that either the ACLU or some wealthy individual doesn't like, for whatever reason, there is instant litigation in the courts. For example, a recent headline read: "ACLU threatens abstinence program [31]." The State of Louisiana is running an abstinence program and has a web site promoting it to young people. On the web site is the testimony of a 15-year old girl who writes, "Virginity is something very special which we have been given by God and we can only have it once. When you give it to someone it will be gone and you can never get it back no matter how rich you are. I'm so thankful to God for being with me and giving me the wise choice — to abstain. I'm 15 and proud to be a virgin and I won't be sorry for that. I think one day my future husband will be very happy for the decision which I made and he'll respect, trust me and feel secure with me." The ACLU threatened to take Louisiana to Federal Court in 30 days if it doesn't remove this and all religious references from the site.

It is time our society stood tall and brought God fully back into our government. I'm not talking about religion. I'm talking about being able to invoke a higher moral calling on all of us, whether or not any of us really understands it. State and Federal governments have an interest in keeping teen pregnancy low. The moral reasons for abstinence are well stated in this teen's testimony. God is a primary basis for motivating moral behavior. Yet today, you are sued for mentioning God on a state web site? If you live in Canada, and publicize the fact that homosexuality is an abomination to God who says such people are "debased" [Rom. 1:28], you wind up in jail?

Myth—Politics Doesn't Matter

Clearly the ACLU has an agenda. When I asked them for assistance on the issue of the denial of my "due process" rights, they expressed no interest in helping me fight this legal battle in court I was unable to fight by myself. The ACLU also didn't care if a thief had orchestrated the theft of a church. That was of no interest to them. Yet, when a 15-year old teen's testimony mentions God on a government supported web site — they go to court within 30 days to protect whose rights? Theirs? Are they a victim? Who forced them to read this teen's testimony? Yet more importantly, why is it offensive in the first place if we have not become a debased society far from the moral moorings that our Founding Fathers set in place?

Often such court legal challenges will get the law "stayed" by the court and then later barred from taking effect or in the case of the web site the perceived offensive material removed. The United States is supposed to be a government "of the people and by the people." Yet everywhere we turn the courts are modifying what the people have ordained. For example, Federal and State Constitutions are under assault and being interpreted by activist courts to approve every form of immorality as some kind of protective right for an individual. Well, what about protecting society from the tyranny of perverse "individual rights?" Why are homosexuals granted the right to teach children that their behavior is moral, when it violates the morality of 98-99% of the population and their right to teach children that it is immoral? The founder's solution is to throw off such an evil government. The question for those who are moral is whether we will have a peaceful transition back to a moral state or whether there will be forced changed or succession or even another civil war. What will a return to morality take?

The legislatures can start impeaching activist judges who legislate from the bench and the country can modify our Constitution to make it clear that this is a moral nation. We can start with a marriage amendment that bans Gay marriage AND Gay civil unions. Moral people should not be forced to pay taxes to support immorality, because it is patented injustice. That would include embryonic stem cell research. Forcing moral people to support immoral policies eventually leads to war if not corrected. This isn't about State's rights; it is about maintaining moral States and a moral nation. Morality bound our nation together at its founding. Immorality in certain states, now threaten to tear our great nation apart from within.

Copyright 2005 Edward G. Palmer, All Rights Reserved.

Myth—Politics Doesn't Matter

King David Has Some *"Biblical"* Advice!

As King David was on his deathbed, he gave Solomon instructions for the next generation of the nation's leadership. His instructions are found in 1 Kings 2 and apply equally well to each successive generation of American leadership. First come God and HIS morality.

"Now the days of David drew near that he should die, and he charged Solomon his son, saying: 'I go the way of all the earth; be strong, therefore, and prove yourself a man. And keep the charge of the LORD your God: to walk in HIS ways, to keep HIS statutes, HIS commandments, HIS judgments, and HIS testimonies, as it is written in the Law of Moses, that you may prosper in all that you do and wherever you turn'; that the LORD may fulfill HIS word which HE spoke concerning me, saying, 'If your sons take heed to their way, to walk before ME in truth with all their heart and with all their soul,' HE said, 'you shall not lack a man on the throne of Israel.' " 1 Kings 2:1-4

You should study this chapter, because the instructions didn't end there. David also instructed Solomon to purge the kingdom of specific evil that would prevent the nation from being godly under his leadership. Solomon complied and his leadership was godly — until his old age.

In Solomon's old age, he succumbed to the evil and vile mores of his Amorite wives. I discussed this in the last chapter. So, what happened? Solomon should have encouraged the "melting pot" idea, which made the U.S. the great nation it was. If any foreigner comes in, they melt in to the local culture. They learn our language and our mores. We used to not accept the changing of our mores to allow "individual rights" at the expense of society's moral health. In other words, what made America the great nation it was needs to become inviolate and built into our Constitution. That includes our basic mores so everyone understands what kind of nation we are, a "melting pot" nation. This is exactly what is being requested of new immigrants to the European Union.

Myth—Politics Doesn't Matter

In an article [32] titled "EU officials implore new immigrants to learn 'European values,' " — "European Union justice and interior ministers agreed … that new immigrants to the 25-nation block should be required to learn local languages, and to adhere to general 'European values' that will guide them toward better integration." It's better societal integration when you've got a "melting pot!" Do you get it? That is what the U.S. had for close to 200 years until we entered into Kennedy's Democrat Party Era of the "Rights of Man." It is what the new EU nations want. Multiculturalism? It only means societal division and the European Union is an example of the conflict it poses and why they are trying to move towards commonality. Multiculturalism is a product of an "individual's rights" mentality that lacks respect for a nation's right to have a united people when it comes to values.

Solomon commingled God's morality with the "morality of rights" of the Amorites and other immoral pagan cultures. He bought into their good sounding "morality of rights" arguments and eventually accepted their perversions as morally equivalent to God's morality. They weren't. God pulled the plug on Solomon by turning HIS back just like HE had done many other times on immoral nations. That is where the United States now finds itself with God. We have a moral choice to make for decades to come.

Politics Matter To Real Christians!

If there is a single message to people of faith from the 2004 election, it is that "politics does matter to Christians." Listen to a few comments found in the news following the election: [33]

1. "The president had the support of 78 percent of white evangelicals, 23 percent of the voters."

2. "Bush won 52 percent of the Roman Catholic vote, and got 56 percent of white Catholics, defeating the first Catholic presidential candidate since John F. Kennedy."

3. "Bush was favored by 61 percent of people from all faiths who attend services weekly; they made up 41 percent of the electorate."

Myth—Politics Doesn't Matter

4. "Democrat John Kerry drew 62 percent of voters who never attend worship, but they only accounted for 14 percent of voters."

5. "Moral values ranked first at 22 percent, surpassing the economy (20 percent), terrorism (19 percent) and Iraq (15 percent)."

6. "This was a high stakes election for those who support traditional moral values."

7. "The Rev. D. James Kennedy of Fort Lauderdale, Fl., said the voters 'have delivered a moral mandate.' "

Yes Christian voters and many others delivered a moral mandate to the government of the United States. However, many who are named Christian do not see it that way. They see a different morality, a "morality of rights" — because for almost 50 years that has been the mantra of the Democratic Party they have listened to. Verily I say unto you that all Christians who did vote for Democrats in 2004 had better dust off the Bible in their closet and return to God Almighty. Or surely they will hear Jesus say, "I never knew you." That's because in the eyes of God — Politics does matter as it shows HIM exactly where your heart's loyalty lies.

Will you be one of those named a Christian who will stand before God rationalizing your support of homosexuality, abortion, lesbianism, multiculturalism, and every other perverse public policy that sounds good but offends God? If so, how will you really defend yourself when HE has provided you with a book of instructions. You know, the B.I.B.L.E. — The "**B**asic **I**nstructions **B**efore **L**eaving **E**arth" that I talked about in the first part of this book! Indeed, it is time to return our nation to the moral moorings of our founders. However, it is unlikely to take place easily unless all of those who are named Christians start becoming real Christians once again. Real Christians represent God's interests in their votes and party politics. Where did your voting interests lie in 2004? Did you vote for God?

Christians need to vote for moral candidates who will uphold God's values. You will not find them in a party that is based on immoral policies. "Good people" *there* are wolves in DEM sheep's clothing [Matthew 7:15].

> *WARNING. If you are a minister, teacher or a named Christian that fails to teach people to participate in the political process on the side of God's righteousness and HIS priorities instead of their own or their political party's, set your house in order with God. Verily I say unto you, it is those who vote in favor of God and HIS perspective that are believers in HIS truth. Only they shall see God's salvation for it is written in the Word, "They did not welcome the truth [God's righteousness] but refused to love it that they might be saved." 2 Thess. 2:10 AMP*

> **"Therefore, whether you eat or drink, or whatever you do, [including politics] do all to the glory of God." 1 Cor. 10:31**

> **"I have found ... a man after MY own heart, who will [also, actually] do all [of] MY [political] will." Acts 13:22**

> *PRAYER. O LORD GOD, free YOUR people from the apostasy that is rampant in the Christian Church today. Surely, if a minister cannot teach their people to vote for YOUR righteousness, they cannot be trusted to teach anything about YOUR Word. They are indeed unfit for anything good and should cease their ministry activities. What should stand true for all concerned is that these false teachers "will perish because they were not lovers of the truth!" Amen.*

"The idea that voting against God's righteousness and HIS priorities is okay with God and that it really doesn't matter to HIM if you vote for your personal priorities and pocketbook is sheer mythology. Those who believe such stuff do not have God and HIS Son dwelling inside their hearts. Verily I say that they lack the ability to correctly *reason*!" The Apostle Edward

If God's Spirit Dwells In Your Heart, Your Spirit-Soul Knows That It's A ...

Myth—Politics Doesn't Matter

Copyright 2005 Edward G. Palmer, All Rights Reserved.

Chapter Twenty One
Myth—Everybody Gets To Go

— Jesus' Astonishing 50% Factor! —

"*THEN* the kingdom of Heaven shall be likened to ten virgins who took their lamps and went out to meet the bridegroom. Now five of them were wise, and five were foolish. Those who were foolish took their lamps and took no oil with them, but the wise took oil in their vessels with their lamps. But while the bridegroom was delayed, they all slumbered and slept. And at midnight a cry was heard: 'Behold, the bridegroom is coming; go out to meet him!' Then all those virgins arose and trimmed their lamps. And the foolish said to the wise, 'Give us some of your oil, for our lamps are going out.' But the wise answered, saying, 'No, lest there should not be enough for us and you; but go rather to those who sell, and buy for yourselves.' And while they went to buy, the bridegroom came, and those who were ready went in with him to the wedding; and the door was shut. Afterward the other virgins came also, saying, 'Lord, Lord, open to us!' But he answered and said, 'Assuredly, I say to you, I do not know you.' Watch therefore, for you know neither the day nor the hour in which the Son of Man is coming." Matthew 25:1-13

— Heaven Has A Selection Process! —

"[Jesus] will separate them one from another, as a shepherd divides his sheep from the goats. And he will set the sheep on his right hand, but the goats on the left. Then the King will say to those on his right hand, 'Come, you blessed of my FATHER, inherit the kingdom prepared for you [righteous people] from the foundation [beginning] of the world.' " Matthew 25:32-34

Myth—Everybody Gets To Go

As I approach the second Christmas without Jackie, I can't help but reflect back on that fateful day when we received notice of her limited time remaining. I remember distinctly being challenged by God with one central question to my soul. "Ed, do you really believe in ME? Can you trust in ME even in the face of the loss of the most precious person your heart has ever loved and known on earth?" I experienced the heart crushing moments of Jackie's impending loss with a distinct personal horror. All of our dreams were suddenly being broken into pieces and I wondered if I could stay alive. Something physical was manifesting itself inside of me in a most destructive way. For the moment I set God's question aside mentally. I didn't know if I could survive Jackie's death or for that matter even if I wanted to survive.

Yet there lies the fundamental question God asks of all of us. "Do you really believe?" Do you? If so, do you likewise believe in obedience or is your faith based on the mythology that obedience doesn't matter? For me, obedience has not been an issue for 26-years. No, the question God had for me to consume was whether given such a loss, did I still believe that HE was real. I have told several people that Jackie's death was a very defining moment for my faith. Verily I say unto you that none of the misery I have suffered on this earth comes remotely close to the pain that I felt losing her.

In the moments of my despair and in the depths of my grief I still felt my LORD walking with me. Deep despair and grief is what the disciples and others felt with the loss of Jesus on the cross. For them it also represented broken dreams. My passion ran deep for Jackie and as we had children I was forced to subdue some of that passion to raise our children. We both acknowledged we had committed to giving up 25-years of our previously intense passion for one another to raise our family. I had always had the dream that after the kids were raised we could return to the passion we once shared before children arrived. Business struggles and other life events delayed that and then, of course, one day it was all over. Our dreams were broken and would never be realized. As I reflected on this human existence, I have come to realize that this is one of the more awful realities of death. Broken dreams. No more future and the hope that was inherent within the potential of human life, then suddenly snuffed out. We survive struggles with the hopes and dreams of the future. What happens when they die?

Copyright 2005 Edward G. Palmer, All Rights Reserved.

Book of Edward—Chapter 21

Myth—Everybody Gets To Go

Songwriter and singer Steve Green has captured this moment of our broken dreams in his song: "People Need The Lord." The song transcends the issue of broken dreams and makes it clear that we all need the LORD at a moment of death to open up a new door of hope. Do you believe? If so, do you know that you *need* the LORD? Maybe the question seems ridiculous. Of course, every believer knows that he or she *needs* the LORD, don't they? Well, strangely, an estimated 50% of those named a Christian do not know that they *really need* the LORD. What? Yes, these people think they have complied with God's requirements by being able to mouth and simply say out loud, "Jesus is my Lord!" They are wrong.

At The End of Broken Dreams, He's The Open Door!

Green's lyrics [1] capture the emptiness of people passing by in life and besides non-believers, also apply to 50% of those named Christian.

> Everyday they pass me by; I can see it in their eye.
> Empty people filled with care, headed who knows where?
>
> On they go through private pain, living fear to fear.
> Laughter hides their silent cries, only Jesus hears.
>
> People need the Lord—people need the Lord.
> At the end of broken dreams, he's the open door.
> People need the Lord—people need the Lord.
> When will we realize—people need the Lord?
>
> We are called to take his light, to a world where wrong seems right.
> What would be too great a cost, for sharing life with one who's lost?
>
> Through his love our hearts can feel, all the grief they bear.
> They must hear the words of life, only we can share.
>
> People need the Lord—people need the Lord.
> At the end of broken dreams, he's the open door.
> People need the Lord—people need the Lord.
> When will we realize that we must give our lives?
> For people need the Lord.
> People need the Lord.

Copyright 2005 Edward G. Palmer, All Rights Reserved.

Book of Edward—Chapter 21

Myth—Everybody Gets To Go

Today almost half of those named Christians believe that they can support evil with impunity from God. That it is somehow okay with God that they kill babies and marry homosexuals and the long laundry list of evils in HIS eyes that I have already discussed. In the United States we are almost evenly split in our political opinions of which side represents evil or good. Why? Consider the moral implications of our recent presidential election. Are we not also likened in the U.S. to ten virgins, five wise and five foolish? Doesn't these prophetic words of Jesus Christ apply to the moral divisions in the United States? What about the moral divisions within Christianity?

Likened To Ten Virgins, Five Wise & Five Foolish!

Presidential Vote	Bush	Kerry
Total U.S. Vote	51%	48%
White Protestants	52%	47%
Catholics	52%	48%

Of course, all of these named Christians believe they are headed towards Heaven and that the other half, are headed towards Hell. It is a spiritual dichotomy. Among these people, are Christian factions that believe in a second chance theology. In order to "rationalize" their false trinity doctrine, they have taken a variety of positions offensive to God.

One position is that no one born human is in Heaven. The dead go into the ground. I've talked about this before. The "Church of God" and "Jehovah Witnesses" have doctrines of this nature. One addition to this doctrine is the idea that no one actually goes to Hell, because Jesus' blood has saved all mankind from damnation. Those who would be destined to Hell without Jesus receive a "second chance" to reconsider after death. Of course, they all do and go to Heaven. Ergo, everybody gets to go! No one goes to Hell. Isn't that quite nice. You can be as evil as you want on earth in this theology and in the end you enjoy the rewards of Heaven just like the righteous are destined to do. Author Neale Donald Walsch in Book 1 of his "Conversations with God" [2] — takes this apostate theology and blends in some New Age thinking. In his god reasoning, "Hitler" is in Heaven. [2]

Myth—Everybody Gets To Go

Is Hitler Really In Heaven?

Walsch writes that God says: "I do not love 'good' more than I love 'bad.' *Hitler* went to Heaven. When you can understand this [fact], you will understand God [ME]." [3]

In Walsch's mind, there is no "good" or "evil" and God doesn't prefer one over the other. Where did such debased spiritual ideas originate? From orthodox trinitarian theology, that's where. It is the genesis that now intellectually excuses all evil as long as you mouth Jesus as your savior. If there is one difference between Walsch's New Age dogma and orthodox trinitarian Christianity, I suspect it is the nuance in orthodox doctrine that a Christian must be able to "mouth" Jesus. I don't think Walsch cares and his writings indicate it is irrelevant. Let's look at the spiritual psychobabble contained in *Book 1* of Walsch's three-volume book set.

"Feelings are the language of the soul." [4]

Comment: If this was true, it negates the need for wisdom and knowledge of God since you simply listen to your feelings. Feelings are a part of our human makeup, but they do not negate the need for reason! I hope this fact is now very clear in your mind from prior chapters.

"The Bible is not an authoritative source of knowledge of God." [5]

Comment: In the first eight pages of his book, Walsch asserts that God tells us to just go with our feelings and to ignore the Bible as a moral guide for our actions. If it feels good, do it!

"There is no Hell." [6]

"There is no evil." [7]

"You have no obligations to anyone in this life." [8]

Myth—Everybody Gets To Go

"Nothing [you can do] is offensive to God." [9]

"Your earthly actions are irrelevant to Heaven." [10]

"Your job on the planet is to decide and experience who you are." [11]

"[Walsch says he] lived hundreds of lives" via reincarnation. [12]

I refer to Walsch's works as spiritual psychobabble for a few reasons. The most obvious reason is that he dismisses the Bible [3] as not being an authoritative basis to know God. Yet on the other hand and throughout his writings, he likes to quote the Bible to reinforce or back up his current statement [13]. Walsch plays on both sides of the spiritual fence and walks a wide path in his writings. It is the broad way that Jesus says leads to our destruction. Note that the implication in Matthew 7:13 is that people do get temporarily into Heaven by entering through the wide gate. It is just that the path is one going to Hell and they don't get to stay. Verily I say unto you that everyone will know whether the choice they've made is right or wrong and will suffer the eternal consequences of their individual spiritual choice.

Jesus said, "Enter by the narrow gate; for wide is the gate and broad is the way that leads to destruction, and there are many who go in by it." Matthew 7:13

Walsch as an author also speaks against his prior writings in what can only be termed "double-speak" [14]. You cannot claim to have it both ways when the positions are polar opposites from a moral or an intellectual perspective. I.E. The technique of first dismissing the Bible as lacking any authority for God and then using it to support spiritual arguments is just plain intellectually dishonest. Yet isn't this what most spiritually debased people want to do? They want to "feel good" spiritually, but do not want to obey a God with an actual set of mores that judge our earthly behavior.

"We are self-created" on our own efforts v. being Spirit-led. [15]

"[Walsch says] I've had dozens of New Age teachers." [16]

Myth—Everybody Gets To Go

"There is no right or wrong, everything is just relative." [17]

"God is the God of Christianity." [18]

Comment: Walsch writes in opposition to a prior statement of his that God is a God with no religions or religious affiliations. It is another example of his Orwellian double-speak.

"Obedience can never produce salvation." [19]

Comment: The issue of obedience is a central theme throughout the Bible. Any assertion obedience doesn't matter is opposite of Jesus' teachings. Obedience is the real issue in all apostasy.

"There is no judgment in the afterlife." [20]

"Reincarnation" is true—[second reference]. [21]

"All illness is self-created." [22]

"Your body was designed to last forever." [23]

Comment: This is also double-speak. Are we designed or did we evolve through evolution? Which is it? It can't be both.

"And in this holy instant came you, out of the sea." [24]

"At the outset, the idea was for you wonderful souls to have a chance to know your Selves as Who You Really Are through experiences gained in the physical body, in the relative world—as I have explained repeatedly here. This was done through the slowing down of the unfathomable speed of all vibration (thought form) to produce matter—including the matter you call the physical body. Life evolved through a series of steps in the blink of an eye that you now call billions of years. And in this holy instant came you, out of the sea, the water of life, onto the land and into the form you now hold." [24]

Myth—Everybody Gets To Go

"There is no male and female, there is no before and after, there is no fast and slow, here and there, up and down, left and right—and no right and wrong." [24]

"There is no devil." [25]

Okay, this is some interesting spiritual stuff. Let's put it all together for an easy view. Neale Donald Walsch in "Conversations With God" teaches the following about God in his *Book 1*.

1. Hitler is in Heaven.
2. There is no good or evil.
3. There is no right or wrong.
4. There is no devil.
5. There is no Hell.
6. Nothing is offensive to God.
7. The Bible is not God's authority.
8. There is no judgment in the afterlife.
9. Feelings are the language of the soul—so go with them.
10. Your earthly actions, good or evil, are irrelevant to God.
11. Reincarnation is a reality for all of those who choose it.
12. Evolution out of the sea is how humans came into existence.
13. We have no earthly obligations except to ourselves.
14. All illness is self-created.
15. Our duty is to decide and experience who we are—what we want.
16. Everything is relative on this earth—there are no moral standards.
17. Obedience is not a part of salvation.

If everything that Neale Donald Walsch teaches is true, why should anyone be concerned about our earthly behavior? In his mind we live in a self-actuated relative world and our only duty is to ourselves to discover and be who we want to be—good or evil. Think about these teachings and ask yourself exactly how many of them you personally believe. In fact put a check mark next to everyone you believe and a check mark next to every one your church teaches. Put a third checkmark against everyone in which your earthly behavior demonstrates a belief even if you won't admit it.

Myth—Everybody Gets To Go

While individually the above list might seem offensive to many who call themselves Christian, the collective list becomes completely acceptable to the Christian who says, "Jesus forgives me of all my sins. Ergo, my sins no longer matter to God." Isn't that the orthodox message of Christianity in many factions today? You can't help yourself? Isn't that why God came down in the flesh and died on the cross? Hello.

What is wrong with such spiritual ignorance is Jesus' astonishing 50% factor cited in Matthew 25 when combined with the selection process also cited in the same chapter. Something terrible is happening in the U.S. culture because half of the country no longer sees an eternal consequence connected to their earthly actions. Same thing with Christians, half of them think there is no eternal consequences to their earthly actions—after they "mouth" Jesus as their Lord. I've already taught you why this salvation doctrine is false. Go back and read chapters 10-12 if you don't understand why. For now, consider that we live in a world where "wrong seems right" to many people. Steve Green captures this present reality with the lyrics—

"We are called to take his light,
To a world where wrong seems right!"

Just look at news headlines on any day. If you know your Bible and U.S. history, you'll recognize that in society—everything seems upside down today. Indeed, today, wrong seems right in biblical and historical terms. One recent headline read, "Banned from Showing Students the Declaration of Independence" [26]. If you think that this means a fifth-grade history teacher was told he couldn't show the United States "Declaration of Independence" document to his students, you are exactly right. Students had asked how "under God" came into the Pledge. To answer the question, the teacher brought in several documents of the Founding Fathers. Of course, one parent "violently" protested the mixing of Church and State at school. Has the "silent" majority succumbed to the idiocy of the "violent" minority? Why is it wrong to teach U.S. history as it happened with the documents of our founders? And why is it right to teach Darwin's evolution in science as it is factual instead of just a theory?

Myth—Everybody Gets To Go

The only reasonable answer is we live in a world where "wrong is right." Another headline read, "Attorney Hopes Texas Court Will Uphold Pastor's Rights" [27]. Unbelievably, a Texas pastor is being sued for "following biblical mandates in administering church discipline." If you don't think that the Church is under assault from within and without, you are a very naïve person. I've already taught you that it is against criminal law in Canada to speak out against homosexuality. That includes reciting in public Bible verses that condemn homosexuality. Now, a pastor is being sued for following biblical instructions in his church. Everything is upside down and wrong is right in too many cases. Satan has a "violent" minority that seeks to impose his evil will on the "silent" moral majority of God.

Another headline reads, "Pelosi: Marriage Amendment Discriminates Against Gays" [28]. House Democrat Minority Leader Nancy Pelosi said, "The proposed constitutional amendment limiting marriage to heterosexual couples would be 'an act of discrimination' against gays." So what! The U.S. Constitution discriminates against many other people as well. Those younger than 25 cannot run for the U.S. House. Those younger than 30 cannot run for the U.S. Senate. Those younger than 35 cannot run for the office of U.S. President. Isn't that also discrimination? And exactly what is wrong with being a little discriminating in our judgment? Don't we also morally discriminate against murderers with laws saying you can't murder? The opposite of discrimination is anarchy, where values have no meaning. Yet isn't that where our society now finds itself? And isn't our language now systematically perverted to support evil in an Orwellian double-speak?

So, exactly how is enforcing the Bible's laws and moral code picking on people? If you've got an answer, let me know. Nobody forces people to live in a moral society. Certainly there are immoral places for those who want to live in an environment of anarchy. Are not the immoral minorities of Satan violently corrupting and taking over our once moral society?

Another headline read, "Methodist Jury Convicts Lesbian Minister." A jury made up of United Methodist Church clergy convicted the Rev. Irene Elizabeth Stroud of violating church law by openly living with her female partner in a committed lesbian relationship. [29]

Copyright 2005 Edward G. Palmer, All Rights Reserved.

Book of Edward—Chapter 21

Myth—Everybody Gets To Go

"Stroud's defense counsel, the Rev. J. Dennis Williams, said in closing arguments that "that heart of the issue is whether all United Methodists, regardless of status, are to be afforded equal rights and equal opportunities." Hello. What's wrong with this argument? These people believe that the church should also be non-discriminating. If so, why not ordain murderers and rapists? Facetious you say? Why? Yes it is, but the simpleminded idea that the Christian Church should not be a discriminating Church that imposes biblical moral standards is just another statement of anarchy. Why should we not discriminate and refuse to accept what God thinks is abominable? We live in an upside down world where what was commonly understood as morally wrong is now taught as okay or right. A violent lesbian sets up a moral conflict by playing innocent, building up a sympathetic church following and then "coming out" on her unsuspecting congregation. Stroud herself, having first built church friendships, imposes spiritual violence on her congregation, which is forced to "understand" her. It is all a spiritual fraud designed to violently alter our morals.

Perhaps capping off the upside down nature of our country is the school principal [30] who was recently admonished and had to apologize for reading a simple poem over the intercom. Of course, and once again, one or more "violent" parents objected on the basis of Church-State separation. Yet the simple poem he read expresses quite eloquently that "wrong is now considered right." With 290 million U.S. citizens, there are now "violent" minorities in abundance to eliminate morals in every single school. They are ready to challenge anything they don't like when it comes to our morals. What is needed is for the "silent" majority to start getting "violent" and take back our morals by spiritual force. That is what our founders did. They took over this country by the force of their spiritual violence!

"The principal of a Georgia high school apologized to parents and students for reading 'The New School Prayer' over the intercom. Tommy Craft, principal of Cedar Shoals High School in Athens, GA., was forced to apologize after fielding complaints about the prayer, which he read the Tuesday before Thanksgiving break, the Associated Press reported." This poem has been on the Internet for years. The last two lines is a prayer? Why should anyone have to apologize for reading this aloud to students?

Myth—Everybody Gets To Go

The New School Prayer [31]

Now I sit me down in school
Where praying is against the rule.
For this great nation under God
Finds mention of HIM very odd.

If Scripture now the class recites,
It violates the Bill of Rights.
And anytime my head I bow
Becomes a federal matter now.

Our hair can be purple, orange or green,
That's no offense; it's a freedom scene.
The law is specific; the law is precise.
Prayers spoken aloud are a serious vice.

For praying in a public hall
Might offend someone with no faith at all.
In silence alone we must meditate,
God's name is prohibited by the state.

We're allowed to cuss and dress like freaks,
And pierce our noses, tongues and cheeks.
They've outlawed guns, but FIRST the Bible.
To quote the Good Book makes me liable.

We can elect a pregnant Senior Queen,
And the 'unwed daddy' our Senior King.
It's 'inappropriate' to teach right from wrong,
We're taught that such 'judgments' do not belong.

We can get our condoms and birth controls,
Study witchcraft, vampires and totem poles.
But the Ten Commandments are not allowed,
No word of God must reach this crowd.

It's scary here I must confess,
When chaos reigns, the school is a mess.
So, LORD, this silent plea I make:
Should I be shot, my soul please take! Amen.

Copyright 2005 Edward G. Palmer, All Rights Reserved.

Book of Edward—Chapter 21

Myth—Everybody Gets To Go

The Violent Take Heaven By Force!

With a world that is truly upside down in moral terms, what's the real cause? The cause is spiritually violent people seeking to "bind" God's values and "loose" Satan's values on the rest of us. When you understand that a small immoral minority of people is "violently" taking over the morals our country, you'll be able to understand why Jesus taught us the following.

> **Jesus said, "And from the days of John the Baptist until now the kingdom of Heaven suffers violence, and the violent take it by force." Matthew 11:12**

To fully understand this teaching of Jesus, consider this one ...

> **Jesus said, "And I will give you the keys of the kingdom of Heaven, and whatever you bind on earth will be bound in Heaven, and whatever you loose on earth will be loosed in Heaven." Matthew 16:19**

Our country is under a moral attack by spiritually "violent" people who intend to try and alter the morality of the nation to their liking. They believe they can bind "morality" and loose "immorality" and have their way in Heaven also. The Catch 22 they don't realize is that this message is "for doing HIS will" — not ours. It doesn't eliminate the Christian duty to seek HIS will and comply with HIS laws. What's the solution to our moral decay in the United States? It is for the "silent majority" to violently take back our morals by confronting the evil people seeking to destroy our mores.

Now with this violent spiritual jockeying for Heaven going on, it would be wise to review once again the primary teaching of Jesus that this book is formulated on. No one gets in that doesn't do HIS will!

> **Jesus said, "Not everyone who says to me, 'Lord, Lord,' shall enter the kingdom of Heaven, *but he who does the will of my FATHER in Heaven.*" Matthew 7:21**

Copyright 2005 Edward G. Palmer, All Rights Reserved.

Book of Edward—Chapter 21

Myth—Everybody Gets To Go

Fifteen items you should have learned so far in this chapter.

1. Jesus says there is 50% factor when it comes to entering Heaven.
2. Jesus says a selection process will weed out the unrighteous.
3. Jesus can open a door of hope at the end of your broken dreams.
4. You will need Jesus and his FATHER at the time of your death.
5. The United States exhibit a 50% factor in voting morals.
6. The Protestants exhibit a 50% factor in voting morals.
7. The Catholics exhibit a 50% factor in voting morals.
8. The U.S. is now likened to five wise & five foolish virgins.
9. Christians are now likened to five wise & five foolish virgins.
10. Apostasy reigns within and without the Christian Church.
11. Those entering Heaven by the wide immoral gate don't get to stay.
12. New Age writers document the full meaning of Christian apostasy.
13. The greatest apostasy is the idea that with Jesus sin doesn't matter.
14. We live in a world where what is wrong is labeled okay or right.
15. Violent servants of Satan are corrupting our nation's moral values.

There is little doubt that almost half of all Christians now have their moral values turned upside down and rationalize that they can have it their own way on the planet earth. I'm here to tell you it isn't so. And, I've got good reason to tell you that. It is the biblically based teachings of Jesus Christ that speak directly against such apostasy. Do you believe the savior you claim gets you into Heaven? If so, then it is your duty to listen to what he has taught us on earth as it relates to our eternal life. The anything goes wide-gate moral beliefs of half of Christianity today only confirm to me that we are indeed in the last days. Everybody gets to go? Hardly, and the three teachings below of Jesus Christ speak directly against such a theology or doctrine. Yet these are not the only teachings of our Lord Jesus Christ, the only human begotten Son of God Almighty. They are just three examples.

1. You don't get into Heaven unless you obey God's will. Mt. 7

2. At least 50% or more of Christians are locked out. Mt. 25

3. God has a selection process that chooses righteous people. Mt. 25

Myth—Everybody Gets To Go

The Bible Teaches Everybody Doesn't Get To Go!

Outside Of Heaven	If God Has Your Heart	Bible Reference
Sexually Immoral	You obey God's sex rules	Rev 22:15
Sorcerers	You do not practice sorcery	Rev 22:15
Murderers	You do not murder	Rev 22:15
Idolaters	You worship only God	Rev 22:15
Lovers of Lies	You are a lover of the truth	Rev 22:15
Practitioner of Lies	You practice truth	Rev 22:15
Unrighteous	You practice righteousness	Rom 1:18, 1Cor 6:10
Ungodly	You practice godliness	Rom 1:18
Fornicators	You obey God's sex rules	1Cor 6:9-10
Adulterers	You obey God's sex rules	1Cor 6:9-10
Homosexuals	You obey God's sex rules	1Cor 6:9-10
Sodomites	You obey God's sex rules	1Cor 6:9-10
Thieves	You do not steal	1Cor 6:9-10
Drunkards	You are temperate	1Cor 6:9-10
Revilers	You do not slander	1Cor 6:9-10
Extortioners	You do not extort	1Cor 6:9-10
Covetous	You do not covet	1Cor 6:9-10

You might remember this table from Chapter 3, page 38. Now is a good time to review again these teachings in Paul's Epistles and in John's Revelation. Apostate believers want to twist Paul's teachings to rationalize their earthly sins. It won't work, because Paul was clear in his teachings. As was John and the other apostles. If you "practice" any of the activities in the left hand column, kiss your eternal life in Heaven goodbye. Likewise, shifting from the left to middle column in your behavior will get you home.

Copyright 2005 Edward G. Palmer, All Rights Reserved.

Book of Edward—Chapter 21

Myth—Everybody Gets To Go

A satanic church has deceived people who practice the items in the left hand column. They have never actually been saved because their heart has not found its "way" back to God's righteousness. You don't have to live there and you don't have to be uncertain about your eternal status. I have placed "A Real Salvation Prayer" in each volume for you to study and take to heart. If you state this prayer with the sincerity of your heart and then back it up with your behavior on earth, you will be saved. Note that this isn't a simplistic "mouthing" prayer. This prayer forces you to acknowledge the fundamental teachings of the Bible in regards to obedience.

Matthew 25

Now that you understand it is not just Jesus that teaches our earthly behavior influences our eternal destination, let's focus on Jesus' teachings about the kingdom of God. It is our Lord's teachings on the kingdom that can set every soul that speaks his name free. That is, IF they will take his teachings to heart and act upon them. Let us look closer at Matthew 25.

In verses 1-13, Jesus teaches the following:

1. The kingdom is likened to five wise and five foolish people.
2. The wise people came fully prepared to shine their "light."
3. The foolish people came unprepared to shine their "light."
4. The Lord came at night, which challenged their "light."
5. The foolish people found themselves "locked out."
6. The Lord responds to the foolish, "I do not know you."
7. We are admonished to have our "light" ready for the Lord.

I don't believe for a moment that Jesus arbitrarily used five wise and five foolish virgins. This 5 of 10 is a 50% factor. In this illustration of the kingdom of Heaven, Jesus makes it clear that 50% of those wanting to get in and who claimed the right to be there, won't actually get in. As I look at the state of Christianity today in the United States, there is little doubt in my spirit that we have come to the point that Christ has referenced. With 50% of Christians supporting policies that kill babies, marry Gays, etc., there is little chance of them gaining permanent entry into Heaven. These Christians have no "light" to shine and the analogy Christ used fits them to a tee.

Myth—Everybody Gets To Go

In verses 14-30, Jesus teaches the following:

1. The kingdom is likened to a man traveling.
2. The traveler gave his three servants his resources to manage.
3. The first servant who received five talents doubled it.
4. The second servant who received two talents doubled it.
5. The third servant who received one talent buried it out of fear.
6. His lord rewarded the first servant saying, "Well done, good and faithful servant, you were faithful over a few things, I will make you ruler over many things. *Enter* into the joy of your lord."
7. His lord rewarded the second servant saying, "Well done, good and faithful servant, you were faithful over a few things, I will make you ruler over many things. *Enter* into the joy of your lord."
8. The third servant said to his lord, "I knew you to be a hard man, reaping where you have not sown, and gathering where you have not scattered seed. And I was afraid, and went and hid your talent in the ground. Look, there you have what is yours."
9. His lord castigated the third servant saying, "You wicked and lazy servant, you knew that I reap where I have not sown, and gather where I have not scattered seed. Therefore you ought to have deposited my money with bankers, and at my coming I would have received back my own with interest."
10. The third servant's returned talent was given to the first servant.
    a. For to everyone who has, more will be given.
    b. From who does not have, even what he has will be taken.
11. "Cast the unprofitable servant into the outer darkness. There will be weeping and gnashing of teeth."

Christ is speaking to his servants and makes it clear that we have a duty to be "obedient and profitable" to God's will — while on earth. We cannot be lazy and claim ignorance. It won't stick in Heaven. All three were servants of a master. In this analogy, only two of the three were allowed to "*Enter* into the joy of the LORD." Jesus teaches the spiritual duty we have to be profitable for God, his FATHER. We cannot claim to be profitable to God if we support immorality. Such behavior is not taking care of HIS business. In the first teaching, the foolish are locked out. In this second teaching the spiritually unprofitable person is thrown into darkness.

Myth—Everybody Gets To Go

If our heart doesn't get it, we won't live it. Those who practice the items in the left hand column of the table above are spiritually unprofitable servants to God from HIS perspective. They never returned to righteousness after claiming to have accepted Christ. They were phonies and insincere believers. They never actually thought of HIS perspective and HIS interests, because they were too busy thinking of their own desire to sin. If they had considered God, they would have *reasoned* differently about their earthly actions. They would have understood that their earthly behavior has eternal consequences. They would have understood "everybody doesn't get in."

In verses 31-40, Jesus teaches the following:

1. Jesus will bring holy angels when he comes.
2. Jesus will sit on his throne of glory.
3. All nations will be gathered before him.
4. Jesus will separate the sheep from the goats, which means that he will separate the righteous from the unrighteous people *for God*.
5. This is a "selection process." The righteous to his "right!"
6. The King [Jesus] will then say to those on his right, "Come, you blessed of my FATHER, inherit the kingdom prepared for you from the foundation of the world."
7. The King [Jesus] will then say to those on his left, "Depart from me, you cursed, into the everlasting fire prepared for the devil and his angels [and all spiritually unprofitable earthly servants]."
8. The unrighteous "go into an everlasting punishment, but the righteous into eternal life."

Not only does Jesus teach the necessity of being prepared and being profitable in Matthew 25, he clearly states the consequences of not being prepared and profitable. Who are those who fall into these categories? They are the unrighteous. Clearly there is a selection process to get into Heaven and it relates to our earthly behavior. As the protests come from the second group, Jesus explains that they never cared about people. Perhaps they had the political mentality that the government should take care of people and that they had no duty to God in these regards. In this case, Jesus makes it clear that we have a duty to care for others less fortunate than ourselves.

Myth—Everybody Gets To Go

Jesus Rejects Those Who Don't Care For Others!

    a. Feed the hungry
    b. Give drink to the thirsty
    c. Take in the stranger
    d. Clothe the naked
    e. Visit the sick
    f. Visit those in prison

Jesus claims he was in these particular needy positions and the second group of unrighteous people never really cared. They protest saying:

"Lord, when did we see you hungry or thirsty or a stranger or naked or sick or in prison, and did not minister to you?"
Matthew 25:44

Jesus responds.

"Assuredly, I say to you, inasmuch as you did not do it to one of the least of these, you did not do it to me."
Matthew 25:45

I am wondering what Jesus will tell the pastor that literally dismantles the food, clothing programs and other ministries that serve the needy? When I joined the Elk River Assembly of God, it had these outreach ministries in place with people serving the needy. I then witnessed Pastor William Neal Matthews systematically dismantle and shut down these ministries. Where does that put him in the eyes of Jesus? *Woe to the pastor who eliminates and shuts down the ministries that God calls all of us in to serve the needy.*

What about politics? Can't we just force the government to take care of the needy with programs paid for by our taxes? No, we can't and that is why liberal politics hold no spiritual weight. God expects us humans to engage in these activities. There is no spiritual cover by claiming you've done your job by supporting a political party that promotes these ideals.

Book of Edward—Chapter 21

Myth—Everybody Gets To Go

I've already talked about two groups of people that God rejects and keeps out of Heaven. The first group is shown above and is defined by their lack of caring for other humans. I just read a statement that the Democratic presidential candidate in 2000 "doesn't give money to charity" [32]. Perhaps this Democrat feels satisfied that his party or the government would do the job? Yet, it doesn't matter to Jesus. He doesn't give people consideration of their political stances. They either personally helped other people or they didn't. *Woe to those who do not care personally and expect others and their government to do the caring for "the least of our brethren."*

Matthew 7

The second group of people tossed out by Jesus are the "lawless" and they will have no excuse for their lack of obedience with God and His Son.

"Many will say to me in that day, 'Lord, Lord, have we not prophesied in your name, cast out demons in your name, and done many wonders in your name?' And then I will declare to them, 'I never knew you; depart from me, you who practice lawlessness!' " Matthew 7:22-23

The group Jesus rejects in Matthew 25 isn't identified by religious affiliation and therefore applies to all of mankind, because Jesus states, "the nations are gathered before him." Ergo, the essence of Christ's rejection relates specifically to non-caring, unrighteous and self-centered individuals. However, there is little doubt that the group Jesus rejects in Matthew 7 is Christian. Who else would dare claim to have "prophesied in your name, cast out demons and done many wonders in your name" [in the name of Jesus]? I've speculated that this statement of Jesus is very representative of Christian leaders who openly speak out and preach apostate doctrines like the leaders in Solid Rock Church. These people seem to take bold spiritual positions for God, but they deny true faith by acts of lawlessness. It takes a bold Christian to do all the things cited in Matthew 7:23. Therefore, Jesus makes it clear that many Christians will be rejected. Indeed, given Jesus' astonishing 50% factor, it is most likely that half or more of all who claim Christ as their savior—will be rejected by him and cast into the lake of fire.

Copyright 2005 Edward G. Palmer, All Rights Reserved.

Book of Edward—Chapter 21

Myth—Everybody Gets To Go

Unprepared Christians. How should the church deal with this issue? Maybe it should start locking the church doors to give Christians practice showing up on time with a Bible? The church could have a few spare Bibles and after they're gone, they could also reject anyone else who shows up without a Bible. Perhaps this would start training Christians that the word of God does matter to their eternal life, because it guides their earthly behavior? That they need to show up on time prepared to shine their light.

That's an interesting thought isn't it? Eventually those serious about God would wake up and those who presently care less would drop out. It would help prescreen the church population for Jesus albeit I don't think the idea would go over well in most churches.

Jesus Defines The Wise And The Foolish!

We do not have to guess about who is wise and who is foolish, as Jesus has defined them in Matthew 7. Consider our Lord's definition of wise and foolish.

Jesus' definition of the wise:

"Therefore whoever hears these sayings of mine, and does them, I will liken him to a wise man who built his house on the rock." Matthew 7:24

Jesus' definition of the foolish:

"But everyone who hears these sayings of mine, and does not do them, will be like a foolish man who built his house on the sand." Matthew 7:26

Wise people are doers of the Word!

Foolish people are not doers of the Word!

Copyright 2005 Edward G. Palmer, All Rights Reserved.

Myth—Everybody Gets To Go

By Jesus definition then, the five wise virgins were obedient to God and were doers of the Word. In contrast, the five foolish virgins were not obedient to God and were not doers of the Word. If you can grasp the obedience requirement that Jesus expounds, you'll understand James.

> **"Therefore lay aside all filthiness and overflow of wickedness, and receive with meekness the implanted Word, which is able to save your souls. But be doers of the Word, and not hearers only, deceiving yourselves. For if anyone is a hearer of the Word and not a doer, he is like a man observing his natural face in a mirror; for he observes himself, goes away, and immediately forgets what kind of man he was. But he who looks into the perfect law of liberty and continues in it, and is not a forgetful hearer but a doer of the work, this one will be blessed in what he does." James 1:21-25**

James admonishes us to "receive with meekness the implanted Word." Immediately afterwards James makes it clear that you need to be a doer of the Word to be saved. Don't deceive yourself by ignoring God and His Son. Verily I say to you that your obedience or lack of it does matter to God!

> **"What does it profit, my brethren, if someone says he has faith but does not have works? Can faith save him? If a brother or sister is naked and destitute of daily food, and one of you says to them, 'Depart in peace, be warmed and filled,' but you do not give them the things which are needed for the body, what does it profit? Thus also faith by itself, if it does not have works, is dead. But someone will say, 'You have faith, and I have works.' Show me your faith without your works, and I will show you my faith by my works. You believe that there is one God. You do well. Even the demons believe—and tremble! But do you want to know, O foolish man, that faith without works is dead? Was not Abraham our father justified by works when he offered Isaac his son on the altar? Do you see that faith was working together with his works, and by works faith was made perfect?" James 2:14-22**

Myth—Everybody Gets To Go

Rapture Statement Contains A 50% Factor!

Before Jesus presented his 50% factor with wise and foolish virgins; the profitable servant criteria; and, the nation selection process shown in Matthew 25, he preceded it with a "Days of Noah" and "Rapture 50% Factor" in Matthew 24. Thus, when Jesus used the word "THEN" in Matthew 25:1, he was referring to the criteria being applied to the situation stated in Matthew 24. It describes how society will be when Jesus returns.

"But as the days of Noah were, so also will the coming of the Son of Man be. For as in the days before the flood, they were eating and drinking, marrying and giving in marriage, until the day that Noah entered the ark, and did not know until the flood came and took them all away, so also will the coming of the Son of Man be." Matthew 24:37-39

Jesus said, "When the Son of Man comes, will he really find faith on the earth?" Luke 18:8

Only eight people survived the flood. Jesus reminds us that the people had no clue. "They did not know" until it was too late to do anything about it. The days of Noah were apostate times and society was debased just like it is today. Even so-called Christians advocate for abortion rights and the right of homosexual marriage. These are debased times just like Noah's time. When Christ comes back will your light be shinning? I hope so. If not, Jesus makes it clear that one will be taken from the field and the other left. Literally 50% will be lifted off the planet in the "rapture" and the other 50% left on the earth to pay the price of their unrighteousness and sin.

50% Raptured Off Earth!

"Then two men will be in the field: one will be taken and the other left. Two women will be grinding at the mill: one will be taken and the other left. Watch therefore, for you do not know what hour your Lord is coming." Matthew 24:40-42

Myth—Everybody Gets To Go

Jesus expounds on the rapture by illustrating two servants. One was found doing what his master [God] wanted. The other was found shirking his responsibilities. It is the illustration of what it means to be sincere or insincere with your God.

"Blessed is that servant whom his master, when he comes, will find so doing." Matthew 24:46

"The master of that [insincere and irresponsible] servant will come on a day when he is not looking for him and at an hour that he is not aware of, and will cut him in two and appoint him his portion with the hypocrites. There shall be weeping and gnashing of teeth." Matthew 24:50-51

Here again is a 50% factor. One servant is faithful and rewarded while the other is unfaithful and is condemned. I read an interesting comment from a renowned atheist who now claims to believe in a God, but he said he did not believe in some kind of cosmic Saddam Hussein figure like many Christians. Of course, Saddam was capricious and killed and slaughtered people over mere whims or even the wrong look on a face, etc. His statement reflects an ignorance of God's character. I serve a God who loves good, but hates evil. That is the God of the Holy Bible. HE is not a capricious God and HE does not engage in any injustice. However, HE is a just God and a punisher of evildoers. If it just takes being a good, caring and faithful person on this planet to obtain eternal life, why is that such a big thing to so many people? Notice I left out mouthing Jesus? The reason will become clear in a moment using Jesus' very own teachings.

When you understand that spiritually violent people are taking over and debasing our nation's mores, when you can understand that Jesus makes it clear that we are to be do-gooders and that is what really matters to God — then you can properly understand the following two statements.

"It is necessary only for the good man to do nothing for evil to triumph." Edmund Burke [33]

Myth—Everybody Gets To Go

> "History will have to record that the greatest tragedy of this period of social transition was not the strident clamor of the bad people, but the appalling silence of the good people." [34]
>
> Rev. Martin Luther King, Jr.

Martin Luther King's statement of the 1960's is just as prophetic as Edmund Burke's statement of the 18th century. And isn't exactly this social phenomenon-taking place today before our very eyes? Isn't a battery of evil lawyers intent on altering the very foundation of our laws supporting this evil effort? Verily I say unto you that silent good people may get repaid with eternal damnation, because good people do speak up against evil. All of us have a duty to God to do what is right in His eyes. We do not have an excuse to remain silent on moral confrontations. When someone allows evil to go forward because they keep their mouth shut, they have committed evil in God's eyes and have failed to meet His minimum righteousness standard. Therefore, the "silence of the good people" is an oxymoron to a God that expects righteousness. Indeed, it too is part of Christian mythology.

Three Groups Judged — One Group Not Judged!

Jesus teaches that three different groups of people will be judged and that one group of people will not be judged. Those that are judged will be raised or condemned on "the last day!" I am not fully sure exactly what the phrase means. I personally believe it means on your last day as "in the day that you physically die." The day you shed our first earthly vessel. That would be consistent with my belief that we are immediately transported into either an eternal life or an eternal damnation upon our earthly death. It would also be consistent with Christ's statement to the thief that, "today you will be with me in Paradise." Others believe that it means the "Day of the Lord" or the day of Christ's return. If you are of that mindset, then you might think it means the moment you come out of the ground and get reunited with Christ. However, there is more to the issue to consider in the "ground debate" as Jesus clearly teaches that one group of people have already received eternal life while on earth in this earthly body. In fact, Jesus states, "they have already passed from death to life."

Myth—Everybody Gets To Go

Perk up now as this teaching may challenge your idea of salvation if you think you can simply claim to be a "believer in Jesus Christ." I might add once more that this is not my teaching. I only now remind you of what our Lord Jesus Christ taught about concerning the kingdom of Heaven. His words were not his own, remember? He only spoke and did what God told him to do. At least that again is what Jesus said. I taught you this earlier.

Already passed from death to life while alive on this earth? Yes. Jesus teaches that there is one group that is not judged but has already passed from death to life. Of course, this teaching of Jesus pokes another huge hole in the doctrine that we all go into the ground. Consider these teachings of Jesus as we continue to explore why everyone doesn't get to go.

Three Groups Judged On The Last Day! Some People Raised, Some People Condemned!

"No one can come to me [Jesus] unless the FATHER who sent me draws him; and I will raise him up at the last day."
John 6:44

"People cannot come to me unless the FATHER who sent me brings them to me. I will bring these people back to life on the last day." John 6:44 GW

"The prophets wrote, 'God will teach everyone.' Those who do what they have learned from the FATHER come to me."
John 6:45 GW

"Then Jesus cried out and said, 'He who believes in me, believes not in me but in HIM who sent me.' " John 12:44

"He who rejects me [Jesus], and does not receive my words [because he is foolish and is not a doer of the Word], has that which judges him—the Word that I have spoken will judge him in the last day." John 12:48

Copyright 2005 Edward G. Palmer, All Rights Reserved.

Book of Edward—Chapter 21

Myth—Everybody Gets To Go

One Group Already Passed From Death To Life!

"Most assuredly, I say to you, he who hears my [Jesus'] word and believes in HIM who sent me [already] has everlasting life, and shall not come into judgment, but has passed from death into life." John 5:24

"I assure you, those who listen to my [Jesus'] message and believe in God who sent me have eternal life. They will never be condemned for their sins, but they have already passed from death into life." John 5:24 NLT

"And we know that the Son of God has come and has given us an understanding, that we may know HIM who is true; and we are in HIM who is true, in HIS Son Jesus Christ. [The FATHER] is the true God and eternal life." 1 John 5:20

Everyone in my Bible study group, including myself, believes in YAHWEH or God the FATHER who sent Jesus. We are taught by Jesus, since we firmly and sincerely hold to that belief, that we already have eternal life and we "shall not come into judgment." Who taught this? Again, Jesus did. Having studied the above verses you should now realize that those who believe in God *and not just HIS Son* already have eternal life. They will not receive judgment. You should also realize that those who sincerely believe in only Jesus would get eternal life when they are picked up on the last day. There is a last day issue here. What does it all mean? I am not completely sure, but this much I know. Those who believe in God belong to HIM and they also go to the King, our Lord Jesus Christ. To use a Monopoly game metaphor, these people bypass jail and collect $200. In this instance it means bypassing Christ's judgment and receiving eternal life before we die. If you believe this teaching of Jesus Christ, then you ought to study more carefully everything he has taught us about the FATHER he serves.

Jesus said, "I am ascending to my FATHER and your FATHER, and to my God and your God." John 20:17

Copyright 2005 Edward G. Palmer, All Rights Reserved.

Book of Edward—Chapter 21

Myth—Everybody Gets To Go

God committed all judgment to Christ.

"For the FATHER judges no one, but has committed all judgment to the Son." John 5:22

But all salvation does not rest in Christ's judgment.

"Salvation belongs to our God who sits on the throne, and to the Lamb!" Rev. 7:10

"For as the FATHER raises the dead and gives life to them, even so the Son gives life to whom he will." John 5:21

"For as the FATHER has life in HIMSELF, so HE has granted the Son to have life in himself, and has given him authority to execute judgment also, because he is the Son of Man [God's only begotten human Son Jesus]." John 5:26-27

There are many sons [and daughters] of God. I myself am a son of God. As such I am a brother of Jesus Christ. However, there is only one who is the human begotten Son of God. That is Christ who came down from Heaven and became Jesus Christ, the incarnate word of God on earth. If you want to understand, then you must recognize how precious the blood of Jesus really was. It was precious enough for God Almighty to transfer all judgment issues to Christ. It was precious enough for God Almighty to grant Christ the authority to give life to "whom he will." Therefore, God has a group of people in Heaven and Jesus also has a group of people in Heaven. In addition there are two other groups that are judged by Christ, but are sent into the lake of fire and second death.

When you reflect back on the moral silence of "good people" and the "political good intentions" of other people—consider the congregation of the church and the influence of its pastors. I've told you about the defrocked lesbian minister in her Methodist church. Certainly she is guilty of spiritual violence against the Church at large and specifically against God Almighty. This and other mainline churches have many "works" directed at the needy.

Myth—Everybody Gets To Go

Yet to God they are only pseudo acts of caring clouded over by the unabashed support of sexual immorality. If you understand the following Bible verse, you'll begin to understand that so-called caring by a church can be wiped out by its support of unrighteousness in God's eyes. Even though the church engaged in acts serving the needy, the church was lawless in God's eyes. In essence, they went through the motions, but it was all for naught. Their "unrighteousness" stunk so much that individually they all wound up headed for Hell instead of in the batch headed for Heaven.

> **"I know your works, love, service, faith, and your patience; and as for your works, the last are more than the first. Nevertheless I have a few things against you, because you allow that woman Jezebel, who calls herself a prophetess, to teach and seduce MY servants to commit sexual immorality and eat things sacrificed to idols. And I gave her time to repent of her sexual immorality, and she did not repent."**
> **Rev. 2:19-21**

Now let me summarize the four groups of people that Jesus teaches about. Two groups (#1-2) wind up in Heaven and two groups (#3-4) wind up in Hell. Three groups (#2-4) will pass through some type of judgment under Christ and one group (#1) will bypass judgment. I have illustrated these four groups in two separate graphics for you. In the first graphic you find God on the top left with an arrow going back and forth to group number one. Jesus teaches that this is a group of people who "believes in God who sent him" and not just in HIS Son. The direct implication is that many who claim belief in Jesus have never come to respect God. Yet those who do respect God have bypassed Christ's judgment and have already, while on this earth, obtained eternal life. This is consistent with the Gospel of Philip's teaching that you need to get your eternal life while alive, which was a previous teaching. It is also consistent with what Christ taught while on earth.

We see in John 6:45 that group one (1) readily embraces and goes to the Son. In the grand scheme of Heaven, Christ is the King, but God is still the only God. In fact, still the only divine if that is supposed to mean God. For me, Christ and all who reflect God are of HIS divine nature.

Myth—Everybody Gets To Go

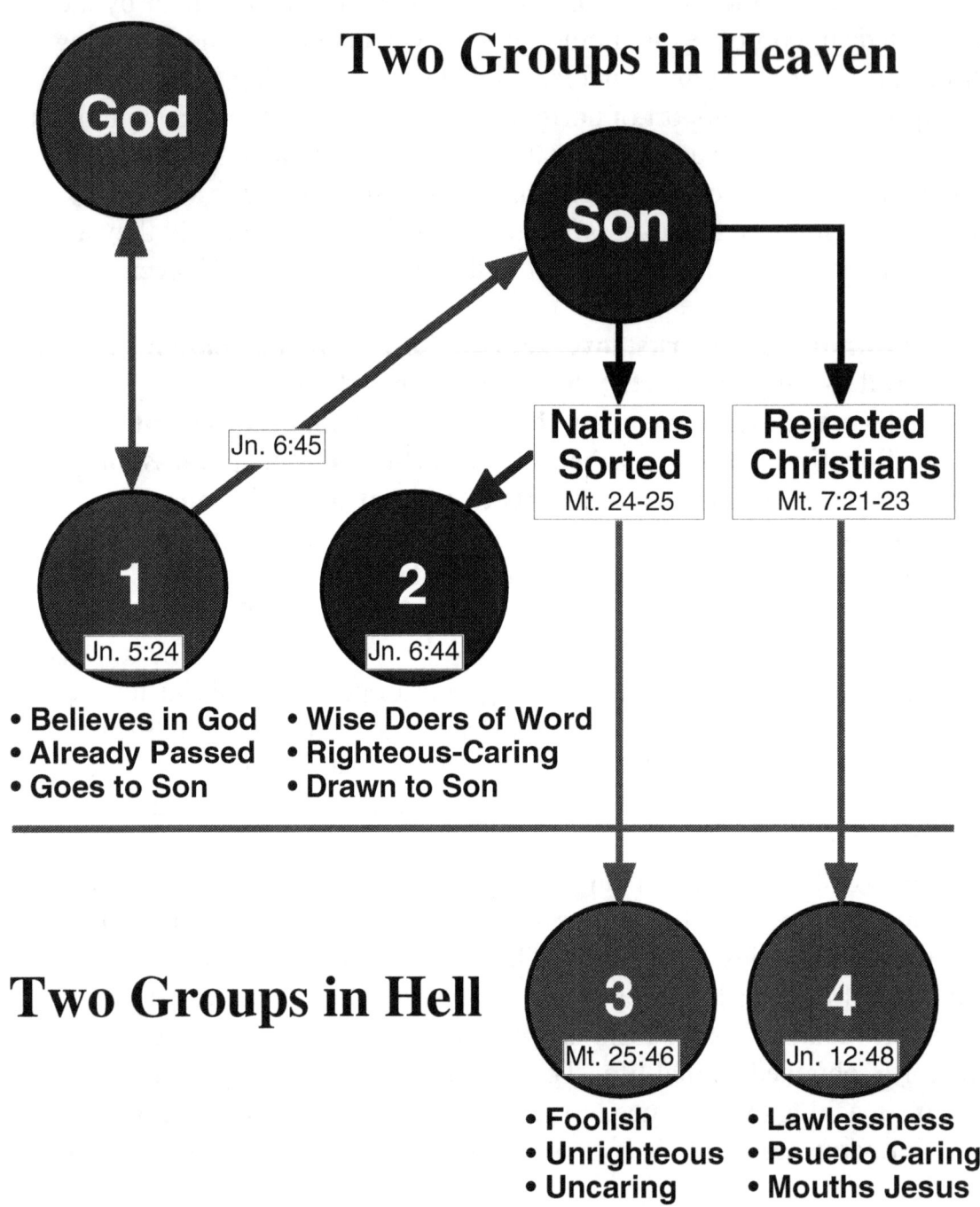

So group one is not judged according to Jesus, but group two (2), three (3) and four (4) face Christ's judgment. Group two (2) is defined in Matthew 24-25 and John 6:44 as wise "doers of the Word." These people are drawn to Christ by the FATHER and are righteous and caring people.

Copyright 2005 Edward G. Palmer, All Rights Reserved.

Book of Edward—Chapter 21

Myth—Everybody Gets To Go

However, both group two (2) and group three (3) are derived from the nations being sorted according to Matthew 25. Within all the nations before Christ's judgment are righteous and unrighteous people. Those who are righteous are caring people who wisely are doers of the Word. In contrast are the unwise who are unrighteous and uncaring. Group two (2) and three (3) constitute an almost even 50/50 division of souls according to Jesus' analogy of the five wise and five foolish virgins.

So group one (1) bypasses judgment and group two (2) and three (3) are the outputs of Jesus' nation sorting. Jesus claims the people in-group three (3) did not care for him by failing to care for those of the least of our brethren. Jesus also marks them [group three] as unrighteous people.

> **"And these [the unrighteous people] will go away into everlasting punishment, but the righteous into eternal life."**
> **Matthew 25:46**

Ergo, group two (2) to Heaven and eternal life and group three (3) to the lake of fire and the second death. Note that Jesus also refers to this as an "everlasting punishment." I'll take Jesus at his word in these regards, but I will point out that many teachers will argue against his language. Would God condone an "everlasting punishment?" Yes, if you believe in a God who also punishes as I previously taught you. In any case, why take a chance and does it really matter from a doctrinal point of view?

The most astonishing fact for Christians may be the teaching of Jesus in Matthew 7:21-23. While the groups sorted out of the nations sort are not identified as to religious affiliation, group four (4) is specifically identified as Christian. The main reason Jesus cites for their rejection to Hell is the fact that they were "lawless." Yes, I believe everyone in this group will claim to have "believed in Jesus" and even "mouthed" his name countless times. Yet these people were the insincere believers Paul talked about. They were the hypocrites that Jesus talked about. They engaged in pseudo caring of the needy while supporting immoral court and legislative actions. Where the rubber meets the road, they above everything else were simply disobedient. They never understood that they had to be wise — doers of the Word.

Copyright 2005 Edward G. Palmer, All Rights Reserved.

Book of Edward—Chapter 21

Myth—Everybody Gets To Go

These four groups can also be thought of as being judged or not being judged. The graphic below illustrates that Christ at the "right hand of God" will do all the judging, but that one group bypassed Christ's judgment. I am inside group one (1). It is the same group my beloved Jackie was in. Which group are you in? Yet in all of these teachings of Jesus, what is absent?

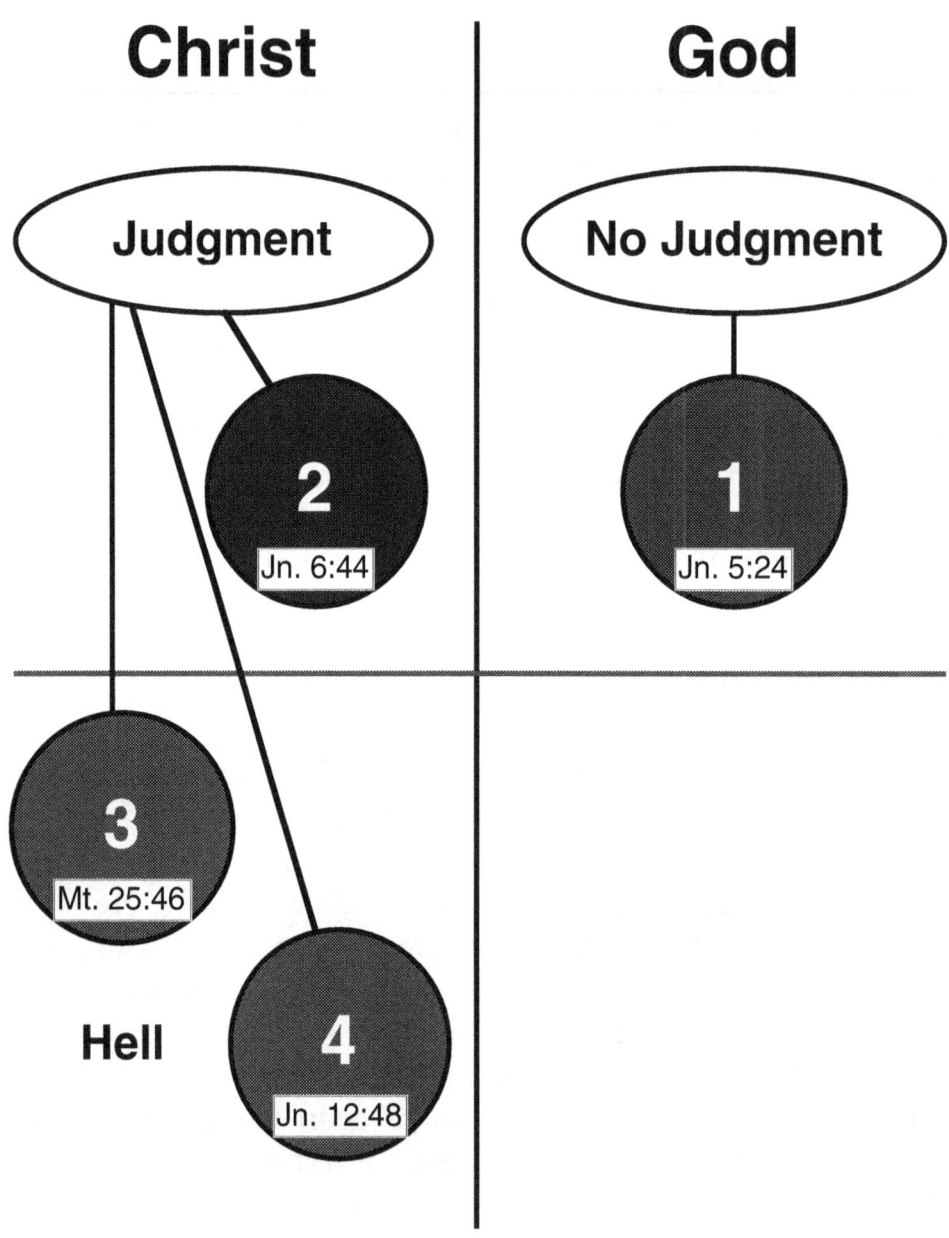

Copyright 2005 Edward G. Palmer, All Rights Reserved.

Book of Edward—Chapter 21

Myth—Everybody Gets To Go

Did you guess that nowhere above did you find that "calling on the name of the Lord" gets you into Heaven? "Mouthing Jesus' name" is flawed when it fails to do to what Jesus commanded. We are taught to be doers of the Word; that is what makes us wise servants. Therefore, the idea of calling upon the name of the Lord or even the LORD God only has meaning to those who are truly obedient to Yashua or Yahweh. Again, this doesn't make us perfect humans. Yet, there is a long way from being a lesbian inside your mind to being a physically practicing lesbian with your body and another lesbian. It is an even further stretch to be "ordained" as a minister and teach a congregation that "lesbianism" is okay. God ignores the good works of helping the needy if congregations and people are purveyors of immorality. In the end, it is only HIS morality that matters when it comes to HIS eternal life. Do you believe? If so, you know we need to obey, because we will all be weighed on HIS balance scales. Many Christians will be found wanting.

50% Of Christians Found Wanting!

God says, "You have been weighed in the balances, and [50% of all of you have been] found wanting [by ME and unacceptable to be given eternal life]." Daniel 5:27

Myth—Everybody Gets To Go

Do you remember the story of King Belshazzar? I taught you this story earlier. It is an example of how a human can so offend God that God would literally slay the human. That night this is exactly what God did and he gave Belshazzar's kingdom to the Medes and Persians. You would do well to restudy this story in Daniel if you do not understand that God is weighing all of us on HIS spiritual balance scales. In the three groups that pass under the judgment of Jesus, that is what is being done. It is December 12, 2004 and while out at dinner tonight, I was reviewing the prior pages. God's Spirit came upon me and reminded me of his balance scales and the fact that our nation as a whole and U.S. Christians fit exactly the criteria that Jesus explained. Consider the 50/50 Christian vote. God reminded me that 50% or more of all Christians would actually go to Hell. HE told me it is the simple difference between being lawful or lawless *unto* HIM.

To understand God's perspective, you only need to reconsider a prior verse I cited, 1 John 5:20. Those who can claim Jesus as savior have come to a full understanding of God. Ergo, they believe in God and are doers of HIS Word. Those rejected in-group four (4) as lawless never did receive an understanding of God the FATHER. Ergo, Jesus never knew them.

> "And we know that the Son of God has come and has given
> us an understanding, that we may know HIM who is true;
> and we are in HIM who is true, in HIS Son Jesus Christ.
> This [FATHER] is the true God and eternal life." 1 John 5:20

Myth—Everybody Gets To Go

So the issue of being a Christian is simple. Real Christians have received an understanding of God the FATHER. They are doers of the Word. Those who never received this understanding are declared unknown by Jesus. The issue of Jesus' nations sorting is just as simple even if it is contradictory to orthodox Christian dogma. With Christ, the sorting boils down to those who are righteous and those who are unrighteous. Our nations' own presidential vote exemplifies a nation morally divided along the lines of Heaven and Hell. Therefore, 50% of the general population may go to Heaven and the other 50% to Hell. This fact has nothing to do with going to church or claiming to know Jesus. It has everything to do with just being a "do-gooder" and righteous person. To understand God's reasoning requires you simply understand the Apostle Peter.

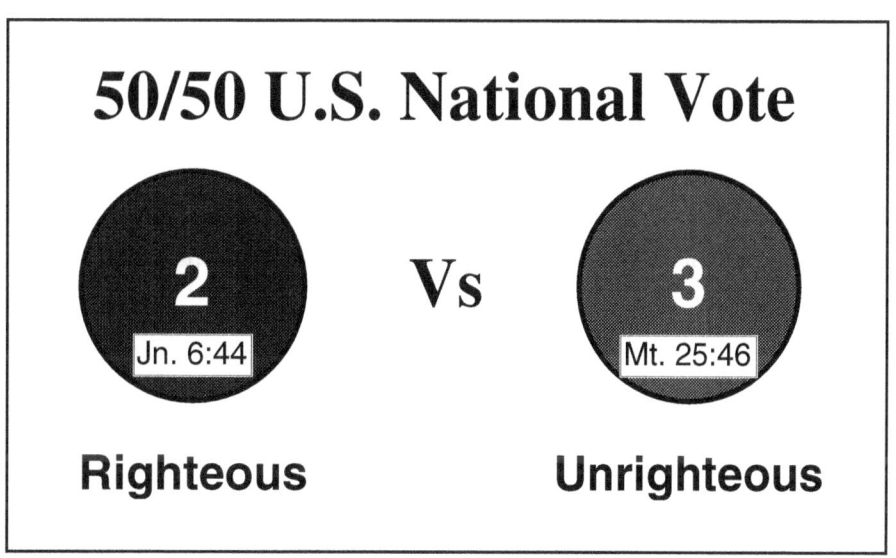

"For the eyes of the LORD are on the righteous, and HIS ears are open to their prayers; but the face of the LORD is against those who do evil." 1 Peter 3:12

"Then Peter opened his mouth and said: 'In truth I perceive that God shows no partiality. But in every nation whoever fears HIM and works righteousness is accepted by HIM.'"
　　　　　　　　　　　　　　　　　　　　Acts 10:34-35

Myth—Everybody Gets To Go

> **"Then Peter began to speak: 'I now realize how true it is that God does not show favoritism but accepts men from every nation who fear Him and do what is right.'"**
> **Acts 10:34-35 NIV**

Do you get the simple message of the Bible concerning salvation? The righteous "do-gooders" who wisely obey God obtain eternal life. The unrighteous "evildoers" are foolish and receive eternal damnation. It isn't about claiming Jesus as Lord, it is about doing what Jesus taught us to do. And what about those who now worship Jesus as their God? Which group are they in? They are part of the lawless group four (4), because they failed the most important commandment of all. "Have no other gods before Me!"

I believe the Qur'an is also a holy book but there are some significant differences with the Holy Bible. Issues such as who Abraham was called on to sacrifice and the issue of Christ's death and resurrection are two of many issues I suspect will be difficult for the religions to bridge an understanding of. However, in the studies I have made of the Qur'an, I found a dialogue between Christ and God worthy of being discussed here. This is because I believe such a dialogue has taken place. Verily I say unto you that many Christian churches have no understanding of God Almighty because they do not worship Him. I bear witness that many churches *now* worship Jesus and in that very act commit idolatry unto God. Why? Consider this dialogue.

> [116]. And behold! Allah [God] will say "O Jesus the son of Mary! Didst thou say unto men 'worship me and my mother as gods in derogation of Allah?' He [Jesus] will say: 'Glory to Thee! Never could I say what I had no right (to say). Had I said such a thing Thou wouldst indeed have known it. Thou knowest what is in my heart though I know not what is in Thine. For Thou knowest in full all that is hidden.' [117]. Never said I to them aught except what Thou didst command me to say to wit 'Worship Allah my Lord and your Lord;' and I was a witness over them whilst I dwelt amongst them; when Thou didst take me up thou wast the Watcher over them and Thou art a Witness to all things.'" Surah 5:116-117 [35]

Myth—Everybody Gets To Go

At least on this point, the Qur'an has it right. We are not supposed to worship anyone other than God Almighty. Jesus' own teachings supports this section of the Qur'an. What will you say to God to explain why you are engaged in idolatry by worshipping Jesus or his mother Mary? How did Christianity devolve into so much apostasy? I don't know, but I do know exactly what is coming down. Jesus explained it all and there exists those people who will listen to the teachings of Jesus and those who will not listen. Don't expect him to know you if you don't know who he is.

> **Then Jesus said to him, "Away with you, Satan! For it is written, 'You shall worship the LORD your God, and HIM only you shall serve.' " Matthew 4:10**

> **"But the hour is coming, and now is, when the true worshipers will worship the FATHER in spirit and truth; for the FATHER is seeking such to worship HIM. God is Spirit, and those who worship HIM must worship in spirit and truth." John 4:23-24**

Yet you say, Edward, people worshipped Jesus in the Bible? So what! Jesus never taught them to worship anyone but God Almighty or in the vernacular of the Qur'an "Allah." Furthermore, Jesus taught us to pray to God, told us that his God was our God and even went so far as to indicate we should stop asking of him [Jesus] and instead ask directly of the FATHER in his name. To honor Jesus, means obeying him. It means worshipping the FATHER, his God and ours. It means asking of the FATHER in Jesus' name. It means praying to God and not to Jesus. The opposite common Christian practices represent idolatry and means that the person committing them has never "received an understanding of HIM who sent Jesus." They did not find "the way" back to God's righteousness, which is the word of God.

> **Jesus said, "And in that day you will ask me nothing. Most assuredly, I say to you, whatever you ask the FATHER in my name HE will give you. Until now you have asked nothing in my name. Ask, and you will receive, that your joy may be full." John 16:23-24**

Myth—Everybody Gets To Go

> **"In that day [I leave earth] you will ask [the FATHER directly] in my name, and I do not say to you that I shall pray [to] the FATHER for you; for the FATHER HIMSELF loves you, because you have loved me, and have believed that I came forth from God. I came forth from the FATHER and have come into the world. [Once] again, I leave the world and go [back] to the FATHER." John 16:26-28**

These are simple teachings of Jesus Christ and he makes seven points crystal clear in these verses of the Holy Bible.

1. You are to go direct to God *now* with all of your petitions.
2. Jesus will not pray the FATHER for you; it is *now* your own duty.
3. Whatever you ask of the FATHER in Jesus' name, believing, you will receive. This assumes you are worshipping God, not Jesus!
4. You receive because in believing Jesus came from God, you have gained an understanding of God and know that Jesus is not God.
5. If you believe Jesus is God, you *still* do not know God or HIS Son.
6. Jesus came from the FATHER, his God and our God.
7. Jesus returned to the FATHER, his God and our God.

Will there be a 50/50 mix of Heaven and Hell bound Christians? I believe that at least 50% of those who refer to themselves as Christian will actually go to Hell. Why? It is simple. In the United States, I bear witness to God that at least 50% of Christians actually support evil in one form or another. I bear witness for God that supposedly good people remain silent and allow our moral values to be compromised. I bear witness for God that the church of HIS Son now has practicing homosexuals and lesbians as both ministers and bishops. The word Christian itself holds little resemblance to the original definition of "followers of Christ." How many get to Heaven, I cannot say. It might be a 20/80 mixture or even a 30/70 mixture. Aside from giving us the "likened to a 50% factor" — Jesus made it clear that only a "few" would find the life, which flows from entering the "narrow gate."

> **Jesus said, "Narrow is the gate and difficult is the way which leads to life, and there are few who find it."**
>
> **Matthew 7:14**

Copyright 2005 Edward G. Palmer, All Rights Reserved.

Book of Edward—Chapter 21

Myth—Everybody Gets To Go

One can hardly think of a 50/50 mix as representing the idea of "many and few" taught by Jesus in Matthew 7:13-14. Many will enter by the wide gate and wind up in Hell. Only a few will enter the narrow gate and obtain life. This teaching of Jesus is similar to the question he poses in Luke 18:8. "When the Son of Man comes, will he really find any faith?" The ideas of being able to "find any faith" and that "only a few find life" are shocking concepts when it comes to eternal life. Both of them are incompatible with 50% of Christians actually gaining entrance to Heaven. Therefore, I believe it will be much worse for Christianity than what is presented in this chapter. Why would that be? Consider for some additional illustration the standards of the Amish as exposed in a recent ABC News special. [36]

The ABC News Magazine 20/20 aired a follow up special on a young Amish woman named Mary who endured a childhood of repeated rape by her brothers. Her mother was made aware of this, but did nothing to stop it. The Amish culture teaches everyone to tell the truth and then to confess his or her sins. After a public confession is made, the church community shuns the sinner for several weeks and then everyone is required to forgive and forget. "Dan Miller, a local Amish bishop, told ABC News that the Byler brothers received the most severe punishment under Amish tradition. Both were banned from church activity for several weeks and made to publicly ask for forgiveness."

"Through the years, by Mary's account, she was raped by several different attackers. But one abused her more often than the others—her brother Johnny. Johnny, one of Mary's eight brothers, began assaulting her when he was 12 and she was 6. The assaults continued into her teen years, she said. I couldn't go to the outhouse because there was always somebody waiting there. I couldn't go anywhere alone."

I relate this story of the Amish, because it illustrates very well the Christian mythology that all should forgive and forget. When does God forgive? After repentance occurs. When one repents, he or she turns the other way and never again does evil. True repentance has not occurred unless the wicked behavior ceases. The Amish like many Christian factions lack the ability to discern and purge evil from among them. *This is evil!*

Myth—Everybody Gets To Go

Christians routinely brush off evil and wickedness under the false belief that they are to endure it through forgiveness and forgetfulness. Yet God has made it clear we are not to condone evil. In Mary's case, she was raped over 100 times by this one brother and over many years. The Amish community imposes a submissive and silent female culture. During the court trial, the Amish community shed tears for the rapist and had no tears for the victim of his rape. The Amish like other Christian factions have their moral values turned upside down. The judge asked the crying Amish crowd, "Where are your tears for Mary?" Indeed, she was the victim of a lifetime of rape. Now, it is she who is shunned because she went outside this closed culture to seek justice and an end to what can only be called torture at the hands of her own community. Christians? Hello. I wonder how God will view the Amish apostasy when we are taught to love our wives like Christ loved the church. The Amish are hypocrites in this instance, because they lack love, charity or honor for the victim. Hypocritical Christianity? Yes!

The Church has many factions that have long since "lost" any pretense of adhering to His Holy Word. Indeed, the few that Jesus says get in through the "narrow gate" may even be 10% or less because of such false beliefs that sanction evil in society instead of getting rid or purging it. So, as God has given me eyes, I bear witness that the church condones and lives with evil, sexual immorality, idolatry, etc. The house of God is in very deep trouble and Peter understood this fact. So do I. Do you?

> **"For the time has come for judgment to begin at the house of God; and if it begins with us first, what will be the end of those who do not obey the gospel of God?" 1 Peter 4:17**

> **And, "If the righteous are barely saved, what chance will the godless and sinners have?" 1 Peter 4:18 NLT**

> **"If the righteous are rewarded here on earth, how much more true that the wicked and the sinner will get what they deserve!" Proverbs 11:31 NLT**

The perverted church doctrines, which allow evil to flourish fits the "hypocrite admonitions" of Jesus.

Myth—Everybody Gets To Go

Christian Church Is Filled With Hypocrites!

Jesus said, "Hypocrites! Well did Isaiah prophesy about you, saying: 'These people draw near to Me with their mouth, and honor Me with their lips, but their heart is far from Me. And in vain they worship Me, teaching as doctrines the commandments of men.' " Matthew 15:7-9

Jesus said, "Hypocrites! You know how to discern the face of the sky, but you cannot discern the signs of the times."
Matthew 16:3

Jesus said, "But woe to you, scribes and Pharisees, hypocrites! For you shut up the kingdom of Heaven against men; for you neither go in yourselves, nor do you allow those who are entering to go in." Matthew 23:13

Jesus said, "Woe to you, scribes and Pharisees, hypocrites! For you devour widows' houses, and for a pretense make long prayers. Therefore you will receive greater condemnation." Matthew 23:14

Jesus said, "Woe to you, scribes and Pharisees, hypocrites! For you travel land and sea to win one proselyte, and when he is won, you make him twice as much a son of Hell as yourselves." Matthew 23:15

Jesus said, "Woe to you, scribes and Pharisees, hypocrites! For you pay tithe of mint and anise and cummin, and have neglected the weightier matters of the law: justice and mercy and faith. These you ought to have done, without leaving the others undone." Matthew 23:23

Jesus said, "Woe to you, scribes and Pharisees, hypocrites! For you cleanse the outside of the cup and dish, but inside they are full of extortion and self-indulgence."
Matthew 23:25

Book of Edward—Chapter 21

Myth—Everybody Gets To Go

> **Jesus said, "Woe to you, scribes and Pharisees, hypocrites! For you are like graves which are not seen, and the men who walk over them are not aware of them." Luke 11:44**

Verily I say unto you that many factions in the Christian Church are filled with hypocrisy of every nature. On the outside they appear to be with God, but on the inside they are with Satan. Indeed, they worship God in vain—because they are not doers of HIS Word. The kingdom of God is something to look forward to for every sincere believer. I certainly do and for good reason. The pain we suffer and endure on this earth is eliminated for the righteous of God. You can be in-group one (1) by getting right with God and HIS Son. By deciding you too will be a doer of HIS Word.

> **"Now I saw a new Heaven and a new earth, for the first Heaven and the first earth had passed away. Also there was no more sea." Rev. 21:1**

> **"And God will wipe away every tear from their eyes; there shall be no more death, nor sorrow, nor crying. There shall be no more pain, for the former things have passed away."**
> **Rev. 21:4**

You Need A Kingdom Focus In Life!

The first thing you should do mentally is to get rid of the idea you go into the ground and get a second chance after this earthly life. This is also Christian mythology. I serve a God of the living, not the dead. This is what Jesus taught us on the subject of the resurrection after our death. These people already died an earthly death, but Jesus says they are the "living."

> **Jesus said, "But concerning the resurrection of the dead, have you not read what was spoken to you by God, saying, 'I am the God of Abraham, the God of Isaac, and the God of Jacob?' God is not the God of the dead, but of the living." Matthew 22:31-32**

Copyright 2005 Edward G. Palmer, All Rights Reserved.

Book of Edward—Chapter 21

Myth—Everybody Gets To Go

Kingdom Requires Repentance!

"From that time Jesus began to preach and to say, 'Repent, for the kingdom of Heaven is at hand.' " Matthew 4:17

Kingdom Belongs To Humble Spirits!

"Blessed are the poor in spirit, for theirs is the kingdom of Heaven." Matthew 5:3

Kingdom Belongs To The Righteous!

"Blessed are those who are persecuted for righteousness' sake, for theirs is the kingdom of Heaven." Matthew 5:10

Kingdom Entry Has A Minimum Righteousness Standard!

"For I say to you, that unless your righteousness exceeds the righteousness of the scribes and Pharisees, you will by no means enter the kingdom of Heaven." Matthew 5:20

Kingdom Belongs To God Almighty, Not Jesus!

Jesus said, "YOUR kingdom come. YOUR will be done. On earth as it is in Heaven." Matthew 6:10

Jesus said, "For YOURS is the kingdom and the power and the glory forever. Amen." Matthew 6:13

First Seek God's Kingdom And HIS Righteousness!

"But seek first the kingdom of God and HIS righteousness, and all these things shall be added to you." Matthew 6:33

Myth—Everybody Gets To Go

Not Everyone Enters Kingdom Of Heaven!
Only those who do the will of the FATHER *enter Heaven!*

> "Not everyone who says to me, 'Lord, Lord,' shall enter the kingdom of Heaven, but he who does the will of my FATHER in Heaven." Matthew 7:21

The Righteous Of All Nations Will Be In Heaven!

> Jesus said, "Assuredly, I say to you, I have not found such great faith, not even in Israel! And I say to you that many will come from east and west, and sit down with Abraham, Isaac, and Jacob in the kingdom of Heaven."
> Matthew 8:10-11

The Unrighteous "Sons" Will Not Be In Heaven!

> Jesus said, "But the sons of the kingdom will be cast out into outer darkness. There will be weeping and gnashing of teeth." Matthew 8:12

Jesus Preached The Gospel Of The Kingdom!

> "Then Jesus went about all the cities and villages, teaching in their synagogues, preaching the gospel of the kingdom, and healing every sickness and every disease among the people." Matthew 9:35

Jesus Commanded We Preach The Kingdom Realities!

> Jesus said, "And as you go, preach, saying, 'The kingdom of Heaven is at hand.' " Matthew 10:7

Copyright 2005 Edward G. Palmer, All Rights Reserved.

Book of Edward—Chapter 21

Myth—Everybody Gets To Go

Everyone In Kingdom Is Greater Than John The Baptist!
Yet, John The Baptist was the greatest human born of a woman!

> "Assuredly, I say to you, among those born of women there has not risen one greater than John the Baptist; but he who is least in the kingdom of Heaven is greater than he."
> Matthew 11:11

Spiritually Violent People Take The Kingdom By Force!

> "And from the days of John the Baptist until now the kingdom of Heaven suffers violence, and the violent take it by force." Matthew 11:12

The Kingdom Of Heaven Is Unified—Not Divided!

> Jesus said, "Every kingdom divided against itself is brought to desolation, and every city or house divided against itself will not stand." Matthew 12:25

Not Everyone Can Understand The Kingdom Mysteries!

> Jesus said, "Because it has been given to you to know the mysteries of the kingdom of Heaven, but to them it has not been given." Matthew 13:11

Satan Snatches Away Loose Kingdom Seeds!

> "When anyone hears the word of the kingdom, and does not understand it, then the wicked one comes and snatches away what was sown in his heart. This is he who received seed by the wayside." Matthew 13:19

Myth—Everybody Gets To Go

Satan Sows Doubt & Corruption About The Kingdom!

> **Jesus said, "The kingdom of Heaven is like a man who sowed good seed in his field; but while men slept, his enemy came and sowed tares among the wheat and went his way."**
> **Matthew 13:24-25**

The Kingdom Is Likened To A Mustard Seed!
The tiny kingdom seed planted in good soil grows strong!

> **Jesus said, "The kingdom of Heaven is like a mustard seed, which a man took and sowed in his field." Matthew 13:31**

The Kingdom Is Likened To Leaven!
The kingdom leaven grows spiritual maturity in the committed heart!

> **Jesus said, "The kingdom of Heaven is like leaven, which a woman took and hid in three measures of meal till it was all leavened." Matthew 13:33**

Jesus Explains The Kingdom Fields, Good Seeds & Tares!

1. Jesus, Son of Man, is *the* sower of good kingdom seeds.
2. Fields represent the world and all of its nations.
3. Good seeds are the sons of the kingdom.
4. Tares [wheat weeds] are the sons of the wicked one [Satan].
5. Satan sowed tare seeds among the good seeds sowed by Jesus.
6. Satan [devil] is the enemy of Jesus' kingdom sowing efforts.
7. Harvest is the end of the age or last days before Jesus returns.
8. Reapers are the angels who accompany Jesus on his return.
9. Tares will be gathered and burned in fire signaling end of this age.
10. Son of Man will send HIS angels to remove all things that are then offensive in HIS kingdom and those who practice lawlessness.

Copyright 2005 Edward G. Palmer, All Rights Reserved.

Book of Edward—Chapter 21

Myth—Everybody Gets To Go

11. Those offensive things removed from the kingdom will be cast into a furnace of fire where there will be wailing and gnashing of teeth.
12. *Then* [at that time] the righteous will shine forth as the sun in the kingdom of their FATHER.

"He who has ears to hear—let him hear!" Matthew 13:37-43

The Kingdom Is Likened To Hidden Treasure!

Jesus said, "Again, the kingdom of Heaven is like treasure hidden in a field, which a man found and hid; and for joy over it he goes and sells all that he has and buys that field."
Matthew 13:44

The Kingdom Is Like A Merchant Seeking Beautiful Pearls!

Jesus said, "Again, the kingdom of Heaven is like a merchant seeking beautiful pearls, who, when he had found one pearl of great price, went and sold all that he had and bought it." Matthew 13:45-46

The Kingdom Is Like A Dragnet Gathering Good & Bad!

Jesus said, "Again, the kingdom of Heaven is like a dragnet that was cast into the sea and gathered some of every kind, which, when it was full, they drew to shore; and they sat down and gathered the good into vessels, but threw the bad away. So it will be at the end of the age. The angels will come forth, separate the wicked from among the just, and cast them into the furnace of fire. There will be wailing and gnashing of teeth." Matthew 13:47-50

The Kingdom Is Like A Householder With Treasures!
Scribes that know the kingdom of God bring forth HIS treasures!

Myth—Everybody Gets To Go

> Jesus said, "Therefore every scribe instructed concerning the kingdom of Heaven is like a householder who brings out of his treasure things new and old." Matthew 13:52

Kingdom Keys Given To Those Who Know Who Jesus Is!
Peter knew Jesus — "You are the Christ, the Son of the living God!"

> Jesus said, "And I will give you the keys of the kingdom of Heaven, and whatever you bind on earth will be bound in Heaven, and whatever you loose on earth will be loosed in Heaven." Matthew 16:19

Kingdom Purged Of Offenders At Time Of Christ's Return!

> Jesus said, "Assuredly, I say to you, there are some standing here who shall not taste death till they see the Son of Man coming in HIS kingdom." Matthew 16:28

Kingdom Entry Requires The Faith Of A Child!

> Jesus said, "Assuredly, I say to you, unless you are converted and become as little children, you will by no means enter the kingdom of Heaven. Therefore whoever humbles himself as this little child is the greatest in the kingdom of Heaven." Matthew 18:3-4

Kingdom Entry Requires Forgiving Those Who Do Repent!

> "Therefore the kingdom of Heaven is like a certain king who wanted to settle accounts with his servants." Matthew 18:23

> "So my heavenly FATHER also will do to you if each of you, from his heart, does not forgive his brother his trespasses."
> Matthew 18:35

Copyright 2005 Edward G. Palmer, All Rights Reserved.

Book of Edward—Chapter 21

Myth—Everybody Gets To Go

Kingdom Has Those Who Chose To Be A Eunuch!

Jesus said, "And there are eunuchs who have made themselves eunuchs for the kingdom of heaven's sake. He who is able to accept it, let him accept it." Matthew 19:12

Kingdom Is Like A Group Of Little Children!

Jesus said, "Let the little children come to me, and do not forbid them; for of such is the kingdom of Heaven."
Matthew 19:14

Kingdom Requires Surrender Of Personal Control!

Jesus said, "Assuredly, I say to you that it is hard for a rich man to enter the kingdom of Heaven. And again I say to you, it is easier for a camel to go through the eye of a needle than for a rich man to enter the kingdom of God."
Matthew 19:23-24

Many Called To Kingdom But Only A Few Chosen!

Jesus said, "For the kingdom of Heaven is like a landowner who went out early in the morning to hire laborers for his vineyard." Matthew 20:1

"Take what is yours and go your way. I wish to give to this last man the same as to you. Is it not lawful for me to do what I wish with my own things? Or is your eye evil because I am good? So the last will be first, and the first last. For many are called, but few chosen." Matthew 20:14-16

Kingdom Receives All Who Are Repentant Of Heart!

Myth—Everybody Gets To Go

> Jesus said, " 'Which of the two did the will of his father?' They said to him, 'The first.' Jesus said to them, 'Assuredly, I say to you that tax collectors and harlots enter the kingdom of God before you [because they received John the Baptist and repented].' " Matthew 21:31

Kingdom Requires That Nation Bears Spiritual Fruit!

> "Therefore I say to you, the kingdom of God will be taken from you and given to a nation bearing the fruits of it."
> Matthew 21:43

Kingdom Likened To A Wedding!
Those who were invited were found not worthy!

> Jesus said, "The kingdom of Heaven is like a certain king who arranged a marriage for his son." Matthew 22:2

Unrighteous Church Leaders Shut Up The Kingdom!

> Jesus said, "But woe to you, scribes and Pharisees, hypocrites! For you shut up the kingdom of Heaven against men; for you neither go in yourselves, nor do you allow those who are entering to go in." Matthew 23:13

Gospel Of Kingdom Will Be Preached In The Entire World!

> Jesus said, "And this gospel of the kingdom will be preached in all the world as a witness to all the nations, and then the end will come." Matthew 24:14

The Kingdom Has A 50% Entry Factor!
Literally 50% of certain groups of people are excluded from Heaven.

Copyright 2005 Edward G. Palmer, All Rights Reserved.

Myth—Everybody Gets To Go

> Jesus said, "Then the kingdom of Heaven shall be likened to ten virgins [five wise and five foolish]." Matthew 25:1

Kingdom Requires Spiritually Profitable Servants!

> Jesus said, "For the kingdom of Heaven is like a man traveling to a far country, who called his own servants and delivered his goods to them." Matthew 25:14

Kingdom Sorts Out And Eliminates Unrighteous People!
Righteous people are rewarded and unrighteous people are condemned!

> Jesus said, "Then the King will say to those on his right hand, 'Come, you blessed of my FATHER, inherit the kingdom prepared for you from the foundation of the world.' " Matthew 25:34

We Will Eat And Drink With Jesus In The Kingdom!

> Jesus said, "But I say to you, I will not drink of this fruit of the vine from now on until that day when I drink it new with you in my FATHER'S kingdom." Matthew 26:29

The Kingdom Of God Is At Hand!
Jesus has fulfilled the time and asks that you repent to enter the kingdom!

> Jesus said, "The time is fulfilled, and the kingdom of God is at hand. Repent, and believe in the gospel [of the kingdom of God]." Mark 1:15

Better To Enter The Kingdom Without A Limb!

> Jesus said, "It is better for you to enter the kingdom of God with one eye, rather than having two eyes, to be cast into Hell fire." Mark 9:47

Myth—Everybody Gets To Go

Jesus' Purpose Was To Preach The Kingdom!
Jesus shifted God's message from the law to the reality of God's kingdom!

> **Jesus said, "I must preach the kingdom of God to the other cities also, because for this purpose I have been sent."**
> **Luke 4:43**

Let The Dead Bury The Dead, You Preach The Kingdom!

> **Jesus said, "Let the dead bury their own dead, but you go and preach the kingdom of God." Luke 9:60**

The Kingdom Is A One-Way Street—Don't Look Back!

> **Jesus said, "No one, having put his hand to the plow, and looking back, is fit for the kingdom of God." Luke 9:62**

It's The FATHER'S Pleasure To Give You The Kingdom!

> **Jesus said, "Do not fear, little flock, for it is your FATHER'S good pleasure to give you the kingdom." Luke 12:32**

People Are "Pressing Into" The Kingdom!
Law and prophets was preached until John the Baptist—Now the kingdom!
John the Baptist was a spiritual dividing line for God!

> **Jesus said, "The law and the prophets were until John. Since that time the kingdom of God has been preached, and everyone is pressing into it." Luke 16:16**

The Kingdom Does Not Come With Visual Observation!

> **"The kingdom of God does not come with observation."**
> **Luke 17:20**

Copyright 2005 Edward G. Palmer, All Rights Reserved.

Book of Edward—Chapter 21

Myth—Everybody Gets To Go

The Kingdom Of God Is Within You!
When your heart chooses God, it activates the kingdom inside of you!

> **"Nor will they say, 'See here!' or 'See there!' For indeed, the kingdom of God is within you." Luke 17:21**

The Kingdom Rewards Those Who Choose To Obey God!

> **Jesus said, "Assuredly, I say to you, there is no one who has left house or parents or brothers or wife or children, for the sake of the kingdom of God, who shall not receive many times more in this present time, and in the age to come eternal life." Luke 18:29-30**

The Kingdom Has Signs—It Is Now Very Close!

> **"So you also, when you see these things happening, know that the kingdom of God is near." Luke 21:31**

You Must Be Born Of The Spirit To Enter The Kingdom!
When your heart sincerely chooses God, you become born of the Spirit!

> **Jesus answered, "Most assuredly, I say to you, unless one is born of water and the Spirit, he cannot enter the kingdom of God." John 3:5**

We Go Through Many Tribulations To Enter The Kingdom!

> **"We must [go] through many tribulations [to] enter the kingdom of God." Acts 14:22**

The Kingdom Of God Is Righteousness, Peace And Joy!
The Spirit manifests the kingdom in righteousness, peace and joy!

Copyright 2005 Edward G. Palmer, All Rights Reserved.

Book of Edward—Chapter 21

Myth—Everybody Gets To Go

> "The kingdom of God is not eating and drinking, but righteousness and peace and joy in the Holy Spirit."
>
> **Romans 14:17**

The Kingdom Is Not In "Words"—But In "Action!"

> "For the kingdom of God is not in word but in power."
>
> **1 Cor. 4:20**

The Kingdom Rejects Categories Of Unrighteous People!

> "Do you not know that the unrighteous will not inherit the kingdom of God? Do not be deceived. Neither fornicators, nor idolaters, nor adulterers, nor homosexuals, nor sodomites, nor thieves, nor covetous, nor drunkards, nor revilers, nor extortioners will inherit the kingdom of God."
>
> **1 Cor. 6:9-10**

Jesus Delivers The Kingdom To God At The End!

> "Then comes the end, when he [Jesus] delivers the kingdom to God the FATHER, when he puts an end to all rule and all authority and power." **1 Cor. 15:24**

Flesh And Blood Cannot Inherit The Kingdom Of God!
Your activated spirit, through a dedicated heart, inherits the kingdom!

> "Now this I say, brethren, that flesh and blood cannot inherit the kingdom of God; nor does corruption inherit incorruption." **1 Cor. 15:50**

Walk Worthy Of God Who Calls You Into HIS Kingdom!

> "That you would walk worthy of God who calls you into HIS own kingdom and glory." **1 Thess. 2:12**

Copyright 2005 Edward G. Palmer, All Rights Reserved.

Myth—Everybody Gets To Go

Be Counted Worthy Of The Kingdom!

> "Which is manifest evidence of the righteous judgment of God, that you may be counted worthy of the kingdom of God, for which you also suffer." 2 Thess. 1:5

The LORD Preserves The Righteous For The Kingdom!

> "And the LORD will deliver me from every evil work and preserve me for HIS heavenly kingdom. To HIM be [the] glory forever and ever. Amen!" 2 Tim. 4:18

Serve God With Reverence And Fear For The Kingdom!
If you've received the kingdom of God, then serve HIM with reverence!

> "Therefore, since we are receiving a kingdom which cannot be shaken, let us have grace, by which we may serve God acceptably with reverence and godly fear." Hebrews 12:28

I have given you highlights on Jesus' kingdom of God and of Heaven teachings. Also are many of Paul's teachings, which mirror those of Jesus. Many of Jesus' cited verses are long parables and it is impractical for me to provide a thorough teaching to you on this subject. It is worthy of an entire book by itself. Still, I have given you the main kernels of truth you need to hear and you are now able to study for yourself the details given in each of the Scripture references.

Why did Jesus preach the kingdom of God? The law and the prophets had become somewhat meaningless teachings and a lot of the spiritual leadership no longer even believed in a resurrection. Christ came back to reinforce two facts. First, God Almighty is real and you should take HIS Word seriously and into your heart. Second, God's kingdom is also real and the righteous will be going there from all nations. And of course, Christ's human sacrifice reconciled "the world" and gave us God's Holy Spirit in abundance for all whose heart is made right with HIM through a choice!

Myth—Everybody Gets To Go

God Created Heaven For Only A Few!

[The angel] answered me and said, "The MOST HIGH made this world for the sake of many, but the world to come for the sake of only a few. But I tell you a parable, Ezra. Just as, when you ask the earth, it will tell you that it provides a large amount of clay from which earthenware is made, but only a little dust from which gold comes, so is the course of the present world. Many have been created, but only a few shall be saved."

[Ezra] answered and said, "then drink your fill of understanding, O my soul, and drink wisdom, O my heart. For not of your own will did you come into the world, and against your will you depart, for you have been given only a short time to live. O LORD above us, grant to your servant that we may pray before YOU, and give us a seed for our heart and cultivation of our understanding so that fruit may be produced, by which every mortal who bears the likeness of a human being may be able to live. For YOU alone exist, and we are a work of YOUR hands, as YOU have declared. And because YOU give life to the body that is now fashioned in the womb, and furnish it with members, what YOU have created is preserved amid fire and water, and for nine months the womb endures your creature that has been created in it. But that which keeps and that which is kept shall both be kept by YOUR keeping. And when the womb gives up again what has been created in it, YOU have commanded that from the members themselves (that is, from the breasts) milk, the fruit of the breasts, should be supplied, so that what has been fashioned may be nourished for a time; and afterwards YOU will still guide it in YOUR mercy. YOU have nurtured it in YOUR righteousness, and instructed it in YOUR law, and reproved it in YOUR wisdom. YOU put it to death as YOUR creation, and make it live as YOUR work. If then YOU will suddenly and quickly destroy what with so great labor was fashioned by YOUR command, to what purpose was it made?"

"And now I will speak out: About all humankind YOU know best; but I will speak about YOUR people, for whom I am grieved, and about YOUR inheritance, for whom I lament, and about Israel, for whom I am sad, and about the seed of Jacob, for whom I am troubled. Therefore I will pray before YOU for myself and for them, for I see the failings of us who inhabit the earth; and now also I have heard of the swiftness of the judgment that is

Copyright 2005 Edward G. Palmer, All Rights Reserved.

Book of Edward—Chapter 21

to come. Therefore hear my voice and understand my words, and I will speak before YOU."

Ezra Prays For Mankind

The beginning of the words of Ezra's prayer, before he was taken up. He said: "O LORD, YOU who inhabit eternity, whose eyes are exalted and whose upper chambers are in the air, whose throne is beyond measure and whose glory is beyond comprehension, before whom the hosts of angels stand trembling and at whose command they are changed to wind and fire, whose word is sure and whose utterances are certain, whose command is strong and whose ordinance is terrible, whose look dries up the depths and whose indignation makes the mountains melt away, and whose truth is established forever — hear, O LORD, the prayer of your servant, and give ear to the petition of your creature; attend to my words. For as long as I live I will speak, and as long as I have understanding I will answer. O do not look on the sins of your people, but on those who serve you in truth. Do not take note of the endeavors of those who act wickedly, but of the endeavors of those who have kept YOUR covenants amid afflictions. Do not think of those who have lived wickedly in YOUR sight, but remember those who have willingly acknowledged that YOU are to be feared. Do not will the destruction of those who have the ways of cattle, but regard those who have gloriously taught your law. Do not be angry with those who are deemed worse than wild animals, but love those who have always put their trust in YOUR glory. For we and our ancestors have passed our lives in ways that bring death; but it is because of us sinners that YOU are called merciful. For if YOU have desired to have pity on us, who have no works of righteousness, then YOU will be called merciful. For the righteous, who have many works laid up with YOU, shall receive their reward in consequence of their own deeds. But what are mortals, that YOU are angry with them; or what is a corruptible race, that YOU are so bitter against it? For in truth there is no one among those who have been born who has not acted wickedly; among those who have existed there is no one who has not done wrong. For in this, O LORD, YOUR righteousness and goodness will be declared, when YOU are merciful to those who have no store of good works."

God Answers Ezra's Petition

Myth—Everybody Gets To Go

God says: "Not all will be saved!"

[God] answered me and said, "Some things you have spoken rightly, and it will turn out according to your words. For indeed I will not concern MYSELF about the fashioning of those who have sinned, or about their death, their judgment, or their destruction; but I will rejoice over the creation of the righteous, over their pilgrimage also, and their salvation, and their receiving their reward. As I have spoken, therefore, so it shall be.

For just as the farmer sows many seeds in the ground and plants a multitude of seedlings, and yet not all that have been sown will come up in due season, and not all that were planted will take root; so also those who have been sown in the world will not all be saved." 2 Esdras 8:1-40 NRSV

I [Ezra] answered and said, "If I have found favor in YOUR sight, let me speak. If the farmer's seed does not come up, because it has not received YOUR rain in due season, or if it has been ruined by too much rain, it perishes. But people, who have been formed by YOUR hands and are called YOUR own image because they are made like YOU, and for whose sake YOU have formed all things—have YOU also made them like the farmer's seed? Surely not, O LORD above! But spare YOUR people and have mercy on YOUR inheritance, for YOU have mercy on YOUR own creation."

"Don't compare yourself to the unrighteous!"

[God] answered me and said, "Things that are present are for those who live now, and things that are future are for those who will live hereafter. For you come far short of being able to love MY creation more than I love it. But you have often compared yourself to the unrighteous. Never do so! But even in this respect you will be praiseworthy before the MOST HIGH, because you have humbled yourself, as is becoming for you, and have not considered yourself to be among the righteous. You will receive the greatest glory, for many miseries will affect those who inhabit the world in the last times, because they have walked in great pride.

Copyright 2005 Edward G. Palmer, All Rights Reserved.

Book of Edward—Chapter 21

Myth—Everybody Gets To Go

But think of your own case, and inquire concerning the glory of those who are like yourself, because it is for you that Paradise is opened, the tree of life is planted, the age to come is prepared, plenty is provided, a city is built, rest is appointed, goodness is established and wisdom perfected beforehand. The root of evil is sealed up from you, illness is banished from you, and death is hidden; Hades has fled and corruption has been forgotten; sorrows have passed away, and in the end the treasure of immortality is made manifest. Therefore do not ask any more questions about the great number of those who perish. For when they had opportunity to choose, they despised the MOST HIGH, and were contemptuous of HIS law, and abandoned HIS ways. Moreover, they have even trampled on his righteous ones, and said in their hearts that there is no God—though they knew well that they must die. For just as the things that I have predicted await you, so the thirst and torment that are prepared await them. For the MOST HIGH did not intend that anyone should be destroyed; but those who were created have themselves defiled the name of HIM who made them, and have been ungrateful to HIM who prepared life for them now. Therefore MY judgment is now drawing near; I have not shown this to all people, but only to you and a few like you."

Then I [Ezra] answered and said, "O LORD, YOU have already shown me a great number of the signs that YOU will do in the last times, but YOU have not shown me when YOU will do them."

Signs Of End Times!

[God] answered me and said, "Measure carefully in your mind, and when you see that some of the predicted signs have occurred, then you will know that it is the very time when the MOST HIGH is about to visit the world that HE has made. So when there shall appear in the world earthquakes, tumult of peoples, intrigues of nations, wavering of leaders, confusion of princes, then you will know that it was of these that the MOST HIGH spoke from the days that were of old, from the beginning. For just as with everything that has occurred in the world, the beginning is evident, and the end manifest; so also are the times of the MOST HIGH: the beginnings are manifest in wonders and mighty works, and the end in penalties and in signs.

Saved By Own Choices!

It shall be that all who will be saved and will be able to escape on account of their works, or on account of the faith by which they have believed, will survive the dangers that have been predicted, and will see MY salvation in MY land and within MY borders, which I have sanctified for MYSELF from the beginning.

Condemned By Own Choices!

Then those who have now abused MY ways shall be amazed, and those who have rejected them with contempt shall live in torments. For as many as did not acknowledge ME in their lifetime, though they received MY benefits, and as many as scorned MY law while they still had freedom, and did not understand but despised it while an opportunity of repentance was still open to them, these must in torment acknowledge it after death.

Therefore, do not continue to be curious about how the ungodly will be punished; but inquire how the righteous will be saved, those to whom the age belongs and for whose sake the age was made."

I [Ezra] answered and said, "I said before, and I say now, and will say it again: there are more who perish than those who will be saved, as a wave is greater than a drop of water."

[God] answered me and said, "As is the field, so is the seed; and as are the flowers, so are the colors; and as is the work, so is the product; and as is the farmer, so is the threshing floor. For there was a time in this age when I was preparing for those who now exist, before the world was made for them to live in, and no one opposed ME then, for no one existed; but now those who have been created in this world, which is supplied both with an unfailing table and an inexhaustible pasture, have become corrupt in their ways. So I considered MY world, and saw that it was lost. I saw that MY earth was in peril because of the devices of those who had come into it. And I saw and spared some with great difficulty, and saved for MYSELF one grape out of a cluster, and one plant out of a great forest."

Myth—Everybody Gets To Go

"So let the multitude perish that has been born in vain, but let MY grape and MY plant be saved, because with much labor I have perfected them." 2 Esdras 8:41-9:22 NRSV

"O LORD, give all who read these words understanding!" Edward

Conclusion

You might have known for a long time that something was amiss and wrong with Christianity. Perhaps you've picked up your Bible and had to put it away, because it conflicted with the pulpit teachings? Secretly, you've wondered what was wrong and what you needed to do about your eternal position with God. Now you know what is wrong with Christianity. You also know what you can do about it. Help your family, friends, church and community get right with God. Start taking a moral stand for HIS truth. It means souls can be saved. Failure to take action can have consequences for your own soul. The basic message of this book is simple. Many Christians are going to Hell. Nothing we can do can stop the mass migration of people towards Hell. However, we can impact those within our sphere of influence about the truth of HIS Word. It starts with recognizing that Jesus is not God.

The first volume of this book was called "Matters Of The Heart" simply because that is how you are going to obtain eternal life. You are going to have to make a choice to engage God and be obedient. It is a choice of the heart because that is where you will find the kingdom of God. The second volume of this book was called "God Does Not Change" and it exposes the mythology of Christianity in regards to the trinity doctrine and the false "mouthing Jesus as Lord" doctrine. You cannot engage God with your heart if you believe that Jesus is God. The third volume of this book was called "Itching Christian Ears" because that is exactly what is happening today. It fulfills prophecy and explains why so many Christians will be found wanting by God. Personally, there is no mystery to me as God has fully explained HIS reasoning in HIS Word. There are only those who refuse to listen to Jesus and those who do listen to him. You can start by reading every word that Jesus spoke in a red letter Bible. It is December 14, 2004. Happy birthday my beloved in Heaven! *PRAYER*: O LORD, have mercy on every soul that reads the words of this book. Open their hearts and minds!

> *WARNING. If you are a minister, teacher or a named Christian that fails to teach people that their earthly behavior has eternal consequences in Heaven or Hell, set your house in order with God. Verily I say unto you, it is those who are obedient to God and HIS morals while on this earth that are the real believers in HIS truth. Only they shall see God's salvation for it is written in the Word, "They did not welcome the truth [of God's morals and righteousness] but refused to love it that they might be saved." 2 Thess. 2:10 AMP*
>
> **"Therefore, whether you eat or drink, or whatever you do, [while on earth] do all to the glory of God." 1 Cor. 10:31**
>
> **"I have found ... a man after MY own heart, who will do all [of] MY [biblical] will [while on earth]." Acts 13:22**
>
> *PRAYER. O LORD GOD, free YOUR people from the apostasy that is rampant in the Christian Church today. Surely, if a minister cannot teach their people to obey YOUR morals while on this earth, they cannot be trusted to teach anything about YOUR Word. They are indeed unfit for anything good and should cease their ministry activities. What should stand true for all concerned is that these false teachers "will perish because they were not lovers of the truth!" Amen.*

"The idea that your earthly behavior has no eternal consequences is a false teaching in factions of the Christian Church. Jesus teaches that 50% + of Christians do not get into Heaven and that a selection process will be used based on earthly behavior. Verily I say that your 'feelings' do not replace your duty of spiritual discernment and *reason*!" The Apostle Edward

If God's Spirit Dwells In Your Heart, Your Spirit-Soul Knows It's A ...

Myth—Everybody Gets To Go

Copyright 2005 Edward G. Palmer, All Rights Reserved.

Book of Edward—Chapter 21

Book of Edward

Epilogue

God awoke me in the middle of my sleep three days after finishing the last chapter. I found myself communicating with God in prayer and spirit. It happens and I've learned to just go with the spiritual flow of the moment. This time, it was a discussion over a song. Was God giving me an epilogue for the book? Yes. Write those words for ME; that's what my spirit heard.

God wants to reassure you that "faith, hope and love" are found in HIS Word. For most of us, life seems like an endless struggle with countless problems and challenges. Even if everything seems to be going quite well on earth, there is always a nagging spiritual feeling that something is not well. In the struggles and despair I have felt in this life, HIS Word has always been the place where I have turned to for hope. I have never failed to find hope when I have turned to HIS Word, not even during Jackie's death.

The beginning of hope starts with a humble heart knowing we serve a mighty God that will extract justice in the end. In that frame of fear you can humbly seek HIS mercy and you will find it. When you find HIS mercy you will also find HIS love and the eternal hope HE offers to all seekers of truth. The single biggest thing missing in Christianity today is the realization that our "earthly behavior has eternal consequences."

This was expressed by the words on a semi truck parked by a local church up town. "Every Body Needs Jesus" — was boldly declared in diagonally large letters spanning the width of the long semi trailer. In those four words lies truth and error. I've already told you that you do need both Jesus and his FATHER at the time of your death. Yet in those four words is the simple message of Christianity that leads many astray and into the wide path that leads to Hell. That is because it is a "Jesus saves" message. Yet I tell you that you need a minimum level of righteousness more than you need the ability to "verbally claim" Christ as savior, with your mouth!

Epilogue

Furthermore, you need to do what Christ told you to do, if you want to claim him as savior. He did not come to earth with a simplistic message of "speak my name" and you're saved. That was not his gospel. Jesus came with a "gospel of the kingdom" message. It was simple, but required action on your part for salvation. Jesus said, "Repent, for the kingdom of God is at hand." Indeed the kingdom is at hand and all who do enter it are repentant souls. The hope that lies for the souls that will enter Heaven is wrapped in action and not words. You'll find the truth of HIS Word in this book, but it is not a substitute for HIS Holy Bible. This book is at best a guide for you to get you back on track with God. It is a guide to surround your hope with the peace and confidence of "being" in HIM, in HIS Son and in doing what they have commanded us to do while on earth. Verily I say unto you there is no peace in "mouthing Jesus" as your savior. Matthew 7:21-23 should dispel that Christian myth.

When you understand your earthly actions have eternal consequences, then you can turn to HIS Word and get the answers you need. This truth is expressed in the song entitled "The Word" by the group "Anointed." You can find this song on the CD titled "Songs From The Book" from Word Music, Inc. © 1999. The CD features various artists and I recommend you get a copy and meditate on all of the songs, especially this one. Indeed, you will find hope in HIS Word and in the truth of needing to be an obedient servant unto God and HIS Son. The song is based on a love chapter verse.

> "There are three things that will endure—faith, hope and love—and the greatest of these is love." 1 Cor. 13:13 NLT

The Word — Anointed
Written by Steve Siler, Steve Crawford, Da'dra Crawford, and Nee-C Walls.

Who am I?
Why am I here?
What can I do, where am I going?
So many doubts
So many fears
Where do I turn to keep on hoping?

Epilogue

The Word is truth the Word is light
It has the power to change your life
Faith, hope, and love is in the Word
When Heaven and earth have passed away
The word of God will remain
And if you take the time to read you'll learn
Whatever you need you can find it in the Word

The world is such
A noisy place
So many things fighting for my attention
I'm overwhelmed
I need some peace
Something to save me from my good intentions
There's got to be
Something more
A place where I can find
What I've been searching for.

The Word is truth the Word is light
It has the power to change your life
Faith, hope, and love is in the Word
When Heaven and earth have passed away
The word of God will remain
And if you take the time to read you'll learn
Whatever you need you can find it in the Word

We all need some direction
Illumination for the winding road
There is food for the soul
It's the place you need to go, it's the Word.

The Word is truth the Word is light
It has the power to change your life
Faith, hope, and love is in the Word
When Heaven and earth have passed away
The word of God will remain
And if you take the time to read you'll learn
Whatever you need you can find it in the Word [Amen!]

Copyright 2005 Edward G. Palmer, All Rights Reserved.

Epilogue

Indeed, you will find whatever you need in HIS Word, but you need to approach it with a committed and humble heart. Christianity has distorted the message of Jesus Christ. He demanded that you "repent" and return to behavior that is consistent with being "righteous" in God's eyes. Why? He gave you the answer. The kingdom of God is at hand. Always shine your light and show that you belong to Jesus and his God. Your own "light" is what Jesus will look for when he returns. Will he find your light shining?

Christ did not come here to give us a pass on God's requirement of being a good person. In my lifetime, I have watched the church distort and pervert Jesus Christ's teachings to the point where an estimated 50-80% of Christians no longer recognize that God *will* hold them accountable for their earthly behavior in spite of claims they belong to Jesus. These people have been duped by a perverted "Jesus saves" message, which distorts our need for repentance. What is true repentance? The answer is in chapters 1-7.

For those who understand the truth of what Jesus taught, there is hope for an eternal rest in the kingdom of God that was prepared [by God] *only* for the righteous from the beginning of time. It's now time for all Christians to "get real" with God and to return to HIS righteousness! But the clock is ticking and indeed the time is short. HE hasn't changed! You need to be a "light" shining in a dark world if you actually want to enter the kingdom of God. Your *hope* in God is only genuine and real when you keep your light shining at all times for HIM. And your *understanding* of God is genuine and real only when you stand firm on HIS Word and not on man-made doctrine.

When God defines something, like the tithe in Deut. 14:22-29, you cannot redefine it for the benefit of your ministry or to rationalize your own belief system. Jesus said, "Why do you break God's commandment in the interest of your [money] tradition?" [Matthew 15:3 REB] And in verse 14, "Let them alone. They are the blind leaders of the blind." To be a part of HIS kingdom, you *have* to embrace HIS truth; the Word *must* take priority over church doctrine or you are lost. May God bless your eternal soul!

Yours in Christ Jesus *and* in his FATHER — OUR GOD,

The Apostle Edward

Book of Edward

Volume III
Notes & Bibliography

Forward section notes are located in the back of Volume I and in Volume IV Appendix H.

Chapter 15

1 — (p504) Ibid.

2 — (p509) Ibid.

3 — (p524) Ibid.

4 — (p542) Vitamin B17 links for cancer related information are on the Internet at http://www.informcentral.org.

5 — (p542) Dr. David Williams Daily Advantage product can be purchased on the Internet at http://www.drdavidwilliams.com.

Chapter 16

1 — (p557) Article was published in the Elk River Star News, Elk River, MN circa 1991.

2 — (p600) Comment: George Orwell's well known book titled "1984" dealt with a perceived evil in the form of double speak. Nothing was what it appeared to be. Hence, euphemistic language would be substituted for the evil reality. Instead of the phrase "let's kill babies" — one might use the terminology "let's be pro choice." Indeed, the Orwellian vision of double-speak has materialized and is widely used in the United States. Matthews

could preach a lesson on righteousness, while at the same time actually be engaged in wickedness. It was just another application of double-speak.

3 — (p608) Jim Kaseman's AFCM is located at http://www.jkmafcm.org.

4 — (p608) Ibid.

5 — (p609) Ibid.

Chapter 17

1 — (p617) (1991) Johnson, David and VanVoderen, Jeff. *The Subtle Power of Spiritual Abuse*. Minneapolis, Minnesota: Bethany House Publishers. <u>Comment</u>: This is an excellent book that explains what is happening in spiritually abusive churches and what you can do about it.

2 — (p654) Ibid.

3 — (p655) Ibid.

4 — (p661) (1989) Martin, Ernest. *The Tithing Dilemma*. Portland, Oregon: ASK Publications. Online at http://www.askelm.com.

5 — (p661) *The Tithing Dilemma, page 33*.

6 — (p662) *The Tithing Dilemma, page 7*.

7 — (p662) *The Tithing Dilemma, page 13*.

8 — (p662) *The Tithing Dilemma, page 14*.

9 — (p663) *The Tithing Dilemma, page 25*.

10 — (p663) *The Tithing Dilemma, page 26*.

11 — (p664) *The Tithing Dilemma, page 32*.

Notes & Bibliography - Volume III

12 — (p674) <u>Comment</u>: Religious organizations are officially recognized by the U.S. government and their gifts and donations are then deemed tax deductible gifts if they register with the IRS and declare themselves to be a 501 (c) (3) corporation. As part of IRS Section 501, these corporations and religious organizations must forgo any actions or statements regarding political candidates or parties. Thus, the government muzzles the church in the guise of allowing you to deduct your offerings on the tax form. Hello. What is wrong with that picture? Not surprising, there are many churches arising that refuse to go along with this. It is an interference in religious freedom and unconstitutional.

Chapter 18

1 — (p681) Information on the market for fetal body parts can be found at http://www.letusreason.org/Curren12.htm. The market for "extracted body parts" is greater than for just the fetus as an "unprocessed specimen."

Fetal Body Part	Body Part Value
Unprocessed Specimen (8 weeks)	$70.00
Livers (8 weeks)	$15.00
Brains (8 weeks)	$999.00
Brains (8 weeks) – If fragmented	$667.00
Bone Marrow (8 weeks)	$250.00
Ears (8 weeks)	$75.00
Eyes (8 weeks)	$75.00
Pituitary Gland	$300.00
Spinal Cord	$325.00

The above table of fetal body part values is from the identified link. Given the strong interest in embryonic stem cell research and other areas of fetal research, I believe this data to be valid and if anything will represent outdated low valuations too soon. Do you think the baby boom generation's quest for a fountain of youth is fueling some of the fetal parts research? Do you think a 16 or 24-week specimen is more valuable than an 8-week fetus? My guess is the answer to both questions is yes. Does this outrage you? If not, why doesn't it?

Notes & Bibliography - Volume III

2 — (p682) Byatt, A.S. (Novel). Hwang, David Henry (Screenplay). The 2002 movie is called *Possession* and stars actors Gwyneth Paltrow and Aaron Eckhart. Information is online at http://www.imdb.com/tt0256276/.

3 — (p688) Eastland, Larry L. (June 28, 2004) *The Empty Cradle Will Rock*. This article appeared online at the Wall Street Journal editorial page and was published in the June 2004 issue of *The American Spectator*. The study showed statistics on how abortion is costing the Democrats voters - literally. It is the first political study of *The Roe Effect* that I have read. Mr. Eastland is managing director of LEA Management Group LLC, a public policy research organization. The tables and information contained in this book were obtained from the Wall Street Journal's Online Opinion Edition published at http://www.opinionjournal.com/extra?id=110005277.

4 — (p693) *Merriam-Webster's 11th Collegiate Dictionary*. Version 3.0 of the software was used for the definitions supplied.

5 — (p696) Hill, Napoleon (1979) *The Law of Success (4th Edition) (Chapter 7)*, Success Unlimited Edition, Success Unlimited, Inc., Chicago, Illinois.

6 — (p699) Data on the names of the framers of the Constitution obtained on the Internet at http://www.usconstitution.net/constframedata.html.

7 — (p700) Jacoby, Susan (2004) *Freethinkers*. New York, New York, Metropolitan Books, Henry Holt and Company LLC.

8 — (p700) The Virginia Constitution found on the Internet at the following address. Http://www.nhinet.org/ccs/docs/va-1776.htm.

9 — (p704) *Eclipse of Reason* (1993). "27-minute video produced by former abortionist Bernard Nathanson, M.D. This video documents the termination of a baby boy at five months gestation, as seen by a camera inside the mother's uterus. Charlton Heston introduces the documentary that is sure to ignite the fires of outrage." Note: Descriptive text shown above found at http://shop.store.yahoo.com/americanlifeleague/ecofreasvid.html where the video can be purchase. Since I first viewed this video, little has

Notes & Bibliography - Volume III

changed in the nature of abortion politics. That is because too many people remain ignorant of the truth of abortion.

10 — (p705) George R. Tiller clinic located in Wichita, Kansas specializes in late term abortions. Material required by Kansas' "Woman's Right to Know" law is presented at http://www.drtiller.com. Along with the detailed descriptions provided in this book, side-by-side ultrasound photos of the baby at each stage of its development are presented. Detailed information on abortion methods and their medical complications for women are also presented. According to Tom Barrett, who publishes an email newsletter from newsletters@conservativetruth.org, George Tiller is an unabashed abortionist who celebrated Roe v. Wade's 30th anniversary in 2003 by giving away free abortions. Mr. Tiller attends the "Reformation Lutheran Church" in Wichita according to the newsletter. It is a testimony of the lack of respect within various churches for the sanctity of life and its CREATOR.

11 — (p709) Abortion info mega site http://www.abortionfacts.com.

12 — (p709) Abortion info mega site http://www.abortiontv.com.

13 — (p710) Campbell, Stuart (2004), *Scans Uncover Secrets of The Womb*. Found at BBC News World Edition on the Internet at the following link. http://news.bbc.co.uk/2/hi/health/3846525.stm.

14 — (p711) Nova (1999) WGBH Boston Video, *The Miracle of Life*, Boston, Massachusetts. Run time 60 minutes. Product information can be found at Amazon.com and other Internet sites.

15 — (p716) Internet baby picture showing tiny baby held in a doctor's hands. Source is http://www.jesusfolk.com/images/BABY.jpg.

16 — (p716-17) Internet baby picture shows spina bifida surgery on Baby Samuel Armas at 23 weeks gestation. Samuel Armas was born later and is doing fine and the extraordinary picture taken has been circulated around the globe. Additional information on Samuel Adams can be found on the Internet at: http://www.tennessean.com/sii/00/01/09/vandyfetal09.shtml. The *Tennessean* first published the photo of Samuel holding the surgeon's finger. The surgeon removed Samuel's hand from the womb to reposition

Notes & Bibliography - Volume III

him for surgery. Spina bifida caused an opening in Samuel's spine, which was then sown shut. Surgery was at the Vanderbilt University Medical Center.

17 — (p719) PETA is the organization of People for the Ethical Treatment of Animals. This organization seeks legislative rights for animals and will revert to violent and destructive actions when they cannot get their way. They clearly believe that animals have a greater right to life than fetuses.

18 — (p720) Amy Richards as told to Amy Barrett (2004). *When One Is Enough.* New York, NY: The New York Times. Article dated July 18, 2004 found online at www.nytimes.com. Commentary and discussion postings found online at www.freerepublic.com.

19 — (p722) Dr. David C. Reardon, Julie Makimaa, & Amy Sobie (2000). *Victims and Victors: Speaking Out About Their Pregnancies, Abortions, and Children Resulting from Sexual Assault.* Acorn Publishing. Found online at http://www.afterabortion.info/Victims.html.

20 — (p722) The Internet site at http://www.afterabortion.info is dedicated to after abortion facts and healing information. Women and their experiences are documenting the real truth about the effects of abortion.

21 — (p728) Article found online at a Kissimmee, Florida Local10 News Internet site. http://www.local10.com/print/3596258/detail.html?use=print. *Teen Gets 50 Years For Sexually Assaulting Girl, 10.*

22-24 (p731-32) Ibid. *Stone's Tanach* page 19 and its footnotes.

25 — (p732) Ibid. *Jewish Study Bible* page 25 footnotes.

26 — (p732) Ibid. The *Talmud* is the authoritative body of Jewish tradition comprising the Mishnah and Gemara.

27 — (p733) Note: Reverend Paul Chaim Benedicta Schenck email letter to Dean Mattila dated July 29, 2004 in reply to question on Genesis 9:6.

Copyright 2005 Edward G. Palmer, All Rights Reserved.

Book of Edward—Notes

Notes & Bibliography - Volume III

28 — (p735) Ibid. Chapter 6, p121.

29 — (p736) Enoch text as found online at Project Timothy. Full Internet address is http://www.projecttimothy.org/book_of_enoch_section_2.htm. The text of the fifth fallen angel teaching mankind to kill the embryo in the womb is found in Richard Laurence's *The Book of Enoch The Prophet* in one chapter earlier than what is shown at the above link [chapter 68 v 69].

30 — (p736) The different chapters and verse references in the two versions of the Book of Enoch reflect different numbering sequences and language nuances. However, both translations contain the same message that the fifth fallen angel Kasyade taught mankind how to kill the embryo in the womb.

31 — (p737) Internet baby picture showing 6-week old fetus. Source is the following: http://abortiontv.com/images/Unborn6Weeks.JPG.

32 — (p738) Hutchinson (2004) Story can be found at http://www.kstp.com. *Doctors Struggle To help Tiny Baby.* Cindy Anderson and Gabriel's story was aired on KSTP-TV on July 28, 2004 at 11:30 a.m.

33 — (p742) The present quote and some Bible references were obtained online at http://www.gospeloflife.net/articles/bible.htm. This site documents Scripture references showing, "The bible teaches that the child in the womb is truly a human child, who even has a relationship with the LORD." Go to site for additional teachings on the subject of life from a Bible perspective.

34 — (p745) Stern, David H. (1998). *Complete Jewish Bible.* Clarksville, Maryland: Jewish New Testament Publications, Inc.

35 — (p746) This exegesis commentary on Exodus 21:22-25 was found at http://www.pilgrimluth.com/library/Abortion_And_The_Bible.htm.

Chapter 19

1 — (p757) Ibid.

2 — (p760) Quote found at http://www.wisdomquotes.com/001422.html.

Notes & Bibliography - Volume III

3 — (p764) M.S. Word 2001 Dictionary

4 — (p766) From Earl Nightingale's success tape series found at Nightingale-Conant online.

5 — (p771) de Becker, Gavin (1997) *The Gift of Fear.* New York, New York: Little, Brown and Company.

6 — (p773) Article titled: "*A New Kind of Spin the Bottle*" accessed at http://www.oprah.com/pastshows/tows_2002/tows_past20020507_b.jhtml on August 17, 2004.

7 — (p774) Article titled: "*Swaggert Sorry for Remark on 'Killing' Gays*" accessed at http://www.foxnews.com on September 22, 2004.

8 — (p778) Tavis Smiley Show, PBS tpt 17 in Minneapolis-St. Paul on August 26, 2004 at 11:53 p.m. *Interview with Bill Maher.*

9 — (p785) Penner, Clifford and Joyce (1981) *The Gift of Sex.* Dallas, Texas: Word Publishing.

10 — (p787) Rate movies at http://movielens.umn.edu/ on the Internet and learn what your real movie preferences are. This is a University of Minnesota study that encompasses a predictive model. The more movies you rate, the more accurate Movielens will predict whether or not you'll like a movie listed on its site that you have not seen. Links to the Internet Movie Database are present to assist you in your movie analysis. The site is highly predictive for the most part.

11 — (p792) "*Homosexual S&M part of Christianity?*" Worldnetdaily.com article posted October 8, 2004 cites perverted sexual presentations scheduled for the American Academy of Religion's 2004 (AAR) Annual Meeting in San Antonio. "Two workshops on the sexual themes are being offered by the *Gay Men's Issues in Religion Group.*" One paper is titled: "Ecstatic Communion: The Spiritual Dimensions of Leathersexuality." In its abstract, author Justin Tanis of Metropolitan Community Church writes: "All of this [is] based within the framework of a belief in the rights of individuals to

Notes & Bibliography - Volume III

erotic self-determination with other consenting adults, rather than apologetics for those practices and lives." The article was accessed at http://www.worldnetdaily.com/news/printer-friendly.asp?ARTICLE_ID=40813 on October 8, 2004. In addition to the many presentations that try to rationalize sexual immorality for Christians, you'd be surprised at who supports the AAR and their efforts. According to the article, the "AAR says it has received support from a number of foundations, including the Lilly Endowment, Inc., The National Endowment for the Humanities, the Henry Luce Foundation, the Booth Ferris Foundation, the William and Flora Hewlett Foundation, and the Fund for the Improvement of Postsecondary Education." AAR is an "organization for professors of religion ... with more than 7,500 scholars expected to gather to share research and collaborate on projects." Indeed, there is a distinct difference between such groups and true believers. Think about it long enough and you'll realize why God and Jesus both said: "They worship me in vain!" Especially Ken Stone of Chicago Theological Seminary who claims that Jeremiah 20:7-18 "can be construed more usefully as a kind of S/M encounter." Hello!

12 — (p793) *Hot Showers #7* is a *Hustler video,* produced by Larry Flynt. This pornography video is readily available in adult video stores or for purchase on the Internet. The video has graphic and lurid depictions of women having sex with other women. This is unsuitable viewing for all, but it is an illustration of what I would classify as a "visual" instructional video for the indoctrination of confused teenage females into the immoral realm of lesbianism. There are equally offensive videos on the shelf or Internet for the indoctrination of confused teenage males into homosexuality.

13 — (p794) *In the Cut (2003)*, directed by Jane Campion and starring Meg Ryan and Mark Ruffalo. This is soft-core pornography that couples Meg Ryan in graphic and nude sex acts along with brutal violence in the killing of women. This is unsuitable viewing for all, but it is an illustration of the way that soft-core porn movies are infiltrating the "family" video stores. Stars with name recognition are coupled with graphic sex into a lame movie plot without any redeeming social value. This movie is an example of lascivious behavior on the part of everyone involved.

Notes & Bibliography - Volume III

14 — (p797) Headline reads: *"Muslim cleric wants women of mass destruction,"* (October 9, 2004) Worldnetdaily.com. "Radical cleric Abu Hamza al-Masri is heard urging Muslim women to breed children for the purpose of creating suicide bombers. — This kind of women, when they miss their killed children, they don't go and look for their graves ... they look for their position in paradise, so they become more happy, more anxious to go and see them, they want to sacrifice more and more." The fact is many Muslim clerics and mullahs are not just silent on the issue of mass murder, they are outright advocates of such evil. The Qur'an recognizes Jesus as a prophet and nothing in the Qur'an will save these people from the *woe* Jesus says is coming their way in Matthew 18:6-7. Nothing in the Qur'an alters the condemnation that God imputes to murderers in Rev 21:8.

15 — (p799) Premier Internet merchant at http://www.amazon.com.

16 — (p801) Premier Internet search engine at http://www.google.com.

17 — (p801) As of October 2004, Google did not have a password feature to their search preferences. One should wonder why this is since it is an easy technology to implement. Perhaps it is too easily defeated without setting up a formal user account. In any case, until some viable password methodology is deployed at Google, parents should be aware of the danger of sexually immoral material and the impact it will have on their children.

18 — (p803, 806) Fancher, Bill (2002) *"White Collar Smut Peddlers' Subject of Pro-Family Report."* Article found at http://www.agapepress.org/archive/ 10/afa/312002e.asp and was accessed on October 7, 2004.

19 — (p804) Burress, Phil (2003), *"It's Not a Privacy Issue!"* Article found at http://www.family.org/cforum/os/p_friendly.cfm?articleurl=/cforum/fosi/pornography/ljaei/a0029600.cfm, which was accessed on October 7, 2004. Burress provides a legal brief on why the distribution of pornography is not protected by the laws even if private use in the home is protected. He lists some of the stats of blue-chip corporation profits.

Notes & Bibliography - Volume III

20 — (p804) Clark, Michael D. (2002), *"CCV Scrutinizes movies at 174 hotels."* Cincinnati, Ohio: The Cincinnati Enquirer. Article found at http://www.enquirer.com/editions/2002/12/17/loc_ccvhotelsurvey17.html and accessed on October 7, 2004.

21 — (p804) The CCV group is sponsoring www.cleanhotels.com "to reward hotels who have chosen not to get involved in the pornography business," according to Phil Burress. On October 7, 2004, the site was not operational and was still being built.

22 — (p806) Associated Press (2004), *"China Offers Rewards for Reporting Porn."* The article states: "China encourages Internet use for education and business but bans sexually oriented content on its own Web sites and tries to block access to foreign sites deemed pornographic or subversive." The article went on to say that China's police ministry offers rewards of up to $240 to people who report such web sites. Comment: It is strange that a communist country realizes the social strain of sexual immorality, but a country like the United States founded on moral grounds does not.

23 — (p806) Ibid.

24 — (p806-807) Ibid.

25 — (p810) Parker, Laurie (2004), *"Church Sign Says God Hates."* Article found at http://www.whnt19.com/global/story.asp?/s=2403511&ClientType=Printable. Accessed on October 9, 2004. WHNT News 19 Channel article describes a sign in front of the St. Luke Missionary Baptist Church, which is close to the Metropolitan Community Church in Huntsville, a predominantly Gay congregation just down the road from the former.

26 — (p813) Ibid. *The Gift of Sex (p230).*

27 — (p815) London, England (2004). *"Study: One in 100 adults asexual."* A survey by Anthony Bogaert, a psychologist and human sexuality expert at Brock University in St. Catherines, Ontario conducted the study and found an estimated 1% of the people to be asexual and not interested in sex. He also stated the there was a 3% homosexual population.

Copyright 2005 Edward G. Palmer, All Rights Reserved.

Notes & Bibliography - Volume III

28 — (p816) Thompson, Jenny (2004) *"Men: Is medicine turning you into a woman?"* Health Science Institute Newsletter. To subscribe to this free premier newsletter, email HSIResearch@healthiernews.com. Author describes Dr. Sear's discoveries that men are in a "vicious cycle of decreasing testosterone and increasing estrogen. You start to look and feel more like a woman but your mind, your culture, still expect you to be a man." The evidence is in and males are having serious hormone issues and this may be one factor in the confused sexual state of males and females.

29 — (p819) Mackinnon, Grace (2004). *"Masturbation: Mortal Sin?"* Found online at http://catholiceducation.org/articles/religion/rre0706.html. Article was accessed on 9/11/04. Writer cites the Catechism of the Catholic Church (CCC# 2352) as a reference source. "Both the Magisterium of the Church, in the course of constant tradition, and the moral sense of the faithful have been in no doubt and have firmly maintained that masturbation is an intrinsically and gravely disordered action."

30 — (p822) Fox, Douglas (2003). Adelaide, Australia. *"Masturbating may protect against prostate cancer."* Article accessed on 9/11/2004 and found at http://www.newscientist.com/news/print.jsp?id=ns99993942.

31 — (p824-825) Johanson, Sue (2004). Provides sex education devoid of spiritual aspects but takes care to invoke sanitation issues of health. Teaches masturbation is acceptable and has instructional lessons on line for a variety of sex topics. Http://www.milkandcookies.com/print.php?sid=1861 is an explanation for women on how to perform oral sex. This Canadian sex therapist is featured prominently on the Oxygen woman's cable network and has a regular show called "Sex Talk With Sue." Caution: graphic dialogue.
32 — (p825) Ibid. *The Gift of Sex (p230-236).*

33 — (p825) Male masturbation is taught at http://www.jackinworld.com.

34 — (p825) Female masturbation is taught at http://www.clitical.com.

35 — (p826) Ibid. *The Gift of Sex (p73).*

Copyright 2005 Edward G. Palmer, All Rights Reserved.

Book of Edward—Notes

Notes & Bibliography - Volume III

36 — (p828) Ibid. *The Gift of Sex (p227-230)*. Note: Penners used the NIV, NASB and LIV Bibles.

37 — (p829) Ibid. *The Gift of Sex (p229)*.

38 — (p832) Boston.com (2004) *"Couple allegedly has sex at the Alamo."* Article at http://www.boston.com/news/nation/articles/2004/10/11/couple_alledgedly_have_sex_at_the_alamo?mode=PF accessed on 10/11/2004. "The [police] report said Kristine Nissel, 18, and Matthew Hotard, 19, were partially clad when the officer apprehended them after several tourists watched the couple and became upset. The pair, both active-duty members of the 232nd Medical Battalion stationed at Fort Sam Houston, was charged with public lewdness ... Bond was set for each at $800."

39 — (p832) Fox News Join the Debate. (2004) *"Streaker Shock."* Article at http://www.foxnews.com/printer_friendly_story/0,3566,77925,00.html and accessed on 10/16/2004. "In response to being banned from his graduation ceremonies, one Pennsylvania high school student chose to wear his birthday suit instead of his cap and gown. Now the teen faces six months to two years of jail time for his streaking stunt."

40 — (p832) WBOC-TV16 (2004). *"Old school days long gone, but not forgotten; Congressman's streaking stunt exposed."* Article accessed on 10/12/2004 and found at http://www.wboc.com/global/story.asp?=2416017&ClientType=Printable. Article states, "Democrats are circulating old newspaper clippings of a 1974 college streaking stunt staged by hundreds of students at what was then called Southwest Texas State University."

41 — (p832) Real Cancun, The (2003). Genre: Documentary per Imdb.com.

42 — (p833) Baker, Andrew R. (2000). *"Cohabitation fails as test for marriage."* Found at http://www.catholic.net/rcc/Periodicals/HPR/May00/marriage.html and accessed on 9/10/2004. Author cites the many studies that show cohabitation is problematic and even a prelude to later marriage failure. "A University of Wisconsin survey found that marriages preceded by living together have a 50% higher disruption rate (divorce or separation) that marriages without premarital cohabitation."

Notes & Bibliography - Volume III

43 — (p834, 842) National Marriage Project (2002). *"The Second Edition of Should We Live Together."* Found online at http//marriage.rutgers.edu/Publications/SWLT@%20TEXT.htm and accessed on 9/10/2004. Among a long list of citations, the study points out "No positive contribution of cohabitation to marriage has ever been found."

44 — (p836) Ibid. Merriam-Webster.

45 — (p841) Males experiencing sexual complications and or ED (erectile dysfunction) can find natural remedies from Dr. Al Sears, M.D. a specialist in male health. You can find information at http://www.vitalmax.com or call the toll free number 800-815-5151 valid as of October 21, 2004. In fact there are many sources of alternative medicine approaches to this issue that are a lot safer that taken prescription drugs that increase nitric oxide levels.

46 — (p846) Ibid. Strong'S Concordance.

47 — (p849) CBSNEWS.com (2004). *"Rosie To Marry Girlfriend."* Article found at http://www.cbsnews.com/stories/2004/02/26/entertainment/printable602385.shtml and accessed on 2/26/04. Discusses Rosie O'Donnell's opinion of Gay marriage of which she is an advocate and her plans to marry her longtime girlfriend Kelli Carpenter.

48 — (p850) U.S. Census Bureau (2003). *"Married-Couple and Unmarried-Partner Households: 2000."* The full report can be accessed online at the Census Bureau site located at http://www.census.gov. Data from the 2000 Census clearly pegs the Gay population at 1% or less.

49 — (p850) Meredith, J. L. (1980). *Meredith's Book of Bible Lists (p176).* Minneapolis: Bethany Fellowship, Inc. Bible references are from the King James Version.

50 — (p851) Ibid. U.S. Census Bureau Data

51 — (p853) Ibid.

Notes & Bibliography - Volume III

52 — (p854) ABC NEWS (2004). *"Primetime Live Poll: American Sex Survey."* Online at http://abcnews.go.com/Primetime/print?id=156921 and accessed on 10/22/2004.

53 — (p854) CBS NEWS (2004). *"For Teens, Sex & Drugs Go Together."* Online at http://www.cbsnews.com/stories/2004/08/19/national/printable 637118.shtml and accessed on 8/19/2004.

54 — (p855) MIRROR.CO.UK (2004). *"Girl, 12, Blamed by Judge for Sex Attack."* Online at http://www.mirror.co.uk/printable_version?method= printable_version_mirror&objectid=14615774&sitrid=50143 and accessed on 8/25/2004.

55 — (p855) FOX NEWS (2004). *"On Breastfeeding, Rights and Good Manners."* Online at http://www.foxnews.com/printer_friendly_story/0, 3566,129908,00.html and accessed on 8/25/2004.

56 — (p856) WorldNetDaily (2004*). "Aborted baby's head left inside woman."* Online at http://www.worldnetdaily.com/news/printer-friendly.asp ?ARTICLE_ID=40024.

57 — (p857) IRISH EXAMINER (2004). *"Bishop: Anglican Church may be beyond repair."* Online at http://www.irishexaminer.com/breaking/ email/printer.asp?j=120021412&p=yzxxzzyy8&n=120022172&x= and accessed on 10/8/2004. Article discusses the Anglican Church split caused by the U.S. Episcopal branch ordaining an active Gay bishop.

58 — (p857) FOX NEWS (2004). *"Anglican Panel Blasts Episcopal Church for Gay Stance."* Online at http://www.foxnews.com/printer _friendly_story/0,3566,135724,00.html and accessed on 10/18/2004. Article states, "Worldwide, Anglican conservatives are heavily in the majority. A 1998 conference of all Anglican bishops declared Gay practices 'incompatible with Scripture' and opposed Gay ordinations and same-sex blessings in a 526-70 vote with 45 abstentions."

59 — (p858) FOX NEWS (2004). *"Housewives Too Hot for Advertisers."* Online at http://www.foxnews.com/printer_friendly_story/0,3566,135873,

Notes & Bibliography - Volume III

00.html and accessed on 10/19/2004. Describes how ABC's "Desperate Housewives" have crossed the decency threshold because of racy content and the fact that advertisers are pulling away from supporting the show.

60 — (p858) Medical News Today (2004). *"Sexually Transmitted Infections continue to increase during 2003 in UK."* Accessed on 7/27/2004 and found at http://www.medicalnewstoday.com/printerfriendlynews.php?/newsid=11335.

61 — (p858) The Desert Sun (2004). *"Not a simple answer for desert's syphilis problem."* Online at http://www.thedesertsun.com/news/stories/2004/health/20041003031904.shtml and accessed on 10/4/2004. Article describes the syphilis epidemic in Palm Spring, California and states it is the highest of any city in the U.S.

62 — (p859) WIRED (2004). *"Google vs. Evil."* Accessed on 10/7/2004 and online at http://www.wired.com/wired/archive/11.01/google_pr.html. Article discusses the moral compromises Google's founders find they are in trying to resolve the corporate core value statement of "Don't be evil." An estimated 80% of all Internet searches are now done by Google. Therefore, for the moment, its search technology is now foundational to the Internet.

63 — (p860) Ibid. *Today's Dictionary of The Bible (p35).*

64 — (p861) Ibid. *Today's Dictionary of The Bible (p428).*

65 — (p863) Ibid. *Meredith's Book of Bible Lists (p177).*

66 — (p877) Ibid. *The Gift of Sex (p78-80).*

67 — (p877) White, Barry -song. *"Can't Get Enough Of Your Love, Babe."* Lyrics and music can be found online at http://www.lyricsondemand.com.

68 — (p879) *The Gift of Sex* (p79) Note: "Helen Singer Kaplan, *The New Sex Therapy* (New York: Brunner/Mazel, 1974), pp. 13-15."

Notes & Bibliography - Volume III

69 — (p879) Carmen, Eric –song. *"Make Me Lose Control."* Lyrics and music can be found online at http://www.lyricsondemand.com.

70 — (p881) Ibid. *Merriam-Webster.*

71 — (p881) *"Asia lags behind Europe in sex, reveals Durex Survey."* Found at http://www.hindustantimes.com/181_1055140,00050004.htm and accessed on 10/13/2004. Article sites frequency of sex in different countries.

72 — (p882) *"We're Not In The Mood."* Found at http://www.nomarriage. Com/articlesexless.html and accessed on 10/27/2004.

73 — (p882) Note: Comment found in *"We're Not In The Mood"* article.

74 — (p883) Holstein, Lana, M.D. *"How To Have Magnificent Sex."* Info can be found at http://www.lanaholsteinmd.com.

75 — (p883) Gray, John, Dr. *"Men are from Mars, Women are from Venus."* Found online at http://www.marsvenus.com.

Chapter 20

1 — (p898) USA TODAY survey states that the most important issue cited by 22% of the 2004 voters was "Moral Values." Survey results found at http://www.usatoday.com/news/graphics/election2004_week/exitpolls/flash.htm and accessed on 11/3/2004. Bush beat Kerry in the total popular vote with 51% of the vote compared to Kerry's 48%.

2 — (p898) StarTribune Editorial Page A24, Friday November 5, 2004. *"Faith works in all ways"* by Cindy Marty, Bloomington, MN.

3 — (p899, 906) Ibid. *Merriam-Webster.*

4 — (p901) Note: States that voted for Bush were called "Red States" and those that voted for Kerry were called "Blue States." However, when a county map of the United States is viewed, the entire United States appears

Notes & Bibliography - Volume III

as a sea of red from coast to coast. Only large metro areas in the Blue States allowed Kerry to carry those states. For example, New York State is almost entirely Red except for New York City. Minnesota is almost entirely Red except for Minneapolis, St. Paul and Duluth. It appears that a significant moral difference exists between large metro areas and the rest of the country.

5 — (p901) THE WEEKLY STANDARD (2004). *"Rove's Secret Weapon: Stupid People."* Found online at http://www.theweeklystandard.com and accessed on 11/13/2004.

6 — (p902) USA TODAY. Race/Ethnicity Voter Graphic shows 89% of blacks voted for Kerry and 11% voted for Bush. Found at http://www.usatoday.com/news/graphics/election2004_week/exitpolls/flash.htm and accessed on 11/3/2004.

7 — (p902) Associated Press, October 19, 2004. *"Poll: Bush Doubles Support Among Blacks."* Article found on Yahoo News. "Exit polls in 2000 showed Gore winning 90 percent of the black vote, with Bush at 9 percent — the lowest support for a Republican presidential candidate since Barry Goldwater garnered 6 percent in 1964."

8 — (p902) Parker, Star (2004). *"How GOP can win the black vote."* Found at http://www.worldnetdaily.com/news/article.asp?ARTICLE_ID=41364 and accessed on 11/13/2004. Parker states: "Black Christians still vote overwhelmingly Democratic."

9 — (p903) FREEDOM WORKS (2002). *"Russia's Flat Tax Reform."* Found at http://www.freedomworks.org/processor/printer.php?/issue_id=890 and accessed on 11/13/2004. "Since January 1, 2001, Russians have enjoyed a 13 percent flat tax ... Revenue has grown as a result following the Laffer Curve: lower marginal tax rates produce higher [tax] revenues."

10 — (p907) Shamir, Shlomo, Haaretz Correspondent (2004). *"Kerry wins 78% of Jewish vote; Bush wins 22%."* Found at http://www.haaretzdaily.com/hasen/objects/pages/PrintArticleEn.jhtml?/itemNo=497277 and accessed on 11/13/2004. Note: Article states that at 78%, Kerry won just

Notes & Bibliography - Volume III

2% less than Al Gore did in the 2000 election. Bush's 22% is a 3% gain over the 19% he received in the 2000 election.

11 — (p907) Gallup Poll News Service (2004). *"How Americans Voted."* Found at http://www.gallup.com/poll/content/print.aspx?/ci=13957 and accessed on 11/2/2004. Note: This is a statistical analysis of voting, which also compared the 2000 election results to the 2004 results.

12 — (p909-910) Religion ETHICS Newsletter (2004). *"Perspectives: Election 2004 Analysis (Episode no. 810)."* Found at http://www.pbs.org/wnet/religionandethics/week810/perspectives.html and accessed on 11/15/2004. This comprehensive PBS news article features Bob Abernethy, as anchor; Professor John Green, a leading expert on religion and politics from the Ray C. Bliss Center for Applied Politics, University of Akron and Kim Lawton from RELIGION & ETHICS NEWSWEEKLY with the exit polls conducted on Election Day by Edison Media Research and Mitofsky International.

13 — (p911) Ibid. U.S. Census Report *"Married-Couple and Unmarried-Partner Households: 2000."* Note: This is extrapolated data from tables 2 and 4 of the report. Table 2 indicates that 301,026 same sex households have male partners and 293,365 same sex households have female partners. Table 4 indicates an average of 22.5% of the male households have kids under 18 and an average of 33.5% of female households have kids under 18. Math is 301,026 x .225 + 293,365 x .335 equals a total of 166,007 underage kids being raised by Gay households.

14 — (p912) FOXNEWS with Chris Wallace as seen on KSMP-TV Fox 9 in Minneapolis on 11/14/2004. In his interview with Chris Wallace, Senate Leader Bill Frist stated, "Morals never changes." Note: This is correct thinking as it is God Almighty who has defined moral values, not mankind.

15 — (p914) Kesler, Charles R. (1961) *The Federalist Papers* (p32-33). New York, New York: Signet Classic Books.

16 — (p918) Note: The concept of Red States vs. Blue States is deceptive in its presentation. When the United States is viewed as a County Map, almost

Notes & Bibliography - Volume III

the entire nation is in "red" save for very large metro areas. This "Red" county-nation map can be found at http://www.newsmax.com.

17 — (p918) Note: List shown are some of the ideas contained in an email my friend Dean received from rorlb@fgn.net and attributed to an email titled *"Separation of Church & State"* written by C-log reader Jim Moore on or about 8/31/2004. The list was not reprinted verbatim, but the originator of the basic thoughts is hereby acknowledged.

18 — (p922) Equal Marriage for same-sex couples (2004). *"Saskatchewan sends message of hope."* Found at http://www.samesexmarriage.ca and accessed on 11/16/2004. Article states, "Saskatchewan became Canada's 7th region to legalize same-sex marriage, this morning, when a court ordered the province to end discrimination against Gay and lesbian couples." In a related article it states *"New York accepts Canadian Gay marriages."*

19 — (p922) WORLDNETDAILY (2004). *"Bible as Hate Speech signed into law."* Found at http://www.worldnetdaily.com/news/article.asp?/ARTICLE_ID=38268 and accessed on 11/16/2004. Article quotes Liberal Party Parliament member John Mckay saying, "Anybody who has views on homosexuality that differ from Svend Robinson's will be exposed rather dramatically to the joys of the Criminal Code [in Canada]." In a related article, a Canadian man was fined $5,000 for taking out a newspaper ad citing Scriptures that condemned homosexuality. Another Canadian was fined $5,000 for refusal to print homosexual materials at his Christian business. Canada's activist homosexual organization EGALE explained it this way. "There's a huge difference between someone being allowed to practice their religion and taking out ads in the newspaper saying that Gay and lesbian people are sick and immoral," said EGALE's Vance. "There is a line there, and it's been crossed." Comment: Christians practicing their faith are required to rebuke sin and wickedness. The only thing Canada did was to abridge freedom of speech and sanctify immorality. *Woe to Canada!*

20 — (p935-939) Daniel, Clifton, Editor in Chief (1987) *Chronicle of the 20th Century.* Mount Kisco, New York: Chronicle Publications Inc. Note: All events listed in the table are newspaper headlines and articles contained in the historical record of this book. See year and date for details.

Notes & Bibliography - Volume III

21 — (p928) Note: Kennedy's acceptance speech is found at http://www.Americanrhetoric.com/speeches/JFK1960dnc.htm and was accessed on 11/19/2004. It is also found at the *American Presidency Project* online where details of all presidential elections are found. This latter resource is an excellent one for students of the U.S. presidency.

22 — (p929) Cass, Connie, AP Writer (2004). *"Addiction to porn destroying lives, Senate told."* Article found at http://www.sfgate.com and accessed on 11/18/2004.

23 — (p930) Hayes, Matt (2004). *"Combating Judicial Political Activism."* Found at http://www.foxnews.com and accessed on 11/13/2004. "Judges do their jobs with surprisingly few checks on the decisions they make, and appellate courts give judges ... wide latitude in sentencing."

24 — (p930) Holland, Gina, AP Writer (2004). *"Supreme Court justice gets racy on talk circuit."* Found at http://www.sfgate.com and accessed on 10/1/2004. "While making the point that judges can have personal moral judgments, it is not the judge's role to impose them on citizens."

25 — (p930) *1960 Democratic Platform* at http://www.presidency.ucsb.edu.

26 — (p941) Note: George Washington's *First Thanksgiving Proclamation* can be found at http://press-pubs.uchicago.edu/founders/documents/amendI_religions54.html and several other places. Accessed on 11/24/2004.

27 — (p950) Note: John Adams quotes are found at http://marksquotes.com/Founding-Fathers/Adams/index2.htm and were accessed on 9/5/2004.

28 — (p953) John Quincy Adams quote found at http://www.quoteworld.Org/search.php?/thetext=john+adams and accessed on 9/5/2004.

29 — (p953) John Quincy Adams quote found at http://christianamerica.com/jqaquotes.htm and accessed on 9/5/2004.

Notes & Bibliography - Volume III

30 — (p971) Grafton, John, Editor (2000) *The Declaration of Independence and Other Great Documents of American History 1775-1865.* Mineola, New York: Dover Publications, Inc.

31 — (p971) Worldnetdaily.Com (2004). *"ACLU threatens abstinence program."* Found at http://www.worldnetdaily.com/news/article.asp?ARTICLE_ID=41544 and accessed on 11/19/2004. Note: State of Louisiana is being threatened with a lawsuit because they have a website promoting abstinence and a 15 year old girl has a testimonial on the site in which she "thanks God" for helping her keep her virginity until marriage.

32 — (p974) SFGATE.COM (2004). *"EU officials implore new immigrants to learn 'European values.' "* Found at www.sfgate.com and accessed on 11/19/2004. Note: EU officials want the melting pot idea to take hold. And they want to hold on to their existing values. Watch what happens as they absorb the "moral" Muslims. Do you think they can get them to not vote for "their morals?" They should therefore codify into their Constitution what they think their EU morals are supposed to be.

33 — (p974) Ostling, Richard N., AP Religion Writer (2004). *"Election Reinforces U.S. Religious Divide."* Found at http://cnn.netscape.cnn.com/news/story.jsp?floc=ne-election-11-115&flok=FF-APO-1130&idq=/ff/story/0001/20041104/1641791322.htm&sc=1130. Note: Good luck on that URL. It may be better to search at cnn.netscape.cnn.com for the story title. Accessed on 11/4/2004. Also note that various stats from different sources quoted may not match up to one another due to different sample groups.

Chapter 21

1 — (p979) Green, Steve — Song: *People Need The Lord.* Lyrics found online at http://www.stlyrics.com.

2 — (p980) Walsch, Neale Donald (1996). *Conversations with God, *An Uncommon Dialogue*, Book 1.* New York: G.P. Putnam's Sons.

3 — (p980) Ibid. Walsch's Book 1, p61.

4 — (p981) Ibid. Walsch's Book 1, p3.

5 — (p981) Ibid. Walsch's Book 1, p8.

6 — (p981) Ibid. Walsch's Book 1, p41.

7 — (p981) Ibid. Walsch's Book 1, p133.

8 — (p981) Ibid. Walsch's Book 1, p135.

9 — (p982) Ibid. Walsch's Book 1, p135.

10 — (p982) Ibid. Walsch's Book 1, p136.

11 — (p982) Ibid. Walsch's Book 1, p138.

12 — (p982) Ibid. Walsch's Book 1, p149.

13 — (p982) Ibid. Walsch's Book 1, p143.

14 — (p982) Ibid. Walsch's Book 1, p153.

15 — (p982) Ibid. Walsch's Book 1, p155.

16 — (p982) Ibid. Walsch's Book 1, p160.

17 — (p983) Ibid. Walsch's Book 1, p162.

18 — (p983) Ibid. Walsch's Book 1, p174.

19 — (p983) Ibid. Walsch's Book 1, p175.

20 — (p983) Ibid. Walsch's Book 1, p183.

21 — (p983) Ibid. Walsch's Book 1, p184.

22 — (p983) Ibid. Walsch's Book 1, p187.

Notes & Bibliography - Volume III

23 — (p983) Ibid. Walsch's Book 1, p193.

24 — (p983-84) Ibid. Walsch's Book 1, p194.

25 — (p984) Ibid. Walsch's Book 1, p205.

26 — (p985) Fox News.com (2004). *"Banned from Showing Students the Declaration of Independence."* Article found online at http://www.foxnews.Com/printer-friendly-story/0,3566,140042,00.html and accessed on 12/1/2004.

27 — (p986) AgapePress.org (2004). *"Attorney Hopes Texas Court Will Uphold Pastor's Rights."* Article found online at http://www.agapepress.org and was accessed on 12/2/2004.

28 — (p986) NewsMax.com (2004). *"Pelosi: Marriage Amendment Discriminates Against Gays."* Article found at http://www.newsmax.com and accessed on 12/5/2004.

29 — (p986) Ostling, Richard N., AP News (2004). *"Methodist Jury Convicts Lesbian Minister."* Available at various Internet sites such as http://www.agapepress.org and accessed on 12/2/2004.

30 — (p987) WorldNetDaily.com (2004). *"Principal apologizes for prayer."* Article found at http://www.worldnetdaily.com/news/article.asp?/ARTICLE_ID=41699 and accessed on 11/20/2004.

31 — (p988) Note: The *New School Prayer* started circulating around the Internet after the Columbine High School shootings and eloquently speaks to the upside down nature of our debased public school system.

32 — (p996) CNSNEWS.COM (2004). *"Why Democrats Will Continue Losing the 'Moral Values' Vote."* Found at http://www.cnsnews.com and accessed on 12/7/2004. Commentary by Sterling Rome states: "Gore railed about representing the 'people versus the powerful' [in 2000] but we later found out that he doesn't give any money to charity. ... Hypocrisy like this is routinely dismissed by the Democrats."

Notes & Bibliography - Volume III

33 — (p1000) Clair, Christopher (2004). *"Burke's quotation does nothing but triumph."* Source: http://scotlandonsunday.scotsman.com/entertainment.cfm?id=1393992004 and accessed on 12/5/2004. Note: Edmund Burke was a famous 18th century political philosopher. The phrase, which is not found in Burke's writings, is widely attributed to him according to this article.

34 — (p1001) AP NEWS (2004). *"March Against Same-Sex Marriage Uses King Quote."* Found at http://www.newsmax.com/archives/ic/2004/12/10/143949.shtml and accessed on 12/10/2004.

35 — (p1012) Ali, Abdullah Yusuf (2001). *The Qur'an* (Text, Translation and Commentary). Elmhurst, New York: Tahrike Tarsile Qur'an, Inc. Note: the phrase "Surah" simply means "book." In the section quoted, it is simply Book 5, Verses 116-117. Ergo, "Surah 5:116-117."

36 — (p1015) ABC News (2004). *"Sexual Abuse in the Amish Community."* Found at http://abcnews.go.com/2020/print?id=316371 and accessed on 12/11/2004. Note: Elizabeth Vargas' report exposed the hellish life of a woman who endured a childhood of repeated rape by her brothers.

Appendix A
A Real Salvation Prayer

OPENING PRAYER: FATHER God, let everyone who utters this prayer of salvation unto YOU, with a sincere heart, immediately feel the presence of YOUR Holy Spirit and equip them with the internal strength of conviction to stand tall for YOUR righteousness at all costs and even unto their own human death. Verily I say unto YOU that this is YOUR expectation of their [my] sincere heart. The Apostle Edward

INSTRUCTIONS: Pray out loud and offer up to God Almighty outstretched arms and the following prayer, on your knees, in the privacy of your prayer closet [private room, alone], and with your sincere heart. Verily I say unto you that your soul will see eternal life in Heaven upon the death of your earthly body if your heart is sincere with God to the point that your behavior turns to righteousness. Mark down the time, date and place of this gift of your heart to God and feel free to share this moment of time when you made a commitment to walk in God's ways with HIS priorities over your life.

PRAY: Heavenly FATHER, the only ONE and True God. YOU, who are also the FATHER and the only ONE and True God of my brother Jesus Christ whom YOU sent down as a living human sacrifice for the sins of all the humans in this earthly realm and world, hear this prayer from my sincere heart. This prayer comes from within the bowels of my spirit-soul and I fully understand that this is a one-way decision of my heart.

A Real Salvation Prayer

FATHER, I believe in YOUR only human begotten Son Jesus Christ. I believe that YOU sent Christ down to this earth and that he became the human being Jesus Christ [Yashua] in the flesh just like the flesh I have. I believe he had bones like I do, flesh like I do and blood like I do. I believe that his body on the cross was no different than any other human body on the cross. I acknowledge Jesus Christ is the Son of God; he is not God.

FATHER, I believe that he only spoke what YOU told him to say and that he only did what YOU told him to do. I believe that he was the final and perfect blood sacrifice for the forgiveness of the sins of mankind. FATHER I believe that includes my sins.

LORD, I fully acknowledge that by accepting Jesus Christ as my personal savior and brother that I am inviting his perfect spirit into my life to share this earthly body with me. Along with his spirit, I understand that you will also give me YOUR Holy Spirit and that YOU also will dwell within me.

I believe that the end result of my sincere acceptance of this gift of YOUR Son is the Oneness that I will share with YOU and him. Christ has taught me that I might live in perfect Oneness, Peace and Joy with YOU and him. O LORD, this is truly the sincere desire of my heart. I no longer want to be spiritually alone.

Therefore, I accept the precious gift of YOUR Son Jesus Christ and I repent of my past sins and sincerely regret every thought, action, behavior or anything that was displeasing unto YOU. I understand that with the precious gift of YOUR Son, YOU expect me to live a righteousness life the rest of my days on this earth.

Such a life entails living up to YOUR expectations and obeying what YOU and YOUR Son taught us in Holy Scripture. LORD, I acknowledge that I cannot be perfect in and of myself. I realize that to be like Christ requires that I "practice" righteousness and that I avoid sin to the best of my ability. I acknowledge that to continue willfully to sin is a tacit rejection of the gift of Jesus.

A Real Salvation Prayer

I also acknowledge FATHER that there will be unintentional and unknown sins that will come in my life. I understand that YOU and Christ will cover those types of sin and function as a guide in my life to keep me on the narrow path to Heaven.

FATHER, I acknowledge that YOUR Son is not a free pass on sins like so many Christians believe. Therefore, when I realize I have sinned against YOU in any way, I promise to confess that sin immediately and to keep a short list of my missteps with YOU. I know YOU are faithful to forgive under such conditions, but I also realize that if any life is filled with such confessions that it will be a testimony of an insincere heart. I recognize YOUR instructions in Ezekiel 18 and that Jesus has not altered YOUR criteria for punishing sinners. Therefore, keep me under YOUR wings O God and give me a pure heart unto YOU.

Having said this FATHER, I pray that you will dwell within me and help me to be the man [or woman] that you want me to be. I ask all of this in the name of Jesus Christ whom I confess with my mouth that he came in the flesh as YOUR only begotten SON. I acknowledge with my heart that YOU expect righteousness, a new life with changed behavior; behavior that glorifies YOU.

FATHER, help me to be an instrument of YOUR will even as Christ was such an instrument. Let this day be the first day of the rest of my life and help me to put away all offensive behavior and sin, which YOU hate. In the name of YOUR only begotten and beloved human Son Jesus, I pray. AMEN

Date and Time of Prayer: _____

Place of Prayer: _____

I First Told To: _____

_____

JVED Publishing

18140 Zane Street NW #410
Elk River, Minnesota 55330

www.jvedpublishing.org

Special Acknowledgements

The Apostle Edward would like to thank Dean and Jackie Mattila along with Vernon Enstad for their spiritual and emotional support during his four plus years of writing. Without their godly personal support and input, this work for God may not have been possible. This book was a spiritual journey for all four of them. A special thanks is also due Brian Mechler for his proof reading assistance. Book updates and errata data will be posted online at http://www.edwardtheapostle.org. For people in countries where the book is not available in print form or for those who prefer, it may be read and searched free online in English via web browsers at this web site.

The Apostle Edward asks ...
Are You Ready?

When he returns for souls, will Christ find you going about God's business? Will he find your spiritual light shining? If not, why? Do you even know why Christ stated those two salvation requirements?

There is an exodus from established churches by Christians who have found out that many churches no longer teach God's truth. The trend is worldwide and was the subject of a recent newsletter I received. These Christians read the Bible and compared what their church taught. They found that the Church supported many evil things that God abhors. In the process, they have asked themselves some fundamental spiritual questions:

- Can we support abortion if God abhors the shedding of innocent blood?
- Can we support Gay rights if God says homosexuality is abominable?
- Can we support a political party that seeks to excise God from everyday life?
- Can we support world friendship when it makes us HIS enemy?

Christian mythology is rampant. The Book of Edward discusses the above and many other important issues that the Church is now confronted with. Will you personally obey God's Word and the teachings of Jesus? If not, you are not saved. This book can reawaken your spirit and save your soul. At the very least, it will educate your heart.

I can remember the first experience in which I felt betrayed and confused by a pulpit teaching that did not line up and match what the word of God actually said. The basic choice you have, as a Christian, is whether you will adhere to God's Word or to the man made doctrines of your social group, your church, its hierarchy or its denomination.

There lies the main issue of salvation. You'll have to decide on God's Word if you want eternal life for in the end analysis you will be held accountable to HIS Word. Christians are leaving the established church and finding small fellowships or home churches as described in the New Testament. God has opened their eyes to HIS truth and if you read and study the Scriptures in this book, HE will open your eyes.

If desired, you may write to me in care of JVED Publishing. May your soul find the true salvation contained in the teachings of Jesus Christ. The Apostle Edward